Civil Liberties Law:
The Human Rights Act Era

...ed on or before
...below.

Civil Liberties Law:
The Human Rights Act Era

Noel Whitty
Law Department, Keele University

Thérèse Murphy
School of Law, University of Nottingham

Stephen Livingstone
School of Law, Queen's University, Belfast

A Member of the LexisNexis Group

Members of the LexisNexis Group worldwide

United Kingdom	Butterworths Tolley, a Division of Reed Elsevier (UK) Ltd, Halsbury House, 35 Chancery Lane, LONDON, WC2A 1EL, and 4 Hill Street, EDINBURGH EH2 3JZ
Argentina	Abeledo Perrot, Jurisprudencia Argentina and Depalma, BUENOS AIRES
Australia	Butterworths, a Division of Reed International Books Australia Pty Ltd, CHATSWOOD, New South Wales
Austria	ARD Betriebsdienst and Verlag Orac, VIENNA
Canada	Butterworths Canada Ltd, MARKHAM, Ontario
Chile	Publitecsa and Conosur Ltda, SANTIAGO DE CHILE
Czech Republic	Orac sro, PRAGUE
France	Editions du Juris-Classeur SA, PARIS
Hong Kong	Butterworths Asia (Hong Kong), HONG KONG
Hungary	Hvg Orac, BUDAPEST
India	Butterworths India, NEW DELHI
Ireland	Butterworths (Ireland) Ltd, DUBLIN
Italy	Giuffré, MILAN
Malaysia	Malayan Law Journal Sdn Bhd, KUALA LUMPUR
New Zealand	Butterworths of New Zealand, WELLINGTON
Poland	Wydawnictwa Prawnicze PWN, WARSAW
Singapore	Butterworths Asia, SINGAPORE
South Africa	Butterworths Publishers (Pty) Ltd, DURBAN
Switzerland	Stämpfli Verlag AG, BERNE
USA	LexisNexis, DAYTON, Ohio

© Reed Elsevier (UK) Ltd 2001

ISBN 0 406 55511 7

Typeset by Doyle & Co, Colchester
Printed and bound in Great Britain by The Bath Press, Bath

Visit Butterworths LexisNexis *direct* at www.butterworths.com

Preface

It is both an exciting and a confusing time to be a civil liberties lawyer. This book tries to work with that tension in a positive, pragmatic way. In particular, it argues for both change *and* continuity in what can loosely be termed the 'civil liberties tradition'.

The text was, of course, prompted by the Human Rights Act 1998 and by other changes in the UK's constitutional culture. It adopts a stance, however, that is neither euphoric nor sceptical about either the legislation or the more general, burgeoning interest in human rights. It also does not place the European Court of Human Rights' jurisprudence at centre-stage. Instead, it focuses on identifying a range of challenges, opportunities and risks that may present themselves in what we call 'the Human Rights Act era'.

In writing this book, we have benefited from help and support provided by our colleagues in the law departments of Keele University, the University of Nottingham and Queen's University Belfast. Our thanks also to our universities for granting sabbaticals which allowed us to research and write the text, and to the law schools at the Universities of Toronto, Harvard and Sydney for their hospitality during those periods of leave. We are very grateful to Butterworths for their unfailing support of this project. Thanks also to Steven Abberley for assistance with the bibliography.

The writing of the book was shared as follows: Thérèse Murphy and Noel Whitty were responsible for Chapters 1, 2, 4, 6, 7 and 8; Stephen Livingstone and Noel Whitty were responsible for Chapters 3 and 5.

The book takes account of major developments up to April 2001 and some developments thereafter.

Noel Whitty
Thérèse Murphy
Stephen Livingstone   July 2001

Contents

Preface   v
Table of statutes   xi
Table of statutory instruments   xv
Table of European instruments   xvii
Table of international instruments   xix
List of cases   xxi

CHAPTER ONE
CIVIL LIBERTIES LAW: THE HUMAN RIGHTS ACT ERA   1
Introduction   1
I.   Why civil liberties law: the Human Rights Act era?   5
       Towards a civil liberties law for the Human Rights Act era: continuity
         and change   6
       Towards a civil liberties law for the Human Rights Act era: deflating
         human rights claims   15
       Civil liberties law: the Human Rights Act era   17
II.   The Human Rights Act: a basic outline   18
       The European Convention on Human Rights   18
       The Human Rights Act   21
III.   Reviewing the Human Rights Act: more doctrinal analysis   23
       The impact on judicial review   27
       The right to a remedy   29
       The definition of 'victim' and standing to litigate   31
       Defining a public authority and public function   33
       Private autonomy and power: the Human Rights Act's horizontal
         effect   35
IV.   'Someone must be trusted. Let it be the judges': whither democracy?
       39
       The judicial record and judges' views on civil liberties, the common
         law and modern constitutionalism   41
       Awaiting the Human Rights Act: two old orthodoxies and a new
         orthodoxy on judges and judging   46
V.   Reconstructing constitutionalism: towards a nonfoundationalist
       approach to law and adjudication   52
Conclusion   55

CHAPTER TWO
PUBLIC ORDER LAW AND PRACTICE   57
Introduction   57
I.   Overview   59
      Public order law and practice and the UK 'rights' tradition   59
      'Law and order' and public order   63
      New directions in public order   66
II.   Outline of public order law   68
III. Protest and order   71
      Protest, disorder and riot   73
      Peace, order and public order   76
IV.   Balance   80
      Public meetings and marches   81
      Public order legislation: 1986–2001   83
      The advent of zero tolerance   85
      Towards balance   87
V.   The decision-makers   94
      The courts   94
      The public order police   95
Conclusion   101

CHAPTER THREE
TERRORISM: RHETORIC AND REALITY   103
Introduction   103
I.   Anti-terrorist law, civil liberties and civil libertarians   105
      The costs of anti-terrorist law and practice   105
      Anti-terrorism and the civil libertarian dilemma   108
II.   The reality of terrorism   112
      The discourse of terrorism   112
      The definitions of terrorism   117
      The extent of the terrorist threat in the UK   121
      Justifying the Terrorism Act 2000   125
III. Responding to terrorism: the lessons of Northern Ireland   128
      Choices in anti-terrorist strategy   128
      Implementing anti-terrorist policy: anti-terrorist
          legislation 1973-2000   131
      Implementing anti-terrorist policy: the role of the military   138
      Implementing anti-terrorist policy: the role of the police   143
IV.   Terrorism and civil liberties: sites of struggle   150
      Parliament   151
      The media   153
      The courts   155
      International forums   159
Conclusion   161

CHAPTER FOUR
FAIR TRIAL VALUES: POLICING, PROSECUTION AND TRIAL PRACTICES   163
Introduction   163
      Fair trial and the Human Rights Act   165
I.   Fair trial in the civil liberties textbook tradition   167

Catalysts for rethinking fair trial values   169
II.   The pre-trial stage: access to legal advice in police custody   180
      Empirical findings on custodial legal advice   181
      Explaining the empirical findings: due process v crime control?   183
      Towards an account of the right to legal advice in context   188
III. The trial stage: rape and the criminal process   192
      Disclosure of evidence to the defence in rape cases   196
      Cross-examination on previous sexual history in the trial   206
      Rape prosecutions, rights discourse and the Human Rights Act   211
Conclusion   213

CHAPTER FIVE
PRISONERS' RIGHTS   **215**
Introduction   215
I.   The changing dynamics of imprisonment   219
      Government officials and policy   220
      Prison staff   227
      Prisoners   232
II.   Legal strategies for protecting prisoners' rights   237
      The 'rule of law' strategy   239
      The 'prison as public body' strategy   240
      The 'human rights of prisoners' strategy   242
III. Sites of legal conflict   244
      (1)   Establishing the accountability of prison authorities   247
      (2)   Maintaining prisoner contacts with the outside world   253
      (3)   Challenging discipline and control policies   261
      (4)   Improving prison conditions   265
      (5)   Reforming prisoner release procedures   268
Conclusion   277

CHAPTER SIX
DEMOCRATISING PRIVACY   **279**
Introduction   279
I.   An overview of privacy law   280
      Parliament, the press and privacy   280
      The judiciary and the 'right to privacy': a special relationship?   283
II.   The European Convention on Human Rights and privacy   292
III. Property and privacy   298
IV.   The value of privacy: searching for a common feature   302
      The public-private divide   304
      Privacy explained?   305
V.   'The way we live now': the information society and privacy   310
      Technology, commerce and governance in information
          society   310
      Media culture and practices in information society   315
VI.   Trumping privacy   317
      Privacy, power and democratic publicity   318
      Privacy in public   320
      Privacy violations and the common good   324
Conclusion   326

CHAPTER SEVEN
BEYOND THE SECRET STATE   329
Introduction   329
I.   Beyond the Secret State   331
II.   Secrecy: the British way   339
III.   A supporting role: the Official Secrets Acts of 1889 and 1911   346
       The 1889 and 1911 Acts: second time lucky?   346
       Offical secrets and national security: creating the link   348
IV.   The Official Secrets Act 1989: 'legislation to last a generation'?   360
V.   Glasnost   361
       Inside the belly of government: sleaze and secrets   362
       Freedom of information: from principle to practice   363
       Changing media practices   365
       'The name is Shayler, David Shayler'   366
VI.   'Mission Impossible'?: new directions for civil liberties law in the
       HRA era   368
       Constitutional vacuum?   369
       War and privatisation   372
Conclusion   375

CHAPTER EIGHT
THE STUFF OF LEGEND: FREEDOM OF EXPRESSION AND EQUALITY   377
Introduction   377
I.   Freedom of expression in the civil liberties tradition   380
II.   Equality and non-discrimination in the civil liberties tradition   387
       Anti-discrimination law: a late starter   389
       Law, law and more law   397
       Article 14, ECHR   403
III.   Expression and equality in the age of recognition   405
       The late-modern way: injury, identity and law reform   405
       Progress denied   421
Conclusion: towards critical pragmatism and imagination   428
       Introducing critical pragmatism and imagination   429

Select bibliography   435
Appendix   449
Index   471

Table of statutes

PAGE

Bail Act 1976
  s 3(6) 71
Children Act 1989 .... 259, 289
Children and Young Persons Act 1933 325
Conspiracy and Protection of Property Act
  1875
  s 7 70
Contempt of Court Act 1981
  s 10 357
Crime and Disorder Act 1998 ...... 65, 67, 68,
                           69, 80, 83, 85, 221
  Pt I (ss 1–27) 70
  s 11–15 84
  Pt II (ss 28–36) 70, 86
  s 28 70
     31 70
     32 70
     82 70
Criminal Appeal Act 1995 164
Criminal Evidence (Amendment) Act
  1997 240
Criminal Justice Act 1991 .... 221, 225, 262
  s 88 252
Criminal Justice and Public Order Act
  1994 .... 65, 83, 85, 180
  s 34 .... 153, 172, 191
     35 172
     36 .... 153, 172
     37 .... 153, 172
     38 .... 153, 172
     39 172
     60 70
  Pt V (ss 61–80) 68, 83, 84
  s 61, 62 70
     63 .... 70, 84
     64–67 70
     68 .... 70, 84
     69 70
     70 .... 69, 81, 84
     76, 77 84
     154 .... 69, 81
Criminal Justice and Police Act 2001 .. 67, 68
  s 44 69
     75 133
Criminal Justice (Terrorism and
  Conspiracy) Act 1998 .... 103, 151

PAGE

Criminal Justice (Terrorism and
  Conspiracy) Act 1998—*contd*
  s 1, 2 134
     5 .... 134, 152
Criminal Procedure and Investigations
  Act 1996 .... 198, 201, 203
  s 3(1) 197
Data Protection Act 1998 281
Defence of the Realm Acts 1914–1915 ... 348
Disability Discrimination Act 1995 . 392, 393
  s 5 398
Disability Rights Commission Act 1999 . 393
Education (No 2) Act 1986
  s 43 59
Electronic Communications Act 2000 311
Emergency Powers Act 1920 348
Equal Pay Act 1970 390
Ethical Standards in Public Life (Scotland)
  Act 2000
  s 25, 26 388
Fair Employment Act 1976 152
Fair Employment Act 1989 152
Football (Disorder) Act 2000 69
Football (Offences and Disorder) Act
  1999 69
Freedom of Information Act 2000 . 337, 364,
                                369, 372, 376
Government of Wales Act 1998 392
Human Rights Act 1998 .... 1, 2, 4, 5, 11, 15,
                             16, 17, 18, 24, 32,
                             39, 40, 41, 47, 48,
                             49, 50, 52, 53, 54,
                           55, 62, 67, 94, 102,
                          103, 165, 166, 167,
                          176, 177, 187, 194,
                          195, 198, 210, 211,
                          214, 244, 258, 277,
                          281, 283, 289, 328,
                          330, 332, 333, 336,
                          367, 376, 380, 387,
                          389, 392, 414, 422,
                             428, 429, 430,
                                 434, 449
  s 1 21
     2 29
     (1) 19

PAGE

Human Rights Act 1998—*contd*
s 3 .... 26, 27, 36
   (2)(b) 28
   4(3), (4) 22
   (6) 22
   5 22
   6 .... 36, 38, 327
   (1) 22, 33, 34, 387
   (2) 23, 28, 33
   (3) 23, 35
   (5) 34
   (6) 22
   7 .... 19, 31
   (1) 387
      (a), (b) 23
   8 .... 29, 37
   (1) 23, 387
   10 22
   11 31
   12 .... 22, 282, 359, 384
   (4) 321
      (b) 284
   13 22
   19 23
   21(5) 134
Immigration Appeals Commission Act
   1997 361
Intelligence Services Act 1994: 334, 337, 355
Interception of Communications Act
   1985 .... 281, 285, 355
Justices of the Peace Act 1361 71
Learning and Skills Act 2000 388
Local Government Act 1986
   s 2A 388
Local Government Act 1988
   s 28 388
Local Government Act 2000
   s 104 388
Magistrates Courts Act 1980 71
Malicious Communications Act 1988
   s 1(1) 415
Misuse of Drugs Act 1971 180
Murder (Abolition of Death Penalty)
   Act 1965
   s 1(1) 269
Northern Ireland Act 1998 .... 2, 393
   s 75, 76 391
   Sch 9 392
Northern Ireland (Emergency Provisions)
   Act 1987 129
Northern Ireland (Emergency Provisions)
   Act 1996 .... 106, 119, 125, 131, 151
   s 11 132
   12 132
   13 132
   17 132
   19 132
   25 132
   27 132
   30, 31 132
   47 192

PAGE

Northern Ireland (Emergency Provisions)
   Act 1996—*contd*
   Sch 1 132
Obscene Publications Act 1959 ...... 168, 382,
                                385, 417, 418
   s 1 418
   3 418
Offences Against the Person Act 1861 286
Official Secrets Act 1889: 331, 339, 346, 347
Official Secrets Act 1911: 329, 331, 339, 343,
                         345, 346, 348, 349,
                         353, 354, 376
   s 1 .... 347, 356
   2 .... 330, 344, 347, 353, 357, 360
Official Secrets Act 1989 ...... 9, 41, 332, 336,
                         339, 357, 366
   s 1 367
   (1)(a), (b) 360
   (3) 360
   2–4 360
   5 361
Police Act 1996 87
   s 89(2) 71, 78
Police Act 1997 355
Police and Criminal Evidence Act
   1984 .... 41, 109, 132, 164, 168,
                  182, 184, 185, 187, 367
   s 1–4 180
   8–19 180
   36–39 180
   40–46 180
   58 .... 179, 180, 183, 188
   (1) 181
   (6), (8) 181
   60 180
   66, 67 180
   76 180
   78 .... 30, 176, 190, 285
   (1) 190
   106 67
   Sch 1 180
Police (Northern Ireland) Act 2000 150
Prevention of Terrorism (Additional
   Powers) Act 1996
   s 13A–13B 133
Prevention of Terrorism (Temporary
   Provisions) Act 1974 .... 41, 103, 151
   s 14 132
   Sch 5 133
Prevention of Terrorism (Temporary
   Provisions) Act 1989 .... 106, 108, 118,
                         119, 125, 135, 168
   s 11–13 133
   16A 158, 176
   18A 133
Protection from Harassment Act 1997 ... 281,
                                415, 416
Protection of Children Act 1999 325
Prison Act 1952 .... 242, 249, 254, 278
   s 6 250
   47 247

PAGE

Private Security Industry Act 2001 100
Protection from Harassment Act 1997 69,
415
Public Interest Disclosure Act 1998 372,
376
Public Order Act 1936 83
Public Order Act 1986 .... 68, 83, 168, 180
  s 1 .... 69, 74, 75
    2 69
    3 69
    4 .... 69, 70, 415
    4A 70
    5 .... 69, 70, 78 , 415
    6 75
    8 74
    11 .... 69, 81
    12 .... 69, 81
      (1)(a), (b) 81
    13 .... 69, 81
    14 .... 69, 81
    14A 69, 81, 82
      (5) 82
    14C 81, 82
    39 70
Public Processions (Northern Ireland)
  Act 1998 148
  s 7(6) 92
    8, 9 92
    10(c) 92
Race Relations Act 1968 393
Race Relations Act 1976 .... 41, 92, 187
  s 1(1)(a) 398
      (b) 399
    19A, 19B 390
    25, 26 390
    32(3) 416
    35–38 400
    71 .... 390, 394
Race Relations (Amendment) Act
  2000 .... 187, 390
Regulation of Investigatory Powers Act
  2000 .... 282, 290, 327, 328, 334, 355
  s 67(8) 283
Representation of the People Act 1983
  s 95, 96 59
Scotland Act 1998 392
Security Service Act 1989 .... 285, 296,
334, 355
Security Service Act 1996
  s 1(1), (2) 334
    2 334

PAGE

Sex Discrimination Act 1975 .. 390, 404, 415
  s 1(1)(a) 398
      (b) 399
    2A(1) 390
    3(1) 390
    41(3) 416
    42 416
Sex Offenders Act 1997 325
Sexual Offences Act 1967 388
Sexual Offences (Amendment) Act 1976
  s 2 208
Special Powers Act 1922 108
Suppression of Terrorism Act 1978 118
Telecommunications Act 1984
  s 43(1) 415
Terrorism Act 2000 .... 69, 103, 104, 112,
120, 127, 131, 136,
160, 180, 181
  s 1 127
    (1) 126
    (2) 126
  Pt II (ss 3–10) 126, 132
  Pt III (ss 14–31) 126, 132, 133
  s 19 133
  Pt IV (ss 32–39) 126
  Pt V (ss 40–53) 126
  s 41–43 132
    44–45 133
  Pt VI (ss 54–64) 126
  s 57 158
    59–61 .... 126, 152
  Pt VII (ss 65–113) 125
  s 65 132
    77 132
    83 132
    89 132
    90, 92 132
    100 .... 125, 149
    108 134
    109 .... 134, 153, 166, 192
  Sch 1 125
  Sch 7 133
  Sch 8 .... 125, 133
  Sch 9 132
Treason Felony Act 1848 392
Youth Justice and Criminal Evidence Act
  1999 .... 193, 206
  s 34 207
    41 .... 209, 214
    58 .... 134, 153, 172, 191
      (1) 166

Table of statutory instruments

PAGE

Prison Rules 1964, SI 1964/388
r   43 .... 264, 267
    47 264
Prison Rules 1999, SI 1999/728 ..... 227, 248,
                                        249, 250,
                                        254, 257, 262
  r 8 253
    12(1) 225
    39(1) 253, 255
      (2)–(4) 255
    41(1) 247
    45 264
    51 264

NORTHERN IRELAND
Criminal Evidence (Northern Ireland)
    Order 1988 153
Criminal Evidence (Northern Ireland)
    Order 1999 134
  art 58 .... 153, 166
Fair Employment and Treatment
    (Northern Ireland) Order 1998,
    SI 1998/3162 .... 152, 397, 400, 401

PAGE

Fair Employment and Treatment
    (Northern Ireland) Order 1998—*contd*
  art 3(2)(a) 398
      (b) 399
    4 391
    50 391
Police and Criminal Evidence (Northern
    Ireland) Order 1989
  art 59 192
  Code C 192
Public Order (Northern Ireland) Order
    1987 92
Race Relations (Northern Ireland) Order
    1997, SI 1997/869 391
  art 3(1)(a) 398
      (b) 399
    37 400
    67 394
Sex Discrimination (Northern Ireland)
    Order 1976, SI 1976/1042 390
  art 3(1)(a) 398
      (b) 399
    46 398
    48, 49 400

Table of European instruments

PAGE

Convention on the Suppression of
Terrorism
Art 13 119
European Convention on the Protection of
Human Rights and Fundamental
Freedoms 1950 .... 2, 5, 6, 18, 22, 25,
27, 31, 34, 36, 39,
44, 45, 46, 47, 53,
54, 79, 106, 152,
241, 242, 308, 311
Art 2 .... 21, 37, 142, 327, 403
3 .... 21, 37, 38, 43, 250, 264,
267, 293, 327, 403
4 21
5 .... 21, 77, 92, 107,
124, 128, 173, 403
(1) 271
(c) 136
(4) 271, 273
6 .... 21, 26, 28, 134, 157, 158,
169, 171, 173, 175, 176,
177, 191, 192, 195, 196,
197, 213, 248, 263, 293,
328, 367, 403
(1) 174, 198, 254, 273
(2) 174
(3) 174
(c) 166, 181
(d) 207
7 .... 21, 403
8 .... 19, 20, 21, 30, 51, 61,
92, 128, 173, 178, 248,
258, 264, 280, 282,
289, 291, **292**, 301,
327, 328, 372, 403
(1) 279, 287, 293, 294, 295
(2) 285, 286, 295, 296, 297, 298
9 .... 20, 21, 43, 403, 405
10 .... 20, 21, 43, **61**, 62, 77, 94,
102, 128, 282, 359, 367,
372, 382, 385, 403

PAGE

European Convention on the Protection of
Human Rights and Fundamental
Freedoms 1950—*contd*
Art 13(1) 384
(2) 80, 332
11 .... 20, 21, **61, 62,** 82, 83,
94, 102, 128, 403
12 .... 21, 293
13 .... 21, 24, 28, 29,
30, 36, 176,
285, 286, 295
14 .... 21, 63, 301, 392, 393,
403, 404, 405
15 .... 107, 123, 124, 160
16 21
17 .... 20, 21
18 21
21 58
27–29 19
34 23
35(1) 19
41 19
44 19
46(2) 19
Protocol 1 61
Art 1–3 21
Protocol 4 135
Protocol 6 134
Art 1, 2 21
Protocol 11 19
Protocol 12 404
European Convention on the Prevention
of Torture 1987 251
European Economic Community Treaty
1957
Art 13 (Ex Art 6a) 395, 402
34 (Ex Art 40) 91
141 (Ex Art 119) 395, 401
EU Charter of Fundamental Rights
2000 .... 2, 396
European Prison Rules 1987 243

Table of international instruments

PAGE

Anglo-Irish Agreement 1985 .... 129, 131
General Agreement on Tariffs and Trade
    1947 (GATT) 67
Geneva Convention on the Status of
    Refugees 1951
    Art 1F(b) 119
International Covenant on Civil and
    Political Rights
    (ICCPR) 6, 105, 279
    Art 2(1) 402
    3 402
    11 58

PAGE

International Covenant on Civil and
    Political Rights—*contd*
    Art 17 303
    26 402
United Nations Convention on the Rights
    of the Child 1989 259
United Nations Standard Minimum
    Rules on the Treatment of
    Prisoners 243
Universal Declaration of Human
    Rights 279
    Art 7 402

List of cases

PAGE

A

A (mental patient: sterilisation), Re (2000), CA 288
A v France (1993), ECtHR 294
A v United Kingdom (1998), ECtHR... 37
ADT v United Kingdom (2000), ECtHR................................ 287, 297, 392
Abdulaziz, Cabales and Balkandali v United Kingdom (1985), ECtHR........ 296, 404
Advocate (Lord) v Scotsman Publications Ltd (1990), HL...................... 358
Ahmad v Inner London Education Authority (1978), CA 393
Ahmad v United Kingdom (1981), ECtHR.................................... 405
Airedale National Health Service Trust v Bland (1993), HL 46
Airey v Ireland (1979), ECtHR 20, 25, 294, 295
Akdivar v Turkey (1996), ECtHR... 294
Aksoy v Turkey (1996), ECtHR 124
Amann v Switzerland (2000), ECtHR 294, 297
American Booksellers Association v Hudnut (1985) 420
Anderson v United Kingdom (1998), ECtHR................................. 90
Andronicou v Cyprus (1996) ECtHR 142
Arbon v Anderson (1943) 237, 247
Ashworth Hospital Authority v MGN Ltd (2001), CA 290
Associated Newspapers Ltd v Wilson (1995), HL............................ 42
A-G v Blake (2000), HL 336, 360
A-G v Guardian Newspapers Ltd (1987), HL 42, 358
A-G v Guardian Newspapers Ltd (No 2) (1990), HL 289, 290, 357, 358, 359, 382
A-G v Jonathan Cape Ltd (1975) 356
A-G v Newspaper Publishing plc (1988), CA 359
A-G v Punch Ltd (2001), CA 333, 359, 366, 384
A-G v Times Newspapers Ltd (1991), HL 359
A-G v Times Newspapers Ltd (2001), CA 333, 359
A-G for the United Kingdom v Heinemann Publishers Australia Pty Ltd (1987), CA;
     affd (1988), HC of A 358
A-G's Reference for Northern Ireland (No 1 of 1975) (1977), HL 139, 158
Averill v United Kingdom (2000), ECtHR 134, 172, 192
Aydin v Turkey (1997), ECtHR 193

B

B v France (1992), ECtHR 294
B v Secretary of State for the Home Department (2000), CA 28, 289
Balfour v Foreign and Commonwealth Office (1994), CA 361
Bamber v United Kingdom (1998), ECtHR 260
Barrett v Enfield London Borough Council (1999), HL........................ 51, 175

PAGE

Barrymore v News Group Newspapers Ltd (1997) 290
Beatty v Gillbanks (1882) 79
Becker v Home Office (1972), CA... 215
Begley, Re (1996) 157
Beldjoudi v France (1992), ECtHR 296
Belgian Linguistics Case (No 2) (1968), ECtHR 404
Botta v Italy (1998), ECtHR 393
Bouchelikia v France (1997), ECtHR 296
Bowers v Hardwick (1986), US SC.. 297
Bowman v United Kingdom (1998), ECtHR 19
Boyle v United Kingdom (1994), ECtHR 296
Boyle and Rice v United Kingdom (1988), ECtHR 258
Bracebridge Engineering Ltd v Darby (1990), EAT 416
Brannigan and McBride v United Kingdom (1993), ECtHR 107, 124
Brind v United Kingdom (1994), EComHR... 117
British Steel Corpn v Granada Television Ltd (1981), HL 42
British Telecommunications plc v Williams (1997), EAT 416
Broadwith v Chief Constable of Thames Valley Police Authority (2000), DC 67
Brogan v United Kingdom (1988), ECtHR... 356
Brogan v United Kingdom (1989), ECtHR.......................... 106, 133, 136, 159
Bromley London Borough Council v Greater London Council (1983), HL.......... 42
Brooks v Home Office (1999) 267
Brown v Board of Education (1954) 108
Brown v Stott (2001), PC 26, 51, 175
Burlington Industries v Ellerth (1998), US SC................................ 415
Burridge v London Borough of Harrow (2000), HL.............................. 51
Burton and Rhule v De Vere Hotels Ltd (1996), EAT 416

C

CR v United Kingdom (1995), ECtHR 196, 294
Campbell v United Kingdom (1992), ECtHR.............................. 254, 294
Campbell and Fell v United Kingdom (1984), ECtHR 174, 262, 295
Carvel v EU Council (Denmark intervening): T-194/94 (1996), CFI 335
Chadee v Comr of Prisons (1999), PC... 267
Chahal v United Kingdom (1996), ECtHR.................... 159, 332, 356, 361
Chandler v DPP (1964), HL... 356
Chappell v United Kingdom (1989) 294
Charleston v News Group Newspapers Ltd (1995), HL............................ 287
Choudhury v United Kingdom (1991), EComHR 392
Christie v United Kingdom (1994), EComHR 296
Ciliz v Netherlands (2000), ECtHR 296
Clark v University of Lincolnshire and Humberside (2000), CA 35
Coco v AN Clark (Engineers) Ltd (1969) 289
Condron v United Kingdom (2001), ECtHR 175, 191
Conegate Ltd v Customs and Excise Comrs: 121/85 (1986), ECJ; apld (1986) 385, 417
Connor v Secretary of State for Scotland (2000), OH 267
Conway v Rimmer (1968), HL... 355
Cornelius v De Taranto (2001) 290
Cossey v United Kingdom (1990), ECtHR 293
Costello-Roberts v United Kingdom (1993), ECtHR 35, 293
Council of Civil Service Unions v Minister for the Civil Service (1985), HL......... 42, 356
Creation Records Ltd v News Group Newspapers (1997) 290
Crown Prosecution Service v Birch (2000) 67
Cyprus v Turkey (1983) 294

D

DH (a minor), Re (1994) 313
Dahlab v Switzerland (2001), ECtHR 405
Daigle v Tremblay (1989), Can SC 32
Dallison v Caffery (1964), CA.................................... 190
Davy v Spelthorne Borough Council (1984), HL.................... 240
Denmark, Norway, Sweden and Netherlands v Greece (1969), EComHR........... 124
Derbyshire County Council v Times Newspapers Ltd (1993), HL 43, 241, 289, 383
De Souza v Automobile Association (1986), CA.................... 415
Deweer v Belgium (1980), ECtHR................................ 20
DPP v Barnard (2000), DC...................................... 70, 84
DPP v Channel Four Television Co Ltd (1993), DC 117, 357
DPP v Fidler (1992) 70
DPP v Jones (1999), HL 62
DPP v Moseley, Woodling and Selvanayagam (1999), DC............ 70
DPP v Orum (1988) 94
Doorson v Netherlands (1996), ECtHR 207
Douglas v Hello! Ltd (2001), CA 38, 52, 292, 327, 384
Dougoz v Greece (2001), ECtHR................................ 267
Driskel v Peninsula Business Services Ltd (2000), EAT........... 424
Dudgeon v United Kingdom (1981), ECtHR 20, 173, 294, 392
Duncan v Cammell Laird & Co Ltd (1942), HL.................... 355
Duncan v Jones (1936), DC 71, 78

E

ELH v United Kingdom (1998) 257
Edwards v United Kingdom (1992), ECtHR....................... 175, 196
Egerton v Home Office (1978) 267
Eldridge v A-G of British Columbia (1997) 34
Ellis v Home Office (1953), CA 237, 248
Entick v Carrington (1765) 298
Esbester v United Kingdom (1993), EComHR...................... 296
Ezelin v France (1991), ECtHR 62

F

F (adult patient), Re (2000), CA 289
Faragher v City of Boca Raton (1998), US SC 415
Findlay v Secretary of State for the Home Department (1985), HL................ 270
Findlay v United Kingdom (1997), ECtHR....................... 174
Florida Star v BJF (1989), US SC 320
Forde v McEldowney (1970), HL................................ 157
Fox, Campbell and Hartley v United Kingdom (1991), ECtHR 106, 159
Foxley v United Kingdom (2000), ECtHR 297
Francome v Mirror Group Newspapers Ltd (1984), CA 289
Freeman v Home Office (No 2) (1984), CA...................... 261
French Estate v A-G of Ontario (1996) 315
Friedl v Austria (1995), ECtHR 294
Funke v France (1993), ECtHR 298

G

Galloway v United Kingdom (1999), EComHR 245

PAGE

Gaskin v United Kingdom (1989), ECtHR 293, 295
Germany v EU Parliament (supported by France, interveners): C-376/98 (2000), ECJ: 385
Gillick v West Norfolk and Wisbech Area Health Authority (1986), HL   42
Golder v United Kingdom (1975), ECtHR 18, 174, 248, 254, 294
Goldsmith v Bhoyrul (1997)   289
Goodwin v United Kingdom (1996), ECtHR 357, 382
Govell v United Kingdom (1998), EComHR 285, 295
Grant v South-West Trains Ltd: C-249/96 (1998), ECJ 402, 411
Greenfield v Secretary of State for the Home Department (2001)   263
Griggs v Duke Power Co (1971), US SC   399
Griswold v Connecticut (1965), US SC   302
Guerra v Baptiste (1995), PC   267
Guerra v Italy (1998), ECtHR   295
Guilfoyle v Home Office (1981), CA   254
Gul v Switzerland (1996), ECtHR   296
Gustafsson v Sweden (1996), ECtHR...   294

H

Hague v Deputy Governor of Parkhurst Prison. See R v Deputy Governor of Parkhurst
    Prison, ex p Hague
Halford v United Kingdom (1997), ECtHR 286, 294
Hallam v Avery (2001), CA...   93
Handyside v United Kingdom (1976), ECtHR 18, 20, 382
Hartshorn v Home Office (1999), CA..   267
Hashman and Harrup v United Kingdom (1999), ECtHR   62
Heinz (H J) Co Ltd v Kenrick (2000), EAT   398
Hellewell v Chief Constable of Derbyshire (1995)   292
Hewitt and Harman v United Kingdom (1992), ECtHR 285, 294
Higgs v Minister of National Security (2000), PC   267
Hill v Chief Constable of West Yorkshire (1988), HL   175
Hill v Church of Scientology of Toronto (1995), Can SC   39
Hoekstra v HM Advocate (No 2) (2000)   24
Holgate-Mohammed v Duke (1984), HL   190
Home Office v Harman (1981), CA; affd sub nom Harman v Secretary of State for the
    Home Department (1983), HL   42
Hughes v Holley (1986)   80
Human Rights Commission (Canada) v Taylor (1990), Can SC   420
Hunter v Canary Wharf Ltd (1997), HL   287
Huntingdon Life Sciences Ltd v Curtin (1998), CA   70
Hurley and South Boston Allied War Veterans Council v Irish-American Gay, Lesbian
    and Bisexual Group of Boston (1995), US SC   91
Hussain v United Kingdom (1996), ECtHR   272

I

Imbrioscia v Switzerland (1993), ECtHR   181
IRC v National Federation of Self Employed and Small Businesses (1982), HL   32
Ireland v United Kingdom (1978), ECtHR............................   106, 124, 159
Irving v Lipstadt and Penguin Books Ltd (2000)   381

J

Jasper v United Kingdom (2000), ECtHR.....................................   198
Jersild v Denmark (1994), ECtHR   385

PAGE

Johansen v Norway (1996), ECtHR 296
John v MGN Ltd (1996), CA 383
Johnston v Ireland (1986), ECtHR 294
Jones v Tower Boot Co Ltd (1997), CA 416
Jordan v United Kingdom (2001), ECtHR 106, 159, 332, 356

K

Katz v New York (1967), US SC 320
Kaya v Turkey (1998), ECtHR 30
Kaye v Robertson (1991), CA 45, 284
Keegan v Ireland (1994), ECtHR 294
Keenan v United Kingdom (2001), EctHR 30, 267
Kelly v United Kingdom (2001), ECtHR 141, 159
Khan v United Kingdom (2000), ECtHR 30, 176, 285, 293, 295
Khorasandjian v Bush (1993), CA 287
Kjeldsen, Busk Madsen and Pedersen v Denmark (1976), ECtHR 18
Klass v Germany (1978), ECtHR 160, 295
Knight v Home Office (1990) 267
Knupffer v London Express Newspaper Ltd (1944), HL 382
Kopp v Switzerland (1998), ECtHR 296
Krocher and Muller v Switzerland (1982), EComHR 267
Kroon v Netherlands (1994), ECtHR 294
Kruslin v France (1990), ECtHR 296
Kuhnen v Germany (1988), EComHR 385

L

L (minors) (sexual abuse: disclosure), Re (1999), CA 288
L (a child) (contact: domestic violence), Re (2000), CA 289
LLA v Beharriell (1995), Can SC 202
Laskey, Jaggard and Brown v United Kingdom (1997), ECtHR 287, 297
Law Debenture Trust Group v Malley (1999) 292
Lawless v Ireland (1960), ECtHR 124
Leander v Sweden (1987), ECtHR 296
Leech v Deputy Governor of Parkhurst Prison (1988), HL 249, 264
Les Editions Vice-Versa Inc v Aubry, Can SC 322
Little Sisters Book and Art Emporium v Minister for Justice (2000), Can SC 425
Liversidge v Anderson (1942), HL 355
Lopez Ostra v Spain (1994), ECtHR 294
Lustig-Prean and Beckett v United Kingdom (1999), ECtHR 297, 392, 395

M

M (sexual abuse allegations: interviewing techniques), Re (1999) 191
M v H (1999), Can SC 411
M (A) v Ryan (1997), Can SC 39, 205
MS v Sweden (1997), ECtHR 297
McCann, Farrell and Savage v United Kingdom (1995), ECtHR 106, 141, 142,
                                                            159, 172, 332, 356
McComb v United Kingdom (1986) 255
McConnell v Chief Constable of the Greater Manchester Police (1990), CA 77
MacDonald v Ministry of Defence (2001), EAT; on appeal (2001), Ct of Sess 392, 415
McGonnell v United Kingdom (2000), ECtHR 174

PAGE

McIlkenny v Chief Constable of West Midlands (1980), CA; affd sub nom Hunter v
    Chief Constable of West Midlands Police (1982), HL 156
McKee v Chief Constable for Northern Ireland (1984), HL 119, 157
McKerr v Armagh Coroner (1988), NICA; revsd (1990), HL 140, 157
McKerry v Teesdale and Wear Valley Justices (2000), CA 320
McLeod v Metropolitan Police Comr (1994), CA 286
McLeod v United Kingdom (1998), ECtHR 78, 286, 298
McMichael v United Kingdom (1995), ECtHR 296
Madrid v Gomez (1995) 266
Malone v Metropolitan Police Comr (1979) 27, 45, 284
Malone v United Kingdom (1984), ECtHR 285, 294
Marcel v Metropolitan Police Comr (1992), CA 288
Marckx v Belgium (1979), ECtHR 294
Mathieu-Mohin and Clerfayt v Belgium (1987), ECtHR 20
Mechanical and General Inventions Co Ltd and Lehwess v Austin and Austin Motor Co
    Ltd (1935), HL 207
Meritor Savings Bank FSB v Vinson (1986), US SC 415
Minister of Justice of Canada v Borowski (1981), Can SC 32
Modinos v Cyprus (1993), ECtHR 297
Monsanto plc v Tilly (2000), CA 67
Moore v Regents of the University of California (1990) 301
Moore and Gordon v United Kingdom (1999), ECtHR 174
Morgans v DPP (2000), HL 285
Moss v McLachlan (1985) 71
Murray v DPP (1994), HL 158
Murray (John) v United Kingdom (1994), ECtHR 294
Murray v United Kingdom (1996), ECtHR 134, 166, 172, 175, 181, 192
Murray v Yorkshire Fund Managers Ltd (1998), CA 290

N

Nicol and Selvanayagam v DPP (1995) 78, 79
Niemietz v Germany (1992), ECtHR 20, 293
Norris v Ireland (1988), ECtHR 19, 295
Nottingham City Council v Amin (1999) 176
Nottingham City Council v October Films Ltd (1999) 287
Nunes v Agrawal (1999), CA 200

O

Observer and Guardian v United Kingdom (1991), ECtHR 320, 359, 382
Observer Publications Ltd v Matthew (2001), PC 383
Olmstead v United States (1928), US SC 310
Olsson v Sweden (No 2) (1992), ECtHR 296
Oncale v Sundowner Offshore Services (1998), US SC 415
Open Door Counselling and Dublin Well Woman v Ireland (1992), ECtHR 32
Osman v Ferguson (1993), CA 175
Osman v United Kingdom (1998), ECtHR 37, 175, 295
Otto-Preminger Institute v Austria (1994), ECtHR 409

P

P v S and Cornwall County Council: C-13/94 (1996), ECJ 390
Paton v Procurator Fiscal (Alloa) (1999) 192
Pauger v Austria (1997), ECtHR 292
Payne v Lord Harris of Greenwich (1981), CA 269

PAGE

Pelle v France (1986), EComHR 263
Pendragon v United Kingdom (1999), ECtHR 69
Percy v DPP (1995) 78
Peterkin v Chief Constable of Cheshire (1999) 79
Pictons (Solicitors), Re (1998), CA 199
Planned Parenthood of SE Pennsylvania v Casey (1992), US SC 303
Plattform Aözte für das Leben v Austria (1988), ECtHR 294
Police v Reid (1987) 83
Poplar Housing and Regeneration Community Association Ltd v Donoghue (2000),
    CA 35, 56
Practice Note (Crown Court: trial of children and young persons: procedure) (2000),
    SC 273
Preston Borough Council v McGrath (2000), CA 288
Procunier v Martinez (1974), US SC 257

Q

Quinn v United Kingdom (1997), EComHR 175

R

R v A (No 2) (2001), HL 26, 51, 194, 208, 214
R v Abdullahi (1992), CA 171, 191
R v Advertising Standards Authority Ltd, ex p Insurance Service plc (1990) 34
R v Alladice (1988), CA 190
R v Anderson (1993), CA 190
R v Andrews and Smith (1990), Can SC 420
R v Argent (1996), CA 191
R v Aubrey, Berry and Campbell (1979) 330, 353
R v Azmy (1996) 199
R v B (2001), HL 300
R v Beycan (1990), CA 190
R v Bingham (1999), HL 158
R v Board of Visitors of HM Prison, The Maze, ex p Hone (1988), HL 262
R v Board of Visitors of Hull Prison, ex p St Germain (1979), CA 248, 262
R v Bow Street Metropolitan Stipendiary Magistrate, ex p Noncyp Ltd (1990), CA . . . 417
R v Bow Street Metropolitan Stipendiary Magistrate, ex p Pinochet Ugarte (No 2)
    (1999), HL 40
R v Bowden (2000), CA 418
R v Brentwood Borough Council, ex p Peck (1998), CA 287
R v BBC, ex p Lavelle (1983) 34
R v Broadcasting Complaints Commission, ex p BBC (2000), CA 284
R v Broadcasting Complaints Commission, ex p Granada Television Ltd (1995), CA . 284
R v Brown (1988), CA 207
R v Brown (1993), HL 46, 284, 286
R v Brushett (2000), CA 198, 199
R v Butler (1992), Can SC 401, 419, 420
R v Cambridge District Health Authority, ex p B (1995); revsd (1995), CA 43
R v Canale (1990), CA 190
R v Carosella (1997), Can SC 202
R v Central Criminal Court, ex p Bright (2001), DC 333, 367, 382
R v Central Criminal Court, ex p West, Blankson and Copeland (2000), DC 325
R v Chief Constable of Avon and Somerset Constabulary, ex p Robinson (1989):   189, 190
R v Chief Constable of Devon and Cornwall, ex p Central Electricity Generating Board
    (1981), CA 78

PAGE

R v Chief Constable of North Wales Police, ex p AB (1997); affd sub nom R v Chief
    Constable of North Wales Police, ex p Thorpe (1998), CA 288
R v Chief Constable of Northumbria, ex p Thompson (2001), CA 190
R v Chief Constable of Sussex, ex p International Trader's Ferry Ltd (1999), HL: 28, 62, 91
R v Chief Constable of the Royal Ulster Constabulary, ex p Begley (1997), HL . . . 158, 192
R v Chief Immigration Officer, Heathrow Airport, ex p Salamat Bibi (1976), CA 19
R v Clegg (1995), HL 140, 155
R v Collins, ex p Brady (2000) 274
R v Condron and Condron (1997), CA 191
R v Coventry City Council, ex p Phoenix Aviation (1995) 79
R v Crown Prosecution Service, ex p Hogg (1994), CA 34
R v Cullen (1990), CA 116
R v Darrach (2000), Can SC 195, 205
R v Davis, Rowe and Johnson (1993), CA 198
R v Department of Health, ex p Source Informatics Ltd (2000), CA 291
R v Deputy Governor of Camphill Prison, ex p King (1985), CA 215, 237, 249
R v Deputy Governor of Parkhurst Prison, ex p Hague (1991), HL 247, 249, 264, 266
R v Derbyshire County Council, ex p Noble (1991), CA 34
R v Director of Government Communications Headquarters, ex p Hodges (1988) . . . 349
R v DPP, ex p Kebilene (1999); revsd (1999), HL 51, 158, 176, 274
R v DPP, ex p Lee (1999) 198
R v DPP, ex p Manning (2000) 248
R v Disciplinary Committee of the Jockey Club, ex p Aga Khan (1993), CA 33
R v Duarte (1990), Can SC 283
R v Dunford (1990), CA 190
R v East Sussex County Council, ex p Tandy (1998), HL 51
R v Elwell (2001), CA 176
R v Emmett (1999), CA 286
R v Ewanchuk (1999), Can SC 194
R v Football Association Ltd, ex p Football League Ltd (1993) 34
R v Frankland Prison Board of Visitors, ex p Lewis (1986) 262
R v Franklin (1994), CA 190
R v Gayme (1991), Can SC 205
R v General Council of the Bar, ex p Percival (1991) 34
R v Gibson (1990), CA 42
R v Gloucestershire County Council, ex p Barry (1997), HL 51
R v Governor of Swaleside Prison, ex p Wynter (1998) 245
R v Governor of Whitemoor Prison, ex p Main (1997), CA 256
R v Greater Belfast Coroner, ex p Northern Ireland Human Rights Commission (2001): 31
R v H (L) (1997) 199
R v Hall (2000), CA 164
R v Headmaster of Fernhill Manor School, ex p Brown (1993) 35
R v Heaton (1993), CA 191
R v HM Prison Service, ex p Hibbert (1997) 262
R v HM Treasury, ex p University of Cambridge: C-380/98 (2000), ECJ 35
R v Hertfordshire County Council, ex p Green Environmental Industries Ltd (2000),
    HL 174
R v Hicklin (1868) 382
R v Hill (1989), CA 197
R v Horne (1999), CA 128
R v Howell (1981), CA 78
R v Hull Prison Board of Visitors, ex p St Germain (No 2) (1979), DC 262
R v Human Fertilisation and Embryology Authority, ex p Blood (1997), CA 40
R v Incorporated Froebel Institute, ex p L (1999) 35
R v International Stock Exchange of the United Kingdom and the Republic of Ireland
    Ltd, ex p Else (1982) Ltd (1993), CA 34
R v Ireland (1997), HL 415
R v Jefferson (1994), CA 75
R v Kalia (1974), CA 207

PAGE

R v Keane (1994), CA 198
R v Keegstra (1990), Can SC 420
R v Khan (Sultan) (1996), HL 27, 30, 43, 176, 285
R v Local Authority in the Midlands, ex p LM (2000) 288
R v Lord Chancellor, ex p Child Poverty Action Group (1998) 31
R v Lord Saville of Newdigate, ex p A (1999), CA 29
R v McCann (1990), CA 116
R v McIlkenny (1992), CA 156
R v McNamee (1998), CA.. 157
R v MacNaughton (1975) 140
R v Martin (1999), CA 118, 206
R v Maze Prison Governor, ex p McKiernan (1985), NICA 249
R v Mental Health Review Tribunal, ex p H (2001), CA 26, 51
R v Miller (1992), CA 171, 191
R v Mills (1999), Can SC.. 195, 201
R v Ministry of Defence, ex p Smith (1996), CA 27, 46, 241, 286, 355, 394
R v Morley (1988), CA 207
R v Mullen (2000), CA 160
R v Nicol and Selvanayagam. See Nicol and Selvanayagam v DPP
R v North and East Devon Health Authority, ex p Coughlan (Secretary of State for
    Health intervening) (2000), CA...................................... 51, 241, 289
R v North West Lancashire Health Authority, ex p A (1999), CA 43
R v Oakes (1986), Can SC 18, 20, 29
R v O'Brien (2000), CA 164, 171
R v O'Connor (1995), Can SC 199, 202
R v Oliphant (1992), CA.. 190
R v Osolin (1993), Can SC 205
R v Panel on Take-overs and Mergers, ex p Datafin plc (1987), CA.............. 33
R v Paris (1992), CA 171, 191
R v Parole Board and Secretary of State for the Home Department, ex p Oyston (2000), CA: 276
R v Ponting (1985) 330, 357
R v Press Complaints Commission, ex p Stewart-Brady (1996), CA 34
R v Reading Justices, ex p Berkshire County Council (1996) 199
R v Ribbans (1995), CA 70
R v Ridley (1999), CA 190
R v Samuel (1988), CA 190
R v Sang (1979), HL 190, 195
R v Seaboyer (1991), Can SC 205
R v Secretary of State for Health, ex p C (2000), CA 288
R v Secretary of State for the Environment, Transport and the Regions, ex p Alconbury
    Developments Ltd (2001), HL 51
R v Secretary of State for the Home Department, ex p Anderson (1984) 254
R v Secretary of State for the Home Department, ex p Anderson (2001), DC 277
R v Secretary of State for the Home Department, ex p Briggs, Green and Hargreaves
    (1997), CA 253
R v Secretary of State for the Home Department, ex p Brind (1991), HL: 42, 43, 117, 361, 382
R v Secretary of State for the Home Department, ex p Cheblak (1991), CA......... 330, 361
R v Secretary of State for the Home Department, ex p Daly (2001), HL 27, 30, 256
R v Secretary of State for the Home Department, ex p Doody (1994), HL 270, 271
R v Secretary of State for the Home Department, ex p Duggan (1994) 268
R v Secretary of State for the Home Department, ex p Fielding (1999) 258
R v Secretary of State for the Home Department, ex p Follon (1996) 276
R v Secretary of State for the Home Department, ex p Gallagher: C-175/94 (1995),
    ECJ; apld sub nom R v Secretary of State for the Home Department, ex p
    Gallagher (1996), CA 133
R v Secretary of State for the Home Department, ex p Hepworth (1998) 264
R v Secretary of State for the Home Department, ex p Herbage (No 2) (1987), CA .. 266
R v Secretary of State for the Home Department, ex p Hickling and JH (a minor) (1986),
    CA 259

PAGE

R v Secretary of State for the Home Department, ex p Hindley (1998); affd (2000), CA;
 affd (2000), HL 40, 241, 272, 273
R v Secretary of State for the Home Department, ex p Hosenball (1977), CA . .   330, 353, 356
R v Secretary of State for the Home Department, ex p Isiko (2001), CA   28
R v Secretary of State for the Home Department, ex p Leech (1994), CA 242, 255
R v Secretary of State for the Home Department, ex p McAvoy (1998), CA 258, 264
R v Secretary of State for the Home Department, ex p McQuillan (1995) 31, 44
R (Mahmood) v Secretary of State for the Home Department (2001)CA   28
R v Secretary of State for the Home Department, ex p Mellor (2001), CA   258
R v Secretary of State for the Home Department, ex p Moon (1995)   43
R v Secretary of State for the Home Department, ex p Northumbria Police Authority
 (1988), CA   42
R v Secretary of State for the Home Department, ex p O'Dhuibhir (1997), CA   255
R v Secretary of State for the Home Department, ex p P and Q (2001)   259
R v Secretary of State for the Home Department, ex p Pearson (2001), DC   260
R v Secretary of State for the Home Department, ex p Pierson (1997), HL 242, 270, 272
R v Secretary of State for the Home Department, ex p Ruddock (1987) 285, 356
R v Secretary of State for the Home Department, ex p Simms (1998), CA; revsd (1999),
 HL 49, 163, 256, 383, 385
R v Secretary of State for the Home Department, ex p Stafford (1998), HL   276
R v Secretary of State for the Home Department, ex p Stitt (1987)   356
R v Secretary of State for the Home Department, ex p Sullivan (1997)   259
R v Secretary of State for the Home Department, ex p Tarrant (1984)   262
R v Secretary of State for the Home Department, ex p Taylor (2001), DC   277
R v Secretary of State for the Home Department, ex p Thompson (1997), HL .   270, 272
R v Secretary of State for the Home Department, ex p Togher (1995), CA   43
R v Secretary of State for the Home Department, ex p Turgut (2000), CA   28
R v Secretary of State for the Home Department, ex p Venables (1998), HL . . .   40, 270, 272
R v Secretary of State for the Home Department and Governor of Frankland Prison,
 ex p Zulfikar (1995), DC   276
R v Secretary of State for the Home Department and Governor of HM Prison Whatton,
 ex p Willis (2000)   276
R v Secretary of State for Trade and Industry, ex p Greenpeace Ltd (1999)   31
R v Secretary of State for Transport, ex p Factortame Ltd (No 2) (1991), HL   40
R v Shanahan (1990), CA   116
R v Sharpe (2001), Can SC 326, 421
R v Sherwood (2000), CA   164
R v Somerset County Council, ex p Fewings (1994); affd (1995), CA   43
R v Stratford Justices, ex p Imbert (1999)   198
R v Taylor and Taylor (1993), CA 171, 197
R v Video Appeals Committee of the British Board of Film Classification, ex p British
 Board of Film Classification (2000)   383
R v W (1999), CA   207
R v W (G) (1997), CA   199
R v Ward (1993), CA   197
R v Weerdesteyn (1994), CA   190
R v Wilkinson (1983), CA   269
R v Wilson (1997), CA   286
R v X (2000), CA   285
RAV v City of St Paul (1992), Can SC   424
RJR-Macdonald Inc v A-G of Canada (1995), US SC   28
Rachid, Re (1997), DC   116
Raimondo v Italy (1994), ECtHR   135
Rantzen v Mirror Group Newspapers (1986) Ltd (1993), CA   383
Raymond v Honey (1983), HL 240, 241, 249, 254
Redmond-Bate v DPP (1999) 62, 383
Reed v Stedman (1999), EAT   424
Rees v United Kingdom (1986), ECtHR   293
Reeves v Metropolitan Police Comr (1999), HL   288

PAGE

Retail, Wholesale and Department Store Union, Local 580 v Dolphin Delivery Ltd
    (1986), Can SC 34
Reynolds v Times Newspapers Ltd (1999), HL 289, 383
Roe v Wade (1973), US SC... 108, 302
Rowe and Davis v United Kingdom (2000), ECtHR............................. 175, 198

S

St George's Healthcare NHS Trust v S (1998), CA 288
Salgueiro da Silva Mouta v Portugal (2001), ECtHR........................... 392
Sander v United Kingdom (2000), ECtHR................................. 176, 385
Saunders v United Kingdom (1996), ECtHR 175
Schering Chemicals Ltd v Falkman Ltd (1982), CA............................ 290
Schmidt and Dahlström v Sweden (1976), ECtHR 404
Secretary of State for Defence v Guardian Newspapers Ltd (1985), HL 357
Secretary of State for the Home Department v Rehman (2000), CA 159
Selmouni v France (1999), ECtHR 264
Service Corpn International plc v Channel Four Television Corpn (1999) 284
Sheffield and Horsham v United Kingdom (1998), ECtHR 294
Shelley Films Ltd v Rex Features Ltd (1994) 290
Sidhu v Aerospace Composite Technology Ltd (1999), EAT; revsd (2000), CA...... 416
Silver v United Kingdom (1983), ECtHR 174, 242, 258, 294
Smith v Gardner Merchant Ltd (1998), CA 382
Smith and Grady v United Kingdom (1999), ECtHR 27, 30, 286, 297,
                                                  355, 392, 395
Society for the Protection of Unborn Children Ireland Ltd v Grogan: C-159/90 (1991),
    ECJ 32, 385
Soering v United Kingdom (1989), ECtHR 20
Stedman v United Kingdom (1997), EComHR 405
Steel v United Kingdom (1998), ECtHR....................................... 62
Stephens v Avery (1988) 289
Stewart v Cleveland Guest (Engineering) Ltd (1994), EAT 416
Stinchcombe v R (1991), Can SC.. 201
Stjerna v Finland (1994), ECtHR.. 293
Strathclyde Regional Council v Porcelli (1986), Ct of Sess 415
Stubbings v United Kingdom (1996), ECtHR 294
Sunday Times v United Kingdom (1979), ECtHR 20, 382
Sutherland v United Kingdom (1998), EComHR 297

T

T v Immigration Officer (1996), HL... 119
TP v United Kingdom (1999), EComHR 296
Thomas v National Union of Mineworkers (South Wales Area) (1985) 42
Thomas v Sawkins (1935), DC 71
Thompson v Home Office (2001), CA 267
Thornburgh v Abbott (1989) 257
Thynne, Wilson and Gunnell v United Kingdom (1990), ECtHR 271
Tinnelly & Son Ltd and McElduff v United Kingdom (1998), ECtHR ... 332, 348, 356, 398
Tolley v JS Fry & Sons Ltd (1931), HL 303
Tolstoy Miloslavsky v United Kingdom (1995), ECtHR........................ 383
Toonen v Australia (1994) 412
Turner v Safely (1987), US SC... 257
Tyrer v United Kingdom (1978), ECtHR 18

PAGE

U

United States v Morrison (2000), US SC   212

V

Venables and Thompson v United Kingdom (1999), ECtHR 39, 174, 207, 273
Venables and Thompson v News Group Newspapers Ltd (2001) 52, 321, 327, 384

W

W v Egdell (1990), CA   290
W v United Kingdom (1987), ECtHR 293, 296
Wakefield v United Kingdom (1990), EComHR   258
Wakely v R (1990), Aus HC   207
Washington v Glucksberg (1997), US SC   302
Webb v EMO Air Cargo (UK) Ltd: C-32/93 (1994), ECJ; revsd sub nom Webb v EMO
    Air Cargo (UK) Ltd (No 2) (1995), HL   390
Weeks v United Kingdom (1987), ECtHR   271
Wheeler v Leicester City Council (1985), HL 42, 394
Williams v Home Office (No 2) (1981); affd (1982), CA   266
Wilson v First County Trust (2001), CA 26, 39, 51
Wilson v Layne (1999), US SC   316
Wingrove v United Kingdom (1996), ECtHR   409
Wolfson v Lewis (1996)   323
Woodward v Hutchins (1977), CA 290, 316
Woolgar v Chief Constable of Sussex Police (1999), CA   288
Wynne v United Kingdom (1994), ECtHR   271

X

X v Bedfordshire County Council (1995), HL   175
X v United Kingdom (1975)   257
X v United Kingdom (1981)   264
X v Y (1988)   290
X and Y v Netherlands (1985), ECtHR 25, 294
X, Y and Z v United Kingdom (1997), ECtHR   294

Z

Z v Finland (1997), ECtHR 199, 294
Z v United Kingdom (2001), ECtHR 30, 37, 51, 175
Zamora, The (1916), PC   355

Chapter One

Civil liberties law: the Human Rights Act era

INTRODUCTION

These appear to be the best of times for civil liberties. There is, for example, a widely held view that we have crossed our 'constitutional Rubicon',[1] and that liberty, so long 'a consequence of the circumstantial silence of the law',[2] is about to have its heyday. Credit for this new constitutional culture generally goes to the New Labour government's constitutional reform programme. This programme – part of a larger drive to 'modernise our society and refresh our democracy'[3] – has already ushered in devolved Parliaments in Scotland and Wales,[4] and forged the basis for a new dialogue between courts and legislatures with the Human Rights Act 1998 (HRA).[5] The latter development, widely anticipated since the publication of *Bringing Rights Home* in December 1996[6] and prodded at least in part by long-term and highly public campaigns for legal institutionalisation of rights protection in the UK, is generally represented as the centrepiece of the reform programme. Not surprisingly, it has generated a flurry of commentary and weighty expectation.[7]

1 582 HL 1298 (3 Nov. 1997) (Baroness Williams).
2 M. Loughlin, 'Rights Discourse and Public Law Thought in the UK' in G. Anderson (ed.), *Rights and Democracy: Essays in UK-Canadian Constitutionalism* (Blackstone, 1999), pp. 193-214, at p. 206. Loughlin goes on to explain that '[liberties were] the freedom we retained after the law had spoken to restrict our actions. In this sense, constitutional development could be understood as a struggle between liberty and the law; unlike in the American system, in which citizens appealed to the law as the source of their liberties, we in Britain appealed to the traditions of our liberties to protect us from the law'.
3 306 HC 782-783 (16 Feb. 1998) (Jack Straw).
4 See generally, R. Blackburn and R. Plant (eds.), *Constitutional Reform: The Labour Government's Constitutional Reform Agenda* (Longman, 1999); R. Hazell (ed.), *Constitutional Futures, A History of the Next Ten Years* (OUP, 1999); and *The English Question* (Fabian Society, 2000).
5 314 HC 1141 (24 Jun. 1998) (Jack Straw). On the issue of dialogue between courts and Parliaments under the HRA, see further T. Campbell, 'Human Rights: A Culture of Controversy' (1999) 26 JLS 6.
6 J. Straw and P. Boateng, *Bringing Rights Home* (Labour Party, 1996) (reprinted at [1997] EHRLR 71). New Labour's commitment to this project became even more evident with the speedy publication of a White Paper detailing their intentions with regard to the HRA: see *Rights Brought Home: The Human Rights Bill* (Cm. 3782, 1997).
7 It is also, of course, generating a body of Convention case law in Scotland and Northern Ireland. Feldman argues that '[b]ecause the interpretation of the Convention rights will be decided simultaneously in three different jurisdictions against the background of different pieces of legislation, one can expect differences of emphasis to emerge which will not be easily resolved by the Privy Council or the House of Lords': 'The Human Rights Act 1998 and Constitutional Principles' (1999) 19 LS 165, 205. It remains to be seen, however, how often the final appeal mechanisms will actually be used; there are obvious political ramifications to the Scottish or Northern Irish authorities (as distinct from individual litigants) appealing to 'London' against decisions of Scottish or Northern Irish judges.

Expectations of the HRA have been heightened even further by evidence of apparently sympathetic emphases in New Labour's wider political platform (in particular its enthusiasm for social inclusion and an ethical foreign policy), and by the promise of more reform in the future. It is also clear that New Labour is not alone in this enthusiasm for human rights institutionalisation and new constitutional cultures. In Northern Ireland, for example, the dynamic of the peace process has been firmly based on official recognition of the primacy of human rights, equality and respecting cultural diversity, and complex structures transcending old dualist debates about sovereignty have already been activated as a result of the Belfast Agreement 1998.[8] The commitment of many senior members of the UK judiciary towards revisioning their role as 'rights guardians' also continues apace.[9] Similarly, both the European Union (in particular in the Treaty of Amsterdam[10] and the more recent Nice EU Charter of Fundamental Rights[11]) and the Council of Europe (in particular via its Protocol 11 overhaul of the creaking machinery of the European Convention on Human Rights (ECHR)[12]) seem keen on deepening their existing commitments to human rights protection. There is also evidence of equivalent trends on an even wider plane. International political discourse, for example, increasingly foregrounds human rights protection in legitimating international treaties, global criminal law jurisdictions and humanitarian interventions.[13] Finally, the fact that intellectual projects have been launched on a range of exciting issues (including cosmopolitanism,[14] citizenship,[15] freedom[16] and accountability[17]) suggests that there is a keenness for a 'new architecture of

8   *The Belfast Agreement* (Cm. 3882, 1998). The Agreement has been incorporated into law via the Northern Ireland Act 1998. For commentaries, see eg, (1999) 22 Fordham Int LJ (a special issue devoted to the NI peace process); C. Harvey and S. Livingstone, 'Human Rights and the Northern Ireland Peace Process' [1999] EHRLR 162; and C. Harvey, 'Governing after the Rights Revolution' (2000) 27 JLS 61.

9   See below, pp. 41-52.

10   See eg, D. O'Keefe and P. Twomey (eds.), *Legal Issues of the Amsterdam Treaty* (Hart, 1999); and G. de Búrca and J. Scott (eds.), *Constitutional Change in the EU: From Uniformity to Flexibility* (Hart, 2000).

11   See House of Lords EU Select Committee Eighth Report, *EU Charter of Fundamental Rights* (May 2000) [www.open.gov.uk] (recommending accession of the EU to the ECHR).

12   The continuing downside is that registered applications before the ECtHR (12,635 in Feb. 2000) have increased by 140% since 1998, with 47,000 provisional files outstanding.

13   A notable example of the last of these was provided by the rhetoric accompanying the UK's intervention in the Kosovo conflict in 1999. See generally, G. Robertson, *Crimes Against Humanity: The Struggle For Global Justice* (Penguin, 2000).

14   See eg, J. Morison, 'The Case Against Constitutional Reform?' (1998) 25 JLS 510; and T. Murphy, 'Cosmopolitan Feminism: Towards a Critical Appraisal of the Late Modern British State' in S. Millns and N. Whitty (eds.), *Feminist Perspectives on Public Law* (Cavendish, 1999), pp. 19-40. More generally, see D. Held, *Democracy and the Global Order: From the Modern State to Cosmopolitan Governance* (Stanford UP, 1995); and U. Beck, 'The Cosmopolitan Perspective: Sociology of the Second Age of Modernity' (2000) 51 BJ Sociology 79.

15   See eg, E. Kingdom, 'Citizenship and Democracy: Feminist Politics of Citizenship and Radical Democratic Politics' in Millns and Whitty, above n. 14, pp. 149-180; J. Shaw, 'The Interpretation of European Union Citizenship' (1998) 61 MLR 293; and C.F. Stychin, *A Nation By Rights: National Cultures, Sexual Identity Politics and the Discourse of Rights* (Temple UP, 1998). More generally, see E.F. Isin and P.K. Wood, *Citizenship and Identity* (Sage, 1999).

16   See eg, W. Brown, *States of Injury: Power and Freedom in Late Modernity* (Princeton UP, 1995); and N. Rose, *Powers of Freedom: Reframing Political Thought* (CUP, 1999).

17   See eg, T. Prosser, 'Theorising Utility Regulation' (1999) 62 MLR 196; and C. Scott, 'Accountability in the Regulatory State' (2000) 27 JLS 38.

legal discourse',[18] one which would allow us to explain, negotiate and critique current and emerging constitutional processes.

It would be foolish, however, to dwell too long on the excitements of the present era; the truth is that these are also testing times for civil liberties. The processes of constitutional modernisation have 'touched many deeply held nerves in public consciousness',[19] spawning new sites of contestation and acting as flashpoints for other bitter debates. Former 'certainties of a robust Britishness'[20] appear to be collapsing, and identity (in particular questions of tradition, difference and dangerousness) has become the lightning rod for myriad debates about political representation, belonging, diversity and multiculturalism within the UK. It is clear that in certain quarters, the ambitions of European law and politics are perceived as potentially fatal threats to the sovereignty of the 'UK nation state' and the revered traditions of the common law.[21] The creeping loss of influence of the Westminster Parliament has also attracted adverse comment and been blamed on the 'constitutional vandalism' of a New Labour modernisation project intent on diffusing power to actors and institutions beyond the traditional parameters. More generally, scorn has been heaped upon the aspirations of an alleged 'liberal establishment' that is said to be intent on destroying the 'British way' which for so long has prioritised '[t]he authority of experience and the continuity of practice'.[22]

Disorientation and dispute are now widespread and quite fundamental; civil liberties itself has been affected. It seems that even the most historic certainties of the 'civil liberties tradition'[23] have been undermined. The locus and forms of governing power are no longer readily identifiable, and old convictions about 'Big Government' or 'The State', as well as familiar accusations of both judicial aimlessness and judicial bias, seem decidedly shaky. Even the standby of faith in representative democracy appears to have taken a battering,[24] as academics, media pundits and opposition parties warn of the increasing dominance of the Prime Ministerial circle of insiders and advisers over both Cabinet and executive,[25] and pinpoint overlapping sites of governing power at local, regional,

---

18   C. Harvey, J. Morison and J. Shaw (eds.), 'Voices, Spaces, and Process in Constitutionalism' (2000) 27 JLS 1, 1.

19   C.F. Stychin, 'New Labour, New "Britain"? Constitutionalism, Sovereignty and Nation/State in Transition' (1999) 19 Studies in Law, Politics and Society 139, 141.

20   N. Whitty, 'Royalty and Identity in Public Law: Diana as Queen of Hearts, England's Rose and People's Princess' in Millns and Whitty, above n. 14, pp. 41-63, at p. 41.

21   See H. Young, *This Blessed Plot: Britain and Europe From Churchill to Blair* (Macmillan, 1998); and N. Davies, *The Isles* (Macmillan, 1999).

22   M. Loughlin, 'Tinkering with the Constitution' (1988) 51 MLR 531, 536. Indeed, as Marshall has pointed out, '[s]ince at least the 1930s there [had] been something approaching an official British article of constitutional faith that Bills of Rights contain abstract or . . . stilted nonsense, fit, perhaps, for the paper constitutions of foreigners and colonials but not suited to the habits and usages of Westminster': see G. Marshall, 'Patriating Rights – With Reservations: The Human Rights Bill 1998' in University of Cambridge Centre for Public Law (ed.), *Constitutional Reform in the United Kingdom: Practice and Principles* (Hart, 1998), pp. 73-84, at p. 73. For a popular account of the alleged decline of 'Britishness', see P. Hitchens, *The Abolition of Britain* (Quartet, 2000).

23   We use this term to describe the spectrum of civil liberties work in the UK, including scholarship, teaching and activism.

24   See eg, Harvey, above n. 8; Morison, above n. 14; and A. Phillips, *Which Equalities Matter?* (Polity, 1999).

25   See eg, T. Nairn, 'Ukania Under Blair' (2000) II(1) NLR 69; and A. Barnett, 'Corporate Populism and Partyless Democracy' (2000) II(3) NLR 48 (comparing the style of the Blair government with that of a large media corporation).

European and global levels. There is also a rising civil liberties anxiety about inherited vocabularies, in particular about the latter's capacity to define the contours of public law amidst increased blurring of state and non-state actors and functions, and more generally about the role of law and legal institutions in regulating a complex administrative state.[26] Finally, historic civil liberties disputes have seemed more intense of late. There appear to be growing cleavages within the broad public law community about the merits and costs of increased judicialisation flowing, since the 1980s, from the rapid expansion of judicial review and, inevitably from October 2000, the UK-wide operation of the HRA. Historic concerns about 'trusting the judges' have been revisited,[27] and there also seems to be a new-found keenness for defining and separating out key terms such as 'civil liberties', 'human rights' and 'values'.[28]

The upshot of all of this is that it is both an exciting and confusing time for the civil liberties tradition. Familiar assertions about whether 'Parliament' or 'the judges' can be said to have the better record on protecting civil liberties appear too small-scale and straightforward for the new constitutional processes. Claims about the automatic dawn of a 'human rights culture' in the UK, the 'caring' nature of government in a post-Thatcher era, and the 'Americanisation'[29] of the judiciary are equally unconvincing. Indeed, all that seems certain is uncertainty and controversy or, to put it more productively, ongoing dialogue and difficult decision-making.[30] This book proposes that the thinking and practices of civil liberties lawyers can and must contribute to the latter. In this regard, and as will become clearer below, it argues for both continuity and change in what can loosely be termed the 'civil liberties tradition'. Successful negotiation of these twin challenges will secure the vitality of civil liberties in the new dialogic era of the HRA,[31] and may help to forge better

---

26   See below, pp. 11-14.

27   See below, pp. 46-52.

28   See eg, K.D. Ewing and C.A. Gearty, *The Struggle for Civil Liberties: Political Freedom and the Rule of Law in Britain, 1914-1945* (OUP, 2000) (esp. pp. 1-35 on the difference between human rights and civil liberties); D. Oliver, 'The Underlying Values of Public and Private Law' in M. Taggart (ed.), *The Province of Administrative Law* (Hart, 1997), pp. 217-242 and her *Common Values and the Public-Private Divide* (Butterworths, 1999) (on the differences between rights, principles and values).

29   See eg, 'US-style Court Role for Lords', *The Times*, 14 Apr. 2000.

30   See eg, T. Campbell, above n. 5 (noting that '[p]ositivization of human rights increases their utility but compromises their moral status . . . [and that] no institutional mechanisms which neglect the existence of radical and reasonable controversy as to the content, form and valence of basic rights can be justified'); and N. Walker, 'Setting English Judges to Rights' (1999) 19 OJLS 133 (arguing that '[d]espite the busy programme, enthusiastic early pace and seductive sound-bites, it remains difficult to discern an overall vision or underlying philosophy' to New Labour's reform programme).

31   References to dialogue or new conversations between legislatures and the judiciary pepper commentaries on the HRA and new constitutionalism more generally: see eg, Harvey et al., above n. 8; or former Home Secretary Jack Straw's description of the HRA's novel model of incorporation of the ECHR ('Parliament and the judiciary must engage in a serious dialogue about the operation and development of the rights in the Bill . . . this dialogue is the only way in which we can ensure the legislation is a living development that assists our citizens' (314 HC 1141 (24 Jun. 1998))). In the Canadian context, Hogg and Bushell have defended the 1982 Charter of Rights and Freedoms against allegations that it has fostered illegitimate forms of judicial review (and thereby an undemocratic constitutional order) by deploying the idea of dialogue between courts and legislatures: see their, 'The *Charter* Dialogue Between Courts and Legislatures (Or Perhaps The *Charter of Rights* Isn't Such a Bad Thing After All)' (1997) 35 Osg Hall LJ 75. See further below, n. 343.

understandings (and better processes or approaches to understanding) of the 'essentially contested concepts'[32] which comprise key elements in the architecture of future legal discourse.

I. WHY *CIVIL LIBERTIES LAW: THE HUMAN RIGHTS ACT ERA?*

Some readers may be surprised that the principal title of this text is *Civil Liberties Law* rather than, for example, 'Human Rights in UK Law' or 'The Human Rights Act'. There are several reasons for this choice, and these reasons go to explain the substance of this book and the thinking that lies behind it. The first reason is the most basic: the Diceyan civil liberties tradition, which promoted the common law's central role in protecting 'liberties', has not necessarily been abolished by the enactment of the HRA; indeed, at present, it seems more likely that both will co-exist in a complex relationship with one another and with a range of other 'high' and 'low' constitutional forces.[33] The senior domestic judiciary may, for example, opt for continued assertions of an identity between the common law and the Convention (thereby deepening their now well-publicised common law constitutionalism[34]), rather than face the controversy and ire that might be drawn by a clearly HRA-grounded constitutionalism. It is also clear that the New Labour government views the HRA as an instrument of balance between two legal traditions – first, judicial review grounded in the Convention rights and secondly, respect for the sovereignty of Parliament[35] – and as a unique, 'British model' of rights incorporation. This raises several large questions about future relationships between courts and Parliaments, and about the increasingly complex ebb and flow of traditional and emerging understandings of constitutionalism. The HRA cannot, therefore, be said unequivocally to represent an obvious abandonment of previous constitutional fundamentals; moreover, it is probably the case that (at least, outside of the Northern Ireland context) it 'will change constitutional assumptions and values *only* if it is applied in a way which secures continuity with previous constitutional fundamentals'.[36]

The second and third reasons for the title's emphasis on civil liberties are no less important than the first one. The second reason is that we seek continuity with the best aspects of the UK *civil liberties* tradition, and the third is

---

32 See discussion in N.J. Hirschmann and C. Di Stefano (eds.), *Revisioning the Political: Feminist Reconstructions of Traditional Concepts in Western Political Theory* (Westview, 1996).

33 See below, pp. 41-46.

34 For a more detailed analysis and critique, see M. Hunt, *Using Human Rights Law in English Courts* (Hart, 1997); and Loughlin, above n. 2.

35 This principle is reflected in particular in ss. 3, 4 and 10, HRA: see below, pp. 21-27.

36 Feldman, above n. 7, p. 173 (emphasis added). In the same passage, he quotes Kentridge who has pointed out that '[the HRA and the ECHR] must be approached with a due sense of proportion. Unlike the Bills of Rights in the German or South African Constitutions [the HRA] does not represent a break with an abhorrent past nor is its object to address great social problems such as those which have faced the United States Supreme Court in the second half of this century. Most of the rights stated in the Convention are to be found in our common law; indeed, most of them may be said to have been derived from the common law of this country': 'The Incorporation of the European Convention on Human Rights' in *Constitutional Reform in the United Kingdom*, above n. 22, pp. 69-71, at p. 69. Cf. Harvey, above n. 8, p. 87 (re the official failure 'to grasp the impact that human rights abuses had on fuelling the conflict').

that we hope that such an emphasis may assist in deflating the unhelpfully swollen status of 'human rights' in some accounts. In concluding this Introduction, we want to try to provide more detail on both of these reasons, as well as offering an overview of the other issues to be discussed in the chapter. We shall first explain our attachment to the UK civil liberties tradition, focusing on two particular strengths which seem to us to merit praise and preservation, and which we aim to carry forward throughout the individual chapters of this book. This will be followed by a section detailing our concerns about the consequences of a singular and non-contextual focus on human rights.

Towards a civil liberties law for the Human Rights Act era: continuity and change

We begin by examining the second reason for the emphasis on civil liberties in this book's title. This reason invokes the desirability of continuity with the civil liberties tradition, but our interest lies, in particular, in carrying forward two strands of that tradition. The first strand is the renowned civil libertarian capacity for argument and debate in the face of apparent hopelessness, widespread opposition and ridicule. The second is the cosmopolitan character of its resourcefulness, in particular the willingness to look beyond the boundaries of the formal constitution and constitutional doctrine (as manifested for example by the fact that there has never been a paradigmatic form of civil liberties pressure through law, and by the early embrace of the ECHR amongst (some) civil liberties scholars and organisations[37]).

Each strand should constitute a considerable virtue in the HRA era, facilitating and giving substance to the era's enthusiastic invocation of the merits of dialogue and, perhaps more importantly, offering a resource for facing the challenges of reinvented government and increasingly powerful non-state actors.[38] Consider, for example, that civil liberties scholarship and activism has historically been an important prompt towards, and key resource for, asking questions about the exercise of *power*, and in particular about the ways in which the structures of law might facilitate control and critique of governing power. There has, admittedly, been a preoccupation with a damagingly narrow range of power brokers, a rather static list of civil liberties 'enemies' and 'victims', and an attachment to a formal concept of law.[39] Overall, however, it seems fair to say that the civil liberties tradition has played an important part in keeping questions about power, freedom and the meaning of democracy on the agenda, irrespective of the political party in power, the sentiments of the judiciary and miscellaneous other influences. It has, for example, helped to politicise both the study and the use of law, by drawing attention to abuses of power and inequalities and suggesting (and deploying) diverse forms of pressure to

37   Until recently, however, this may have been more appearance than substance: see C. Harlow and R. Rawlings, *Pressure Through Law* (Routledge, 1992), p. 267 (concluding that, by transatlantic standards, pressure group performance in the ECtHR has been 'desultory and unenterprising'). Similar views have long been expressed about the ECtHR itself: see C.A. Gearty, 'The European Court of Human Rights and the Protection of Civil Liberties: An Overview' (1993) 52 CLJ 89, 89-91 (referring to the 'impression of busy success' arising from the ECHR's 'almost revolutionary assertion of judicial power extending over 27 governments and hundreds of millions of people').

38   See below, pp. 11-14 and 35-39.

39   See below, pp. 8-17 for more detail on these criticisms.

address injustice. 'Unpopular' causes have also generally found a valuable – indeed, sometimes their only – ally in the civil liberties tradition; civil liberties lawyers have, for example, been to the forefront in seeking redress for prisoners and in attempting to influence public debate and policy-making on issues such as the Northern Ireland conflict and racist policing.

Civil liberties' historic cosmopolitanism is evident from its diverse influences, resources and strategies.[40] The civil liberties student, teacher or scholar (and the civil liberties-minded judge) commonly ignores boundary classifications, and instead surfs across legal theory, constitutional, administrative, criminal, evidence, labour, European and human rights law, perhaps drawing upon comparative constitutional analysis or empirical studies for additional ideas or supporting evidence.[41] Civil liberties courses in law schools have typically evidenced shifting subject-matters (and indeed appear in the first place under a range of labels including constitutional law, administrative law, public law, human rights law as well as civil liberties itself). Topics such as obscenity, terrorism and official secrecy helped to encourage panoramic perspectives, and a reaching beyond law's external boundaries towards 'literature', 'history' and 'politics' respectively.[42] Furthermore, whether in print, in the classroom or courtroom (or indeed elsewhere), civil liberties advocates have been fairly adept at searching out and promoting the use of a diverse range of legal resources, either via comparative constitutional analysis,[43] or by an embrace of international treaties (for example, the International Covenant on Civil and Political Rights (ICCPR))[44] and supranational institutions (such as European and UN bodies). A similar propitious diversity is evident in civil liberties' choices in relation to possible forms of redress for injustice and inequality. Finally, the blanket-effect of the HRA – in particular the queue of lawyers, textbook writers, and politicians seeking to proclaim human rights credentials and praise the new constitutional order – should not be allowed to erase the past. Although faced with contempt, ridicule and disinterest, numerous civil liberties advocates upheld a long-term and highly public commitment, first, to highlighting the uniqueness and inadequacy of UK law's protection for human rights,[45] and secondly, to securing the 'mainstreaming' or institutionalisation of rights over and above the traditional protections derived from the mix of common law presumptions, rules of statutory interpretation, and convoluted judicial review procedures and remedies. In so doing, they broke significant amounts of new ground, most notably perhaps by encouraging recourse to international human rights

40 The lack of certainty about the boundaries of the discipline has also attracted comment and criticism: see eg, Ewing and Gearty, above n. 28, p. 1.

41 See eg, the expanding content of Harry Street's classic text, *Freedom, The Individual and the Law* (Penguin) from the first edition in 1963 onwards.

42 See eg, G. Robertson, *Obscenity* (Weidenfeld and Nicolson, 1979); and K. Boyle, T. Hadden and P. Hillyard, *Law and State: The Case of Northern Ireland* (Martin Robertson, 1975). We do not, however, wish to overplay the extent or impact of this 'reaching beyond'.

43 See eg, successive editions of S.H. Bailey, D.J. Harris and B.L. Jones, *Civil Liberties: Cases and Materials* (Butterworths); or D. Feldman, *Civil Liberties and Human Rights in England and Wales* (Clarendon, 1993).

44 See eg, D.J. and S. Joseph (eds.), *The International Covenant on Civil and Political Rights and United Kingdom Law* (Clarendon, 1995).

45 See eg, Street, above n. 41; A. Lester, *Democracy and Individual Rights* (Fabian Society, 1968); L. Scarman, *English Law: The New Dimension* (Stevens, 1974); and P. Wallington and J. McBride, *Civil Liberties and A Bill of Rights* (Cobden Trust, 1976).

norms, and this cosmopolitanism (in what was, for the most part, an era of overt legal provincialism) should not be forgotten.[46]

Of course, building on the strengths or virtues of the civil liberties tradition also requires a cutting away of weaknesses or omissions. We would argue that the tradition's principal vice is atheoreticism, and that this vice, although by no means unique to civil liberties,[47] needs to be purged. The fact that the latter is long overdue (and still largely undiscussed in certain quarters) may perhaps be attributed to the grip on civil liberties of an extended, and sometimes piercing, debate on the juridification of governing power. This debate is undeniably significant,[48] but its longstanding pre-eminence within the civil liberties tradition may also have served to squeeze out or foreclose attention to normative thinking on other issues. Another major contributory factor has been the resilience of legalism within the civil liberties tradition. By legalism, we mean the preoccupation with statute law, common law doctrine and judicial discourse that has dominated civil liberties textbooks and other civil liberties analyses[49] (and has been a pre-eminent characteristic of law teaching and legal scholarship more generally[50]). In contrast, there has been little attention to issues such as the role of discretion, the importance of social and cultural contexts, and the prevalence of non-legal forms of regulation. Whilst recognising that civil liberties lawyers and activists sometimes have *no* choice about whether to use law (for example, where individuals or groups face criminal prosecution), the tradition as a whole appears to have given insufficient attention to *strategic choices*, such as whether in any particular instance one should 'stand outside the courtroom and criticise the legal system . . . [or] stand inside the courtroom and use the law to further one's political goals'.[51] Indeed in some contexts,

46   For more details, see Hunt, above n. 34.

47   See eg, the compelling critiques of the criminal law tradition provided, inter alia, by N. Lacey, 'Contingency and Criminalisation' in I. Loveland (ed.), *Frontiers of Criminality* (Sweet & Maxwell, 1995), pp. 1-27; N. Lacey, 'Criminology, Criminal Law, and Criminalization' in M. Maguire, R. Morgan and R. Reiner (eds.), *The Oxford Handbook of Criminology* (Clarendon, 1997), pp. 437-450; and N. Lacey and C. Wells, *Reconstructing Criminal Law* (Butterworths, 1998). Extended examples of critical criminal law are provided by L. Farmer, *Criminal Law, Tradition and Legal Order* (CUP, 1996); and A. Norrie, *Crime, Reason and History* (Butterworths, 1993). Jo Shaw has provided a similar critique of the European Law tradition: see eg, her 'Constitutionalism in the European Union' (1999) 6 JEPP 579.

48   See below, pp. 41-52.

49   See Tomkins' review of Feldman, above n. 43 and McCrudden and Chambers, below n. 56, wherein it is argued that these authors 'seek to find out what the law states and how the law's statements have altered over the past few decades. They present the law as a series of such statements, which may be (but do not have to be) rules. While the books contain passages in which it is briefly acknowledged that there may be more to life than law (and even that there may be more to human rights scholarship than law) such passages are presented as merely background or even afterthought': A. Tomkins, 'Inventing Human Rights Law and Scholarship' (1996) 16 OJLS 153, 155.

50   See eg, the criticisms of criminal law in the works cited above n. 47; D. Sugarman, 'A Hatred of Disorder: Legal Science, Liberalism and Imperialism' in P. Fitzpatrick (ed.), *Dangerous Supplements: Resistance and Renewal in Jurisprudence* (Pluto, 1991), pp. 34-67 (arguing that 'the "black letter" tradition continues to overshadow the way we teach, write and think about law. Its categories and assumptions are still the standard diet of most first-year law students and they continue to organise law textbooks and casebooks . . .'); and W. Twining, *Blackstone's Tower: The English Law School* (Sweet & Maxwell, 1994).

51   M. Davies, *Asking the Law Question* (Sweet & Maxwell, 1994), p. 204 paraphrasing M. Matsuda, 'When the First Quail Calls: Multiple Consciousness as Jurisprudential Method' (1988) 11 Women's Rights L Reporter 7, 8.

rights discourse and litigation may *be* the problem, as Smart, for example, has highlighted in relation to the rape trial and abortion politics.[52]

Law and social change

Legalism has also both contributed to and been aggravated by a general atheoreticism about the relationship between law and social change.[53] It is surely telling that there has been little civil liberties interest in examining the use that pressure groups have made of litigation and other methods of encouraging reform (such as media strategies). The void in UK literature in this respect has been described as a 'black hole':[54] the omission seems even more surprising when considered in the light of the extensive literature on the issue in other jurisdictions,[55] and the fact that at least two of these jurisdictions – Canada and the US – are common resources for comparative constitutional analysis by UK civil libertarians. This is not to suggest that the civil liberties tradition has shown no interest in such questions. Empirical studies on, for example, police arrest powers, detention periods, Official Secrets Acts prosecutions, and Obscene Publications Act seizures have influenced the teaching and analysis of legal rules.[56] The strategic and symbolic nature of litigation has also been hinted at in a range of contexts (most especially, in connection with 'taking the case to Strasbourg').[57] The overall picture, however, is one that evidences clear neglect of the resource offered by the range of empirical and theoretical studies which are available on the relationship between rights cultures, patterns of social behaviour and social transformation.[58]

One of the important lessons of the scholarship on 'rights politics' is the need to avoid the import of legal concepts and strategies from other jurisdictions without an awareness of the different historical, social and political factors which are at work in those jurisdictions.[59] A good example is provided by the advocacy of First Amendment free speech doctrine for the UK context, whilst apparently oblivious to the culture of neo-liberalism from which this jurisprudence springs.[60]

52　C. Smart, *Feminism and the Power of Law* (Routledge, 1989). See also, Ch. 4.
53　For a discussion of these limitations in relation to civil libertarian positions on 'police powers' and the concept of a fair trial, see Ch. 4.
54　The choice of phrase is from C. Harlow and R. Rawlings, *Pressure Through Law* (Routledge, 1992), p. 2: this book provides a notable exception to the general pattern.
55　See eg, W.A. Bogart, *Courts and Country* (OUP, 1994); D. Herman, *Rights of Passage: Struggles for Gay and Lesbian Legal Equality* (Toronto UP, 1994); *The Anti-Gay Agenda and the Christian Right* (Chicago UP, 1997); W.A. Rosenberg, *The Hollow Hope: Can Courts Bring About Social Change?* (Chicago UP, 1991); and J. Bakan, *Just Words: Constitutional Rights and Social Wrongs* (Toronto UP, 1997).
56　See eg, C. McCrudden and G. Chambers, 'Individual Rights and British Law: Some Conclusions' in C. McCrudden and G. Chambers (eds.), *Individual Rights and British Law* (Clarendon, 1994), pp. 535-587.
57　See generally, Harlow and Rawlings, above n. 54.
58　We discuss adjudication, and the extent to which judicial behaviour and the development of legal doctrine is determined by wider social forces, in more detail below: see pp. 52-56.
59　See S. Engle Merry, 'Global Human Rights and Local Social Movements in a Legally Plural World' (1997) 12 CJLS 247; and J. Fudge, 'What Do We Mean By Law and Social Transformation?' (1990) 5 CJLS 47.
60　This point also applies to the wholesale importation of reform strategies, such as US anti-pornography and anti-abortion legal campaigns.

Emphasis on context is crucial here: however, the central role of advertising in consumer culture has had little influence on the legal theorisation of freedom of expression and regulation of texts and images;[61] and the dominant social and economic foundations of 'official secrecy' have also generally been ignored amidst the focus on legal doctrine.[62] More generally, UK civil liberties lawyers could profit from examining analyses of law and social change from jurisdictions, such as Canada, where human rights litigation regularly and dramatically impacts on the social and political life of the country, as reflected in extensive media coverage.

In recent decades, Canada has been riddled with vociferous claims that 'the Charter was a mistake'[63] and that litigation 'can corral legislative, bureaucratic and administrative initiatives' to the detriment of disadvantaged groups.[64] Other criticisms point to the public loss of faith in the traditional democratic process; the growth of pressure groups; and the fact that rights discourse is now so ubiquitous that the 'same rights-based demands made on courts will inevitably be brought to bear on legislatures'.[65] The adverse impact on pressure groups of devoting significant effort to engaging in litigation strategies has also been highlighted, including alienation of non-professional supporters, the creation of legal elites, expenditure of resources, de-radicalisation of demands, and the fracturing of group identity in the aftermath of narrow legal 'victories'.[66] There is, however, one major problem with a great deal of this debate about the 'legalisation of politics', 'excessive' judicial activism and 'legal reform' – its lack of context and specificity:[67]

> [T]he Charter has different potentials, depending on who is claiming what and why. [It] has not been deployed to undermine corporate power. Similarly, there is little evidence that any dents have been made in institutional racism in the wake of the Charter's advent. Yet, the extent to which it can be used to challenge or at least highlight other forms of power, perhaps that which exists between women and men, may be different, and there is some indication that this is so. What is needed is a comparative analysis – one which examines what different groups have achieved, or not, and why.[68]

---

61   See eg, I. Ramsey, *Advertising, Culture and the Law* (Sweet & Maxwell, 1996).

62   See D. Vincent, *The Culture of Secrecy: Britain 1832-1998* (OUP, 1998); and Ch. 7.

63   Bogart, above n. 55, p. 309. See also, A. Hutchinson, *Waiting for Coraf: A Critique of Law and Rights* (Toronto UP, 1995); and below, n. 331.

64   Ibid., p. 306.

65   K. Roach, Review of Bogart, above n. 55, (1995) U Tor LJ 105.

66   The US anti-pornography strategy initiated by Catharine MacKinnon is a particularly instructive campaign as it has been one of the most influential in recent years. By setting an agenda (law reform), building a movement (feminist and conservative), publicising its demands (writings and meetings), MacKinnon succeeded in irreversibly transforming the debate on pornography from a sole focus on obscenity to a focus on women's equality. Whether or not the strategy was a success depends on context: for some, it was a failure because law reform did not occur; for some, it was a dangerous alliance with conservative forces and damaging for feminism; and for others, it was a catalyst for personal transformation and resistance, and a disruption of dominant ideologies.

67   A recent example is F.L. Morton and R. Knoff, *The Charter Revolution and the Court Party* (Broadview, 2000) (identifying a Court Party of 'national unity advocates, civil libertarians, equality-seekers, social engineers, and postmaterialists' and 'university-based intellectuals').

68   D. Herman, 'The Good, the Bad, and the Smugly: Perspectives on the Canadian Charter of Rights and Freedoms' (1994) 14 OJLS 589. The *perception* of how courts behave may sometimes be more significant for some than the ideological and practical impact of court decisions. In jurisdictions such as the US, Canada and Ireland, the Christian Right believe that liberal forces have 'captured' the law on gay rights and abortion.

This appeal for more attention to be devoted to critiquing the *effects* of human rights claims deserves to become a clarion call for civil liberties in the UK (now that the HRA has effectively resolved the debate over the existence of rights in UK law). Moreover, helpful examples of sophisticated 'rights and social change' critiques – which recognise the limitations, risks and benefits of rights discourse, but neither essentialise rights nor exaggerate their potential – are available (albeit not in significant quantities). These critiques indicate that awareness of the 'cultural variability [of rights] must be combined with an appreciation that the function of rights can shift over time within cultures'.[69] Thus, they highlight how the achievement of rights claims by historically marginalised groups, while important both in symbolic and substantive terms, can lead to the 'normalisation' of more radical claims, and how prevailing (and deeply problematic) social norms may remain unchallenged because 'minority' claims are eventually subsumed into dominant political and legal cultures. Canadian Charter jurisprudence on the family, for example, points to apparently contradictory results – legal losses for 'welfare mothers', and legal victories for lesbian mothers and 'spouses' – which can only be made sense of if law is recognised as one of several sites for the construction and regulation of the family and gender relations.[70] Equally, however, these critiques also point to examples of the upside of rights discourse's contingent and unpredictable characteristics, and the increasing deployment of rights claims in novel ways and arenas (particularly at the international level).[71]

The state and governing power

A second obvious weakness in the civil liberties tradition which can be attributed to the vice of atheoreticism concerns understandings, and representations, of the state and state power. The latter are some of the most difficult, and hotly debated, issues in theoretical, and other, work today; they are also amongst the most crucial, in part, because of the widespread acknowledgement of pronounced shifts in forms of governance over the last two decades and the prospect of further shifts in the future. Civil liberties, however, can only enter this debate (if it does so at all) from a compromised position. This is because its history places it in a debilitating paradox, such that it is commonly both enamoured with, and mistrustful of, the state and state power.[72] The dominant civil liberties paradigm has been sovereign state versus the individual, with the former presented as the enemy (or, at least prone towards knowing neglect) of civil liberties. Thus, 'the traditional article of faith [is] that civil liberties are concerned only with the distribution of power between the individual and the

---

69   Stychin, above n. 15, pp. 16-17.
70   See S.A.M. Gavigan, 'Legal Forms, Family Forms, Gendered Norms: What is a Spouse?' (1999) 14 CJLS 127; and S. Boyd, 'Family, Law and Sexuality: Feminist Engagements' (1999) 8 SLS 369.
71   See eg, N.J. Beger, 'Queer Readings of Europe: Gender Identity, Sexual Orientation and the (Im)potency of Rights Politics at the European Court of Justice' (2000) 9 SLS 249 (re the 'dilemma of rights politics').
72   Admittedly, this history also provides evidence of the fact that, for many years, the 'Bill of Rights debate' almost single-handedly focused attention in the UK on the proper relationship between the different branches of government, the absence of foundational values in public law, and the legitimacy of judicial activism in protecting human rights: see eg, the successive editions of M. Zander, *A Bill of Rights* (Sweet & Maxwell); and of J.A.G. Griffith, *The Politics of the Judiciary* (Fontana).

state, and that the regulation of relations between citizens is a matter for substantive law and conventional politics'.[73] But this general mistrust of state power co-exists with an 'unresolved tension' as regards the circumstances in which state intervention or regulation is appropriate in public and private spheres, which has sometimes manifested itself in a paradoxical 'belief in the power of state policy as the promoter of social change and, especially, social progress'.[74]

This civil liberties paradox is of considerable lineage. It has, however, been aggravated by the stranglehold of an 'oppositional politics'[75] that became characteristic of some civil liberties positions in reacting to Thatcherism from 1979 onwards. Attempts to broach the paradox have also tended to be derailed by a further characteristic of the civil liberties tradition: the fear that change might lead to increased juridification of governing power. It seems clear therefore that civil liberties will not be able either to procure or develop a more nuanced state tradition 'overnight'.[76] Equally, however, its current position is becoming more and more of a liability, amidst a new era of governance in the UK where diverse and overlapping spheres of power are obvious, and where New Labour policies and discourses have collapsed former certainties of Left and Right. The advent of the 'contracting state',[77] particularly when seen as part of a larger package of reinvented government, requires civil liberties' responses of immense sophistication, rendering state theory a perilous enterprise even for the alert and highly experienced. In this new age of governance, state functions are both more dispersed and more concentrated:

> with the systematic dispersal of the sites of power beyond the confines of what we had learned to recognise as the state, the old certainties . . . are no longer there. Even so, for many of the retained core functions of the state . . . less means more: more invigilation of the undeserving, more surveillance of the unrespectable, more suspicion of the uninvited.[78]

These shifts suggest that there would be even less to be gained today than heretofore from conventional civil liberties perspectives on the state, and also that it will be extremely difficult to capture 'the state we're in'.[79] Neither looking

---

73   S. Sedley, 'The Spider and the Fly: A Question of Principle' in L. Gostin (ed.), *Civil Liberties in Conflict* (Routledge, 1988), pp. 136-144, at p. 140. See also, S. Sedley, 'Law and State Power: A Time for Reconstruction' (1990) 17 JLS 234.

74   E. Frazer and N. Lacey, *The Politics of Community* (Toronto UP, 1993), p. 47.

75   D. Dixon, *Law in Policing: Legal Regulation and Police Practices* (Clarendon, 1997), p. 162 (criticising the skewed nature of some responses to Thatcherism).

76   M. Loughlin, 'Sitting on a Fence at Carter Bar: In Praise of J.D.B. Mitchell' [1991] Juridical Review 133, 151. For an extended account of the neglect of the state in the English common law tradition, see J.W.F. Allison, *A Continental Distinction in the Common Law: A Historical and Comparative Perspective on English Public Law* (Clarendon, 1996); and his, 'Theoretical and Institutional Underpinnings of a Separate Administrative Law' in Taggart, above n. 28, pp. 70-89.

77   This clever phrase is taken from I. Harden, *The Contracting State* (Open UP, 1992) and refers to the contractualisation of public administration and services to private actors (such as utility companies) and quasi-public actors (such as agencies).

78   S. Sedley, 'Foreword' in Taggart, above n. 28, pp. vii-viii, at p. vii. For discussion of the impact on women of this concentration of state power, see eg, Brown, above n. 16.

79   This phrase is taken from W. Hutton, *The State We're In* (Cape, 1996). For extended discussion of the challenges reinvented government poses for other areas, see: C. Harlow and R. Rawlings, *Law and Administration* (Butterworths, 1997) or Taggart, above n. 28 (administrative law); Murphy, above n. 16 (feminism); and Harvey et al., above n. 18 (constitutionalism).

'forward' (towards a prioritisation of the local and the supranational), nor looking 'back' (to a discourse of sovereign states) will do.[80] Theories, teaching and strategies now need to accommodate a multifaceted phenomenon of governing power operating at different and overlapping levels. First, the 'indistinctness of modern state administration'[81] presents obvious challenges as traditional state functions are continually pared down, hybrid institutional forms proliferate, and government contracting powers increasingly blur the boundaries between state and private actors (for example, security firms and corporate-run schools). The classic public/private tool of state analysis simply lacks the sophistication to cope with this restructuring of social and economic relations, the fluidity of the political process, and the new forms of social control and exclusion.[82] Secondly, the expanding province of supranational institutions such as the United Nations (UN), the European Union (EU),[83] NATO,[84] the Council of Europe (in particular, its flagship, the ECHR) and other increasingly global actors (such as corporations[85]) open up complex relationships between the 'sovereign' nation state and other systems of governance, as well as impacting on notions of cultural and political identities.[86] Thirdly, the internal devolution of power to Scotland, Wales and Northern Ireland[87] (especially the latter, with its binational arrangements) has created new political spheres of autonomy and law-making, which present deep challenges to the historically dominant constructions of sovereignty and nationhood.[88] Finally, despite talk about the decline of state power and the need to think 'beyond the state', the cruel paradox remains that, in certain fields, state power has a rising potency and 'historically unparalleled prominence'.[89] The shift from a 'welfare' to 'control' perspective in government policies – emphasising public safety, dangerousness, risk management, economic choice/incentives and personal responsibility – has resulted in increasingly repressive legislation and practices in the social

80   See N. MacCormick, 'Beyond the Sovereign State' (1993) 56 MLR 1, 17.

81   Allison, above n. 76, p. 89.

82   See D. Garland and R. Sparks, 'Criminology, Social Theory and the Challenge of Our Times' (2000) 40 BJ Crim 189; S. Boyd (ed.), *Challenging the Public/Private Divide: Feminism, Law and Public Policy* (Toronto UP, 1997); and M. Thornton (ed.), *Public and Private: Feminist Legal Debates* (OUP, 1995).

83   See J. Weiler, *The Constitution of Europe* (CUP, 1999); and de Búrca and Scott, above n. 10.

84   See eg, S. Wheatley, 'The NATO Action Against the Federal Republic of Yugoslavia: Humanitarian Intervention in the Post-Cold War Era' (1999) 50 NILQ 478.

85   The Michael Mann film on the tobacco industry, *The Insider*, vividly illustrates how multinational corporations are a network of political and economic power that can easily influence both governments and mainstream media.

86   See generally, N. MacCormick, *Questioning Sovereignty: Law, State and Nation in the European Commonwealth* (OUP, 1999); E. Darian-Smith, *Bridging Divides: The Channel Tunnel and English Legal Identity in the New Europe* (California UP, 1999); and J. Steans, *Gender and International Relations* (Polity, 1997).

87   On devolution, see eg, *Constitutional Reform in the United Kingdom: Practice and Principles* (Hart, 1998), above, n. 22, pp. 7-58; R. Rawlings, 'The New Model Wales' (1998) 26 JLS 461; *The English Question* (Fabian Society, 2000); and G. Evans and B. O'Leary, 'Northern Irish Voters and the British-Irish Agreement: Foundations of a Stable Consociational Settlement?' (2000) 71 Pol Q 78.

88   See Stychin, above n. 15; P. Craig and M. Walters, 'The Courts, Devolution and Judicial Review' [1999] PL 274; T. Nairn, *After Britain* (Granta, 2000); and A. Marr, *The Day Britain Died* (Profile, 2000).

89   Brown, above n. 16, p. 168.

welfare, criminal justice, mental health and political asylum fields.[90] Apart from the gendered, racialised and class-based dimensions of these new techniques, increased 'state' surveillance and control is usually not feasible without a new nexus of government and corporate actors, with the latter providing the necessary technological and managerial resources[91] (for example, computerised data collection, CCTV monitoring, neighbourhood security patrols, and private detention centres).

If civil liberties lawyers are going to be effective in influencing any of these developments, they must cast off some of their historical 'anti-state' baggage and come to terms with the contemporary nature of governing power. Only then can a debate about appropriate modes of governance, and where the balance is to be struck between judicial control and deference to other regulatory regimes, take place.[92] A more sophisticated understanding of state power is also required in order to influence the burgeoning debate on the appropriate reach of the HRA in the regulation of private power and actors,[93] as well as comprehending the increasing blurring between the public and private spheres in late modern lifestyles.[94] Finally, recognising how the state can resemble 'a coherent actor purposefully carrying out objectives and policies' and, at the same time, 'a schismatic terrain across which forces struggle for hegemony and control'[95] is crucial for the successful furtherance of civil liberties politics.

Identity and citizenship

A further notable consequence of civil liberties' atheoreticism has been the absence of detailed scrutiny of issues of identity. This omission is more obvious now than before, not least because of the vogue for 'citizenship'-based arguments amongst politicians, social movements and academic commentators. Civil liberties' references to citizenship seem linear, partial and gauche in comparison with the analyses of the politics of 'recognition' and 'redistribution',[96] representative or participatory democracy[97] and transnational citizenship[98] which dominate the work of both critical lawyers and critical theorists more generally. This is not to deny that 'race' and 'sex' equality have been important sites of civil libertarian engagement in the UK, but understandings of 'race', 'sex' and indeed of 'equality' have generally lacked sophistication, and engagement with other identities has been indefensibly

---

90   See J. Young, *The Exclusive Society* (Sage, 1999); J. Braithwaite, 'The New Regulatory State and the Transformation of Criminology' (2000) 40 BJ Crim 222; and N. Rose, 'Government and Control' (2000) 40 BJ Crim 321.
91   See M. Lianos and M. Douglas, 'Dangerization and the End of Deviance' (2000) 40 BJ Crim 261.
92   See Scott, above n. 17.
93   See eg, A. Clapham, 'The Privatisation of Human Rights' [1995] EHRLR 20; and R. Abel, *Speech and Respect* (Sweet & Maxwell, 1996); and below, pp. 35-39.
94   See T. Murphy and N. Whitty, 'What is a Fair Trial? Rape Prosecutions, Disclosure and the Human Rights Act' (2000) 8 FLS 1 (arguing for the development of the concept of 'democratic publicity').
95   D. Cooper, *Power in Struggle* (New York UP, 1995), p. 59.
96   See eg, S. Boyd, 'Family, Law and Sexuality: Feminist Engagements' (1999) 8 SLS 369; N. Fraser, *Justice Interruptus: Reflections on the 'Postsocialist' Condition* (Routledge, 1997), pp. 11-39; and a range of articles by Fraser and others in (1997) 223 NLR and (1997) 52/53 Social Text.
97   See eg, the works cited above nn. 14 and 15.
98   See eg, the work of critical European lawyers such as Jo Shaw, above n. 15. See also, S. Sassen, *Globalization and Its Discontents: Essays on the New Mobility of People and Money* (New Press, 1999).

limited.[99] 'British' identity has too often been equated with an under-theorised 'multiculturalism', and concepts such as 'less favourable treatment' have been allowed to drown out more penetrating and wide-ranging analyses.[100] The civil liberties tradition has also failed to attend to the potential underside of citizenship discourses (now more prevalent in 'Fortress Europe'), in particular the way in which citizenship can prop up undemocratic practices by offering 'a significant marker in the international system of population management' and providing states with:

> an internationally acceptable rationale for regulating the movements of those who appear (or threaten to appear) on or within their borders as refugees from war and other forms of institutionalised violence, or simply in search of what they believe will be a better life. It helps to keep the poor in their place and, by promoting discrimination against the foreigner, it appears to offer some benefits even to the poorest of citizens who remain at home.[101]

Towards a civil liberties law for the Human Rights Act era: deflating human rights claims

This brings us to the third and final reason why we choose to emphasise civil liberties in the title of this text: we do so in an attempt to deflate the sometimes swollen status of 'human rights' in both HRA-eulogies and more generally. As Harvey has argued, the 'voice of the legal profession defending its "professional faith"' and the 'misguided wave of euphoria'[102] (in some quarters) that has greeted the enactment of the HRA need to be countered. We want to highlight a number of points that should be cause for reflection (and which should accord with the political realism and sense of history of the civil liberties tradition). First, institutionalisation of human rights has been a primary component of the new world order of reinvented government; indeed, the collapse of communism has cemented (neo)liberal democracy, capitalism and rights as the only conceivable world order:

> 'liberal democracy' is being touted as the *ne plus ultra* of social systems for countries that are emerging from Soviet-style socialism, Latin American military dictatorships, and southern African regimes of racial domination.[103]

The perceived 'end of history'[104] has, thus, dovetailed with the rise of human rights and the 'norm of democratic governance'. This makes it all the more

---

99 Path-breaking engagements with identity have been provided by a range of critical legal theorists: see eg, Cooper, above n. 95 and her *Governing Out Of Order: Space, Law and the Politics of Belonging* (Rivers Oram, 1998); and Stychin, above n. 15.

100 See eg, R. Langlands, 'Britishness or Englishness? The Historical Problem of National Identity in Britain' (1999) 5 Nations and Nationalism 53; R. Dyer, *White* (Routledge, 1997); and A. Phillips, *Equality Matters* (Sage, 1999). See generally on equality, Ch. 8.

101 B. Hindess, 'Divide and Rule: The International Character of Modern Citizenship' (1998) 1 EJST 57, 68. See also, C. Harvey, *Seeking Asylum in the UK: Problems and Prospects* (Butterworths, 2000); and C. Dauvergne, 'Citizenship, Migration Laws and Women' (2000) 24 Melb Univ LR 280.

102 Harvey, above n. 8, p. 96.

103 Fraser, above n. 96, p. 69.

104 A phrase commonly used now to refer to the rise of neo-liberalism: see F. Fukayama, *The End of History and the Last Man* (Free Press, 1992). For an interesting international law theorist's perspective on this phenomenon, see S. Marks, *The Riddle of All Constitutions: International Law, Democracy, and a Critique of Ideology* (OUP, 2000).

important to acknowledge that, as set down in Bills of Rights or international documents, human rights are 'only paper, dead tree, with ink on it';[105] in other words, in and of themselves 'they do not change the world'.[106] The most productive understandings of rights make it clear that rights are fundamentally 'difficult, complicated tools', not least because of their political indeterminancy. Thus, '[r]ights claims are neither inherently radical rearticulations nor dangerous and diversionary. More often than not they are neither, occasionally they may be both'.[107] Furthermore, there appears to be a considerable increase in both the risks and the opportunities of 'rights talk' when rights are 'invoked within an intersection of regional, national, transnational and international legal orders':

> [Such a] deployment of rights can 'trouble' or disturb 'traditional' conceptions of national sovereignty and jurisdiction based on fixed and legally enforceable boundaries of state power. In this moment, the power of rights may lie in its capacity to generate constitutional 'conversations' between an array of different legal and political actors. Rights illustrate that jurisdiction and sovereignty, rather than being fixed, immutable, or 'natural', are instead subject to ongoing political contestation. Yet, at the same time, rights can also facilitate the construction of judicial and political value judgments in the language of universalism, legalism, and positivism. [This then is what is meant by] the political indeterminancy of 'rights talk'.[108]

Rights claims, however, are more likely to facilitate 'radical rearticulations' if they are treated as a 'problematic'; that is, as a prompt towards asking questions, rather than as an end in themselves.[109] Similarly, rights-thinking and rights-holders seem more likely to benefit from what has been described as 'the age of the individual'[110] if rights are regarded 'not as personal possessions but as part of a pattern of social obligations'.[111]

These conclusions should force civil liberties lawyers to revisit their understanding of rights. They need, for example, to review the iconic subjects of the human rights protectorate (such as the dissenter and the accused), as well as favoured 'enemies'.[112] Secondly, they need to guard against the promotion of an elite of human rights 'experts' (who would then dominate debates on interpretation of human rights and the meanings of human rights culture). Thirdly, they should take note of the accusations that 'HRA-talk' (and constitutional reform more generally) has generated a cloaking effect which foregrounds classic institutions of 'big government' and the formal constitution, and thus further submerges acknowledgement of the rise of 'fugitive power'.[113] In other words, society and governance are just too complex and dynamic to take seriously some of the posturing about future human rights lawyering. Fourthly, attention must not be diverted from the crucial, wider issues of how to democratise

---

105 J. Bakan, *Just Words: Constitutional Rights and Social Wrongs* (Toronto UP, 1997), p. 3.
106 S. Sedley, 'What Bill and What Rights?', *LRB*, 5 Jun. 1997, 35, at p. 39.
107 D. Herman, 'Beyond the Rights Debate' (1993) 2 SLS 25, 40.
108 C.F. Stychin, 'Relatively Universal: Globalisation, Rights Discourse, and the Evolution of Australian Sexual and National Identities' (1998) 18 LS 534, 535.
109 See D. Herman, Review of J. Bakan, *Just Words: Constitutional Rights and Social Wrongs* (1997) 35 Osg Hall LJ 407, 407.
110 See T. Franck, *The Empowered Self: Law and Society in the Age of Individualism* (OUP, 2000).
111 Sedley, above, n. 106.
112 For an account of the need for such a review in the context of the right to a fair trial and rape prosecutions, and in understanding of police cultures, see Ch. 4.
113 See eg, Morison, above n. 14; and G. Monbiot, *Captive State* (Macmillan, 2000).

processes of modern governance which are imbued with 'complex relationships at regional, national, and global levels and across political institutions, agencies, networks and associations in the economy and in civil society at each level'.[114] As has been recognised, one cannot 'pretend that the [HRA] will supply anything approaching a comprehensive set of ethics for public life in the twenty-first century':

> A more comprehensive set of values will need to be internalised by public authorities if a more principled attitude to public duties is to take effect generally. If public authorities do not become more open, the potential benefits of the Act will not be realised. Even if public authorities come to take seriously their responsibilities under the Act, it is likely to have little impact on private undertakings which use their economic power in ways which affect the public. The responsibility of public authorities to enforce publicly responsible behaviour on the part of commercial and industrial entities is likely to become one of the key tests of the state in the next century. The Act may help to being that responsibility to the notice of public authorities, but the authorities themselves must work out how to respond.[115]

This realisation that law, lawyers and courts have an important role to play in the new landscape of civil liberties is uncontroversial; recognising, however, that other social and economic forces and actors are equally important may be harder (at least for some) to accept.

Civil liberties law: the Human Rights Act era

To sum up then: the first thing to say is that this text starts from the position that there is a great deal to be mined from the civil liberties tradition's rich brew of unfathomable optimism and deep pessimism, and from its versatility and resourcefulness. A second tenet is that, here and now in the UK, civil liberties faces a 'constitutional moment', one of those 'fleeting junctures of opportunity for radical redesign of a polity'.[116] Thirdly, we take the view that both premises require a text that is neither classic civil liberties nor human rights euphoric. Similarly, they would be ill-served by a Convention-centred approach or exclusive focus on the formal constitution. The text, therefore, aims to position itself in the borderlands, and this we would argue is the space one must occupy in the HRA era.[117] Civil liberties in the HRA era requires close attention to the HRA,

---

114 J. Morison, 'The Government-Voluntary Sector Compacts: Governance, Governmentality, and Civil Society' (2000) 27 JLS 98, 99. See also, his 'The Case Against Constitutional Reform?' (1998) 25 JLS 510; and C. Harlow, 'Accountability, New Public Management and the Problems of the Child Support Agency' (1999) 26 JLS 150.

115 Feldman, above n. 7, pp. 204-205. Scott, above n. 17, p. 57, also argues that the 'challenge for public lawyers is to know when, where, and how to make appropriate strategic interventions in complex accountability networks to secure appropriate normative structures and outcomes'.

116 We take this idea from N. MacCormick, 'Democracy, Subsidiarity, and Citizenship in the "European Commonwealth"' (1997) 16 L&P 331, 333.

117 This idea of 'space' has also been alluded to by the Lord Chancellor, who noted that '[t]he design of the [HRA] is to give courts as much space as possible to protect human rights, short of a power to set aside or ignore Acts of Parliament': 582 HL 1228 (3 Nov. 1997). A further allusion is provided by Willis' reference to the need for administrative lawyers to traverse 'the shadowy and arduous borderland between law, political science and public administration [,] where you have to use your feet as well as your head': see 'Canadian Administrative Law' (1961) 6 JSPTL 53, 54. See similarly, Harlow and Rawlings, above n. 79.

but it is also about more than that Act. Similarly, it requires engagement with human rights but is not just about human rights. The HRA era demands an appreciation of contemporary and evolving constitutional processes, a going-beyond of the traditional concerns of legal doctrine, and a deep engagement with the social and cultural contexts from which human rights abuses occur – and from which civil liberties activism springs.

The rest of the chapter is in various parts. First, in Part II, we provide an outline of the statute at the centre of the new constitutional culture, the Human Rights Act 1998 (HRA). Then, in Part III, we aim for a better understanding of the HRA by concentrating on the views of those commentators who, while apparently in favour of a domestic Bill of Rights, have identified deficiencies and ambiguities in the content and probable scope of the HRA. Much of this commentary has been expressed in 'pragmatic' terms (focusing 'on the text of the Act' and the 'case-law'[118]), eschewing engagement with contested issues of judicialisation, constitutional values and rights discourses. In Part IV, we explore the central debate over the role of judges in the pre- and post-HRA era, examining the contributions of academics, practitioners and senior judges. We argue that the hold of the 'politics' of the civil liberties tradition, and the 'orthodoxy' of the Diceyan legal tradition, have both contributed to a failure openly to face up to the changed constitutional landscape in the UK and the reinvigorated role of the judiciary. Finally, in Part V, we outline a proposal for a different civil liberties law account of adjudication, one which recognises the importance both of judicial experience and the ideological nature of law.

II.   THE HUMAN RIGHTS ACT: A BASIC OUTLINE

The HRA is designed 'to give further effect to rights and freedoms guaranteed under the European Convention on Human Rights'.[119] The ECHR is the flagship of the Council of Europe. It was adopted by the Council's Member States in 1950, and ratified by the UK in 1951. It is 'an instrument designed to maintain and promote the ideals and values of a democratic society',[120] and is also 'a living instrument which . . . must be interpreted in the light of present-day conditions'.[121]

The European Convention on Human Rights

Article 34 allows for complaints of alleged breach of the ECHR to be lodged either by other contracting states or by any person, non-governmental organisation or group of individuals (situated within the jurisdiction of a

---

118 See N. Bamforth, 'The Application of the Human Rights Act 1998 to Public Authorities and Private Bodies' (1999) 58 CLJ 159, n. 4.

119 As stated in its Long Title. Extended discussion of the ECHR is available from D.J. Harris, M. O'Boyle and C. Warbrick, *Law of the European Convention on Human Rights* (Butterworths, 1995). Convention case law is also examined in A. Lester and D. Pannick (eds.), *Human Rights: Law and Practice* (Butterworths, 1999); and K. Starmer, *European Human Rights Law* (LAG, 1999).

120 *Kjeldsen, Busk, Madsen and Pedersen v Denmark* (1976) 1 EHRR 711, para. 53. The ECtHR has identified pluralism, tolerance and broadmindedness, as well as the rule of law and access to the courts, as key values for democratic societies: see respectively, *Handyside v UK* (1976) 1 EHRR 737, para. 49 and *Golder v UK* (1975) 1 EHRR 524, para. 34. For a similar approach, see Dickson CJ's judgment in the Canadian SCt case of *R v Oakes* [1986] 1 SCR 103.

121 *Tyrer v UK* (1978) 2 EHRR 1, para. 31.

contracting state with a right of individual petition to the European Court of Human Rights) who claims to be a 'victim'[122] of an alleged breach of the Convention.[123] Under Article 35(1), however, an individual petitioner is obliged first to exhaust all effective or potentially effective domestic remedies before applying under the ECHR.[124]

Following a substantial and belated overhaul in 1998, the Convention operates with a single, full-time court.[125] A three-judge committee of the Court (which must act unanimously) determines the threshold question of admissibility, and cases ruled admissible are then generally heard by a chamber of seven judges (although exceptionally, for example in cases involving serious questions of interpretation of the ECHR, a grand chamber of 17 judges will adjudicate).[126] The Court can grant declaratory relief, and, under Article 41, it also has the power to award 'just satisfaction'[127] to the victim of a violation and to make a full award of costs. The Court's decisions are final and binding, and may be enforced by the Committee of Ministers.[128]

The ECHR seeks to protect a range of rights (including, for example, the right to life, the right to protection of private life and the right to liberty), but this protection is not guaranteed without limit or restriction.[129] Understanding the scope of protection requires an appreciation of the principles of interpretation which have been developed by the Strasbourg Court (and, formerly, by the European Commission on Human Rights). Acquiring such an understanding has become all the more important since the onset of the New Labour project for 'bringing rights home': the HRA requires UK courts and tribunals to 'take account of' ECHR jurisprudence,[130] which means that Convention principles of interpretation will be of considerable relevance in the interpretation of the Act.

122 S. 7, HRA provides that a person may rely on a Convention right only if they are or would be a 'victim' for the purposes of Art. 34, ECHR. The ECtHR uses a broad, facilitative understanding of 'victim' (see eg, *Norris v Ireland* (1988) 13 EHRR 186; *Bowman v UK* (1998) 26 EHRR 1).

123 The right extends to legal as well as natural persons, and is not confined to those with a lawful right to be present in the state of a contracting party. On the history of the UK's acceptance of the right of individual petition, see A. Lester, 'UK Acceptance of the Statutory Jurisdiction: What Went on in Whitehall' [1998] PL 237.

124 Art. 35(1), ECHR also requires that a petition be filed within six months of the date of the violation, or the date of the final relevant domestic remedy.

125 The vehicle for this overhaul was Protocol 11, ECHR. Previously, the ECHR operated a two-tier enforcement system, with a commission (the European Commission of Human Rights) and a court. Protocol 11 also removed the Committee of Ministers' responsibility for adjudication.

126 Arts. 27-29, ECHR. If the three-judge committee is not unanimous in its decision to declare a case admissible or strike it out, the case will be referred to chamber which will determine the admissibility and the merits of the application.

127 A. Mowbray, 'The European Court of Human Rights' Approach to Just Satisfaction' [1997] PL 647.

128 Art. 44 and Art. 46(2), ECHR.

129 The 'style' of the ECHR was, at one time, the subject of judicial criticism: see most famously the view expressed by Lord Denning MR that '[the ECHR] is drafted in a style very different from the way which we are used to in legislation. It contains wide general statements of principle. They are apt to lead to much difficulty in application: because they give rise to much uncertainty. They are not the sort of thing which we can easily digest. Art. 8 is an example. It is so wide as to be incapable of practical application. So it is much better for us to stick to our own statutes and principles, and only look to the Convention for guidance in case of doubt' (*R v Chief Immigration Officer, Heathrow Airport, ex p Bibi* [1976] 1 WLR 979, 985).

130 S. 2(1), HRA.

What, then, are the relevant Convention principles of interpretation? First, as noted earlier, the ECHR is to be treated as a 'living instrument' which has as a key goal the maintenance and promotion of the ideals and values of a democratic society.[131] Secondly, it is relevant to take account of the existence of any 'generally shared approach' amongst the contracting states (but 'absolute uniformity is not required'). Thirdly, because ECHR rights are intended to be 'practical and effective', the conditions imposed for the exercise of a right must not 'impair their very essence and deprive them of their effectiveness'; moreover, courts are encouraged to 'look behind the appearances and investigate the realities of the procedure in question'.[132] Fourthly, there is the general principle of striving for a 'fair balance' as between 'the demands of the general interest of the community and the requirements of the protection of the individual's fundamental rights'.[133] This principle is brought to life by the doctrine of proportionality, which provides that restrictions on Convention freedoms must be 'proportionate to the legitimate aim pursued'.[134] It is generally accepted that three criteria must be met before the proportionality test will be satisfied: first, the legislative objective must be sufficiently important to justify limiting a right; secondly, the measure(s) designed to meet that objective must be rationally connected thereto (ie, they must not be arbitrary, unfair, or based on irrational considerations); and finally, the means used to impair the right must be no more than is necessary to achieve the legitimate objective (ie, there should be as little as possible interference with the right).[135]

Account must also be taken of the explicit directions on interpretation which are contained in the ECHR. Article 17, for example, prevents interpretations which might allow abuse of rights.[136] A second example is provided by the express limitations which are laid down in respect of the rights guaranteed in Articles 8 to 11. These limitations are drafted in similar terms, and provide that, where there is a prima facie interference with one of these rights, it is for the state to demonstrate that any restriction on the exercise of such a right is prescribed by law (or in accordance with law) and is necessary in a democratic society for the advancement of one of a list of specified objectives (including the protection of public order, health or morals, or the interests of others).[137] Reference must be made to the principle of proportionality in determining the meaning of 'necessary'.

---

131 Above nn. 120 and 121.

132 See respectively: *Airey v Ireland* (1979) 2 EHRR 305, para. 24; *Mathieu-Mohin v Belgium* (1987) 10 EHRR 1, para. 52; and *Deweer v Belgium* (1980) 2 EHRR 439, para. 44.

133 *Soering v UK* (1989) 11 EHRR 439. On the doctrine of proportionality under the ECHR, see generally, Harris, O'Boyle and Warbrick, above n. 119, pp. 283-301; and Lester and Pannick, above n. 119, pp. 68-69.

134 *Handyside v UK* (1976) 1 EHRR 737, para. 49.

135 For a very clear identification of the three criteria, see the opinion of the SCt of Canada in *R v Oakes* [1986] 1 SCR 103.

136 Art. 17 provides that: '[n]othing in this Convention may be interpreted as implying for any State, group or person any right to engage in any activity or perform any act aimed at the destruction of any of the rights and freedoms set forth herein or at their limitation to a greater extent than is provided for in the Convention'.

137 The ECtHR has bolstered the protection for rights by providing that exceptions to rights 'must be narrowly interpreted', and that the rights themselves are to be construed using a broad, purposive construction, taking account of the importance of the right(s) in issue: see respectively, *Niemietz v Germany* (1992) 16 EHRR 97, para. 31; *Sunday Times v UK* (1979) 2 EHRR 245, para. 65; and *Dudgeon v UK* (1981) 4 EHRR 149, para. 52.

Finally, brief mention needs to be made of what has come to be known as the doctrine of the 'margin of appreciation'. This doctrine promotes the merits of restrained review at the international level; in other words, it offers support to the idea that national authorities may have the pre-eminent role in determining rights protection, and that the ECHR mechanism is 'subsidiary to [such] national systems'.[138] As will be discussed further below, the relevance of this doctrine to UK courts when applying the HRA is currently the subject of some dispute.

The Human Rights Act

This brings us to the text of the HRA itself.[139] Its Long Title states that it is designed 'to give further effect to the rights and freedoms guaranteed under the European Convention on Human Rights'.[140] This rather bland-sounding objective, and the repeated references in the debates on the Human Rights Bill to 'bringing rights home',[141] would seem to suggest that the Act is nothing special, that it is just another 'ordinary law'. But to adopt this view would be to make a grave mistake. However one looks at it, '[t]he HRA is no ordinary law'.[142] It is a highpoint of the New Labour constitutional reform programme and 'the culmination of an aggressive campaign for the incorporation into domestic law of the [ECHR], a campaign in which the judges joined forces with other political activists'.[143] It gives individuals the opportunity to argue for their Convention rights[144] in the UK's own courts and tribunals, allows judges to adjudicate directly on Convention issues and seeks a new dialogue between

138 *Handyside*, above n. 120, at para. 48.
139 Overviews of the HRA are provided by: K.D. Ewing, 'The Human Rights Act and Parliamentary Democracy' (1999) 62 MLR 79; S. Grosz, J. Beatson and P. Duffy, *Human Rights: The 1998 Act and the European Convention* (Sweet & Maxwell, 1999); Lester and Pannick, above n. 119; B.S. Markesinis (ed.), *The Impact of the Human Rights Bill on English Law* (Clarendon, 1998); S. Palmer, 'The Human Rights Act 1998: Bringing Rights Home' (1998) 1 YELS 125; and J. Wadham and H. Mountfield, *Blackstone's Guide to the Human Rights Act 1998* (Blackstone, 1999).
140 The full text of the long title indicates that the HRA is also designed to make provision with respect to the holders of certain judicial offices who become judges of the ECtHR and for connected purposes. For an explanation of the intended meaning of 'further', see the comments of the Lord Chancellor, Lord Irvine, at 583 HL 478 (18 Nov. 1997) and 585 HL 755 (5 Feb. 1998).
141 See J. Straw and P. Boateng, *Bringing Rights Home* (Labour Party, 1996) (reprinted at [1997] EHRLR 71). This policy document was reinforced by an election manifesto pledge that '[c]itizens should have statutory rights to enforce their human rights in the UK courts. [New Labour] will by statute incorporate the European Convention on Human Rights into UK law to bring these rights home and allow our people access to them in their national courts': see *New Labour: Because Britain Deserves Better* (Labour Party, 1997). New Labour's commitment to this project became even more evident with the speedy publication of a White Paper (*Rights Brought Home: The Human Rights Bill* (Cm. 3782, 1997)) which detailed their intentions with regard to the HRA and explained that the aim of the legislation 'is a straightforward one. It is to make more directly accessible the rights which the British people already enjoy under the Convention. In other words, to bring those rights home' (para. 1.19).
142 Lester and Pannick, above n. 119, p. 18.
143 Ewing, above n. 139, p. 79.
144 S.1, HRA specifies the Convention rights which are to be given further effect in domestic law: they are the rights guaranteed under Arts. 2-12 and 14, ECHR; Arts. 1-3 of the First Protocol to the ECHR; and Arts. 1 and 2 of the Sixth Protocol to the ECHR. These rights are to be read in the light of the general protections contained in Arts. 16-18, ECHR. The Convention rights do not include Art. 1, ECHR (because the HRA itself gives effect to it by 'securing to people in [the UK] the rights and freedoms of [the ECHR]' (583 HL 475 (18 Nov. 1997) (Lord Irvine)), or Art. 13, ECHR (on which, see below pp. 29-30).

the judges and government so as to transform the protection of human rights in the UK and 'strengthen representative and democratic government'.[145]

The HRA is centred around four key innovations. First, in section 3, it provides that '[s]o far as it is possible to do so, primary and subordinate legislation must be read and given effect in a way which is compatible with the Convention rights'. This obligation applies to all courts and tribunals, and imposes an interpretative obligation which is alleged to go 'far beyond'[146] the previous rule which allowed courts to take the ECHR into account in resolving ambiguities in statutory provisions.

Secondly, where it is impossible to read a provision of primary legislation compatibly with a Convention right (or rights), the higher courts may make a declaration of incompatibility.[147] Any such declaration 'will encourage the government and Parliament to consider urgent amendments to the relevant legislative provision by remedial action'.[148] If 'compelling reasons' exist, the government may bring forward a remedial order to amend the incompatible legislation to the extent necessary to remove the incompatibility; such an order may also be used in order to respond to a decision of the European Court of Human Rights.[149] However, the HRA evidences a clear preference for 'the principle that primary legislation should be amended or repealed only by primary legislation'.[150] It also needs to be emphasised that a declaration of incompatibility cannot force a change in the law: Parliament has a discretion whether to remove an incompatibility,[151] and, unless and until, there is a legislative amendment, the legislative provision which has been declared incompatible remains valid and effective.[152] If Parliament refuses to make an amendment, the victim of the Convention right violation could then seek redress in the European Court of Human Rights. One example of a law in respect of which the New Labour government would not be willing to introduce an amendment was given by then Home Secretary, Jack Straw, during debates on the Human Rights Bill. Citing a scenario wherein a higher court issued a declaration of incompatibility in respect of the abortion law, he insisted that:

> [I]t would be wrong simply to accept what the committee [of the House of Lords] had said and that a right to abortion, albeit quite properly limited and developed in this country over a period of thirty years should suddenly be cast aside.[153]

The government did consider the possibility of giving the courts the power to set aside or strike down an Act of Parliament deemed to be incompatible with

---

145 306 HC 769 (16 Feb. 1998) (Jack Straw). Cf. below n. 343.
146 Above n. 141, para. 2.7.
147 Ss. 4 and 5, HRA. The power also applies in relation to delegated legislation in respect of which primary legislation prevents the removal of an incompatibility with Convention rights (s. 4(3) and (4)). Where primary legislation does not so require, judges must interpret delegated legislation compatibly with Convention rights or, if not possible, set it aside under s. 6(1).
148 Lester and Pannick, above n. 119, p. 17. The Bill's original proposals on remedial action (cl. 10) met with significant opposition and criticism, and were amended during the course of the parliamentary debates. Ss. 12 and 13, HRA are further examples of parliamentary amendments to the Human Rights Bill.
149 S. 10, HRA.
150 Ewing, above n. 139, p. 93.
151 S. 6(6), HRA.
152 S. 4(6), HRA. See further, 583 HL 546 (18 Nov. 1997).
153 317 HC 1301 (21 Oct. 1998).

the Convention rights, but rejected the idea on the basis that it would constitute an unwanted and potentially dangerous development. In so doing, it emphasised the value of parliamentary sovereignty, the risks of drawing judges into serious conflict with Parliament, and the fact that there was 'no evidence to suggest that [the judges] desire this power, nor that the public wish them to have it'.[154]

The third key feature of the HRA is contained within section 6. This makes it unlawful for public authorities (which include courts and tribunals and 'any person certain of whose functions are functions of a public nature')[155] to act in a manner which is incompatible with a Convention right.[156] A person who claims that a public authority has acted (or proposes to act) in a manner which is unlawful under the HRA may bring legal proceedings (section 7(1)(a)) or may rely on a Convention right in any legal proceedings (section 7(1)(b)), so long as they are or would be a 'victim' of the unlawful act for the purposes of the ECHR.[157] Courts are empowered to grant such relief or remedy, or make such orders as are considered just and appropriate, where they find that a public authority has acted (or proposes to act) in an unlawful manner (section 8(1)).

The final novel feature of the HRA is section 19. This section obliges a Minister of the Crown in charge of a Bill in either House of Parliament to make a written statement, before the second reading, about the compatibility of the proposed legislation with Convention rights. Where a Minister cannot confirm that the Bill is compatible with these rights, they must explain that the government nevertheless wishes to proceed with the Bill.

It is clear, therefore, that the HRA is 'no ordinary law'. The more pressing question, however, is: just how extraordinary or special is it likely to be in practice? Will it succeed in 'bringing rights home'? And, more fundamentally, what exactly is covered by such a goal?

III. REVIEWING THE HUMAN RIGHTS ACT: MORE DOCTRINAL ANALYSIS

The Act has generated an abundance of commentaries, and, not surprisingly, these commentaries have tended to range across the spectrum of possible reactions and approaches. Equally, however, closer examination suggests a preponderance of doctrinal analysis. The purpose of this Part, therefore, is to outline the issues which have been the most heavily discussed in those commentaries that adopt this perspective. This is an important task, not just because many of the points raised by individual commentators will be of crucial importance for legal strategies in the HRA era, but also because the focus and substance of these commentaries reveals the 'mindset'[158] of contemporary public lawyers and human rights lawyers in the UK. Part III should, however, be read alongside the one following, wherein 'judicialisation', the pre-eminent and more wide-ranging anxiety about the HRA era, is discussed.

---

154 Above n. 141, para. 2.13. Cf. the account of judical activism, below pp. 41–52.
155 S. 6(3). See further below pp. 33–35.
156 S. 6(2), HRA adds the proviso that an incompatible act will not be unlawful if primary legislation compels a public authority to act in a manner inconsistent with a Convention right.
157 See above n. 122 for the Art. 34, ECHR position on 'victims'.
158 This idea is taken from C. Harlow, 'Changing the Mindset: The Place of Theory in English Administrative Law' (1994) 14 OJLS 419.

Many overview, or general, commentaries, as provided by sections of the media and by academics, practitioners and pressure groups, have been positive (in contradiction to the pessimism of one Law Lord who dismissed the HRA as 'a field day for crackpots, a pain in the neck for judges, and a gold mine for lawyers'[159]). Individual journalists have, for example, drawn attention to alleged popular support for a Bill of Rights and increased judicialisation (although others, citing the volume of litigation in Scotland since the HRA came into force there in 1998, prefered to warn of the chaos and uncertainty which lay ahead for the UK legal systems).[160] A positive tone is also evident in a range of more academic general accounts of the HRA: Anthony Lester, for example, has suggested that there are 'only three imperfections in [this] otherwise brilliant Bill'[161] and welcomed it as 'a turning point in the UK's legal and constitutional history' and 'the beginning of a new era of greater executive accountability and greater domestic respect for human rights under the rule of law'.[162] Similar views have been expressed by other leading figures, including the administrative lawyer, William Wade (who visualised 'a quantum leap into a new legal culture of fundamental rights and freedoms'[163]), and Anthony Barnett, founder of Charter 88 (who heralded the onset of 'our constitutional revolution', noting that '"we the people" – to use a long-coined phrase that may finally become currency in Britain – have changed, especially in our relationship to authority'[164]). And, as noted earlier, the importance of the HRA to the Northern Ireland peace process has also received favourable comment.[165]

Positivity about the HRA, however, is not unanimous, and a significant proportion of the academic literature generated by the passage of the Act has

---

159   582 HL 1269 (3 Nov. 1997) (Lord McCluskey). See *Hoekstra v HM Advocate* (2000) SCCR 367 (repeat of comments by sitting judge in newspaper article breached right to fair trial).

160   See eg, H. Young, 'Politicised Judges May Now Learn to Keep Out of Politics', *The Guardian*, 20 Apr. 2000 ('The Human Rights Act is part of a wider public appetite to settle more by law than politics'); M. Linklater, 'A Judicial Iceberg That Threatens Our Rulers', *The Times*, 16 Mar. 2000 ('a massive legal iceberg heading our way from Strasbourg'); and M. Berlins, 'Writ Large', *The Guardian*, 24 Apr. 2000 ('The abolition of assistant recorders is the fault of the Human Rights Act . . .'). The former Home Secretary, Jack Straw, urged organisations 'not to panic' about the future and to use the HRA as an opportunity to develop the concept of 'corporate citizenship': *The Guardian* 1 Oct. 1998.

161   584 HL 1264 (19 Jan. 1998). The 'three imperfections' are the omission of Art. 13, ECHR, the absence of a Human Rights Commission, and the narrow standing rules: see Ewing, above n. 139, p. 85, n. 38.

162   A. Lester, 'The Impact of the Human Rights Act on Public Law' in *Constitutional Reform in the United Kingdom*, above n. 22, pp. 105-107, at p. 105. Particular optimism seemed to surround the HRA's potential for progressive impact on certain individual rights, with the issues of free speech, privacy, fair trial and sexual orientation generating headline-grabbing media coverage: see eg, L. Ward, 'Section 28 Violates Human Rights Act, Lawyers Claim', *The Guardian*, 30 Mar. 2000; and D. Pannick, 'Rape: Could it be a Case of Guilty Until Proven Innocent', *The Times*, 25 Apr. 2000 ('to reverse the burden of proof on consent . . . would breach the [ECHR]').

163   W. Wade, 'Human Rights and the Judiciary' [1998] EHRLR 520, 532.

164   A. Barnett, *This Time: Our Constitutional Revolution* (Vintage, 1997). The enthusiasm of others has been a great deal more contained: see eg, the speech delivered by the Home Secretary at the end of the Bill's passage through the House of Commons (arguing that '*over time*, the Bill will bring about the creation of a human rights culture in Britain' (317 HC 1358 (21 Oct. 1998) (emphasis added))).

165   See eg, Harvey, above n. 8; and B. Dickson, 'Northern Ireland' in Lester and Pannick, above n. 119, pp. 287-308.

concentrated on highlighting alleged omissions, deficiencies or other potential working problems.[166] One strand of these critiques is characterised by generalised disappointment with the chosen 'British model of incorporation'. Marshall[167] and Wade,[168] for example, have both argued the case for an entrenched Bill of Rights (as in the US and Canada), whereunder judges would have full powers of constitutional review of incompatible legislation. Other commentators within this broad strand have pointed to the limitations of the ECHR, emphasising that it 'is a mid-century bill of rights, designed to accommodate a number of countries with a variety of legal systems and political histories'[169] and that a home-grown, British Bill of Rights might have had a different, less individualist civil and political rights slant.[170]

The ECHR is undoubtedly a product of the circumstances surrounding its creation, in particular the fact that '[i]ts authors were not only looking over their shoulders at the tyranny of Nazism; they were looking ahead at a Europe in which strong pro-Communist parties were bidding for power'.[171] It is unsurprising then that 'for these and no doubt other reasons, the states that put together the European Convention placed their faith in the 19th-century liberal paradigm of the autonomous individual whose natural antagonist is the state; and that the European Convention therefore treats the state as a necessary evil in whose favour exceptions have to be made in what are otherwise the absolute rights of individuals'. Understanding the reasons for the structure and content of the ECHR does not, of course, offer an answer to the critics who point to the Convention's 'pre-modern' characteristics, notably the fact that it contains 'no underlying collectivist notion that the state may have positive obligations as a guarantor, if not a source, of individual security and opportunity, and no bedrock of fundamental duties of respect that individuals may owe one another'.[172]

A second, and far larger, strand of criticism of the HRA focuses not on generalised disappointment but on specific omissions, deficiencies and ambiguities. Particular sections of the Act have been subjected to intense

---

166 Critical commentaries started to appear once it became clear that the Labour Party planned to incorporate the ECHR (see eg, [1997] EHRLR 115-160) and have continued unabated (see eg, Grosz, Beatson and Duffy, above n. 139, pp. 133-152 on the HRA's impact on the range and nature of legal remedies).

167 Marshall, above n. 22. See also, T.H. Jones, 'The Devaluation of Human Rights Under the European Convention' [1995] PL 430.

168 W. Wade, 'The United Kingdom's Bill of Rights' in *Constitutional Reform in the United Kingdom*, above n. 22, pp. 61-68.

169 S. Kentridge, 'The Incorporation of the European Convention on Human Rights' in *Constitutional Reform in the United Kingdom*, above n. 22, pp. 69-72, at p. 69.

170 See eg, K.D. Ewing, 'Social Rights and Constitutional Law' [1999] PL 104. Three different non-governmental organisations, Liberty, the Institute for Public Policy Research (IPPR) and the Committee on the Administration of Justice (CAJ), were amongst those who produced 'home-grown' Bills of Rights in the early 1990s.

171 S. Sedley, 'A Bill of Rights for the United Kingdom: From London to Strasbourg by the Northwest Passage?' (1998) 36 Osg Hall LJ 63, 67. Similar arguments can be made with respect to the origins of UN human rights instruments.

172 Ibid. However, as Sedley goes on to explain, the ECtHR, which came into being in 1959, 'has not been idle': in particular, it has taken some steps towards the development of a concept of positive state obligation, ie, a duty to legislate to protect individuals' ECHR rights, in addition to the duty to refrain from infringing them (at p. 68 citing *Airey v Ireland* (1979) 2 EHRR 305 and *X and Y v Netherlands* (1985) 8 EHRR 235).

scrutiny in terms of their parliamentary origins, choice of wording and likely judicial interpretations. This ooze of doctrinal analysis is not in the least surprising; it is, however, extremely partial and also rather short-sighted. Consider, for example, the section 3 obligation to interpret legislation in accordance with Convention rights '[s]o far as it is possible to do so'. This obligation has been one of the most notable victims of doctrinal analysis, generating a literature which would satisfy even the most ardent fan of the rules of statutory interpretation.[173] The merits of such analyses, however, are surely questionable:

> The intended effect of s. 3 is quite unequivocal. It explicitly requires courts to use their interpretive ingenuity to avoid an incompatibility with Convention rights. Moreover, by making a declaration of incompatibility [under section 4] available in cases where a compatible interpretation is not possible, the scheme of the Act cleverly binds courts into a scheme which gives them every incentive to discover the interpretive flexibility to avoid granting such declarations. This makes them likely to reach compatible interpretations which they might not otherwise have reached by more traditional interpretive techniques. As the White Paper makes clear, the interpretive obligation imposed by s. 3 goes far beyond merely taking the Convention into account in resolving ambiguity in legislation.[174]

If this is correct, then the meaning of section 3 will not be found within the framework of traditional rules and principles of statutory interpretation; indeed, to adopt such an approach would be to 'mischaracterise the nature of the new interpretative obligation'. Section 3 also has the capacity to contribute to a reformulation of the doctrine of precedent: courts and tribunals will not be bound by previous interpretations of existing legislation, even by higher courts, if such interpretations did not consider the issue of compatibility with Convention rights.[175] However, as with statutory interpretation, this opportunity-value of section 3 may also be compromised and 'effectively neutralized by the prevailing legal culture if [the section] is understood, not as a transformative provision in its own right, but in terms of the very culture in reaction to which it is being introduced'.[176]

---

173 See eg, F. Bennion, 'What Interpretation is "Possible" Under Section 3(1) of the Human Rights Act 1998?' [2000] PL 77; G. Marshall, 'Interpreting Interpretation in the Human Rights Bill' [1998] PL 167; Lord Irvine, 'Activism and Restraint: Human Rights and the Interpretative Process' [1999] EHRLR 350; A. Lester, 'The Art of the Possible: Interpreting Statutes Under the Human Rights Act' [1998] EHRLR 665; Lord Steyn, 'Incorporation and Devolution: A Few Reflections on the Changing Scene' [1998] EHRLR 153; and Wade, above n. 168. On the range of interpretative approaches to s. 3, see Grosz, Beatson and Duffy, above n. 139, pp. 29-52.

174 M. Hunt, 'The Human Rights Act and Legal Culture: The Judiciary and the Legal Profession' (1998) 26 JLS 86, pp. 97-98. This view is confirmed by several cases interpreting s. 3: see eg, *Brown v Stott* [2001] 2 WLR 817 (PC) (Road Traffic Act 1988, s. 172 *compatible* with Art. 6); *R v A (No 2)* [2001] UKHL 25, [2001] 3 All ER 1 (HL) (Youth Justice and Criminal Evidence Act 1999, s. 41 *incompatible* with Art. 6); *R v Mental Health Review Tribunal, ex p H, The Times*, 2 Apr. 2001 (CA) (Mental Health Act 1983, ss. 72 and 73 *incompatible* with Art. 5); and *Wilson v First County Trust* [2001] 3 WLR 42 (CA) (Consumer Credit Act 1974, s. 127 *incompatible* with Art. 6).

175 *Bringing Rights Home* (Cm. 3782, 1997), para. 2.8.

176 Hunt, above n. 174, p. 97. See *R v A*, above n. 174, para. 108 (per Lord Hope): 'The rule of construction which section 3 lays down is quite unlike any previous rule of statutory interpretation.'

In the sections which follow, we shall outline the other main concerns of initial (largely doctrinal) studies of particular aspects of the HRA. These sections are complemented by, and should be seen as part of a package with, Part IV, wherein views on the impact of the HRA on judging and judges in the UK are examined and critiqued.

The impact on judicial review

There is considerable uncertainty as to how the new processes of judicial reasoning required under the HRA will impact on traditional standards of judicial review of public authority acts and subordinate legislation.[177] Some commentators predict 'a major departure from the conventional methodology of judicial review'[178] and 'significant changes'[179] of procedure, substance and culture. These changes may occur in several related ways. First, in considering whether there has been, or is likely to be, a breach of Convention rights, UK courts will have to take account of the more analytical ECHR jurisprudence on the justification for interference with rights, thereby facilitating the ousting of the haphazard common law approach,[180] in favour of a requirement that restrictions must satisfy the key Convention criteria: that is, be prescribed by law; pursue a legitimate aim; be necessary in a democratic society; and be non-discriminatory.[181] Secondly, the principle of proportionality (the 'necessity test') will be applied in a much wider range of contexts than before and may come to be recognised as a fundamental legal norm in UK law (as is already the case in the jurisprudence of the European Court of Human Rights and the European Court of Justice).[182] Furthermore, in assessing the proportionality of public authority action, a much more intrusive standard of review may have to be developed and applied than under the traditional *Wednesbury* test of unreasonableness or irrationality.[183] This is because interference with a Convention right must not only be necessary to meet a 'pressing social need', but the means used to achieve a legitimate aim must be proportionate.[184] Thirdly, as noted above in the discussion on section 3, the courts will have the opportunity (and indeed, should consider themselves obliged) to apply a new principle of statutory interpretation when considering 'whether an act of a public authority otherwise contrary to section 6 can be saved by primary legislation which is

177 For discussion of the impact on devolution of courts' interpretations of their powers of judicial review, see P. Craig and M. Walters, 'The Courts, Devolution and Judicial Review' [1999] PL 274.
178 M. Supperstone and J. Coppel, 'Judicial Review After the Human Rights Act' [1999] EHRLR 301.
179 Grosz, Beatson and Duffy, above n. 139, p. 106. See also, I. Leigh and L. Lustgarten, 'Making Rights Real: The Courts, Remedies, and the Human Rights Act' (1999) 58 CLJ 507, 522-542 (arguing, inter alia, that '[t]he requirement that public law cases raising human rights issues be brought exclusively by means of judicial review is likely to have a significant and adverse impact on the ability of individuals to enforce their rights effectively').
180 See eg, *Malone v Metropolitan Police Comr* [1979] Ch 344; and *R v Khan* [1996] 3 All ER 289 (HL).
181 See *R v Secretary of State for the Home Department, ex p Daly* [2001] UKHL 26, [2001] 3 All ER 433, para. 27.
182 On proportionality in EU law, see G. de Búrca, 'Proportionality and Wednesbury Unreasonableness: The Influence of European Legal Concepts on UK Law' (1997) 3 EPL 561; and F.G. Jacobs, 'Public Law: The Impact of Europe' [1999] PL 232.
183 See eg, the hopelessness of the *Wednesbury* standard in interrogating a ban on lesbians and gays serving in the armed services: *R v Ministry of Defence, ex p Smith* [1996] 1 All ER 257 (CA).
184 Contrast the approach of the CA in *Smith*, ibid., with that of the ECtHR in *Smith v UK* (1999) 29 EHRR 493.

itself incompatible with Convention rights . . .'.[185] Finally, in order to satisfy the requirements of Article 6 of the ECHR in relation to a full and fair hearing (and of Article 13 in relation to an effective remedy), there may be some shift in the traditional common law distinction between courts acting in a 'supervisory' rather than an 'appellate' role in judicial review proceedings. As a consequence of this, 'the sharp distinction between the approach to questions of law and that to questions of fact, and the general unwillingness to go behind the facts found or the inferences drawn by the decision-maker will require reconsideration where a case involves Convention rights'.[186] There is also likely to be a shift in legal culture in relation to the amount of evidence disclosed by public authorities, including a move towards the provision of reasons demonstrating the alleged justification for interference with Convention rights.[187]

The fundamental issue, however, is the depth of judicial scrutiny in individual cases, in particular the actual test of proportionality applied and the extent of any 'area of discretion' (howsoever that may be labelled) left to a public authority when reaching a decision.[188] Recent judgments suggest that this is a matter of some sensitivity amongst the judiciary. Certain judges in the Court of Appeal have openly applied a heightened standard of judicial review, requiring a public authority to explicitly justify interference with Convention rights and thereby involving judges in a genuine examination of the process and merits of the decision.[189] The Law Lords, however, have been rather more guarded about their approach(es), as evidenced for example by the majority opinion in *International Trader's Ferry*,[190] which was described as 'the clearest expression of an implicit test of proportionality as a ground of review in general administrative law, while never explicitly labelling it as such'.[191] The approach which eventually emerges will depend on how judges perceive their role in the HRA era. Thus, as Supperstone and Coppel have pointed out, '[j]udicial deference or not, as the case may be, is, accordingly, the key ingredient which must be added to the bare bones of the three-stage analysis in order to produce a complete picture of the proportionality test':

> [P]roportionality is not, in and of itself, a more intensive standard of review than the *Wednesbury* test. It entails a different analytical approach, but, so far as the intensity

---

185 Supperstone and Coppel, above n. 178, p. 312 (discussing the likely judicial approach under ss. 6(2) and 3(2)(b)).

186 Grosz, Beatson and Duffy, above n. 139, p. 124.

187 See eg, *RJR-MacDonald Inc v Canada* [1995] 3 SCR 199 (re Canadian government's failure to provide sufficient evidence to justify tobacco advertising restrictions which violated the right to freedom of expression under the Charter).

188 See generally, H. Fenwick, 'The Right to Protest, the Human Rights Act and the Margin of Appreciation' (1999) 62 MLR 491; D. Pannick, 'Principles of Interpretation of Convention Rights Under the Human Rights Act and the Discretionary Area of Judgment' [1998] PL 545; R. Singh, M. Hunt and M. Demetriou, 'Is There a Role For the Margin of Appreciation in National Law After the Human Rights Act?' [1999] EHRLR 15; and Jones, above n. 167.

189 See the endorsement of this approach in *B v Secretary of State for the Home Department* [2000] Imm AR 478 (deportation breached principle of proportionality as interference with free movement of EU national and Art. 8, ECHR). Contrast *R v Secretary of State for the Home Department, ex p Turgut* [2000] Imm AR 306; *R (Mahmood) v Secretary of State for the Home Department* [2001] 1 WLR 840; and *R v Secretary of State for the Home Department, ex p Isiko* [2001] 1 FCR 633 (CA).

190 *R v Chief Constable of Sussex, ex p International Trader's Ferry* [1999] 1 All ER 129.

191 G. Wong, 'Towards the Nutcracker Principle: Reconsidering the Objections to Proportionality' [2000] PL 92, 109. See Lord Bingham's 'common law' approach in *Daly*, above n. 181.

or intrusiveness of review is concerned, it is an empty vessel. Proportionality may be a highly intensive standard of review, or it may be as deferential as the *Wednesbury* test, depending upon the extent to which the courts defer to the decision-maker's view of proportionality in any particular case.[192]

Judicial deference, or not, is also, of course, of relevance outside the terrain of the proportionality test; it will be the determining factor more generally on the extent of the discretion accorded to decision-makers in judicial review. Presently, however, all of this is distinctly grey area. Moreover, recourse to the range of different tests which exist for assessing the justification of state interference with fundamental human rights will not clarify matters.[193] The application of such tests is as dependent on the broad social and political contexts in which the adjudication occurs as it is on any prescribed legal criteria.[194] The upshot is that, as we discuss below in relation to the changing nature of judicialisation, and as evidenced throughout this book (on issues as diverse as police powers, prisoners, sexual orientation and national security), the role of the judiciary needs to be recognised as complex and contingent, and as not easily captured by prediction.[195]

The right to a remedy

A further focal point for criticism is the omission of Article 13 of the ECHR – which guarantees everyone whose rights have been violated 'an effective remedy before a national authority' – from the list of Convention rights in the HRA.[196] Government ministers used the debates on the Bill to insist that Article 13's inclusion would be superfluous as the very passing of the HRA satisfied the obligation imposed by the provision.[197] These insistences do not, however, provide a complete response to the complexities created by the omission.

It is clear that pursuant to section 2 of the HRA, the courts will be able to take account of the ECHR jurisprudence on Article 13 in the same way as that on any other Article.[198] Furthermore, as Phillipson has pointed out, the right to a remedy provided by section 8 of the HRA is much more restrictive than Article 13; a remedy is only available against any 'act (or proposed act) of a public authority'.[199] Most crucially, perhaps, the casual assumption that the

---

192 Above n. 178, pp. 314-315. See *R v Lord Saville, ex p A* [1999] 4 All ER 860.

193 See eg, the Canadian SCt approach in *R v Oakes* [1986] 1 SCR 103.

194 For detailed argument along these lines, see eg, A. Hutchinson, 'The Rise and Ruse of Administrative Law and Scholarship' (1985) 48 MLR 293; M. Loughlin, 'The Underside of Law: Judicial Review and the Prison Disciplinary System' (1993) 46 CLP 23; S. Halliday, 'The Influence of Judicial Review on Bureaucratic Decision-Making' [2000] PL 110; and D. Cooper, *Sexing the City: Lesbian and Gay Politics Within the Activist State* (Rivers Oram, 1994).

195 Even the dynamics of an individual court make generalisations problematic: see eg, D. Robertson, *Judicial Discretion in the House of Lords* (Clarendon, 1998).

196 See eg, Marshall, above n. 22, p. 77; Grosz, Beatson and Duffy, above n. 139, pp. 5-6. Art. 13, ECHR reads: 'Everyone whose rights and freedoms as set forth in the Convention are violated shall have an effective remedy before a national authority notwithstanding that the violation has been committed by persons acting in an official capacity.'

197 See eg, 582 HL 1308 (3 Nov. 1997) (Lord Williams of Mostyn); 583 HL 475 (18 Nov. 1997) (Lord Irvine).

198 583 HL 475-477 (18 Nov. 1997) (Lord Irvine); and 312 HC 978-981 (20 May 1998) (Jack Straw).

199 See below, pp. 35-39 on the possible significance of this limitation in relation to the HRA's application to the acts of private bodies and individuals.

requirements of Article 13 will be satisfied by the fact that a human rights complaint can be articulated before a domestic court, and also that such a court will always be capable of providing an effective remedy, would appear to be contradicted by the European Court of Human Rights in several important judgments.

The first of these judgments is *Smith v UK*,[200] where a Ministry of Defence blanket ban on lesbians and gays in the armed forces was successfully challenged. The Strasbourg Court ruled that the applicants did not have an effective domestic remedy as required by Article 13 because the test of irrationality ('outrageous in its defiance of logic') was set at such a high level that the UK courts were precluded from even considering whether the alleged interference with private lives could be justified on the basis of social need, national security or public order. Similarly, while the House of Lords in *R v Khan*[201] considered that the discretion of the trial judge to exclude evidence obtained illegally or improperly (a tape-recorded conversation obtained by a police listening device) under section 78 of the Police and Criminal Evidence Act 1984 (PACE) ensured the fairness of the trial – and thus provided an effective remedy for an alleged violation of the Article 8 right to privacy – the Strasbourg Court ruled to the contrary:

> The Court would note at the outset that the courts in the criminal proceedings were not capable of providing a remedy because, although they could consider questions of the fairness of admitting the evidence in the criminal proceedings, it was not open to them to deal with the substance of the Convention complaint that the interference with the applicant's right to respect for his private life was not 'in accordance with the law' [as required by Article 8 of the ECHR]; still less was it open to them to grant appropriate relief in connection with the complaint. . . . As regards the various other avenues open to the applicant in respect of the Article 8 complaint [such as the Police Complaints Authority] . . . the Court finds that the system of investigation of complaints does not meet the requisite standards of independence needed to constitute sufficient protection against the abuse of authority and thus provide an effective remedy within the meaning of Article 13.[202]

These judgments will have significant implications for UK courts when assessing the extent of the 'practical and effective' nature of remedies. Courts and tribunals under the HRA cannot refuse to consider the substance of alleged human rights violations, and must provide 'appropriate relief' if the complaint is well-founded. It is also clear that the composition and procedures of other investigatory authorities are vulnerable to challenge (especially where allegations of serious human rights violations such as death, torture or serious injury are in issue[203]).

---

200 (1999) 29 EHRR 493. See *R v Secretary of State for the Home Department, ex p Daly* [2001] UKHL 26, [2001] 3 All ER 433.

201 [1996] 3 All ER 289.

202 *Khan v UK* (2000) 8 BHRC 310, paras. 44-47. See also *Keenan v UK* (ECtHR, 3 April 2001) (violation of Art. 13 as no remedy available for mentally-disturbed prisoner to challenge additional punishment; and to examine liability of prison authorities for suffering caused to prisoner prior to death, or for failing to prevent prisoner's death by suicide).

203 See *Kaya v Turkey* (1998) 28 EHRR 1 (violation of Art. 13 as 'serious deficiencies' in autopsy and forensic examinations and no 'thorough and effective' investigation by authorities into disputed killing by state forces). See also, *Z v UK* [2001] 2 FLR 246 (ECtHR).

The definition of 'victim' and standing to litigate

The question of who qualifies as a victim under the HRA has also attracted critical attention. Only a person who claims that they are or would be a victim of an unlawful act by a public authority may bring a claim under section 7 of the Act.[204] This contrasts with the wider 'sufficient interest' test in judicial review proceedings where the courts have adopted an 'increasingly liberal approach'[205] to the question of standing. It also contrasts with the ECHR case law on the meaning of 'victim', which evidences a similarly broad approach.[206]

Concern has been voiced as to whether the section 7 definition will prevent non-governmental organisations (NGOs), which commonly fund, and provide legal advice for, judicial review challenges, from fronting litigation under the HRA.[207] In response, however, it has been suggested that the 'rigours of the victim test' may be mitigated by NGOs using a suitable victim as the named applicant, whilst still funding the legal action themselves, and by courts increasingly allowing the participation of NGOs in human rights litigation through the filing of *amicus* briefs.[208] It has also been pointed out that section 11 of the HRA[209] expressly preserves all other legal avenues for 'non-victims' to challenge alleged violations of human rights; that is, 'pressure groups and others who are not victims remain entitled to mount challenges in judicial review proceedings based upon a violation of fundamental rights conferred by the common law and by European Community law'.[210] Furthermore, given that respect for the ECHR is also a general principle of EC law, and the standing rule for alleging a breach of Community law is close to the 'sufficient interest' test in domestic judicial review proceedings, it seems unlikely that the UK courts, if they were so minded, would be able to sustain a 'dual-track system of public law litigation'[211] in relation to the 'victim' test under the HRA.

The issue of standing is also, however, closely connected with the broader question of the legitimate scope of a Bill of Rights in regulating the activities of private individuals and bodies. As will be discussed below, there remains a large question mark over the extent to which the UK courts will extend the reach of the HRA into the private sphere. Moreover, although there has been considerable academic discussion about the possible 'legality' (under section 6

---

204 See Grosz, Beatson and Duffy, above n. 139, pp. 75-88.

205 *R v Foreign Secretary, ex p World Development Movement Ltd* [1995] 1 WLR 386, 395 (per Rose LJ).

206 See Harris, O'Boyle and Warbrick, above n. 119, pp. 632-638.

207 See eg, *R v Lord Chancellor, ex p Child Poverty Action Group* [1998] 2 All ER 755; and *R v Secretary of State for Trade and Industry, ex p Greenpeace (No. 2)* [2000] 2 CMLR 95. Cf. *R v Greater Belfast Cononers, ex p Northern Ireland Human Rights Commission*, *The Times*, 11 May 2001 (NIHRC refused intervenor status).

208 Supperstone and Coppel, above n. 178, p. 308.

209 S.11 provides that '[a] person's reliance on a Convention right does not restrict: (a) any other right or freedom conferred on him by or under any law having effect in any part of the United Kingdom; or (b) his right to make any claim or bring any proceedings which he could make or bring apart from sections 7 to 9'.

210 Supperstone and Coppel, above n. 168, p. 309. Cf. Grosz, Beatson and Duffy, above n. 119, p. 82 (noting the risk that s. 7 may be interpreted as a 'statutory removal of standing from public interest groups disabling them from making appropriate, important human rights challenges').

211 S. De Smith, H. Woolf and J. Jowell, *Judicial Review of Administrative Action* (Sweet & Maxwell, 1998), p. 613. See also, *R v Secretary of State for the Home Department, ex p McQuillan* [1995] 4 All ER 400 (Sedley J).

of the HRA) of extended judicial regulation of private action, little attention
has been directed at the political aims or merits of such a development.
Awareness of the strategic use of human rights discourse by pressure groups
and individuals in other jurisdictions such as Ireland and Canada would cast a
pall over uncritical advocacy of wide rules of standing. In particular, the
traditional exclusion of 'busy-bodies and mischief makers'[212] from seeking
judicial review of public authority action takes on a much sharper focus where
private groups are able to target *private individuals* for allegedly violating
fundamental human rights. Anti-abortion campaigners, for example, were
successful in convincing the Irish courts to award them standing in order to
'police' state abortion law, and to seek the closure of counselling services
providing abortion information, on the basis that the right to life of the 'unborn'
was threatened.[213] Several other jurisdictions have had similar experiences with
private parties seeking to undermine abortion legislation or to prevent individual
women securing terminations of pregnancy.[214] Such recourse to the courts has,
on occasion, resulted in the immediate issue of injunctions restraining the
freedom and autonomy of individuals. Expensive and lengthy litigation can
ensue before eventual resolution of the issue.[215] Furthermore, as many feminist
commentaries on anti-abortion politics have highlighted, the use of legal (rights)
discourse in this context can skew important debates on consent, autonomy
and reproductive health.

Critical attention, therefore, needs to be directed to the difficult questions
surrounding the permitted standing of private individuals and groups. While
the right of access to court is clearly to be cherished (particularly, in light of
the historic exclusion of prisoners from challenging state power[216]), it is a mistake
to accept it as an apolitical procedural right and universal good. Instead, the
risk of judicial bias, in the narrowing of the rules of standing to suit judicially
desired political outcomes, has to be weighed against the equal risk that
(sometimes internationally) well-funded and partisan groups will seek to use
the HRA as a tool for regressive ends, in particular for targeting vulnerable and
historically disadvantaged groups. A context-sensitive application of rules of
standing would offer one potential safeguard against pressure-group litigation
which has as its aim the deliberate undermining of other core rights and values
protected by the HRA (such as the privacy and equality rights of women, lesbians
or gays). Moreover, although one government minister revealed in
parliamentary debates that the aim of the restricted standing rule under the

---

212 See eg, *IRC v National Federation of Self-Employed* [1982] AC 617.
213 See M. Fox and T. Murphy, 'Irish Abortion: Seeking Refuge in a Jurisprudence of Doubt and
     Delegation' (1992) 19 JLS 454; N. Whitty, 'Law and the Regulation of Reproduction in Ireland:
     1922-1992' (1993) 43 U of Toronto LJ 851; G. de Búrca, 'Fundamental Human Rights and
     the Reach of EC Law' (1993) 13 OJLS 283; R. Fletcher, 'Silences: Irish Women and Abortion'
     (1995) 50 Fem R 44; and her '"Pro-Life" Absolutes, Feminist Challenges: The Fundamentalist
     Narrative of Irish Abortion Law 1986-1992' (1998) 36 Osg Hall LJ 1.
214 See *Minister of Justice of Canada v Borowski* [1981] 2 SCR 575 (plaintiff seeking a declaration
     that abortion provisions were inoperative); and *Daigle v Tremblay* [1989] 2 SCR 530 (plaintiff
     seeking injunction against former girlfriend to prevent her having an abortion).
215 The legal claims of Irish anti-abortion campaigners (to which the Irish Attorney General
     became a party) were eventually rejected in both the ECJ and the ECtHR: see *Society for the
     Protection of Unborn Children v Grogan* [1991] 3 CMLR 849; and *Open Door Counselling and
     Dublin Well Woman Centre v Ireland* (1992) 15 EHRR 244.
216 More generally on prisoners' rights, see Ch. 5.

HRA was to prevent 'interest groups from SPUC to Liberty . . . [venturing] into frolics of their own in the courts',[217] it should be possible for judges to distinguish between the purposes and expertise of an anti-abortion group and respected NGOs such as Liberty, Amnesty International or the Joint Council for the Welfare of Immigrants.

In suggesting this, however, we do not wish to be seen as advocating a strict division between those groups attempting to appropriate state power to interfere with the rights of private individuals and groups attempting to reverse direct state interference with human rights. As we highlight in other chapters, straightforward accounts of the public/private divide, and the traditional civil libertarian distrust of state power, are challenged by campaigns against racism, pornography or live animal exports which make appeals for the use of state power against respectively National Front marchers, the pornography industry and ferry companies. What we are arguing for is a more explicit politicisation of public law terminology (such as 'public interest', 'responsible challenger' and 'unmeritorious application') at all stages of the legal process. This can only be achieved if more attention is paid to the historical, social, political and cultural contexts in which human rights violations occur, and the relative powerlessness of certain groups and perspectives in society is openly acknowledged. It also requires judges to be aware both of the personal consequences of litigation for the parties involved (including the fundamental interests at stake where, for example, a court delays a pregnancy termination or compels medical intervention or detention), and of the symbolic importance of a 'day in court' (which may be crucial in diffusing political tension, or threatened public disorder).

Defining a public authority and public function

The duty imposed by section 6(1) of the HRA on every 'public authority' to act in a manner compatible with Convention rights (save where exempted under section 6(2) because of the unambiguous obligation of other primary legislation) has provided another fruitful source of commentary and critique, and offered a new site for a re-run of familiar arguments about the correct parameters of the jurisdiction of judicial review: that is, what is a 'public' body, and when does it perform a 'public function'?[218] Parliamentary debates on the Human Rights Bill implied that government Ministers would be content to let judges determine the reach of the HRA in this area. But how should the judiciary make such a determination? They could build on their existing administrative law jurisprudence and fix a public/private divide according to criteria such as the identification of 'a public element, which can take many different forms',[219] the source of a body's authority (statute, prerogative power or contract), or the exercise of powers classed as 'governmental' in nature.[220] The combination of these criteria has, however, produced somewhat inconsistent definitional

---

217 314 HC 1086 (24 Jun. 1998).

218 See eg, N. Bamforth, 'The Scope of Judicial Review: Still Uncertain' [1993] PL 239; M.J. Beloff, 'Judicial Review – 2001: A Prophetic Odyssey' (1995) 58 MLR 143; H. Woolf, 'Droit Public – English Style' [1995] PL 57; and the essays in Taggart, above n. 28.

219 *R v Panel on Take-Overs and Mergers, ex p Datafin* [1987] QB 815, 838 (per Donaldson MR).

220 *R v Disciplinary Committee of the Jockey Club, ex p Aga Khan* [1993] 1 WLR 909 (per Hoffmann LJ).

outcomes[221] (although the general direction of the courts has been towards expanding the range of 'government' activities subject to judicial review – for example, the Bar Council, the Stock Exchange, the Advertising Standards Authority[222]). Certain actions of public authorities, such as employment disputes, remain immune from judicial review;[223] contractual functions of public authorities (such as government departments) may be considered private commercial functions; and the Jockey Club (despite its powerful position at the head of the state-funded racing industry) is considered a private body, whereas the Press Complaints Commission (a voluntary organisation of media personnel) is not.[224]

The former Home Secretary, Jack Straw, argued that the test under the HRA 'must relate to the substance and nature of the act, not to the form and legal personality'.[225] The obvious category of public authorities will, therefore, continue to be historic 'state actors' (government departments, local authorities, police, prisons); the less obvious will be those 'borderline' public authorities that have a mix of public and private functions (privatised utilities, security companies, private nursing homes, housing associations). For example, the Lord Chancellor has stated:

> Railtrack would fall into that category because it exercises public functions in its role as a safety regulator, but it is acting privately in its role as a property developer. A private security company would be exercising public functions in relation to the management of a contracted-out prison but would be acting privately when, for example, guarding commercial premises. Doctors in general practice would be public authorities in relation to their National Health Service functions, but not in relation to their private patients.[226]

It remains to be seen, however, whether and how the courts will reshape the definitions of 'public' and 'private' body; a conceptual distinction developed in an era where human rights considerations were either not an issue, ignored or only sporadically acknowledged in litigation. As Bamforth has pointed out, the parliamentary discussion about the definition of a public authority under section 6(1) does not square with the current parameters of judicial review where courts use a variety of criteria relating both to the source of a body's power and the nature of its functions.[227] Neither does it square with the ECHR

---

221 See generally, T. Prosser, 'Journey Without Maps? Review of Martin Loughlin: *Public Law and Political Theory*' [1993] PL 346; C. Harlow, 'Changing the Mindset: The Place of Theory in English Administrative Law' (1994) 14 OJLS 419; and Harlow and Rawlings, above n. 79.

222 *R v General Council of the Bar, ex p Percival* [1991] 1 QB 212; *R v ISE of the UK and Ireland, ex p Else* [1993] QB 534; and *R v ASA, ex p Insurance Service* (1990) 2 Admin LR 77.

223 *R v CPS, ex p Hogg* (CA) [1994] 6 Admin LR 778; *R v Derbyshire CC, ex p Noble* [1991] CLY 59; and *R v BBC, ex p Lavelle* [1983] 1 WLR 23.

224 *R v Press Complaints Commission, ex p Stewart-Brady* (1996) 9 Admin LR 274. See also *R v Football Association, ex p Football League* [1993] 2 All ER 833.

225 314 HC 433 (17 Jun. 1998).

226 583 HL 811 (24 Nov. 1997). Where bodies have mixed functions, s. 6(5) of the HRA explicitly provides that a person is not a public authority if 'the nature of the act is private'.

227 N. Bamforth, 'The Application of the Human Rights Act 1998 to Public Authorities and Private Bodies' (1999) 58 CLJ 159, 161. Canadian law in this area is also complex: see the Canadian SCt's early attempt to resolve the issue in *Retail, Wholesale and Department Store Union v Dolphin Delivery* [1986] 2 SCR 573 (where it was held that a court order, when issued in *private* party litigation and when based on common law, is *not* governmental action and thus Canadian Charter does not apply). However, where the state is a party to litigation, or where legislation governs the issue, the Charter will apply: see *Eldridge v British Columbia* [1997] 3 SCR 624 (re hospitals bound by Charter when implementing government policy or programmes). For more detail, see P. Hogg, *Constitutional Law of Canada* (Carswell, 1999), pp. 683-711.

case law involving private schools and UK state obligations; while the UK government has been liable in Strasbourg for human rights violations in private educational facilities (for example, the use of corporal punishment[228]), domestic judicial review is not available where the relationship between private school and fee-paying parents is purely contractual.[229] An ongoing issue to be clarified in the HRA era, therefore, is how judges resolve the apparent inconsistencies between the test for determining a 'public authority' under section 6 and the old test for judicial review purposes.[230] Most importantly, from a civil liberties perspective, it remains to be seen how judges will react to the statutory immunity against HRA scrutiny afforded to certain state activities, even though clearly performed by public authorities – with a long history of 'misuse' of state power.[231]

Private autonomy and power: the Human Rights Act's horizontal effect

A much more intense debate about the effect of the HRA on private autonomy and power has been sparked by the meaning of section 6(3) of the Act. This section explicitly includes courts (and tribunals) in the definition of a public authority and raises the question of the extent of the general obligation on *courts* to act compatibly with the Convention – regardless of whether public authorities *or* private parties are involved in litigation. The shorthand for the resulting debate, which has so far generated a more diverse range of commentaries than any other section of the Act, is the potential *horizontal effect* of the HRA on private parties.[232] Three main perspectives have been put forward, with various academics and practitioners lining up behind each position. The first perspective, and the catalyst for the entire debate, is provided by Wade's dramatic contention that section 6(3) in effect binds judges *never* to act incompatibly with the Convention.[233] His argument flows both from the 'letter of the law' and the 'spirit' of the Act:

> Since the courts are themselves made 'public authorities' and since it is unlawful for a public authority to act in a way which is incompatible with Convention rights, a court will be unable to give a lawful judgment, if a Convention rights point arises, except in accordance with that right. . . . In the Parliamentary debates much was

---

228 See *Costello-Roberts v UK* (1993) 19 EHRR 112.

229 *R v Inc Froebel Educational Institute, ex p L* [1999] ELR 488; *R v Fernhill Manor School, ex p Brown* (1993) 5 Admin LR 159. Cf. *Clark v University of Lincolnshire and Humberside* [2000] 3 All ER 752; and *R v HM Treasury, ex p University of Cambridge* [2000] 1 WLR 2514 (ECJ).

230 See the leading decision by Woolf LCJ in *Poplar Housing and Regeneration Community Association Ltd v Donoghue* [2001] EWCA Civ 595. See G. Morris, 'The Human Rights Act and the Public/ Private Divide in Employment Law' (1998) 27 ILJ 293; and D. Oliver, 'The Frontiers of the State: Public Authorities and Public Functions under the Human Rights Act' [2000] PL 476.

231 Complaints about alleged violations of privacy due to the interception and surveillance actions of MI5, MI6, GCHQ and police agencies must be directed to a special tribunal rather than in the form of legal action under the HRA in a court: see Regulation of Investigatory Powers Act 2000; and Chs. 6 and 7.

232 *Vertical* effect describes the HRA's primary purpose in protecting the citizen's rights against state power. See generally, I. Leigh, 'Horizontal Rights, the Human Rights Act and Privacy: Lessons from the Commonwealth?' (1999) 48 ICLQ 57; and A. Clapham, *Human Rights in the Private Sphere* (Clarendon, 1993).

233 See W. Wade, 'The United Kingdom's Bill of Rights' in *Constitutional Reform in the United Kingdom: Practice and Principles* (Hart, 1998), pp. 61-68; and Wade [1998] EHRLR 520.

said about the definition of 'public authorities' and about the bodies which might or might not fall within it. But horizontality will eliminate such problems altogether, since Convention rights will take effect against public and private persons equally, thus saving a great deal of litigation. . . . [A] new culture of human rights has developed in the Western world, and the citizen can legitimately expect that his human rights will be respected by his neighbours as well as by his government.[234]

The second perspective on horizontal effect is provided by Murray Hunt. He too argues for an unequivocal duty on the courts to ensure that all existing law is compatible with Convention rights, but not to the extent of totally collapsing the public/private divide through the creation of new causes of action (as appears to have been advocated by Wade[235]). Thus, while the HRA does not permit *direct* horizontal effect, there is an *indirect* horizontal effect flowing from the courts' duty under section 6:

> Law which *already exists* and governs private relations must be interpreted, applied and if necessary developed so as to achieve compatibility with the Convention. But where no cause of action exists, and there is no therefore no law to apply, the courts cannot invent new causes of action, as that would be to embrace full horizontality.[236]

The third perspective is provided by Phillipson. Unlike the above two accounts, it suggests a much narrower scope of application for section 6 based on a consideration of the origins and full text of the HRA, the parliamentary debates, and the jurisprudence of the European Court of Human Rights. Phillipson accepts that the HRA will clearly have some form of horizontal effect: the section 3 duty to interpret *all* legislation in accordance with Convention rights applies whether the legislation regulates public or private activity; and section 6 defines all courts and tribunals as public authorities who must act compatibly with the Convention. However, he goes on to insist that 'the attempt to deduce from the HRA a general and absolute duty to achieve conformity of the common law with Convention rights is unpersuasive and will not be accepted by the courts . . .'.[237]

In a detailed analysis, he identifies six factors which he suggests indicate that the courts will have a *discretion* as to whether to adopt a 'strong' or 'weak' version of indirect horizontal effect. First, he rejects arguments (such as Wade's) that the clear legislative intention only to bind public authorities under section 6 of the HRA, and to provide procedures and remedies specifically for this purpose, will be blatantly short-circuited by courts adopting an expansive role in litigation involving private bodies. Secondly, the fact that Convention rights are not *directly* incorporated into domestic law (for example, a right of privacy is not created by the HRA itself) means that the courts cannot be under a duty under section 6(1)

---

234 W. Wade, 'Horizons of Horizontality' (2000) 116 LQR 217, 220 and 223-224.
235 'Whether this is called direct or indirect effect or a new cause of action seems to be a matter of words and to make no intelligible difference': ibid., p. 222.
236 M. Hunt, 'The Horizontal Effect of the Human Rights Act' [1998] PL 423, 442. See also, R. Singh, 'Privacy and the Media after the Human Rights Act' (1998) EHRLR 712; B. Markesinis, 'Privacy, Freedom of Expression and the Horizontal Effect of the Human Rights Bill: Lessons from Germany' (1999) 115 LQR 47, 72-74 (arguing that the question 'is not *whether* we can privatise human rights but *to what extent* we should do so'); and Lester and Pannick, above n. 119, p. 32 (stating that 'the HRA 1998 will have an indirect but powerful influence upon private law rights and obligations in tort, contract and other contexts in which the Convention imposes minimum standards which the United Kingdom must guarantee').
237 G. Phillipson, 'The Human Rights Act, "Horizontal Effect" and the Common Law: A Bang or a Whimper?' (1999) 62 MLR 824, 845.

to uphold Convention rights that do not legally exist in the private sphere.[238] Thirdly, section 8 of the HRA requires the courts only to grant remedies against the acts of public authorities; not against the acts of private bodies.[239] Fourthly, if the courts are under an absolute *duty* (rather than having a freedom) to develop all law in accordance with Convention rights, many existing rules and values in the common law will have to be refashioned – an outcome so radical that it contradicts clear parliamentary statements on the purpose of the HRA and jettisons the incremental nature of common law development:

> Courts under the Hunt [and Wade] model[s], would thus simply have to disregard the rules of the relevant current tort and the values underpinning it and change automatically all its pre-existing rules into compliance with whatever the relevant Convention Article demanded. . . . It would be a startling thing if a Human Rights Act which conspicuously omits any mention of private common law were to be found by this indirect route, to require this potentially radical and wholesale revision of it.[240]

Fifthly, while the imposition of liability on public authorities (for example, injunctions or damages[241]) for violation of Convention rights is clearly intended by the HRA, the potentially onerous nature of widespread court-sanctioned regulation of private bodies and individuals is not mandated either by legislation or parliamentary debate. Finally, even assuming that the courts are under a duty to interpret the common law in accordance with Convention rights, the actual jurisprudence of the European Court of Human Rights on a state's obligations to protect rights in the private sphere is easily satisfied because of the doctrine of the margin of appreciation.[242] No Strasbourg case law suggests that courts are under a *general* duty to intervene to prevent human rights violations in the private sphere and, where state intervention is expressly required,[243] specific remedial outcomes are not prescribed but left to the discretion of the individual state.

Phillipson concludes by predicting that the HRA will have a minimal general horizontal effect on the common law affecting private individuals and organisations; that Convention rights will gradually, over time, inform principles and values in litigation; and that any judicial willingness to apply the same HRA standards to public authorities and private parties (for example, in relation

---

238 Some commentators have stressed the significance of the omission from the HRA of Art. 1, ECHR (which secures 'to everyone within their jurisdiction the rights and freedoms in . . . this Convention').

239 The specific exclusion of Art. 13, ECHR (which guarantees everyone whose rights have been violated 'an effective remedy before a national authority') from the HRA reinforces the view that the courts are under no obligation always to provide a remedy where violations are not committed by public authorities.

240 Phillipson, above n. 237, p. 839. Cf. Wade, above n. 234, p. 223 (arguing that this 'benign effect does not seem to have been appreciated, so that no Parliamentary intention can be discerned'). See *Z v UK* [2001] 2 FCR 246 (ECtHR) (re negligence claims).

241 See Bamforth, above n. 228, p. 159 (discussing possible remedies available against judicial and non-judicial public authorities).

242 Harris, O'Boyle and Warbrick, above n. 119, pp. 12-15, 321-322.

243 See eg, *A v UK* (1998) 27 EHRR 611 (violation of Art. 3, ECHR because UK law in effect permitted 'inhuman or degrading treatment or punishment' in relation to parental corporal punishment of child); and *Osman v UK* (1998) 29 EHRR 245 (state could in principle be liable under Art 2, ECHR for failure to intervene where life at risk from the criminal acts of another). See also S. Sedley, *Freedom, Law and Justice* (Sweet & Maxwell, 1999), p. 24 (national courts 'may be under an obligation to take legal steps to prevent interference by non-state actors with a Convention right').

to similar violations of an individual's privacy by police, media, employer or neighbour) will be an incremental process.

These conclusions resonate with those in other academic commentaries, including for example Grosz, Beatson and Duffy who argue that 'such development may be slow, as it is likely, at least in the early stages of the development of HRA jurisprudence, that the courts will adhere to their traditional incremental approach to the judicial development of the common law'.[244] There has also been a strong rejection of the Wade view (and, implicitly, of Hunt's[245]) in the extra-judicial writing of Buxton, a Lord Justice of the Court of Appeal. Buxton emphasises that the HRA is 'an orthodox English Act of Parliament' in contrast to Canadian or New Zealand human rights documents with '"constitutional" status', or European Community law where 'the underlying treaty itself creates rights between private citizens'.[246] Basing the first leg of his argument on the nature of the ECHR as an international treaty, with the state/citizen relationship as the exclusive focus, he finds no support for the claim that the ECHR affects legal relationships between private parties (especially as Article 1 is omitted from the HRA). Drawing on the facts of *A v UK*, where the Strasbourg Court found a violation of Article 3 because the defence of 'reasonable chastisement' in UK law permitted violent parental corporal punishment of a child, Buxton argues:

> This case would seem to come closer than any other to recognising an effect of the E.C.H.R. between private citizens. Nevertheless, the E.C.H.R. right is still stated to be a right to protection by the state, rather than a right directly against the ill-treating person. . . . If A's E.C.H.R. right was that there should be an effective system of national law, the respondent to that right being the national state, that right cannot translate into a Convention right under the H.R.A. directly against the stepfather. . . . [Furthermore] the Convention rights brought into national law by the H.R.A. do not include the rights set out in article 1 of the E.C.H.R.: so whatever right that was recognised in *A v United Kingdom* is not in any event a Convention right under the H.R.A.[247]

In the second leg of his argument, dealing with the text of the HRA, Buxton discounts Wade's claim that the HRA will have *direct* horizontal effect on the grounds that the legislative intent behind section 6 is clear and, in any event, several procedural obstacles confront any private law action alleging breach of Convention rights (as argued also by Phillipson). He then quotes the following well-known passage from Canadian Supreme Court jurisprudence on the limited relationship between the Canadian Charter of Rights and the common law, but finds it 'very doubtful' that the HRA will have such a limited role:

> Private parties owe each other no constitutional duties and cannot found their cause of action upon a Charter right. The party challenging the common law cannot allege that the common law violates a Charter *right* because, quite simply, Charter rights

---

244 Grosz, Beatson and Duffy, above n. 139, p. 95. See also, Bamforth, above n. 228, p. 168 (courts 'might use the [ECHR] cases to inform the development of the common law'); Ewing, above n. 139, p. 90 (re 'more extravagant claims' about HRA's impact on common law); and Leigh, above n. 232, pp. 82-83 ('may be a change of atmosphere post-incorporation).

245 Wade acknowledges the differences between Hunt's view and his own but has wondered why Hunt 'is not targeted by the Lord Justice along with myself' (above n. 234, p. 222).

246 R. Buxton, 'The Human Rights Act and Private Law' (2000) 116 LQR 48, nn. 1 and 5.

247 Ibid., p. 54. Cf. the open-ended discussions re the right to privacy in *Douglas v Hello! Ltd* [2001] 2 All ER 289 (CA); and Ch. 6.

do not exist in the absence of state action. The most that the private litigant can do is to argue that the common law is inconsistent with Charter *values*.[248]

His view is that Convention values 'remain, stubbornly, values whose content lives in public law' (as distinct from private law) and also that, in any event, such values are 'already recognised in English courts by the use made of the terms of the E.C.H.R. as an articulation of such values'.[249] Rejecting assumptions of 'a high level of English judicial activism' in future litigation involving private parties, he concludes by arguing that the spotlight should remain on the actions of public authorities: 'the courts will thus be freed to devote their attention to the very important task of working out the effect of the H.R.A. in the sphere of public law where it, and the E.C.H.R., properly belong'.[250]

The question which arises, therefore, is what conclusions ought to be drawn on the extent of the horizontal effect of the HRA given the diversity of views on the subject? One route towards a conclusion may be to ask why broader questions about the purpose and scope of the HRA have not received comparable publicity or discussion. This is the route we shall follow in the next part of the chapter.

IV. 'SOMEONE MUST BE TRUSTED. LET IT BE THE JUDGES':[251] WHITHER DEMOCRACY?

The issue of judicialisation of governing power has been a staple of academic inquiry over recent decades and the resulting slew of commentaries makes it clear that judges, practitioners, academics, politicians and the media have sharply divergent views about the legitimate role of judges in general and, specifically, in relation to human rights adjudication.[252] In some respects, these inquiries have been a reflection of, and sometimes catalyst for, wider shifts in the UK's institutional, political and social landscape over the last 20 years. The period has been characterised by increasing prominence and controversy around the activities of judges, both in and outside court.[253] Warnings about a crossing of 'constitutional' boundaries have become commonplace;[254] senior

---

248 *Hill v Church of Scientology of Toronto* [1995] 2 SCR 1130, 1170-1171 (Cory J) (re common law of defamation held to be compatible with Charter values). See also, *M(A) v Ryan* [1997] 1 SCR 157 (re common law on disclosure of privileged communications between patient and psychiatrist held to be compatible with Charter values).

249 Buxton, above n. 246, p. 59. Cf. *Wilson v First County Trust* [2001] 3 WLR 42 (CA).

250 Ibid., pp. 64-65. Cf. *Venables and Thompson v News Group Newspapers* [2001] 1 All ER 908; and Ch 6.

251 Lord Denning, *What Next in the Law* (Butterworths, 1982), p. 330 (and paraphrased as follows by a government minister during debates on the Human Rights Bill: 'we have to trust someone, so why not trust the judges' (306 HC 857 (16 Feb. 1998) (Michael O'Brien)).

252 See eg, J.A.G. Griffith, *The Politics of the Judiciary* (Fontana, 1997); and his 'The Brave New World of Sir John Laws' (2000) 63 MLR 150; Ewing and Gearty, above n. 28; A. Lester, 'English Judges as Law Makers' [1993] PL 269; G. Robertson, *The Justice Game* (Vintage, 1998); Sedley, above n. 243; and F. Klug, *Values for A Godless Age* (Penguin, 2000).

253 D. Williams, 'Bias: The Judges and the Separation of Powers' [2000] PL 45. See further, R. Stevens, 'A Loss of Innocence?: Judicial Independence and the Separation of Powers' (1999) 19 OJLS 365. Historical examples of once-controversial extra-judicial writing include Lord Hewart's 1929 book, *The New Despotism* (Ernest Benn); Lord Denning's 1949 book, *Freedom Under the Law* (Stevens); and more recently Lord Scarman's 1974 book, *English Law: The New Dimension* (Stevens).

254 Cherie Booth, QC, reported in *The Times*, 15 Oct. 1999 (referring to 'a special responsibility on judges not to stray too readily into politics').

judges have been asked to chair high-profile inquiries on prison riots, arms sales to Iraq, police racism and the 'Bloody Sunday' shootings;[255] public and media interest in the law has increased (as exemplified by cases such as *Factortame, Blood, Venables and Thompson, Pinochet,* and *Hindley*[256]); and the New Labour constitutional reform programme has placed a spotlight on the composition of the House of Lords and the method of appointing senior judges,[257] and fuelled an already-appreciable stream of extra-judicial writing.

In recent years, the role of senior judges in promoting or creating a (human) rights jurisdiction as intrinsic to the English common law tradition has preoccupied many judicial observers, as well as the judges themselves.[258] This is unlikely to change in the coming years and will probably become even more widespread: the enactment of the HRA may have effectively resolved the issue of *whether* there is a human rights basis to UK law, but the broader debate about *what* judges are doing (and should do) when using rights discourse remains unresolved. Two strands of commentary have traditionally dominated this field of inquiry (although, as we shall explain below, they must now be seen as intersecting with a broader range of more recent HRA-influenced perspectives).[259] The first strand may loosely be termed as 'classic' civil libertarian, both in terms of its origins and historical influences and its primary concern with the ideological nature of law and the 'politics of the judiciary'.[260] The second strand is less easily labelled, and examples of the scholarship which fall within it can be found scattered amongst constitutional, administrative and European law literatures (which together comprise contemporary 'public law' scholarship). It has been characterised by adherence to the goal of explaining and legitimating the expanding judicial role in public law litigation, and has had no uniform stance on, or special interest in, human rights protection.

Increasingly, however, these two strands have to be seen through the lens of HRA-inspired commentaries on appropriate judicial roles. These latter commentaries are illuminating not only for their various interpretations of traditional constitutionalism, but also for the sense they give of the different political goals and expectations of the HRA's supporters, sceptics and detractors. They have a significant overlap with the historically dominant strands;

---

255 See eg, *Prison Disturbances April 1990: Report of an Inquiry by the Rt Hon Lord Justice Woolf (Parts I and II) and his Honour Judge Stephen Tumim (Part II)* (Cm. 1456, 1991) (The Woolf Report). For details of and commentaries on other prominent recent inquiries, see eg: A. Tomkins, *The Constitution After Scott: Government Unwrapped* (Clarendon, 1998); L. Bridges, 'The Lawrence Inquiry: Incompetence, Corruption and Institutional Racism' (1999) 26 JLS 298; and B. Hadfield, '*R. v Lord Saville of Newdigate, ex p Anonymous Soldiers*: What is the Purpose of a Tribunal of Inquiry?' [1999] PL 663.

256 See respectively, *R v Secretary of State for Transport, ex p Factortame (No. 2)* [1991] 1 AC 603 (HL); *R v Human Fertilisation and Embryology Authority, ex p Blood* [1997] 2 All ER 687 (CA); *R v Secretary of State for the Home Department, ex p Venables* [1997] 3 All ER 97 (HL); *R v Bow Street Metropolitan Stipendiary Magistrate, ex p Pinochet (No. 2)* [1999] 1 All ER 577 (HL); and *R v Secretary of State for the Home Department, ex p Hindley* [2000] 2 All ER 385 (HL).

257 See eg, D. Woodhouse, 'The Office of Lord Chancellor' [1998] PL 617; and A. O'Neill, 'The European Convention and the Independence of the Judiciary: The Scottish Experience' (2000) 63 MLR 429.

258 A path-breaking analysis is provided by Hunt, above n. 34. For an account of the development of a human rights jurisprudence by the Australian High Court, see G. Williams, *Human Rights Under the Australian Constitution* (OUP, 1999).

259 See below, pp. 46-52.

260 The pre-eminent account is Griffith's, *The Politics of the Judiciary*, above n. 252.

indeed, in many respects, they are only a continuation (albeit more insistent and wide-ranging in character) of the soul-searching sparked by the growth of judicial review in the 1980s, the reception of European law and shifts in governance in the UK. What the emergence of these commentaries shows is that human rights litigation is inevitably a battleground in terms of assessing what counts as a 'win' and as a 'loss': this is the case not just in the sense of particular litigant outcomes, but also, more broadly, in relation to the deep contestation over foundational norms, institutional legitimacy, and appropriate modes of governance and adjudication.[261]

This part of the chapter engages with the vogue for commenting on the judicial record and the predictions of 'judicialisation of democracy'. First, it will examine the judicial record on civil liberties and common law constitutionalism more generally, as well as the academic commentaries thereon. The growing willingness of some judges, in the decade prior to the HRA 1998, to articulate their dissatisfaction with the orthodox doctrinal framework of the common law will be given particular emphasis. This will be followed by an outline of the three dominant reactions to the recent judicial shift towards a jurisprudence of individual rights in the UK and expectations of further judicial activism under the HRA. The final part of the chapter will outline our view on the best approach to law and adjudication for civil liberties law in the HRA era.

The judicial record and judges' views on civil liberties, the common law and modern constitutionalism

Most students of civil liberties since the 1970s will have been exposed to a similar account of freedoms and rights in the UK. This account will have identified the weakness of the common law as a bulwark against parliamentary and executive erosion of fundamental rights and liberties, and the general inability or refusal of the judiciary to do much to further the cause of civil liberties.[262] It may also have represented the period of Conservative rule from 1979-97 as a highpoint of the threat to the 'culture of liberty' in Britain (Northern Ireland providing an awkward, but usually undiscussed, exception to this culture[263]). Furthermore, although Parliament's record may have been described in a number of ways (with final judgment withheld on the basis that the record is mixed[264]), the judiciary's record will almost certainly have been

---

261 For more details on the 'culture of controversy' engendered by rights litigation, see Campbell, above n. 5; and Stychin, above n.15.

262 See eg, K.D. Ewing and C.A. Gearty, *Freedom Under Thatcher: Civil Liberties in Modern Britain* (OUP, 1990) and successive editions of G. Robertson's, *Freedom, The Individual and the Law* (Penguin). For accounts offering less sceptical perspectives on the judicial record, see eg, D. Feldman, *Civil Liberties and Human Rights in England and Wales* (Clarendon, 1993); and H. Fenwick, *Civil Liberties* (Cavendish, 1998).

263 For a notable exception, see J. Morison and S. Livingstone, *Reshaping Public Power: Northern Ireland and the British Constitution* (Sweet & Maxwell, 1995).

264 See eg, the Race Relations Act 1976 as compared with the Prevention of Terrorism Act 1974 (Labour government), or the Police and Criminal Evidence Act 1984 as compared with the Official Secrets Act 1989 (Conservative government). For more details on the parliamentary record on civil liberties, see McCrudden and Chambers, above n. 56.

roundly condemned; the most common technique being to provide a litany of infamous cases, preceded by a rhetorical question:[265]

> Are we seriously asked to rely on the ethical values and political wisdom of those who in recent years have given us (for select example) the following judgments? In *ex parte Brind*[266] the courts upheld a nation-wide ban on freedom of expression by a recognised political party with elected members in Parliament and in local authorities. In *CCSU*[267] they upheld a ban on trade union membership. In *Bromley v GLC*,[268] a blatantly party political decision of the Court of Appeal was upheld by the Law Lords who, it is said, thought 'economic' and 'economical' bore the same meaning. In *Spycatcher*,[269] at a crucial stage, the Law Lords upheld an injunction banning publication of material already in the public domain. In *Home Office v Harman*[270] the solicitor for the National Council for Civil Liberties was held guilty of contempt of court for disclosing to a journalist material that had been read in open court. In *British Steel Corpn v Granada*,[271] and other like cases, courts ordered the disclosure of journalists' sources. In *Associated Newspapers v Wilson*[272] the courts ruled in favour of employers who sought, contrary to statute, to replace collective bargaining with individual contracts of service. Alongside these examples is the series of judicial failures to set aside miscarriages of justices resulting in long terms of imprisonment.[273]

The question which arises is, to what extent, if at all, should this account be accepted? It appears to be challenged by developments from the early 1990s onwards, in particular the emergence of an increasingly explicit commitment on the part of certain judges (many of whom have been elevated to the Court of Appeal and House of Lords) towards revisioning their role through the reformulation of the common law. This latter 'common law' constitutionalism evolved quietly, even stealthily, through a series of cases and an expansive corpus of extra-judicial writing, and until recently discussion of it was eclipsed by debates on the incorporation of the ECHR (which attracted broader political and public

---

265 Or via an emphatic conclusion: see eg, Ewing and Gearty, above n. 262 (concluding that '[i]t should now be clear that civil liberties in Britain are in a state of crisis. . . . [The] concern is that in the hands of the English judges a bill of rights would make very little difference to the conditions of political freedom in this country. . . . The harsh reality is that we need to be protected by Parliament from the courts, as much as we need to be protected from the abuse of executive power' (pp. 255, 270-271)); and their *The Struggle for Civil Liberties*, above n. 28 (stating that '[i]t can be claimed with confidence that there is not a single example throughout [the period 1914-1945] of a judicial decision in Britain at High Court or appellate level which can be said to have served to protect or to promote civil liberties against the hostile attentions of the State' (p. 403)).

266 *R v Home Secretary, ex p Brind* [1991] 1 AC 696.

267 *Council of Civil Service Unions v Minister for the Civil Service* [1985] AC 374.

268 [1983] 1 AC 768.

269 *A-G v Guardian Newspapers Ltd* [1987] 1 WLR 1248.

270 [1981] 2 QB 534.

271 [1981] AC 1096.

272 [1995] 2 AC 454.

273 Griffith, above n. 252, p. 164 (original references). Other 'infamous' cases are *Thomas v NUM* [1985] 2 All ER 1 (re common law right to use the highway without unreasonable interference and injunction against demonstrating miners); *R v Secretary of State for the Home Department, ex p Northumbria Police Authority* [1988] 1 All ER 556 (re prerogative power to keep the peace and issuing of plastic bullets and CS gas to police); and *R v Gibson* [1990] 2 QB 619 (re common law offence of outraging public decency). Needless to say, some cases contradictory of the general civil libertarian thesis exist in this period: see *Gillick v West Norfolk and Wisbech HA* [1986] AC 112 (re provision of contraceptives to minors); and *Wheeler v Leicester CC* [1985] 2 All ER 1106 (re emphasising 'fundamental freedoms of the individual', albeit to play rugby in apartheid South Africa).

interest over this period – particularly, from 1993 onwards, following on from the Labour Party's shift of position from historic opposition towards Bills of Rights).[274]

The most significant feature of this body of judicial and extra-judicial writing was its emphasis on the (new) foundational role of the common law in the evolving rights jurisdiction. For example, in 1993, Lord Bingham MR boldly reconstructed the judicial function in terms rarely seen in traditional English constitutional law doctrine, insisting that there was 'no task more central to the purpose of a modern democracy, or more central to the judicial function, than that of seeking to protect, within the law, the basic human rights of the citizen, against invasion by other citizens or by the state itself'.[275] The House of Lords in *Derbyshire CC v Times Newspapers*[276] was adamant that the non-availability of defamation actions for local authorities was to be based on the common law right to free speech, and (unlike the Court of Appeal) refused to pursue the relevance of Article 10 of the ECHR. The *Derbyshire* stance evolved into a pattern, whereby judges held that Convention rights merely reflected the content of the common law.[277] For example, in *Re B*, Laws J (reflecting views expressed in a series of articles[278]) argued that:

> certain rights, broadly those occupying a central place in the ECHR and obviously including the right to life, are not to be perceived merely as moral or political aspirations nor as enjoying a legal status only upon the international plane . . . [b]ut are to be vindicated as sharing with other principles the substance of the English common law.[279]

A new activist role for the judiciary was advocated, moving judicial review away from the narrow issue of powers and remedies towards notions of rights:[280] 'the principles by which [judicial review] is conducted are neither unitary nor static . . . for example, while the Secretary of State will be largely left to his own devices in promulgating national economic policy . . . the court will scrutinise

---

274 Writing in 1999, Walker referred to its 'emergent and still subordinate status and its relative neglect in the academic literature': 'Setting English Judges to Rights' (1999) 19 OJLS 132, 142. For detailed accounts of the emergence of common law constitutionalism, see Hunt, above n. 34; and Loughlin, above n. 2.

275 T. Bingham MR, 'The European Convention on Human Rights: Time to Incorporate' (1993) 109 LQR 390, 390.

276 [1993] AC 534.

277 See eg, *R v Home Secretary, ex p Togher* (CA), 1 Feb.1995 (Art. 3); *R v Khan* [1996] 3 All ER 289 (Art. 6); and *R v Home Secretary, ex p Moon* (1995) 8 Admin LR 477 (Art. 9). This is not to suggest that progressive outcomes always followed, or were intended by, such judicial claims: see eg, its use as an excuse for insularity by Lord Donaldson MR in *R v Secretary of State for the Home Department, ex p Brind* [1991] 1 AC 696, 717 (CA) ('You have to look long and hard before you can detect any difference between the English common law and the principles set out in the Convention, at least if the Convention is viewed through English judicial eyes').

278 J. Laws, 'Is the High Court the Guardian of Fundamental Constitutional Rights?' [1993] PL 67; 'Judicial Remedies and the Constitution' (1994) 57 MLR 213; 'Law and Democracy' [1995] PL 72; 'The Constitution: Morals and Rights' [1996] PL 622; 'Public Law and Employment Law: Abuse of Power' [1997] PL 455; and 'The Limitations of Human Rights' [1998] PL 254. A review of Laws LJ's judicial and extra-judicial writing is offered by Griffith, above n. 252.

279 *R v Cambridge District Health Authority, ex p B* [1995] 1 FLR 1055. Laws J's decision was reversed by the CA on the ground that allocation of NHS resources was generally non-justiciable: [1995] 1 WLR 898. Cf. *R v NW Lancashire HA, ex p A* [1999] Lloyds Rep Med 399 (CA).

280 *R v Somerset CC, ex p Fewings* [1994] 92 LGR 674. On appeal, the CA upheld Laws J's decision without endorsing all of his reasoning: [1995] 3 All ER 20.

the merits of his decision much more closely when they concern refugees or free speech'.[281] Even more explicitly, as advocated by (then) Sedley J, where EU law was implicated, the judicial obligation to further the new legal order of human rights was inevitable:

> Once it is accepted that the standards articulated in the European Convention are standards which both march with those of the common law and inform the jurisprudence of the EU, it becomes unreal and potentially unjust to continue to develop English public law without reference to them.[282]

Most remarkably, judges such as Lord Woolf openly challenged the constitutional lodestar of parliamentary supremacy by suggesting a refashioning of the relationship between courts and executive where fundamental rights or principles were at stake:

> [I]f Parliament did the unthinkable, then I would say that the courts would be required to act in a manner which would be without precedent . . . [because] ultimately there are even limits on the supremacy of Parliament which it is the courts' inalienable responsibility to identify and uphold.[283]

The implications of this constitutional sea-change were also pointed out extra-judicially, most controversially by John Laws who suggested that 'the concept of fundamental rights ought in principle to affect the reach and length of democratic power' – *whether or not* the ECHR was incorporated.[284] Laws' view was grounded in a belief that an electoral mandate did not give Parliament absolute power to interfere with rights (such as freedom of expression) as there was a 'higher-order law'[285] which the courts were bound to observe. Other judges did not accept Laws' view on 'higher-order' norms, choosing instead to ground their 'human rights project' in pragmatism and placing emphasis on the fact that 'at its present stage of development our society happens to articulate some of its most fundamental needs in terms of individual rights, and . . . judges should recognize this in refining their constitutional jurisprudence'.[286] Whatever the justification, however, it soon became clear that:

---

281 J. Laws, 'Is the High Court the Guardian of Fundamental Constitutional Rights?' [1993] PL 59, 69. See also, Lord Irvine, 'Judges and Decision-Makers: The Theory and Practice of Wednesbury Review' [1996] PL 59.

282 *R v Secretary of State for the Home Department, ex p McQuillan* [1995] 4 All ER 400, 422. For commentary on the European legal order in this period, see eg, G. de Búrca, 'Fundamental Human Rights and the Reach of EC Law' (1993) 13 OJLS 283; and her 'The Language of Rights and European Integration' in J. Shaw and G. More (eds.), *New Legal Dynamic of European Union* (Clarendon, 1995), pp. 29-45.

283 'Droit Public – English Style' [1995] PL 57, 68-69. He went on to say: 'I do see advantages in this country having a Bill of Rights of its own. . . . A British Bill of Rights would avoid the difficulty which exists at present in protecting some of our basic rights' (p. 70).

284 'Law and Democracy' [1995] PL 72, 81-82. He continued: 'While, along with many others, I would welcome incorporation I am not concerned . . . merely to add my name to the call . . . the idea of incorporation is beset by conceptual difficulties so long as we adhere to what I believe to be the out-dated, or perhaps misunderstood, notion of sovereignty of Parliament'.

285 Ibid., p. 84.

286 Walker, above n. 274, p. 149. Sedley's views can be traced in a series of extra-judicial writings: see eg, 'Free Speech for Rupert Murdoch: The Limitations of a Bill of Rights' *LRB*, 19 Dec. 1991; 'The Sound of Silence: Constitutional Law without a Constitution' (1994) 110 LQR 270; and 'Human Rights: A Twenty First Century Agenda' [1995] PL 386.

[s]elf-characterized as a species of the common law, the new approach [was] well placed to draw on its long traditions, but with the partial exception of the . . . judicial tendency to 'discover' an identity between the deep-rooted values of the common law and international human rights standards, the trend [was] towards a more overt statement of the courts' pioneering role.[287]

As suggested above, the courts sought to give effect to their 'pioneering role' in a range of overlapping ways. First, they forged a presumption of statutory interpretation whereunder Parliament was assumed not to have intended to legislate in a manner which would be inconsistent with fundamental rights. Secondly, they reoriented judicial review such that there was more detailed review of decisions which interfered with fundamental rights. Thirdly, courts pursued the idea of an 'identity' between the common law and the ECHR, thereby indirectly facilitating the development of the common law. Fourthly, judicial discretions were carefully exercised so as to ensure compatibility with the ECHR. And finally, a more relaxed attitude towards European Community law allowed for a greater appreciation of 'European' legal concepts such as proportionality.

This evolution of judicial enthusiasm for a rights jurisdiction was motivated by different concerns; moreover, in many cases, the exact reasons for dissatisfaction with the historic position remained submerged. At the same time, however, a post-1990s vantage point allows one to see that there was a range of possible explanations for the emergent 'modern constitutionalism': 'the changing texture of executive government',[288] in particular the dawning realisation that under the Westminster system a government could easily interfere with rights and values; the inadequacies and 'ethical aimlessness' of the common law framework;[289] governmental refusal to give further effect to the ECHR in domestic law, despite myriad lengthy legal campaigns leading to UK government defeats in Strasbourg; the growing impact of EU law in human rights contexts such as sex discrimination, and more generally on approaches to statutory interpretation; and the expansion of judicial review to cope with new forms of governance (albeit with the recognition that it was deficient as a human rights-mechanism).[290] The judicial embrace of rights discourse was also, of course, a reaction to the increasing currency of 'rights-style' claims in litigation and 'rights-talk' more generally in popular discourse: while legal claims might not have been articulated in these terms, in the litigant and public mind, high-

---

287 Ibid., p. 143.
288 Ibid., p. 146.
289 The cases of *Malone v Metropolitan Police Comr* [1979] Ch 344 (re telephone tapping) and *Kaye v Robertson* [1991] FSR 62 (re media intrusion in a hospital ward) were considered prime examples of the deficiencies of the common law.
290 Loughlin, above n. 2, suggested that '[t]he traditional beliefs which lawyers have held about the nature of the political order no longer seem able to sustain unconditional respect. The judiciary, as a consequence, are searching for a more appropriate way of comprehending the universe of civic rights and responsibilities. At the heart of their endeavours, it would appear is the attempt to reconstruct the political order on the foundation of rights' (p. 200-201). Hunt invited the judiciary to accept the 'mission' of 'modern constitutionalism', and thereby to provide 'a more mature version of constitutionalism capable of co-existing with the modern administrative state' which would not be derailed by Diceyan constitutionalism: see his 'Constitutionalism and the Contractualisation of Government in the United Kingdom' in Taggart, above n. 28, pp. 21-39.

profile cases like *Brown*[291] and *Bland*[292] were clearly perceived as being about *human rights.*

Whatever the exact catalysts, however, it is undeniable that the doctrinal shift which took place over the course of the 1990s was a fundamental one; it could be argued that this is the common law, but not as we have known it. Diceyan constitutionalism still generally held sway, most notably where it appeared that the politics of the situation so demanded. Thus, in 1995, in *R v Ministry of Defence, ex p Smith* (wherein the Court of Appeal upheld the government's ban on lesbians and gays serving in the armed forces), Lord Bingham MR insisted that '[judges] owe a duty . . . to remain within their constitutional bounds and not trespass beyond them'; if the ECHR 'were part of our law . . . then clearly the primary judgment . . . would be for us and not others: the constitutional balance would shift'.[293] Similarly, in 1999, his judgment in *Hindley* (as well as that of Lord Woolf in the Court of Appeal), upholding the Home Secretary's increase of Myra Hindley's tariff to 'whole life', reverted to Diceyan orthodoxy on parliamentary intention and separation of powers – with 'fundamental' common law rights or the 'equivalent' ECHR standards seemingly of no relevance.[294]

Yet, just as Wade argued in 1991 in relation to the judicial absorption of EC law – '*Factortame* shows how . . . smoothly the courts may discard fundamental doctrine without appearing to notice'[295] – the 1990s transformation to 'common law' or 'rights-regarding'[296] constitutionalism was ultimately triumphant. Indeed from certain vantage points, enactment of the HRA can be viewed as an attempt to *contain* judicial power as much as a legitimating or reforming constitutional measure.[297]

Awaiting the Human Rights Act: two old orthodoxies and a new orthodoxy on judges and judging

We move now to consideration of the broad concerns articulated in the outpouring of commentaries generated since New Labour announced its plan to incorporate the ECHR and published the Human Rights Bill. Earlier in this chapter we examined commentaries on specific aspects of the HRA (such as its indirect horizontal application); what follows has a different focus and thus is intended to serve a different purpose – in particular, it is intended that it should

---

291 *R v Brown* [1993] 2 All ER 75.
292 *Airedale NHS Trust v Bland* [1993] 1 All ER 821.
293 [1996] 1 All ER 257.
294 See further Ch. 5. The *Hindley* litigation makes the press conference statements by the Lord Chief Justice, Lord Woolf, all the more revealing: he predicted that the role of the executive in the sentencing process would be challenged under the HRA and that the courts would then decide on the issue as 'a matter of law'. He also expressed reservations about claims that 'any given case is so lacking in aspects of redemption that one can anticipate that throughout the natural life of the individual concerned, it will never be proper to release that person': see *The Times*, 7 Jun. 2000.
295 W. Wade, 'What Has Happened to the Sovereignty of Parliament?' (1991) 107 LQR 1, 4.
296 See Walker, above n. 274.
297 Williams, above n. 253, p. 53, suggests that Lord Irvine's initiation of a House of Lords debate in 1996 on the judiciary (at which time Irvine was effectively Lord Chancellor 'in-waiting') was 'intended to be a pre-emptive strike to dampen down extravagant assumptions about the response of the judiciary to prospective constitutional change'.

complement the previous section on judges and the judicial record in the immediate pre-HRA period, and provide an appreciation of three prevailing understandings of adjudication in the HRA era.

(1) Enduring distrust: democracy sullied by the Human Rights Act

Adherents to the first strand of reactions to the HRA exhibit what might be described as 'enduring distrust'. They point to the relevance for the HRA era of the classic civil liberties emphasis on problematising the role of the judiciary, promoting the need for a continuing – and indeed, increased – focus on the judicial track record. Their key concern is that democracy will be sullied by the massive transfer of governing power inherent in the HRA model, and they generally have little truck with voguish notions of a 'new dialogue' or 'conversation' between courts and Parliaments.

Ewing and Gearty are examples of adherents to this first strand. They have, for example, strongly argued against the apparently infectious enthusiasm for the HRA and put forward the view that the historical record holds the key to future developments. They criticise judges, who 'can now be liberal because liberalism is in the air', and insist that civil liberties law must not be deflected from uncovering 'the real face of our new constitutional masters'.[298] They themselves push ahead with this task and draw the following conclusions. First, Gearty alleges that '[t]hroughout this century, the courts have been the most reactionary and illiberal branch of the democratic state. This has been true whether or not the citizens of the state concerned have been the possessors (proud or otherwise) of "human rights"'. He dismisses the recent enthusiasms for 'common law' constitutionalism amongst members of the senior judiciary, noting the high levels of 'revisionism' associated with this project:

> It was not statute but judge-made law which allowed the police to roadblock the motorways to prevent striking miners from exercising their freedom to picket. Nor was it any statute which required the then Lord Chief Justice, Lord Lane, to uphold the automatic imposition of draconian bail conditions on striking miners. . . . It was not statute which compelled the courts to assist the Tory Government's suppression of Peter Wright's allegations in Spycatcher, or to uphold the media ban against Sinn Féin and others holding Republican views.[299]

Ewing has carried forward this theme by identifying reasons for deep anxiety about the 'massive judicialisation' of democracy which may be ushered in by the HRA, in particular the way in which 'quasi-entrenchment of liberal icons [of the ECHR], particularly when secured in a manner which allows courts . . . to question Acts of Parliament' represents a drift from Labour's traditional 'principles of democratic socialism'.[300] Griffith picks up this idea, pointing out that the HRA and the judicial celebration of the liberal individualism of 'rights' compromises the vision of the 'socialist [who] looks first to the inequalities in society and to the human casualties created'.[301] Griffith also pursues other familiar themes, emphasising the relevance for the HRA era of historic concerns

298 C. Gearty, 'Here Come The Judges' *LRB*, 4 Jun. 1998, p. 10.
299 Ibid., p. 12. Cf. C. Gearty, 'What Are Judges For?' *LRB*, 25 Jan. 2001, pp. 10–13.
300 'The Human Rights Act and Parliamentary Democracy' (1999) 62 MLR 79, 98-99.
301 Griffith, above n. 252, pp. 159, 163, 174, 176. See also, his 'Judges and the Constitution' in R. Rawlings (ed.), *Law, Society and Economy* (Clarendon, 1997), pp. 289-310.

about the 'politicisation of the judiciary', their 'unelected' mandate, and their narrow educational and professional backgrounds, as well as the fact that 'they are less well equipped than politicians' to make 'political' judgments. The Ewing, Gearty and Griffith axis has also received support from what may seem an unexpected quarter. Writing from a feminist perspective, McColgan endorses their deep distrust of judicial power and rights, and warns that the HRA represents a 'false promise' for women.[302]

These reactions have a certain compelling power (and considerable case law resources). They also provide a corrective to the excesses of HRA euphoria and unreflexive court-centredness; they prompt us to focus on depth not surface in giving effect to the 'drive to modernise our society and refresh our democracy',[303] and offer an incentive for engagement with the broad critical interest in forms of participatory or deliberative democracy.[304] Equally, however, these reactions to the HRA seem unlikely to garner a long-term audience or to hold the attention of critically pragmatic constitutionalists. Obvious flaws include the following: first, there is insufficient acknowledgement of the changed constitutional landscape and the legal, social and political catalysts which led to the creation of a rights-regarding constitutionalism in the UK; secondly, the principal battlelines are drawn along a class axis with no discussion of the complex intersections of struggles for recognition and redistribution in a range of constitutional democracies in recent years;[305] thirdly, the contingency of human rights discourse is largely ignored; and finally, adjudication tends to be presented as being about nothing more than judges acting ideologically.

(2) 'The English Constitution': down but not out in the Human Rights Act era

Like those in the first strand, adherents to the second HRA grouping are the disciples of an old orthodoxy. They strive to fulfil the goal of the sovereignist mind set, and (re)interpret the new constitutional (and more generally, public law) landscape through orthodox foundationalist lenses of the 'English Constitution'. Their work is preoccupied with matters such as defence of the ultra vires principle as the central doctrine of judicial review[306] in the face of a flood of judicial and academic indicators which point to the fact that 'compatibility with the (hierarchially superior) [HRA] and its values is part of future legal life'.[307] Some adherents to this second strand contend that, although 'increasingly perceived as redundant', 'the constitutional utility of the ultra

---

302 A. McColgan, *Women Under the Law: The False Promise of Human Rights* (Longman, 2000) (identifying a gender bias within rights discourse and highlighting negative political outcomes of human rights litigation for women in jurisdictions such as Canada and the US).

303 306 HC 782-783 (16 Feb. 1998) (Jack Straw).

304 On a dialogic model of law and democracy, see especially J. Habermas, *Between Facts and Norms: Contributions to a Discourse Theory of Law and Democracy* (Polity, 1997) (as well as Habermas' earlier work). See also, Harvey, above n. 8; and Morison, above n. 14.

305 For discussion of the recognition/redistribution issue, see Ch. 8.

306 See eg, M. Elliott, 'The Ultra Vires Doctrine in a Constitutional Setting: Still the Central Principle of Administrative Law' [1999] CLJ 129 (re avoiding 'the heterodoxy of challenging legislative supremacy'). See also, C.F. Forsyth, 'Of Fig Leaves and Fairy Tales: The Ultra Vires Doctrine, the Sovereignty of Parliament and Judicial Review' [1996] CLJ 122, 134 (arguing that '[t]he upshot of all this is that . . . to abandon ultra vires is to challenge the supremacy of Parliament').

307 Markesinis, above n. 139, p. 85 (note omitted).

vires doctrine is capable of surviving contemporary reformulations of the interrelationship of the legislative and judicial branches'.[308] The HRA is also said to 'pose no threat to the traditional conception of Parliamentary sovereignty in theoretical terms'.[309] Furthermore, in contrast to the first strand of HRA-inspired commentaries, this perspective constructs judges as 'neutral' arbiters outside the fray of politics who are committed to the non-political task of upholding the 'rule of law'.

The perspective sidesteps a slew of evidence demonstrating the seismic changes wrought by the changing role of the state, European integration, devolution and the centrality of human rights discourse. Not only this, it also never makes it entirely clear *why* 'rescuing' allegedly-foundational Diceyan principles of constitutional law should be a priority for public lawyers. However, perhaps the most interesting aspect of this position is that judicial and political actors still uncritically endorse the virtues and persuasiveness of Diceyan orthodoxy. Some of this advocacy seems designed for strategic purposes.[310] Thus, Lord Irvine, in opposition in 1996, famously condemned challenges to parliamentary supremacy as smacking of 'judicial supremacism'[311] and, subsequently, as Lord Chancellor, argued that the declaration of incompatibility mechanism in section 4 of the HRA does not compromise the supremacy principle.[312] Total judicial deference to the sovereignty principle is even less believable given that the history of the judicial development of a rights-foundation for the common law demonstrates that judges played a key role in *forcing the hand* of government in enacting the HRA. Nevertheless, some judges are clearly uncomfortable with the new order. Lord Hoffmann's sentiments, for example, seem very clear: 'For [two centuries] we have entrusted our most fundamental liberties to the will of a sovereign Parliament and, taken all in all, Parliament has not betrayed that trust'.[313] This stance receives support and further clarification from his judgment in *Simms* where he explicitly emphasised that the legislative power to *violate* human rights standards will not be diminished in the new constitutional culture, that much of the ECHR 'reflects the common law', and that the HRA is 'unlikely to involve radical change in our notions of fundamental human rights':

> Parliamentary sovereignty means that Parliament can, if it chooses, legislate contrary to fundamental principles of human rights. The Human Rights Act 1998 will not detract from this power. The constraints upon its exercise by Parliament are ultimately political, not legal.[314]

---

308 M. Elliott, 'The Demise of Parliamentary Sovereignty? The Implications for Justifying Judicial Review' (1999) 115 LQR 119, 120.

309 Ibid., p. 126.

310 Perhaps because 'it is not good enough to say, as is repeatedly said in this debate in the [UK], that a fundamental law to which other statutes must yield is contrary to our tradition of democracy. One reason why this is so is that we do already have a fundamental law to which all others must yield. . . . [I]t is the European Communities Act 1972' (S. Sedley, 'A Bill of Rights for the United Kingdom: From London to Strasbourg by the Northwest Passage' (1998) 36 Osg Hall LJ 63, 70). See also, Lord Nolan and Sir Stephen Sedley, *The Making and Remaking of the British Constitution* (Blackstone, 1997).

311 'Judges and Decision-Makers: The Theory and Practice of Wednesbury Review' [1996] PL 59, 77.

312 See eg, Lord Irvine, 'The Development of Human Rights in Britain Under an Incorporated Convention on Human Rights' [1998] PL 221.

313 Lord Hoffmann, 'Human Rights and the House of Lords' (1999) 62 MLR 159, 160. See also, his comments in *R v Chief Constable of Sussex, ex p International Trader's Ferry Ltd*, above n. 190.

314 *R v Secretary of State for the Home Department, ex p Simms* [1999] 3 All ER 400, 412.

(3) Pragmatism and zeal: the new foundationalism?

Pragmatism characterises a majority of judicial, academic and practitioner scholarship on the HRA and is, thus, the emergent orthodoxy. Its adherents are generally not interested in debating how or why the ECHR has been incorporated into UK law. They seem content to cleave to human rights norms as the new foundational base of UK constitutionalism and, cushioned perhaps by the pre-HRA 'common law' constitutionalism discussed earlier, have experienced few of the transition pains which have affected adherents to both of the old orthodoxies. HRA 'zealots' pursue a similar line to pragmatists in dispensing with the need for lengthy investigations of justifications for the new constitutional framework or exposés of political contradictions or obstacles: they differ from them in the fact that their commitment to a rights culture is generally more explicit (and often rather longer-term).[315]

Pragmatism is more widespread than zeal and tends to manifest in a range of forms. In one such form, where it seeks to give effect to the idea of pragmatism as 'getting on with things', it dominates the outpouring of practitioner perspectives which set out to 'explain' the HRA in terms of procedural rules, remedies and 'relevant' ECHR case law. The stated goal of such accounts is to predict substantive outcomes in order to prepare individuals and institutions for any increased litigation, costs, procedural reforms or dramatic 'cultural' changes. Furthermore, as suggested by article titles such as 'Do Taxpayers Have Human Rights?', minimal practitioner interest tends to be directed at interpreting the underlying values or political choices in human rights litigation. And where specific rights (such as privacy or freedom of expression) are discussed, the debate has got not much further than assertions about ECHR case law and undeveloped references to ideas such as 'democratic society' and 'pressing social need'.[316]

Pragmatism is also evident in the academic scholarship which reduces the HRA to just one more (albeit a very important) Act of Parliament. Following a pattern familiar from early academic responses to the European Communities Act 1972, this approach foregrounds non-critical, detailed explication of the provisions of the HRA and the judgments of the European Court of Human Rights. It makes few references to the contested nature of human rights or the historical contexts which have generated human rights claims and activism. Yet, as Leigh and Lustgarten have pointed out, interpretations of Convention rights 'if they are not to remain either vacuous or wholly subjective require grounding in some articulated theory which draws explicitly upon concepts and conceptions of morality and political legitimacy'.[317] And, no less a figure than Lord Browne-Wilkinson has pointed to the necessary sea-change in legal methodology: 'Moral attitudes which have previously been the actual, but unarticulated, reasoning lying behind judicial decisions will become the very

---

315 See eg, the work (that is, the published scholarship, human rights practice and parliamentary role) of Anthony Lester, a long-time advocate of a Bill of Rights for the UK and eminent rights-practitioner.

316 'Journalists are right to be concerned about Her Majesty's judiciary taking greater powers to decide, in the interests of protecting privacy, what should be included in tomorrow's *Times* or *Sun*': Lester and Pannick, above n. 119, p. 46.

317 I. Leigh and L. Lustgarten, 'Making Rights Real: The Courts, Remedies and the Human Rights Act' (1999) 58 CLJ 507, 543.

stuff of decisions on [ECHR] points . . . [and the] silent true reason for a decision will have to become the stated *ratio decidendi*.'[318] Overall, however, the prevailing atheoreticism and apoliticism of much of the new HRA-pragmatist orthodoxy raises serious questions about the extent to which law schools and the legal profession are poised and willing to alter established habits, embrace the value of critique and comparative rights jurisprudence, or recognise the contested nature of rights politics.[319]

Some judges have recognised these issues. Lord Justice Brooke, in appealing for the legal profession to embrace information technology, argued that 'in cases raising a European Convention issue, the whole of English law could be up for grabs'.[320] Similarly, Lord Woolf has predicted that the HRA 'will energise the whole of the United Kingdom's legal system . . . [and] the landscape of UK law will be transformed'.[321] In case law where the HRA has been raised, most notably in the House of Lords, early references to impending 'fundamental' change have given way to more cautious approaches which emphasise the need for 'balance'.[322] Yet, there is little sense of the Law Lords strategically preparing the ground for the future impact of ECHR reasoning: for example, case law on two evolving and politically controversial areas – negligence actions against public authorities,[323] and adjudication on resource allocation[324] – continues to reflect a diversity of legal approaches. The Court of Appeal's approach to Convention rights appears to be less cautious. Pre-HRA, for example, it was said to be important to 'pay particular attention' to Article 8 of the ECHR in *Coughlan*[325] – concerning a health authority's closure of a promised 'home for life'. Post-HRA, several of the Court's judges have confidently embraced the new interpretive freedom under sections 3 and 4 of the Act. For example, in both *Wilson v First County Trust* and *R v Mental Health Review Tribunal, ex p H*, the issuing of declarations of incompatibility was done in an almost routine manner.[326] Likewise, the elaboration of a right to privacy in *Douglas*

318 'The Impact on Judicial Reasoning' in Markesinis, above n. 139, pp. 21-23, at p. 22. For a sense of the cultural change required of the Law Lords, see W.T. Murphy and R. Rawlings, 'After the Ancien Regime: The Writing of Judgments in the House of Lords 1979-1980' (1981) 44 MLR 617. See also, Lord Hope, 'Human Rights: Where Are We Now' [2000] EHRLR 439 ('We reached a watershed . . . but we have yet to climb the mountain').

319 Leigh and Lustgarten, above n. 317, p. 544 ('[I]t is hard to see how a three year university education can possibly prepare the next generation of lawyers with the intellectual tools necessary to enable the full potential of the HRA to be realised.'). See also, C. Bell et al., *Teaching Human Rights* (National Centre for Legal Education, 1998).

320 'Judges Go Hi-Tech to Cope with Human Rights Act', *The Times*, 16 May 2000.

321 'Preface' in Lester and Pannick, above n. 119, pp. vii-viii, at p. vii.

322 See respectively, *R v DPP, ex p Kebilene* [1999] 4 All ER 801 ('It is now plain that incorporation of the [ECHR] into our domestic law will subject the entire legal system to a fundamental process of review and, where necessary, reform by the judiciary' (per Lord Hope)); *Brown v Stott* [2001] 2 WLR 817; *R v Secretary of State for the Environment, ex p Alconbury* [2001] UKHL 23, [2001] 2 All ER 929; and *R v A (No 2)* [2001] UKHL 25, [2001] 3 All ER 1.

323 *Barrett v Enfield London BC* [1999] 3 All ER 193 (HL); and *Z v UK* [2001] 2 FCR 246 (ECtHR).

324 See E. Palmer, 'Resource Allocation, Welfare Rights: Mapping the Boundaries of Judicial Control in Public Administrative Law' (2000) 20 OJLS 63; *R v Gloucestershire CC, ex p Barry* [1997] 2 All ER 1 (HL); *R v East Sussex CC, ex p Tandy* [1998] 2 All ER 769 (HL); and *Burridge v London Borough of Harrow* [2000] 1 All ER 876 (HL).

325 *R v North & East Devon HA, ex p Coughlan* [1999] Lloyds Rep Med 306 (CA).

326 [2001] EWCA Civ 633, [2001] 3 All ER 229; and *The Times*, 2 April, 2001.

v Hello! Ltd and *Venables and Thompson v News Group Newspapers* generated little judicial angst, and left the 'horizontal effect' debate wide open.[327]

Similar problems are evident in the 'zeal' camp. Its adherents promote the new political culture of liberal constitutionalism, which is said to 'give overwhelming priority to judicially enforced human rights and shift the main focus of political activity from representative institutions to the courts',[328] but rarely explain *why* better forms of democracy will follow as a consequence of this culture. They also appear to have engaged only minimally with critical evaluations of rights discourses, and with the literature suggesting that the relationship between law and social change is as complex and variable in rights-respecting legal cultures as it is in other legal cultures. This is not to suggest that zeal has no place in human rights activism, or that it is necessarily ineffective as a campaigning tool or media strategy. Rather, the point is that it may easily become the dominant discourse of a human rights elite, founded on problematic assumptions and exclusionary in practice and outcomes.[329]

V. RECONSTRUCTING CONSTITUTIONALISM: TOWARDS A NONFOUNDATIONALIST APPROACH TO LAW AND ADJUDICATION

It seems to us that civil liberties law in the HRA era needs to be able to make sense of the above commentaries if it is to engage the radical potential of the Act and further the scope for progressive politics. There is a 'new entwinement of law and politics'[330] in the UK – does this mean that adjudication will be more politics than law after the HRA? If so, this would appear to be a confirmation of the traditional civil liberties critique of judges as pure political actors (only now with expanded opportunities under the HRA). In contrast, mainstream 'public law' insists that the judicial task in the HRA era, albeit using a different foundational norm (namely human rights), remains a distinctively *legal* enterprise, and the 'rule of law' is not just politics by another name.

Using Allan Hutchinson's recent work,[331] it is possible to move beyond the range of commentaries on the HRA and, before that, on 'common-law' constitutionalism, towards the identification of two dominant approaches to law and adjudication: *foundationalist* and *antifoundationalist*. The foundationalist perspective generally views law and judicial reasoning as rational, principled, determinate and as different from 'politics'.[332] Law is recognised as 'thoroughly political in context and consequence', but this is not deemed to preclude the promotion or endorsement of an account of law 'in which adjudication not only should be but also can be and is largely performed in a qualitatively distinctive and democratically legitimate style'.[333] Hence, the argument is put

---

327 [2001] 2 All ER 289 (CA); and [2001] 1 All ER 908 (Fam).

328 See discussion in M. Malik, 'Governing After the Human Rights Act' (2000) 63 MLR 281, 293.

329 See generally, Hunt, above n. 174; and Lustgarten and Leigh, above n. 317, pp. 542-545.

330 H. Young, 'Politicised Judges May Now Learn to Keep Out of Politics', *The Guardian*, 20 Apr. 2000.

331 The analysis in this section is influenced by A.C. Hutchinson, *It's All In The Game: A Nonfoundationalist Account of Law and Adjudication* (Duke UP, 2000). Our thanks to David Fraser for drawing our attention to this text.

332 See eg, the classic accounts of R. Dworkin: *A Matter of Principle* (Duckworth, 1984); and *Law's Empire* (Fontana, 1986).

333 Hutchinson, above n. 331, p. 11.

forward that, in a democracy, there must be a 'division of constitutional labor between legal and political institutions' and there must be 'some real difference between what adjudication entails and what ideological debate involves'.[334]

Much of the HRA-inspired debate and scholarship on 'judicialisation' fits within this foundationalist perspective. This is evidenced by its insistence that parliamentary sovereignty and separation of powers must be respected to prevent judges acting 'politically' as they lack a democratic mandate. Thus, although judges in the HRA era will continue to deal with political issues, take account of political values and interpret legal rules, adjudication must remain a non-ideological process. Even the unique interpretive openness of section 3 of the HRA – 'so far as it is possible to do so' legislation must conform with Convention rights – has been accommodated within the foundationalist framework by placing emphasis on the fact that it merely provides judges with the tool (and legitimacy) to give effect to substantive human rights norms. The legitimate task of the judge, therefore, is always one of *legal* interpretation and this process is never open-ended but constrained by objective rules and conventions.

In contrast, the antifoundationalist perspective generally emphasises the ideological nature of law and views adjudication as subjective exercises of judicial power. 'Whereas foundationalist jurists locate truth and authority primarily in legal doctrine, the antifoundationalist critics confer that interpretive privilege almost exclusively on judges.'[335] The classic civil liberties scholarship arguing that 'law is politics' (using, for example, the history of anti-trade union law), or that the 'politics of the judiciary' is the determinative factor in adjudication, is firmly in the antifoundationalist camp.[336] Moreover, as seen above, its more recent manifestation in HRA-prompted scholarship perpetuates these emphases by noting the ideological leanings of the judiciary and the dangers of 'trusting the judges'. The antifoundationalist sees judgments (whether expressed in sophisticated or crudely partisan terminology) as predictable and as the direct imposition of the ideological values of the judge. This is in stark contrast to the foundationalist who views the judge as engaged in a good faith process of legal reasoning which will produce coherent and determinate answers – even when dealing with the particularly open texture of ECHR guarantees (such as the 'right to privacy') or difficult policy factors (for example in relation to media freedom or national security).

One way beyond this dichotomy of theories of adjudication (and meriting, we would argue, close attention from civil liberties law) is to adopt what Hutchinson terms a *nonfoundationalist* approach. This combines insights from the two dominant perspectives in a quest for greater recognition of 'both the professional and ideological character' of law and adjudication. It proposes,

---

334 Ibid., pp. 10-11.
335 Ibid., p. 13.
336 Antifoundationalism is also evident in those strands of scholarship which provide totalising accounts of, for example, gender or race. This scholarship represents law, legal institutions and rights discourse as irrevocably conditioned by wider social, economic and political forces, and adjudication is reduced to the external forces operating on the judge or, alternatively, the appointment of (for eg) a woman judge is treated as *necessarily* leading to more progressive legal judgments: see eg, the scholarship and activism of Catharine MacKinnon on the relationship between law and pornography (although her work can also be interpreted as deliberately polemical), including *Feminism Unmodified: Discourses on Life and Law* (Harvard UP, 1987) and *Only Words* (Harper Collins, 1994).

first, that adjudication is not an 'objective exercise in the neutral application of given rules' but rather that judicial experience is always crucial; and secondly, that whilst it is true that 'law is politics', there is no fixed and determinate essence to this link.[337]

We believe that this nonfoundationalist approach is better able to capture the potential of the HRA, and the role of judges in the interpretation of legal texts. It enables the transformative effect of adjudication to be recognised, thereby facilitating the use of law as progressive politics in the HRA era:

> [L]egal adjudication is indeterminate and ideological in that it inevitably and inescapably involves choosing among values in contingent circumstances; it is as much about playing with the rules as it is about playing within the rules. As such, adjudication is an ideological game that is played within law's political stadiums. This does not mean that law is reduced to only the play of political forces but that legal intellectual interests mediate the ideological projects and impulses that are at large in society at any particular time. As such, adjudication is a game that must be appreciated from both an internal perspective (according to the professional self-understandings of its active participants) and an external perspective (according to the ideological lights of its social spectators).[338]

This means that the movement to represent the HRA and the judgments of the European Court of Human Rights as a collection of fixed legal rules is deeply flawed; these legal norms are contingent and can only be understood in their socio-political contexts. Similarly, the recurring plea for 'values' and 'principles' in public law theory would benefit from moving beyond a foundationalist search for a fixed set of liberal icons and moral criteria.

A nonfoundationalist approach would also oblige civil liberties law to accommodate the reality that adjudication in the HRA era will be contingent; while judges work within a framework of legal reasoning and conventions, legal outcomes are never rigid but are influenced by a multitude of (legal, social, political, economic, historical, cultural, personal) variables. Thus, judges 'do follow and apply rules, but what is the relevant rule and what it means to follow it or apply it are always up for grabs'.[339] In many respects, there is little in this which will startle an alert contemporary public lawyer: the elaborate and elegant manoeuvrings of the judges in reconciling the common law tradition with European law and a positive rights jurisprudence, and in pushing out the boundaries of judicial review, are already obvious to most commentators. So too is the fact that what the judges were doing and what they said they were doing were sometimes very different things.

A civil liberties law theory of adjudication grounded in nonfoundationalism therefore seems the best prospect for capturing the judicial project in the HRA era. The 'intention' of Parliament in passing the HRA is not reducible to one concrete meaning, nor is there a 'Founding Father' meaning to the text of the ECHR. Too much of the discussion about the new form of judicial reasoning required in the HRA era has shied away from stating the obvious: there is no one adjudicative approach shared by all judges and different judges will adopt different approaches depending on the contexts and the desired

---

337 Hutchinson, above n. 331, p. 13.
338 Ibid., p. 11.
339 Hutchinson, above n. 331, p. 184.

results. The personal experiences, backgrounds and 'politics' of senior judges are relevant factors, but they should not be considered conclusive. Similarly, commentaries which seek to use Convention case law or common law 'principles' so as to predict how courts must interpret, for example, the rights to privacy or fair trial, are missing the point or engaging in wishful thinking. Adjudication is always and inevitably a dynamic and contingent process: civil liberties law in the HRA era needs to hold tight to this if it is successfully to explain, negotiate and critique the new constitutional culture. And, perhaps most importantly, this approach to adjudication also makes it possible to see rights discourse as neither inherently progressive nor regressive, emancipatory nor debilitating. '[I]t depends on what you make of it':[340] human rights campaigns may have transformative potential in certain contexts but not in others; and rights discourse can hide structural inequalities and privilege regressive individualism, but it can also be a site of empowerment and a catalyst for social change.[341]

CONCLUSION

The HRA provides new and exciting opportunities for the civil liberties tradition. In this opening chapter, we have sought to emphasise the Act's origins, potential and limitations, while also placing it within the wider context of shifting constitutionalism and governance in the UK. We have also tried to show how, if civil liberties law is to negotiate, explain and critique this new era, it must discard its history of legalism and atheoreticism, and embrace literature which is still most often outside the mainstream law curriculum.

We have sought to provide a range of pointers for the new civil liberties law. We emphasised the need to pay attention to context and comparative inquiry, but also indicated the unique character of human rights discourse: rights litigation is contingent and complex, and the diversity of social, economic and cultural factors influencing outcomes compromises predictive ability. We have also emphasised the need for a better civil liberties law theory of adjudication for the HRA era. The foundationalists' attempt to ground public law on some *universal* principle such as ultra vires or parliamentary sovereignty is flawed, and an unwelcome distraction. Similarly, their attempt to explain the shift to a rights-regarding constitutionalism in pure doctrinal terms is unconvincing and fails to recognise the 'constitutional moment' which we are experiencing in the UK. We also rejected anti-foundationalist claims that law is pure politics and that judges are purely ideological actors or dupes of the executive. Judicial history varies and adjudication in the HRA era will be influenced both by the professional sense and experience of individual judges, and by wider social and political forces.

Thus, civil liberties law for the HRA era is about recognising that the HRA does not have one fixed interpretation, and that adjudication is more complex

---

340 D. Herman, Review of *Just Words* (1997) 35 Osg Hall LJ 407, 411.
341 See eg, Bakan, above n. 55; Herman, above n. 55; and Stychin, above n. 15.

and contingent than usually represented by academics or judges.[342] Of course, this is not to suggest that judges will throw off their doctrinal straitjackets overnight or that progressive legal change is inevitable.[343] Equally, however, the HRA era may encourage a much more explicit process of adjudication (wherein ideological values and political choices cannot easily be hidden) and, thus, open up possibilities for new legal strategies and political campaigns. Engaging the opportunities of the HRA era, while retaining awareness of the costs of rights discourse and the difficulties of achieving meaningful social change, is therefore the best starting-point for the civil liberties lawyer today.

342 There is a welcome renewed focus on the issue of adjudication. See eg, the texts by D. Kennedy, *A Critique of Adjudication (Fin De Siècle)* (Harvard UP, 1998); W. Lucy, *Understanding and Explaining Adjudication* (OUP, 1999); M. Loughlin, *Sword and Scales: An Examination of the Relationship Between Law and Politics* (Hart Publishing, 2000); and N. Duxbury, *Jurists and Judges: An Essay on Influence* (Hart Publishing, 2001). See also, A.C. Hutchinson, 'Casaubon's Ghosts: The Haunting of Legal Scholarship' (2001) 21 LS 65, 93 ('legal reasoning is as much about political oppression as it is about ethical consensus'); J. Limbach, 'The Concept of the Supremacy of the Constitution' (2001) 64 MLR 1, 8–9 ('there is no binding constitutional theory or catalogue of useful criteria that could serve as a signpost in the ridge-walking between law and politics'); C. Harlow, 'Disposing of Dicey: From Legal Autonomy to Constitutional Discourse?' (2000) 48 Pol Studies 356, 365 ('Law cannot endure as a world neutrally detached from the contests of political argument'); and G.W. Anderson, 'The Danger of (Un)Making Assumptions: A Legal Pluralist Critique of Contemporary Constitutional Scholarship' (2000) 50 U of Toronto LJ 443, 466 ('it is assumed that there should and can be no politics in adjudication').

343 See the comments of Lord Bingham to the Houses of Parliament Joint Committee on Human Rights, 26 March 2001, Question 78: 'I would not myself think in terms of dialogue at all. The business of the judges is to listen to cases and give judgment. In doing that, of course, they will pay attention to the arguments that are addressed to them and one hopes they will be alive to the currents of thought which are prevalent in the community, but I do not myself see it as the role of the judges to engage in dialogue'. See also, *Poplar Housing and Regeneration Community Association Ltd v Donogue* [2001] EWCA Civ 595, para. 75 (per Woolf LCJ): 'section 3 [of the HRA] does not entitle the court to *legislate*; its task is still one of *interpretation* . . .'.

Chapter Two

Public order law and practice

INTRODUCTION

There is a startling conclusion to the chapter on Protest and Public Order in David Feldman's *Human Rights and Civil Liberties in England and Wales.*[1] According to Feldman, it is '[t]his field, *perhaps more than any other*, [that] makes manifest the consequences of a constitutional and political ethos which values pragmatism above principle, and has little or no room for rights'.[2] We suspect that many readers will be surprised by Feldman's conclusion; some may dismiss it outright. Moreover, it is easy to see why the conclusion might provoke such reactions: the range of liberties that have been undermined by the residual approach to freedom in UK law makes it difficult to see any basis for singling out public order law and practice for particular odium.

The reality, however, is that there is a great deal to back up Feldman's argument that, in the UK, public order law and practice are in deep trouble. One reason for the current difficulties is that the democratic value of protest, and more broadly the related freedoms of assembly and expression, have gone largely undiscussed. In part, this has been because, historically, the freedoms of assembly and expression have not been legally secured. It may also be a result of freedom of assembly's low profile in the civil liberties, public law, criminal law and criminal justice arenas. Or it may be a consequence of the fact that the deployment of public order arguments – often the nemesis of freedom of assembly and expression – has 'generally been marked by an uncanny absence of overt contention'.[3] All of this evidence suggests that Feldman is right: public order law and practice is a troubled arena, one characterised by assumed consensus on the demands of 'order' as well as pervasive ambiguity. It is also an arena that is replete with little-managed discretionary powers, prey to party-political short-termism, and protected by grand-sounding, but potentially empty, metaphors like 'balance'.

A second issue regarding the currently troubled status of public order law and practice which deserves particular attention is the popularisation and continued ascent of 'law and order' in party-political, pressure group and media circles. This development has further compromised the already precarious standing of public protest; it has also extended the criminalisation of low-level disorder. As Downes and Morgan explain, it has done this largely by blurring the boundaries

---

1 D. Feldman, *Civil Liberties and Human Rights in England and Wales* (OUP, 1993).
2 Ibid., p. 842 (emphasis added).
3 C. Townshend, *Making the Peace: Public Order and Public Security in Modern Britain* (OUP, 1993), p. 191.

between public order transgression and straightforward criminality, or between order-defiance and law-breaking,[4] making it much harder to argue for the democracy-enhancing capacities of public protest. 'Law and order' has meant that those who seek to present, or use, public protest as an expression of, rather than a threat to, democracy, and those who question the increasing use of the criminal law in this area, or ask about common understandings of 'public order', are immediately put on the defensive. Moreover, in the current climate of 'active citizenship' and ahistoricity, their arguments or actions can easily be represented as irresponsible, selfish posturing and then dismissed without serious consideration.

Part I of this chapter will outline the troubled status of public order law and practice, focusing on the two issues highlighted above. Part II will offer an outline of current public order law. In Part III, we shall examine 'protest' and 'order', two core concepts in constructing a democratic law of public order. The material in this section draws attention to the amorphous nature of these ubiquitous concepts and, thus, to the importance of understanding different standpoints if definition and regulation is to claim the authority of informed consensus. In Part IV, we shall attempt to deepen our understanding of public order law and practice by examining another fundamental issue: 'balance', the metaphor of choice in this field. This Part will be structured around a case study of state power to impose conditions on, and to ban, public gatherings. It will also chart the recent repackaging of public order law (most notably in the Criminal Justice and Public Order Act 1994), so as to highlight the burgeoning preoccupation with 'quality-of-life' crimes and disorderly groups. Finally, because public order law is about enforcement and interpretation practices as much as it is about formal rules, we shall conclude in Part V by considering the decision-makers who dominate this area, in particular the police and the judiciary.

In setting out this account of the troubled status of freedom of assembly in the UK, we do not mean to eulogise all forms of public protest, or to dismiss the 'democracy-forcing'[5] virtue of order. Nor we do mean to single out the UK as uniquely culpable in this area; questions of protest and order are difficult for all democracies. As we see it, assembly and expression are freedoms that cannot be without limit: if they were without limit, protesters' communicative aims would most likely go unachieved, and disruption, violence, and loss of life might also ensue. Public protest has to be recognised not just as an area where freedoms connect but also as one where they collide. Just such a recognition probably lies behind the fact that it is a right to *peaceful* assembly (and then only subject to certain qualifications) which is protected in international and national rights-protecting instruments.[6] Thus, the key to a democratic law and

---

4   D. Downes and R. Morgan, 'Dumping the "Hostages to Fortune"? The Politics of Law and Order in Post-War Britain' in M. Maguire, R. Morgan and R. Reiner (eds.), *The Oxford Handbook of Criminology* (OUP, 1997), pp. 87-134, at p. 88.

5   C.R. Sunstein, 'Foreword: Leaving Things Undecided' (1996) 110 Harv LR 6.

6   On the international front, see eg, Art. 21, ICCPR and Art. 11, ECHR. There is a similar emphasis on peaceful assembly in national instruments; moreover, '[t]hose jurisdictions which provide constitutional protection for free expression have generally accepted that the protection will extend to some but not all forms of public protest. The distinction is based on the classification – in the US – of some forms of protest as outside the meaning of "speech" or arises because the threat posed by the conduct element outweighs the significance of the speech. These distinctions may reflect perceptions that the well known free speech justifications are not all equally applicable to public protest and that not all forms of protest participate equally in those which are applicable': H. Fenwick, 'The Right to Protest, the Human Rights Act and the Margin of Appreciation' (1999) 62 MLR 491, 492.

practice of public order lies in achieving an optimum 'balance'. It also has to be accepted that order is necessary for the existence of society, and that it is neither intrinsically anti-democratic nor conservative. Thus, borrowing a phrase from Sunstein, we would argue that order is democracy-forcing:[7] that is, it can, and does, nourish democracy and clear space for positive, peaceful social change. Unfortunately, it can also tip over into a democracy-foreclosing quietism and, as will be argued throughout this chapter, it is this latter outcome which must be guarded against in the HRA era.

I. OVERVIEW

In this Part, we shall examine the issue of the troubled status of public order law and practice in the UK, exploring the two points identified above in greater detail. We begin with the lack of discussion on the democratic merit of freedom of assembly and the assumed consensus on the demands of order.

Public order law and practice and the UK 'rights' tradition

As with the other rights discussed in this book, assembly and expression traditionally had no constitutionally declared status in UK law. Thus, in accordance with the British way, these freedoms were residual rather than overt and legally secured.[8] This status has compromised their capacity to watch over public gatherings, particularly public protest, in at least three ways. First, it has ceded a near-monopoly to public order concerns in this field of law. Second, it has veiled the neglect of consultation on, and periodic review of, the demands of public order, and cloaked the potential for discrimination inherent in assumed consensus and unguided discretion. Third, and finally, assembly and expression's residual status has inhibited the quality and quantity of judicial review in this area, blunting inquiry into broad questions (such as the meaning of public order, and whether a state's obligation to preserve the freedom to assemble extends to providing access to protesting space) as well as narrower ones (such as whether individual public order offences have been drafted with sufficient clarity).

Public protest is obviously not the sole victim of the traditional UK approach to liberty; as this book illustrates, other freedoms have also been burdened. But, following Feldman, we would argue that it has lost out especially heavily as a result of UK traditions. Discussion on freedom of expression has not really touched on protest issues. Moreover, freedom of assembly has tended to be overshadowed by its affiliates, the freedoms of expression and association. In part, this may be because the emphasis on public order has elided assembly's connection with expression and association. It may also be a consequence of the civil libertarian romance with the latter rights: assembly can seem a rather

---

7 See above n. 5.
8 Ss. 95-96 of the Representation of the People Act 1983 (providing parliamentary candidates with limited rights to hold public meetings prior to a general election) and s. 43 of the Education (No. 2) Act 1986 (placing university and college authorities under a positive duty to 'ensure that freedom of speech within the law is secured for members, students and employees of the establishment and for visiting speakers') are notable exceptions to this general rule.

pallid subject of inquiry when pitted against expression and association's popular characterisation as the source of newsworthy tussles, and their capacity to accommodate favourite stereotypes (such as the Secret State or the anti-union employer).

The marginalisation of freedom of assembly, and the failure to explore expression's links with public protest, has left us particularly ill-prepared as regards difficult protest and parading claims. These claims often involve expression/equality trade-offs, similar to those generated in Northern Ireland where the Orange Order maintain a 'right to march' using traditional routes, and in the US where GLIB (Boston's Irish-American Gay, Lesbian and Bisexual Group) went to the US Supreme Court to argue that they should be allowed to march in Boston's annual St. Patrick's Day parade despite the contrary wishes of the parade's organisers.[9]

The civil libertarian romance with particular aspects of expression and association, and the general neglect of assembly, has not been public protest's only enemy, however. It has also been marginalised by the lack of attention to public order in the fields of criminal law and criminal justice. As regards the criminal law, Lacey and Wells observe that, although 'practically every area of criminal law has a "public order" aspect' and 'public order problems might be seen as constituting the very core of crime as socially constructed',[10] public order law is not commonly studied in criminal law courses and criminal lawyers are tempted to dismiss it as peripheral to, or tangibly different from, the core concerns of their subject. Moreover, even if one shifts the focus to criminal justice – in particular to law enforcement and interpretation practices – interest in public order remains fairly low-level. For the most part, it seems to have lost out to 'serious' crimes in criminal justice discussions, thereby subverting another possible source of democratic engagement.

Public order *policing* has had a greater degree of visibility, both within the force and outside. Inside the force, 'lay theories' of disorder have tended to dominate, emphasising criminogenic explanations for disorder: as Peter Waddington reminds us, 'senior police officers cannot afford the luxury of too much time spent theorising about public order . . . and understandably they fall back on the basis of their own experience as a means of understanding'.[11] There is also a rich seam of academic work on public order policing,[12] which debates historical trends in this field (for example, has there been a drift towards paramilitarism?) while also charting the particular challenges thrown up by the paradoxical nature of the police force's current mandate (which involves 'hard' order-maintenance and crime control *and* 'soft' community policing), and by changing patterns of dissent, policing and the social order itself.

Public order policing's higher profile, however, has not succeeded in bringing it to the attention of public lawyers in any consistent way. Moreover, 'policing research [itself] too often presents policing as if it is isolated from changes in

---

9   See below, pp. 91-93. Such 'trade-offs' continue to provoke immense controversy in many countries: see the argument in the US over prominent civil libertarians' defence of the Ku Klux Klan's right to demonstrate.

10   N. Lacey and C. Wells, *Reconstructing Criminal Law* (Butterworths, 1998), pp. 219, 150.

11   P.A.J. Waddington, *Liberty and Order: Public Order Policing in a Capital City* (UCL, 1994), cited in D. Waddington, 'Key Issues and Controversies' in C. Critcher and D. Waddington (eds.), *Policing Public Order: Theoretical and Practical Issues* (Avebury, 1996), pp. 1-36, at p. 5.

12   For an overview of these studies, see ibid.

public administration'.[13] The upshot is that, in an era characterised by surging interest in public law powers and the impact of privatisation and public/private partnerships,[14] the exercise of discretion in the public order field is rarely commented upon. There has also been remarkably little work connecting law in policing with broader debates about regulation.[15] Admittedly, there have been some flurries of academic interest (for example, around the policing, prosecutorial and sentencing policies during the 1984-85 miners' strike), but by and large, the political power which is exercised throughout the public order process – from individual officers (or, increasingly, private security) to chief constables, from magistrates to legislative enactments and Home Office Circulars – has been little analysed.[16] We are unclear about why this has happened and consider that the question asked over ten years ago by Dennis Galligan is still relevant today: '[g]iven that the same issues of accountability occur in this area as in other arenas of official discretion, what has stalled the application of principles that have been developed in public law?'[17]

Of course, it might be argued that this lament for public protest is now out of date and that things will surely change for this freedom as a result of the Convention rights to expression and assembly contained within the HRA. These rights provide that:

Article 10[18]
  1. Everyone has the right to freedom of expression. This right shall include freedom to hold opinions and to receive and impart information and ideas without interference by public authority and regardless of frontiers. This Article shall not prevent States from requiring the licensing of broadcasting, television or cinema enterprises.
  2. The exercise of these freedoms, since it carries with it duties and responsibilities, may be subject to such formalities, conditions, restrictions or penalties as are prescribed by law and are necessary in a democratic society, in the interests of national security, territorial integrity or public safety, for the prevention of disorder or crime, for the protection of health or morals, for the protection of the reputation or rights of others, for preventing the disclosure of information received in confidence, or for maintaining the authority and impartiality of the judiciary.

Article 11
  1. Everyone has the right to freedom of peaceful assembly and to freedom of association with others, including the right to form and to join trade unions for the protection of his interests.
  2. No restrictions shall be placed on the exercise of these rights other than such as are prescribed by law and are necessary in a democratic

---

13 D. Dixon, *Law in Policing: Legal Regulation and Police Practices* (Clarendon, 1997), p. 24.
14 See C. Harlow and R. Rawlings, *Law and Administration* (Butterworths, 1997); and M. Taggart (ed.), *The Province of Administrative Law* (Hart, 1997).
15 Dixon, above n. 13.
16 For notable exceptions, see L. Lustgarten, *The Governance of Police* (Sweet & Maxwell, 1986); and N. Walker, *Policing in a Changing Constitutional Order* (Sweet & Maxwell, 2000).
17 D. Galligan, 'Preserving Public Protest: The Legal Approach' in L. Gostin (ed.), *Civil Liberties in Conflict* (Routledge, 1988), pp. 39-64, at p. 47.
18 The ECHR's protection for property rights also needs to be taken into account: see Art. 8 and the First Protocol.

society in the interests of national security or public safety, for the prevention of disorder or crime, for the protection of health or morals or for the protection of the rights and freedoms of others. This article shall not prevent the imposition of lawful restrictions on the exercise of these rights by members of the armed forces, of the police or of the administration of the State.

It seems unlikely that public protest and assembly more generally will achieve a less troubled status as a result of Articles 10 and 11 alone, at least in the short term. As emphasised in Chapter 1, it is foolish to assume that rights inevitably lead to positive social change. There is also scant Convention case law on public protest:[19] applications under Article 11 of the ECHR have tended to be dismissed as manifestly ill-founded by the Commission;[20] there is only one judgment, *Ezelin v France*,[21] where the European Court of Human Rights has found an infringement of the Article; and 'due to the existence of Article 11, . . . Strasbourg has not . . . developed a distinct Article 10 jurisprudence on the use of speech as public protest'.[22]

Of course, this gloomy outlook may be unjustified. Recent judgments of the Court of Appeal, the House of Lords and the European Court of Human Rights have laid down some support for public protest.[23] In a Divisional High Court judgment, *Redmond-Bate v DPP*, Lord Justice Sedley issued a powerful reminder that:

Free speech includes not only the inoffensive but the irritating, the contentious, the eccentric, the heretical, the unwelcome and the provocative provided it does not tend to provoke violence. Freedom only to speak inoffensively is not worth having. What Speakers' Corner (where the law applies as fully as anywhere else) demonstrates is the tolerance which is both extended by the law to opinion of every kind and expected by the law in the conduct of those who disagree, even strongly, with what they hear. From the condemnation of Socrates to the persecution of modern writers and journalists, our world has seen too many examples of state control of unofficial ideas. A central purpose of the European Convention on Human Rights has been to

19 See D.J. Harris, M. O'Boyle and C. Warbrick, *The European Convention on Human Rights* (Butterworths, 1995), Ch. 12. See also, Fenwick, above n. 6; B. Fitzpatrick and N. Taylor, 'Trespassers Might Be Prosecuted: The European Convention and Restrictions on the Right to Assemble' [1998] 3 EHRLR 292; and J. Wadham and H. Mountfield, *Blackstone's Guide to the Human Rights Act 1998* (Blackstone, 1999), pp. 101-107. For discussion of *DPP v Jones* against a backdrop of ECHR case law, see H. Fenwick and G. Phillipson, 'Public Protest, the Human Rights Act and Judicial Responses to Political Expression' [2000] PL 627.

20 Fenwick, above n. 6, argues that where an adverse Commission decision on admissibility based on manifest ill-foundedness seems relevant in a domestic case under the HRA, it may be interpreted as 'virtually conclusive' by inexperienced practitioners, magistrates and judges 'since on its face it appears to mean that the case was almost unarguable' (p. 504).

21 (1991) 14 EHRR 362.

22 Fenwick, above n. 6, p. 496.

23 See respectively, *DPP v Jones* [1999] 2 All ER 257 (below, pp. 82-83); *Redmond-Bate v DPP* [1999] Crim LR 998 (below, p. 79); *Steel v UK* (1998) 28 EHRR 603; and *Hashman and Harrup v UK* (1999) 30 EHRR 241 (below, pp. 79-80). However, another case, *R v Chief Constable of Sussex, ex p International Trader's Ferry Ltd* [1999] 1 All ER 129 (below, p. 91), suggests that at least some members of the senior domestic judiciary may not see the HRA, or 'European concepts of proportionality and margin of appreciation', as providing any new basis on which to interfere with senior police officers' discretion: 'in this case I think that the Chief Constable must enjoy a margin of discretion that cannot differ according to whether its source be found in purely domestic principles or superimposed European principles' (per Lord Hoffmann).

set close limits to any such assumed power. We in this country continue to owe a debt to the jury which in 1670 refused to convict the Quakers William Penn and William Mead for preaching ideas which offended against state orthodoxy.[24]

Several academic commentators have been upbeat about the impact of rights-based protection on the status of protest and assembly. Writing in 1988, Galligan highlighted two advantages of such protection: first, it would provide guaranteed status to rights to free protest which could be of enduring value, particularly in novel and contentious cases; and secondly, judicial review would be an obvious companion to such a system, permitting decisions as to scope and content of the right to be considered by the courts.[25] These are still sound arguments;[26] moreover, as Fenwick has pointed out, the non-discrimination provision in Article 14 of the ECHR may also be relevant here, offering a potentially important tool for curbing any tendency towards higher levels of state interference in relation to *minority* public protests.[27]

'Law and order' and public order

We turn now to the second feature which seems to us to support Feldman's hunch that public order law and practice is in deep trouble: the prominence of 'law and order', in particular 'the stridency of the appeals to fear'[28] in party political, pressure group and media circles. The 'law and order' phenomenon is hard to pin down; it is also all too easy to overplay the state's malign intent and deviousness in this context.[29] That said, however, it does seem fair to say that, as far as public protest is concerned, the politics of 'law and order' has proved to be a nasty form of anti-politics. The reason for this lies in a paradox: 'law and order's' rise to prominence has flattened out public contestation of the relationship between protest, crime and democracy.

Admittedly, there has never been a rich discourse on this issue in the UK; in fact, 'the deployment of the concept of public order has generally been marked by an uncanny absence of overt contention'.[30] That said, the outpouring of disorder in the 1980s (for example, St. Paul's in Bristol, Brixton, Greenham

---

24 Ibid.
25 Galligan, above n. 17.
26 See below pp. 94-95.
27 Above n. 6, p. 497. Art. 14 of the ECHR provides that '[t]he enjoyment of the rights and freedoms set forth in this Convention shall be secured without discrimination on any ground such as sex, race, colour, language, religion, political or other opinion, national or social origin, association with a national minority, property, birth or other social status': see Harris, O'Boyle and Warbrick, above n. 19, pp. 462-488.
28 A. von Hirsch and A. Ashworth, 'Law and Order' in A. von Hirsch and A. Ashworth (eds.), *Principled Sentencing* (Hart, 1998), pp. 410-424, at p. 411.
29 The 'authoritarian state thesis' is the subject of lively academic debate. Crudely, it proposes that the British state has responded to significant challenges to it over the last three decades with 'an overtly co-ordinated alliance between the police, mass media, judiciary and governments of the day' (Waddington, above n. 11, p. 8). However, as is illustrated by the wide variations in accounts of police behaviour and attitudes during the 1984-85 miners' strike, proving or disproving the thesis is difficult. This thesis may have more relevance in the context of terrorism (see Ch. 3) and the security services (see Ch. 7).
30 Townshend, above n. 3. See, however, the recent revival of the debate on the 'flashpoints' for public disorder in Britain in the 1980s: D. Waddington, 'Waddington Versus Waddington: Public Order Theory on Trial' (1998) 2 Theor Crim 373; and P.A.J. Waddington, 'Orthodoxy and Advocacy in Criminology' (2000) 4 Theor Crim 93.

Common and the 1984-85 miners' strike) did seem poised to challenge and define civic virtue in a more truly consensual way, one more appropriate to a modern democracy which has to 'try harder to preserve or rebuild the convention of orderliness and reasonableness'.[31] It is now clear that the government did 'try harder' after the disorder of the 1980s; however, as we see it, the value of public protest, and more generally, of the freedom to assemble and express oneself, got lost in that effort.

The question which arises therefore is: what went wrong for public order law in the 1980s and early 1990s? As noted above, Downes and Morgan argue that, '[i]t was the achievement of "Thatcherism" to blur the difference between [public order legislation and its enforcement and straightforward criminality], and even to fuse them symbolically to political effect'.[32] These authors go on to illustrate how this blurring, and ultimate fusion, of crime, protest and disorder spun out from the early 1970s, documenting the means by which the state justified each new move in beguilingly pragmatic terms. Their account identifies three features of particular note. First, the destruction of industrial conflict, particularly strikes and picketing, which began in the 1970s and continued through the 1980s.[33] This destruction was implemented by Conservative policies, at times aided by naïve union attitudes to militancy and law-breaking. It ravaged an entire tradition of protest and exaggerated negative associations between public protest and crime and disorder. Importantly, it also left the Labour Party (which has a history of strong trade union associations) electorally vulnerable on protest and, more generally, on law and order, vis-à-vis the Conservative Party.

Secondly, in the 1980s, a more general souring of protest occurred, nurtured in large part by the mediagenic horror of late 1970s/early 1980s riots in English cities like Bristol and London.[34] As Lord Scarman explained in one of his oft-cited reports on public order, television brought the spectacle of this disorder directly into people's homes:

> [T]he British people watched with horror and incredulity an instant audio-visual presentation on their television sets of scenes of violence and disorder in their capital city, the like of which had not previously been seen in this century in Britain . . . the petrol bomb was now used for the first time on the streets of Britain . . . .[35]

Similar scenes had previously occurred in other UK cities – Belfast and (London)Derry were more than familiar with 'scenes of violence' and with the 'petrol bomb' – but the 'mainland' disorder of the late 1970s and early 1980s was seen as something altogether different. As Townshend argues, it was as if

---

31   Ibid., p. 192.
32   Downes and Morgan, above n. 4.
33   See eg, M. Adeney and J. Lloyd, *Loss Without Limit: The Miners' Strike of 1984-5* (Routledge, 1986); R. Geary, *Policing Industrial Disputes* (CUP, 1985); D. Waddington, *Contemporary Issues in Public Disorder: A Comparative and Historical Approach* (Routledge, 1992); and P. Wallington, 'Policing the Miners' Strike' (1985) 14 ILJ 145.
34   See eg, J. Benyon (ed.), *Scarman and After: Essays Reflecting on Lord Scarman's Report, the Riots and their Aftermath* (Pergamon, 1984); J. Benyon and J. Solomos (eds.), *The Roots of Urban Unrest* (Pergamon, 1987); G. Gaskell and R. Benewick (eds.), *The Crowd in Contemporary Britain* (Sage, 1987); J. Lea and J. Young, 'Urban Violence and Political Marginalisation: The Riots in Britain; Summer 1981' (1982) 1 CSP 59; and C. Unsworth, 'The Riots of 1981: Popular Violence and the Politics of Law and Order' (1982) 9 JLS 63.
35   Lord Scarman, *The Scarman Report: The Brixton Disorders 10-12 April 1981* (Penguin, 1982), pp. 13-14.

'Red Lion Square [had] opened a wound in the body politic'[36] which could not heal itself. Ultimately, these disorders tarnished protest itself, not just particular classes of protesters (like rioters or striking workers), or particular places (like Northern Ireland) in relation to which it was assumed that consensus on public order was impossible, and where militarisation and other special police powers were presented as the price of day-to-day life. Furthermore, although the 'mainland' disorders of the 1980s did provoke policing reforms, they also generated distrust of public order policing – especially within communities that had been subjected to racist policing patterns.[37] Finally, they raised the stakes for future media coverage of protest and demonstration.

Third, and finally, in the early to mid-1990s the democratic virtues of public protest slid even further out of view as a new 'right' – the right to order – achieved a remarkable ascendancy. This 'right' was levered into position by means of a double move. On the one hand, there was further investment (both in terms of political rhetoric and legislative enactment) in criminalisation, thereby boosting the state's command-and-control stance and confirming its tough, 'no-nonsense' line on law-breaking. A prime example of this is the Criminal Justice and Public Order Act 1994 which amended the earlier public order legislation of 1986 to bring trespass, and other acts disrupting lawful activities, within the grip of the criminal law.[38] In addition, the change of name in a later legislative development in this area – the *Crime and Disorder* Act 1998 – represented a further powerful signifier of the stranglehold of criminalisation and the increasing difficulty in separating public order transgressions from straightforward criminality.

This increasing criminalisation did not stand alone, however. As suggested above, it was one part of a double move initiated by the Conservative government in the early 1980s. They chose to twin it with the concept of 'community':

> The ground shifted, imperceptibly at first but now quite markedly. The much-vaunted toughness remained – enhanced police capacity to deal with public disorder – but was joined by 'community' – with all its imprecise aura of vacuous virtue.[39]

As deployed, the concept of 'community' stressed the limits of police power to impose order, and championed privatisation, particularly the volunteer spirit of 'active' citizens, as the way forward on public order. In the 1983 General Election, the Conservative Party manifesto explained this development as follows:

> Dealing with crimes, civil disobedience, violent demonstrations and pornography are not matters for the police alone. It is teachers and parents – and television producers too – who influence the moral standards of the next generation. There must be close co-operation and understanding between the police and the communities they serve.[40]

---

36   Townshend, above n. 3, p. 145. Kevin Gately died during a political demonstration in Red Lion Square, London on 15 Jun. 1974. He was the first person to be killed in a political demonstration in England since 1919.

37   B. Bowling, *Violent Racism: Victimisation, Policing and Social Context* (Clarendon, 1998).

38   For more detail, see eg, S.H. Bailey, D.J. Harris and B.L. Jones, *Civil Liberties: Text and Materials* (Butterworths, 1995), pp. 237-239; and M. Wasik and R. Taylor, *Blackstone's Guide to the Criminal Justice and Public Order Act 1994* (Blackstone, 1995).

39   R. Reiner and M. Cross, 'Introduction: Beyond Law and Order – Crime and Criminology into the 1990s' in R. Reiner and M. Cross (eds.), *Beyond Law and Order: Criminal Justice Policy and Politics into the 1990s* (Macmillan, 1991), at p. 5. See also, D. Garland, 'The Limits of the Sovereign State: Strategies of Crime Control in Contemporary Society' (1996) 36 BJ Crim 445.

40   *The Challenge of Our Times* (Conservative Party, 1983).

The Conservatives' deployment of 'community' and 'active citizenship' was political gold; unfortunately, it has proved less than supportive of a democratic law of public order.[41] Four particular problems have emerged. First, by fuelling the blurring of crime and public disorder noted earlier, the concepts of community and active citizenship have rendered public order law and practice far more amorphous than before. Secondly, these concepts seem to have fed a fascination with particular types of public disorder. Traditional concerns around the regulation of marches and meetings have been supplanted by a preoccupation with 'quality-of-life' crimes, crimes which disturb the peace of urban neighbourhoods, disrupt consumerism or hinder the enjoyment of 'traditional' rural pursuits. Thirdly, dissenting voices (and perhaps dissent itself) have been marginalised by the characterisation of order-maintenance as a matter not simply of crime, disorder and their control, but of 'present and future morality',[42] and as something for which all of us ('teachers and parents – and television producers too'[43]), not just the police, must take individual responsibility. For some – road construction companies, for example – taking individual responsibility has meant investing in private security. The latter is now a growth industry, filling a 'market opportunity' in 'protecting vested interests from the activities of protestors',[44] and creating a rather worrying 'privatisation of public order'.[45] Finally, because the emphasis on 'community' can be understood as implying that police authority with respect to public order should derive not from law but from the communities served, it has raised complex, and as yet unanswered, questions about the source and scope of police discretion in on-the-spot encounters, and about appropriate judicial responses to that discretion.[46] Moreover, emphasising 'community' surely involves an enormous sleight-of-hand when the UK is a 'two-thirds' society with an increasingly excluded 'underclass'[47] and it is less and less clear that there is a single, undifferentiated 'public' who are served by public order law, and from whom public order policing can derive legitimacy.

New directions in public order

Admittedly, 'community' and 'active citizenship' are not wholly unmeritorious concepts. As explained in Chapter 1, they do contain welcome potential for

41   Zedner has argued that the deployment of 'community' and 'active citizenship' parallels 'prison works' rhetoric; thus, the latter is 'not reflective of some new-found faith in the instrument of the prison but rather reproduces a significant change in the perceived goals of incarceration. The prison "works", but in one limited sense only: it excludes from society those who threaten its security. In this respect, the prevailing political rhetoric is explicitly and avowedly disintegrative' (L. Zedner, 'In Pursuit of the Vernacular: Comparing Law and Order Discourse in Britain and Germany' (1995) 4 SLS 517). See also, below Ch. 5, p. 217.
42   Above n. 40, p. 191.
43   Ibid.
44   P.A.J. Waddington, 'Public Order Policing: Citizenship and Moral Ambiguity' in F. Leishman, B. Loveday and S.P. Savage (eds.), *Core Issues in Policing* (Longman, 1996), at p. 128.
45   Waddington, above n. 11, p. 31. See below, pp. 99-101.
46   See below, pp. 96-98. See also, D. Livingston, 'Police Discretion and the Quality of Life in Public Places: Courts, Communities and the New Policing' (1997) 97 Col LR 551.
47   R. Reiner, 'Have the Police Got a Future?' in Critcher and Waddington, above n. 11, pp. 261-267.

greater participative democracy.[48] However, their recent deployment in the sphere of public order indicates that they are also perilous concepts.[49] In addition, developments in this sphere (such as the approach to children and young people's 'anti-social' behaviour in the Crime and Disorder Act 1998[50] and the Criminal Justice and Police Act 2001) give little hope that criminalisation will stop under the New Labour administration. They also offer little indication of what it would take to initiate democratic negotiation of criminalisation's proper limits or, as Reiner and Cross have put it, what it would mean even to start to unpick 'community's' 'imprecise aura of vacuous virtue'?[51]

Against this backdrop, it is hard to raise much enthusiasm about the democratising potential of the rights to assembly and expression contained within the HRA. Moreover, late-1990s public order developments may well raise new issues in the HRA era, in particular because it now seems that '[b]oth the dominant forms of public disorder and the corresponding police strategies and tactics of control are in the midst of important transition'.[52] Contemporary protesters – Reclaim the Streets; The Land is Ours; and protests about genetic engineering, animal exports, asylum law, petrol prices and the world economic order – have given up on the 'pendulum of protest'[53] that swung between left and right. Instead, 'protest today is against neo-liberalism, global financial interests, international corporations and all politicians – right, left or centre – who support them; protest involves graduates and professionals, the un- and underemployed, ex-squaddies, sometimes the homeless':

> Protestors are ripping up genetically modified crops and simulating car crashes on a London motorway to stop traffic and hold a party, deckchairs, sound-systems and all. They filled Claremont Road with sofas, snooker tables and giant chess games to fight the M11 extension; they are protesting against GATT . . . ; they are campaigning against quarries; they fought for every inch of the nine-mile route of the Newbury by-pass; did a Lady Godiva in Coventry Cathedral to draw attention to 'the seventeen million people killed directly by the motor car'.[54]

Thus, of late, it seems that '[t]here is a new kind of politics, that of social movements'.[55] This politics is most often centred on long-term protest around

48   See further J. Morison, 'The Case Against Constitutional Reform?' (1998) 25 JLS 510.
49   'Community' involvement in criminal justice has also been double-edged; eg, the public consultations under s. 106 of the 1984 Police and Criminal Evidence Act have been described as unbalanced, tightly constrained and, overall, 'little more than a forum for consensual impression management': see M. Weatheritt, 'Community Policing: Rhetoric or Reality' in S.D. Mastrofski and J.R. Greene (eds.), *Community Policing* (Praeger, 1989), p. 172 (cited in D. Dixon, *Law in Policing: Legal Regulation and Police Practices* (Clarendon, 1997), p. 313). See also, A. Crawford, *The Local Governance of Crime: Appeals to Community and Partnership* (Clarendon, 1997).
50   See C. Piper, 'The Crime and Disorder Act 1998: Child and Community "Safety"' (1999) 62 MLR 397; and B. Vaughan, 'The Government of Youth: Disorder and Dependence?' (2000) 9 SLS 347.
51   Reiner and Cross, above n. 39.
52   Waddington, above n. 11, p. 2. For recent judicial attempts to grapple with 'new' forms of protesting, see eg, *Broadwith v Chief Constable of Thames Valley Police* [2000] Crim LR 924; *Monsanto plc v Tilly* [2000] Env LR 313 (CA). See also the discussion by F. Donson, 'Limiting the Freedom to Protest: Legal Responses to Direct Action' in P. Smith (ed.), *Making Rights Work* (Ashgate, 1999), pp. 209-228.
53   See B. MacArthur (ed.), *The Penguin Book of 20th-Century Protest* (Penguin, 1998).
54   J. Griffiths, 'Noddy is on Page 248' *LRB*, 10 Jun. 1999, p. 35. See also, G. McKay (ed.), *DIY Culture: Party and Protest in Nineties Britain* (Verso, 1998).
55   Waddington, above n. 11, p. 30.

environmental or ecological issues. It also tends to involve people from across the socio-economic spectrum: press reports placed particular emphasis on the participation of the 'middle-class' in the Newbury by-pass and live animal export protests, and Greenpeace claims mass public support for its anti-GM protests. Forms of protest are also different today. 'Stealth' protest, using cell-based organising structures and Internet recruitment, is reported to be on the increase, supplanting the more familiar industrial picket or mass demonstration.[56] Furthermore, the traditional line between peaceful protest and criminal activity is actively challenged by the fact that the aim of some of this new protesting is to damage (as in the smashing of Hawk aircraft destined for Indonesia) or remove (as in the 'rescue' of laboratory animals) property.

Police responses to these contemporary protests, and to the increase in statutory public order powers, also raise new issues. Overall, 'public order policing no longer seems quite so monolithic and uncompromising in character than it was in the previous decade'.[57] We have already noted the emphasis on 'community' involvement in policing in general: in the public order field, this new emphasis is beginning to raise important questions about managing police discretion in addressing low-level public misconduct, and judicial responses to that discretion.[58] Other public order policing trends include the heightened profile of pre-emptive measures, ranging from intelligence gathering and surveillance[59] to co-operation and negotiation with protest organisers. More general developments in policing, including the increased localisation and centralisation, and the burgeoning emphasis on managerialism and efficient resource allocation have also had an impact.

Overall, it seems that today's public order policing is far more tentative. Divergences in local practice are also much more apparent, as for example in relation to the 1995 live animal export protests at ferry terminals and airports throughout the South of England.[60] Taken together, all of these developments suggest the need to rethink the relationship of legal rules, courts, communities and the newer forms of policing in public order. Given this, the remainder of this chapter will focus on the pros and cons of these developments in greater detail. Prior to that, however, we offer a snapshot of the current law on public order in England and Wales.

II.   OUTLINE OF PUBLIC ORDER LAW

In England and Wales,[61] the Public Order Act 1986, as amended by Part V of the Criminal Justice and Public Order Act 1994 and supplemented by the Crime

---

56   See eg, the press reports following the Jun. 1999 'City of London' protest and the May Day 2000 and 2001 protests.
57   Waddington, above n. 11, p. 2.
58   See Livingston, above n. 46. See Criminal Justice and Police Act 2001 (CJPA), re on the spot penalties.
59   By a range of actors, including traditional 'national security' agencies such as MI5.
60   See also, D. Rose, 'PC PC Plod', *The Observer*, 18 Jan. 1998, contrasting the tactics of the Cambridge and Oxford police forces in respect of the decision to withdraw rather than disperse protesters; and M. King and M. Brearley (eds.), *Public Order Policing: Contemporary Perspectives on Strategy and Tactics* (Perpetuity, 1996).
61   For an outline of public-order law in Northern Ireland, see B. Dickson (ed.), *Civil Liberties in Northern Ireland* (CAJ, 1997), pp. 140-161.

and Disorder Act 1998, occupies centre-stage in the legal regulation of public order.[62] This Act seeks to close down the risks of public disorder in two ways: first, by creating a series of regulatory powers to control the routes and other incidents of processions and the terms on which meetings may be held (if at all); and secondly, by stacking up a series of criminal offences with attendant powers of arrest to enhance on-the-spot control. The Act is bolstered by the trademark of common law control in this area: the aged, but wily, power to prevent breaches of the peace. Finally, there is a ragbag assortment of other statutory, common law and prerogative powers, including specialist provisions on football and alcohol-related disorder.[63]

Sections 11-14 of the 1986 Act contain the key powers for advance control of public processions and assemblies. Section 11 imposes an advance-notice requirement on the organisers of any public procession which is to demonstrate support for or opposition to the views or actions of any person(s), or to publicise a cause or campaign, or to mark or commemorate any event. Section 12 provides for the imposition of conditions on public processions where, for example, a senior police officer reasonably believes, having regard to the time, place, circumstances, and route of the procession, that it may result in 'serious disruption to the life of the community' or 'serious damage to property'. Section 13 provides a power to ban public processions where it seems that section 12 conditions are unlikely to prevent 'serious public disorder'. The power to impose conditions on public assemblies (or static demonstrations) is laid down in section 14, and backed up by section 14A which allows for the banning of 'trespassory assemblies'.[64]

The regulatory powers for advance control of processions and assemblies are accompanied by a series of 'moment-of-crisis' criminal offences with attendant powers of arrest. Sections 1-5 of the 1986 Act replaced common law dinosaurs of public order such as rout and unlawful assembly with new statutory crimes, ranging from riot and affray through to section 5's 'horseplay'[65] offence of using threatening, abusive or insulting words or behaviour, or disorderly conduct, within the hearing or sight of a person likely to be caused harassment, alarm or distress thereby. Together, sections 1-5 generated an 'index of fright',[66] based on offences of descending severity. The index was extended by section 154 of the Criminal Justice and Public Order Act 1994, which sought to plug a perceived gap between sections 4 and 5 of the original Act by inserting a new

---

62 See also, Protection from Harassment Act 1997 (PHA); Terrorism Act 2000; and CJPA 2001. For a fuller account of public-order law powers, see Bailey, Harris and Jones, above n. 38. See also, Feldman, above n. 1; H. Fenwick, *Civil Liberties* (Cavendish, 1998), pp. 275-316; and T. Murphy, 'Freedom of Assembly' in D.J. Harris and S. Joseph (eds.), *The International Covenant on Civil and Political Rights and United Kingdom Law* (Clarendon, 1995), pp. 439-464. On the 1994 and 1998 Acts, see respectively, Wasik and Taylor, above n. 38 and R. Leng, R. Taylor and M. Wasik, *Blackstone's Guide to the Crime and Disorder Act 1998* (Blackstone, 1998).

63 See Football (Offences and Disorder) Act 1999; Football (Disorder) Act 2000; and CJPA 2001. See also CJPA 2001, s. 44 amending PHA 1997 allegedly in response to animal rights protests at Huntingdon Life Sciences lab and other similar premises.

64 This latter power was added by s. 70, Criminal Justice and Public Order Act 1994. See also, *DPP v Jones*, below pp. 82-83; and *Pendragon v UK* [1999] EHRLR 223.

65 Feldman, above n. 1, p. 808.

66 A. Sherr, *Freedom of Protest, Public Order and the Law* (Blackwell, 1989), p. 85.

offence of causing intentional harassment, alarm or distress by using threatening, abusive or insulting words or behaviour or disorderly behaviour, or displaying any writing, sign or other representation which is abusive or insulting.[67] More recently, the Crime and Disorder Act 1998 has introduced racially-aggravated versions of the section 4, 4A and 5 offences,[68] and extended the power to control 'anti-social' behaviour by adults and children through specialist orders and curfews.[69] The 1998 Act also supplemented the special powers of stop and search contained in section 60 of the Criminal Justice and Public Order Act 1994 by providing the police with new powers to require the removal of masks or other items which conceal a person's identity.[70]

Other aspects of modern 'anti-social' behaviour are tackled elsewhere in the 1994 Act. Thus, there are sections allowing control of raves (a quintessential early-1990s assembly),[71] and also what the legislation describes as 'aggravated trespass' (in practice, provisions targeted at particular groups of protesters, including hunt saboteurs and road-building protesters).[72]

The Public Order Act 1986 is not the only source of moment-of-crisis powers for controlling public disorder: it and other repackagings of public order law left undisturbed a medley of other significant statutory powers, as well as the formidable capacity of the common law to prevent breaches of the peace. Furthermore, public order law has tended to throw up unexpected arguments: for example, there have been attempts to use the Protection from Harassment Act 1997 against animals rights protesters,[73] and archaic 'watching and besetting' powers were revived for use against anti-abortion protesters.[74]

The common law power of breach of the peace will be discussed in more detail in Part III of this chapter, where it features as one aspect of a broader inquiry into the dividing lines between legitimate and illegitimate protest. In practice, it is often combined with the statutory offence of wilful obstruction of

---

67   S. 4A of the Public Order Act 1986.
68   Part II of the 1998 Act, in particular s. 28 (defining 'racial aggravation'); s. 31 (setting out the 'racially aggravated' versions of ss. 4, 4A and 5 of the Public Order Act 1986); and s. 32 (setting out the 'racially aggravated' versions of ss. 2 and 4 of the Protection from Harassment Act 1997). S. 82 puts *R v Ribbans* (1995) 16 Cr App Rep (S) 698 on a statutory footing by providing that racial aggravation must be taken into account as an aggravating factor in sentencing in relation to any offence in which it is proved. (The offence of inciting racial hatred is set out in ss. 18-23 of the Public Order Act 1986.)
69   Part I of the 1998 Act, in particular ss. 1, 5, 6, 8, 9, 11, 14, 16 and 17. See also, CJPA 2001 extending the curfew power to under 16s and allowing the police to initiate curfew schemes.
70   For more detail, see Taylor and Wasik, above n. 38, pp. 63-66.
71   Ss. 63-66.
72   Ss. 68-69; see *DPP v Barnard* [2000] Crim LR 371. Other trespass powers are contained in ss. 61-62, Criminal Justice and Public Order Act 1994, replacing s. 39 of the Public Order Act 1986 (originally drafted with the purpose of checking 'hippy convoys').
73   See eg, *Huntingdon Life Sciences Ltd v Curtin* (1998) 3 J Civ Lib 37; and *DPP v Moseley, Woodling and Selvanayagam, The Times*, 23 Jun. 1999. For an account of the Act, see T. Lawson-Cruttenden and N. Addison, *Blackstone's Guide to the Protection from Harassment Act 1997* (Blackstone, 1998).
74   *DPP v Fidler* [1992] 1 WLR 91. The power is set down in s. 7 of the Conspiracy and Protection of Property Act 1875.

a police officer in the execution of their duty.[75] In court, it can lead, inter alia, to a binding over order,[76] or the imposition of restrictive bail conditions.[77] When viewed separately, breach of the peace and these other common law and statutory powers appear unexceptional; it needs to be remembered, however, that they have a powerful, unpredictable flexibility, as well as considerable, and unnecessary, overlap with the powers set down by recent public order legislation.

III. PROTEST AND ORDER

In this Part, we examine two icons from the public order field: first, public protest and secondly, public order. As we see it, securing public protest,[78] while also minimising unwarranted incursions on public order, requires discussion and debate on these foundational concepts and their respective values. One should not assume that existing legal rules tell the whole story (or, for that matter, an accurate one) on these matters; it is also not safe to rely on arid conceptualisation or commonsense. Rather, a fuller account will require historical sensitivity, an openness to different perspectives and a willingness to question fundamental, and allegedly apolitical, tenets.

We can begin by noting that public protest and public order share a number of characteristics. Both are appealing and are commonly cited as part and parcel of democracy. Both also share generally respectable, if incompatible, historical lineages. So, for example, once one looks beyond contemporary concerns about increased societal breakdown and adopts an historical perspective, several things become clear: first, the prevalence and diversity of both protest and disorder,

75 S. 89(2), Police Act 1996. The police have a duty to prevent reasonably apprehended and imminent breaches of the peace, therefore the offence of obstruction may be made out where a person fails to obey instructions reasonably directed towards that goal. The case law on obstruction of an officer contains some of public-order law's most troubling decisions, including *Duncan v Jones* [1936] 1 KB 218 (described by Sedley LJ in *Redmond-Bate*, above n. 23, as a case where the court 'cast its reasoning somewhat wider than . . . is consonant with modern authority') and *Moss v McLachlan* [1985] IRLR 76. Moreover, until the decision in *Redmond-Bate*, case law was unclear on the status of the 'heckler's veto', in particular the question of who ought to be moved on: the heckler or those being heckled who wish to exercise their freedoms of assembly and expression? Breach of the peace and obstruction powers have also generated an extensive 'on-the-spot' capacity to disperse assemblies and processions, and to impose conditions. These powers operate not only in relation to demonstrations and assemblies held in public, but also those held in private, and appear to include a wide general right of entry to private premises: *Thomas v Sawkins* [1935] 2 KB 249.

76 Binding-over powers stem from the common law, the Justices of the Peace Act 1361 and the Magistrates Courts Act 1980. They allow a person to be required to undertake to 'keep the peace' or be 'of good behaviour' (*contra bonos mores*), on pain of forfeiting a 'recognisance' (a sum of money) if a breach is made out. Refusal to be bound over can lead to a prison sentence of up to six months. For more details, see the Law Commission Report No. 222, *Binding-Over* (HMSO, 1994). Their lawfulness under the ECHR has recently been ruled upon by the ECtHR: see *Steel v UK* and *Hashmann & Harrup v UK*, above n. 23, and discussed below, pp. 79-80.

77 S. 3(6), Bail Act 1976.

78 Clearly, it might objected that 'protest' is not broad enough to cover the range of gatherings controlled by public-order law and policing. However, there is no brightline between political and non-political activity on the part of citizens: thus, '[a] ceremonial occasion, such as the State Opening of Parliament may be considered to be no more than a secular pageant, unless protesters seek to use the occasion to demonstrate opposition to government policy' (P.A.J. Waddington, 'The Politics of Public Order Policing: a "Typographical Analysis!"' in Critcher and Waddington, above n. 11, pp. 129-144).

and the contribution which they have made to positive social change;[79] and secondly, as even the briefest historical inquiry demonstrates, '[t]here seems always to have been a "golden age" [of orderliness] about twenty years ago'.[80]

It is also clear that we tend to fear extreme versions of both protest and order. So, for example, although '[o]rder maintenance is probably seen as the elemental task of government',[81] the concept of a police state has few supporters, and emergency powers are generally perceived as requiring greater justification than ordinary ones. Similarly, public protest is usually viewed in less positive terms if it involves, or collapses into, riot or looting. It is also worth noting here that fear of disorder, particularly massive social breakdown, tends to distort perception and memory: consider, for example, the lasting appeal of accounts of daily life in World War II Britain depicting a time of tremendous national orderliness, despite contrary historical evidence indicating that looting was widespread throughout the period.[82]

The final characteristic shared by protest and order which deserves mention is that they are both difficult to pin down. Dictionary definitions inject little clarity, offering 'both negative and positive formulations, and . . . a flood of synonyms'.[83] In part, this definitional elusiveness may derive from the myriad forms that public protest and public order can take. It may also be an unfortunate historical inheritance, flowing from the failure to argue out the substance of 'the Queen's Peace' (a particularly culpable omission given the latter's centrality to common law powers such as breach of the peace), and also from the enduring, but surely misguided, attachment to the notion that an organic, non-political consensus on public order existed at one time, and that it can be rebuilt.[84]

However, the most important reason why definitions of protest and order are difficult to pin down is that, in this sphere, the act of definition is itself highly political. In short, definitions of protest, disorder and order can never be neutral or simply descriptive; instead, the meanings ascribed to particular manifestations of protest, disorder and order depend on perspective, although authoritative perspectives – like the law – do tend to elide all others (and also the importance of perspectivity itself).[85]

In what follows, we shall explore the meanings of protest and order in more detail. In looking at protest, we shall consider the common assumption that violent protest is to be deplored, even though 'by checking violent protest, it is possible that the law checks the very kind of protest which is most likely to obtain fundamental change'.[86] This will be followed by an examination of the concept of order, concentrating on the power to arrest for breach of the peace, the trademark of common law control in the policing of public order.

---

79   G. Pearson, *Hooligan: A History of Respectable Fears* (Macmillan, 1983).
80   Townshend, above n. 3, p. 133.
81   Ibid., p. 4.
82   Pearson, above n. 79.
83   Townshend, above n. 3, p. 7. See also, R. Sparks, A.E. Bottoms and W. Hay, *Prisons and the Problem of Order* (Clarendon, 1996), pp. 70-71; and the discussion of national security in Ch. 7.
84   Townshend, ibid., Ch. 1.
85   See generally, Lacey and Wells, above n. 10, pp. 114-115.
86   Bailey, Harris and Jones, above n. 38, p. 168. See Ch. 5 for a discussion of the role of prison riots as a catalyst for improved prison conditions.

Protest, disorder and riot

We begin with protest. Protesting has numerous faces and, as should be manifestly clear, not all of them are attractive.[87] Yet, it enjoys a robust popularity such that it has been suggested that, worldwide, we have entered a phase of 'extraordinary politics':

> All ... around the globe, millions of people have decided that protest offers the best opportunity to put pressure on the political and economic system. Millions ... have decided that the ordinary system of politics lacks legitimacy and that the only way to practice democratic politics is to operate outside that system.[88]

This phenomenon of 'extraordinary politics' should be recognisable to anyone who has lived in the UK in recent years. The 1996 Newbury by-pass protest, the protests against live animal exports at seaports and airports in the south of England in 1995, and the 1998 Countryside March were all examples of practices of dissent by emergent social movements. These examples show the wide-ranging appeal of the notion of 'extraordinary politics', or people power. The notion conjures images of an active, engaged citizenry and widespread democratic participation. It also has welcome historical resonance: there is a lot of evidence of how protest made ordinary politics work better, opening up opportunities for greater democracy as in the civil rights struggles of the US in the 1960s, or more recently, those in South Africa and Eastern Europe.

But protest, however essential or virtuous, is not enough to guarantee stable democracy: in short, '[d]emocracy needs more than anti-politics if it is to flourish'.[89] Moreover, people-power protests do not always have happy endings or noble beginnings.[90] They can lead to human tragedy and increased state authoritarianism (for example, Tiananmen Square), and they can manifest ugly, threatening and profoundly anti-egalitarian sentiments (for example, neo-Nazi street protests in post-unification Germany or violent anti-abortion protests in the US). In addition, it is sometimes difficult to ascribe meaning to a particular display of people power. A good example of this is the difference of opinion in Northern Ireland on the Orange Order's summer marching season: as the North Review explained in its account of the 1996 marches, '[t]he meaning and interpretation of the experience of parades differs radically according to the perspectives of those taking part and those who are looking, listening and reacting'.[91]

It seems then that we need a way to harness the democracy-forcing character of public protest, whilst also controlling for unwanted side-effects. This will be a delicate and intricate task. It will require a thorough understanding of 'balance', an idea that is increasingly central to public order law. 'Balance' will be examined in the next Part of this chapter. Moving forward will also require an understanding of how the social definition of 'public order' is affected by

---

87   See Fenwick, above n. 6, pp. 494-495 for a categorisation of forms of protest.
88   C.C. Euchner, *Extraordinary Politics* (Westview Press, 1996), p. xi.
89   Ibid.
90   P.A.J. Waddington, *Liberty and Order: Public Order Policing in a Capital City* (UCL Press, 1994), p. 1.
91   *Independent Review of Parades and Marches* (Stationery Office, 1997), p. 3 (chaired by Peter North, Faculty of Law, Oxford University). See also, N. Jarman, 'Regulating Rights and Managing Public Order: Parade Disputes and the Peace Process, 1995-1998' (1999) 22 Fordham Int LJ 1415.

the form of protest, and the nature of the space used; by the participants themselves (and their audiences (hostile or otherwise)); by the motivation behind a protest; and by the handling of protest (whether by the protesters, the police (whether public and/or private), the media, or government). These issues will be discussed in more detail in later sections. Finally, securing public protest may also oblige us to contest fundamental, even apparently incontestable, tenets; what we might call the 'innocent space' of public order law.[92] One such foundational tenet is that protest should be peaceful and that violence as part of protest is unacceptable. As Bailey, Harris and Jones note, two justifications are commonly advanced for this belief: first, 'any violence in society is unacceptable' and secondly 'violence in this context distorts the "proper" democratic political process for obtaining reform'.[93] But how foundational is this belief in reality? Might there in fact be some instability to what we consider to be firm and fixed?

Taking the example of civil disobedience and riot; at first glance, they would appear to occupy different ends of the protest spectrum. Civil disobedience has a high degree of respectability. It evokes historical greats like Martin Luther King and Gandhi, and closer to home, it has been a 'substantial and generally honourable strand in the history of the Labour Party. . . . No left-wing cause had street credibility without a march, demonstration, or occupation'.[94] Riot also occupies a substantial strand in the history of the UK, ranging from the food riots of the seventeenth century to the urban riots of the 1970s and 1980s, and the poll tax riot in 1990. However, the similarity ends there because riot, unlike civil disobedience, is generally condemned as obvious lawlessness and criminal activity, and very rarely seen as a form of public protest.

But how accurate is this representation? It would seem to give rise to at least four problems.[95] First, the criteria and preconditions of civil disobedience mean many different things to many different people; moreover, with hindsight, the once illegitimate may be reread as necessary and justifiable, if unfortunate. Secondly, civil disobedience itself illustrates the blurry line between non-violence and violence, particularly if one tries to hold to a distinction between 'moral' and 'physical' coercion. Thirdly, the question of when disorder constitutes or becomes a riot is a difficult one. Everyday usage of the term 'riot' is often indiscriminate, and the legal definition of riot in section 1 of the Public Order Act 1986 is also extraordinarily opaque:

(1) Where 12 or more persons who are present together use or threaten unlawful violence[96] for a common purpose and the conduct of them (taken together) is

---

92   J. Flax, 'The End of Innocence' in J. Butler and J. Scott (eds.), *Feminists Theorize the Political* (Routledge, 1992), pp. 445-463.
93   Above n. 38.
94   Downes and Morgan, above n. 4, pp. 107-108.
95   See more generally, T.R.S. Allan, 'Citizenship and Obligation: Civil Disobedience and Civil Dissent' (1996) 55 CLJ 89.
96   'Violence' is defined in s. 8 of the Public Order Act 1986: ' . . . "violence" means any violent conduct, so that –
    (a) except in the context of affray, it includes conduct towards property as well as violent conduct towards persons, and
    (b) it is not restricted to conduct causing or intended to cause injury or damage but includes any other violent conduct (for example, throwing at or towards a person a missile of a kind capable of causing injury which does not hit or falls short).'

such as would cause a person of reasonable firmness present at the scene to fear for his personal safety, each of the persons using unlawful violence for the common purpose is guilty of riot.[97]

(2) It is immaterial whether or not the 12 or more use or threaten unlawful violence simultaneously.

(3) The common purpose may be inferred from conduct.

(4) No person of reasonable firmness need actually be, or be likely to be, present at the scene.

(5) Riot may be committed in private as well as in public places.

(6) A person guilty of riot is liable on conviction on indictment to imprisonment for a term not exceeding ten years or a fine or both.

There are several problems with this definition.[98] First, it is hard to see how it fits with common understandings of riot: it requires only 12 people to be involved, it can be committed in a private place, and no 'person of reasonable firmness' need actually be present. More worryingly, the definition vests a remarkably wide discretion in the courts,[99] and, as Lacey and Wells note, one has to wonder about an adjudicator's ability to be fair to a defendant who has been involved in (or got caught up in) a politically controversial event which led to disorder (and subsequent negative coverage in the media) and is now charged with the undeniably serious offence of riot:

> Can such a tribunal distinguish between the person who was defending herself in a disordered situation, one who was fighting with the police, or one who was simply trying to remove herself from the situation? Can a clear distinction between liability for acts and for omissions be maintained in a context where initial presence may already invoke the court's opprobrium and a willingness to interpret a defendant as having certain predispositions? Is 'subjective' 'mens rea' any real guarantee of fairness to the defendant?[100]

Finally, law's preoccupation with individual responsibility intensifies the difficulties in understanding and defining riot because it tends to obscure the existence of social conditions which might help to explain rioting.[101] By contrast, historians and criminologists have been more willing to recognise and explore a discourse of riot based on determinism.[102] These latter accounts are less concerned with individual agency, responsibility and blame, and more interested in examining the 'ordered' and political nature of (at least some) riots and the associated social conditions (for example, high unemployment, political powerlessness and exclusion, and racial discrimination and

---

97 S. 6 provides that a person will be guilty only if they intend to use violence or are aware that their conduct may be violent.

98 Following a demonstration in the City of London on 18 Jun. 1999, one commentator queried whether a claim for riot damages can be made if the elements of a riot are present but a riot is not declared: *The Times*, 13 Jul. 1999, p. 45.

99 Moreover, although the riot offence applies only to those who are shown to have used unlawful violence, a defendant who has not used unlawful violence may be convicted of riot as an aider and abettor if they are shown to have encouraged the use of violence by others: *R v Jefferson* [1994] 1 All ER 270.

100 Lacey and Wells, above n. 10, p. 151.

101 However, convictions for riot following outbreaks of serious disorder have largely eluded the authorities, indicating evidential problems in the law of riot and also (possible) juror sensitivity to issues of determinism.

102 Compare P.A.J. Waddington, above n. 90, pp. 2-6 with D. Waddington, *Contemporary Issues in Public Disorder: A Comparative and Historical Approach* (Routledge, 1992).

disadvantage),[103] as well as explaining the circumstances by which some flashpoints ignite into riot while others are defused.[104]

In recent years, these sorts of accounts have struggled to make themselves heard amidst the politicisation of 'law and order'. 'Law and order' emphasises that '"explanation" amounts to "excuse"' – hence, Margaret Thatcher's claim that 'rioting can never be justified by unemployment' – and, as Downes and Morgan explain, this populist rhetoric can easily overpower 'the logical objection – rarely voiced – that nevertheless such realities may help to explain it'.[105] Moreover, the New Labour government's allegedly more expansive approach – 'tough on crime, tough on the causes of crime' – has yet to prove itself in any real way with respect to the latter part of the claim.[106]

There is another feature of riot which is often missing from legal, or other official, stories: the 'racialisation' of riot, and disorder more generally.[107] This is part of a more general tendency of associating disorder with 'outsiders' and thereby distancing it from 'mainstream' society, which in turn helps to prop up the notion of societal consensus on public order. It frequently evokes discriminatory ideas about cultural proclivities and generational, or familial, breakdown.[108] It also feeds off an historical amnesia that allows accounts of a mythical past free of unrest and disorder to flourish. The phenomenon is evident not just in the treatment of the urban 'race' riots of the 1980s in St Paul's, Brixton, Toxteth, Handsworth and Broadwater Farm, but also in accounts of how 'inferior "Continental" street politics'[109] led to the un-British disorder at meetings of Mosley's British Union of Fascists in the 1930s.[110] A more contemporary example is the construction of the new urban 'underclass' who populate Britain's 'sink' estates, and who came to public attention following the mid-1990s riots in cities like Newcastle and Cardiff.[111]

Peace, order and public order

We turn now to the second concept in this section: 'public order'. This is very murky ground: one need only recall the contention of some criminologists and historians that riots are 'ordered', to get a feel for the problems in defining 'order'. 'Order' evokes inconsistent images – peacefulness and tranquillity but also coercion and imposition – and competing interpretations have been multiplied by recent 'law and order' politics. Furthermore, if we set about

103 See eg, J. Walter, 'Grain Riots and Popular Attitudes to the Law: Maldon and the Crisis of 1629' in J. Brewer and J. Styles (eds.), *An Ungovernable People* (Hutchinson, 1980). A key 'flashpoint' in Northern Ireland was the transformation of the 1969 civil rights agitation into sectarian strife and paramilitary-state violence from 1970 onwards: see Ch. 3.

104 D. Waddington et al., *Flashpoints: Studies in Public Disorder* (Routledge, 1989).

105 Downes and Morgan, above n. 4, p. 100.

106 Ibid. See Piper, above n. 50, p. 408.

107 M. Keith, *Race, Riots and Policing: Lore and Order in a Multi-Racist Society* (UCL Press, 1993); and M. Rowe, *The Racialization of Disorder in Twentieth Century Britain* (Ashgate, 1998).

108 On the 'criminalisation' of black youth in media and popular narratives, see J. Pines, 'Black Cops and Black Villains in Film and TV Crime Fiction' in D. Kidd-Hewitt and R. Osborne (eds.), *Crime and the Media: The Postmodern Spectacle* (Pluto, 1995), pp. 67-77; and L. Young, *Fear of the Dark: 'Race', Gender and Sexuality in the Cinema* (Routledge, 1996).

109 Rowe, above n. 107, p. 93.

110 The reality is that racist far-right organisations have been centrally involved in rioting in English cities, as in London in 1958, and in modern forms of racist violence: see B. Bowling, *Violent Racism: Victimisation, Policing and Social Context* (Clarendon, 1998), pp. 23-57.

111 See B. Campbell, *Goliath* (Metheun, 1993).

defining '*public* order', we are immediately confronted by 'the question of *whose* view of order "public" order is':[112]

> Most criminal laws define acts . . . people may disagree as to whether the act should be illegal . . . but there is little disagreement as to what the behaviour in question consists of. Laws regarding disorderly conduct and the like assert, usually by implication, that there is a condition ('public order') that can be diminished by various actions. The difficulty, of course, is that public order is nowhere defined and can never be unambiguously defined because what constitutes order is a matter of opinion and convention, not a state of nature.[113]

Townshend argues that, even though public order law has mushroomed over the last two decades, '[p]ublic order is an odd, and in a sense un-English, concept'. He charts a void in the representation of 'the public' in British history, explaining that the concepts of 'public order' and 'public security' were subsumed in common law language as 'the rule of law' and 'keeping the peace'. Yet, when one turns to the common law, the lack of authoritative definition is not remedied, despite the fact that common law powers to deal with breaches of the peace have long been a centre-piece of British public order law, and the concept of 'breach of the peace' is itself 'about as old as English law'.[114]

These breach of the peace powers have tended to provoke significant disquiet in academic circles. Thus, commentators have noted how judges disagree over the meaning of the concept 'breach of the peace', as well as the extent of the preventive power it accords to the police. They have also noted the ongoing questions about the breadth of the bind over powers often used against persons arrested in connection with a breach of the peace: a court can bind over any person before it to 'keep the peace' and/or to be of good behaviour towards another person (*contra bonos mores*) by requiring him or her to enter into a recognisance (basically, a conditional debt) to this effect.[115] In 1994, the Law Commission recommended the repeal of the bind over powers, citing procedural defects, the availability of alternative sanctions and the likelihood that these powers breach obligations under Articles 5 (the right to liberty) and 10 (the right to freedom of expression) of the ECHR.[116]

---

112 Lacey and Wells, above n. 10, p. 94 (their emphasis).
113 J.Q. Wilson, *Varieties of Police Behaviour* (Harvard UP, 1968).
114 *McConnell v Chief Constable of the Greater Manchester Police* [1990] 1 All ER 423, 425.
115 See generally on binding-over, Law Commission Report No. 222, *Binding Over* (HMSO, 1994). For criticism of the use of these powers during the miners' strike, see S. McCabe and P. Wallington, *The Police, Public Order and Civil Liberties* (Routledge, 1988).
116 The Commission, ibid., para 4.34, said: 'We regard reliance on contra bonos mores as certainly, and breach of the peace as very arguably, contrary to elementary notions of what is required by the principles of natural justice when they are relied on as definitional grounds justifying the making of a binding-over order. Because an order binding someone to be of good behaviour is made in such wide terms, it fails to give sufficient indication to the person bound over of the conduct which he or she must avoid in order to be safe from coercive sanctions'. More specifically, at para. 6.27, it said that: 'We are satisfied that there are substantial objections of principle to the retention of binding over to keep the peace or to be of good behaviour. These objections are, in summary, that the conduct which can be the ground for a binding-over order is too vaguely defined; that binding-over orders when made are in terms which are too vague and are therefore potentially oppressive; that the power to imprison someone if he or she refuses to consent to be bound over is anomalous; that orders which restrain a subject's freedom can be made without the discharge of the criminal, or indeed any clearly defined, burden of proof; and that witnesses, complainants or even acquitted defendants can be bound over without adequate prior information of any charge or complaint against them'. See also below, pp. 79-80 for an account of two recent ECtHR judgments on binding-over.

Since *R v Howell* in 1981, 'breach of the peace' has generally been considered to be limited to violence or the threat of violence.[117] Despite this, concern about breach of the peace has not really abated. In 1983, the Law Commission recommended against the use of the concept in any new criminal offences legislation.[118] It has also been argued that the definition of 'peace' remains 'fluid, shifting and malleable', and seems most often to be 'centred according to the subjectivity of the speaker'.[119] Thus, in the 1980s, in a nice (but ineffective) twist, women protesters from Greenham Common asked the magistrates they appeared before to reflect on who was really breaching the peace, introducing witnesses who testified that the women had not been 'breaching the peace', but rather had been attempting to save and keep the peace.[120]

There has also been concern about the breadth of police powers to prevent or stop a breach of the peace. Case law indicates that these powers are threefold: first, a power to take steps short of arrest to defuse the situation; second, a power to arrest and detain; and third, a power to enter or remain on private premises for the purpose of preventing or stopping a breach of the peace. Case law also indicates that, before any of these powers can be exercised, there must either be a breach of the peace in progress or a reasonable apprehension of an imminent breach of the peace.[121] However, there are still myriad problems with these powers. They have been described as 'the invisible force of the criminal law',[122] mostly because the extent and nature of discretion that they accord to individual officers remains unstructured and under-checked. Generally, the choices made by patrolling officers have had an extremely low visibility, reducing the chances of any form of review. This problem has been compounded by the slippery nature of legal concepts such as 'reasonableness' and 'imminence' (as set out in the need for an officer to have a reasonable apprehension of an imminent breach of the peace). The upshot has been

---

117 '[E]ven in these days when affrays, riotous behaviour and other disturbances happen all too frequently, we cannot accept that there can be a breach of the peace unless there has been an act done or threatened to be done which either actually harms a person, or in his presence his property, or is likely to cause such harm, or which puts someone in fear of such harm being done': [1981] 3 All ER 383. See also, *Percy v DPP* [1995] 1 WLR 1382 and *R v Nicol and Selvanayagam* [1996] Crim LR 318. However, Lord Denning MR managed to cause a definitional flutter when he appeared to assign a significantly wider meaning to the concept in *R v Chief Constable of Devon and Cornwall Constabulary, ex p Central Electricity Generating Board* [1981] 3 All ER 826, at 832 by suggesting that '[t]here is a breach of the peace whenever a person who is lawfully carrying out his work is unlawfully and physically prevented by another from doing it'. For the ECtHR's view, see *McLeod v UK* (1998) 27 EHRR 493.

118 Law Commission Report No. 123, *Criminal Law: Offences Relating to Public Order* (HMSO, 1983), pp. 7-8. The now-repealed s. 5 of the Public Order Act 1936 used this formula.

119 A. Young, *Femininity in Dissent* (Routledge, 1990), p. 20. On protest and the peace movement generally, see J. Hinton, *Protests and Visions: Peace Politics in Twentieth-Century Britain* (Hutchinson Radius, 1989). See R. Stone, 'Breach of the Peace: The Case for Abolition' [2001] 2 Web JCLI arguing for abolition of the common law offence.

120 Young, ibid.

121 Failure to obey instructions reasonably directed to the latter end may lead to a charge of obstructing a constable in the execution of his or her duty under s. 89(2) of the Police Act 1996. 'Failure' has generally been very broadly defined, including, for example, verbal disobedience as well as physical non-compliance (*Duncan v Jones* [1936] 1 KB 218). But for a more robust approach to the use of the power, see *Redmond-Bate*, above n. 23.

122 K.D. Ewing and C.A. Gearty, *Freedom under Thatcher: Civil Liberties in Modern Britain* (OUP, 1990), p. 93.

minimal scrutiny of police action, even where the latter has involved the use of disproportionately expansive exclusion zones around suspected problem areas (for example, picket sites),[123] or a direction that a public meeting protesting against unemployment was to move to another site on the basis that, one year earlier, a similar meeting at the chosen site had ended in disorder.[124] Lower courts (in particular) have also taken a less than robust approach in reviewing police decisions to restrain protesters who are acting lawfully but where there is violent opposition, or police apprehension thereof, from other persons.[125] The recent decision by Sedley LJ in *Redmond-Bate* appears however to create the opportunity for a change of direction in this field. The judgment revisits the classic authority of *Beatty v Gillbanks*, and by dismissing *Duncan v Jones'* description of it as 'somewhat unsatisfactory' and emphasising the importance of 'the constitutional shift which is now in progress' vis-à-vis the interpretation of breach of the peace powers, it suggests the possibility of more robust judicial scrutiny of police decision-making.

In 1998, in *Steel v UK*,[126] the European Court of Human Rights offered general support for current 'breach of the peace' powers, indicating that domestic law on bind overs is largely compatible with the ECHR, so long as the response of the relevant authorities is not disproportionate. The case itself involved three different applicants, all of whom had been arrested on the grounds of preventing a breach of the peace and subsequently detained by the police. The first applicant, Steel, had taken part in a protest against a grouse shoot, standing in front of the participants to obstruct their shots; the second applicant, Lush, had taken part in a protest against road-building, standing in front of a JCB digger in order to obstruct its path; and the final applicants, had taken part in a protest against the arms trade outside a fighter helicopter conference, handing out leaflets and displaying banners. The Court found a Convention violation in the case of the final applicants, holding that their protests had been 'entirely peaceful' and had not involved any behaviour justifying police fears of a likelihood of a breach of the peace. However, the Court took a harder line in relation to Steel and Lush, the first two applicants: by a five-four majority, it held that Steel's arrest, detention and imprisonment had been proportionate to the risk of disorder (indeed, the Court pointed explicitly to the dangers inherent in her particular form of protest), and it was unanimous in holding that Lush's arrest had been proportionate to the aim of preventing disorder (irrespective of the fact that the risk of immediate disorder was lower than in Steel's case).

The Court's holding in favour of the final applicants in *Steel* (particularly when viewed alongside the domestic court judgments in *Jones* and *Redmond-Bate*)[127] may signpost more effective judicial control in this sphere in the future. However, following through on this promise will require the courts, and others, to face several thorny issues. As noted earlier, one issue which will demand rigorous and clear-headed thought is that of 'balance', in particular the idea of

---

123 For a more robust approach, see *Peterkin v Chief Constable of Cheshire*, *The Times*, 16 Nov. 1999.
124 *Duncan v Jones*, above n. 75.
125 But, for evidence of a more robust approach brushing aside *Duncan v Jones*, see the decision of the Divisional Court in *R v Coventry City Council, ex p Phoenix Aviation* [1995] 3 All ER 37.
126 Above n. 23.
127 Above n. 23, and for further details see below, pp. 82-83.

achieving a proper balance between competing rights and interests. It is to this that we shall turn in Part IV.

Subsequently, in *Hashmann and Harrup v UK*, the Strasbourg Court took a dimmer view of the power to bind over to be of good behaviour (*contra bonos mores*).[128] The applicants were 'hunt saboteurs' who had been bound over to keep the peace and to be of good behaviour following activities at a hunt in 1993. The Court noted that their protest impeded the hunt, but held nonetheless that it constituted an expression of opinion under Article 10. The Court went on to hold that authorities' interference with the protesters' right to freedom of expression via the imposition of a binding over order violated their Article 10 rights. In particular, the Court found that the concept of behaviour *contra bonos mores* was not adequately defined for the purposes of Article 10(2), holding that '[c]onduct which is "wrong rather than right in the judgment of the majority of contemporary citizens" is conduct which is not described at all, but merely expressed to be "wrong" in the opinion of a majority of citizens'.

IV.   BALANCE

Public protest may have proven democratic credentials but it is also an activity that imposes burdens on others: even peaceful protest can disrupt, annoy and intimidate communities and individuals (indeed, protesters sometimes rely on these outcomes in order to raise the profile of their cause). Protest also diverts and absorbs limited police resources. It can cause economic harm and, in some circumstances, it may even threaten the fabric of democracy itself.

These attributes mean that regulation of protest is inevitable. They also suggest that great care should be taken over the values and processes which determine the extent and nature of such regulation. The metaphor of choice in this area tends to be 'balance'. At first glance, it seems a reasonable enough option: 'balance' has a respectable profile in human rights reasoning (as noted in Chapter 1, it underpins the entire ECHR[129]) and, in this jurisdiction, ever since '[t]he stress of the 1970s' in the field of public order, it has triumphed over the earlier allegiance to a 'specifically English' synergy of tranquillity and tolerance.[130] Its most notable champion has been Lord Scarman, and it was one of Scarman's 'beautifully written'[131] reports on public order which yielded the following oft-cited passage:

> A balance has to be struck, a compromise found that will accommodate the exercise of the right to protest within a framework of public order which enables ordinary

---

128 Above n. 23. Behaviour *contra bonos mores* was described as 'conduct which has the property of being wrong rather than right in the judgment of the majority of contemporary fellow citizens' in *Hughes v Holley* (1986) 86 Cr App Rep 130, per Glidewell LJ.

129 See D. Feldman, 'The Human Rights Act 1998 and Constitutional Principles' (1999) 19 LS 165, 173-178.

130 Townshend, above n. 3, p. 148. But see Piper's scepticism about the 1998 Crime and Disorder Act's introduction of the idea of 'balance' into the child and youth criminal justice sphere in the form of child safety orders (above n. 50), and more generally, see Dixon, above n. 13, p. 284, who cautions against the allure of the concept: 'Certainly, experience suggests that it provides an often irresistible temptation to degenerate into crude and unhelpful formulations. Its superficial utilitarianism trivializes important interests and inappropriately treats them as if they can be weighed off against each other'.

131 A chief constable, c. 1986 quoted in R. Reiner, *Chief Constables: Bobbies, Bosses or Bureaucrats?* (OUP, 1991), p. 120.

citizens, who are not protesting, to go about their business and pleasure without obstruction or inconvenience. The fact that those who at any time are concerned to secure the tranquillity of the streets are likely to be the majority must not lead us to deny the protesters their right to march; the fact that the protesters are desperately sincere and are exercising a fundamental human right must not lead us to overlook the rights of the majority.[132]

Public meetings and marches

The above passage – part of Lord Scarman's 1975 report on the Red Lion Square disorders – was characteristically prescient; with the enactment of the Public Order Act 1986, 'balance' emerged as an avenging angel, poised to soothe conflicts of freedom and order in modern society. Its central role is most apparent in sections 11-14 of the Act, where the powers to impose conditions on or ban public meetings and marches are set out.[133] These powers work on what Fenwick calls a system of 'triggers':[134] for example, section 12 allows the imposition on a procession of any condition which appears necessary to the senior police officer in order to avert serious public disorder, serious damage to property, serious disruption to the life of the community (section 12(1)(a)); or intimidation of others with a view to compelling them not to do an act they have a right to do, or to do an act they have a right not to do (section 12(1)(b)). In addition, in making a determination as to the existence of a section 12 'trigger', the senior police officer is directed to have regard to the time and place at which, and the circumstances in which, any public procession is being held or is intended to be held and to its route or proposed route.[135]

The 1986 Act also allows the banning of marches and one particular type of static demonstration, the 'trespassory assembly'. Thus, section 13 obliges the chief officer of police to apply to the local district council for a banning order against all public processions (or a specified class thereof) if they reasonably believe that the condition-powers under section 12 will not be sufficient to avert 'serious public disorder'. Recently, however, it has been the power to ban trespassory assemblies (which was added to the 1986 Act by section 70 of the Criminal Justice and Public Order 1994) which has generated the most interest and controversy. The banning power is laid down in section 14A. It provides that a chief officer of police may apply for a banning order if they reasonably believe that an assembly is likely to be trespassory and may result in serious disruption to the life of the community or damage to certain types of buildings and structures.[136] It is reinforced by a stop-and-turnback power in section 14C which allows the police to stop persons within a radius of five miles from the assembly if an officer reasonably believes that such persons are on their way to

---

132 *The Red Lion Square Disorders of 15 June 1974: Report of Inquiry by the Rt. Hon. Lord Scarman,* Cmnd. 5919 (HMSO, 1975), para. 5.

133 The Act provides that an assembly consists of 20 or more persons in a public place (a 'public place' is defined as one which is wholly or partly open to the air). It defines a public procession as one in a place to which the public have access.

134 H. Fenwick, *Civil Liberties* (Cavendish, 1998), p. 291.

135 S. 14 of the Act, which uses the same triggers as s. 12, allows a more limited range of conditions to be imposed on assemblies.

136 The ban can subsist for no longer than four days and must operate within a radius of no more than five miles around the area in question.

the assembly and that it is subject to a section 14A order. Non-compliance with a police direction under section 14C will expose a person to arrest and a possible fine if convicted.

Section 14A was considered in *DPP v Jones*. On 22 May 1995, the police obtained a section 14A order prohibiting the holding of assemblies within a four-mile radius of Stonehenge between 29 May and 1 June of that year. The latter date was the ten-year anniversary of the 'Battle of the Beanfield', a violent confrontation between the police and members of a travelling convoy at the Stonehenge monument, and, because they anticipated a commemorative protest, the police sought out a section 14A banning order. But a protest did take place, despite the order, on 1 June. On this date, a small group (numbered at 21 persons by the police) assembled on a grass verge on the roadside beside the perimeter fence of the monument. Their purpose was to register a peaceful and non-obstructive protest against restrictions on access to the site, and on public assemblies more generally. Ultimately, two of the protesters, Margaret Jones and Richard Lloyd, were arrested after failing to disperse following a police request. They were convicted at the magistrates' court, appealed successfully to the Crown Court, and then lost on appeal by way of case stated by the DPP to the Divisional Court, before finally winning on appeal to the House of Lords.

The *Jones* case turned on the interpretation of section 14A(5). This section provides that once a banning order is in effect it prohibits any assembly which is held on land to which the public has no, or only a limited, right of access and which takes place without the permission of the owner of the land, or exceeds the limits of the permission or of the public's right of access. Thus the key question in the *Jones* appeal was, what were the limits of the public's right of access to the highway? In particular, did the right of access to the highway include use of it by a peaceful and non-obstructive assembly, irrespective of the operation of a section 14A order?

The Divisional Court said that the highway was to be used for passing and repassing, and although it noted that meetings and demonstrations on the highway were sometimes tolerated, it insisted that there could be no legal *right* to engage in these activities. By breaching the banning order, this assembly had exceeded the limited right of access to the highway, and Jones and Lloyd were rightly convicted. Moreover, the Divisional Court saw no need to refer to Article 11 of the ECHR as it considered the legislation to be clear and unambiguous. Thus, it seemed that simply assembling in a group of 20 or more in breach of a banning order could, *without more*, exceed the public's right of access and render participants liable to arrest and conviction.

Fortunately, a bare majority of the House of Lords saw things differently. Lord Irvine, the Lord Chancellor, delivered the most expansive of the majority opinions, arguing that older civil cases on the public's right to use a highway had to be viewed in the light of 'commonplace and well accepted' modern-day practices:

> [T]he public highway is a public place which the public may enjoy for any reasonable purpose, provided the activity in question does not amount to a public or private nuisance and does not obstruct the highway by unreasonably impeding the primary right of the public to pass and repass: within these qualifications there is a public right of peaceful assembly on the highway.

Lord Irvine considered that the common law recognition of this right was clear and unambiguous. However, his opinion also included a fall-back position based on Article 11 ECHR, in which he argued that if the common law in this area was considered uncertain, it should be clarified by reference to the Convention, thereby producing an identical right of peaceful assembly on the public highway.

Overall, *Jones* is a decent enough outcome for 'balance'. Balancing is never going to be like magic; nor is it going to be scientific or apolitical, and difficult questions as to the interests to be weighed and the procedures to be followed are inevitable. Still, the strength of opinion in the Divisional Court decision in *Jones* (and the two dissenting judgments in the House of Lords emphasising the rights of private landowners) does force one to ask whether, in fact, the odds are largely stacked *against* protest under the 1986 Act?

Public Order Legislation: 1986–2001

Academics writing about civil liberties have been suspicious of the 1986 Act's potential for some time. They have argued that it is replete with attractive but dangerously loose ideas; in addition to 'balance', there is 'community', 'serious disruption', 'intimidation' and 'coercion'. They have also claimed that insufficient attention has been paid to underlying principles,[137] and to issues of accountability in the process of decision-making. Townshend, for example, has pointed out that the White Paper which preceded the 1986 Public Order Act appeared merely to assert that added restrictions were necessary to prevent serious disorder. He also notes a significant change from earlier public order legislation: '[w]hereas the 1936 Act was mainly confined to quite narrow means of dealing with a specific political mode of collective violence, the 1986 Act had a pedagogical strain: it told people they would have to try harder to preserve or rebuild the convention of orderliness and reasonableness.' Ewing and Gearty have argued that the Act itself 'threatens to permit only those demonstrations that are so convenient that they become invisible'. They also remind us that 'community' admits of vastly different interpretations,[138] a point picked up by Fitzpatrick and Taylor who argue that the Act conceives of the community as monolithic and capable of having a unitary 'life'.[139] Fitzpatrick and Taylor ask: what happens if a community is patently divided (as for example the residents of Newbury were in relation to the environmental protests against the planned road by-pass)? Moreover, do protesters not comprise a community (a community of shared interests), and is public assembly not a type of communal activity?

Adverse commentaries on the 1986 Act increased in the wake of the amendments introduced by the Criminal Justice and Public Order Act 1994. The more recent Crime and Disorder Act 1998 has also engendered significant disquiet, especially as regards its provision for anti-social behaviour orders, and child and young person curfews and safety orders. The public order provisions of the 1994 Act, mostly contained within Part V, met with particularly biting criticism: for example, Smith argued that 'Parliament has given us . . . a mean-

---

137 See eg, D. Bonner and R. Stone, 'The Public Order Act 1986: Steps in the Wrong Direction?' [1987] PL 202.
138 See above n. 122, p. 121 (however, in *Police v Reid* [1987] Crim LR 702, it was emphasised that the words were not to be diluted).
139 See above n. 19, p. 298.

spirited, intolerant, ungenerous piece of work that may, if equally ungenerously implemented, lay trouble in store for years to come'.[140] The Act was ushered in by a Conservative Home Secretary, Michael Howard, amidst widespread angst about the breakdown of the 'British way' and an intense politicisation of 'law and order' and 'active citizenship'. For the most part, it presents disorder as the deviant choice of outsiders (in particular, hunt saboteurs, ravers, road protesters, 'peace' convoys and other travelling people), severing any possible connection between these people's 'choices' and state (in)action on social issues. In order to stem this 'disorder', the Act's public order provisions set about 'topping-up' existing powers: it introduced a new criminal offence of aggravated trespass (section 68),[141] and powers in relation to 'raves' (section 63), one of the quintessential forms of early-1990s assemblies; it supplemented police powers to remove trespassers from land (sections 61-62), and deal with threatening, abusive and insulting words or behaviour (section 154); and it targeted squatters (section 76) and 'unauthorised campers' (sections 77 and 80).[142]

The Crime and Disorder Act 1998, introduced by a New Labour Home Secretary, Jack Straw, had a similar feel and it too has met with mixed reactions: indeed, one commentary suggests that it would 'not be surprising, if the heightened awareness of human rights issues in legal circles [as a result of the Human Rights Act 1998] required the Government to reconsider some of the provisions in the Crime and Disorder Act in the face of challenge in the courts'.[143] Many of the 1998 Act's provisions are aimed at minors, in particular 'the perceived threat from children "out of control"'.[144] Thus, sections 11-15, which provide for child safety orders and child curfew schemes and notices, are targeted at the under-tens; and section 1 creates an 'anti-social behaviour order' which is available to courts in England and Wales in relation to anyone aged ten or over. Concern over these provisions results in part from the ambivalence of government policy; the Act's 'mixed messages' about the relationship between child and community 'safety' mean that, to date, it has been 'all things to all people'.[145] Without careful interpretation and enforcement, the Act has the potential to conflate child and community safety, moving away from a child-centred system, grounded in rights, welfare and need, towards an emphasis on 'discipline', community protection and curbing 'youth' crime. In Standing Committee, the responsible Minister claimed that the Bill

---

140 A.T.H. Smith, 'The Public Order Elements' [1995] Crim LR 19, p. 27. See also, M.J. Allen and S. Cooper 'Howard's Way – A Farewell to Freedom?' (1995) 58 MLR 364, 378-389; A. Tomkins, 'Public Order Law and Visions of Englishness' in L. Bently and L. Flynn (eds.), *Law and the Senses* (Pluto, 1996), pp. 80-93; and P. Vincent-Jones, 'Squatting and the Recriminalisation of Trespass' in I. Loveland (ed.), *The Frontiers of Criminality* (Sweet & Maxwell, 1995), pp. 219-247.

141 In *DPP v Barnard* [2000] Crim LR 371, it was held under s. 68 CJPO 1994, that the occupation of land could only constitute an act intended to intimidate or obstruct if that act was distinct from the original act of trespass.

142 Part V, s. 70 also introduced the 'trespassory assembly' power, discussed by the House of Lords in *Jones*: see above, pp. 82-83. For details on all of these sections, see Smith, above n. 140; Bailey, Harris and Jones, above n. 38; or Wasik and Taylor, above n. 38.

143 Leng, Taylor and Wasik, above n. 62, p. 2. Cf. the CJPA 2001.

144 Piper, above n. 50, p. 399.

145 Ibid., pp. 403, 408.

was concerned with protecting 'both the child and the community'; he insisted that the aim of the new child safety orders was 'to facilitate a balance'.[146]

The advent of zero tolerance

The 1994 and 1998 Acts also hint at 'zero-tolerance', a term conventionally associated with a particular style of policing in New York and, crucially, with New York City's plummeting crime rate (down by 36% in the three years 1993-96).[147] This version of 'zero-tolerance' is informed by the *Fixing Broken Windows* philosophy of US academic, George Kelling;[148] as such, it is characterised by increased criminalisation and an insistence that individual citizens must accept responsibility both for their own behaviour and for helping to ensure the safety of fellow citizens. It propounds particular understandings of 'order' and 'disorder': thus, order arises out of 'small change' of urban life, that is the day-to-day respect with which we deal with others and the concern that we exercise for their privacy, welfare, and safety'.[149] Disorder is defined in broad terms, placing particular emphasis on 'incivility, boorish and threatening behavior [sic] that disturbs life, especially urban life'.[150] It is also worth noting that, in this version of 'zero-tolerance', it is civil libertarians, social liberals and advocates for the homeless who end up taking most of the flak for the recent breakdown of social order; with claims that disorder 'proliferated with the growth of an ethos of individualism and increasing legislative and judicial support for protecting the fundamental rights of individuals at the expense of community interest'.[151]

The idea of 'zero-tolerance' has been a hit in the UK in recent years, attracting interest from across the political spectrum.[152] The criminologist, Jock Young, however, criticises the philosophy as one half of the new 'criminology of intolerance', pairing it with the increased use of imprisonment.[153] Dixon has warned against its increasing popularity in Australian political and media discourses. Not only is the effect of street policing on the crime rate contestable, but the costs of aggressive, interventionist strategies and increased criminalisation are profound:

---

146 *H.C. Debs.*, vol. 311, cols. 273, 270 (7 May 1998). In April 2001, an anti-social behaviour order was imposed on a 15-year-old boy in Manchester for a period of 10 years.

147 The link between 'zero-tolerance' street policing and the drop in the crime rate is hotly contested: see D. Dixon, 'Broken Windows, Zero Tolerance and the New York Miracle' (1998) 10 Current Issues in Crim J 96 (eg, crime rates dropped in several US cities where different police strategies were used; the crack cocaine epidemic declined in New York around the same time; police numbers expanded significantly and intelligence-led policing was adopted; and the pattern of violent crime is different in the US).

148 G.L. Kelling and C.M. Coles, *Fixing Broken Windows* (Free Press, 1997).

149 Ibid., p. 12.

150 Above n. 148, p. 14.

151 Ibid.

152 For example, it reverberated through a Labour Party report entitled *Tackling disorder, insecurity and crime*, drawn up by Jack Straw, the former Home Secretary, whilst in opposition, and the term featured explicitly in his first speech to a party conference after New Labour came to power: see J. Young, *The Exclusive Society* (Sage, 1999), pp. 121-140. The London Metropolitan Commissioner, John Stevens, has also expressed support for the concept: eg, in relation to the controversial policing of the May Day 2001 protest.

153 Young, ibid. See further Ch. 5 on the issue of imprisonment.

Zero tolerance is a policy designed for a [US] society which regards criminal justice and punishment as its primary tools of social policy. Zero tolerance is a policy for a society divided by chasms of class and particularly race, in which the fear of the 'underclass' permeates. In contrast, Australian society retains (despite growing challenges) a commitment to a broader state capacity in welfare and public health and to inclusive policies of multiculturalism and reconciliation. . . . [E]ven if serious disorder is not instigated, zero tolerance is likely to worsen relations between police and the communities whose activities are no longer tolerated. . . . [Another] cost of zero tolerance is a substantial expansion of the prison population.[154]

The concept of 'zero tolerance' also invokes an unobtainable condition of 'public order', where no crimes occur because law and policing operate to prevent them. As we highlight in Chapter 4, this is a flawed view of the impact of law on policing.

As Young points out, there are some parallels between the *Broken Windows* approach and feminism's discourse of 'zero-tolerance' against crimes against women.[155] These parallels make snap and total dismissals of the concept rather problematic:

Both wish to reduce tolerance – to, in the phrase, 'define deviancy up'. And both are concerned with a range of infractions: that is they are worried by both what are regarded by all as serious offences and by the more minor 'quality of life' crimes.[156]

Unfortunately, the lack of emphasis on the *differences* between these two 'zero-tolerance' discourses has led to the neglect of valuable feminist (and realist) insights about the continuum of violence.[157] It has also, somewhat ironically, contributed to the popularisation of allegedly 'feminised' criminal justice programmes which prioritise 'safety', but do so largely by separating crime from the causes of crime, and opting for child curfews and anti-social behaviour orders rather than genuine debate about 'community safety', 'inclusiveness' and 'accountability'.

It is difficult to discern what happened to 'balance', supposedly the metaphor of choice in this area. We have seen that recent Acts, and successive Home Secretaries' pronouncements, are certainly intolerant of 'crime', but the New Labour government stated that it would be just as intolerant of 'the causes of crime'. Increasingly, however, the political climate is such that there is little official enthusiasm for the idea that '[z]ero-tolerance of crime must mean zero-tolerance of inequality if it is to mean anything . . . [that] it is necessary not merely to punish offenders for breaking windows, but to actually mend the windows. That is to engage in a thorough programme of social reconstruction in our cities'.[158]

---

154 Dixon, above n. 147, pp. 99-101.
155 See J. Mooney, *Gender, Violence and Social Order* (Macmillan, 1999).
156 Young, above n. 152, p. 138.
157 Eg, it is arguable that such insights provide democratic justification for penalising forms of hate speech, allowing such developments to be separated out from regressive aspects of the new 'criminology of intolerance'. See further below, Ch. 8 (but for an argument cautioning against over-ambitious use of the criminal law in improving multiculturalism, see M. Malik, '"Racist Crime"; Racially Aggravated Offences in the Crime and Disorder Act 1998 Part II' (1999) 62 MLR 409).
158 Young, above n. 152, p. 140.

Towards balance

Clearly, if balance is to be more than an empty metaphor, changes will have to be made.[159] In the following paragraphs, we shall consider several possible options. Galligan, for example, has proposed two measures: first, delving beneath surface assumptions or abstractions to ensure that there are real, meritorious interests in conflict; and secondly, where principles and policies to measure the relative importance of competing values and interests are elusive, greater emphasis must be placed on accountability in the process of decision-making. With respect to the latter, Galligan insists on two *de minimis* requirements: first, important issues of policy and principle should be decided upon by authorities suitably accountable to the democratic process; and secondly, decision-makers of all types must make every effort to explain and justify the principles and policies behind their decisions.[160]

Giving effect to these proposals will require imaginative and wide-ranging thought about the parameters of judicial review (including the ways in which they differ as between the decision-making of senior and lower-ranked officers);[161] the utility of other tools of public law (for example, Ombudsmen, rights of consultation and participation, auditing and monitoring, and guidelines); and the lessons that can be learnt from the new attention to issues of regulation. It will also require us to take heed of the need for increased *political* accountability with respect to public order policy-making at senior levels. This is likely to be a tall order: as Barnard and Hare explain, 'clarity has never been a characteristic of the relationship between chief constable, local police authority and Home Secretary', and although the Police Act 1996 'seeks to preserve an area of constabulary independence while securing a measure of local and national accountability', the Home Secretary's greater financial clout means that in practice 'the balance of power shifts tangibly to the centre'.[162] The Home Secretary can alter police funding simply by laying a report before Parliament stating the considerations which have been taken into account in the particular instance; the Secretary of State also has extensive powers in respect of special financial assistance:

> The resulting structure gives rise to the legitimate fear that the Home Secretary may be influenced by party political considerations when making decisions concerning special financial assistance. By this mechanism, central government can ensure that the full coercive force of the state is used against groups or causes which it may regard as undesirable, while preserving a veneer of neutrality and distance.[163]

Other changes will also be required if we are to give effect to the idea of 'balance'. Three things come to mind. First, greater attention must be paid to

---

159 Several commentators have argued for a move away from the 'balance' metaphor in the wider criminal justice field, claiming that it has been the 'scourge of many debates about criminal justice policy': A. Ashworth, *The Criminal Process* (Clarendon, 1994), p. 292. See also, D. Feldman, 'Protest and Tolerance: Legal Values and the Control of Public-Order Policing' in R. Cohen-Almagor (ed.), *Liberal Democracy and the Limits of Tolerance* (Michigan UP, 2000), pp. 43-69.

160 Above n. 17, p. 47.

161 For eg, '[c]onsiderations of local responsiveness and cost allocation [may] quite properly modify the manner in which a court will review the formulation of [senior] police policy': C. Barnard and I. Hare, 'The Right to Protest and the Right to Export: Police Discretion and the Free Movement of Goods' (1997) 60 MLR 394, 400.

162 Ibid., pp. 400-401.

163 Barnard and Hare, above n. 161, p. 402.

the impact of police preventive practices on assemblies and marches. We need to avoid what Reiner has called a 'spook's view of policing', in particular the assumptions that the police view their primary role as the enforcement of the law of public order, and that 'because a legal or coercive capacity exists, that capacity will be used to the full'.[164] Secondly, cherished ideals under the public/ private divide deserve fresh consideration in the light of shifting patterns of public and private space and property-ownership in contemporary society, and the impact which these shifts may have on the nature of policing, protest, and regulation.[165] Thirdly, the question of whether there are other values which should be weighed in the balance alongside public order and freedom of assembly needs to be addressed. In the following paragraphs, we shall introduce each of these issues in turn.

Police preventive practices

First, police preventive practices. Lawyers are constantly blinded by legal rules, neglecting the broader nature of controls – for example, dominant social mores or institutionalised political pressure – determining access to public protest and, more generally, the exercise of police discretion. It has to be remembered, however, that there may be 'places where, and occasions on which, the police are prepared to "die in a ditch" (although the legal basis may be ambiguous)', such that '[t]he principal institutions of state are inviolable; the police do not need to be told this and therefore act on this assumption'.[166] It is also clear that the police *under-enforce* public order law: Peter Waddington's study of policing in London cited neither the threat of law nor force, but 'police guile' as the key reason why a city with at least three major protest demonstrations each week rarely experiences associated disorder.[167] Basically, for the patrolling police officer, 'the law is one resource among many that he [sic] may use to deal with disorder, but it is not the only one or even the most important. . . . Thus, he approaches incidents that threaten order not in terms of enforcing the law but in terms of "handling the situation"'.[168]

The under-enforcement of public order law should be no real surprise: limited resources, the low visibility of the exercise of street-level discretion, and crucially, the open-endedness of key public order law concepts, make full enforcement a 'chimera'.[169] However, this reality needs to seep far deeper into the civil liberties tradition, such that in thinking about how best to construct a democratic concept of 'balance', we pair criticism of bad law-making and inquiry into the significance of legal rules with a far better understanding of 'the aims

---

164 P.A.J. Waddington, *Liberty and Order: Public Order Policing in a Capital City* (UCL, 1994), p. 40.
165 See T. Jones and T. Newburn, *Private Security and Public Policing* (Clarendon, 1998), pp. 41-53. The growth of private policing will be discussed below, pp. 99-100.
166 P.A.J. Waddington, 'Dying in a Ditch: The Use of Police Powers in Public Order' (1993) 21 Int J Soc Law 335, 350.
167 P.A.J. Waddington, 'Public Order Policing: Citizenship and Moral Ambiguity' in F. Leishman, B. Loveday and S.P. Savage (eds.), *Core Issues in Policing* (Longman, 1996), p. 126.
168 J.Q. Wilson, *Varieties of Police Behaviour* (Harvard, 1968), p. 31 (cited in D. Dixon, above n. 13, p. 12). See also, E. Bittner, 'The Police on Skid-Row: A Study of Peace Keeping' (1967) 32 Am Soc Rev 699.
169 Dixon, above n. 13, pp. 12-13.

of police officers, the obstacles they face and the resources they are able to utilise'.[170]

There is a positive side to the culturalist insight that law is simply one resource for the patrolling police officer. We have seen that much recent public order law is heavy-handed and ill-drafted: it can be difficult for the police to apply (even if for the most part they use it only as a resource); their efforts may be challenged (whether through the courts or havoc on the streets); and 'mistakes' create 'in-the-job' and 'on-the-job' trouble for officers involved,[171] with potentially serious, long-term repercussions for police-community relations. We have also suggested that the police's broad order-maintenance function can probably never be captured by legal regulation, no matter how carefully drafted. These problems with public order law mean that police preventive practices can avert ugly, unnecessary confrontation. However, we still need to scrutinise these practices. For example, do they measure up to 'policing by consent',[172] or do the police negotiate so far, and then no further, such that a majority of protests take place on their terms? Is pre-demonstration negotiation 'less a process of "give and take" and more of the organiser giving and the police taking', such that protest organisers are 'had over' by experienced officers who take full advantage of 'home ground advantage' and the police 'monopoly of expertise' on suitable routes, traffic flow, etc?[173]

Ownership and space

The second issue that deserves attention in the quest for a better understanding of 'balance' in public order policing and protest is the altered geography of modern towns and cities. Urban space, in particular, has become a complex amalgam of different types of ownership and space.[174] More public life is taking place on private property; privately-owned areas are being designed to imitate

---

170 Waddington, above n. 90, p. 40. See also, A. Sanders, 'Criminal Justice: The Development of Criminal Justice Research in Britain' in P.A. Thomas (ed.), *Socio-Legal Studies* (Dartmouth, 1997), pp. 185-205, at p. 196: '[m]uch Home Office research . . . has moved on from the early days of purely descriptive or statistical administrative criminology to do more sensitive work. A study of public order policing, for instance, recognised and used some of the insights and advances outlined here: McBarnet is cited on the permissiveness of the criminal law, and arrest is seen as a resource for enforcing order and authority. Although little is made of these insights, here or elsewhere in Home Office work, there is sometimes, enough for a secondary analyst to use' (citing D. Brown and T. Ellis, *Policing Low-Level Disorder* (Home Office Research Study No. 135, 1994).

171 See M. Chatterton, 'Police Work and Assault Charges' in M. Punch (ed.), *Control in the Police Organization* (MIT, 1983) (cited in Waddington, above n. 90, p. 41). In crude terms, 'on-the-job' trouble arises from problems faced whilst on patrol, and 'in-the-job' trouble refers to the need to explain oneself to one's superiors within the force and in the courts. Cf. Jefferson and Grimshaw's alternative explanation in terms of the 'audiences' (eg, legal, local community and fellow police) that impact of police decision-making on public order issues: T. Jefferson and R. Grimshaw, *Controlling the Constable: Police Accountability in England and Wales* (Cobden Trust, 1984).

172 See below, pp. 97-102.

173 Waddington, above n. 164, pp. 101, 198.

174 Rural space is increasingly contentious: see eg, the debates around the 'right to roam' and the Countryside and Rights of Way Act 2000. See generally on uses of public space, D. Cooper, *Governing Out of Order: Space, Law and the Politics of Belonging* (Rivers Oram, 1998); and D. Cooper, 'Regard between Strangers: Diversity, Equality and the Reconstruction of Public Space' (1998) 57 CSP 465.

'public space'; and (paradoxically) some publicly-owned space is being given a private look and feel (for example, crime prevention features of modern housing developments).[175] The modern shopping centre is a good example of the changing nature of space. In public order terms, it is a fascinating and complex space. It is subject to routine access by very large numbers of people (who may perceive and use it as public space), but it tends to be privately-owned. It is usually patrolled by private security but the public police may have jurisdiction to enter (and indeed their presence may be actively encouraged by the owners).[176] The question which arises is what does this complex space mean for freedom of assembly, policing and the alleged centrality of 'balance'?

> Does one have freedom of speech in a shopping mall? . . . [W]hat about in the 'food court' of a shopping mall – a privately-owned space designed to look like a public space? What if that is the only real meeting place in the community?[177]

These developments oblige us to think again about cherished understandings of public and private, in particular whether there needs to be affirmative governmental action to facilitate expression and assembly. Historical protections for private property and privacy (which set out to guard the citizen from the state) assumed a congruence between private property and private space; today, property ownership and access to space do not fit in any neat way into categories like 'public' and 'private' (indeed, 'hybrid' property, that is 'spaces which in some sense are neither unambiguously public nor unambiguously private'[178] may be a better description of much current ownership and access). This means that we need to revisit earlier assumptions about privacy and owner's rights.[179]

Public space also requires fresh consideration, including what exactly counts as public space today, as well as the principles that should guide those who decide claims of access to public property for expressive activity.[180] One pressing issue is the need for 'lasting and socially just resolutions' of young people's collective use of public space, in particular their experience of being 'moved on' by police who 'feel organizationally compelled to respond to public complaints about noise and nuisance':

> [At present,] what is in effect disputation about the legitimate use of public space is enacted as an issue for the police, and 'resolved' by imposing an un-negotiated order

---

175 See Jones and Newburn, above n. 165.
176 The relationships between the public and private police are discussed below, pp. 99-101.
177 P. Kasinitz (ed.), *Metropolis: Centre and Symbol of our Times* (Macmillan, 1995), p. 278. See *Anderson v UK* [1998] EHRLR 218 (Art. 11 does not include a right to assemble for social purposes in a shopping centre). For commentary, see K. Gray and S.F. Gray, 'Civil Rights, Civil Wrongs and Quasi-Public Space' [1999] EHRLR 46.
178 Jones and Newburn, above n. 165, pp. 227-228.
179 On rethinking privacy more generally, see further Ch. 6.
180 The US Supreme Court has an elaborate jurisprudence on this topic via its 'public forum' case law which holds that restrictions on speech should be subject to higher scrutiny when, all other things being equal, that speech occurs in areas with strong traditional links to the expressive activity of ordinary citizens (eg, streets and parks). The merits of this jurisprudence are contested, however; US constitutional lawyer, Laurence Tribe, has complained of 'the blurriness, the occasional artificiality, and the frequent irrelevance, of the categories within the public forum classification', arguing that the Court uses the entire classification scheme as a shield for conclusions reached on other grounds, and that 'it might be considerably more helpful if the Court were to focus more directly and explicitly on the degree to which the regulation at issue impinges on the first amendment interest in the free flow of information': see, *American Constitutional Law* (Foundation, 1988), p. 987.

that adversely affects the interests of the young people concerned, and significantly undermines police-youth relations. . . . The issue needs to be constituted outside of a 'law and order' paradigm and subject to processes of mediation in which all interested parties can endeavour to produce resolutions that do not constantly threaten to criminalize the social practices of young people.[181]

More generally, Cooper highlights the political importance of creating and maintaining public spaces in order to foster community relations. Emphasising the *public* in public space, she directs us to ask: 'what kinds of spaces create geographic communities that are heterogeneous, open and equality-oriented?'[182]

Weighing interests

The final issue we want to raise as deserving attention in any attempt to give substance to the idea of 'balance' is the question of weighing competing interests in public order decision-making. It can be difficult for even the best-intentioned state, or individual police force, to know where and how to intervene, or to see a way to achieve 'balance'. For one thing, the parameters of negotiations can broaden out quite unexpectedly. For example, in *International Trader's Ferry*, a policy decision by the Chief Constable of Sussex to limit exports of live animals from the port of Shoreham by reducing policing was challenged as an unlawful restriction on the free movement of goods under (then) Article 34 of the Treaty of Rome.[183] Ultimately, the challenge was unsuccessful,[184] but it flags up the potential for 'collision between national constitutional traditions and the fundamental economic freedoms promoted by the market-orientated EC Treaty', and, more importantly, the possible 'vulnerability of civil and political rights (such as those of expression and protest) to being overridden by fundamental economic rights'.[185]

The question of balancing competing interests is also thrown up in an interesting and difficult way by the Northern Ireland Orange Order's traditional summer marching season, and by *Hurley*,[186] a case concerning Boston's annual St. Patrick's Day parade which came before the US Supreme Court in 1995. In

---

181 I. Loader, 'Democracy, Justice and the Limits of Policing: Rethinking Police Accountability' (1994) 3 SLS 521, p. 524. See also, I. Loader, *Youth, Policing and Democracy* (Macmillan, 1996).

182 Above n. 174, at p. 484.

183 *R v Chief Constable of Sussex, ex p International Trader's Ferry Ltd* [1999] 1 All ER 129 (HL). Quantitative restrictions on exports, and all measures having equivalent effect, are prohibited between Member States, unless justified under (previous) Art. 36 EC.

184 The HL adhered to its traditional policy of showing restraint when faced with requests to interfere with the discretion of senior police officers.

185 Barnard and Hare, above n. 161, pp. 410, 411. In the case itself, Lord Hoffman made it clear that 'on the particular facts . . . the European concepts of proportionality and margin of appreciation produce the same result as what are commonly called Wednesbury principles . . . in this case I think that the Chief Constable must enjoy a margin of discretion that cannot differ according to whether its source be found in purely domestic principles or superimposed European principles'. See C. Barnard and I. Hare, 'Police Discretion and the Rule of Law: Economic Community Rights versus Civil Rights' (2000) 63 MLR 581.

186 *Hurley and South Boston Allied War Veterans Council v Irish-American Gay, Lesbian and Bisexual Group of Boston* (1995) 115 Supreme Court Reporter 2338. See also, C.F. Stychin, *A Nation By Rights: National Cultures, Sexual Identity Politics, and the Discourse of Rights* (Temple UP, 1998), pp. 21-51.

Northern Ireland, the North Review body was charged with the task of creating a mechanism which would mediate the impasse between the Orange Order and local residents. At first, this must have seemed an impossibly tall order: in the Review team's public consultation, '[s]ome submissions suggested that . . . the "right to march" was predominant, while others put the proposition that what some have described as being a "right for residents to withhold consent" for a parade to proceed should be paramount'; interestingly, a 'third group of submissions – the largest – argued that a balance must be struck between competing rights'.[187]

The Review team resolved on a novel way of striking a balance. Their proposal – subsequently adopted in the Public Processions (Northern Ireland) Act 1997 – involved the creation of an independent body, the Parades Commission. This new body has three functions, namely: promoting greater understanding by the general public of issues concerning public processions; promoting and facilitating mediation as a means of resolving disputes over parades; and finally, and most importantly, determining what, if any, conditions should be imposed on disputed parades.[188] The 1997 Act also broadens out the statutory criteria on which conditions can be imposed on public processions, so as to allow regard to any impact which a procession may have on relationships within the community, and the desirability of allowing a procession customarily held along a particular route to be held along that route.[189] The Act is supplemented by guidelines on the factors which the Commission will take into account in deciding on whether to impose conditions, as well as a Code of Conduct for parade organisers and participants.

The Parades Commission is a laudable attempt to think through one of Northern Ireland's toughest public order issues; it is also an 'interesting prototype' for public order decision making more generally. However, the Commission will still need to address the question of why freedom of assembly 'is valued and the role and function it plays, or should play, in Northern Ireland', in particular 'how should freedom of assembly be defined and applied in order to bring about a more tolerant society based on equality and parity of esteem'.[190] Difficult questions about the nature and role of the police in a divided society like Northern Ireland also continue to loom large, although the report of the Patten Commission on the future of the RUC provided pioneering insights on how policing might be grounded in a human rights culture.[191] The North Review

187 Above n. 91, p. 13.
188 See www.paradescommission.org. The Commission's determinations are subject to review by the Secretary of State on application by the Chief Constable (s. 8). S. 9 of the Act emphasises that the common law powers of a constable to take action to deal with or prevent a breach of the peace are unaffected by this new regime (raising the disturbing possibility of Commission-police conflict (eg, if police on the spot were to use their common law powers to overturn or subvert a Commission determination)). See, T. Hadden and M. Donnelly, *The Legal Control of Marches in Northern Ireland: Report for the Community Relations Council* (Belfast, 1997), p. 49 arguing that if police action to protect the rights of loyalists to march imposed a curfew on local residents this would amount to 'an unacceptable denial of the rights of those residents to liberty under Article 5 of the Convention and to respect for their private and family life under Article 8'.
189 S. 7(6). The original criteria were set down in art. 4(1) of the Public Order (NI) Order 1987. The power to ban parades remains with the Secretary of State (s. 10); however, here the statutory criteria are extended to require consideration of 'any serious impact which the procession may have on relationships within the community' (s. 10(c)).
190 I. McAuley, 'Reforming the Law on Contentious Parades in Northern Ireland' [1998] PL 44, 55.
191 See Independent Commission on Policing for Northern Ireland, *A New Beginning: Policing in Northern Ireland* (HMSO, 1999) (www.belfast.org.uk).

grasped the nettle of individual or group responsibility for handling contentious parades, and made the welcome proposals that requests by the Orange Order to organise specific parades must be accompanied by the Order's own policing plans and that the Order should be required to have trained marshals in place during any parade or march. As O'Leary has pointed out, these proposals are 'a splendid example of combining a right – freedom of assembly – with a duty – the obligation to preserve the peace, law and order in a democratic society'.[192]

Hurley concerned Boston's annual St Patrick's Day parade held on 17 March, a celebration dating back to 1737 in Boston. In 1992, a number of gay, lesbian and bisexual descendants of Irish immigrants joined together with other supporters to create 'GLIB', for the purpose of marching in the annual parade. The parade's organisers, the Veterans Council, refused GLIB permission to march and the parties went to court. The US Supreme Court framed the issue as a question of free speech: 'whether Massachusetts may require private citizens who organize a parade to include among the marchers a group imparting a message the organizers do not wish to convey?'[193] The Court went on to uphold the rights of the Veterans Council, characterising the parade as *private* speech activity and emphasising the First Amendment rights of the organisers to decide on the content of their parade's message.

Hurley could have had a very different outcome. For example, emphasising the idea of 'balance' might have allowed the case's underlying free speech/ equality clash to come into obvious focus. A rethinking of understandings of 'public' and 'private', as suggested earlier, might also provide a rather different framing of the issue at stake, such that the question for the court would be:

> whether a group of *private* citizens who help a city administer a *public* event commemorating a *public* holiday, an event first established by the City which has received *public* funding and support throughout its long history and which takes place on the *public* streets of that city, can exclude a group of city residents because of the sexual orientation of the group's members.[194]

In the next Part, we shall increase the spotlight on public order decision-makers. Our focus will be the courts and the police. We realise that these are not the only decision-makers in this field: we have already commended the Parades Commission as a worthwhile experiment in public order decision-making. Protesters themselves are also decision-makers; so too is the Home Secretary, in particular because of the impact that central government police-funding powers can have on the exercise of discretion by senior police officers.[195]

---

192 B. O'Leary, 'A Bright Future – and Less Orange', *THES*, 19 Nov. 1999, p. 22. The self-policing of marches is now a feature of several major cultural events, which historically have been the focus for community/police tensions: see eg, London's Notting Hill Carnival and Sydney's Lesbian and Gay Mardi Gras.

193 *Hurley*, above n. 186, pp. 2340-2341.

194 Stychin, above n. 186, p. 44 (references omitted). See also, Cooper, above n. 174, p. 473 arguing that: '[a]lthough common spaces are subject to processes of exclusion, they also form sites for reclamation, affirmation and resistance . . . [F]eminist and gay movements have used open space as a place of political expression to assert the "public" character of identities or practices that appear to have been shunted off into the private domain' (references omitted). See also, *Hallam v Avery* [2001] 1 WLR 655 (HL) (local authority breached Race Relations Act 1976 by imposing extra conditions on hire of building for Romany gypsy wedding after police alleged risk of public disorder).

195 See generally, Walker, above n. 16, pp. 111-112.

All of these decision-makers require further study, and our decision to focus on the police and the courts should not detract from this.

V.   THE DECISION-MAKERS

Our primary interest here is in the police, but we shall start with some brief comments about the role of the domestic courts – past, present and future.

The courts

Historically, the courts – from magistrates to the House of Lords – have bowed to the alleged needs of 'public order', discarding numerous opportunities to uphold the freedom of assembly and to pin down the weasel words that characterise this area of legal regulation.[196] At times, the courts have clearly endorsed the use of the police and public order law in enforcing government policy on industrial relations, as for example, in magistrates' approval of police turn-back powers and liberal use of suspect bail conditions and bind over orders during the 1984-85 miners' strike. More recently, however, there have been glimpses of a developing respect for freedom of assembly, via higher court judgments in *Jones* and *Redmond-Bate*, as well as several robust lower court rulings.

With the coming into force of the HRA, it seems likely that the courts will be asked increasingly to adjudicate on human rights challenges to aspects of public order law. As a result, we shall have further and better opportunity to see what the judiciary makes of the trend towards increased criminalisation in the public order field, in particular its compatibility with human rights values. The outcomes of such challenges are not predictable, however. As noted earlier, there is little ECHR case law on Article 11, and Article 10 has not been developed in this area. The long-standing deference of the domestic courts towards the decision-making of senior police officers,[197] and the relative invisibility of the routine exercise of police discretion in relation to low-level street disorder, also obscure the picture. There may also be procedural obstacles to change given that only the higher courts have the power to issue declarations of incompatibility and few public order cases go beyond the lower courts. Moreover, inappropriate reliance on the courts could stymie the possibility of positive change arising out of the newer, community policing, given that '[c]ourts cannot "solve" the problem of police discretion by invalidating reasonably specific public order laws . . . without seriously impairing legitimate community efforts to enhance the quality of neighborhood [sic] life'.[198] More generally, it has to be remembered that '[t]he potential for the development of legal remedies is a matter of controversy: strong arguments for and against judicial review can be found among leading public lawyers'.[199] The marginality of law to policing in certain circumstances also has to be remembered; judicial decisions do not automatically translate into police working practice.[200] As a result, a rounded

---

196 For discussion, see K.D. Ewing and C.A. Gearty, *The Struggle for Civil Liberties: Political Freedom and the Rule of Law in Britain 1914–1945* (OUP, 2000), Chs. 5 and 6.
197 See eg, *ITF*, above n. 23.
198 Livingston, above n. 46, p. 561.
199 Dixon, above n. 13, p. 312.
200 See Ch. 4.

response to public protest, and more importantly to the recent legislative trend towards increased criminalisation of low-level disorder, may require a widening of the traditional public lawyers' circle, including a 'renewed focus upon those political, administrative, and other "subconstitutional" controls that might assist in constraining arbitrary police enforcement'.[201]

It also seems likely that the courts will be invited to revisit conventional understandings of 'public' and 'private' in the light of the changing nature of ownership, access to space and policing. The rise of private policing or, more accurately, the legal tools of private policing, may cause particular problems for them. Private police powers stem from the civil law, including 'the law of property, (governing, for instance, the rights of property owners to control access to, and conduct on, their property), employment and industrial-relations laws (defining the rights of management to control activities in the work place and the conduct of workers), and the law of contract (whereby submission to various security procedures can be made a condition of access to various facilities and resources)'.[202] As Shearing and Stenning note, these powers are 'quasi-legal'; in other words, 'they are exercised in relation to persons who, through the use of various legal fictions, are often deemed in law to have "consented" to their exercise'.[203] Therefore, it seems likely that increased use of private police will oblige the courts to face difficult questions about the quality and meaning of consent, especially given the broader cultural shift to public police-community 'partnerships', 'consultation', and 'accountability'.

The public order police

These shifts may also force the courts and others to think about how to legitimate public order policing more generally. As Peter Waddington explains, if we take protest seriously as a rational activity, then we must also take the policing of protest seriously. To date, however, analysis of this aspect of public order policing has been patchy and crisis-driven, such that '[i]n so far as the police are included amongst the *dramatis personae* of protest episodes, they are restricted to an occasional walk-on part, usually swinging clubs'.[204] The single exception to this profile has been the policing of riots, but this coverage has largely presented public order policing as synonymous with police in riot-gear battling with defenceless, ordinary citizens, thereby heightening the lament for a fictional 'Golden Age of policing'.

Not surprisingly, '[t]he real [policing] story is more complex and less sensational': the past was not so golden, the present is much tougher for all sorts of police work, and overall it is arguable that the police 'are now in a healthier state than before'.[205] The lack of attention to public order policing

---

201 Livingston, above n. 46, p. 561. Changing media representations of popular protests (as in the focus on 'Swampy', an anti-roads protester at Newbury) also merits attention given the influence of media narratives in (de)legitimating political activity.
202 C.D. Shearing and P.C. Stenning, *Private Security and Private Justice* (Quebec: Institute for Research on Public Policy, 1982), pp. 21-22 (cited in Dixon, above n. 13, p. 122).
203 Ibid.
204 Above n. 90, p. 8.
205 Downes and Morgan, above n. 4, pp. 220-221. The authors go on to argue that the police 'look worse [today] because far more is known about their shortcomings, thanks to a mixture of scandals, research, and the gradual move towards more stringent forms of both legal and political accountability'. See also, I. Loader and N. Walker, 'Policing as a Public Good: Reconstituting the Connections Between Policing and the State' (2001) 5 Theor Crim 9.

has obscured this; it has also flattened out interest in strategies to manage the routine exercise of discretion; the relationship between routine and riot policing; the increasingly volatile policing mix; and the question of how to harness the new emphasis on community, problem-oriented and managerialist philosophies in policing as a tool of positive change. In the following paragraphs, we shall consider these latter issues in more detail.

Towards structured discretion

First, discretion. We have already noted the trend towards preventive policing in public order, characterised by negotiation with protest organisers and community consultation, and backed up by increased use of intelligence-gathering and surveillance. We have also emphasised that policing and law co-exist in a complex relationship whereby legal rules are a 'resource' for patrolling officers and 'the dimensions of police discretion are not delineated by officers' authority to apply legal sanctions'.[206] In addition, we have noted the open-endedness of key public order concepts, the difficulty of 'legalising' the police's order-maintenance function, and the low visibility of street policing of minor misconduct. Taken together, these factors suggest not only that we need to focus on the exercise of discretion in the public order field, but also that our analysis must reach beyond the question of whether legal rules can control discretion. As Dixon has pointed out:

> Rules may provide a 'framework and focus', but they are not enough. They are just one of the 'tools of government'. Rules are likely to have their place in any governmental strategy, but they must be used in thoughtful and original ways. Their objective must be clear, they must be designed and chosen carefully, they must be appropriate to the specific subject matter, their potential relationship with existing regulation by other normative systems (such as police cultures) must be appreciated, and supplements and alternatives to rules need to be considered.[207]

Importantly, Dixon goes on to explain that this approach is not rule-sceptic; rather, it is a call for 'intelligent rule-making'. This latter distinction is crucial in light of the recent upsurge in 'crime control' arguments, which cite the ineffectiveness of traditional forms of regulation as evidence of the need to dispense with legal restraints, in favour of a 'new policing' based on the 'expert use' of discretion and reported 'community' needs.[208] The overall goal of the human rights lawyer must be to *manage* discretion; it is futile to seek to eliminate discretion through legal rules and very dangerous to allow it to operate without legal authority. Civil libertarian outcomes must balance 'policing by consent' with 'policing by law' or, to put it differently, they must render community policing (with its emphasis on neighbourhood needs and quality-of-life crimes) consistent with the rule of law.

---

206 R.E. Worden, 'Situational and Attitudinal Explanations of Police Behaviour' (1989) 23 Law and Society Review 668, 668 (cited by Dixon, above n. 13, p. 314). See also, A. Sanders, 'From Suspect to Trial' in Maguire, Morgan and Reiner (eds.), above n. 4, pp. 1051-1093, at pp. 1054-1056.

207 Dixon, above n. 13, p. 311 (references omitted). See also, D.J. Galligan, *A Reader on Administrative Law* (1996, OUP); and K. Hawkins (ed.), *The Uses of Discretion* (OUP, 1992).

208 Ibid., p. 315.

Developing this concept of managed or structured discretion will not be easy. It will be an ongoing task, not a one-off or panic response to crisis. It will require an understanding of police culture.[209] It will also demand sustained inquiry into the respective merits of a range of sub-judicial controls, including police guidelines to inform the exercise of discretion, and ongoing internal and external monitoring and audit to deepen police-community relationships.[210]

Historically, there have been two particular obstacles to police-community consultation and public participation: first, the age-old (although now rather tattered) rhetoric that presents the police as ordinary citizens 'in blue'; and secondly, the doctrines of 'constabulary independence' and, more recently, 'professionalism' and 'managerialism'. We have already noted the way in which continued attachment to the idea of 'constabulary independence' obscures the lack of balance as between chief constables, local police authorities and the Home Secretary, thereby hindering the development of appropriate channels of political accountability in respect of the impact of central government funding powers on decision-making by senior police officers.[211] The doctrine also appears to have curtailed thinking on how to render street policing of minor misconduct more accountable.

More recently, government emphasis on managerialism and service provision within policing has thrown up new barriers to police-community relations and the end-goal of democratic accountability.[212] For the most part, this emphasis has presented policing as 'an unproblematic and clearly defined product' and policing problems as 'a series of technical issues'.[213] Both government and police leaders have foregrounded 'the language and style of consumerism',[214] including performance indicators, mission statements and codes of ethical service. One result of this has been that attention has been shifted away from 'the issue of the state's accountability for its use of coercive force towards an altogether safer terrain concerned with the quality of service provision and the most efficient means of service delivery'.[215] There has also been remarkably little acknowledgement of the tensions within the new approach: for example, the pressure to be 'tough on crime' and to produce tangible results, measured by indicators such as number of arrests and clearance rates, may reduce the time available for ordinary street policing and strain police-community partnerships.

The new emphasis on efficiency and service is not, however, totally without value. Although it promotes police accounting rather than accountability,[216] it

---

209 See J. Chan, *Changing Police Culture: Policing in a Multicultural Society* (CUP, 1997); and Ch. 4. See also, F. Heidensohn, '"We Can Handle It Out Here": Women Officers in Britain and the USA and the Policing of Public Order' (1994) 4 Policing and Society 293, on the impact of using women officers in public-order policing.

210 See Livingston, above n. 46.

211 See Walker, above n. 16, pp. 97-149.

212 Ibid., pp. 261-274. See also, I. Brownlee, 'New Labour – New Penology? Punitive Rhetoric and the Limits of Managerialism in Criminal Justice Policy' (1998) 25 JLS 313; Leishman, Loveday and Savage (eds.), above n. 44; Loader, above n. 181; and Waddington, above n. 11, at pp. 26-29.

213 Loader, above n. 181, p. 522. On the Canadian experience with managerialism, see W. De Lint, 'New Managerialism and Canadian Police Training Reform' (1998) 7 SLS 261, arguing that 'police occupational culture . . . continues to reframe reform according to entrenched traditions . . .'.

214 R. Reiner, 'Policing a Postmodern Society' (1992) 55 MLR 761, 778.

215 Loader, above n. 181, p. 522.

216 Weatheritt, above n. 49.

presents the public as far less passive and seeks to find out and fulfil their policing needs. The new consumerist ethos may also have the capacity to infuse older doctrines of constabulary independence with important concepts of good practice which, in turn, may assist in the development of managed discretion in public order policing.

Towards paramilitarism?

Of course, discretion is not the only tool of public order policing. Since the widespread public disorder of the 1970s, militarisation has given the police an arsenal of 'peace-keeping' equipment including shields, visored crash-helmets, and flame-retardant overalls, as well as armoured Land Rovers, CS gas and 'rubber bullets'. There have also been shifts in the training of police officers, including the establishment of special groups and increased paramilitary command of public order policing. There are also mutual aid arrangements, which facilitate the movement of police from their usual beat to work against people they do not know, by allowing one chief officer of police to provide assistance to a fellow chief whose force is under pressure. Together, these developments have led to fractious debates about the pros and cons of a paramilitaristic approach to policing public disorder, and anxiety about the *de facto* emergence of a specialist public order 'third force'.[217]

As usual, the reality is more complex than most descriptions of it.[218] We have already noted that recent trends in public order policing emphasise pre-emption and prevention, rather than paramilitarism. Moreover, the recent 'tooling up' of the police (particularly when viewed alongside the more recent emphases on community policing, professionalism and managerialism) appears to have forged a force that has multiple roles, rather than the much-feared 'third force'. Such a multiplicity of roles is nothing new to the police in certain parts of Northern Ireland, and their experience may help in gauging whether such roles are sustainable within a single police force. For the most part, it suggests that a single force will find it difficult to sustain both militarised and community-oriented policing. Indeed, few would describe the following account of a police inspector's preparations prior to an armoured-vehicle, army-covered patrol of the Falls Road area of West Belfast in the early 1990s as 'routine policing':

> First he put on his gun, then his flakjacket; he put his baton into his pocket; he then put on his radio, attaching a microphone from the radio to the flakjacket and putting on an ear-piece, so that messages would not be blurted out in public and only he would hear them. Finally he put on his hat and we were ready.[219]

217 Bailey, Harris and Jones, above n. 38, p. 176. Cf. the contrasting arguments of T. Jefferson, *The Case Against Paramilitary Policing* (Open, 1990) and P.A.J. Waddington, *The Strong Arm of the Law: Armed and Public Order Policing* (Clarendon, 1991).
218 See eg, J. Morgan, *Conflict and Order* (Clarendon, 1987) arguing that recent anxieties about policing styles are simply a contemporary manifestation of a longer historical tradition.
219 Reiner and Cross, above n. 39, at p. 82. See also, J.D. Brewer and K. Magee, *Inside the RUC* (Clarendon, 1991); G. Ellison, '"Reflecting All Shades of Opinion": Public Attitudinal Surveys and the Construction of Police Legitimacy in Northern Ireland' (2000) 40 BJ Crim 88; A. Mulcahy, 'Visions of Normality: Peace and Reconstruction of Policing in Northern Ireland' (1999) 8 SLS 277; and A. Mulcahy, 'Policing History: The Official Discourse and Organizational Memory of the Royal Ulster Constabulary' (2000) 40 BJ Crim 68.

Northern Irish experience also alerts us to the fragility of other accepted boundaries. Northern Ireland has had 'hard' and 'soft' areas, and the RUC has had 'routine' and 'emergency' powers, but everywhere the police '[have worn] flakjackets, patrolled in landrovers, [carried] handguns and occasionally machine guns'.[220] It is obvious that 'normalising' the RUC will be 'a stupendous job';[221] in certain parts of Northern Ireland, developing police-community reciprocity will also be a mammoth task, dependent on a range of forces including wider political events such as the peace process.

This is not to argue for the establishment of a separate, elite public order force. There is evidence that 'flying squads' have brutalising effects on their members; these squads also tend to display autocratic tendencies towards their local counterparts.[222] At present, the conclusion can only be that more research is needed; such research would be particularly valuable if it managed to be as open-minded and thoughtful as the recent Patten Report on policing Northern Ireland.[223] Thus, we need more information on street policing in divided societies. We also need sustained inquiry into the pros and cons of paramilitarism in public order policing, as well as an agreed definition of the techniques, tactics and equipment associated with this style of policing.

Towards a new public order 'police'

More research is also needed on the increasing range of actors participating in modern order-maintenance policing. Contemporary public order policing is a co-production, involving the public police, private security (some of whom may be public police 'moonlighters'), and a range of 'active', self-policing citizens. We need to consider how these various types of 'policing' relate to one another if we are to understand the range of the legal rules affecting order-maintenance today, as well as the nature of enforcement practices.

'Loss prevention' rather than 'crime prevention' is the primary concern of private police; their task is to prevent damage to clients' assets, not order-maintenance *per se*. But 'client loss' is a broadly defined concept in private policing; in the US, for example, it encompasses 'protection' for clients and employees in public places:

> At the New Jersey Bell Telephone Company in Newark . . . a cordon of private security guards rings the building each night at 5.00pm. Guards stand at twenty-five-yard intervals for three blocks in order to provide safe passage for commuters wishing to reach railway stations.[224]

Increased 'privatisation' of public order policing also opens up other complex questions. First, what is the role of the public police in relation to protests on private property? During the 1996 Newbury road by-pass protest, the public police's role 'became restricted to that of monitoring interactions between the parties to the conflict'; '[e]ven the physical safety of the protesters was the

---

220 Ibid., p. 82.
221 W. Hart, 'Waging Peace in Northern Ireland' (1980) 3 Police Magazine, p. 30.
222 This was a common feature of the 1984-85 miners' strike when police were bussed in from outside police forces to a site of industrial conflict.
223 See C. Shearing, '"A New Beginning" for Policing' (2000) 27 JLS 386.
224 L. Johnston, 'Privatisation and the Police Function: From "New Police" to "New Policing"' in Reiner and Cross, above n. 39, at pp. 25-26.

technical responsibility of [a] government quango, the Health and Safety Executive'.[225] This fact alone gives rise to serious questions about accountability; when combined with allegations that the public police at Newbury covertly sided with the private security personnel (by ignoring improper action by the latter and also by asking for severe bail restrictions in respect of arrested protesters), it suggests a very worrying trend in public order policing.[226]

Secondly, it has been argued that mass private policing raises 'troubling questions of equity' given that only the wealthy – whether individuals, neighbourhoods or businesses – can afford such services.[227] Policing for hire may also 'ghettoise' public policing, leaving the public police with responsibility for policing only parts of society, most likely the deprived parts.[228] And, if the public police's remit is narrowed, this in turn might make it difficult to counter arguments for reduced public police funding.

Thirdly, concerns have been raised about private policing's reliance on civil law powers. To date, anxiety has tended to centre on the nature and scope of authority provided to private police by the explicit or implied consent that underpins private law relationships.[229] But increased reliance on private law could also lead to a situation where 'consent' is used to get around conventional restrictions on *public police* powers. Thus, as Dixon has pointed out:

> The neat allocation of private powers to private police and public powers to public police is not the whole story. . . . Public police, too, may use private powers . . . in Chicago, Housing Department and city police may carry out sweep searches for weapons in public housing project apartments on the authority of consent provisions in housing leases. If signing such a lease is in practice a precondition of access to public housing, then the implications for police powers are considerable.[230]

An account of contemporary order-maintenance policing would also need to examine self-policing. This can range from the officially-sanctioned Special Constabulary and Neighbourhood Watch, to the pure self-policing of Northern Ireland punishment squads and others who move against drug-dealers, prostitutes, kerb-crawlers and other 'neighbourhood offenders' engaged in 'anti-social' conduct.

At present, it is difficult to assess the merits of the Special Constabulary in the public order context. Their traditional role in policing has been reduced in recent years; however, this may change given the continued emphasis on 'active citizenship' and community involvement in policing issues, and the changing nature of protest and public order policing more generally. One benefit of using special constables is that they tend to be more representative of the population where they carry out their duties; moreover, their relative heterogeneity in terms of gender and ethnicity stands in contrast to the traditionally more uniform (white, male, working-class) backgrounds of regular rank-and-file officers.[231]

---

225 Waddington, above n. 11, p. 31.
226 Ibid.
227 Livingston, above n. 46, p. 569.
228 See G. Hughes, *Understanding Crime Prevention: Social Control, Risk and Late Modernity* (Open UP, 1998), pp. 130-153.
229 See attempt at regulation in the Private Security Industry Act 2001.
230 Dixon, above n. 13, p. 122-123.
231 See Leon in Critcher and Waddington, above n. 11. See also, Rose, above n. 205, pp. 211-259 on changing police culture.

But specials are not the only form of 'active citizens'; as noted above, 'self-policing' also encompasses groups and individuals who act without any form of official authority, relying instead on claims of 'community morality' or 'the wishes of the majority'. This form of order-maintenance policing is very dangerous. Questions arise about who will be drawn to these groups, and about the relationship between participation and accountability. Self-policing groups may also be susceptible to hijack, and individuals may be swept into group membership, without training, and risk breaking the law.

At the same time, however, abandoned communities may feel that 'self-help' is the best, or only, option available to them.[232] This feeling of social exclusion needs to be changed if the excesses of vigilantism are to be avoided. The risks of 'self-policing' suggest the need to emphasise police-community reciprocity, as well as the ongoing need for external legal regulation, rather than pure community-driven 'solutions' to order-maintenance problems (for example, the 'community' action against prostitution in areas of Birmingham city). 'Active citizenship' has to have clear and agreed limits. This holds true for police-community interactions on public order policing as well as 'self-policing': otherwise, attempts at democratising public order policing through greater community consultation and participation may end up reproducing or aggravating local tyrannies, and they may also stymie public protest.[233] As Livingston explains, communities do not speak with a single voice, '[n]eighborhoods [sic] are not homogenous and problems of disorder sometimes emerge by virtue of racial, cultural and economic tensions that arise among those who legitimately live, work, and recreate in a given area'.[234] Thus, although the recent interest in police accountability through greater community involvement is a welcome development, it must not end up sanctioning forms of police practice whereby community majorities push out already-excluded minorities. The risk of this should not be underestimated: as Reiner has explained, one of the key problems of policing in a liberal democratic polity is how to protect vulnerable minorities from police oppression sanctioned by 'communal morality'; a problem which 'limits the potential of "democratic accountability" as a panacea against abuse'.[235] As a result, far more thought needs to be given to the question of accountability through police-community reciprocity, in particular the mechanisms for bringing it into being and securing it in practice.[236]

CONCLUSION

'We all have a problem.' These are the opening words of the North Review on public processions in Northern Ireland and they are admirably prescient, not just as regards parading conflicts, but in connection with the status of public order law and practice more generally. At the same time, however, we are currently in a period of transition as regards protesting, policing and public

---

232 See generally, R. Abrahams, *Vigilant Citizens* (Polity, 1998).

233 Ss. 12 and 14A, Public Order Act 1986.

234 Above n. 46, pp. 655-656 (references omitted).

235 R. Reiner, *The Politics of the Police* (Wheatsheaf, 1992), p. 216. See also, R. Reiner and S. Spencer (eds.), *Accountable Policing: Effectiveness, Empowerment and Equity* (IPPR, 1993).

236 See eg, W. Lyons, *The Politics of Community Policing: Rearranging the Power to Punish* (Michigan UP, 1999), arguing that, in one area of Seattle, community policing was more disciplinary than democratising and left the community more disempowered.

order law. The causes, tactics and identities of protesters have shifted in recent years. So too have the arguments they make in court: increasingly they suggest that criminal activity associated with protesting is justifiable in the public interest. Policing is also in flux, with both positive and negative indicators. A key example of the former is the pioneering approach of the Patten Report on policing in Northern Ireland, and it is to be hoped that its recommendations will be considered throughout the UK.[237] If they are, then, there is a chance that we may be able to alleviate the negative consequences of conceptions of policing as a 'force' or a 'service'.

Fundamentally, however, the future of protesting and assembly in the HRA era depends on whether and how we face up to the challenges of two key concepts: first, limits and second, legitimation.[238] As regards the former, we need to think in terms of the limits of the traditional approach to regulating protesting and assembly and the limits of public order law. This chapter has argued against the recent trend towards increased criminalisation of low-level disorder. A number of these new legal rules may be vulnerable under Articles 10 and 11. More fundamentally, there is little evidence that such laws achieve their aims. Law is simply one resource for the patrolling police officer; senior officers seem to prefer preventive public order policing, opting to negotiate and consult with protest organisers. We also need to think in terms of the limits of conventional understandings of public and private if we hope to face the challenge of changing patterns of ownership, access to space and policing. The increased use of private law is a potential problem, especially the reliance on notions of consent. Finally, we need to think more generally about the limits of legal regulation in the public order field. Discretion is inevitable in policing, particularly public order policing, and legal rules alone do not, and cannot, control discretion. Thus the aim should be justifiable managed, or structured, public police discretion.

This brings us to 'legitimation', the second key concept that will need to be tackled in dealing with public order law and practice over the coming years. The aim here must be to legitimate protest and other democratic forms of assembly, as well as public order policing. As this chapter has argued, achieving such legitimation requires further normative reflection and debate on the role of both protest and policing in a democratic society. Balance, consent, community, and active citizenship will have to be examined as part of any such reflection. There is also a need to take a closer look at definitions of order and disorder more generally. Finally, achieving legitimation will require an identification of the possibilities of practical change, and the potential for legal and non-legal regulation to facilitate such changes. This chapter has emphasised the limits of traditional legal regulation in public order policing, and it seems inevitable therefore that other methods of regulation – both legal and non-legal – will need to be utilised. This might seem like a very tall order. Recent progressive indicators – including the Parades Commission, the Patten and North Reports, senior judicial pronouncements in *Jones* and *Redmond-Bate*, and the European Court of Human Rights' judgment in *Hashman and Harrup* – allow for some, albeit very limited, optimism that some, if not all of the above, can be achieved.

---

237 Cf. P. Hillyard and M. Tomlinson, 'Patterns of Policing and Policing Patten' (2000) 27 JLS 394.
238 See more generally, Lacey and Wells, above n. 10.

Chapter Three

Terrorism: rhetoric and reality

INTRODUCTION

When introducing the Prevention of Terrorism (Temporary Provisions) Act 1974, then Home Secretary Roy Jenkins described it as a 'draconian measure'.[1] Twenty-four years later, Prime Minister Tony Blair supported the creation of fresh anti-terrorist legislation, the Criminal Justice (Terrorism and Conspiracy) Act 1998, with the claim that these were 'desperate measures for desperate times'.[2] Most recently, then Home Secretary, Jack Straw, justified the Terrorism Act 2000 (TA 2000), the new permanent UK-wide legislation, because of the need 'to combat current and future threats from all kinds of terrorist groups'.[3] That Labour politicians with liberal credentials – the first devised Britain's initial anti-discrimination legislation, the second and third belong to the government that introduced the HRA – should advocate such measures demonstrates the fragile position of civil liberties when faced with claims of terrorist threats. It is perhaps not surprising then that, for much of the past 30 years, anti-terrorist law has been the nadir of civil liberties in the UK.

In this chapter, we shall examine the relationship between civil liberties and efforts, primarily legal, to prevent and punish terrorism. The task is a particularly important one given the effect that the anti-terrorist imperative has had on a wide range of human rights. Criminal law and procedure, national security provisions, public order law and policing practices all bear the mark of counter-terrorist strategy. Institutions, notably the courts and Parliament, which have been the hope of civil libertarians in relation to other areas have been severely tested, and usually found wanting, when it comes to protecting human rights in the face of the perceived terrorist threat.

Yet, the situation is more complex than a straightforward critique of the repressive nature of anti-terrorist law suggests. Perhaps paradoxically, anti-discrimination law and human rights institutions in Northern Ireland – advocated partly on the grounds that they would undercut support for terrorism

---

1   *H.C. Debs.*, vol. 882, col. 35 (25 Nov. 1974). See R. Jenkins, *A Life at the Centre* (Papermac, 1994).
2   See generally, C. Walker, 'The Bombs in Omagh and their Aftermath: The Criminal Justice (Terrorism and Conspiracy) Act 1998' (1999) 62 MLR 879; and C. Campbell, 'Two Steps Backwards: The Criminal Justice (Terrorism and Conspiracy) Act 1998' [1999] Crim LR 941.
3   Home Office Press Release 393/99, 2 Dec. 1999 (www.open.gov.uk). See generally, *Legislation Against Terrorism: A Consultation Paper*, Cm. 4178 (HMSO, 1998); *A Summary of the Government's Proposals*; at the Home Office's 'Legislation' website at: www.homeoffice.gov.uk/leg.htm.

– are now a potential model for the rest of the UK.[4] The Patten Report on the future of policing in Northern Ireland has been welcomed as an incisive critique of the legitimacy and accountability of policing institutions.[5] The work and influence of human rights NGOs within Northern Irish civil society also provides lessons for comparable organisations in other parts of the UK.[6] Even more broadly, it has been argued that the 'problem' of Northern Ireland has exposed the limitations of traditional British public law theory, especially Diceyan concepts of rights and parliamentary representation, in ways that may have contributed to the wider desire for constitutional change in the UK.[7] A focus on terrorism and its consequences, therefore, has wide implications for the HRA era: it can provide us with a range of general insights on the possibilities and limits of creating a human rights culture throughout the UK.

Part I of this chapter begins by noting some of the damaging effects which anti-terrorist law and policy have had on civil liberties in the UK. It will then move on to explore the challenges which the problem of terrorism poses for human rights advocates. We reject the idea that civil libertarian arguments are rendered pointless or impotent in the face of the terrorist threat and contend that they still have an important role to play in this sphere. Indeed, one of the features of the Northern Ireland peace process in recent years has been the extent to which human rights language has become a common currency of debate, and source of agreement, amongst the different actors.[8] Part II will examine one of the central grounds for restricting human rights as part of an anti-terrorist strategy: that terrorism poses a particular threat to liberal democratic society and requires the curtailment of 'the liberty of a few to protect the liberty of the many'. We shall argue that use of the term 'terrorism' is politically loaded and confusing, and while political violence may pose a threat to democracy, there is no evidence that it is as great as claimed or that emergency legislation is needed.[9] We shall also highlight how a dominant feature of anti-terrorist strategy has been the promotion of legal measures antithetical to civil liberties, often as much for their symbolic as practical effects.

Part III will explore some of the state's responses to the terrorist threat. The content of the specific anti-terrorist legislation which has been in force in the different parts of the UK since the 1970s – now consolidated and extended by the TA 2000 – is first described in this section. We shall then analyse some of the practices of the police, army and security services in anti-terrorist actions, and the extent of the relationship between law and policy in the field of counter-

---

4   See eg, S. Spencer and I. Bynoe, *A Human Rights Commission: A Blueprint* (IPPR, 1998); and, more generally, see C. Harvey and S. Livingstone, 'Human Rights and the Northern Ireland Peace Process' [1999] 3 EHRLR 162.

5   See the Report of the Independent Commission on Policing for Northern Ireland at www.belfast.org.uk; and J. McGarry and B. O'Leary, *Policing Northern Ireland* (Blackstaff, 1999).

6   See eg, L. Whelan, 'The Challenge of Lobbying for Civil Rights in Northern Ireland: The Committee on the Administration of Justice' (1992) 14 HRQ 149.

7   See C. McCrudden, 'Northern Ireland and the British Constitution' in J. Jowell and D. Oliver (eds.), *The Changing Constitution* (Clarendon, 1994), pp. 323-375; and J. Morison and S. Livingstone, *Reshaping Public Power: Northern Ireland and the British Constitutional Crisis* (Sweet & Maxwell, 1995).

8   See eg, G. Mitchell, *Making Peace* (Heinemann, 1999); and the text of the Northern Ireland Good Friday Agreement 1998 (available at: www.nio.gov.uk).

9   See the UK statistics for terrorism offences in S. Livingstone and N. Whitty, *Still 'Temporary' After 22 Years: The Case Against Permanent Anti-Terrorism Legislation* (IPPR, 1996).

terrorism. We shall also highlight how, in tandem with these legislative and military/policing responses, the UK government has increasingly adopted diplomatic and political initiatives (in recent years, strategically co-ordinated with the Irish government) designed to undercut support for terrorism in Northern Ireland.

Our overall conclusion is that, historically, state anti-terrorist policy has been largely reactive and frequently contradictory. The repressive nature of state responses has both perpetuated the political conflict and created the conditions in which abuses of human rights have occurred, especially through the lack of adequate accountability mechanisms. One particularly negative side-effect of these anti-terrorist strategies has been the way in which once-exceptional powers and practices have become normalised throughout the UK; for example, the changes to evidence law (such as limiting the right to silence), the (paramilitary) policing of large demonstrations, and the increased use of covert surveillance have all been influenced by state responses to the Northern Ireland conflict.[10] Most obviously, the New Labour government's adoption of *permanent* anti-terrorist legislation, with the implication that terrorism will always be a part of the social and political landscape in the UK, highlights how human rights norms and concepts of institutional accountability can be eroded over time.

In Part IV, the final section of the chapter, we shall examine some of the usual accountability mechanisms and how civil liberties arguments have fared in the face of the anti-terrorist policies of several key institutions. We shall highlight the limited influence of human rights discourse on courts, Parliament and international organisations as well as the varied nature of media responses to political violence. From this history, we shall evaluate what lessons can be learned in relation to what form human rights claims should take, and in what forum they should be presented. Our conclusion will be a pessimistic one: the HRA is unlikely to have a significant impact in the arena historically most hostile to a civil liberties agenda.

I.   ANTI-TERRORIST LAW, CIVIL LIBERTIES AND CIVIL LIBERTARIANS

The costs of anti-terrorist law and practice

In many of the areas discussed in this book, aspects of UK law and practice have been found wanting before the European Court of Human Rights. Equally, however, the UK has rarely been the focus of sustained criticism by UN human rights monitoring bodies or international human rights NGOs such as Amnesty International. There is, however, one main exception to this: anti-terrorist legislation and policy. In its concluding observations on the UK's fourth periodic report in 1995 (under the International Covenant of Civil and Political Rights), the UN Human Rights Committee called upon the government to 'dismantle the apparatus of laws infringing civil liberties which were designed for periods of emergency'.[11] The UN Committee Against Torture has expressed 'grave

---

10   See eg, P. Norman, 'The Terrorist Finance Unit and the Joint Action Group on Organised Crime: New Organisational Models and Investigative Strategies to Counter "Organised Crime" in the UK' (1998) 37 Howard J 375; J. Jackson, 'Curtailing the Right to Silence' [1991] Crim LR 404; and T. Jefferson, *The Case Against Paramilitary Policing* (Open UP, 1990).

11   CCPR/C/79/Add.55 (1995).

concern' as to the treatment of detainees arrested under anti-terrorist provisions in Northern Ireland in its 1991, 1995 and 1998 reports on the UK.[12] In 1996, the UN Special Rapporteur on the Independence of Judges and Lawyers, Dato Param Cumaraswamy, published a report indicating concern that defence lawyers in Northern Ireland were subjected to police harassment and called for a number of changes in law and practice to ensure their safety and independence.[13]

International NGOs have, as one might expect, been even more critical of the UK's record on anti-terrorism. Amnesty International has issued several reports in this area, raising concern about matters such as the treatment of detainees, the use of lethal force and the fairness of trials.[14] Its 1978 report on the mistreatment of detainees in Northern Ireland's Castlereagh Holding Centre (the main centre for questioning of terrorist suspects) led directly to a government inquiry[15] and to subsequent changes in the detention regime. In more recent years, other international human rights NGOs, such as Human Rights Watch and Lawyers Committee for Human Rights, have also devoted attention to anti-terrorist policy in the UK. Their reports highlight concerns that international human rights norms have been infringed in respect of matters such as the regulation of public demonstrations, abuse of children by security forces, freedom of movement and the right to a legal defence.[16]

The Council of Europe human rights institutions have not been silent in this regard either. The European Court of Human Rights has found certain anti-terrorist practices to be in violation of the most fundamental rights protected by the ECHR, such as the right to life[17] and the right to freedom from inhuman and degrading treatment.[18] Elements of the two key pieces of anti-terrorist legislation, the Prevention of Terrorism (Temporary Provisions) Act 1989 (PTA)[19] and the Northern Ireland (Emergency Provisions) Act 1996 (EPA),[20] have also been found to be in breach of the Convention and a number of other cases are currently pending.[21] After its first visit to Northern Ireland in 1993, the European Committee for the Prevention of Torture called for the Holding Centre at Castlereagh police station to be closed down. The Committee concluded that the operation of this facility created an unacceptable risk that those detained there would be subjected to inhuman or degrading treatment.[22]

---

12   See respectively CAT/C/SR.133 (1991); A/51/44 (1995); and CAT/C/UK (1998).
13   E/CN.4/1998/39/Add.4.
14   See eg, *Political Killings in Northern Ireland* (1994). (Amnesty International's reports on the UK are available at: www.amnesty.org/).
15   *Report of the Committee of Inquiry into Police Interrogation Procedures in Northern Ireland* (Cmnd. 7497, 1979).
16   See eg, Human Rights Watch, *Human Rights in Northern Ireland* (1991), *Children in Northern Ireland* (1992) and *To Serve Without Favor* (1997) (available at: www.hrw.org); and Lawyers Committee for Human Rights, *Human Rights and Legal Defense in Northern Ireland* (1993) and *At the Crossroads: Human Rights and the Northern Ireland Peace Process* (1996) (available at: www.lchr.org).
17   *McCann, Farrell and Savage v UK* (1995) 21 EHRR 97; and *Jordan v UK* (4 May 2001).
18   *Ireland v UK* (1978) 2 EHRR 25.
19   *Brogan v UK* (1989) 11 EHRR 439.
20   *Fox, Campbell and Hartley v United Kingdom* (1991) 13 EHRR 157.
21   See the ECtHR website at: www.echr.coe.int.
22   CPT/Inf (94) 17. The Centres were not closed until Dec. 1999 following a further CPT visit: CPT/Inf (2001) 6.

Overall, this record adds up to a crescendo of international concern about the human rights implications of anti-terrorist law and practice in the UK. The police, military and prison service have all faced exacting international scrutiny, and subsequent adverse media coverage.[23] It is important, however, to retain a sense of perspective for two reasons. First, the extent to which legal rules (and court decisions) actually influence the attitudes, policies and practices of police and security services in some operational areas is unclear. As we highlight in the chapters dealing with public order, fair trial and prisoners, the relationship between law and policing or order-maintenance is extremely complex. In the context of terrorism, a culture of 'rule-breaking' or 'rule-avoidance' may be the norm, depending on the particular policy of the time (as, for example, in relation to interrogation techniques in the 1970s, the 'shoot to kill' controversy in the 1980s, or the denial of lawyers' access to detainees). The preference of some soldiers for 'Big Boys' Rules' rather than legal norms constraining the use of lethal force, and the policy of deliberate deception of the media and courts – both of which are highlighted in Urban's account of the involvement of elite military and intelligence services in Northern Ireland – clearly reveals a particular institutional mindset.[24] In other contexts, however, adverse rulings of the European Court of Human Rights and criticism by human rights organisations appear to have had a positive impact on policy-making and led to reforms, including, for example, the creation of an Independent Commissioner for Holding Centres in Northern Ireland.[25] However, in the absence of access to detailed information on the origins of particular anti-terrorist policies – a category of information embargoed for up to 100 years in the Public Records Office – one can only speculate as to when and where *human rights* institutions have *decisively* influenced successive UK government policy.

Secondly, it must be emphasised that the UK has actually won more cases than it has lost in Strasbourg relating to anti-terrorist policy.[26] Moreover, the European Court of Human Rights consistently upheld the UK government's argument that the level of terrorist violence in Northern Ireland justified its derogation (under Article 15 of the ECHR) from aspects of the right to liberty of the individual under Article 5 of the Convention.[27] The 'risk' of adverse rulings from the Court in relation to anti-terrorism powers is, therefore, not substantial. Furthermore, where violations of the Convention have been found, as in *McCann v United Kingdom*, the consequences have been adverse media publicity rather than serious, long-term restrictions on the operational freedom of state agencies.

---

23   See eg, Amnesty International's 1997 report on Special Secure Units in UK prisons, *Special Security Units: Cruel, Inhuman or Degrading Treatment* (AI Index EUR 45/06/97). The need to contain IRA prisoners was one of the main justifications for the development of such units.

24   See M. Urban, *Big Boys' Rules: The SAS and the Secret Struggle Against the IRA* (Faber & Faber, 1993); and below, pp. 139-143.

25   See C. Walker and B. Fitzpatrick, 'The Independent Commissioner for the Holding Centres: A Review' [1998] PL 106; and their, 'Holding Centres in Northern Ireland, the Independent Commissioner and the Rights of Detainees' [1999] EHRLR 27.

26   For an overview of Northern Irish cases in Strasbourg, see S. Livingstone, 'Reviewing Northern Ireland in Strasbourg 1969-1994' [1995] Irish HR Yearbook 15; and B. Dickson, 'Northern Ireland and the European Convention' in B. Dickson (ed.), *Human Rights and the European Convention* (Sweet & Maxwell, 1997), pp. 169-182; and his 'Northern Ireland and the Human Rights Act' in A. Lester and D. Pannick (eds.), *Human Rights Law and Practice* (Butterworths, 1999), pp. 287-308.

27   See *Ireland v UK* above n. 18; and *Brannigan and McBride v UK* (1993) 17 EHRR 539.

Anti-terrorism and the civil libertarian dilemma

The above history highlights a UK record of *fundamental* rights violations in respect of anti-terrorist law and practice. One might expect, therefore, that a study of anti-terrorist law would be at the heart of most civil liberties texts, courses and activism in the UK. Yet, this is far from being the case. Terrorism is referred to in civil liberties texts, but it is rarely given the prominence of topics such as freedom of expression or privacy.[28] Similarly, while anti-terrorist law is the central focus of the work of many human rights NGOs in Northern Ireland, those operating in Britain, with the notable exception of Liberty,[29] have engaged with it more gingerly. Indeed, it has often seemed that human rights advocates in Britain have avoided entanglement with the issue of Northern Ireland, lest their proposals for reform in other areas be tarnished by association.[30]

Apart from the historical and personal factors which may explain such distancing (for example, a lack of expertise or issues of identity), there is also of course the common political hurdle faced by all civil liberties advocates working in jurisdictions where terrorism is a reality: the need to justify supporting the rights of individuals who reject the legitimacy of the state and are prepared to use political violence to further that aim. Throughout this book we highlight how much of the energy behind civil liberties struggles comes through identification with the character or objectives of those whose liberty is being asserted. Thus, although human rights may be presented as abstract ideas such as freedom of expression or freedom from discrimination, it also has its paradigm cases, its heroes and heroines whose stories shape the key principles.[31] The courageous journalist seeking to expose government corruption or the gay rights activists seeking freedom to go about their daily lives, for example, provide concrete images which civil liberties activists and lawyers can draw upon to provide points of reference and inspire action.[32] Terrorism provides few such role models. It may often provide the appearance of glamour[33] but rarely, for those whose commitment is to democracy and pluralism, a sense of value which should be supported. At best, it may offer cases of those wrongly accused of involvement in terrorism around whom wider campaigns may be mobilised, the Birmingham Six and the Guildford Four being obvious infamous examples.[34]

---

28   For example, the topic is discussed only as an aspect of arrest powers and media restrictions by H. Fenwick, *Civil Liberties* (Cavendish, 1998) and D. Feldman, *Civil Liberties and Human Rights in England and Wales* (Clarendon, 1993). There is a short discussion, mainly focused on the Prevention of Terrorism Act 1989, in E. Shorts and C. de Than, *Civil Liberties: Legal Principles of Individual Freedom* (Sweet & Maxwell, 1998). Only S.H. Bailey, D.J. Harris and B.L. Jones, *Civil Liberties: Cases and Materials* (Butterworths, 1995) devote a chapter to the issue of terrorism, focusing primarily on anti-terrorist law in Northern Ireland.

29   One of the first reports of the National Council for Civil Liberties (Liberty's predecessor) was on the use of the Special Powers Act 1922 in Northern Ireland in 1936.

30   For a discussion of this point, see eg, P. Hillyard, 'The Politics of Criminal Injustice: The Irish Dimension' in M. McConville and L. Bridges (eds.), *Criminal Justice in Crisis* (Edward Elgar, 1994), pp. 69-79.

31   See R. Cover, 'The Supreme Court 1982 Term-Foreword: Nomos and Narrative' (1983) 97 Harv LR 4.

32   Famous US examples used in many teaching contexts are the school desegregation case *Brown v Board of Education* (1954) and the abortion case *Roe v Wade* (1973).

33   Individual terrorists such as 'Carlos the Jackal' or, more recently, the Saudi exile Osama bin Laden, have been the focus of extensive media attention.

34   The film, *In the Name of the Father*, focusing on those wrongly convicted of the 1974 Guildford bombing, is one of the few examples of popular culture seeking openly to garner support for those labelled terrorists.

Campaigning on behalf of someone to whom it is argued a law has wrongly been applied (albeit that it can often provide the impetus for a critique of aspects of the law itself) is, however, rather different from endorsing the actions of someone who has clearly violated the criminal law.

Civil liberties activism, though, has never just required appealing victims or deserving causes. Curbing police powers is a standard focus of civil liberties courses and human rights practitioners and, often, this entails asserting the rights of those who have been involved in undesirable activities such as assault or robbery. Civil libertarians in this field will frequently stress that their concern is less with the individual defendant than with ensuring the integrity of the criminal justice system and that the police and prosecution agencies remain accountable to the rule of law. 'Slippery slope' arguments will frequently be invoked to suggest that once the police are allowed to fabricate evidence against known drug-dealers or paedophiles, they may do the same, for example, to African-Caribbean teenagers on racist grounds.

Such arguments are also available in respect of anti-terrorist law and, as already noted, there are growing concerns about police forces transferring the powers and methods used in anti-terrorist activity to other spheres of policing. However, these points never seem to carry quite the same weight in this context. One reason may be that placing primary emphasis on whether police officers obey legal rules appears somewhat insensitive when those officers and their families may be the target of terrorist attack, something which is unlikely when dealing with 'ordinary' criminals. Secondly, whereas those involved in 'crime' can often be presented as deprived or dysfunctional, the dominant myth of 'the terrorist' tends to emphasise his or her skilled, ruthless and cunning nature. Human rights activists can, thus, often end up being portrayed as legal fetishists who are indifferent to human suffering or as naïve humanitarians. The frequent alliance of media organisations with state interests when national security is perceived to be threatened (exacerbated by the control of journalistic access to police/military sources) also results in the downplaying or ignoring of civil liberties viewpoints.[35]

Consequently, much of the legal writing on anti-terrorist law from a human rights perspective appears somewhat hesitant and muted in its ambitions. Walker, for example, after an extensive study of British anti-terrorist law in 1986, offered proposals which he hoped would be a 'modest improvement on emergency legislation current in the United Kingdom'.[36] In 1992, Dickson provided a trenchant critique of the EPA as primarily motivated by a government desire to appease the electorate rather than to tackle political violence in Northern Ireland, but concluded by recommending the 'ordinary' criminal law as an adequate substitute.[37] Yet, as we have explored in other chapters, the 'ordinary' law of the Police and Criminal Evidence Act 1984 (PACE) is also flawed in criminal justice terms and, more importantly, one cannot just assume that statutory rules ('law in books') and actual policing practices ('law in action') are the same. Thus, the theme of the adequacy of the ordinary criminal law to deal with political violence appears to be more strategic than seriously analytical; essentially conservative, it perhaps reflects a feeling amongst some activists that in the face of frequent calls for even more extreme measures (including internment and the return of the death penalty), it may result in a limited victory.

35　See generally Ch. 7 on the role of media in national security contexts.
36　C. Walker, *The Prevention of Terrorism in British Law* (Manchester UP, 1986), p. 216.
37　B. Dickson, 'Northern Ireland's Emergency Legislation – The Wrong Medicine?' [1992] PL 592.

Some commentators, however, have argued that the cautious and tentative nature of activism in relation to anti-terrorism policy is the product of problems in the civil libertarian tradition itself. Tomlinson and Rolston, for example, argue that civil libertarians seek to position themselves as neutral umpires between the state and the individual asserting rights.[38] Normally this position is adequate and the civil libertarian critic may advance arguments for law reform which are designed to improve the position of all citizens within the state. However, this position becomes untenable in the face of political violence which aims to change or overthrow the state. Such violence clearly rejects the legitimacy of the state which civil libertarian arguments presuppose. The use of force by the state (which includes arrests, trials and imprisonment) against groups involved in political violence in turn poses questions as to the legitimacy of the state itself, since the force cannot be legitimate if the state is not.[39] Some respond to the terrorist threat by nailing their colours firmly to the mast of the legitimacy of the state and are prepared to accept draconian measures to protect it (as evidenced by the comments from Labour politicians such as Roy Jenkins and Tony Blair with which we began this chapter). Others will accept the view of those who reject the legitimacy of the state and may even join them: Nelson Mandela, perhaps the most famous example of a civil liberties lawyer, took the view that only overthrowing the apartheid South African state would ensure that it became a multi-racial democracy and protected the rights of all citizens.[40] Most advocates of civil liberties in the UK context (and particularly NGOs working in Northern Ireland), however, seek to avoid either position. Continually protective of their neutral position, they will avoid criticising state actors too heavily, lest this be seen as endorsing the views of those who physically attack them, but they will also reject the claim that the state should be immune from accountability for its actions in an anti-terrorist context. As a result, some argue that 'in terms of political effects, the recommendations from the civil liberties stable seem to achieve little more than being fed into the files of "options" lining the walls of the Cabinet Office'.[41]

We reject this characterisation of the civil libertarian approach for a number of reasons. First, we agree with Hillyard that a focus on human rights has an immediate and practical value:

[I]t is important to challenge the use of arbitrary power as a cause in its own right irrespective of the origins of the law. Abuses of power affect people's daily lives; the struggle to improve their lot is sufficient justification in itself to pursue a civil libertarian approach.[42]

---

38   M. Tomlinson and B. Rolston, 'Spectators at the Carnival of Reaction: Analysing Political Crime in Ireland' in M. Kelly, L. O'Dowd and J. Wickham (eds.), *Power, Conflict and Inequality* (Turoe, 1982), pp. 21-43.

39   See D. Dyzenhaus, *Hard Cases in Wicked Legal Systems: South African Law in the Perspective of Legal Philosophy* (OUP, 1991); and M. Walzer, *Just and Unjust Wars* (Basic Books, 1992).

40   There are many other examples of conflicts worldwide where political violence has been used as part of liberation struggles, with consequent dispute over its legitimacy and the labelling of 'freedom fighters'/'terrorists' (for example, Rhodesia/Zimbabwe, Nicaragua, Palestine/Israel, Spain/Basque region). See generally, C. Gearty (ed.), *Terrorism* (Dartmouth, 1996).

41   See Tomlinson and Rolston, above n. 38, at p. 33.

42   P. Hillyard, 'Political and Social Dimensions of Emergency Law in Northern Ireland' in A. Jennings (ed.), *Justice Under Fire: The Abuse of Civil Liberties in Northern Ireland* (Pluto, 1988), pp. 191-212, at p. 207.

Anti-terrorist law has resulted in some of the most serious abuses of human rights in the UK over the past 30 years, it has often undermined mechanisms of accountability, and has corrupted even those institutions otherwise protective of civil liberties. Challenging these effects alone is an important task, and a common cause which people sharing a variety of political perspectives might support.

Secondly, we would go further than such an instrumental defence of civil libertarian strategy in this area to suggest that the above criticism is valid only in respect of a narrowly focused version of rights. The approach we outlined in Chapter 1 goes beyond a rights culture limited to a list of proscriptions on state interference. Instead, it seeks to follow an approach which views the promotion of human rights norms as an aspect of a broader project of advancing democratic pluralism and encouraging political transition and conflict resolution. Far from pursuing an abstract fetishism of law and rights, this approach is sensitive to issues of power and context. In the difficult area of anti-terrorist law, it means avoiding the reification of both 'the state' and 'the terrorist' as either presumptively legitimate or illegitimate. Instead, there is a requirement to look more closely at the conduct of those who actually represent the state and those who actually seek to overthrow or change it using violence. In respect of both, there are two conditions. First, that any use of force in the name of others must be based on some sort of democratic mandate and, secondly, such use of force respects the limits of fundamental human rights guarantees.[43] The governments of democratically elected states will normally find it easier to satisfy the first condition and often the second. However, *sometimes* major changes in the character of the state will be necessary to achieve either and *sometimes* those opposing the state by violent means will be able to claim that they are closer to satisfying them.[44]

Third and finally, as we have already noted, the relationship between law/ human rights discourse and social change is complex.[45] Even in the hostile arena of anti-terrorist policy, there have been occasions when government actors have responded to findings of human rights violations and the lobbying of human rights activists: in Northern Ireland, anti-discrimination law, the regulation of marches, the video-monitoring of police interviews, the creation of a Northern Ireland Human Rights Commission, and the Patten policing reforms all point to the success of human rights activism. On the other hand, however, such 'reforms' can camouflage the continuation of other more repressive practices (such as stop and search, the intimidation of defence lawyers, or the coercion of informers). Equally, legislative changes may alter the procedure but not the substance of state action; for example, the transfer of the power to authorise detention up to seven days from the Home Secretary to

---

43   See generally, R. Mullerson, 'International Humanitarian Law in Internal Conflicts' (1997) 2 J Armed Conflict Law 109; L. Moir, 'The Implementation and Enforcement of the Laws of Non-International Armed Conflict' (1998) 3 J Armed Conflict Law 163; and H. Wilson, *International Law and the Use of Force by National Liberation Movements* (OUP, 1998).

44   The Algerian military's cancellation of elections in 1992, after the Islamic Salvation Front (FIS) won 3.25 million votes out of an electorate of 13 million in the first round, is a clear illustration of this point.

45   See S. Livingstone, 'Using Law to Change a Society: The Case of Northern Ireland' in S. Livingstone and J. Morison (eds.), *Law, Society and Change* (Dartmouth, 1990), pp. 51-70; and K. McEvoy, 'Law, Struggle and Political Transformation in Northern Ireland' (2000) 27 JLS 542.

a judicial authority under the TA 2000 *may* not in practice result in the curtailment of lengthy police interrogations. Our general point, therefore, is that one-dimensional accounts of the success or failure of human rights strategies in this field are inadequate; it depends on the context.

It is in this spirit that we shall examine the issue of anti-terrorist law and practice in the UK. While the content of legislation and case law is important, there is a need to move beyond this narrow focus and assess the wider social and political contexts which influence the direction of state policy. In particular, civil liberties scholarship needs to engage more with the literature on policing and military cultures,[46] the institutional reforms within Northern Ireland,[47] and the broader political and diplomatic measures generated by the conflict.[48] Only then can a proper assessment be made of the role of human rights law and lawyers in relation to state responses to terrorism in the UK.

II.   THE REALITY OF TERRORISM

The discourse of terrorism

Despite the very different historical and political factors affecting individual situations of political violence worldwide, there is a remarkable consistency to the representation of terrorism and terrorists. In place of serious analysis, government, media and academic discourses tend to share a general perception about the groups involved, their methods and their ultimate aims. Even Northern Ireland-related terrorism, a conflict which has generated more literature than any other[49] – and where successive UK governments have been in secret contact with the main terrorist organisation, the IRA, since the early 1970s[50] – has not escaped simplistic analysis.[51]

Two main factors have contributed to the myth of all terrorists as clever, ruthless and indifferent killers, prepared to cause chaos to advance their cause: first, academic writing on terrorism and secondly, media representations.

Academic discourse on terrorism

In the 1970s and 1980s, there was an enormous growth in academic and journalistic writing about terrorism, and in particular on 'international

---

46   See eg, A. Mulcahy, 'The Official Discourse and Organizational Memory of the Royal Ulster Constabulary' (2000) 40 BJ Crim 68; and his 'Visions of Normality: Peace and the Reconstruction of Policing in Northern Ireland' (1999) 8 SLS 277.

47   See eg, E. Meehan, 'The Belfast Agreement: Its Distinctiveness and Points of Cross-Fertilization in the UK's Devolution Programme' (1999) 52 Parl Affairs 19; Morison and Livingstone, above n. 7; and J. McGarry and B. O'Leary, *Explaining Northern Ireland* (Blackwell, 1995).

48   See eg, C. O'Clery, *The Greening of the White House* (Gill & Macmillan, 1997).

49   See the survey of literature in J. Whyte, *Interpreting Northern Ireland* (Clarendon, 1991).

50   See P. Bishop and E. Mallie, *The Provisional IRA* (Corgi, 1988); and T. Coogan, *The IRA* (Harper Collins, 1995). For accounts of the IRA's shift to a political strategy, see P. Taylor, *Provos* (Bloomsbury, 1998); and J. Major, *John Major: The Autobiography* (Harper Collins, 1999).

51   Clearly, however, although politicians, diplomats and security agencies adopt the uncompromising language of condemnation of terrorists in public, behind-the-scenes perceptions of the 'terrorist' and awareness of political solutions may be very different.

terrorism' as a phenomenon in its own right.[52] A whole academic sub-genre developed around the topic of terrorism, with its own journals and research institutes. Some of this writing sought to explore difficult questions around definitions and responses, often coming to no firm conclusions. The literature also stressed continuity between contemporary terrorism and political violence throughout history, and focused on terrorism as a tactic which could be resorted to by states as well as groups.[53]

However, another line of analysis eschewed academic aspirations to neutrality in favour of a much more partisan approach. Perhaps most vividly captured in the title of a book edited by future Israeli Prime Minister Benjamin Netanyahu, *Terrorism: How the West Can Win*,[54] this approach called explicitly for a 'war' on terrorism and urged Western governments to adopt repressive legislative and military responses. In this writing genre, terrorism was represented as a distinct modern phenomenon limited to the actions of armed opposition groups acting against Western democratic interests. Less attention was given to the definition of terrorism than to sketching out the main characteristics of the terrorist, attributes which were presented as unvarying across the different armed opposition groups under examination. As Netanyahu comments:

> The terrorist represents a new breed of man which takes humanity back to prehistoric times, to the times when morality was not yet born. Divested of any moral principle, he has no moral sense, no moral controls and is therefore capable of committing any crime, like a killing machine, without shame or remorse.[55]

This approach avoided examining the causes of terrorism or the question of resorting to any strategy to deal with it other than state repression. It stressed military and security responses to terrorism, with legislation playing a supportive, instrumental role. Furthermore, since terrorism was seen as an international phenomenon – indeed in some accounts it was viewed as an international communist conspiracy co-ordinated by the Soviet Union in the 1980s – it also stressed the need for an international response and railed against those states who refused to take the prescribed anti-terrorist measures (often because of constitutional constraints) as affording terrorists a safe haven.[56]

The development of this academic literature helped to legitimise the view that terrorism was a specific problem which states had thus far been insufficiently attentive to and, most crucially, that it required fresh legal and security initiatives. This view proved particularly influential with some key policy makers: Brian Jenkins, commenting on the reception of the journalist Claire Sterling's book *The Terror Network* in the early 1980s, observed that there were 'three kinds of people in Washington: those who have always believed the Soviet Union is responsible for international terrorism; those who want to believe it; and those who, in order to maintain their influence in government, must pretend to

---

52   International terrorism is normally defined in terms of violence directed at state X but conducted on the territory of state Y, although nationals of state X may be the primary targets.

53   See eg, W. Laquer, *Terrorism* (Abacus, 1977); or G. Wardlaw, *Political Terrorism* (CUP, 1989).

54   B. Netanyahu (ed.), *Terrorism: How the West Can Win* (Weidenfeld & Nicholson, 1986).

55   Ibid., p. 27.

56   Examples of some of the leading critics of this mindset, and the role of US foreign policy in supporting 'terroristic' regimes (particularly, Central American in the 1980s), are N. Chomsky, *The Culture of Terrorism* (Pluto, 1988) and *World Orders, Old and New* (Pluto, 1997); and E. Said and C. Hitchens (eds.), *Blaming the Victims: Spurious Scholarship and the Palestinian Question* (Verso, 1988).

believe'.[57] This perception clearly influenced US policy in relation to Northern Ireland, for example, as the Reagan administration tightened extradition rules in the 1980s in respect of IRA suspects who had fled there.[58] In addition to reinforcing the view that suspected terrorists would not be able to escape justice by crossing international boundaries, the move was also aimed at securing the US-British political alliance in actions (such as aerial bombing) against 'terrorist-supporting' states (such as that against Libya in 1986).[59] Moreover, even where this genre of anti-terrorist scholarship failed to see its objectives realised, it succeeded in setting the future agenda for official definitions and responses to the problem of political violence.

Media representations of terrorism

Academic scholarship and terrorism institutes alone, however, were not responsible for the broader public acceptance of the claims that democracies were under threat worldwide from violent political groups: the role of the media was also crucial in the wider representation of the terrorist. Many commentators have highlighted the fascination that violence holds for media outlets, particularly individual/group violence directed against state institutions or sections of the public.[60] This 'symbiotic' relationship between the media and terrorism results in actions such as bombings and hijackings leading news bulletins, with the resulting state response (including air-strikes, special forces and bomb-disposal units) providing further follow-up dramatic copy.[61] For example, during a 17-day hostage crisis in 1985 following the hijack of a TWA flight, the three main US television networks broadcast nearly 500 news segments relating to the event. Similar saturation coverage has been observed in Italy, Germany and the UK.[62] Perhaps one of the most dramatic accounts broadcast on British television was the use of the SAS to enter the Iranian Embassy in London in 1980, an event central to the mythology of that unit as a ruthless, efficient anti-terrorist force.[63]

In turn, however, at least some of those involved in political violence have stressed the importance of capturing the media spotlight. For example, Black September members involved in the 1972 Olympics kidnapping acknowledged that they sought a target which would guarantee them maximum publicity, leading some commentators to argue that 'terrorist attacks are often carefully choreographed to attract the attention of the electronic media and the international press'.[64] For many anti-terrorism 'experts' and government

---

57   Quoted in A. Schmid, *Political Terrorism* (Transaction, 1983), p. 214.
58   See M. Simon, 'The Political Offense Exception: Recent Changes in Extradition Law Appertaining to the Northern Ireland Conflict' [1988] Arizona J of Int & Comp L 244; and J. Speer, 'Asylum – Extradition – Political Offense or Serious Nonpolitical Crime Committed in Northern Ireland' (1991) 85 AJIL 345.
59   See P. Thornberry, 'International Law and Its Discontents: the US Raid on Libya' (1986) Liverpool LR 53.
60   See generally, D. Kidd-Hewitt and R. Osborne (eds.), *Crime and the Media: The Post-Modern Spectacle* (Pluto, 1995).
61   See Wardlaw, above n. 53, at pp. 76-87; and R. Farren 'Terrorism and the Mass Media: A Systematic Analysis of a Symbiotic Process' (1990) 13 Terrorism 99.
62   See B. Hoffman, *Inside Terrorism* (Gollancz, 1998), pp. 132-135.
63   See J. Newsinger, *Dangerous Men: The SAS and Popular Culture* (Pluto, 1997).
64   See B. Jenkins, 'International Terrorism: A New Mode of Conflict' in D. Carlton and C. Schaerf (eds.), *International Terrorism and World Security* (Croom Helm, 1975), p. 16.

officials, the implications of this phenomenon are clear. Media coverage is said to promote terrorism, enabling its protagonists to spread their message to a wider audience, while undermining the capacity of the state to respond to it. In particular, pictures of hostage victims or their families sap the will of a government to stand firm in response to terrorist demands. It has also been argued that media coverage helps to legitimise terrorists, especially if they are interviewed, and often raises public doubts about the correctness or proportionality of state responses. To counter these effects, some governments have attempted, in former Prime Minister Margaret Thatcher's famous phrase, to starve terrorist groups of the 'oxygen of publicity'. Where this has happened, the media have been limited in their reporting of certain events, and the interviewing of representatives of certain political groups, primarily through the influence of self-regulatory codes and informal government briefings,[65] but sometimes by means of legislation.[66] The primary aim of such media manipulation is to prevent any legitimising of terrorist actions, particularly the drawing of an equivalence between the terrorist and the responding state.

The reality of UK media coverage of political violence, however, does not lend itself to an approach which legitimises terrorism. Mainstream newspapers and television programmes overwhelmingly reflect an instinctive, pro-state bias in their reporting of terrorism, with many (wittingly or otherwise) playing an important propaganda role.[67] Yet, apart from the political ideologies that influence the output of media organisations – consider, for example, the contrast between *The Daily Telegraph* and *The Guardian* – the changing nature of news reporting itself, with its emphasis on personalities, 'soundbites, public opinion survey results and news-as-entertainment for a global audience',[68] rarely produces serious and thoughtful coverage. At the tabloid level, most forms of political violence are simply represented as 'terrorism' and the work of 'terrorists'. Where media coverage does go beyond reporting the 'event' (for example, a bombing and reactions to it), the analysis of those responsible often degenerates into psychological speculation on the nature of the 'men of violence', or cloak-and-dagger tales as to meetings with terrorists face-to-face, rather than serious political critique. Thus, far from legitimising political violence and the causes that inspire it, much daily media representation engages in the demonisation of those responsible for it.

This demonisation is even more apparent in fictional film coverage of political violence. Terrorism has most frequently been portrayed in the thriller, a popular genre which easily lends itself to simplified conflicts and one-dimensional characters. It is also (and increasingly so since the 1980s) a genre where spectacular representations of violence often overwhelm whatever analysis or perspective may be contained in the story. In successful box office Hollywood productions such as *Die Hard*, *Patriot Games* and *Speed*, or to take a British example *Who Dares Wins*, those involved in political violence are portrayed as glamorous

---

65 On the close relationship between government and media in the area of national security, see P. Taylor, *War and the Media* (Manchester UP, 1998); and Ch. 7.

66 The UK, Irish and German governments, for example, have used legal powers to order broadcasters to refrain from broadcasting certain categories of 'political' material from dissent/terrorist groups.

67 This is particularly true of the Northern Ireland conflict: see L. Curtis, *Ireland: The Propaganda War* (Pluto, 1985); and D. Miller, *Don't Mention the War* (Pluto, 1994).

68 S. Redhead, *Unpopular Cultures: The Birth of Law and Popular Culture* (Manchester UP, 1995), p. 87.

intelligent outlaws at best, cruel deranged psychopaths at worst.[69] The standard storyline pits the terrorist against courageous police officers or agents, whose aim is not just to annihilate the terrorist but also to protect the general public from the threat of indiscriminate violence. Even more politically aware films about the Northern Ireland conflict find it difficult to avoid the use of stereotypes: in *The Crying Game*, Miranda Richardson's IRA volunteer is represented as psychologically unstable and a sexual predator.[70] Male characters involved in political violence are only ever cinematically represented as three-dimensional figures when, as in *The Crying Game* or *Cal*, they are haunted individuals seeking to renounce their violent past and in as much danger from their former comrades as the security forces. Only in *Michael Collins*, a biographical account of a former IRA leader who became an Irish statesman and was eventually assassinated by his former colleagues, is there any attempt to explain the roots of political violence and the personal motivations of the members of a terrorist group.[71]

Such representations of terrorists, in academic and popular media forms, are highly relevant to the study of civil liberties law. Representations of groups have a profound impact on societal responses to such groups.[72] Images from popular culture – including the terrorist as evil, intelligent fanatic – are highly influential on public opinion, which in turn is often mirrored by the attitudes and practices of police, judges and politicians. In the UK, such images have helped to perpetuate sensationalist media coverage of political violence;[73] their pervasiveness has also raised questions about the role of judges and juries in 'terrorist' cases,[74] and the ease with which politicians and security forces have justified extraordinary, repressive legislative and policy initiatives.[75]

The civil libertarian approach to terrorism that we advocate in this chapter would interrogate such images as a first step towards challenging the claim that terrorism poses a unique threat to the UK requiring unique measures. If a

---

69   Films detailing the human rights violations associated with state (usually US-aided) 'counter terrorism' policy – such as *Missing* (Chile), *Salvador* (El Salvador) and *Under Fire* (Nicaragua) – are now a rare genre in Hollywood, and usually centred on a US (media) personality rather than the indigenous targets of the violence.

70   See S. Edge, '"Women are Trouble, Did You Know That Fergus?" Neil Jordan's *The Crying Game*' (1995) 50 Fem Rev 173; and K. Ayers, 'The Only Good Woman isn't a Woman at All: *The Crying Game* and the Politics of Misogyny' (1997) 20 Women's Studies International Forum 329.

71   See comments of the film's producer, S. Woolley, 'When is a Film Not a Film? When British Journalists Don't See It' (1996) 125 New Statesman, p. 38 (8 Nov.).

72   See eg, J. Millbank, 'From Butch to Butcher's Knife: Film, Crime and Lesbian Sexuality' (1996) 18 Sydney LR 451; and L. Young, *Fear of the Dark: 'Race', Gender and Sexuality in the Cinema* (Routledge, 1996).

73   See *R v Cullen, McCann and Shanahan* (1990) 92 Cr App Rep 239 (Court of Appeal quashed convictions of three suspected terrorists on grounds that media comments by Northern Ireland Secretary and Lord Denning prejudiced a fair trial); and *In Re Rachid*, *The Independent*, 27 Jun. 1997 (Div Ct refused to accept that racist French media coverage of Algerians was a ground for refusing extradition to France to face bombing charges).

74   See description in G. Conlon, *Proved Innocent: The Story of Gerry Conlon of the Guildford Four* (Hamish Hamilton, 1990).

75   See eg, the speech of Prime Minister Tony Blair to the UN General Assembly in Sep. 1998: 'The fight against terrorism has taken on a new urgency. The past year's global roll call of terror includes Luxor, Dar es Salaam, Nairobi, Omagh and many others. Each one is a reminder that terrorism is a uniquely barbaric and cowardly crime. Each one is a reminder that terrorists are no respecters of borders. Each one is a reminder that terrorism should have no hiding place, no opportunity to raise funds, no let-up in our determination to bring its perpetrators to justice.'

democratic society is to respond adequately to the threat of political violence, it is vital that substantial, politically informed research on the composition, methods and motives of terrorist groups should form the basis of policy. Moreover, challenges to government and standard mass media accounts are crucial not only in influencing public debate, but also in allowing journalists to maintain lines of communication with the representatives of all terrorist/ political groups. This is why civil libertarians viewed the restrictions on media coverage of Northern Irish paramilitary groups and their supporters from 1988 to 1994 with such alarm.[76] As feared, the 'Broadcasting Ban' was interpreted by cautious broadcasters in ways that went well beyond limiting the direct advocacy of support for such groups.[77] Legal challenges to these measures were rejected by the House of Lords[78] and, with disturbing ease, by the European Commission on Human Rights,[79] in a manner which once again showed the difficulties of making human rights claims in the face of anti-terrorist rhetoric. Only after the IRA and loyalist paramilitary ceasefires came into effect in 1994, did the UK government conclude that this particular anti-terrorist measure was no longer necessary. The repercussions of the 'Broadcasting Ban' are, however, still being felt, not just in relation to the type of media coverage that prevails and its negative influence on government policy, but also in the increasing shift towards targeting journalists to reveal their sources: instead of recognising the democratic importance of an independent media in conflict situations,[80] police and prosecution agencies continue to represent certain journalists as 'aiding the terrorist' and use legal powers to censor stories and discourage investigative reporting.[81]

The definitions of terrorism

If terrorism is such a major problem for democratic societies as to justify a whole range of repressive measures in response, one might expect some clarity on the question of how it is to be defined. Definition has, however, proved elusive. One major study considered 109 different definitions of terrorism and concluded that 'the search for an adequate definition is still on'.[82] Comments on the difficulties of defining terrorism appear frequently in the opening

---

76 Introduced by way of a direction from the Home Secretary to the broadcasting authorities, this provision required them to refrain from broadcasting the spoken words of those who represented or invited support for a range of organisations. Some, such as the IRA and UFF, were proscribed organisations. Others, including Sinn Féin and the UDA, were (at that time) legal organisations.

77 An official circular even banned a song by the music group, *The Pogues*, because it expressed sympathy with the cause of the imprisoned Birmingham Six. See generally, ARTICLE 19, *No Comment: Censorship, Secrecy and the Irish Troubles* (ARTICLE 19, 1989).

78 *R v Secretary of State for the Home Department, ex p Brind* [1991] 1 All ER 720 (HL).

79 *Brind v UK* (1994) 77-A D & R 262.

80 The role of the media has been central, for example, in the investigation of the events of Bloody Sunday in 1972, now the subject of an official inquiry headed by Lord Saville: see www.bloody-sunday-inquiry.org.uk/. See also, B. Hadfield, '*R. v Lord Saville of Newdigate, ex p. Anonymous Soldiers*: What is the Purpose of a Tribunal of Inquiry?' [1999] PL 663 (on the question of anonymity for the soldiers to give evidence).

81 See *DPP v Channel 4* [1993] 2 All ER 517 (£75,000 fine imposed for refusal to disclose sources for a programme on terrorism); and p. 157 below.

82 A. Schmid and A. Jongman, *Political Terrorism: A New Guide to Actors, Authors, Concepts, Data Bases, Theories and Literature* (Transaction Books, 1988).

chapters of books on terrorism. The editor of one recent collection brushed aside such questions as unlikely to yield much insight:

> The authors who contributed to this book did not become bogged down in a morass of verbiage in trying to craft the universal definition of terrorism. They chose instead to discuss terrorism without detailed discussions about the problem with the problem definition.[83]

Such a confident dismissal of the difficulties of defining terrorism, however, is available only to those who believe they 'know it when they see it', or to those who are attempting to score political points. Most legal commentators find the issue troubling. Usually, attempts at defining terrorism focus either on objectives or methods. Definitions which focus on objectives normally conceptualise terrorism in terms of violence directed at the destabilisation and overthrow of the government in power. However, this is frequently criticised on the grounds that it leaves no space for legitimate rebellion and hence ends up as an apology for the (repressive) status quo. It also creates difficulties for distinguishing terrorism from war: the defeat of governments is the exact aim of states in wartime, yet, many of those who advocate strong anti-terrorist measures would not, for example, see NATO's action against Serbia in 1999 as amounting to 'terrorism'. Moreover, attempts to nuance this sort of definition to allow some scope for legitimate rebellion against an oppressive state tend to only lead to relativistic arguments that 'one person's terrorist is another's freedom fighter'.[84]

Definitional attempts which focus on methods are more promising. These define terrorism in terms of random violence designed to create terror and (in some versions) garner publicity for the terrorists' cause. Such an approach, however, turns out to be both over- and under-inclusive. It is over-inclusive as much criminal activity (such as armed robbery or mugging) might fall within it. It appears under-inclusive as it might not include much of the violent activity undertaken by groups popularly seen as terrorist: such violence is often planned rather than random and is designed to achieve very specific goals (such as removing a policing presence from an area or securing the release of prisoners) rather than to create terror generally or obtain publicity.[85]

Given these problems with defining terrorism, it is not surprising that legal provisions are confused and contradictory. UK law has employed several different definitions of terrorism for different purposes.[86] The Suppression of Terrorism Act 1978 (which was passed to give effect to the UK's legal obligations under the 1977 European Convention on the Suppression of Terrorism) has nothing to say on the subject as agreement could not be reached amongst the signatories to the treaty on a satisfactory definition of terrorism. The 1978 Act achieves its objective of providing that extradition shall be refused for terrorist offences by simply listing a number of offences in respect of which defendants may not plead the political offence exception.[87] The Prevention of Terrorism

---

83   H. Kushner (ed.), *The Future of Terrorism: Violence in the New Millennium* (Sage, 1998), p. vii.
84   See eg, D. Rapoport and Y. Alexander (eds.), *The Morality of Terrorism: Religious and Secular Justifications* (Pergamon, 1982).
85   See *R v Martin* [1999] Crim LR 97 where the Court of Appeal reduced a sentence of 35 years to 28 against an IRA member who planned to plant 37 bombs at six electricity stations. It was accepted that, even though crimes which threatened democracy and the general public were especially serious, the primary aim of the campaign was to cause damage to property rather than take human life.
86   See generally, Bailey, Harris and Jones, above n. 28, pp. 265-320.

(Temporary Provisions) Act 1989 and the Northern Ireland (Emergency Provisions) Act 1996 both defined terrorism as 'the use of violence for political ends', although this was then qualified by indicating that such violence must either 'relate to the affairs of Northern Ireland' or to anywhere but the UK apart from Northern Ireland (that is, it must be 'international terrorism').

In the UK courts, judicial comment on the definition of terrorism has been limited, but it seems clear that judges favour a broad construction of the term.[88] Asylum law has also provided an interpretation in *T v Secretary of State for the Home Department*,[89] where the House of Lords had to decide whether an Algerian asylum applicant had committed a 'serious non-political crime' within the meaning of Article 1F(b) of the 1951 Geneva Convention on the Status of Refugees. The House of Lords took the view that it was possible to draw a distinction between a political crime and a terrorist offence. Lord Lloyd ruled that where a crime was committed for a political purpose, the court must then assess whether there was a sufficiently close and direct link between the crime and the political purpose. Where, as here, the act in question was likely to result in the indiscriminate killing or injuring of members of the public, it could be seen as insufficiently related and, hence as, a terrorist rather than a political offence.[90] That such a pluralism of definitions has not led to legal chaos is largely due to a political consensus, which we shall discuss in greater detail below, among government, the security forces and the judiciary as to who the 'terrorist' groups are, and when legal intervention against them is justifiable.

These difficulties in defining terrorism reflect the normative status of the term. As we outlined above, the dominant discourse of terrorism emphasises its wickedness. Moreover, not since the members of the Russian Narodnaya Volya published pamphlets in favour of 'pure terror' in the late nineteenth century, have many individuals or groups been willing to openly refer to themselves as terrorists.[91] On the contrary, groups involved in political violence tend to use other terminology to define themselves – for example, rebels, guerillas, armies or liberation forces – and to emphasise their historical legitimacy. In response, opponents of such groups use the labelling 'terrorist' as a first step towards isolating and defeating them. Consequently, the highly charged and politically loaded character of the term (which, of course, those involved in 'counter-terrorism' have a self-interest in maintaining) gets in the way of attempts at appropriate definition.

With writers such as Gearty and Sederberg, we would argue that a narrow and precise definition of terrorism is both possible and desirable.[92] This would focus on the use of serious violence for political ends against members of the

---

87   This effectively means that all these offences are regarded as terrorist. The Convention on the Suppression of Terrorism provides a loophole to states to continue to distinguish 'terrorist' from 'political' offences in the Art. 13 provision which allows a Member State to reserve the right to refuse extradition in respect of any one of the listed offences which it considers to be a political offence.

88   *McKee v Chief Constable for Northern Ireland* [1984] 1 WLR 1358; and below, n. 294.

89   [1996] 2 All ER 865.

90   The applicant, an acknowledged member of the FIS, was involved in planning an attack on an Algiers airport in which ten people died.

91   For a discussion of the actions of the Narodnaya Volya, see Laquer, above n. 53, pp. 44-55.

92   See C. Gearty, *Terror* (Faber, 1991); and P. Sederberg, *Terrorist Myths: Illusion, Rhetoric and Reality* (Prentice Hall, 1989).

public (that is, non-state actors or 'non-combatants' as Sederberg puts it), such as the 1988 Lockerbie bombing or the 1998 Omagh bombing. Such a definition might be valuable in that it would fit with humanitarian law developments which seek to impose internationally recognised limits on the conduct of both states *and* armed opposition groups in times of armed conflict.[93] It would also provide the basis of international criminal responsibility and would have an impact on questions of impunity and amnesty at the end of armed conflicts.[94]

Such a definition might also provide scope for debate as to whether racist, sexist or homophobic violence should be brought within the scope of terrorism.[95] This violence is frequently specifically, and always generally, pursued with the political aim of striking fear into a particular group of people.[96] Yet, it is rarely mentioned in discussions of what sorts of activity should be included within the definition of terrorism. While concerns as to the wisdom of giving greater credence to such a politically unstable term as 'terrorism' are substantial, it is worth highlighting the significance of the failure of official discourse to even consider, at least prior to the London Soho bomb of 1999, that homophobic violence might constitute a form of terrorism.[97]

We are not so naïve as to believe that such a limited definition would prove unproblematic in practice,[98] or that it would satisfy everyone. In excluding killings of state actors, such as police officers or judges, it leaves out much of what is currently captured by the TA 2000 (discussed below) and, to some, it may seem that this amounts to a failure to treat such violence and the suffering it causes with sufficient seriousness. We would argue, however, that such a response falls into the trap of defining terrorism purely in terms of what is legitimate or illegitimate. We have no difficulty with characterising the use of political violence in a functioning democracy such as the UK as illegitimate and something against which that society is entitled to protect itself. Our point is that indiscriminately describing all political violence as *terrorist* serves only to

---

93   See A. Eide, A. Rosas and T. Meron, 'Humanitarian Standards and Grey Zone Conflicts' (1995) AJIL 215. Some governments resist such a development precisely because it suggests equivalence between the state and groups using violence.

94   See eg, N. Roht-Arriaza and L. Gibson, 'The Developing Jurisprudence on Amnesty' (1998) 20 HRQ 843.

95   As feminist writers such as MacKinnon have observed, analogising rape with torture may significantly alter society's perception of the seriousness of the activity in question: see C. MacKinnon, 'On Torture: A Feminist Perspective on Human Rights' in K. Mahoney and P. Mahoney (eds.), *Human Rights in the Twenty First Century* (Kluwer, 1993), pp. 21-31. See also, R. Morgan, *The Demon Lover: On the Sexuality of Terrorism* (Norton, 1989); S. Gibson, 'The Discourse of Sex/War: Thoughts on Catharine MacKinnon's 1993 Oxford Amnesty Lecture' (1993) 1 FLS 179; and D. Buss, 'Women at the Borders: Rape and Nationalism in International Law' (1998) 6 FLS 171.

96   See P. Panayi (ed.), *Racial Violence in Britain in the Nineteenth and Twentieth Centuries* (Leicester UP, 1996); Human Rights Watch, *Racist Violence in the United Kingdom* (1997); and B. Bowling, *Violent Racism* (OUP, 1999).

97   See generally, G. Mason and S. Tomsen (eds.), *Homophobic Violence* (Hawkins Press, 1997); and E. Stanko and P. Curry, 'Homophobic Violence and the Self "At Risk": Interrogating the Boundaries' (1997) 6 SLS 513.

98   The policy for release of those involved in politically motivated violence during South Africa's apartheid era attempted to use such a criteria to distinguish between those who should and should not be granted early release. Negotiations broke down when the ANC sought the release of a key negotiator, Robert McBride, who had been convicted of planting a bomb that killed five people. See R. Keightley, 'Political Offences and Indemnity in South Africa' (1993) 9 SAJHR 334.

obscure, and avoids the political motivation behind such acts and the social problems (and state action) that may have given rise to them.

Acknowledging the political origins of such violence does not mean that those involved in it are absolved of responsibility,[99] but it does mean that those who seek to respond to it have an obligation to examine the reasons behind it, even if they disagree with them. In light of the indisputable reality that worldwide many of the most infamous 'terrorist' groups have now been acknowledged as primarily *political* actors (for example, the ANC, PLO and Sinn Féin/IRA) – often first entering (secret) negotiations with governments during the period of continued armed resistance – our suggested approach can no longer be easily dismissed as likely to be counter-productive. On the contrary, the lesson of the dominant 1970s and 1980s 'counter-terrorism' strategy is how wrong it was in its refusal to engage with the necessity for political solutions and, arguably, its own role in prolonging the periods of violent conflict.[100]

The extent of the terrorist threat in the UK

Terrorism is popularly seen as a threat to democratic societies. For some, it justifies the commitment of significant military, police, diplomatic, legislative and media efforts to defeat it. Civil liberties lawyers, however, must question the level of any threat and assess the type of state measures in response: both historical experience of anti-terrorist policies and the 'benchmarks' provided by the standards of international human rights law require such a questioning.

As we see it, civil libertarians have at least three good reasons to be sceptical of claims that the level (or even the potential level) of terrorism justifies extraordinary measures. First, unscrupulous governments may utilise the existence of a fairly low level of terrorist activity to justify a broad range of repressive powers. South Africa's apartheid government in the 1960s, for example, responded to a limited and infrequent level of ANC military activity by enacting a draconian anti-terrorist law whose scope extended to any damage to property, providing it was carried out with the intent to bring about constitutional change or a political aim.[101] Amnesty International country reports contain many similar examples of repressive governments fabricating or exaggerating 'terrorist' threats leading to states of emergency.[102]

Secondly, even democratic governments with good human rights records may find themselves panicked into over-reacting, thereby generating far more substantial infringements of the rights of citizens than the terrorist group was ever able to achieve. As Gearty comments 'once they are fully mustered, the forces of even the purest nation will inevitably dwarf in both breadth and impact all the energetic subversion that rebellious opponents will have managed to contrive in years of hectic lawlessness'.[103] Canada and Ireland, for example, are

---

99 For a classic discussion of issues of responsibility and political violence, see A. Camus, *The Rebel* (Penguin, 1971).

100 The Russian military 'anti-terrorist' strategy in Chechnya is an obvious example of this approach.

101 A. Mathews, *Freedom, State Security and the Rule of Law* (Sweet & Maxwell, 1988), pp. 33–38.

102 See www.amnesty.org.

103 See Gearty, above n. 92, p. 131.

both jurisdictions where government/police reaction to minimal political violence in the 1970s led to significant human rights abuses.[104]

Thirdly, over-reaction by state actors to a limited level of terrorist violence may only provoke a higher level of violence in response. The introduction of internment (that is, mass detentions without trial) in Northern Ireland in 1971 is the most notorious UK example. In the first eight months of that year, 27 people died in Northern Ireland as a result of terrorist violence. In the four months after the introduction of internment, another 147 people were killed and the following year turned out to be the most violent of Northern Ireland's recent history.[105] Similarly, commentators on contemporary US efforts to respond to right-wing militias have expressed concern that exaggerating the threat posed by such groups may only serve to unify and embolden them, as well as generating sensationalist media coverage.[106]

Ultimately, therefore, the decision as to the seriousness of any threat of terrorist violence, and the type of state response, is a *political* one. In a democracy, it is crucial that this issue is open to public debate and, for this reason, most international guidelines on when a 'state of emergency' (the most dramatic response to a situation of terrorist violence) may be declared provide for the decision to be taken by the legislature.[107] Clearly, however, in the immediate aftermath of a bomb attack or an assassination attempt, civil libertarians may find it extremely difficult to persuade politicians and media that a terrorist threat is not sufficient to justify particular measures in response. Fortunately, a number of 'limiting principles' are available to challenge claims that extraordinary and repressive measures are necessary.

Limiting principles and terrorist threat

The first principle is that there must be some credibility to the threat. To take a common example, there is always a risk that terrorists might 'go nuclear', that they might obtain the technology and resources to make a nuclear bomb and threaten to use it unless certain demands are met.[108] Leaving aside the fact that the conduct of states who already possess nuclear weapons poses a much greater risk to the public and to environmental safety, it must be acknowledged that this is a terrifying prospect. It is a prospect which justifies very stringent controls over the use and transfer of nuclear material and technology. However,

---

104 The 'October Crisis' of 1970, where a violent Quebec separatist group kidnapped a politician and diplomat, led to the invocation of the War Measures Act by the Canadian federal government and the arrest and detention of 497 people: see P. Hogg, *Constitutional Law of Canada* (Carswell, 1992), p. 458. The activities of the Irish Special Branch during the 'Heavy Gang' period in the 1970s resulted in police assaults on suspects and led to an official inquiry (the 'O'Brian Report' in 1978).

105 See the account of all 3,600 deaths in D. McKittrick, S. Kelters, B. Feeney and C. Thornton, *Lost Lives: The Stories of the Men, Women and Children Who Died as a Result of the Northern Ireland Troubles* (Mainstream, 1999).

106 See T. Mijares and W. Mullins, 'Prosecuting Domestic Terrorists: Some Recommendations' in Kushner, above n. 83, pp. 157-163.

107 See generally, J. Fitzpatrick, *Human Rights in Crisis: The International System for Protecting Rights During States of Emergency* (Pennsylvania UP, 1994).

108 See B. Jenkins, 'Will Terrorists Go Nuclear? A Reappraisal' in Kushner, above n. 83, pp. 225-249. Jenkins concludes that the possibility has increased over the past 20 years but remains unlikely.

it remains so low a risk as to be unable to support claims, for example, that extensive surveillance powers on every suspect political group are justified.

In relation to Northern Ireland-related terrorism, however, the difficulty of challenging official claims about the credibility of any future threat is that no background information is placed in the public domain on national security grounds. Thus, civil libertarian critics of proposed measures will often be at a disadvantage, especially when outflanked by the selective leaking of 'secret' surveillance details to pro-establishment media outlets. This further reinforces the argument made earlier about the need for independent and politically-informed journalistic accounts of the motivations and methods of groups suspected of political violence, and also the need for public awareness of international human rights norms and comparative human rights cultures. One further obstacle is the likely lack of any significant parliamentary opposition, regardless of the political party in power, to anti-terrorism proposals. In part this is because independent politicians are subject to the same public and media pressures as party politicians; increasingly, however, it is also due to the reality of near-absolute government control of parliamentary business more generally (and particularly of 'headlining' initiatives by Ministers).[109]

A second limiting principle is the need for government to demonstrate that the threat is one which overwhelms the capacity to respond of existing law enforcement strategies and institutions. Gearty and Kimbell conceptualise this limitation as an aspect of the broader principle of equality before the law. They argue that special anti-terrorist measures will usually afford fewer rights to those targeted under such powers and, thus, 'at its very least the principle [of equality] would require a very clear case that there was no alternative other than reliance on these wide powers'.[110] This perspective is most often lost sight of in the rush to introduce new powers after a terrorist outrage. For example, following the Omagh bombing of August 1998, new legislation was rushed through both UK and Irish parliaments with little explanation as to why existing anti-terrorist powers were insufficient to enable the police to apprehend those involved. In many respects, such legislative action is often purely symbolic, providing governments with an easy opportunity to appear to take 'decisive' action and satisfy media demands. While the co-ordinated nature of both government responses in 1998 suggest that this step was taken as part of the wider peace process (that is, to further marginalise dissident groups who rejected any ceasefire), the long-term effects of such strategies are often severe – as the history of the 'temporary' Prevention of Terrorism Acts makes clear.

A third limiting principle is provided by the jurisprudence of international human rights institutions, such as the European Court of Human Rights. This is the closest one comes to an independent forum giving an objective appraisal of the extent of a terrorist threat in a particular jurisdiction. Article 15 of the ECHR allows states to derogate from some of the provisions of that treaty, where there exists a situation of war or 'public emergency

---

109 See P. Riddell, *Parliament Under Pressure* (Orion, 1998); and P. Cowley and M. Stuart, 'Parliament: A Few Headaches and A Dose of Modernisation' (2001) 54 Parl Affairs 238.

110 C. Gearty and J. Kimbell, *Terrorism and the Rule of Law* (Civil Liberties Research Unit, Kings College London, 1995), p.13.

threatening the life of the nation'.[111] On a number of occasions, the Strasbourg organs have examined the issue of whether such an emergency exists in a particular state, and whether that state has adopted a legitimate response to it.[112] Indeed, the first case ever to be decided by the European Court of Human Rights, that of *Lawless v Ireland*, focused on the issue of whether Ireland was justified in entering a derogation to Article 5 of the ECHR (the right to liberty) in response to an IRA campaign in the mid-1950s. The Court concluded that conditions in Ireland did amount to a state of emergency threatening the life of the nation. It also offered guidelines as to when the Article 15 criteria would be satisfied: any terrorist threat must be 'current or imminent', must affect the whole of the state in question, and must have produced a situation where the normal mechanisms of law enforcement were unable to function. While the Court indicated that it was initially for the defendant state to determine whether these conditions were satisfied, and also that in coming to this determination the state had a 'margin of appreciation', it did emphasise that this margin of appreciation was subject to European supervision and that, ultimately, it was for the Court itself to decide whether the conditions set out in Article 15 were satisfied.

The *Lawless* criteria provide a good set of democratic 'benchmarks' for civil libertarians to draw upon in identifying when a terrorist threat requires specific and extraordinary action. However, as we highlight below when we examine the judicial approach to anti-terrorist law, *in practice*, the European Court of Human Rights has not interpreted the criteria in a rigorous way and has usually concluded that the state's claims as to the existence of a state of emergency is made out.[113] As always, judicial scrutiny is very much an ex-post facto event and it has proven difficult to challenge political decisions that terrorism poses a major threat (not least because the Court has seen its role as establishing only *minimum* standards of human rights protection within a diversity of countries). While the UK courts might have been more robust in interpreting Article 15 – the derogation was withdrawn in February 2001 – comparative evidence suggests that the judicial role in challenging anti-terrorist law will be limited. Thus, civil liberties arguments are most likely to prove successful in limiting a

---

111 See generally, D.J. Harris, M. O'Boyle and C. Warbrick, *Law of the European Convention on Human Rights* (Butterworths, 1995), pp. 489-507. No derogation is possible from the right to life; protection from torture or inhuman or degrading treatment or punishment; freedom from slavery; and the right not to be subject to retrospective criminal penalties or punishments. Not all terrorist threats will warrant, or will be seen by states as requiring, a derogation. Indeed in cases such as *Klass* and *Brogan*, the ECtHR has recognised that the context of a legitimate terrorist threat may entitle states to a wider 'margin of appreciation' in taking actions short of what would be permitted under a derogation. In such decisions, though, the existence of a significant terrorist threat is presumed. The cases involving Art. 15 (see n. 112 below), therefore, offer a better insight into the Court's approach when that existence is problematised.

112 See, for example, *Lawless v Ireland* (1960) 1 EHRR 1; *Denmark, Norway, Sweden and Netherlands v Greece* [1969] Yearbook of the European Commission on Human Rights 1; *Ireland v UK* (1978) 2 EHRR 25; *Brannigan and McBride v UK* (1993) 17 EHRR 539; and *Aksoy v Turkey* (1996) 23 EHRR 553.

113 For criticism of the ECtHR's decisions, see J. Hartman 'Derogation from Human Rights Treaties in Public Emergencies' (1981) 22 Harv ILJ 1; S. Marks 'Civil Liberties at the Margin: The UK Derogation and the European Convention on Human Rights' (1995) 15 OJLS 69; and O. Gross '"Once More unto the Breach": The Systematic Failure of Applying the European Convention on Human Rights to Entrenched Emergencies' (1998) 22 Yale JIL 437. More generally, see S. Cohen, 'Human Rights and Crimes of the State: The Culture of Denial' (1993) 26 ANZ J Crim 97.

state's response if they can prevent the perception of a terrorist threat from arising in the first place or, alternatively, being exaggerated. Unfortunately, however, the New Labour government's enactment of the permanent TA 2000 is a prime example of the latter, and it suggests a bleak future for human rights in this field at least in the short term.

Justifying the Terrorism Act 2000

The proposal for a permanent counter-terrorism law was first officially mooted by the then Conservative government in the wake of the Northern Ireland ceasefires of 1994. The then Home Secretary charged a House of Lords judge, Lord Lloyd, with the task of inquiring into 'the future need for specific counter-terrorism legislation in the United Kingdom if the cessation of terrorism connected with the affairs of Northern Ireland leads to a lasting peace'.[114] Lloyd's eventual report exemplified several of the themes and processes that we have highlighted in this chapter. First, there was a heavy reliance on academic work in the field of 'terrorism studies', with Lloyd commissioning Professor Paul Wilkinson to write a report on the nature of the terrorist threat that became central to his analysis of terrorism.[115] Secondly, the views of the police and security services were given considerable weight, certainly much greater than those of people primarily concerned with civil liberties and international human rights law. For example, Lloyd convened a two-day expert seminar in the process of researching his report which was attended by six senior members of the security forces, but only one person to 'represent the civil liberties viewpoint' as the report puts it. Thirdly, where the final report does make reference to human rights standards, it does so mainly in relation to the perceived difficulties of complying with cases that the UK has lost in Strasbourg – that is, where the UK has been found to have violated *fundamental* human rights.[116]

Given this background, it is not surprising that Lloyd concluded that there was a need for new and permanent counter-terrorist law, a view unambiguously adopted by the then Home Secretary, Jack Straw.[117] Significantly, Lloyd based this perception of need on potential future threats, whether from 'religious fundamentalists' from the Middle East or 'individuals with fanatical leanings' in Britain.[118] The resulting legislation, the TA 2000, draws upon the now-repealed Prevention of Terrorism (Temporary Provisions) Act 1989, albeit with significant modifications.[119] Notable positive aspects of the new Act are the abolition of the Home Secretary's power to make exclusion orders, the introduction of video-recording of police interviews in Holding Centres (section 100), and the transfer of the power to authorise extended detention following arrest, for up to seven days, from the Home Secretary to a judicial authority (Schedule 8).

---

114 *Inquiry into Legislation Against Terrorism* (Cm. 3420, 1996), p. 1.
115 Wilkinson's paper is published in full as Vol. 2 of the Report. See also, P. Wilkinson, *Terrorism and the Liberal State* (Macmillan, 1995).
116 This mindset is replicated by the subsequent Home Office consultation paper, *Legislation Against Terrorism* (Cm. 4178, 1998), which was published *after* the HRA had been passed.
117 See 'Straw Launches Broader Laws Against Terrorism', *The Guardian*, 18 Dec. 1998.
118 See above n. 114, paras. 1.21-1.24. See H. Fenwick, *Civil Rights* (Longman, 2000), Ch. 3.
119 The full text of the Act is available at: www.legislation.hmso.gov.uk. The EPA 1996 is also repealed, but certain provisions are to be kept in force by the 2000 Act (see Sch. 1) until Part VII is brought into force.

The Act, however, is more notable for the extension of legal power than for any reforms. The power to proscribe organisations, and the range of offences related to membership and fundraising, are extended beyond groups concerned with Northern Ireland to other domestic and international groups (Parts II and III). Powers to stop and search vehicles and pedestrians, to set up police cordons and (a new power) to arrest without warrant are also included (Parts IV and V). New offences of weapons training, directing terrorist organisations, possession and collection of information throughout the UK are created (Part VI). Controversially, sections 59-61 make it an offence for a person to 'incite terrorism' anywhere outside of the UK. The centrepiece of the Act, however, is the new definition of terrorism in section 1(1):

> . . . the use or threat, for the purpose of advancing a political, religious or ideological cause, of action which: (a) involves serious violence against any person or property; (b) endangers the life of any person; or (c) creates a serious risk to the health or safety of the public or a section of the public.[120]

There are numerous civil liberties objections to the TA 2000, but we shall concentrate on three main points. First, while some critics of anti-terrorist law, notably Walker, have argued that permanent legislation is a desirable alternative to 'panic' emergency-law type provisions, we see this step as a dangerous development. The introduction of *permanent* legislation in the UK involves the symbolic rejection of the idea that terrorism tends to be either a small-scale problem, which can best be dealt with through the use of ordinary criminal law and democratically accountable police and security services, or a large-scale political problem, which may require strictly *temporary* emergency legislation coupled with intensive political initiatives. Instead, terrorism has now been conceptualised as a constant part of the social and political landscape in the UK, an eternal problem which can only ever be 'managed' through the use of specialist laws, agencies and expertise. In the words of the Home Office paper, 'the nature of terrorism is ever changing with new methods and technologies being deployed within and across national boundaries'.[121] The concomitant dangers of a permanent erosion of accountability of state agencies and a lowering of human rights standards are obvious.

Secondly, it is clear that no convincing evidence exists at the time of writing to support the claim that political violence is an ongoing threat and that special legislation is essential. Both Northern Ireland-related and other terrorist incidents have been steadily declining in the UK since the early 1980s.[122] When the Lockerbie bombing is omitted from statistics, only 36 deaths can be attributed to 'international terrorism' since 1985. Moreover, as Gearty and Kimbell point out, many of the successes of the police and security agencies in dealing with foreign terrorist groups could have occurred without using PTA powers.[123] The Lloyd inquiry itself acknowledges that 'domestic terrorism', whether from animal rights groups or Welsh nationalists, is too insignificant to justify special legislation. Thus, the only justification remains some unspecified

---

120 S. 1(2) also makes clear that this new definition extends to intended 'terrorist' action outside of the UK (that is, even the threat of violence). In March 2001, the Home Secretary banned 21 groups (such as ETA and PKK) under the TA 2000.
121 *Legislation Against Terrorism: A Summary of the Government's Proposals* (1999), above n. 116, p. 1.
122 See Livingstone and Whitty, above n. 9.
123 See Gearty and Kimbell, above n. 110, pp. 24-25.

future threat from figures such as the 'religious fundamentalist' or the 'lone fanatic'.[124] There is, however, no evidence of either threat within the UK and, just as importantly, no evidence that ordinary policing powers and strategies would be insufficient in response if such a threat did arise.

The importance of this evidentiary approach is that it highlights how legislative powers, universally acknowledged in 1974 as 'draconian', can become 'normalised' as domestic law in the twenty-first century. In many respects, however, actual statistics as to terrorist incidents are irrelevant: wider social and political forces dictate the direction of national security policies. The coalition of interests and agencies involved in counter-terrorism – what might be described as the 'national security state' – is incredibly difficult to challenge, both for the government in power (if it ever wished to do so[125]) and for all other sites of opposition, such as parliament, media and civil liberties groups. This may be one reason why, apart from obvious easy electoral and media approval (and regardless of the opportunities provided by the Northern Ireland peace process), the New Labour government has so enthusiastically embraced permanent anti-terrorist legislation. But an important civil liberties battle has been lost with the passage of this Act: no future UK government is likely voluntarily to repeal anti-terrorism legislation. For this reason, challenges to the effects of the TA 2000 might best be directed to other forums, including the domestic and European courts, adverse media publicity, and the (limited) opportunities for establishing political accountability for the actions and policies of the police and security service agencies.

The third and final key objection to the TA 2000 is that its definition of terrorism is so broad as to cast doubt on whether police and security service attention could ever be directed at all the possible activities that come within its ambit. While some commentators view this legislative development as a strategy to 'find a role' for otherwise redundant security personnel (especially with the decline of IRA terrorism), it seems likely that economic and managerial considerations, as much as legal and political factors, will result in some prioritisation of 'threats'. At its widest, the Home Office paper suggests that 'using serious violence' should include 'serious disruption, for instance resulting from attacks on computer installations or public utilities'.[126] Thus, the diverse range of individuals involved in 'hacking' could potentially be classed as 'terrorists'. Similarly, organisations involved in lobbying and civil disobedience campaigns (for example, against the World Trade Organisation or polluting oil companies) could easily trigger the use of extensive arrest and search powers by the police. Even more politically contentious are the numerous groups based in the UK who campaign against repressive governments abroad, and support various 'terrorist'/liberation forces in those countries, who have now been brought within the definition of terrorism in section 1 of the Act. The likelihood of any prosecution, and subsequent conviction, in such contexts raises some doubts about the future operational scope of the TA 2000 (although, this does not

---

124 As Gearty comments: 'Anything might happen: Parliament might be blown up, Prince Charles might be injured by a letter bomb, the water supply might be poisoned by a Japanese terrorist angry about the length of the queue for Madam Tussauds' ('Terrorism and Human Rights: A Case Study in Impending Legal Realities' (1999) 19 LS 367, 371).

125 On the actual extent of Ministerial awareness and oversight of UK security services' activities, see L. Lustgarten and I. Leigh, *In From the Cold: National Security and Parliamentary Democracy* (Clarendon, 1994); and generally, Ch. 7.

126 See above n. 116, para. 3.17.

mean that extensive surveillance powers will not continue to be used against such groups for information-gathering purposes).[127] In the end, *political* choices will dictate the use of the new Act, a point made in an (unsuccessful) parliamentary attack on the change of direction in UK anti-terrorist policy:

> Terrorism law exists precisely to cover areas that cannot be dealt with by criminal law. It is bad law, as well as bad politics, to sweep people into the definition of 'terrorist', when they are just straightforward criminals. . . . People who attack an animal testing laboratory in Oxfordshire, for example, could be dealt with by criminal law. They should not even be considered for inclusion under terrorist legislation; the fact that they hear ideological voices or have strong ideological views is irrelevant. If something can be dealt with by criminal law, it should be.[128]

III.   RESPONDING TO TERRORISM: THE LESSONS OF NORTHERN IRELAND

Choices in anti-terrorist strategy

As noted earlier, perceptions of the nature and extent of a terrorist threat play a key role in how a society responds to it. If the threat is perceived as minimal, there is a good chance that the state response to it will be minimalist in character. Thus, responsibility will be placed on the police to focus on the criminal behaviour and separate it from the political activity which surrounds it (for example, distinguishing between animal liberation groups and animal rights protesters). Even where the threat is perceived as significant, if it stems from visible grievances, there may be some scope for a response which is not purely repressive. However, once the perception takes hold that a terrorist threat is substantial (particularly, if the legitimacy of the state or government is questioned), and that it is posed by groups whose primary aim is to use violence, then even the most cogent argument for a restrained response is likely to be swept aside.[129]

Where there is a perception of a substantial terrorist threat, three standard 'solutions' tend to be considered: a military solution, which treats terrorism as a form of war; a policing response, which sees terrorism as criminal activity; and a political response, which views political violence as a form of rebellion or uprising. Most societies, especially if a terrorist problem lasts for a significant period of time, tend to adopt a mixed approach. The response of successive

---

127 Government legal officers may also seek to avoid certain legal 'opponents' and likely challenges to the legislation under the HRA. For example, there are question marks over whether the broad nature of the definition of terrorism is in conformity with the ECHR standards of Art. 5 (in relation to arrests), Art. 8 (in relation to searches), Art. 10 (in relation to the expression of political opinion) and Art. 11 (freedom of association).

128 S. Hughes, Liberal Democrat MP (Terrorism Bill 1999, Standing Committee D, 18 Jan. 2000). The Court of Appeal has also distinguished between animal rights extremism and terrorism by recommending lower levels of sentencing in the former: see *R v Horne* (unreported, 26 Feb. 1999, CA).

129 The US air strikes on Sudan and Afghanistan, following bombings of US embassies in Africa in 1998, is a policy manifestation of a perception of terrorists as beyond reason or, at least, of a perception that US Presidents will rarely suffer domestically by treating foreign terrorists as such. See generally, J. Lobel, 'The Use of Force to Respond to Terrorist Attacks: The Bombing of Sudan and Afghanistan' (1999) 24 Yale JIL 537; and R. Wedgwood, 'Responding to Terrorism: The Strikes Against bin Laden' (1999) 24 Yale JIL 559.

UK governments to the conflict in Northern Ireland has been to pursue such an approach, with all the contradictions that entails.[130] Northern Ireland has primarily been viewed as a political problem requiring a political solution. Thus, initiatives have included reform measures, generally endorsed by civil libertarians, such as the introduction of extensive anti-discrimination legislation and the Parades Commission. Since the Good Friday Agreement 1998, several other significant reforms such as the Northern Ireland Human Rights Commission, the Equality Commission and proposed changes to policing and the criminal justice system have also been acted upon.[131]

Such periods of reform, however, have alternated, and even overlapped, with periods of repression. UK governments have always viewed terrorism relating to Northern Ireland as requiring an aggressive policing response and, at times, as requiring military-type solutions. The most visible evidence of this approach has been the extensive range of emergency legislation designed to make it easier for security forces to prevent, apprehend and imprison people involved in terrorism.[132] For certain periods, especially between 1975 and 1985, UK governments appeared to believe that only a security response was likely to bring terrorism to an end, or at least reduce it to a 'manageable level' as a precondition of any political negotiations. Even when political strategy shifted, as with the signing of the Anglo-Irish Agreement 1985 (which amongst other things increased the role of the Irish government in Northern Irish affairs)[133] and modifications to the Northern Ireland (Emergency Provisions) Act in 1987, events could produce a sudden change in direction. For example, following the killing of eight British Army soldiers engaged in a charity run in 1988, the then Thatcher government swiftly introduced the 'Broadcasting Ban' on the media,[134] restrictions on the right to silence,[135] and a requirement that all local councillors take an oath foreswearing violence.

The result of adopting mixed counter-terrorist strategies, arguably, has placed most strain on the development of policing, and the position of the Royal Ulster Constabulary (RUC), within Northern Ireland. As many historians have highlighted, the violent reaction of the RUC to the civil rights movement in the 1960s, and the adverse publicity it created worldwide, raised serious questions about the legitimacy of the RUC as a cross-community police force.[136] Once violence escalated in the 1970s, the political status of the RUC and its security strategies (and, thus, anti-terrorism law) became permanent central issues in the conflict. As Mulcahy argues:

> Given the RUC's intrinsic character as a key state agency, nationalists' and republicans' rejection of the state's legitimacy implied a *de facto* rejection of the RUC's legitimacy. Relatedly, the primacy of the RUC's security role gave it a wide licence in terms of

---

130 See P. O'Malley, *The Uncivil Wars: Ireland Today* (Beacon, 1997); and J. McGarry and B. O'Leary, *Explaining Northern Ireland* (Blackwell, 1995).
131 See Dickson, above n. 26. On the NI Human Rights Commission, see S. Livingstone, 'The Northern Ireland Human Rights Commission' (1999) 22 Fordham Int LJ 1465.
132 See extracts from the legislation and references in Bailey, Harris and Jones, above n. 28.
133 See B. Hadfield, 'The Anglo-Irish Agreement 1985: Blue Print or Green Print?' (1986) 37 NILQ 1; and W. Harvey Cox, 'Managing Northern Ireland Intergovernmentally: An Appraisal of the Anglo-Irish Agreement' (1987) 40 Parl Affairs 80.
134 For more detail, see Bailey, Harris and Jones, above n. 28, pp. 338-339.
135 See J. Jackson, 'Inferences From Silence: From Common Law to Common Sense' (1993) 44 NILQ 103; and below, p. 153.
136 See N. O'Dochartaigh, *From Civil Rights to Armalites* (Cork UP, 1997).

the strategies it could pursue to maintain state security. Because republican paramilitaries have represented the most visible threat to the state, historically the RUC has concentrated its energies on policing those communities. This offered vast scope for the aggressive policing of nationalist areas.[137]

Faced with allegations of human rights abuses (for example, during police interrogation), and subsequent proposals for law reform or new methods of accountability, the official RUC discourse (often shared by politicians and media) has been to characterise all advocates of change as 'politically motivated'. Civil liberties campaigners, therefore, have had to work in a climate where law reform aimed at protecting human rights is commonly represented as 'concessions to terrorism' and also as an attack on the institution and history of the RUC itself.

One commentator has noted that '[r]emarkable inconsistencies or contradictions . . . have characterised the Northern Irish policy-making and implementation of the four Conservative governments since 1979'.[138] However, it can be said that contradiction has been a feature of British policy in Northern Ireland regardless of the party in government.[139] While some have seen a Machiavellian project either to reinforce Unionism or impose a united Ireland (depending on their political persuasion), government policy has always been the product of a variety of influences whose strength waxes and wanes in different contexts. Thus, the viewpoints of Northern Ireland's political parties are clearly one influence, and since they have often taken diametrically-opposed positions on civil liberties questions, efforts to promote the protection of human rights have generally carried a political price.[140] The tactics and level of support for organisations engaged in terrorism has been another influence. For example, police interest in law reform allowing for inferences to be drawn from silence grew after the IRA's switch to a cell structure, and a policy of silence during interviews reduced the benefits to be gained from lengthy interrogations of suspected terrorists.[141] The vagaries of British politics have also played a role. Frequently, policy measures for Northern Ireland have been as much about proving political parties' credentials to voters in Britain than impacting on terrorism.[142] As noted above, the police and military have been particularly influential in the development of security policy, not least because they have been prime targets of terrorist attacks.[143] The role of the security services, heavily shrouded in secrecy, has been a constant and controversial factor in the Northern Ireland conflict.[144] Influences outside the UK have also

---

137 Mulcahy, above n. 46, p. 70.
138 B. O'Leary, 'The Conservative Stewardship of Northern Ireland, 1979-97: Sound-Bottomed Contradictions or Slow Learning?' (1997) 45 Pol Studies 663, 663.
139 For general accounts of the complexity of public administration, see C. Harlow and R. Rawlings, *Law and Administration* (Butterworths, 1997); and T. Daintith and A. Page, *The Executive in the Constitution* (OUP, 1999).
140 Consider, for example, the reaction of Ulster Unionist Party leader, David Trimble, to the report of the Patten Commission on policing in Northern Ireland: he described it as the 'most shoddy piece of work I have seen in my entire life' (*The Irish Times*, 10 Sep. 1999).
141 Bishop and Mallie observe that the cell structure was never rigidly adopted by the IRA and that volunteers might belong to several cells: see above n. 50, pp. 256-258.
142 The former 'Broadcasting Ban' on media interviews with Sinn Féin representatives is, arguably, one such measure.
143 See C. Ryder, *The RUC: A Force Under Fire* (Mandarin, 1997).
144 See Urban, above n. 24.

played an important role. While the Irish government, especially since the signing of the Anglo-Irish Agreement 1985, is clearly the most prominent actor, the role of US governments and politicians,[145] as well as European institutions (such as the European Court of Human Rights), has been very significant.[146] With such a combination of forces, therefore, it seems unrealistic to generalise about the origins of all counter-terrorist strategies.

Having outlined the complex character of the influences on Northern Irish anti-terrorist strategy, we shall now briefly describe the relevant legislation and assess the role of various agencies in its implementation. Our focus will be more on overall critique than detailed description of the content of individual Acts (which have now mostly been supplanted by the TA 2000). In particular, we shall draw attention to the way that legislative changes have mirrored changing security policies and the dominant institutional role of the army and police in counter-terrorism strategy. Two features have been particularly prominent: first, the broad discretion granted by legislation to the security forces with consequent minimal judicial oversight; and secondly, the controversies generated by the 'extra-legal' nature of certain state practices (such as interrogation techniques and the use of lethal force). This has resulted in highly politicised debates about policing and the level of human rights abuses, with (law) reforms often occurring as a consequence of 'external' forces (such as Amnesty International reports or European Court of Human Rights rulings) rather than proactive government initiatives.

Implementing anti-terrorist policy: anti-terrorist legislation 1973-2000

Two key pieces of legislation have been central to anti-terrorist policy in the UK. First, the EPA, which was first enacted in 1973 and was re-enacted several times up to its last version in 1996.[147] The EPA, which replaced the 50-year-old Special Powers legislation of the former Northern Irish Parliament, only ever applied in Northern Ireland. The second key piece of legislation is the Prevention of Terrorism (Temporary Provisions) Act (PTA), which was first enacted in 1974 and was last re-enacted in 1989, and applied throughout the UK. Both statutes overlapped on some points, for example, with respect to the proscription of organisations and attendant criminal offences. However, they also reflected slightly different underlying approaches to dealing with terrorism: whereas the PTA, as its name suggested was primarily concerned with measures to prevent terrorism, the EPA focused more on enhancing the capacity of law enforcement authorities to apprehend and prosecute those responsible for it.

The TA 2000 repeals the EPA and the PTA, but replicates and extends powers from both, and it also applies throughout the UK. It also keeps in force certain provisions of the EPA, in some cases with amendment, until the date when Part VII (which deals only with Northern Ireland) is brought into force. Thus, in the following description of the PTA and EPA, we shall continue to use the present tense for the EPA powers, but use the past tense for the PTA; in every case, we shall reference the corresponding sections of the new legislation in the footnotes.

---

145 See O'Clery, above n. 48.
146 For a discussion of such external influences, see Morison and Livingstone, above n. 7, pp. 179-203.
147 In 1978, 1987 and 1991.

The Northern Ireland (Emergency Provisions) Acts 1973-96[148]

At the heart of the EPA is the provision for those accused of 'scheduled offences' to be tried by a single judge without a jury.[149] The Act also provides that in trials of those charged with scheduled offences, confessions may be admitted providing that they have not been obtained by 'torture, inhuman or degrading treatment or by violence or the threat of violence'.[150] When first introduced this provision departed significantly from the voluntariness standard of 'ordinary' criminal law, raising further concerns about the conduct of police interrogations, but the language is now much closer to the corresponding provisions of the Police and Criminal Evidence Act 1984 (PACE).[151] The onus of proof in bail hearings is reversed for those charged with scheduled offences and there are a number of changes in the burden of proof as regards possession of firearms offences.[152] In addition to these departures from the general criminal law as regards the mode of trial and evidence used at it, the EPA gives the police a power to stop and question any person as to their movements and identity[153] and includes powers to enter premises[154] and close roads.[155] It also enables the Secretary of State for Northern Ireland to proscribe organisations, and makes it a criminal offence to be a member of, or solicit support or money for, such an organisation.[156] Finally, it should be noted that the effect of the EPA is not limited to an extension of the powers of the police and prosecution authorities. It is also the key legislative instrument for conferring power on the army to stop and question, conduct searches and make arrests.[157]

The Prevention of Terrorism (Temporary Provisions) Acts 1974-89[158]

While the PTA also contained proscription powers, it did not effect any changes in the admissibility of evidence or mode of trial, nor did it confer any powers on the army. Instead, the main 'benefit' of the PTA was the arrest power contained in section 14 of the Act which enabled a police officer to arrest anyone they suspected of involvement in the 'commission, preparation or instigation of acts of terrorism'.[159] Anyone detained under this provision could

---

148 See generally, Bailey, Harris and Jones, above n. 28, pp. 267-300.
149 EPA 1996, s. 11 and Sch. 1 (TA 2000, s. 65 and Sch. 9). The 'Scheduled Offences' include common law offences such as murder, manslaughter, riot and kidnapping as well as a wide range of statutory offences. On the Diplock courts, see J. Jackson and S. Doran, *Judge Without Jury* (Clarendon, 1995).
150 EPA 1996, s. 12 (TA 2000, s. 108).
151 On the PACE provisions, see eg, K. Lidstone and C. Palmer, *Investigation of Crime: A Guide to Police Powers* (Butterworths, 1996), pp. 552-586.
152 EPA 1996, s. 13 (TA 2000, s. 77).
153 EPA 1996, s. 25 (TA 2000, s. 89).
154 EPA 1996, s. 17 (TA 2000, s. 90).
155 EPA 1996, s. 27 (TA 2000, s. 92).
156 EPA 1996, ss. 30-31. Parts II and III of the TA 2000 now deal with proscription and terrorist property.
157 EPA 1996, s. 19 (TA 2000, s. 83) The army may arrest on reasonable suspicion that someone has, or is about to commit, any offence, and may detain a suspect for up to four hours. In the early 1970s, much of the army's activity under the EPA was directed at identifying and apprehending people for detention without trial.
158 See generally, Bailey, Harris and Jones, above n. 28, pp. 301-320.
159 The TA 2000 now provides the powers to arrest without warrant (s. 41), to search premises (s. 42) and to search persons (s. 43).

be held for up to seven days in police custody (at least in respect of terrorism connected to Northern Ireland),[160] before either being charged or released. The Home Secretary, a politician, was solely responsible for granting the authorisation to extend detention.[161] The PTA arrest power thus appeared to treat terrorism as criminal activity; however, the departure from permitting arrest only on reasonable suspicion of committing an offence represented a different approach in that the power was justified as necessary to permit the police to take *preventive* action.

Other key provisions of the PTA were the power to make exclusion orders[162] and port powers. The former allowed the Secretary of State to make orders excluding people from Britain to Northern Ireland, or from Northern Ireland to Britain, or from the UK altogether. Such exclusion did not require any judicial finding of criminal guilt or even involvement in terrorism; a suspicion of involvement in the commission, preparation or instigation of acts of terrorism was sufficient. Moreover, the port powers allowed people to be detained for up to 12 hours without even the need for such suspicion.[163] In addition to the above, the PTA also contained powers to investigate and seize what were believed to be terrorist assets,[164] stop and search powers,[165] and offences in respect of withholding information about any suspected involvement in terrorism.[166]

When first introduced in 1974, the PTA was given the title '(Temporary Provisions)' and lapsed after two years. Following several re-enactments, the final 1989 version provided that the Act would continue in force providing Parliament passed a resolution supporting this (which became an annual rubber-stamping exercise). Although the Act applied to both Northern Ireland-related and international terrorism, it was overwhelmingly utilised against the former. Thus, over 90% of those detained under the PTA since 1974 have been detained in connection with Northern Irish terrorism.[167] Furthermore, while the Act was initially generally used only in Britain, as the RUC moved to the forefront of anti-terrorist strategy in Northern Ireland the PTA became the prime UK-wide legal tool because of the scope for interrogation under the seven-day detention period.

160 Following the ECtHR decision in *Brogan v UK* (1989) 13 EHRR 439 (discussed below), the UK government announced that those arrested in respect of 'international terrorism' should either be charged or released within four days.
161 The power to authorise extended detention is now transferred to a judicial authority (TA 2000, Sch. 8). See also Criminal Justice and Police Act 2001, s. 75.
162 Exclusion orders are now abolished by the TA 2000. A procedural aspect of exclusion orders was successfully challenged in the European Court of Justice in 1995: see *R v Home Secretary, ex p Gallagher* Case C-175/94 [1995] ECR I-4253.
163 Sch. 5 to the PTA allowed an examining officer to detain for up to 12 hours 'to determine' whether the person 'appears to be . . . a person involved in terrorism'; only after this period was reasonable suspicion of such involvement required for further detention. No statistics are kept on those detained for less than one hour, even though an examination for 55 minutes can be a traumatic experience for most people. Between 1974-1994, an annual average of over 200 people were questioned for between one and 12 hours, although less than 5% of these were subsequently charged with an offence or excluded. See generally, P. Hillyard, *Suspect Community: People's Experience of the Prevention of Terrorism Acts in Britain* (Pluto, 1993), pp. 39-43. Sch. 7 to the TA 2000 has reduced the maximum period of port detention to nine hours.
164 PTA 1989, ss. 11-13 (TA 2000, Part III).
165 PTA (AP) 1996, ss. 13A-13B (TA 2000, ss. 44-45).
166 PTA 1989, s. 18A (TA 2000, s. 19).
167 See Hillyard, above n. 163, p. 5.

Supplementary anti-terrorist legislation

Supplementary anti-terrorist legislation in the UK has primarily focused on the sphere of criminal procedure. For example, in 1988 restrictions on the right to silence in Northern Ireland were introduced,[168] a provision which the police had long argued for. However, allowing the prosecution to draw inferences from a defendant's silence increased the pressure on the right to a fair trial in the anti-terrorist context, and when combined with EPA-based restrictions on a suspect's access to a defence lawyer while in police custody, the provision was held by the European Court of Human Rights to breach Article 6 of the ECHR in the *Murray* case.[169]

Secondly, although UK anti-terrorism law, unlike its counterparts in western Europe and the US, has traditionally not created new criminal offences, the Criminal Justice (Terrorism and Conspiracy Act) 1998 (CJTCA 1998) (introduced after the Omagh bomb) marked a departure. This Act introduced a new offence of conspiring to commit terrorist acts abroad.[170] The justification for such legislative action was alleged international concern about the UK as a 'haven for terrorists', a claim that seems to have more ideological value than any basis in reality (as no prosecutions have occurred). Similarly, the other key provision introduced in the 1998 Act, that which enables defendants to be convicted of membership of a proscribed organisation simply on the testimony of a senior police officer,[171] seems to be a mere symbolic gesture. The exercise of such a power would also arguably raise question marks about its compatibility with Article 6 of the ECHR.

Analysis of anti-terrorist legislation

The first thing worth noting about UK anti-terrorist legislation is what it does not do. It does not introduce an *offence* of terrorism (as distinct from a definition), though it has created some new offences such as membership of a proscribed organisation and directing terrorism. Nor, contrary to anti-terrorist legislation in the US and some continental European countries, does it affect the penalties for offences committed in a terrorist context.[172] Although political demands for the return of the death penalty for terrorist killings are frequently heard,[173] UK governments have resisted this and, indeed, have not prescribed

---

168 Criminal Evidence (NI) Order 1988.
169 *Murray (John) v United Kingdom* (1996) 22 EHRR 29. A right of access to a lawyer is now provided where adverse inferences from a suspect's silence may be drawn: see Youth Justice and Criminal Evidence Act 1999, s. 58; Criminal Evidence (NI) Order 1999, s. 58; and TA 2000, s. 109. See also *Averill v UK* [2000] Crim LR 682.
170 CJTCA 1998, s. 5. See Campbell, above n. 2.
171 CJTCA 1998, ss. 1-2 (TA 2000, s. 108).
172 See A. Vercher, *Terrorism in Europe* (OUP, 1992), pp. 297-302; and J. Beall 'Are We Only Burning Witches? The Anti-Terrorist and Effective Death Penalty Act of 1996's Answer to Terrorism' (1998) 73 Indiana LJ 693.
173 Arts. 1 and 2 of the Sixth Protocol to the ECHR abolish the death penalty in peacetime. S. 21(5) of the HRA implements the abolition of the death penalty for military offences, and liability to the death penalty under the Armed Forces Act is replaced by liability to imprisonment for life or some other lesser penalty. During debates on the Human Rights Bill, Lord Williams of Mostyn, then Minister of State for the Home Office, said that the UK's ratification of the Sixth Protocol makes it 'impossible for Parliament to reintroduce the death penalty in future, except for acts committed in time of war or imminent threat of war, without denouncing the Convention itself': see *H.L. Debs.*, vol. 593, col. 2084 (29 Oct. 1998).

minimum sentences for terrorist offences (though prisoner remission periods have been altered by the PTA on occasions).

The main focus of anti-terrorist policy has been on preventing terrorist action taking place, and on making it easier for law enforcement authorities to apprehend and convict those involved in it. Legislative changes have followed changing views on the most effective anti-terrorist strategy. In the 1970s, at the height of internment and extensive intelligence-gathering operations, the EPA permitted police and soldiers to arrest someone simply on the suspicion that they were a terrorist, and to search their house on a mere suspicion that arms might be found there. By 1987, when the army was playing a less prominent role and the police were concentrating on more lengthy interrogations of suspects under PTA conditions, requirements of 'reasonable suspicion' were introduced into such powers. Similarly, changes in 1987 reinstating judicial discretion to exclude evidence, and providing that judges could refuse to admit confessions based on violence or the threat of violence, may have been influenced by judicial reluctance to admit confessions where the level of coercion fell just short of 'torture, inhuman or degrading treatment'. It may also have been related to the shift in police methods of evidence-gathering, with a reduction in exclusive use of confessions in favour of forensic evidence in terrorist trials.[174] The introduction, in the 1989 PTA, of an offence of 'directing terrorism' and provisions to seize terrorist assets clearly resulted from a policy of targeting the 'godfathers' of terrorism who, it was perceived, were proving immune to existing forms of investigation.

Not surprisingly, the content and effects of anti-terrorist legislation have been the subject of substantial civil libertarian criticism (albeit that, as noted earlier, much of the criticism has come from Northern Ireland-based academics and organisations).[175] In the main, this scholarship has tended to focus on the nature of the legal powers. This was most obviously manifest in the critique of the (now abolished) exclusion order power under the PTA, which appeared to be in clear contravention of international treaty provisions on freedom of movement and conspicuously failed to respect due process guarantees.[176] Proscription powers are similarly suspect, although most civil liberties lawyers seem to have accepted these as a justifiable, if largely irrelevant, restriction on freedom of expression and association.[177] Not surprisingly, suspension of jury trial has also attracted substantial criticism; to many common lawyers, suspension

---

174 See C. Walker and E. Stockdale, 'Forensic Evidence and Terrorist Trials in the United Kingdom' (1995) 54 CLJ 69.

175 In addition to substantial NGO criticism of anti-terrorist powers and their use, there has been a broad range of academic writing in the same vein. See eg, K. Boyle, T. Hadden and P. Hillyard, *Law and State: The Case of Northern Ireland* (Martin Robertson, 1975); A. Jennings (ed.), *Justice Under Fire: The Abuse of Civil Liberties in Northern Ireland* (Pluto, 1988); D. Walsh, *The Use and Abuse of Emergency Legislation in Northern Ireland* (Cobden Trust, 1983); P. O'Higgins and J. Hayes, *Lessons from Northern Ireland* (SLS, 1990); C. Gearty and K. Ewing, *Freedom Under Thatcher* (OUP, 1990), pp. 209-254; and D. Schiff, 'Managing Terrorism the British Way' in R. Higgins and M. Flory (eds.), *Terrorism and International Law* (Routledge, 1997), pp. 125-143.

176 The UK did not ratify the Fourth Protocol to the ECHR, which guarantees freedom of movement. However, Walker notes that in *Raimondo v Italy* (1994) 18 EHRR 237, the ECtHR upheld restrictions on the movement of suspected Mafia members as being consistent with Protocol 4 and suggests that exclusion orders might be viewed in a similar light: see C. Walker, 'Constitutional Governance and Special Powers Against Terrorism: Lessons from the United Kingdom's Prevention of Terrorism Acts' (1997) 35 Columbia J of Transnational L 1, 47.

177 See the discussion in Gearty and Kimbell, above n. 110, pp. 37-40.

of jury trial is a measure that should be opposed in principle.[178] However, it is not something which contravenes international human rights law *per se* and, as highlighted in Chapter 4, assumptions about the fairness of jury trial may be simplistic and misleading given the ways in which the criminal justice process operates. The curtailment of the right to silence, and the 'Broadcasting Ban' on the media in 1988, were also opposed from the start by civil liberties organisations and academics.

For other powers, however, criticism has focused as much on the exercise of the powers as their content. The PTA (now TA 2000) arrest power is a good example. If its use were limited to those against whom reasonable suspicion of involvement in terrorist violence existed, then little concern would arise. Indeed, in the *Brogan* case the European Court of Human Rights was prepared to find this power consistent with Article 5(1)(c) of the ECHR on the grounds that reasonable suspicion of involvement in terrorism required reasonable suspicion of the commission of an offence.[179] However, arrest statistics clearly show that over 80% of those arrested under the PTA were released without charge, compared with less than 50% of suspects arrested under PACE. This suggests that the primary use of the arrest power was not to target those suspected of involvement in terrorism and to facilitate arrests; rather, its use has been focused more on intelligence-gathering and, sometimes, on harassment of certain individuals. This was confirmed (albeit unintentionally) by a former Home Secretary in 1985, when Leon Brittan rejected the argument that the low rate of prosecution indicated a minimal usefulness:

> What the figures do not tell you is about how much information was obtained, not only about the people concerned but about others, and how many threats were averted as a result of obtaining information from those who were detained. The object of the exercise is not just to secure convictions but to secure information.[180]

Hillyard has highlighted how one effect of this 'useful' police power, especially when combined with the PTA port powers to question, was the creation of a large 'suspect community' of individuals and groups who lived in Britain and had any family, business or social connections with Ireland or Northern Ireland.[181] In Northern Ireland itself, similar perspectives have been expressed in relation to police and army use of stop and question powers, and the power to search premises. In each context, law has been both a symbolic and practical means of oppression of those who are suspected, not of political violence, but of political dissent.

Some anti-terrorist practices have generated particularly intense scrutiny and controversy, namely the RUC interrogation of paramilitary suspects during the 1970s, allegations of a 'shoot to kill' policy in the 1980s, and allegations of collusion with loyalist paramilitaries in the 1990s. We shall discuss the issue of lethal force in more detail below in relation to the institutional role of the police and military in anti-terrorist strategy but, in terms of the relevance of

---

178 See S. Greer and A. White, *Abolishing the Diplock Courts: The Case for Restoring Jury Trial for Scheduled Offences in Northern Ireland* (Cobden Trust, 1986).

179 However, it is important to note that in *Brogan* (1989) 13 EHRR 439 the ECtHR also observed that the applicants were questioned about specific bombing and shooting incidents. It is not clear whether arrests for questioning without a link to a specific offence would comply with Art. 5(1)(c).

180 Interviewed on *This Week*, RTE Radio, Jun. 1985.

181 See Hillyard, above n. 163.

law in such contexts, it seems arguable that it was the width of anti-terrorist powers, the officially accepted culture of violation of such powers, and the lack of any meaningful accountability mechanisms that contributed to the most serious human rights abuses. To illustrate this point, we shall focus on the use of interrogation methods, which the European Court of Human Rights examined in *Ireland v United Kingdom*.[182]

From the mid-1970s, the RUC replaced the army as the primary security force in Northern Ireland and, as part of a 'criminalisation' policy, the conviction of paramilitary suspects on the basis of confessions obtained during interrogation assumed a central role. Allegations of abuse of detainees became a regular occurrence yet no official action was taken until a damning Amnesty International report in 1978.[183] The subsequent Bennett Inquiry and Report led to the introduction of safeguards for detainees in police detention (such as video-monitoring of corridors), with the result that the number of complaints of ill-treatment dropped (but did not disappear).[184] While one can point to no law mandating such police conduct – although, in the immediate aftermath of internment, policy directives to utilise sensory-deprivation techniques existed – the combination of over-use (by police and prosecution authorities) of confessions in Diplock court trials,[185] extended statutory periods of police detention, and denial of immediate access to lawyers,[186] all contributed to the culture of abuse. Just as importantly, the lack of any accountability mechanisms exacerbated the problem, despite the assertions of the police and government officials to the contrary. As Mulcahy highlights, the official discourse of the RUC was to emphasise *its* commitment to investigating all complaints, and to deny the validity of allegations by stressing the terrorists' policy of lying and self-infliction of injury.[187] The Bennett Report explicitly endorsed such a discourse in its conclusions, pointing out that 'the major benefit of increased safeguards for prisoners would not be the better protection of prisoners from their interrogators, but the better protection of the interrogators . . .'.[188] Thus, mirroring an official pattern which has continued since the 1970s, 'law reform' is never primarily represented as a necessary constraint upon *state* action.

Concerns that human rights abuses are almost inevitable when repressive legal powers become permanent, coupled with persistent government rhetoric about the need for security strategies to deal with 'all forms of terrorism', have led to a significant constituency calling for repeal or amendment of such anti-terrorist legislation. In Part IV, we shall explore the outcome of such campaigns in traditional sites of civil liberties struggle such as Parliament and the courts. In the next two sections, however, we shall focus on the role of the military and police. Our aim will be is to highlight a number of factors important to a deeper analysis of the role of (human rights) law: first, the changing

---

182 Above n. 18.
183 See P. Taylor, *Beating the Terrorists? Interrogation in Omagh, Gough and Castlereagh* (Penguin, 1980); and Amnesty International, *Report of an Amnesty International Mission to Northern Ireland* (1978).
184 See above n. 22 and accompanying text.
185 Walsh, above n. 175, notes that confessions were obtained in 90% of the cases he studied in 1981.
186 Up to the early 1990s, over 50% of requests for immediate access were denied and access was delayed for up to 48 hours.
187 Mulcahy, above n. 46, pp. 79-82.
188 Ibid., p. 81.

roles of institutions in anti-terrorist strategies, often because of a revised *political* view of a particular terrorist organisation and its aims; secondly, the (in)ability of law to regulate or influence state agencies in certain contexts; and, thirdly, the conditions or catalysts which may generate institutional reforms. We shall use a case study of use of lethal force by the military, and the RUC 'shoot to kill' controversy, to develop this analysis.

Implementing anti-terrorist policy: the role of the military

In Britain, implementing anti-terrorist law and policy has largely fallen to the police and security services. The army have been deployed at airports on occasion and specialist units have been available to provide back-up to the police. They have also been utilised to deal with terrorist activity outside the UK, the use of the SAS in Gibraltar in 1988 being one particularly notable example. In general, however, the army has not been significantly involved in anti-terrorist activity.

The position is very different in respect of Northern Ireland. First deployed in 1969, army strength in Northern Ireland has varied between 10-22,000 soldiers for most of the last 30 years. It was originally deployed 'in support of the civil power'[189] (and politically welcomed by nationalists) but, in the wake of a deteriorating security situation after the introduction of internment, it assumed the primary anti-terrorist role between 1971-75. The military strategy in this period treated terrorism primarily as a problem of counter-insurgency and drew on the lessons of anti-colonial campaigns in Kenya and Cyprus in the 1950s.[190] Hence, there was less interest in collecting evidence for use in criminal trials than on extensive intelligence-gathering, notably through a massive increase in arrests and house searches.[191] Such intelligence was directed towards controlling territory, drawing suspected terrorists into armed conflict and identifying people for internment. The criminal law was not ignored and army strategists continued to stress the ideological value of obtaining convictions and maintaining the rule of law; however, it was clearly marginalised in favour of a strategy which promoted proactive and interventionist state action.

This period was witness to the worst violence of the Northern Ireland conflict in terms of deaths and injuries.[192] The army suffered significant losses but was also responsible for many killings, most notably and controversially, the shooting of 13 people in (London)Derry in January 1972.[193] Although some observers argue that by mid-1975, the army was gaining control of the situation militarily and was close to defeating the IRA,[194] government officials appear to have taken

---

189 See S. Greer, 'Military Intervention in Civilian Disturbances: The Legal Basis Reconsidered' [1983] PL 573.

190 See F. Kitson, *Low Intensity Operations* (Faber, 1971).

191 The number of searches rose from 17,262 in 1971 to 74,556 in 1973, before falling to 20,724 in 1977, and less than 7,000 by 1979.

192 The number of conflict-related deaths averaged 270 a year in this period, but fell to 136 between 1976-80.

193 See above n. 80. A secret memo from the officer in command of troops in Northern Ireland in 1972 has apparently revealed that a policy of shooting rioters was under consideration: see *The Guardian*, 13 Mar. 2000. See generally, D. Walsh, *Bloody Sunday and the Rule of Law in Nothern Ireland* (Macmillan, 2000).

194 See P. Wilkinson, 'British Policy on Terrorism: An Assessment' in J. Lodge (ed.), *The Threat of Terrorism* (Wheatsheaf, 1988), pp. 29-56.

the view that the conflict was more long-term and that a different strategy was required. Following the Gardiner Report, policing and the use of criminal law again came to the fore, with the army losing overall control of security operations.[195]

Army involvement in anti-terrorist operations, therefore, has changed in the period since 1969. Today, most soldiers in Northern Ireland are a part of, what Urban has termed, the 'Green Army' and are engaged in providing support to police patrols, search or arrest operations (particularly in areas where it is considered too dangerous for the RUC), and policing demonstrations.[196] Army personnel have, however, also played another more crucial and less visible role through the deployment of specialist surveillance, intelligence and bomb disposal units. The SAS, first deployed in Northern Ireland in 1976, is perhaps the best known unit but it is by no means the only one.[197]

Use of lethal force by the military

From a human rights perspective, the most controversial aspect of army operations has been its involvement in the use of lethal force. This has been true of the army in both its covert and overt manifestations, although the most serious problems have arisen in regard to the latter. Of the more than 3,500 people killed during the Northern Ireland conflict, 357 have been killed by state forces, and, although the police have been involved in the use of lethal force, the majority of these killings (294) have been ascribed to the army. The killings have tended to occur largely in two different types of circumstances. The first can be described as 'encounter killings' where someone is shot in the course of a riot, or after breaking through a roadblock, or running away when the army have sought to apprehend them for questioning.[198] Most of these incidents involve regular 'Green Army' units conducting patrols or roadblocks. The second category of killings results from planned operations, often involving specialist units who have placed suspected terrorists under surveillance and subsequently move in to intercept them. Classic examples are the SAS's killing of three IRA members in Gibraltar in March 1988, and of eight IRA members and one bystander in Loughgall in May 1987. No special emergency or anti-terrorist law regulates the use of such force. The applicable legal regime is that of self-defence and, specifically, that of section 3(1) of the Criminal Law Act 1967 which provides:

> [A] person may use such force as is reasonable in the circumstances in the prevention of crime, or in affecting or assisting the lawful arrest of offenders or suspected offenders or of persons unlawfully at large.[199]

This regime, however, was designed to cover the occasional use of force by individuals in self-defence or, at most, the regular use of non-lethal force by

195 *Report of a Committee to Consider, in the Context of Civil Liberties and Human Rights, Measures to Deal with Terrorism in Northern Ireland* (Cmnd. 5847, 1975).
196 See generally, Urban, above n. 24.
197 Others have included the Field Research Unit and 14 Intelligence Company.
198 The facts of the *A-G for Northern Ireland's Reference (No. 1 of 1975)* [1977] AC 105 are typical. Soldiers stopped and questioned a man and then let him proceed. The commander of the patrol wanted to question him again, but when shouted at the man ran away, and was then shot by a soldier who claimed that he believed he was shooting a terrorist.
199 See generally, J.C. Smith and B. Hogan, *Criminal Law* (Butterworths, 1999), Ch. 10.

the police; it is inadequate for regulating the conduct of armed soldiers. As Lord Chief Justice Lowry observed in 1975, 'the security forces are operating in conditions with which the ordinary law was not designed to cope, and in regard to which there are no legal precedents'.[200]

Incidents involving the use of lethal force give rise to sharp tensions between soldiers and their supporters, who do not feel they should be facing criminal charges for doing their duty in difficult circumstances, and the relatives of those who have been killed, who accuse the soldiers of literally 'getting away with murder'.[201] The law has generally resolved such tensions firmly in favour of the military. In a crucial decision in 1976, the House of Lords indicated that the issue of reasonableness as regards the use of force should be left to the jury. Acknowledging that a key question was whether the soldier perceived himself to be in 'imminent danger' when he opened fire, Lord Diplock also suggested that the jury might take the view that such danger existed if a suspected terrorist was allowed to escape given that they were likely 'sooner or later to participate in acts of violence'.[202] In offering such an expanded time frame of imminent danger to security force members, this and other similar decisions contrast markedly, for example, with the judicial emphasis on the need for an 'immediate threat' in the case of women who kill abusive partners. Moreover, as Jennings has pointed out, 'the law's vagueness and imprecision [leads] to the security forces being granted a virtually unlimited licence to kill'.[203]

This legal framework explains why, apart from wider political calculations, so few prosecutions of security force members for murder have ever been brought in Northern Ireland. Additionally, as Amnesty International has pointed out, inadequate police work in the immediate aftermath of a killing has played an important role in depriving the prosecution of a full account of the surrounding events.[204] Even when prosecutions have been initiated, only four have resulted in convictions and all but one has been reversed on appeal, with the courts often showing, at least, sympathy for the soldiers accused. Once the legal process has ended, influential media and political campaigns have usually secured swift release for those few soldiers who have been convicted and imprisoned. The use of lethal force by the military was further insulated from legal and political scrutiny following changes in the inquest rules in Northern Ireland in 1980, which prevented inquests from bringing in a verdict or even calling those responsible for a death to give evidence. Soldiers have, therefore, been allowed to submit written evidence alone to the inquest or, where they choose to appear in person, to preserve their anonymity. Such rules have also withstood legal challenge in the House of Lords.[205]

A noteworthy feature of the small number of prosecutions that have occurred is that they generally relate to 'encounter killings'. Deaths resulting from pre-planned operations have been almost entirely immune from legal scrutiny, at

---

200 *R v McNaughton* [1975] NI 203, 208.
201 See particularly the facts of *R v Clegg* [1995] 1 All ER 334.
202 See generally, J. Rogers, 'Justifying the Use of Firearms by Policemen and Soldiers: A Response to the Home Office's Review of the Law on the Use of Lethal Force' (1998) 18 LS 486.
203 A. Jennings, 'Shoot to Kill: The Final Courts of Justice' in Jennings, above n. 42, pp. 104-130, at p. 112.
204 See generally, F. Ní Aoláin, *The Politics of Force: Conflict Management and State Violence in Northern Ireland* (Blackstaff, 2000).
205 *McKerr v Armagh Coroner* [1990] 1 All ER 865. Cf. *Jordan v UK*, above n. 17.

least where the army have been the responsible agency. Urban has argued that in such cases there is an implicit 'bargain' between the active soldiers and the army hierarchy: soldiers are only willing to become involved in dangerous undercover work if they are protected from prosecution. This policy also appears to extend to the provision of legal advice to soldiers, and to the production of witness statements – such as, when challenged the suspect 'spun round and appeared to be reaching for a weapon' – which appear regularly at inquests when undercover soldiers explain their decision to open fire.[206]

Such cases raise especially difficult issues in the context of anti-terrorist policy and the type of response of human rights NGOs. On the one hand, most of those killed were acknowledged to be involved in terrorist activity (although there are exceptions) and were frequently killed, as at Loughgall, when on their way to carry out a shooting or bombing. Thus, there is a serious debate about the risks to state actors when confronted with lethal force.[207] The official planning of such operations is also often based on the evidence of informers who may be compromised if the incident is exposed to detailed scrutiny in judicial proceedings. On the other hand, however, it fundamentally offends basic democratic principles and human rights norms when the policy of state security forces is to plan operations which are aimed at causing people's deaths (rather than, for example considering the possibility of arrest), and where politicians often (secretly) acquiesce. Urban has described the operations planning process that was adopted in the 1980s and shown how a plan to conduct an operation against suspected terrorists would be developed by intelligence co-ordinating groups and referred to the army's commander of land forces for approval:

> He may then refer it up to the GOC and chief constable and they in turn may tell the Secretary of State. There is likely to be a brief conversation in which the Secretary of State is told that there is an opportunity to deal a significant blow to the terrorists. If asked the Secretary of State usually responds that the general or senior police officer should do what they think is right.[208]

One consequence of this process, of course, is that ministers may deny any direct knowledge if events do not go as planned. Such compromises have been said to be 'typical of British government, in which real power is exercised by those who are not responsible to Parliament or the electorate who, in return, shield those who *are* responsible from painful decisions'.[209] However, from a human rights perspective, such a general state policy does not meet the requisite legal threshold; in particular, it does not meet the principles of necessity, proportionality and respect for human right values that are required under the ECHR. This legal threshold was established by the European Court of Human Rights in *McCann, Farrell and Savage,* and has subsequently been reinforced by the decisions in *Jordan and Kelly.*[210]

---

206 See Urban, above n. 24, pp. 72-76.
207 See P. Waddington, '"Overkill" or "Minimum Force"?' [1990] Crim LR 695; and R. Parent and S. Verdun-Jones, 'Deadly Force: Police Firearms Use in British Columbia' (1999) LXXII Police J 209.
208 Urban, above n. 24, p. 170.
209 Ibid., p. 168.
210 (1995) 21 EHRR 97; and ECtHR, 4 May 2001.

Significantly, the Northern Irish courts have failed to respond to this category of state killings in any way that enhanced accountability of state agencies, improved cross-community confidence in the legal or political processes, or sought to confirm that human rights principles might have a role in political conflicts. There are several possible reasons for this failure: judicial uncertainty about their function; institutional loyalty to state actors; personal political bias; or an intrinsic inability of legal processes to interpret and respond to highly contested state action. Unfortunately, however, the price of such failure has been high, as the opening statement of the Bloody Sunday Inquiry, now investigating the shooting of 13 civilians in 1972, recognises:

> [I]t would be foolish for us to ignore the fact that there are allegations that some of those concerned in the events of Bloody Sunday were guilty of very serious offences, including murder. Whether there is any substance in those allegations remains, of course, to be seen. . . . We are enquiring into matters that have given rise to very strong emotions. Those emotions are wholly understandable, for whatever the circumstances, people were killed and wounded. There are also, undeniably, strong political views.[211]

Security force killings by British military forces – from Bloody Sunday in 1972 up to the 'shoot to kill' controversies of the 1980s – have thus been centre-stage in a wider ideological battle over the legitimacy of the state, its institutions and its laws. For many constitutional nationalists, as well as militant republicans and the family relations of those killed, the apparent official immunity of soldiers in such contexts has confirmed long-held views about the ongoing political subordination of one section of the community. Furthermore, such incidents have provided easy propaganda opportunities for paramilitary groups to represent the Northern Ireland conflict as a genuine 'war', requiring them to engage in defensive and reactive violence.

In contrast to domestic courts, the European Court of Human Rights, in the *McCann, Farrell and Savage* decision, did feel able to interrogate the process that led to the use of lethal force. In so doing, it injected some notion of political accountability into such operations, significantly, at the senior level of command.[212] In a decision heavily criticised by some sections of the UK media – perhaps, an illustration of the perceived vulnerability of the state's 'democratic' credentials on the international stage where state policy leads to loss of life – the Court, by ten votes to nine, found a violation of Article 2 of the ECHR. Recognising that the actions of individual soldiers in such contexts are often pre-determined, the Court shifted its focus to the overall planning of the operation. It concluded that the UK government had had opportunities to arrest the suspected terrorists before they posed a threat to life; that the planning of the military operation had treated hypotheses about possible events as definite facts; and that the soldiers had been placed in a situation where their perception of risk was increased, with the greatly increased likelihood of lethal force being used.[213]

---

211 Opening Statement of Lord Saville (3 Apr. 1998): see www.bloody-sunday-inquiry.org.uk/opening.htm. The role of former Lord Chief Justice Widgery in the first official inquiry has been the subject of sustained criticism, not least because of the perception that judicial impartiality is suspect in matters relating to Northern Ireland.

212 *McCann, Farrell and Savage v UK* (1995) 21 EHRR 97. See also, *Andronicou v Cyprus* (1996) 6 EHRLR 661 (re Cypriot police's use of force).

213 Subsequently, in *Jordan*, above n. 210, the Court found flawed investigatory procedures to be in breach of Art. 2.

The Court's focus on the planning of military operations and the methods of accountability is important. In an area where judicial abstention has been the norm,[214] the ability of a legal institution (albeit at the international level) to challenge and investigate state action in the context of lethal force is important. Whether it is likely to counter the range of political factors which make prosecutions of soldiers a rare event is debatable; however, where such events do lead to litigation, the decision might be valuable in providing a focus on the overall policy-making apparatus, the need for accountability, and the responsibility of state actors to adopt proportionate responses to terrorist threats. It may also present opportunities for renewed challenges, using the HRA, to the limitations on inquests in obtaining information about such operations.

Overall, though, it cannot be disputed that the reassertion of *political* control over military strategy and the activities of undercover military units is the most effective means of reducing the likelihood of such killings occurring. Not surprisingly, when the use of such methods declined in Northern Ireland after 1990, it had more to do with the government's revival of political initiatives and the desire to negotiate with the IRA than a diminished capacity on the part of specialist units.[215] This is confirmed by a recent account of a military operation against the IRA in April 1997, from a journalist with obvious access to official documents and sources:

> If members of an IRA sniper team preparing to kill a soldier had come up against the SAS a decade earlier, they would almost certainly have been shot dead rather than restrained and handed over to the RUC for arrest and questioning. This time the SAS team inserted into South Armagh was directed to carry out the 'arrest option' by swooping on the farm complex before [the IRA members] had brought out their weapons. . . . [W]ith MI5 briefing the Government that a second IRA ceasefire was possible, the prevailing philosophy was that the creation of four republican martyrs would be counter-productive.[216]

Implementing anti-terrorist policy: the role of the police

As noted earlier, the police have also been central to anti-terrorist policy throughout the UK, producing significant changes in the organisation and operational ethos of different police forces. In neither Britain nor Northern Ireland, however, have they enjoyed total control over the implementation of anti-terrorist policy. In the former, the police lost primacy to the security service, MI5, after the IRA's bombing of the City of London in 1992. In the latter, as we highlighted above, the army gained control of anti-terrorist policy in the early 1970s, at a time when the RUC was under sustained criticism for its lack of impartiality and demoralised by the rapid growth of terrorist violence.

The main change that anti-terrorism policies have wrought in policing throughout the UK is the shift to intelligence-based and proactive methods. Such an approach has the primary aim of preventing terrorist attacks, rather than responding to events and attempting to solve crimes after they occur. It is based on a significant investment in surveillance (whether human or electronic),

---

214 See below, pp. 155-159.
215 See the discussion in J. Holland and S. Phoenix, *Phoenix: Policing the Shadows* (Coronet, 1996), pp. 257-258 (based on the diaries of a deceased RUC anti-terrorist intelligence officer).
216 T. Harnden, *'Bandit Country': The IRA and South Armagh* (Hodder & Stoughton, 1999), p. 303.

placement of agents within terrorist organisations, and cultivation of informers from such organisations, rather than reliance on co-operation from the public in providing information (often not a likely prospect because of the covert nature of terrorism). The approach has not been confined to anti-terrorist policing, but now plays a major role in countering organised crime, football violence and other activities.[217] Moreover, as the technical resources available to the police for surveillance, data-retention and data-matching increase, all forms of policing are likely to be affected.[218]

This 'surveillance' approach, with its emphasis on producing knowledge of suspect populations and assessing risk,[219] has come to the fore in anti-terrorist policing for a number of reasons. First, the significant risk to the public, including the lives of police officers themselves, if terrorist attacks are not prevented lends a particular urgency to the need to gather advance information. Secondly, the fact that terrorist groups act in an organised way, rather than as a collection of individuals, lends itself to a form of policing which seeks to gather information about all aspects of an organisation. Thirdly, especially in Northern Ireland, the police may find that fear or hostility results in the absence of co-operation from the public in solving crimes. This means that other sources of information must be found. Finally, legislative changes in respect of stop, search and arrest powers have facilitated the surveillance approach to policing. Even where legal powers may not have been designed to enable extensive surveillance operations, in practice, the police have adapted them to suit such purposes. Often, the legislative intention is clear, as in the (former PTA) 'carding' power requiring any passenger travelling to and from Ireland and Northern Ireland to complete a card giving their personal details.[220]

One consequence of these developments has been a move away from a 'policing by consent' model to a security/military type model in certain sectors of UK policing.[221] Of course, in many respects, the latter model has always been operated by the RUC:

> Unlike the situation in Britain, the issue of consent for the police role and function in Northern Ireland (and Ireland under British colonial rule) has been a historically peripheral issue. From the earliest days of the Northern state, the institutional relationship between the RUC and the Unionist government – direct political subordination and direction – meant that while public support for the force may have been desirable, it was in fact, immaterial. Political exigencies, in particular the control of political dissent, were prioritized over that of courting the support of the nationalist/Catholic community and their relationship to the new Northern state.[222]

---

217   See M. Innes, '"Professionalizing" the Role of the Police Informant: The British Experience' (2000) 9 Policing and Society 357.

218   See Norman, above n. 10.

219   See generally, R. Ericson and K. Haggerty, *Policing the Risk Society* (Clarendon, 1997); and M. Maguire, 'Policing by Risks and Targets: Some Dimensions and Implications of Intelligence-Led Crime Control' (2000) 9 Policing and Society 315.

220   See now TA 2000, Sch. 6.

221   There is a large literature on the extent of consent to policing within Britain. See eg, G. Pearson, *Hooligan: A History of Respectable Fears* (Macmillan, 1983); T. Jefferson, *The Case Against Paramilitary Policing* (Open UP, 1990); and R. Reiner, *The Politics of the Police* (OUP, 2000).

222   G. Ellison, '"Reflecting All Shades of Opinion": Public Attitudinal Surveys and the Construction of Police Legitimacy in Northern Ireland' (2000) 40 BJ Crim 88, 90 (references omitted).

This tension between the RUC's historical role as a paramilitary force and its contemporary role as a 'police service' has manifested itself in many ways. The involvement of the RUC in unlawful interrogation tactics against paramilitary suspects in the 1970s is one example. A similarly controversial example is the 'shoot to kill' (or Stalker) affair in the 1980s.

The RUC 'shoot to kill' controversy

This controversy came to prominence after the RUC shot dead six people in alleged confrontations at road-blocks over a period of several weeks in late 1982. Five of these were acknowledged IRA or INLA (Irish National Liberation Army) members, the other was universally accepted as having no involvement in terrorism. All were found to have been unarmed at the time of their death, although the police officers who fired the fatal shots indicated that they had believed them to be armed and had fired in self-defence. Very unusually, in the context of the historical use of lethal force by state actors in Northern Ireland, the Director of Public Prosecutions decided that there *was* sufficient evidence to mount a criminal prosecution in respect of the officers. Although all were subsequently acquitted, the trials exposed a number of fabrications in the original RUC accounts. Far from being random encounters between the police and suspected terrorists, each of the shootings followed extensive surveillance operations, involved the use of an elite police unit trained in 'speed, firepower and aggression',[223] and was followed by an elaborate cover-story for the media on the detail of the confrontation.

Following media and political pressure, the RUC Chief Constable appointed Manchester Deputy Chief Constable John Stalker to conduct an investigation into the shootings. Stalker's inquiry, however, was obstructed by disputes over his terms of reference, resistance from within the RUC and, ultimately, an investigation against Stalker himself in connection with alleged corruption in Manchester – an allegation which proved baseless and is still shrouded in controversy.[224] As a consequence, Stalker did not complete his inquiry; it was taken over by another English police officer who produced a report that was never placed in the public domain, and the Attorney-General subsequently decided, on 'public interest' grounds, not to pursue its recommendations of prosecutions of a number of RUC officers for conspiracy to pervert the course of justice.

In Stalker's own subsequent published account of the entire affair, the RUC policy is described in terms which highlight the way that non-legal norms often dictate the circumstances in which lethal force is used:

> There was no written instruction, nothing pinned upon a noticeboard. But there was a clear understanding on the part of the men whose job it was to pull the trigger that that was what was expected of them.[225]

---

223 The comments of RUC Deputy Chief Constable Michael McAtamney at the trial of Constable Robinson: *Irish News*, 5 Jun. 1984.

224 In Sep. 1998, the Home Affairs Select Committee called for all police compensation awards to be publicly disclosed. This followed a pay-out of £1.4 million to Kevin Taylor, who had claimed that Greater Manchester Police had maliciously prosecuted him for fraud to discredit his friend, the former Deputy Chief Constable John Stalker.

225 *The Times*, 9 Feb. 1988; and J. Stalker, *Stalker* (Penguin, 1988).

Such a policy is clearly more akin to a military strategy than any form of policing role. Yet, it is noteworthy how the RUC went to great lengths to justify its actions in terms of their legal legitimacy (using the discourse of self-defence) and their acceptance by public opinion (through extensive fabrication of stories for the media). Other aspects of the Stalker affair are also revealing both in terms of the institutional rivalry between anti-terrorist agencies, and the circumstances in which a particular policing strategy becomes so undermined that it leads to changes in police practices. Thus, for example, although the role of the security services in 'shoot to kill' operations, and their relationship with the RUC, has remained immune from any form of public scrutiny, the political, media and legal 'fall out' from such operations did force a change in RUC strategy. Within the RUC, the view was formed that such undercover operations were best left to elite military units, who were better trained (especially in the use of firearms), able to leave Northern Ireland swiftly after an incident and more likely to gain immunity from judicial proceedings.[226] Thus, it was no surprise that, from 1983 onwards, the number of incidents in which the RUC was engaged in shooting suspected terrorists declined significantly.[227]

This change in policy, however, did not necessarily represent a total RUC rejection of a military approach to anti-terrorism. Even after 1983, RUC personnel remained heavily involved in the planning of operations in which military undercover units were deployed. The primary role of police officers in such operations was to gain intelligence which facilitated the military actions discussed earlier in this chapter. Moreover, recurrent allegations of collusion between the RUC and loyalist paramilitaries in Northern Ireland suggest that some police officers may have concluded that passing information to non-state actors, who have a proven record of using lethal force against republican suspects, avoids some of the legal and political pitfalls outlined above. Although some of the most extensive collusion allegations have proved groundless, there remain several incidents – such as the killings of solicitors Pat Finucane in 1989 and Rosemary Nelson in 1999 – where the extent of RUC knowledge of, and acquiescence in, the fatal attacks remains unclear.[228]

Intelligence-led policing

The main anti-terrorist RUC strategy, however, has been focused on gathering evidence to seek criminal convictions. As we outlined above, the history of legislative changes generally points to more permissive police powers and pro-prosecution amendments in criminal procedure. Some of these changes, as with the curtailment of the right to silence, the extension of detention periods and the restrictions on raising funds for terrorist organisations, have proved successful. In other instances, the outcomes have been more mixed, as, for example, with the use of 'supergrasses' in the mid-1980s. This latter policy

---

226 See Urban, above n. 24, pp. 159-160.

227 Ironically, it was the London Metropolitan Police Force which was involved in the most recent killing of a suspected terrorist by the state when Dairmuid O'Neill was shot in Sep. 1996: see 'IRA Suspect Killed Lawfully, Inquest Rules', *The Guardian*, 18 Feb. 2000.

228 Following a new inquiry led by John Stevens, (now) London Metropolitan Commissioner, a loyalist RUC Special Branch informer, William Stobie, was prosecuted in relation to the Finucane murder; see further, below n. 283 and accompanying text.

arose when, between November 1981 and November 1983, a total of 18 republican and seven loyalist paramilitaries agreed to name nearly 600 people as being involved in terrorism. Several of those who became supergrasses were granted legal immunity or shortened sentences, and were subsequently provided with the financial resources to adopt a new identity outside Northern Ireland. The RUC's use of supergrasses to generate evidence against secretive criminal organisations was not an entirely new police tactic – the London Metropolitan Police had used a similar tactic several years earlier[229] – but the number of supergrasses and the scale of the operation suggest that it could only have been instigated with considerable advance planning (perhaps, involving the DPP and the Northern Ireland Office, as well as the RUC).

The supergrass strategy largely collapsed when the Northern Irish courts overturned convictions on appeal and some supergrasses proved obviously unreliable witnesses. It may, however, still have achieved related police objectives of creating tensions over loyalty in terrorist groups.[230] Multiple objectives are commonplace in police anti-terrorist strategy. For example, the extensive use of arrest and search powers cannot just be explained by a desire to initiate prosecutions; often, the purpose of frequent arrests is directed at low-level intelligence gathering, recruiting informers or notifying suspected terrorists that the police are aware of their activities.

It is difficult to draw firm conclusions about the success of such intelligence-based policing.[231] The RUC points to the large number of people successfully prosecuted for terrorist offences and also claim to have averted a significant number of terrorist attacks. However, it is clear that such policing has not, and arguably cannot, 'defeat' terrorism relating to Northern Ireland – an objective only attainable through the ongoing political process. Furthermore, one of the clear costs of anti-terrorist law and practices has been the number of civil liberties controversies generated, which in turn has led to questions about the extent to which law and policing have created and perpetuated the use of political violence by paramilitary groups and prolonged political paralysis in Northern Ireland. Whatever the answer to such questions, the enactment of the TA 2000 as a permanent piece of legislation (retaining intact once 'temporary' and 'draconian' powers), means that the impetus for change in anti-terrorist strategy now lies with reforming key institutions (such as the RUC) and revitalising other fora of accountability (such as the courts and police authorities).

One consequence of this is that debate on and implementation of the Patten Report on the future of policing in Northern Ireland assumes a central importance. For some critics of the RUC, policing (and human rights abuses) have been a major contributing factor to the conflict and can be traced directly to sectarianism – the fact that over 90% of the RUC are from the Protestant community as opposed to less than 60% of the population whom they police. Law is thus seen as a cover for ideological and practical domination of the non-Unionist communities. At the other extreme, the RUC has sought to emphasise

---

229 See S. Greer, 'Supergrasses and the Legal System in Britain and Northern Ireland' (1986) 102 LQR 198.

230 One terrorist organisation, the Irish National Liberation Army (INLA), conducted a violent internal feud leading to the deaths of several members.

231 See generally, R. Heaton, 'The Prospects for Intelligence-Led Policing: Some Historical and Quantitative Considerations' (2000) 9 Policing and Society 337.

its own impartiality by pointing to the number of loyalist terrorists imprisoned, its role (at least, in recent years) in policing loyalist marches in nationalist areas and its rejection of a flawed policing history (which, when it is acknowledged, tends to be explained by a 'few bad apples in the barrel' theory).

Such monolithic views of any institution, particularly policing ones, are unconvincing.[232] The truth lies somewhere between these two discourses. The RUC has clearly evolved and professionalised when compared with its violent reactions to the civil rights movement in the late 1960s. There is, however, evidence of sectarian attitudes amongst RUC officers[233] (but this is perhaps not surprising where a police force is drawn exclusively from one community/culture).[234] Indeed, until 1998 when the decision on whether a contentious march should take place became the responsibility of the Parades Commission,[235] there was annual evidence of police failure to maintain impartiality in the 'resolution' of parading conflicts: the RUC frequently showed a willingness to uphold the rights of Orange Order marchers along 'traditional routes', often necessitating a considerable deployment of policing force, against any objections of nationalist residents. It is also the case that the RUC has a higher clear-up rate in respect of loyalist than republican terrorist incidents, and that successive chief constables have sought to insulate the RUC from direct political influence.[236] At the same time, however, although the extent of collusion between the RUC and loyalist paramilitary groups remains unclear, suggestions of systematic high-level collusion need to be treated with great caution.

The 'few bad apples' explanation for human rights violations by the RUC must also be rejected, both because there is concrete evidence of the systematic nature of such abuse (as in relation to interrogation in the 1970s) and because it ignores the repressive paramilitary history of policing in Northern Ireland. Moreover, as we have argued throughout this chapter, the *nature* of anti-terrorist law and policing, especially where it is heavily intelligence-dependent, inevitably increases the risk of human rights abuses. One institutional danger of such policing is the increase in power and prestige (and, thus, non-accountability) of elite intelligence units within the police, military and security services: indeed, the Patten Report makes clear that there are significant concerns as to the extent to which RUC Special Branch has become a 'force within a force', a culture which sees itself as exempt from the normal rules of policing.[237] Furthermore, as greater emphasis is put on surveillance and intelligence, what started out as a strategy to cope with the absence of public support may become a strategy indifferent to public support. One manifestation of this phenomenon can be found in complaints that RUC officers who arrest young street criminals in nationalist parts of Northern Ireland are more interested in 'turning' them for intelligence purposes than protecting the community from theft or violence.

232 See generally, D. Dixon, *Law in Policing: Legal Regulation and Police Practices* (Clarendon, 1997).

233 See M. Farrell, *Arming the Protestants* (Brandon, 1983); and G. Ellison and J. Smyth, *The Crowned Harp: Policing Northern Ireland* (Pluto, 2000).

234 See the discussion of the influence of Afrikaner culture on the South African police in C. Shearing, 'Transforming the Culture of Policing: Thoughts from South Africa' (1995) ANZ J Crim 54.

235 See Public Processions (NI) Act 1998. This followed the recommendations of the North Report on public processions in 1997: see Ch. 2.

236 See Ryder, above n. 143, pp. 262-264.

237 See Patten Report, *A New Beginning: Policing in Northern Ireland* (1999), pp. 72-73.

Unsurprisingly, constant pressure to get quick results creates a risk of abuse in any form of policing. Given the higher stakes (in terms of death or injury) involved in anti-terrorist policing, that risk is much greater, as the history of torture by the Israeli security forces or killings by Spanish anti-terrorist police demonstrates. Moreover, efforts to reduce the influence of politics on the police can actually lead to the police becoming reluctant to enter into any contact with the public. From the early 1980s onwards, the RUC appeared to turn inwards and to match pride in its own sense of professionalism with a deep suspicion of the criticism of outsiders. Such an attitude provides a breeding ground for the view that the police know best and, hence, that even cover-ups are legitimate. The importance of the RUC adopting a different approach, accepting and responding to the challenges to its 'official' history, cannot be overstated. As Mulcahy has argued:

> While the RUC nominally views a preoccupation with the past as an obstruction to the improvement of police-community relations, the RUC itself relies heavily on the organizational memories articulated in its official discourse as a strategy of legitimation. This discourse comprises a highly circumscribed account of the RUC's history that privileges specific and favourable memories of it. ... These constructions and reconstructions of the past have profoundly material consequences. They are not limited to decorative or incidental roles; instead they underlie the very basis of debates about the legitimacy of the RUC, as well as the ongoing debate about police reform in Northern Ireland.[238]

From a human rights law perspective, therefore, it should be clear that the nature of anti-terrorist policing always carries a high risk of a substantial disregard of legal/human rights norms. What has helped turn a risk into reality, especially in Northern Ireland, has been the lack of adequate safeguards against the police abusing their enhanced powers (although, this is not to suggest that 'safeguards' are always possible, or always likely to be effective). For example, criticism of the lack of legal redress in respect of soldiers involved in disputed killings could equally be applied to police officers. In addition, the RUC has successfully resisted proposed reforms which might have provided important safeguards, such as a suspect's immediate right of access to a lawyer, taping of interviews,[239] a requirement that detainees be brought quickly before a judge, and an adequate system of inquests.

At a more structural level, there has been a lack of adequate complaints and accountability mechanisms. Despite several efforts at reforming the system of police complaints in Northern Ireland, there remains a significant lack of public confidence in its operation, not least because no complaint of police assault has ever been sustained. In 1998, the UK government decided to abolish the Police Complaints Commission (modelled closely on the Police Complaints Authority in Britain) and replaced it with a Police Ombudsman, who it is hoped will have sufficient powers to examine alleged police malpractice. Ensuring police accountability has also been a constant problem within Northern Ireland. Learning from what were perceived to be mistakes of the past, the UK government has sought to remove the RUC from direct political control. However, this poses the risk that the police will then find themselves exempt

---

238 Mulcahy, above n. 46, p. 69.
239 Although provided for in Britain since 1984, even in respect of PTA arrests, this safeguard was resisted in Northern Ireland until 1998. See TA 2000, s. 100.

from any form of supervision. This appeared to be the reality in relation to the Police Authority for Northern Ireland (PANI),[240] which struggled to exercise any control over the police force for which it was legally responsible. Thus, although PANI appointed the Chief Constable, thereafter he or she could remove issues from the scrutiny of the Authority by claiming that they pertain to 'operations', rather than 'policy' matters. It is arguable that a more independent Authority might have challenged this stance but, in any event, nationalist politicians were so hostile to PANI as to refuse to serve on it. For these reasons, the Patten Report recommended that civilian oversight be conducted by a board which includes representatives of all political parties.[241]

At time of writing, the future of policing in Northern Ireland remains uncertain, despite the passing of the Police (Northern Ireland) Act 2000, which came into force in November 2000. The Act provides for a new name for the police, which henceforth is to be entitled the 'Police Service of Northern Ireland', though it provides that this incorporates the RUC as opposed to disbanding it. PANI is replaced by a new oversight body, the Policing Board. This is to be comprised of up to 19 members, of whom 10 are to be drawn from the Assembly according to party strength. New district policing partnerships are also to be established to facilitate greater local oversight of policing. There are provisions to allow 50 per cent of new recruits to be chosen from the pool of applicants who have identified themselves as Catholics and the Chief Constable, in consultation with the policing Board, is required to issue a new code of ethics for police officers. Further changes, including the appointment of a human rights adviser for the police, are provided for in an operating plan and the legislation requires the creation of an independent Commissioner to oversee the policing changes. Although the Act incorporates most of the changes recommended by Patten, human rights groups have remained unhappy about the proposed changes which were omitted, notably the extent to which the Chief Constable or Secretary of State will be able to block the Policing Board from holding an inquiry into incidents concerning allegations of police abuses of human rights. Politically, while the Act has been a source of great concern to Unionists, it has failed to win the support of Nationalist parties, with neither Sinn Féin nor the SDLP showing a willingness as yet to nominate party members to the Policing Board, though large numbers of Catholics have applied to join the new force. Further negotiations regarding policing are inevitable: these may focus on matters such as the powers of the Policing Board, the Police Ombudsman, the ability of district policing partnerships to raise revenue for 'additional' policing services and the future of the RUC Reserve.[242]

IV.   TERRORISM AND CIVIL LIBERTIES: SITES OF STRUGGLE

In our introduction to this chapter, we placed anti-terrorism law and practice at the heart of the struggle for civil liberties within the UK since the early 1970s. Human rights abuses, the increased power of key national security institutions

---

240 See www.pani.org.uk.
241 See Patten Report, above n. 237, pp. 28-34.
242 For commentary on the Patten Report, see the articles by Shearing, and Hillyard and Tomlinson, at, respectively: (2000) 27 JLS 386 and 394.

such as the police and security services, and international condemnation of the UK have been constant features of this history. We believe that the role of law in creating and perpetuating some of the causes of the Northern Ireland conflict – as well as its role in resolving the conflict – provides wider lessons about the creation of a human rights culture in the UK. While obviously not unique to this area, the ideological, discursive and practical effects of law (and legal institutions and actors) appear much more stark in the context of anti-terrorism strategy – for example, at its extreme, when suspected paramilitaries are killed by an elite military unit. Indeed, the 'repressive state' rhetoric of traditional civil liberties discourse is much more convincing in this context than many others.

In this final Part, we shall examine the successes and failures of civil liberties strategies and human rights discourse in a number of key forums. Focusing on Parliament, the media, the courts and international bodies, we argue that bodies which have offered space for the promotion of human rights in other areas have often been uneasy and hostile actors in the context of anti-terrorism.

Parliament

In some parts of the world, governments' first response to any terrorist threat is to suspend Parliament itself.[243] Apart from a brief period in the early 1920s when martial law was declared in parts of Ireland,[244] the UK has retained legislative control of anti-terrorist policy. Major statutes have set the overall direction of anti-terrorist policy and, often, politicians have used the theatre of Parliament to dramatically demonstrate a national commitment to 'tough' responses to terrorism. In addition, legislation has been required to respond to 'losses' in the European Court of Human Rights (for example, the *Brogan* case) and has been used for most of the 'reforming' initiatives by government (for example, the limiting of the right to silence).[245] Parliament, therefore, has had multiple opportunities to influence and control the character of anti-terrorist policy.

The reality, however, is that the general domination of Parliament by the executive is most pronounced in this area. The PTA (1974) and CPTA (1998) were both rushed through all legislative stages with a minimum of debate. Although, at least in respect of the former, an atmosphere of moral panic might be offered as some explanation, it is a feature of such legislation that parliamentary attempts to revisit the issues and mitigate the harshness of any provisions are rare. In terms of political party support, this is also an issue where cross-party consensus has become the norm – often, it appears, to avoid the accusation of being 'soft on terrorism'. The Conservative Party supported both the PTA and EPA while in opposition in the 1970s. During their 18 years in power between 1979-97, they expanded the former and made few changes to the latter. In so doing, Conservative Ministers frequently justified legislative change on the basis of intelligence information which could not be made accessible to Parliament, a common government tactic in the area of national

---

243 See J. Fitzpatrick, *Human Rights in Crisis* (Pennsylvania UP, 1994), pp. 29-35.
244 Martial law was introduced in some parts of Ireland between Dec. 1920 and Jul. 1921: see C. Campbell, *Emergency Law in Ireland: 1918-25* (OUP, 1994), pp. 30-38.
245 The exceptions are diplomatic initiatives, whether with the Irish government in relation to Northern Ireland, or other governments in relation to international terrorism.

security.[246] During this period, the Labour Party initially opposed the annual renewal of the PTA[247] but was unable to secure any significant amendments to it. It subsequently abandoned such opposition for fear that it was an electoral liability against the Conservatives.[248] When Labour returned to power in 1997, it again abandoned its earlier policy position on the repeal of anti-terrorist legislation. In 1998, it introduced a new anti-terrorism statute, which included one provision that the previous government had dropped in the face of parliamentary opposition.[249] Most recently, with the TA 2000, it has done what no other government has ever done and introduced a permanent statute with powers that have been internationally condemned as contributing to human rights violations.

This is not to suggest that anti-terrorism legislation has remained unchanged since the early 1970s or that government has always dominated the agenda. Some of the broadest search and arrest powers in the EPA have been curbed, and provisions like the 'Broadcasting Ban' have been rescinded. There has also been a significant amount of reforming legislation, although this seems to stem as much from international and media pressure, or ECHR 'losses' in the European Court of Human Rights, as from any need to satisfy Parliament. Prominent among broader political initiatives is the introduction of extensive legislation on religious discrimination in Northern Ireland.[250] Such legislation permits affirmative action on a greater scale than other forms of anti-discrimination legislation in the UK and creates a powerful enforcement regime.[251] Concerns about curbing religious discrimination also led to significant legislation on housing and local government in the early 1970s in Northern Ireland. Although such legislative reforms have not been without their critics, the view of most human rights advocates is that they have produced a legal environment conducive to the achievement of equality in principle, and that they have encouraged moves towards equality in fact.[252] Given this, it seems remarkable that there has been so little parliamentary interest in such models within Britain.

Where Parliament has had an opportunity to draw upon wider public concern and to lobby government for greater human rights safeguards, it has usually

---

246 For example, in a PTA debate on amendments to exclude lawyer/client privilege from the scope of the offence of withholding information about a terrorist offence, then Home Office Minister of State Douglas Hogg claimed that he had information that certain lawyers were 'unduly sympathetic to the cause of the IRA' (*Hansard*, Standing Committee B, col. 508, 17 Jan. 1989). When challenged, Hogg refused to offer names or withdraw the remarks. Defence lawyer Patrick Finucane was killed by loyalist terrorists less than a month later.

247 From its inception, the EPA provided for annual renewal and the PTA required the same since 1989. However, attendance at these debates was notoriously poor and it became little more than a rubber-stamping exercise.

248 See J. Sopel, *Tony Blair: The Moderniser* (Michael Joseph, 1995), pp. 166-169.

249 S. 5 of the Criminal Justice (Terrorism and Conspiracy) Act 1998 made it an offence to conspire to commit terrorism abroad (now TA 2000, ss. 59-61).

250 The history of the legislation is the Fair Employment Act 1976; the Fair Employment Act 1989; and currently the Fair Employment and Treatment (Northern Ireland) Order 1998.

251 See A. McColgan, *Discrimination Law: Text, Cases and Materials* (Hart Publishing, 2000); and C. McCrudden, 'Mainstreaming Equality' (1999) 22 Fordham Int LJ 1696.

252 In its 1998-99 Annual Report, the Fair Employment Commission (now part of the Equality Commission) observed that the Catholic composition of the monitored workforce had risen by 3.9% in the period 1990-99; in organisations investigated by the FEC, the rise was 7%: see Fair Employment Commission, *Tenth Annual Report* (FEC, 1999), p. 25.

not been able to achieve statutory reform. For example, after Amnesty International and the media exposed mistreatment of suspects during interrogation in Northern Ireland Holding Centres in the late 1970s, Parliament had an increased opportunity to press for amendment of the EPA to make it more difficult to admit confessions, or to guarantee access to lawyers during detention. Unfortunately, however, all the government felt the need to offer were administrative guidelines to ensure suspects access to doctors and to impose time limits on periods of interrogation.

At the same time, however, government legislative initiatives can have unpredictable and positive consequences. For example, when police campaigns against 'abuse' of the right to silence resulted in changes in the law of evidence permitting the drawing of inferences from silence,[253] RUC officers interviewing suspects continued with their practice of delaying or discouraging access to a legal adviser until a confession was forthcoming. In the *Murray* case, however, the European Court of Human Rights ruled that the right to silence provision only complied with Article 6 of the ECHR if a suspect had access to a legal adviser in certain circumstances. Paradoxically, therefore, the consequence of the largely symbolic campaign of the police against the 'right to silence' resulted in a strengthened legal right of access to a defence lawyer prior to the drawing of inferences from a suspect's silence.[254]

Ultimately, however, and perhaps even more than some of the other areas we explore in this book, the record of anti-terrorism legislation shows that a confident UK government, armed with a comfortable majority, can force measures antithetical to civil liberties through Parliament with a minimum of difficulty. One consequence of this – and of the growing trend of marginalisation of backbench politicians, and the decreasing influence of the House of Commons over the executive generally – has been a shift in lobbying tactics. Human rights groups campaigning in this field are now more likely to seek media coverage, international pressure and direct access to government Ministers than to rely on parliamentary intervention. However, in light of the ideological and practical importance of anti-terrorism law for governments, the success rate for such efforts is not high.

The media

While Parliament has had little influence on government-sponsored anti-terrorist legislation, it has also not played any major role in exposing the abuses of power associated with anti-terrorist strategies. The main actor in raising public awareness of such human rights violations and exerting significant influence over reform campaigns has been the media. Yet, as noted earlier, it has also played a dominant role in constructing the terrorist threat and legitimising the repressive responses of state institutions.[255] The contradictions and complexity of these media practices and representations are a standard feature of the media studies literature, highlighting how issues such as ownership, control,

253 See the Criminal Evidence (NI) Order 1988; and Criminal Justice and Public Order Act 1994, ss. 34, 36-38.
254 See now Youth Justice and Criminal Evidence Act 1999, s. 58; Criminal Evidence (NI) Order 1999, art 58; and TA 2000, s. 109; and discussion in Ch. 4.
255 See the discussion of media representations of terrorism, above pp. 114-117.

professional identity, news sources and audience research – as well as discourses of nationality, race, gender, etc – affect media coverage.[256] Thus, accounts of media portrayals of terrorism which identify pro- and anti-state positions are often too simplistic.[257] At the same time, however, it can also be argued that there have been common features to much of the coverage of Northern Ireland-related human rights abuses in the last 30 years.

In its 'campaigning' mode, the media has exposed such abuses of human rights as the mistreatment of suspects in police custody, the wrongful convictions of the Birmingham Six, the 'shoot to kill' controversies, and paramilitary 'punishment beatings'. Media coverage of the annual marching confrontations in Northern Ireland was, arguably, influential in forcing the UK government to devise a regulatory mechanism that removed the RUC from the initial decision-making process. Dogged investigative reporting, by individual journalists and television programmes, continues to shed light on issues such as Bloody Sunday in 1972[258] and the harassment of defence lawyers in Northern Ireland. In addition, the willingness of some journalists to seek out and communicate the views of those labelled terrorists, whether in respect of Northern Ireland or elsewhere, has played an important part in keeping open some channels of communication and, hence, suggesting that non-military approaches to terrorism were a political option.

In its 'national security', reactionary mode, however, sections of the media have played a key role in manufacturing public outrage against terrorism and support for harsh anti-terrorist measures.[259] Some newspapers (such as *The Daily Telegraph*) have consistently campaigned to increase anti-terrorist powers and penalties, and have been willing to label people as terrorists against whom action must be taken. A related feature of this journalism has been attacks on other journalists or newspapers (such as *The Guardian*) which are seen as 'sympathetic' to the terrorist cause or who draw attention to the abuses of human rights by state actors.[260] At times, this zeal has interfered with the legal process, as in 1988, when three people were acquitted of charges of conspiring to kill the then Northern Ireland Secretary of State after the Court of Appeal ruled that prejudicial publicity had interfered with their right to a fair trial.[261] *The Sunday Times* newspaper was also involved in a bitter personal attack on witnesses who gave evidence at the Gibraltar Inquest into the SAS killings of three IRA members.[262] Similarly, the television documentary on these events,

---

256 See eg, D. Kidd-Hewitt and R. Osborne (eds.), *Crime and the Media: The Post-Modern Spectacle* (Pluto, 1995); and C. Carter, G. Branston and S. Allan (eds.), *News, Gender and Power* (Routledge, 1998).

257 See, similarly, the range of issues raised by the media and legal representations of a female killer of another woman in Northern Ireland: C. Bell and M. Fox, 'Telling Stories of Women Who Kill' (1996) 5 SLS 471.

258 Veteran journalist Peter Taylor made the documentary, *Remember Bloody Sunday*, in 1992; and Channel 4 News won the Royal Television Society's award for news story of the year in 1998 for its coverage of new evidence.

259 See generally, E. Herman and N. Chomsky, *Manufacturing Consent* (Vintage, 1995).

260 See S. Glover, 'The Republican Cell at the Heart of the Guardian', *The Spectator*, p. 29 (19 Feb. 2000): 'What is less widely known is that the *Guardian* has become "green" to the point of being pro-IRA. . . . Alone in the British press, the *Guardian* is a bit too close for its own good to a terrorist organisation that has still not laid down a single weapon.'

261 See *R v Cullen, McCann and Shanahan*, above n. 73.

262 See J. Tweedie and T. Ward, 'Why the Verdict isn't the End of the Matter' (1988) 138 NLJ 744; and their 'The Gibraltar Shootings and the Politics of Inquests' (1989) 16 JLS 464.

Death on the Rock, which challenged official accounts of the shootings, was heavily criticised by both government Ministers and sections of the media, yet was vindicated in a subsequent inquiry and by the eventual decision of the European Court of Human Rights in *McCann, Farrell and Savage v UK*.[263] The tabloid media, in particular, have played a key role in denigrating efforts to protect human rights in the anti-terrorism context. Civil liberties groups campaigning against the miscarriages of justice committed in the 1970s faced hostile media reaction for many years until the Court of Appeal finally released the Guildford Four and Birmingham Six.[264] It is also notable that very different media responses were forthcoming in the campaigns to free soldiers convicted of the unlawful use of lethal force in Northern Ireland.[265]

While the reality of much mainstream media coverage of terrorism, therefore, is that it reflects an instinctive, pro-state bias, and the propaganda role of some media outlets is overwhelmingly obvious, the issues are not always entirely clear cut. For example, crucial legal and ethical questions, involving several journalists and television broadcasters, have been raised by the Bloody Sunday Inquiry's order that confidential journalistic sources must be disclosed so that soldier witnesses can be identified and questioned as to the events of 1972. Yet, the types of journalism which led to the setting up of the Inquiry would not be possible if sources could not trust a journalist's assurances of confidentiality. The Inquiry, however, has justified its stance by arguing that it cannot fulfil its role without this evidence, and that the evidence cannot be obtained in any other way.[266]

The courts

Lawyers often place their faith in the courts to protect civil liberties and 'going to court' is a central tenet of civil liberties strategies and rhetoric. The level of public and political support for harsh anti-terrorist measures, however, means that courts generally represent a forum of limited potential for civil libertarians. Liberal theory holds that judges are impartial and independent protectors of rights, but the judicial performance in national security contexts provides stark evidence of the partiality of *all* government institutions in the face of perceived threats to their legitimacy.[267] In the Northern Ireland context, the fact that judges are on the list of 'legitimate targets' for terrorist organisations, live under armed police protection and have experienced the killings of some of their colleagues has also naturally hardened such attitudes.

Studies of the role of the judiciary in relation to civil liberties generally focus on the appellate bench. However, as Lobban's study of political trials in apartheid South Africa demonstrates,[268] the role of the trial judge is also worthy of examination when the state seeks to counter challenges to its authority through

---

263 For more detail, see Bailey, Harris and Jones, above n. 28, pp. 340-341.
264 See C. Mullin, *Error of Judgment* (Poolbeg, 1990).
265 See eg, *R v Clegg* [1995] 1 All ER 334.
266 See J. Mullin, 'Taking a Liberty', *The Guardian*, 4 Oct. 1999; and the Inquiry rulings at: www.bloody-sunday-inquiry.org.uk/.
267 See eg, A.W.B. Simpson, *In the Highest Degree Odious: Detention Without Trial in Wartime Britain* (Clarendon, 1994); and Ch. 7.
268 M. Lobban, *White Man's Justice* (OUP, 1996). See also, D. Dyzenhaus, *Judging the Judges, Judging Ourselves* (Hart, 1998).

the use of the criminal law. This is especially so where, as in anti-terrorist trials in Northern Ireland non-jury courts, the trial judge is solely responsible for deciding on both guilt and sentence. At the same time, however, although some studies have raised concerns as to the predominantly unionist background of the Northern Irish judiciary,[269] most commentators have concluded that the Diplock court judges have displayed impartiality and integrity.[270] Moreover, given the scale of the conflict and the questionable practices of the RUC highlighted earlier in this chapter, there have been remarkably few claims of miscarriages of justice in Northern Ireland.[271] Judges have been prepared to exclude confessions they regard as having been achieved through police coercion and have dismissed charges against suspected terrorists for want of evidence. Acquittal rates in Diplock court trials are lower than jury trials, but not that much lower. And on the main occasion when the integrity of the judiciary at the trial level did become an issue of significant concern, during the 'supergrass' saga in the 1980s, it was the judiciary itself who removed any suspicions as to judicial independence with a number of acquittals and reversals on appeal. The major area in which there is ongoing concern as to the impartiality of Northern Irish trial judges is prosecutions of security force members. As highlighted above, there have been few convictions in such cases, often because those cases which have gone to trial turned out to be evidentially weak. However, the comments of some judges when delivering verdicts of acquittal have done little to reassure the public about standards of judicial impartiality.[272]

While we would argue that, on the whole, trial judges in Northern Ireland have acted to protect the right to a fair trial, the same cannot be said with such confidence about the conduct of terrorist trials in Britain. As we observe in Chapter 4, one of the primary catalysts for re-examination of the entire criminal justice process was the series of miscarriages of justice associated with the trials of suspected terrorists in the 1970s. The main responsibility for these miscarriages lay in serious police misconduct and inadequate safeguards for suspects in custody (as well as false forensic evidence, questionable prosecution tactics and sensationalist media coverage),[273] but the role of individual trial judges was also significant, most obviously in biased summings-up to juries. Moreover, the senior judiciary subsequently became vigorous opponents of any effort to re-examine verdicts: a judicial attitude that government actors must be believed in terrorist contexts is clearly revealed in Lord Denning's infamous remark that claims of police malpractice in the Birmingham Six case disclosed an 'appalling vista', which simply 'could not be'[274] – as well as the hostile comments of former Lord Chief Justice Lane that 'the longer these cases continue, the more convinced we are of their guilt'.[275]

---

269 See Boyle, Hadden and Hillyard, above n. 175, pp. 12-13.
270 See Jackson and Doran, above n. 149.
271 See B. Dickson, 'Miscarriages of Justice in Northern Ireland?' in C. Walker and K. Starmer (eds.), *Miscarriages of Justice: A Review of Justice in Error* (Blackstone, 1999), pp. 287-303.
272 The most controversial example was Lord Justice Gibson's observation that police officers had brought terrorist suspects to the 'final court of justice' in one of the Stalker-related trials. In 1987, the judge and his wife were killed by a car bomb planted by the IRA.
273 See generally, Walker and Starmer, above n. 271.
274 *McIlkenny v Chief Constable of West Midlands* [1980] 2 All ER 227, 240.
275 *R v McIlkenny* [1992] 2 All ER 417, 93 Cr App Rep 287.

When the decisions of the judiciary at the appellate level are examined, one finds a dominant executive-minded and deferential approach.[276] Judges have followed the parliamentary trend of always widening the scope of anti-terrorist legislation both in the interpretation of wording and the exercise of discretionary powers. Once again, it is arguable that the Northern Irish judiciary has been slightly more positive in its approach. Thus, the Court of Appeal in Northern Ireland has given some significant decisions limiting the scope of emergency law arrest powers,[277] and preserving a judicial discretion to exclude confessions obtained in an oppressive manner in the face of EPA changes which seemed to exclude this possibility.[278] However, the first of these decisions was reversed by the House of Lords and the second, arguably, made little impact on the actual treatment of suspects. Moreover, the same Court of Appeal has demonstrated a willingness to uphold broad powers to proscribe organisations,[279] to delay suspects access to lawyers,[280] and to limit the scope of inquests resulting from security force killings.[281] Overall, while the Northern Ireland Court of Appeal may have seen itself as neutrally applying the law, there is little sense of it regarding itself as having a duty to protect the human rights of individuals.[282] The decision of Lord Chief Justice Carswell in the *Moloney* case in October 1999 could, however, be interpreted as a sign of a more robust approach in the future to promoting human rights standards in Northern Ireland. Moreover, in ruling that Ed Moloney, the Northern Editor of *The Sunday Tribune*, did not have to disclose his journalistic notes to the RUC where the latter had failed to show that they would be of substantial value to a murder investigation, an important principle of media freedom in situations of political conflict has been established.[283]

In relation to the English Court of Appeal, it is also evident that a sea-change in judicial attitudes has taken place in relation to the likelihood of wrongful convictions. Particularly since the establishment of the Criminal Cases Review Commission (which investigates suspected miscarriages of justice), individual judges have been highly critical of failings in police, forensic and prosecution practices. In numerous cases, convictions have been quashed on the grounds of suspect evidence, and it has been made clear to trial judges that their primary responsibility is to ensure a suspect the right to a fair trial (with increased references also being made to the significance of Article 6 of the ECHR).[284]

---

276 See S. Livingstone, 'The House of Lords and the Northern Ireland Conflict' (1994) 57 MLR 333.
277 See *McKee v Chief Constable for Northern Ireland* [1984] NI 169.
278 See D. Greer, 'The Admissibility of Confessions under the Northern Ireland (Emergency Provisions) Act' (1980) 31 NILQ 205.
279 See *Forde v McEldowney* [1970] NI 11.
280 *Re Begley* (1996) 5 BNIL 39.
281 See *McKerr v Armagh Coroner* (1988) 14 NIJB 70.
282 For an overall assessment of the Northern Ireland judiciary, see B. Dickson, 'Northern Ireland's Troubles and the Judges' in B. Hadfield (ed.), *Northern Ireland: Politics and the Constitution* (Open UP, 1992), pp. 130-147.
283 Moloney had conducted interviews with a loyalist RUC Special Branch informer, William Stobie, about the circumstances of the murder of solicitor Pat Finucane in 1989, in particular, the claims that the RUC was aware of the assassination plan. Following a new inquiry led by John Stevens, Deputy Metropolitan Commissioner, in 1999, Stobie was arrested and charged in relation to the Finucane murder. Moloney subsequently ordered to hand over his notes to the Stevens Inquiry. See J. Mullin, 'Journalist's Notes Denied to Police', *The Guardian*, 28 Oct. 1999; and L. Hickman, 'Press Freedon and New Legislation' (2001) 151 NLJ 716.
284 See eg, *R v McNamee* (CA), 17 Dec. 1998 where the conviction of the 'Hyde Park Bomber' was quashed because of the non-disclosure of evidence and unreliable forensic evidence; and Ch. 4.

In many respects, the most deficient judicial forum in the anti-terrorist context has been the House of Lords. Although the Law Lords are heavily criticised in a number of fields of case law,[285] not least for their hostility to the development of human rights principles, the UK's highest court has been especially conservative and executive-minded when analysing the use of anti-terrorist powers.[286] There has been a pattern of endorsing broad and vague interpretations of legal provisions, such as the definition of terrorism and the guidelines on the use of lethal force by state actors. Other judicial decisions on issues such as when adverse inferences may be drawn from silence,[287] or a suspect's right of access to a lawyer[288] have also offered little for advocates of civil liberties. Distinguishing features of these decisions include their short length and the lack of any detailed engagement with common law principles of liberty, let alone international human rights standards. Even more striking is the depoliticised tone of this body of case law; there is no indication that anti-terrorist legislation and practices are heavily contested in Northern Ireland or that judicial discourse might expand beyond the rules of statutory construction. Overall, therefore, although references to 'Crown forces' are no longer included in judgments, as in the 1970s,[289] the political role of the Law Lords in reinforcing the legitimacy of state action in Northern Ireland is still paramount.[290]

Optimists may argue that this judicial record once again demonstrates the absence of fundamental rights guarantees in UK law, and that the HRA era will be different. Some commentators have taken heart from the *Kebilene* decision where the Divisional Court (including then Lord Chief Justice Bingham) invoked Article 6 of the ECHR via the HRA to adopt a narrow interpretation of section 16A of the PTA.[291] The House of Lords overruled the decision on the ground that the HRA was not yet in force and could not be used to circumvent the criminal appeal system, but it left open the issue of the compatibility of the anti-terrorism provision with the ECHR.[292] The hope of civil liberties lawyers remains that, as the HRA becomes an established part of the legal and political landscape, it will be used by judges to restrict the scope of anti-terrorist powers. Thus, for example, arrest powers, interference with lawyers' access to suspects, the use of lethal force, media restrictions, and inquest procedures may all be ripe for re-examination.

While we would welcome such judicial reappraisal, it is unrealistic to view the HRA alone as being the catalyst for such change. The key issue appears to

---

285 See D. Robertson, *Judicial Discretion in the House of Lords* (Clarendon, 1998); and Ch. 1.

286 In a study conducted in 1994, it was found that the government had only lost two of 13 cases before the Law Lords in relation to Northern Ireland: see Livingstone, above n. 276.

287 See *Murray (Kevin) v DPP* [1994] 1 WLR 1; and *R v Bingham* [1999] 1 WLR 598.

288 See *R v Chief Constable of the RUC, ex p Begley* [1997] 4 ALL ER 833.

289 *A-G's Reference (No. 1 of 1975)* [1977] AC 105, 136 (per Lord Diplock).

290 This is an interpretation which Lord Saville, the head of the Bloody Sunday Inquiry, appears to be aware of; his inclusive language in official statements and press conferences is very different from the approach of his predecessors, Lords Diplock and Widgery, who conducted official inquiries (on the criminal justice system and Bloody Sunday, respectively) in Northern Ireland in the early 1970s.

291 S. 16A of the PTA 1989 (now TA 2000, s. 57) deals with possession of an article for terrorist purposes and places the burden of proof on the accused: see Gearty, above n. 124.

292 *R v DPP, ex p Kebilene* [1999] 4 All ER 801 (HL).

be whether the wider political climate is favourable to a more interventionist judicial approach in historically contentious areas. It may be no accident that *Kebilene* occurred after several years of ceasefires in Northern Ireland. Studies of the judiciary in several countries during times of crisis suggest that the appellate bench will generally show deference to the state in such periods.[293] Moreover, regardless of the content of Bills of Rights, the judicial branch has generally proven reluctant to act in ways which may (or even appear to) hinder the executive's suppression of rebellion or terrorism. As a result, several years of 'post-conflict' peace may be necessary before the UK judiciary closely examines anti-terrorist law and practices for conformity with human rights standards.[294]

International forums

In challenging UK anti-terrorist law, human rights campaigners have often had more satisfaction in international forums than domestic ones. There are several reasons for this success, most notably that national politicians, judges and media do not have the reflective distance of international organisations. The most significant international actor, the European Court of Human Rights, has played a valuable role in challenging UK government claims about the necessity of certain legal powers and the lawfulness of certain state actions.[295] Thus, although criticism of the European Court of Human Rights for its 'minimalist' and over-cautious jurisprudence is a common and valid perspective, it should not be forgotten that, in the anti-terrorism context, the Court has often provided the *only* judicial forum to challenge state practices since the 1970s. In one of its earliest decisions on anti-terrorist law and policy, that of *Ireland v UK* in 1978, it stated clearly that combating terrorism could not justify breaches of fundamental rights.[296] Its decision in *McCann, Farrell and Savage* further stressed that even when dealing with known terrorists, the state has an obligation to conduct law enforcement in a way which minimises the threat to life.[297] Decisions in cases such as *Brogan*,[298] *Fox, Campbell and Hartley*,[299] and *Chahal*[300] have all upheld the value of the right to liberty, even in the context of combating terrorism, and have stressed the need to retain judicial oversight of any deprivation of liberty. In addition to the decisions of the European Court of Human Rights, there has been extensive recognition by other Council of Europe and UN bodies that anti-terrorist law and policy in the UK over the past 30 years has given rise to significant human rights violations. Pressure by governments in Ireland and

---

293 See G. Alexander 'The Illusory Protection of Human Rights by National Courts During Periods of Emergency' (1984) 5 HRLJ 1.

294 See C. Walker, 'The Commodity of Justice in States of Emergency' (1999) 50 NILQ 164 (on the marginalisation of judicial adjudication as a force for change). Cf. *Secretary of State for the Home Department v Rehman* [2000] 3 All ER 778 (re deportation and international terrorism).

295 See Livingstone, above n. 26; and P. Jean, 'The Jurisprudence of the European Commission and Court of Human Rights with Regard to Terrorism' in Higgins and Flory, above n. 175, pp. 217-250.

296 (1978) 2 EHRR 25.

297 (1995) 21 EHRR 97. See also *Jordan and Kelly v UK* (4 May 2001).

298 (1989) 13 EHRR 439.

299 (1991) 13 EHRR 157.

300 (1996) 23 EHRR 413.

the US, as well as EU bodies, has also played an important role in curbing the excesses of such policies and devising political and economic initiatives to reduce support for terrorism.

This is not to suggest, however, that international forums can provide a panacea for human rights critics of anti-terrorist strategy. Many cases have been rejected at the initial stage by the (former) European Commission on Human Rights, including the application relating to the 'Broadcasting Ban' on the media which would have provided an obvious test for exploring the limits of freedom of expression in a situation of political violence.[301] Also, the Court itself has consistently upheld the right of the UK to derogate (under Article 15 of the ECHR) from some of its human rights obligations in view of the alleged emergency situation prevailing in Northern Ireland.[302] Furthermore, in many of its decisions on anti-terrorist law, from the UK and other countries, the Court has accepted that 'some compromise between requirements for defending democratic society and individual rights is inherent in the system of the Convention',[303] a compromise which inevitably reinforces state power.

It should, however, be noted that the international forum is not exhausted by the actions of inter-governmental institutions and organisations. Human rights NGOs, arguably, have been a leading catalyst in sparking media and public debate on anti-terrorism policy and, sometimes, have been instrumental in achieving reforms. The international prestige of Amnesty International or Human Rights Watch, and their influence on members of UN bodies such as the Human Rights Committee, has resulted in a significant 'external' pressure being applied to the UK government. This was most obvious during the period of introduction of the 'MacBride Principles' in the US, when state legislatures enacted laws preventing US companies from investing in Northern Ireland unless fair employment practices were first observed.[304] More recently, the need for national governments to observe human right standards, even in the face of 'terrorism threats', appears to be slowly becoming a baseline principle influencing (if not determining) the response of the 'international community' of states, global organisations, media and NGOs to certain conflicts – as the cases of Kosovo and East Timor generally indicate.[305]

Government co-operation at the international level, however, can often play a decisive role in the opposite direction, generating national anti-terrorism policies and rhetoric which place significant strain on the development of a human rights culture.[306] The recurrent theme of the need for greater international harmonisation and co-operation against 'terrorism', which appears both in academic writing and in the influential counter-terrorism discourse of the US State Department, is largely a negative force. In a replication of the growth of academic and media coverage in the 1970s focusing on aviation bombings and liberation groups, the late 1990s brought a similar construction

---

301 See Bailey, Harris and Jones, above n. 28, pp. 338-340.

302 The Art. 15 derogation was withdrawn in Feb. 2001 after TA 2000 came into force.

303 *Klass v Germany* (1978) 2 EHRR 214, para. 59.

304 See L. Currier, 'Religion and Employment in Northern Ireland: US Influence on Anti-Discrimination Legislation' (1990) 12 Comp Lab LJ 73; and Ch. 8.

305 See generally, S. Wheatley, 'The NATO Action Against the Federal Republic of Yugoslavia: Humanitarian Intervention in the Post-Cold War Era' (1999) 50 NILQ 478.

306 See *R v Mullen* [2000] QB 520 where the Court of Appeal quashed the conviction of an alleged IRA bomber as an abuse of process because of the unlawful collusion between British and Zimbabwean authorities as to his deportation back to the UK.

of threats from 'post-communist organised crime', 'eco-terrorism', 'cults' and 'Internet crime'. The political offence exception in extradition law has also been rendered virtually extinct, and there are increasing efforts to prevent those alleged to have been involved in terrorism from seeking asylum.[307] In other developing areas, such as the right of law enforcement authorities to access emails, demands for international harmonisation in order to combat terrorism may well make it impossible for domestic legislatures to act to protect human rights.[308] Beyond such legislative initiatives, daily co-operation of law enforcement and security bodies is a reality – for example, the TREVI group in Europe, where information is gathered and exchanged on the basis of a number of rationales, including counter-terrorism.[309] In light of the democratic deficit within the justice structures of the EU, such international law enforcement co-operation occurs in an environment beyond most national or European accountability mechanisms. Without more effective scrutiny of such 'post-national' surveillance, whether by legal, political and media structures, the current (limited) safeguards at state level are likely to be ignored or bypassed.

CONCLUSION

Defending the cause of human rights in the context of a perceived terrorist threat, especially when that threat is credible, remains a difficult task. There is likely to be significant public support for harsh anti-terrorist measures and many of the traditional forums of resistance to state power prove hostile or ineffective. However, as we have demonstrated throughout this chapter, human rights discourse has a role to play even in the most hostile environments, and can operate simultaneously at different local, national and international levels.

In some respects, the history of UK anti-terrorism strategy is the history of UK government policy on Northern Ireland since the early 1970s. This has been one long journey from state denial of human rights to the recognition of their relevance in a final political solution. We have argued that this history proves that the adoption of repressive anti-terrorist rhetoric and tactics is inevitably counter-productive: it increases the opportunities for human rights violations by state actors, further 'militarises' the environment, and marginalises the option of political solutions.[310] Anti-terrorism law was both a symbolic and practical means of oppression throughout this period and, thus, became another component perpetuating the conflict.

More recently, however, and despite the fact that the UK government has now made it clear that a Terrorism Act will always be a part of the legal landscape,

---

307 See generally, S. Kemp, 'Refugee Law as a Source in Extradition Cases' [1998] Crim LR 774.

308 See JUSTICE, *Under Surveillance: Covert Policing and Human Rights Standards* (1998), pp. 101-107.

309 For a discussion of the activities of TREVI, see C. Gueydan, 'Co-Operation Between Member States of the European Community in the Fight Against Terrorism' in Higgins and Flory, above n. 175, pp. 97-122, at p.105. See also, S. Peers, *EU Justice and Home Affairs Law* (Longman, 2000), Ch. 9.

310 This is not to suggest that the republican movement did not pursue an exclusive 'military' approach to its goal of Irish unification up until the 1980s when it adopted its dual 'armalite and ballot box' electoral strategy, which led eventually to serious political negotiations with the UK government in the early 1990s. Our point is that political rather than military or policing initiatives by the UK government achieved this outcome. It should also be noted that, even during apparent 'hardline' Thatcher administrations, secret talks with the IRA were authorised.

there appears to be an official recognition at the political level that a lasting peace in Northern Ireland can never be achieved through the adoption of the oppressive anti-terrorist strategies of the past. Thus, it seems to have been accepted that the *approach* of the Good Friday Agreement – with reviews of policing and the criminal justice system, the creation of powerful new Human Rights and Equality Commissions, and the attempt to devise representative government structures[311] – is the only viable means of reducing support for politically motivated violence long term.[312]

Unfortunately, however, there is no guarantee that UK government policy will persist with this approach, particularly if the main paramilitary groups decide to use violence again in an attempt to strengthen their negotiating positions. As we have highlighted throughout this chapter, the tragic human costs of terrorist attacks can easily generate a 'wartime', defensive mentality within state institutions, mainstream media and the general public, such that 'human rights' and 'terrorism' are seen as incompatible and unrelated terms. In a fundamental sense, therefore, anti-terrorism law will always be a tool available in any political struggle between the state and those who challenge its legitimacy.[313] This may explain why the role of human rights discourse – which provides one means of transcending, and helping to resolve, political conflict – has always been marginal in the responses of state institutions in the UK.[314] Only after the paramilitary ceasefires has this discourse come to the fore in official responses. Yet, to date, it seems that this shift has been (at least outside of Northern Ireland itself) very much at the level of 'high' government policy – the stuff of Anglo-Irish government initiatives and negotiations, with an acquiescent Parliament and British media following in tow. It remains to be seen whether attitudes to anti-terrorism law and strategy, and to the primacy of human rights discourse, have been fundamentally altered because of the lessons of Northern Ireland.

311 For a summary of these developments see Harvey and Livingstone, above n. 4; Dickson, above n. 26, pp. 301-308; the Special Issue at (1999) 22 Fordham Int LJ; and C. Shearing, '"A New Beginning" for Policing' (2000) 27 JLS 386.

312 See G. Evans and B. O'Leary, 'Northern Irish Voters and the British-Irish Agreement: Foundations of a Stable Consociational Settlement?' (2000) 71 Pol Q 78.

313 This is one reason why ordinary police powers and legislation, which *are* adequate to counter most terrorist threats, are claimed to be insufficient compared with extraordinary anti-terrorism powers.

314 See also McEvoy, above n. 45, p. 571: 'Engagement in legal struggle has both circumscribed and deepened Republican analysis. Isolated from political dialogue because of violence and their abstentionist policy until the 1980s, Republicans were insulated from the reality that Unionists could not be militarily coerced into a united Ireland. Dialogical engagement, in legal and other arenas, has necessitated a tacit acceptance of the *rights* of Unionists to a British identity, a recognition now enshrined in the Good Friday Agreement signed by Sinn Fein'.

Chapter Four

Fair trial values: policing, prosecution and trial practices

INTRODUCTION

This chapter examines the concept of a right to a fair trial or, more broadly, fair trial values. At first glance, this may appear to be a straightforward task; a right to a fair trial – so the words imply – is about what happens *in* the courtroom, in particular the composition and behaviour of the relevant tribunal and the procedural rules governing the adversarial process. The general expectation – bolstered by the centrality of the jury trial in both law books and media representations[1] – is that the 'classic' components of a fair trial, including presumption of innocence, an impartial tribunal, legal representation, the rules of evidence and contempt laws, will operate to ensure that, first and foremost, innocent persons are acquitted, and also that guilty defendants are fairly treated and (perhaps) convicted.

Trust in fair trial safeguards has, however, taken a serious battering in recent years. In a long string of cases, the Court of Appeal has confirmed miscarriage after miscarriage of justice;[2] for some, these admissions of error have come too late. In February 1998, the Court of Appeal acknowledged its 'very profound regret that in 1952 [Mahmood Hussein Mattan] was convicted and hanged, and that it has taken 46 years for that conviction to be shown to be unsafe'.[3] In July 1998, a former Chief Justice, Lord Goddard, was criticised by the Court of Appeal for the hanging of Derek Bentley after denying him 'that fair trial which is the birthright of every British citizen'.[4] For Mattan and Bentley's families and friends, and for the innocent women and men who have walked free from court after long years of imprisonment – the Guildford Four, the Birmingham Six, the Maguire Seven, Judith Ward, Stefan Kiszko, the Cardiff Three, the

---

1   See N. Lacey and C. Wells, *Reconstructing Criminal Law: Text and Materials* (Butterworths, 1998), pp. 1-90; and N. Padfield, *Text and Materials on the Criminal Justice Process* (Butterworths, 1995), pp. 195-305. Lord Devlin, for example, argued that the jury 'is the lamp that shows that freedom lives': *Trial By Jury* (Stevens, 1966), p. 64.
2   According to Lord Steyn in *R v Secretary of State for the Home Department, ex p Simms and O'Brien* [1999] 3 All ER 400, 402 the term 'miscarriage of justice' is 'apt where a conviction was at first upheld on appeal but subsequently, after the defendant had perhaps served years in prison, the case was re-opened and the conviction found to be unsafe'.
3   *The Times*, 5 Mar. 1998.
4   [1998] Crim LR 330.

Taylor sisters, numerous West Midlands Serious Crime Squad defendants, Patrick Nicholls, the Bridgewater Four, Kevin Callan, and Iain Hay Gordon, to name only some[5] – the concept of a right to a fair trial has most likely appeared shallow and meaningless.

The realisation that miscarriages of justice cannot be confined to a particular time period, or specific police force, or type of offence or defendant, appears to have nurtured a growing public awareness that the trial process may be fatally flawed in certain contexts. Even senior members of the judiciary, in contrast to earlier eras of indifference and denial (particularly in the Court of Appeal), acknowledge this deficiency: in *Simms and O'Brien*, a case involving restrictions on prisoners' access to investigative journalists, Lord Steyn accepted that '[t]he risk of such miscarriages is ever present'.[6] The most obvious manifestation of institutional acceptance of the limitations of the trial process is provided by the Criminal Cases Review Commission, an independent body established under the Criminal Appeal Act 1995 to investigate suspect convictions (in England, Wales and Northern Ireland): since it commenced work in April 1997, the Commission has received 3,193 applications claiming miscarriages of justice, with over 77 cases currently referred to the Court of Appeal.[7]

Common assumptions about 'fair trial' safeguards have not, however, been undermined only by infamous miscarriages of justice. Increasing overlap between the fields of criminal law, criminal justice and criminology, for example, has contributed to a shift in understandings of how the criminal justice process actually operates. Thus, a growing body of research indicates that the different social constructions of criminal behaviour by the media, parliaments, police and courts – in relation to tax fraud, prostitution, terrorism, drug-taking, domestic violence or rape – result in very different responses to 'crime'.[8] Increased awareness of the need to focus on the *pre-trial* stage of the criminal justice system, in particular 'the mass production of guilty pleas', has also contributed to the challenge to common assumptions about 'fair trial' safeguards.[9] Statistics show that only a small percentage of all crimes committed are reported, recorded and investigated. Moreover, if a prosecution does occur '[t]he vast majority of cases – over 90 per cent in magistrates' courts and some two-thirds in the Crown Court – proceed on a plea of guilty, which means that no trial of guilt ever takes place'.[10] A further major challenge to conventional thinking on 'fair trial' has been provided by extensive research findings on the effects of the Police and Criminal Evidence Act 1984 (PACE). These findings have generated a sophisticated debate about the nature of policing and police cultures, their relationship to the criminal justice process, and the effects of

5   See the list of cases in C. Walker and K. Starmer (eds.), *Miscarriages of Justice: A Review of Justice in Error* (Blackstone, 1999), pp. 45-52. For more recent quashed convictions on the basis of false confessions or fabricated evidence, see *R v Hall, O'Brien & Sherwood* [2000] Crim LR 676; and J. Dein, 'Police Misconduct Revisited' [2000] Crim LR 801.

6   Above n. 2.

7   CCRC, *Annual Report 1999-2000* (available at http://ccrc.gov.uk). The Scottish Criminal Cases Review Commission was established in Apr. 1999. See S.M. Keegan, 'The Criminal Cases Review Commission's Effectiveness in Handling Cases from Northern Ireland' (1999) 22 Fordham Int LJ 1776; and R. Nobles and D. Schiff (2001) 64 MLR 280.

8   N. Lacey, 'Contingency and Criminalisation' in I. Loveland (ed.), *Frontiers of Criminality* (Sweet & Maxwell, 1995), pp. 1-27.

9   A. Sanders and R. Young, *Criminal Justice* (Butterworths, 2000), pp. 395-482.

10   A. Ashworth, *The Criminal Process: An Evaluative Study* (OUP, 1998), p. 302.

legal and administrative rules in governing policing.[11] In many studies, policing practices have been shown to vary depending on the specific context: on the street; in the police station; with the category of crime; or when the goal is prosecution. Questions have also been raised about the assumption that law enforcement is the primary motivation of policing; a growing number of people are being arrested and released without any further action, suggesting that:

> the police are increasingly pursuing police-defined objectives and have expanded a 'shadow' system of police punishment. The key feature is that the police lack interest in legal or factual guilt and are more concerned with imposing control and maintaining order.[12]

Often, the targets of such policing are vulnerable, historically marginalised groups (such as African-Caribbean people) leading to debates about whether police racism is a reflection of institutionalised racism within the UK, or whether the 'occupational culture' of policing (which is not *necessarily* static) lends itself to stereotyping, harassment and violence against certain groups. In recent years, the complexity of the criminal justice process has been further highlighted by the development of research on the impact of managerialism on police forces, the Crown Prosecution Service (CPS), and the court system.[13] A particular focus of contemporary research is the impact of the new populist drive towards punitive criminal justice policies which emphasise 'zero tolerance', 'public protection' and 'victims' rights'; a trend that places the police, court and prison systems as the primary and proactive agents in combating (certain) crime and the consequences of social exclusion.[14]

Fair trial and the Human Rights Act

It is against this complex backdrop that we examine how the civil liberties lawyer, in the era of *Bringing Rights Home*, should respond to the operation of the criminal justice system. It is undoubtedly true that fair trial issues will generate a significant body of case law throughout the UK in the Human Rights Act era; in post-Charter of Rights Canada, the Supreme Court delivers some 60 decisions annually on criminal procedure.[15] Predicting and assessing the outcomes of such cases, however, is a much more difficult matter; it requires close contextual analysis of many variables and cannot be simplistically equated with legal 'victories' or 'losses' under the provisions of the Convention right to

---

11 See generally, D. Dixon, *Law in Policing: Legal Regulation and Police Practices* (OUP, 1997); and J. Chan, *Changing Police Culture: Policing in a Multicultural Society* (Cambridge UP, 1997).

12 P. Hillyard and D. Gordon, 'Arresting Statistics: The Drift to Informal Justice in England and Wales' (1999) 26 JLS 502, 519. See also, R. Reiner, 'Policing and the Police' in M. Maguire, R. Morgan and R. Reiner (eds.), *The Oxford Handbook of Criminology* (Clarendon, 1997), pp. 997-1049.

13 See eg, C. Jones, 'Auditing Criminal Justice' (1993) 33 BJ Crim 187; N. Lacey, 'Government as Manager, Citizen as Consumer: The Case of the Criminal Justice Act 1991' (1994) 57 MLR 534; and W. De Lint, 'New Managerialism and Canadian Police Training Reform' (1998) 7 SLS 261.

14 See eg, I. Brownlee, 'New Labour – New Penology? Punitive Rhetoric and the Limits of Manageralism in Criminal Justice Policy' (1998) 25 JLS 313; A. Sanders, 'What Principles Underlie Criminal Justice Policy in the 1990s?' (1998) 18 OJLS 533; and T. Hope and R. Sparks (eds.) *Crime, Risk and Insecurity* (Routledge, 2000).

15 R. Delisle and D. Stuart, *Learning Criminal Procedure* (Carswell, 1994), p. v.

a fair trial (Article 6). In this chapter, we shall argue that the HRA will generate mixed outcomes in the criminal justice field: thus, although promotion of the values underpinning the Act has the potential to transform aspects of the criminal justice process, it also must be recognised that legal norms (whether derived from PACE, Strasbourg jurisprudence or the HRA itself) may have little or no impact on a system composed of actors who are subject to a range of competing political, economic, bureaucratic and cultural influences.

Our argument will be developed in three sections. Part I will provide an overview of 'fair trial' in the civil liberties textbook tradition, arguing that historically the main focus has been on the narrow issue of safeguarding personal liberty in the face of 'abuses' of police powers rather than on the details of the criminal justice process. Part I will also highlight a series of catalysts that have generated a more critical perspective on 'fair trial' and a heightened awareness of the potential of using human rights norms to challenge policing, prosecution and judicial practices and attitudes. Parts II and III will examine the substance of the right to a fair trial. In these parts, we shall focus on two key phases of the criminal justice process in order to draw out the implications of some of the procedural guarantees in Article 6.

In Part II, we shall examine access to a legal adviser at the pre-trial stage, as generally guaranteed by section 58 of PACE and protected under Article 6(3)(c) of the Convention.[16] Our case study on this right demonstrates the complex relationship between a formal legal guarantee and the actual practices of police, suspects and legal advisers, as well as the role of judges in supervising the criminal justice process. It also suggests that the civil liberties tradition will need to engage more fully with critical scholarship on 'criminalisation' and policing if it hopes to assess the likely ideological and practical impact of the HRA and engage it in favour of progressive ends. Part III shifts attention to the trial stage. Using a case study on rape prosecutions, it aims to highlight how key principles underpinning the right to a fair trial – in particular the right to disclosure of evidence to the defence and the right to cross-examination – have been interpreted in practice. Particular attention will be paid to the downside of such interpretations and the need for a revisioning of the concept of 'fairness' within the idea of a 'right to a fair trial'.

Our overall argument is that the concept of 'fairness' requires more detailed scrutiny as an 'essentially contested concept'[17] and that the rhetoric about the importance of (largely procedural) fair trial safeguards needs to be placed in context. Civil liberties textbook scholarship in this area has tended to confine itself within the parameters of traditional criminal law/evidence doctrine with the result that there is an over-emphasis on statutory wording and case law,

16   S. 58(1) provides: 'A person arrested and held in custody in a police station or other premises shall be entitled, if he so requests, to consult a solicitor privately at any time'. Art. 6(3) provides: 'Everyone charged with a criminal offence has the following minimum rights: . . . (c) to defend himself in person or through legal assistance of his own choosing or, if he has not sufficient means to pay for legal assistance, to be given it free when the interests of justice so require'. Following the ECtHR decision in *Murray (John) v UK* (1996) 22 EHRR 29, a right of access to a lawyer is now guaranteed where adverse inferences from a suspect's silence may be drawn: see Youth Justice and Criminal Evidence Act 1998, s. 58; Criminal Evidence (NI) Order 1999, s. 58; and TA 2000, s. 109.

17   The phrase is from W.B. Gallie. See N.J. Hirschmann and C. Di Stefano (eds.), *Revisioning the Political: Feminist Reconstructions of Traditional Concepts in Western Political Theory* (Westview, 1996).

rather than any serious engagement with the process and institutions of criminal justice. While the growing interest in rights discourse is long overdue, there are already signs that the HRA is being interpreted in the criminal justice context as a mere 'procedural tool' for practitioners to integrate into their established legal and cultural practices. At the level of political discourse, there is also a need – while still celebrating the right to a fair trial as a legitimate core value – to move beyond both the civil libertarian 'aura of due process'[18] and the 'commonsense' but often retributionist clamour of 'crime victims'. In particular, in light of the centrality of the rape trial in current debates, it means that 'superficial portrayals of clashes or conflicts' – for example, of 'lawyers being concerned solely with fairness and feminists with prosecution' – need to be exposed and avoided.[19]

I.   FAIR TRIAL IN THE CIVIL LIBERTIES TEXTBOOK TRADITION

Today, the words 'fair trial' are part and parcel of the civil liberties vocabulary but, strange as it may seem, this was not always so. Traditionally, civil liberties texts have either avoided analysis of the criminal justice process or addressed only very specific aspects. The standard approach has been to focus on diverse topics – such as arrest and detention (police powers), the role of the jury in prosecutions under the Official Secrets Acts (national security), and restrictions on media reporting of legal proceedings (free speech) – in different chapters, rather than offering any systematic account of fair trial. There has also been a 'reverence for jury trial ... [as] the lynch-pin of an adversarial system of criminal justice'.[20] Robertson commented on these practices in the seventh edition of *Freedom, The Individual and the Law*, published in 1993, noting how 'remarkable' it was 'that none of the present "casebooks" on civil liberties have any section devoted to the right to fair trial'.[21] Thus, while Bailey, Harris and Jones,[22] Ewing and Gearty,[23] Shorts and de Than,[24] Stone,[25] Fenwick,[26] and Feldman[27] all provide accounts of PACE, the analysis does not move beyond arrest and detention powers (pre-trial stage), or the power of judges to exclude evidence (trial stage). In *The Three Pillars of Liberty*,[28] presented as an audit of 'key democratic rights' in the UK against international human rights standards, there is no examination of the right to fair trial. To date, Robertson is the only textbook writer within

---

18   W.A. Bogart, *Courts and Country: The Limits of Litigation and the Social and Political Life of Canada* (Toronto UP, 1994), p. 211.
19   C. Fennell, 'Review of S. Edwards, *Sex and Gender in the Legal Process*' (1999) 50 NILQ 254, 269.
20   Below n. 21, p. 339.
21   G. Robertson, *Freedom, The Individual and the Law* (Penguin Books, 1993), p. xi.
22   S.H. Bailey, D.J. Harris and B.L. Jones, *Civil Liberties: Cases and Materials* (Butterworths, 1995).
23   K.D. Ewing and C.A. Gearty, *Freedom Under Thatcher* (OUP, 1990).
24   E. Shorts and C. de Than, *Civil Liberties: Legal Principles of Individual Freedom* (Sweet & Maxwell, 1998).
25   R. Stone, *Textbook on Civil Liberties* (Blackstone, 2000).
26   H. Fenwick, *Civil Liberties* (Cavendish, 1998).
27   D. Feldman, *Civil Liberties and Human Rights in England and Wales* (OUP, 1993).
28   F. Klug, K. Starmer and S. Weir, *The Three Pillars of Liberty: Political Rights and Freedoms in the United Kingdom* (Routledge, 1996). Cf. Liberty, *Criminal Justice and Civil and Political Liberties* (NCCL, 1993).

the civil liberties tradition to have attempted an account of the concept of a fair trial in light of actual policing, prosecution and judicial practices.[29]

Ironically, one possible explanation for the general omission of fair trial from the civil liberties canon can be found in the origins of the Robertson text itself. Early editions of this text, *Freedom, the Individual and the Law* – authored by Street – illustrate how the subject was constructed from very specific concerns; the main one being 'the Englishman's [sic] cherished idea that he does not live in a police state'.[30] This concern led to a focus on police powers and the best means of protecting an individual's right to liberty; thus, Street's own approach was to 'follow the police from their powers of arrest to the restrictions imposed on the searching and entering of premises, to police questioning, then to bail and *habeas corpus*. . .'.[31] This approach was underpinned by the popular and academic belief that 'the policeman's [sic] main task is to detect and catch people suspected of crime so that the courts may try them',[32] and, overall, little attention was paid to the nature of policing or the fact that jury trial is an exceptional occurrence in the criminal justice process.

A second possible explanation for the omission of fair trial from the civil liberties canon can be found by examining the impact of conventional subject divisions within the law curriculum. Criminal law and evidence scholarship have been viewed as the primary reference point on many issues relating to the criminal process: several civil liberties commentaries on PACE and the trial process make reference to the leading criminal law texts and cases in explaining policing, prosecutorial and judicial behaviour. The problems with this practice, however, have become evident in recent years with the growth of a 'critical' criminal law scholarship that exposes the shortcomings of the doctrinal tradition in criminal law textbook writing. Farmer, for example, criticises the 'Criminal Law Textbook' for raising and dismissing the 'moral, political and social dimensions of the law . . . in a single movement in favour of grinding technical discussions of legal minutiae'.[33] An obvious criticism of the Criminal Law Textbook has been that its discussion of key statutes, such as PACE, the Public Order Act 1986, the Prevention of Terrorism Act 1989 or the Obscene Publications Act 1959, is often an exercise in statutory interpretation and doctrinal exposition. The political origins of legislation, its effects (if any) on social groups, police, and prosecution practices, and the wider functioning of the criminal justice process tend to remain unaddressed: as Dixon has argued, 'accounts of what the police ought to do are presented as if they are descriptions of practice: in the cruder formulations, what the law says is what the police do'.[34] Criticism of

29　Above n. 21. See also the essays: S.H. Bailey, 'Rights in the Administration of Justice' in D.J. Harris and S. Joseph (eds.), *The ICCPR and UK Law* (Clarendon, 1995), pp. 186-241; and J. Jackson, 'Due Process' in C. McCrudden and G. Chambers (eds.), *Individual Rights and the Law in Britain* (Clarendon, 1994), pp. 109-144.

30　H. Street, *Freedom, the Individual and the Law* (Penguin Books, 1972), p. 15. See also, S. Hall, *Drifting into a Law and Order Society* (Cobden Trust, 1980), p. 17 ('in its widest sense, the question of who polices the police is a matter which has been, historically, at the very heart and centre of our civil liberties').

31　Ibid.

32　Ibid.

33　L. Farmer, 'The Obsession with Definition' (1996) SLS 57, 57. See also, A. Norrie, *Crime Reason and History: A Critical Introduction to Criminal Law* (Weidenfeld & Nicolson, 1993); and Lacey and Wells, above n. 1.

34　D. Dixon, *Law in Policing: Legal Regulation and Police Practices* (OUP, 1997), p. 1. See eg, the approach of K. Lidstone and C. Palmer, *The Investigation of Crime: A Guide to Police Powers* (Butterworths, 1996).

the impact of traditional subject divisions in the law curriculum on the nature and content of criminal law teaching and scholarship has also come from the mainstream *Criminal Law Review*: a 1997 editorial noted that 'human rights has too often been regarded as a separate subject, rather than being integrated into teaching and books on criminal law, evidence, criminal justice and so on', and concluded that '[c]hange is now needed'.[35] The narrowness and legalism of civil liberties textbook scholarship on the form and function of the criminal trial can also be linked to the evidence textbook tradition. In the latter, rule-based categories of evidence have tended to be the main focus of inquiry. In addition, not only is the trial given centre stage, it is depicted using doctrinal accounts of trial procedures and idealised portrayals of judicial, jury and lawyer functions, rather than accounts of actual courtroom practices and experiences.[36]

Catalysts for rethinking fair trial values

The limitations of the civil liberties *textbook* tradition have not, however, stymied reflection on the concept of a 'right to fair trial'. The growth of criminal justice research, political lobbying and litigation strategies by civil liberties groups, and the evolution of human rights norms in UK courts (often prompted by the European Court of Human Rights), have led to important shifts in understanding of fair trial values. In this section, we shall identify and examine four broad (and overlapping) catalysts that have played a significant role in this process. These are: (1) the extraordinary scale of miscarriages of justice and the resulting focus on the merits of PACE in controlling police malpractice; (2) the draconian 'emergency law' framework of Northern Ireland, in particular the absence of jury trial in the 'Diplock courts' and the rewriting of evidence laws; (3) the Strasbourg jurisprudence on the right to a fair trial under Article 6 of the ECHR; and (4) the general turn towards critical theory, particularly feminism, in the criminal law, criminal justice and criminology fields.

(1)   Miscarriages of justice and the impact of PACE

The issue of wrongful convictions in high-profile 'terrorism' cases such as the Guildford Four, Maguire Seven, Birmingham Six and Judith Ward forced the concept of a fair trial into the public spotlight in a spectacular way: from the dramatic televised release of the Guildford Four in 1989 onwards, the sense of fallibility, if not crisis, in the criminal justice system could not be denied.[37] Significantly, it was the campaigning work of many civil liberties organisations and investigative journalists that was crucial in persuading successive Home Secretaries to refer suspect convictions back to the Court of Appeal – a forum traditionally very hostile to claims of systematic police fabrication of evidence and abuse of suspects.[38] Furthermore, the future prominence of 'fair trial' issues

---

35   [1997] Crim LR 461.
36   For critical commentary on the evidence textbook tradition, see eg, P. Roberts, 'Review of Hunter and Cronin, *Evidence, Advocacy and Ethical Practice: A Criminal Trial Commentary* (Sydney: Butterworths, 1995)' (1996) 1 E&P 92; and J. Jackson, 'Analysing the New Evidence Scholarship: Towards a New Conception of the Law of Evidence' (1996) 16 OJLS 309.
37   See eg, C. Walker and K. Starmer (eds.), *Justice in Error* (Blackstone, 1993); and M. McConville and L. Bridges (eds.), *Criminal Justice in Crisis* (Edward Elgar, 1994).
38   See eg, C. Mullin, *Error of Judgment* (Poolbeg, 1990).

within civil liberties discourse was secured by the setting up of a Royal Commission on Criminal Justice in 1991 (the Runciman Commission), in direct response to concerns about these miscarriages of justice.

Commentators have identified a number of factors common to the 'terrorism' miscarriages: the arrest and prosecution of people with Irish backgrounds;[39] sensationalist media coverage; police willingness to take 'investigative shortcuts'; charges supported solely by (coerced) confessional evidence and, in some cases, faulty scientific material; prosecution failures to disclose relevant materials; biased judicial summing-up; and the reluctance of appeal mechanisms (judicial and political) to recognise errors and reverse convictions.[40] While the Court of Appeal in quashing the verdicts only tended to emphasise one particular flaw in each prosecution (such as false forensic evidence), a more systematic cause seems more convincing.

It is arguable that this category of miscarriages 'subvert[ed] justice to political expediency'[41] in a most exceptional way: one obvious distinguishing feature from other miscarriages was police reliance on the Prevention of Terrorism Act and its seven-day detention power.[42] As we argue in Chapter 3, the 'lawlessness' and brutality of the state response to IRA terrorist threats in the 1970s can be attributed to a mixture of police prejudices, media over-reaction and official policy to 'win the war' at all costs: police, prosecution lawyers, scientists, judges, juries, the media and the public all played their part in the wider process of demonising the 'terrorist' and reinforcing the legitimacy of the state.[43] It is also true, however, that the factors that led to the 'terrorism' miscarriages (for example, reliance on confessions, racism and non-disclosure of evidence) are evident in other types of police investigation and prosecution. Moreover, numerous miscarriages of justice have occurred outside the context of terrorist offences: infamous cases such as *Bentley* (1952), *Hanratty* (1962) and *Confait* (1972) have become shorthand for historical concern about police 'rule breaking' and the failure of the trial process to identify unreliable or fabricated evidence.[44] In the 1970s, many commentaries on the criminal justice system concentrated on the need for a statutory code of police powers in order to curb police malpractices. The courts were, to put it mildly, not viewed as

---

39   Evidence of the extent of racism in this period can be found in unexpected sources. 'No doubt the first reaction of the Englishman, if not of the Irishman, is to do as a policeman asks': Street, above n. 30, p. 22. It needs also to be emphasised that a suspect 'Irish' identity in practice encompassed people with Irish, Northern Irish and British backgrounds and familial connections. On the social construction of black criminality in this period, see S. Hall et al., *Policing the Crisis* (Macmillan, 1978).

40   See McConville and Bridges, above n. 37; Walker and Starmer, above n. 5; and R. Nobles and D. Schiff, *Understanding Miscarriages of Justice* (OUP, 2000).

41   P. Hillyard, 'The Politics of Criminal Injustice: The Irish Dimension' in McConville and Bridges, above n. 37, pp. 69-79, at p. 78.

42   See P. Hillyard, *Suspect Community: People's Experience of Prevention of Terrorism Acts in Britain* (Pluto, 1993).

43   Some actors behaved much more culpably and illegally than others – for example, police assaults on defendants and the fabrication of evidence. See the account of police interrogation provided by Gerry Conlon: 'The questioning and the beating began again. I was told to stand a couple of feet from the wall, and then put my hands on it. They bent down to my ear and yelled into it, punching my kidneys. "You'll make a statement, because you're guilty. You're guilty, so you'll make a statement"': *Proved Innocent: The Story of Gerry Conlon of the Guildford Four* (BCA, 1994), p. 78.

44   C. Walker, 'Miscarriages of Justice in Principle and Practice' in Walker and Starmer, above n. 5, pp. 31-62, at pp. 45-46.

effective guardians of suspects' rights; quite apart from the gradual extension of police common law powers, there was a pervasive willingness amongst the senior judiciary to ignore or condone police illegality. As Choongh points out, the main concern of judges at that time was the reliability of evidence rather than questioning the circumstances in which it was obtained: 'many judges accepted police claims that they could be trusted with broader powers, and that the fight against crime necessitated such an increase in police powers.'[45]

A major shift in the debate occurred with the coming into force of PACE in 1986. The Act prescribes a statutory list of police powers and suspects' rights, and contains very detailed Codes of Practice.[46] One of the most pressing dilemmas for the civil liberties lawyer has been knowing how to respond to the miscarriages of justice that have occurred in the PACE era. Diverse cases such as the *Cardiff Three* (1990),[47] the *Taylor Sisters* (1992),[48] and *O'Brien* (1988)[49] – as well as the ongoing quashed convictions involving the West Midlands Police Serious Crime Squad – highlight the failure of PACE safeguards for suspects in police custody and the failure of the trial process to recognise and acquit innocent defendants. This dilemma has left civil liberties lawyers mired in a debate (conducted since the 1960s in the criminal justice literature[50]) about the capacity of legal rules to promote a 'due process' model of criminal justice; in particular, the ability of PACE and judicial regulation to transform a 'crime control' culture of policing. This debate is set to further intensify with the coming into force of the HRA, increased judicial reference to Article 6 of the ECHR, and the growing concerns about the New Labour government's criminal justice policies.[51]

(2)   Fair trial in Northern Ireland

The second catalyst that has raised the profile of the right to a fair trial both within civil liberties discourse and more generally is Northern Ireland's historical emergency law framework. The abolition of jury trial in the 'Diplock courts' for terrorism-related offences, for example, represents a most dramatic curtailment of a 'core' civil liberty.[52] These courts, and other 'emergency-led' changes in policing, prosecution practices and criminal/evidence law, provoked a civil liberties critique of criminal justice, despite the 'long-standing reluctance among academics living in England, Scotland and Wales to examine the situation in Northern Ireland when writing about policing and criminal justice in

---

45   S. Choongh, *Policing as Social Discipline* (Clarendon, 1997), p. 18. See generally, S. Sharpe, *Judicial Discretion and Criminal Investigation* (Sweet & Maxwell, 1998).
46   See below pp. 180-181.
47   *R v Paris, Abdullahi and Miller* (1992) 97 Cr App Rep 99.
48   *R v Taylor and Taylor* (1993) 98 Cr App Rep 361.
49   [2000] Crim LR 676.
50   See P.A. Sanders, 'Criminal Justice: The Development of Criminal Justice in Britain' in A. Thomas (ed.), *Socio-Legal Studies* (Dartmouth, 1997), pp. 185-205.
51   See eg, the debate over the Criminal Justice (Mode of Trial) Bill which aimed to remove a defendant's ability to elect for jury trial in re certain offences; D. O'Brien and J.A. Epp, 'Salaried Defenders and the Access to Justice Act 1999' (2000) 63 MLR 394; and Criminal Defence Service (Advice and Assistance) Act 2001.
52   See S. Greer and A. White, *Abolishing the Diplock Courts* (Cobden Trust, 1986); J. Jackson and S. Doran, 'Diplock and the Presumption Against Jury Trial' [1992] Crim LR 755; and J. Jackson and S. Doran, *Judge Without Jury* (Clarendon, 1995).

Britain'.[53] The principal drive towards critique was provided by Northern Ireland-based organisations (such as the Committee on the Administration of Justice (CAJ) and the former Standing Advisory Commission on Human Rights (SACHR)) and academics.[54] Issues which they have highlighted include the use of lethal force, the oppressive nature of police interrogation centres, the hostile relationships between police and defence lawyers, the use of 'supergrasses' as prosecution witnesses, the impact of exclusion orders under the Prevention of Terrorism Act, and journalists' rights to protect their sources.[55]

The catalytic effect of Northern Ireland's criminal justice system has intensified in recent years. This has happened in part because of the ease with which successive Home Secretaries have replicated Northern Ireland police powers on the 'mainland'. Former Home Secretary, Michael Howard, for example, succeeded in extending the terms of the Criminal Evidence (Northern Ireland) Order 1988 to England and Wales, using claims that 'Government will never put the civil rights of terrorists before the lives of the British people', and that the right of a suspect to remain silent was being 'ruthlessly exploited by terrorists'.[56] A second reason for the increased catalytic effect of Northern Ireland's criminal justice system is the shift away from an internal Northern Ireland critique of anti-terrorism provisions towards a broad human rights perspective on criminal justice. This shift has been facilitated by the close links between organisations such as CAJ, Amnesty International and Liberty in lobbying, litigation and publicity strategies:[57] these organisations have also been quick to take advantage of the development of international human rights standards, using them to highlight the treaty commitments of the UK government under the Strasbourg and UN mechanisms. Important victories have been secured in cases such as *Murray (John) v UK*[58] (on the freedom from self-incrimination and access to legal advice) and *McCann, Farrell and Savage v UK*[59] (on the use of lethal force). UN reports, such as that of the Special Rapporteur on the Independence of Judges and Lawyers,[60] have also helped to highlight the importance of legal advice for detainees and to place criminal justice issues on a broader human rights footing.

Institutional reforms in Northern Ireland have also been justified as necessary for the creation and promotion of a human rights culture with the aim of resolving

---

53   Hillyard, above n. 41, p. 69.

54   See eg, B. Dickson (ed.), *Civil Liberties in Northern Ireland: The CAJ Handbook* (CAJ, 1997); B. Dickson, 'Miscarriages of Justice in Northern Ireland' in Walker and Starmer, above n. 5, pp. 287-303; and P. Maguire, 'The Standing Advisory Commission on Human Rights: 1973-80' (1981) 32 NILQ 31.

55   See Ch. 3. See generally, A. Jennings (ed.), *Justice Under Fire: The Abuse of Civil Liberties in Northern Ireland* (Pluto, 1990); and C. Gearty, 'Political Violence and Civil Liberties' in Harris and Joseph, above n. 29, pp. 145-178. On a journalist's right to protect their sources in the context of anti-terrorist investigations, see Ch. 3, n. 283.

56   See ss. 34-39 of the Criminal Justice and Public Order Act 1994 (now amended by the Youth Justice and Criminal Evidence Act 1999, s. 58) re guaranteed access to legal advice.

57   See L. Whelan, 'The Challenge of Lobbying for Civil Rights in Northern Ireland: The Committee on the Administration of Justice' (1992) 14 HRQ 149; and P. Hunt and B. Dickson, 'Northern Ireland's Emergency Laws and International Human Rights' (1993) 11 Neth Q of Human Rights 173. More generally, on Amnesty International's interest in the right to a fair trial, see its Fair Trials Manual at: www.amnesty.org/ailib/themes/fair.tria.htm.

58   (1996) 22 EHRR 29. See also *Averill v UK* [2000] Crim LR 682.

59   (1995) 21 EHRR 97.

60   E/CN.4/1998/39/Add.4. See also, Human Rights Watch, *To Serve Without Favor: Policing, Human Rights and Accountability in Northern Ireland* (1997).

the wider political conflict. Thus, the mechanism for determining the routes and policing of historically contentious marches has been transformed by the establishment of the Parades Commission, with its powers to ban and regulate public processions.[61] A new Human Rights Commission distinguishes Northern Ireland as closer to the human rights cultures of countries such as Canada and South Africa than any other part of the UK.[62] Finally, the opportunities for institutional and occupational reforms of policing, with the emphasis on promoting human rights values and democratic governance, have been highlighted and debated as a result of the Patten Report on the future of the Royal Ulster Constabulary (RUC).[63]

(3)   Article 6 of the European Convention on Human Rights

The third obvious catalyst has been the influence of the ECHR. Fair trial questions under Article 6 have been the most common type of application under the Convention system.[64] This is not surprising as much criminal and civil litigation, as well as the proceedings of some administrative tribunals, raises potential questions about the guarantee of a right to a fair hearing.[65]

The lengthy wording of Article 6 indicates the broad nature of the right to a fair trial. It reads:

1. In the determination of his civil rights and obligations or of any criminal charge against him, everyone is entitled to a fair and public hearing within a reasonable time by an independent and impartial tribunal established by law. Judgment shall be pronounced publicly but the press and public may be excluded from all or part of the trial in the interest of morals, public order or national security in a democratic society, where the interests of juveniles or the protection of the private life of the parties so require, or to the extent strictly necessary in the opinion of the court in special circumstances where publicity would prejudice the interests of justice.
2. Everyone charged with a criminal offence shall be presumed innocent until proved guilty according to law.
3. Everyone charged with a criminal offence has the following minimum rights:
   (a) to be informed promptly, in a language which he understands and in detail, of the nature and cause of the accusation against him;
   (b) to have adequate time and facilities for the preparation of his defence;

---

61 See N. Jarman, 'Regulating Rights and Managing Public Order: Parade Disputes and the Peace Process: 1995-1998' (1999) 22 Fordham Int LJ 1415.

62 For information on the Northern Ireland Human Rights Commission, see www.nihrc.org.

63 See Chs. 2 and 3.

64 For detailed accounts of Art. 6 case law, see eg, D.J. Harris, M. O'Boyle and C. Warbrick, *Law of the European Convention on Human Rights* (Butterworths, 1995), pp. 163-273; A. Lester and D. Pannick (eds.), *Human Rights Law and Practice* (Butterworths, 1999), pp. 133-160; and S Grosz, J. Beatson and P. Duffy, *Human Rights: The 1998 Act and the European Convention* (Sweet & Maxwell, 2000), pp. 219-261. According to a chronological survey of English cases where judges have made reference to the ECHR, Art. 6 was first cited in 1975: see M. Hunt, *Using Human Rights Law in English Courts* (Hart, 1997), p. 326. In the area of criminal justice, other provisions of the ECHR overlap with Art. 6, such as Art. 5 (right to liberty) in relation to arrest and detention powers, and Art. 8 (right to privacy) in relation to police surveillance and evidence-gathering. Art. 8 has also been influential in promoting criminal law reform on gay sexual relations: see *Dudgeon v UK* (1981) 4 EHRR 149; and Ch. 6.

65 See D. Galligan, *Due Process and Fair Procedures: A Study of Administrative Procedures* (Clarendon, 1996), pp. 214-222.

(c) to defend himself in person or through legal assistance of his own choosing or, if he has not sufficient means to pay for legal assistance, to be given it free when the interests of justice so require;

(d) to examine or have examined witnesses against him and to obtain the attendance and examination of witnesses on his behalf under the same conditions as witnesses against him;

(e) to have the free assistance of an interpreter if he cannot understand or speak the language used in court.

The Strasbourg authorities – historically, the Commission and the Court – have emphasised the overall need for *procedural* fairness in legal proceedings in their approach to the general guarantee of Article 6(1), and to the specific guarantees of Articles 6(2) and (3) in criminal cases.[66] Thus, for example, delay beyond 'a reasonable time', the absence of an 'independent and impartial tribunal', or the violation of the principle of 'equality of arms' between litigants (such as equal access to evidence or cross-examination) may breach the right to a fair trial. However, as the main focus of Article 6 is the trial process rather than pre-trial proceedings, it must be shown that the fairness of the proceedings *as a whole* are impugned in order to establish a violation of the Convention. This means that the opportunity to challenge any 'defects' at the trial stage, or on appeal, will often satisfy the requirements of Article 6.[67] In practice, therefore, the European Court of Human Rights – which tends to be very conscious of the differences between common and civil law systems, and of the need to defer to national courts' assessment of the facts of cases – often impacts only marginally on the actual criminal justice process in Member States.

There have, however, been several important strands of cases where the UK has been found to breach the 'fair trial' standards of the ECHR.[68] The prosecution of children in adult criminal courts has been condemned for its impact on defendants' comprehension of the conduct of proceedings and because the intimidating surroundings interfere with their ability to consult with lawyers (*V and T*[69]). A particularly successful area of litigation concerns challenges to prison and military disciplinary proceedings.[70] Cases in this area have established a prisoner's right of access to lawyers and courts (*Golder; Silver; Campbell and Fell*[71]), and revealed the lack of independence and impartiality of the court-martial system (*Findlay; Moore and Gordon*[72]) and of the Home Secretary's role in setting prisoner tariffs (*V and T*[73]). The UK courts'

---

66   See generally above n. 64; D. Cheney, L. Dickson, J. Fitzpatrick and S. Uglow, *Criminal Justice and the Human Rights Act 1998* (Jordans, 1999), pp. 75-106; and A. Ashworth, 'Article 6 and the Fairness of Trials' [1999] Crim LR 261.

67   See S.D. Sharpe, 'The European Convention: A Suspects' Charter?' [1997] Crim LR 848. See *R v Hertfordshire CC, ex p Green Environment Industries Ltd* [2000] 2 AC 412 (HL) (jurisprudence underpinning Art. 6 concerned with fairness of trial and not extra-judicial inquiries).

68   See generally the works cited above n. 64.

69   (1999) 30 EHRR 121.

70   See Ch. 5.

71   See respectively (1975) 1 EHRR 524; (1983) 5 EHRR 347; and (1984) 7 EHRR 165.

72   See respectively (1997) 24 EHRR 221; and (1999) 29 EHRR 728. For a commentary on the former, see A. Lyon, 'After *Findlay*: Aspects of Military Justice' [1998] Crim LR 109. The continued role of the Lord Chancellor as an occasional Law Lord is now in question as a result of the decision in *McGonnell v UK* (2000) 30 EHRR 289 (Art. 6 breached where Guernsey judge was also a member of the executive and legislature).

73   Above n. 69. In Mar. 2000, the Home Secretary responded to the ECtHR ruling by transferring the decision to set tariffs in children's cases to the Lord Chief Justice.

development of more rigorous standards of judicial review in this field and the growing emphasis on 'prisoners' rights' can also be attributed to the influence of the Strasbourg authorities.[74]

A third area of case law concerning the UK deals with challenges to aspects of criminal investigatory practices. The Strasbourg case law in this field displays a range of outcomes. In *Saunders*, the power of Department of Trade and Industry inspectors to compel a fraud suspect to answer questions was held to infringe the freedom from self-incrimination.[75] In *Murray (John)*, denial of access to a legal adviser during police questioning was held to breach Article 6 but, on the particular facts, the drawing of adverse inferences from a terrorist suspect remaining silent in police custody and refusing to testify was upheld.[76] In *Edwards*, a police failure to disclose relevant information to the defence at the trial stage was held to have been sufficiently remedied at the appellate stage by the Court of Appeal's assessment of the effects of that non-disclosure.[77] However, in *Rowe and Davis*, where the prosecution decided, without notifying the trial judge, to withhold relevant evidence on public interest grounds, the Court of Appeal review of the undisclosed evidence in an ex parte hearing was considered inadequate to meet the standards of Article 6.[78] Only the trial judge was in a position to assess the full relevance of the evidence in light of the testimony of witnesses and lawyers' cross-examination tactics as the trial progressed.

The influence of Strasbourg has also been felt in a controversial and ongoing line of civil cases concerning House of Lords decisions not to allow negligence actions against public authorities on public policy grounds.[79] The European Court has ruled that such a procedural limitation infringes Article 6 in the context of compensation claims against the police for allegedly failing to prevent a fatal shooting (*Osman*[80]), and claims against a local authority for allegedly failing to prevent child abuse (*X v Bedfordshire County Council*[81]).

These and other cases concerning the UK have led to conflicting perspectives on the role of the ECHR and the Strasbourg Court in relation to the criminal justice system. Some criminal and evidence lawyers have applauded the 'very positive view of the value and importance' of the right to a fair trial in the *Murray* and *Saunders* cases, noting how it 'contrasts starkly with the negative view implicit in recent Parliamentary incursions'.[82] Civil liberties activists, in particular, have emphasised the potential for strengthening fair trial values in the criminal justice process, for example, in relation to the right to silence, extending prosecution disclosure of evidence to the defence, the police use of

---

74   See Ch. 5.
75   (1996) 23 EHRR 313. Cf. *Brown v Stott* [2001] 2 WLR 817 (HL).
76   (1996) 22 EHRR 29. See also *Quinn v UK* [1997] EHRLR 176 (challenge in another 'right to silence' case from Northern Ireland failed on its facts at Commission level). The first similar jury trial case from England and Wales was successful: see *Condron v UK* [1999] Crim LR 984; (2001) 31 EHRR 1 (drawing of adverse inferences from refusal to answer questions in police interview on legal advice breached Art. 6).
77   (1992) 15 EHRR 417.
78   (2000) 30 EHRR 1. See Part III below on disclosure in rape prosecutions.
79   See eg, *Hill v Chief Constable of West Yorkshire* [1989] AC 53. For an analysis of this area, see L. Hoyano, 'Policing Flawed Police Investigations: Unravelling the Blanket' (1999) 62 MLR 912.
80   [1993] 4 All ER 344; [1999] 1 FLR 193 (ECtHR). See C.A. Gearty (2001) 64 MLR 159.
81   [1995] 3 All ER 353; *Z v UK* [2001] 2 FCR 246, ECtHR; and *Barrett v Enfield London Borough Council* [1999] 3 WLR 79.
82   P. Mirfield, *Silence, Confessions and Improperly Obtained Evidence* (Clarendon, 1997), p. 304.

informers, and increased covert surveillance.[83] However, more sceptical views on Article 6 and the HRA have also been expressed. There has, for example, been some concern about Article 6's influence on the 'pro-defendant' bias of several recent debates, as exemplified by negative reactions to the new restrictions on cross-examination on a complainant's past sexual history in rape cases.[84] There have also been commentaries which have sought to dampen down what is seen as excessive enthusiasm for Article 6: Sharpe has challenged 'any expectation that Article 6 . . . will rectify those deficiencies which currently exist in the protection of suspects and defendants in this jurisdiction',[85] and Ashworth has described the detailed provisions of PACE and its Codes of Practice as 'an advance' on the text of the ECHR, while also conceding that the HRA 'is the best we are likely to get, and certainly preferable to remaining without even the safeguards it promises'.[86]

The judicial position on Article 6 is more difficult to discern. References to the 'right to a fair trial' and 'fairness' are a standard feature of UK case law. At the same time, however, the criminal courts have traditionally ignored the relevance of persuasive ECHR jurisprudence and, where it has been cited, individual judges have tended to conclude that the provisions of the common law or PACE are comparable, if not superior.[87] The current views of senior English judges appear to be rather diverse: Lord Hoffmann, for example, has been very hostile towards the European Court of Human Rights' judgment in *Osman*, and has questioned the 'suitability, at least for this country, of having questions of human rights determined by an international tribunal made up of judges from many countries'.[88] Apart from the Northern Ireland-related cases, the decision of the House of Lords in *Khan*, arguably, best reflects the approach of the Law Lords to the ECHR where police powers are challenged. Thus, despite the illegal bugging of private property to gain prosecution evidence, the obvious relevance of Article 8 privacy jurisprudence was discounted while Article 6 fair trial jurisprudence was considered to be indistinguishable from English law on the exclusion of unfair evidence (PACE, section 78).[89] The more recent case of *Kebeline*[90] demonstrated a greater variety of judicial responses to the ECHR: while Lord Chief Justice Bingham was willing to rule that the reversal of the burden of proof in section 16A of the Prevention of

---

83   See J. Wadham and H. Mountfield, *Blackstone's Guide to the Human Rights Act 1998* (Blackstone, 1999), pp. 76-90.

84   See below, pp. 206-211.

85   Sharpe, above n. 67, p. 848. Cf. *Sander v UK* [2000] Crim LR 767.

86   A. Ashworth, 'The Impact on Criminal Justice' in B. Markesinis (ed.), *The Impact of the Human Rights Bill on English Law* (OUP, 1998), pp. 141-157, at pp. 150, 157.

87   See eg, *R v Sultan Khan* [1996] 3 All ER 289. The Scottish courts have started to develop a body of case law dealing with the right to a fair trial under Art. 6. For an overview of Scottish criminal justice, see P. Duff and N. Hutton (eds.), *Criminal Justice in Scotland* (Ashgate, 1999); and C. Walker, 'Miscarriages of Justice in Scotland' in Walker and Starmer, above n. 5, pp. 323-353. An account of the application of the HRA in Scotland is provided in Lester and Pannick, above n. 64, pp. 267-285 and Scottish human rights case law is available at: www.scotcourts.gov.uk. For Northern Irish judges' reaction to the ECHR, see Ch. 3. See also, *R v Elwell* (CA, 18 May 2001) (re entrapment).

88   L. Hoffmann, 'Human Rights and the House of Lords' (1999) 62 MLR 159, 164.

89   The ECtHR found a violation of Arts. 8 and 13: *Khan v UK*.

90   *R v DPP, ex p Kebeline* [1999] 4 All ER 801. See also, *Nottingham CC v Amin* [2000] 2 All ER 946 (magistrate wrong to refuse to admit police evidence on ground that contrary to the intention of the HRA and unfair under Art. 6); and *Brown v Stott*, above n. 75.

Terrorism Act 1989 violated an accused's presumption of innocence under Article 6 (indicating that the Director of Public Prosecutions (DPP) was under an obligation to anticipate the effect of the HRA *prior* to its coming into force), the House of Lords reversed his ruling on the ground that judicial review should not be used to replace the remedies available to defendants within the criminal justice system. The most remarkable aspect of the House of Lords decision was the diversity of views on the future effect of the HRA and the uncertainty surrounding individual Law Lords' perception of their role.

(4)   The impact of critical theory

The final catalyst for rethinking traditional accounts of criminal justice has been provided by the growth of critical theory. Critical commentators tend to argue for an approach that integrates different perspectives in order to gain fuller insight into the complexity and diversity of the criminal justice system, in particular the nature of policing.[91] They also attempt to reach beyond the empiricism that has dominated some criminal justice research,[92] and atheoreticism of many legal accounts. One branch of critical theory – feminist scholarship and activism— has had a particularly profound impact on thinking about criminal justice. The need to situate legal critique within wider social and political contexts has been a central goal of feminist theory, as well as highlighting the limitations of law reform and rights discourse in achieving progressive social change.[93] Analysis of women's interactions with the criminal process in the context of domestic violence, prostitution and other forms of offending, as well as imprisonment, has presented a deep challenge to the rhetoric of 'fair trial'.[94] Feminist critiques of the laws on sexual assault and courtroom practices in rape trials have been particularly important in exposing problems within dominant understandings of 'crime' and 'criminal justice': for example, 'the sexual overtone of the trial . . . as a pornographic spectacle; . . . the [focus on] admission and scrutiny of the sexual history of the complainant; . . . [and] the contribution of the sentencing stage of the trial to the construction of the "ideal" rape victim'.[95]

Current themes within critical theory – both feminist and other strands – include the impact on criminal justice policy of punitive 'law and order' rhetoric and 'new' managerialism. Brownlee, for example, has argued that the New Labour government's 'tough on crime' stance, which fuels public expectations that crime can be controlled by heavier punishments, is at odds with its commitment to managerialism and the securing of increased efficiencies

---

91   See eg, N. Lacey, 'Criminology, Criminal Law and Criminalization' in Maguire, Morgan and Reiner, above n. 12, pp. 437-450; J. Muncie, E. McLaughlin and M. Lagan, *Criminological Perspectives: A Reader* (Sage, 1996); R. van Swaaningen, *Critical Criminology: Visions from Europe* (Sage, 1997); and S. Walklate, *Understanding Criminology: Current Theoretical Debates* (Open UP, 1998).

92   See Dixon, above n. 11.

93   N. Lacey, *Unspeakable Subjects: Feminist Essays in Legal and Social Theory* (Hart, 1998), pp. 98-124.

94   Leading feminist texts include C. Smart, *Law, Crime and Sexuality* (Sage, 1995); F. Heidensohn, *Women and Crime* (Macmillan, 1996); and N. Naffine, *Feminism and Criminology* (Temple UP, 1996).

95   J. Bridgeman and S. Millns, *Feminist Perspectives on Law: Law's Engagement With the Female Body* (Sweet & Maxwell, 1998), p. 427.

throughout the criminal justice system.[96] The growth in surveillance within criminal justice agencies, with its emphasis on 'knowledge of risks, communication skills and good records', has also been a source of academic interest.[97] This growth is associated with a 'New Penology' based on a paradigm of 'actuarial justice': '[i]nstead of a concern with individuals and a preoccupation with guilt, responsibility, and treatment, the new paradigm is concerned with techniques for identifying, classifying, and managing groups assorted by levels of dangerousness'.[98] A further area of inquiry within critical scholarship concerns the increased centrality of the concept of 'community'[99] in discourses about criminal justice, and the repressive potential contained within its ambiguities.[100] The retributive goals of some 'victim' support groups have also drawn the attention of critical scholars interested in the growing public prioritisation of 'the rights of the victim'.[101]

One strand of critical scholarship which seems of particular interest to a human rights constituency is concerned with exploring the impact of ideas of regulation, accountability, openness and democratic mandate in the fields of criminal law and criminal justice. Dixon, for example, has argued that '[t]he relevance to policing of the new public law which has positive state regulation as its central project would seem to be clear'.[102] Lacey has taken up this theme, arguing in favour of reconceiving criminal law 'as a form of public law':

> both in the sense that it is involved in rendering certain kinds of publicly relevant behaviour accountable, and also in the sense that criminalising practices generate and deploy a wide range of public powers, in both formally public and private bodies and officials.[103]

She suggests that such a reconceptualisation of criminal law would have two aims: first '. . . to find a central place for criminalisation in [a] critical theory of governance, and to begin to think about the democratisation of all aspects of criminalisation practices'; and secondly, to question 'what these practices tell us about our society, about its modes of governance, about its conception of citizenship, about its idea of and degree of regard for the people who make it up'.[104] Keith pursues a similar aim in highlighting the 'sheer scale of criminalization of Afro-Caribbean people in Britain' and how the criminal justice

---

96 Above n. 14. See also, I. Taylor, *Crime in Context: A Critical Criminology of Market Societies* (Polity, 1999).

97 R.V. Ericson, 'The Royal Commission on Criminal Justice System Surveillance' in McConville and Bridges, above n. 37, pp. 113-140, at p. 138. See generally, R.V. Ericson and K.D. Haggerty, *Policing the Risk Society* (Clarendon, 1997); and D. Garland, 'The Limits of the Sovereign State: Strategies of Crime Control in Contemporary Society' (1996) 36 BJ Crim 445.

98 Hillyard and Gordon, above n. 12, p. 504. See generally, M. Feeley and J. Simon, 'Actuarial Justice: The Emerging New Criminal Law' in D. Nelken (ed.), *The Futures of Criminology* (Sage, 1994), pp. 173-202.

99 See Ch. 2 for a discussion of 'community' in the context of public order law.

100 See eg, N. Lacey and L. Zedner, 'Discourses of Community in Criminal Justice' (1995) 22 JLS 301; and N. Lacey, 'Community in German Criminal Justice: A Significant Absence' (1998) 7 SLS 7.

101 See eg, B. Hudson, *Understanding Justice* (Open UP, 1996); and L. Zedner, 'Victims' in Maguire, Morgan and Reiner, above n. 12, pp. 577-612. Cf. B. Bowling, *Violent Racism: Victimisation, Policing and Social Contexts* (Clarendon, 1998).

102 Dixon, above n. 11, p. 300.

103 Lacey, above n. 8, p. 25.

104 Ibid., p. 26.

system has become a key racialising institution: 'the process of criminalization itself now constitutes a significant racializing discourse'.[105] Loader echoes the concerns about regulation by drawing attention to the diversity of public and private agencies that now undertake policing functions and the importance of subjecting this new 'network' of policing to some form of democratic governance.[106]

We believe that the civil liberties tradition needs to pursue this 'drift to theorizing'[107] in criminal law and criminal justice research. This is more than a plea for civil liberties and human rights texts to become 'contextual' and take account of the empirical findings on PACE and prosecution practices when discussing the right to a fair trial. Leading textbooks, such as Bailey, Harris and Jones, have always referenced socio-legal research on issues such as stop and search powers or custodial detention times, and the impact of 'civil liberties-inspired' academics who 'aimed to expose how the system worked in inegalitarian or non-libertarian ways with a view to legal reform'[108] is evident in the development of British criminal justice research. Our argument is that these existing forms of contextualisation need to be supplemented by a full civil liberties engagement with the new ways of theorising criminal justice and the move to transcend disciplinary boundaries. We also believe that without such an engagement, discussion of 'fair trial' in the HRA era will be one-dimensional, ignoring the wider social and political contexts that influence policing, prosecution and judicial practices.

In Parts II and III of this chapter – as well as in the chapters on public order and terrorism – we aim to give some indication of how civil liberties/human rights lawyers might begin to contextualise criminal justice issues and move beyond a narrow, legalistic focus on police powers and rhetoric about human rights. Part II examines the pre-trial process via a case study of access to legal advice in police custody under section 58 of PACE. By using this case study, we aim to show how policing practices at the custodial stage may affect the outcome of the criminal process, thereby demonstrating the need to examine police culture and practices as well as legal rules and rhetoric on fair trial. Part III focuses on the trial stage. It examines two core elements of the right to a fair trial – first, disclosure of evidence to the defence and secondly, the right to cross-examination – by means of a case study on rape trials. The aim here is to show how current interpretations of these aspects of the right to a fair trial can end up distorting the fairness of trials. It also highlights how law interacts with other social and cultural forces in constructing the meaning of 'rape', reinforcing gender relations and stereotypes, and (often) disempowering women who pursue criminal prosecutions. Drawing upon human rights discourse in relation to prosecutions for sexual assault, therefore, is problematic and, in certain contexts, may even be counter-productive. Equally, however, women's rights discourse can provide a site of resistance and a tool for progressive reforms.

---

105 M. Keith, 'Criminalization and Racialization' in Muncie, McLaughlin and Langan, above n. 91, pp. 271-283, at pp. 271-272.
106 I. Loader, 'Plural Policing and Democratic Governance' (2000) 9 SLS 323.
107 Dixon, above n. 11, p. 48.
108 Sanders, above n. 50, p. 185.

II.   THE PRE-TRIAL STAGE: ACCESS TO LEGAL ADVICE IN POLICE CUSTODY

The enactment of PACE in 1984 rooted the exercise of police powers within a single, detailed statutory framework. The Act and its operation have been the focus of extensive research and commentary ever since, generating a lively, and sometimes fractious, debate. Some (principally police) commentators have represented the Act and its Codes of Practice as a 'sea-change' in policing, arguing that it has radically altered criminal investigations, ushering in 'a supposedly American model of due process'.[109] Others, by contrast, have emphasised the Act's *non-impact* on police practices, arguing that it has been absorbed into police culture and that there have been few substantive changes (although they do acknowledge the plethora of post-PACE bureaucracy, including new recording practices via custody sheets and stop and search forms).[110] A third position builds on the tensions between the other two strands of commentary, and on the evidence that the Act is 'being applied differently in some respects in various locations'. It steers away from general conclusions about the Act, arguing instead that 'the inconsistencies revealed should make us question suggestions that there has been a unitary response to PACE, based on police culture, and that policing cannot be changed by legal reform'.[111]

The most important features of the Act are as follows.[112] First, it provides and codifies powers to stop and search persons (sections 1-4); to search and seize property on premises (sections 8-19 and Schedule 1); and to arrest (sections 24-26).[113] Secondly, it sets out the powers of the police to detain and question in custody, while also providing a series of safeguards for the suspect such as imposing welfare and record-keeping duties on a 'custody officer' (sections 36-39); prescribing detention time limits and reviews (sections 40-46); requiring the taping of interviews (section 60); and guaranteeing a right to legal advice (section 58). Thirdly, detailed Codes of Practice attached to the Act (sections 66-67) provide guidance on how to exercise the statutory powers in relation to stop and search (Code A); conducting searches and seizures of property (Code B); detention and questioning (Code C); identification of persons (Code D); and recording of interviews with suspects (Code E). Finally, the Act does not introduce a general exclusionary rule for evidence obtained in breach of it and its Codes of Practice; courts have a duty, however, to exclude a confession where it has been obtained in 'oppressive' or 'unreliable' circumstances (section 76), and a discretion to exclude evidence that adversely affects the 'fairness' of the proceedings (section 78).

Our focus here will be on section 58 of the Act and a person's access to legal advice. The section provides that a person arrested and held in custody 'shall be entitled, if he so requests, to consult a solicitor privately at any time'

---

109 D. Dixon, 'Legal Regulation and Policing Practice' (1992) 1 SLS 515, 518. Dixon summarises this strand of commentary at pp. 518-521.

110 M. McConville, A. Sanders and R. Leng, *The Case for the Prosecution* (Routledge, 1991), p. 189.

111 Dixon, above n. 109, p. 527.

112 For a more detailed account of PACE and references, see Bailey, Harris and Jones, above n. 22, pp. 32-165; and N. Padfield, *The Criminal Justice Process* (Butterworths, 2000).

113 Additional stop and search, seizure and arrest powers are contained in other legislation, including the Misuse of Drugs Act 1971, Public Order Act 1986, Criminal Justice and Public Order 1994, and Terrorism Act 2000. For an account of some of these powers, see eg, Lidstone and Palmer, above n. 34; and Sanders and Young, above n. 9.

(section 58(1)).[114] Code C of PACE further provides that the custody officer must inform a suspect of the right to free legal advice. Section 58 has been represented as a key due process 'right', one which recognises the vulnerability of suspects in the police station and the problematic nature of confession evidence provided in the absence of legal advice.[115] The section also fits with the right to fair trial under Article 6(3)(c) of the ECHR which has been held to guarantee a right of access to a solicitor during police detention in particular circumstances.[116] Several research studies have, however, revealed a gap between the formal section 58 right and its operation in practice. In the following paragraphs, we shall examine the empirical findings and the conclusions of these studies.

Empirical findings on custodial legal advice

Research suggests that a whole range of variables may affect the nature and quality of legal advice in individual cases. The range includes the following: geographical location of the police station; the seriousness of the offence; the fact that 'ethnic minority suspects and adults request advice more often than do white suspects and juveniles';[117] the experience, motivation and remuneration of the solicitors' firms and the legal advisers; the professionalism of the custody officer; and the actions of individual investigating officers. The attitude of the suspect is a further key variable; many suspects decline the opportunity to obtain legal advice citing reasons such as the perceived triviality of the offence, confidence in their own ability to defend themselves, or distrust or dislike of solicitors (particularly duty solicitors).[118] There is also, of course, the fact that 'the pressure of confinement is such that the vast majority of suspects find it difficult to contemplate waiting . . . for a solicitor to arrive'.[119]

Despite these variables in the nature and quality of legal advice, three broadly similar empirical findings have been documented by research studies on section 58. The first common finding is that there has been a consistently low take-up rate for legal advice. Prior to PACE, a majority of suspects did not exercise the right even when informed of it; various studies have shown that, after PACE, only 25-38% request legal advice.[120] Furthermore, even the 50% take-up rate discovered in one smaller research sample 'means that almost half of all suspects decline a free offer of legal advice designed to assist them'.[121]

---

114 S. 58(6) and (8) allow the police to delay access to legal advice in certain restricted circumstances. For the position of suspects detained under the Terrorism Act 2000, see Ch. 3.

115 According to the Royal Commission on Criminal Procedure: '[o]nly an experienced lawyer can give . . . [legal] information and advise . . . how best to proceed' ((Cm. 8092, 1981), para. 4.89).

116 *Imbrioscia v Switzerland* (1993) 17 EHRR 441; and *Murray (John) v UK* (1996) 22 EHRR 29. See generally, Harris, O'Boyle and Warbrick, above n. 64, pp. 256-266.

117 A. Sanders and L. Bridges, 'The Right to Legal Advice' in Walker and Starmer, above n. 5, pp. 83-99, at p. 85

118 Ibid., pp. 85-87. For new Criminal Defence Service, see references above n. 51.

119 Choongh, above n. 45, p. 149.

120 See eg, A. Sanders et al., *Advice and Assistance at Police Stations and the 24 Hour Solicitor Scheme* (Lord Chancellor's Department, 1989); D. Brown et al., *Changing the Code – Police Detention Under the Revised PACE Codes of Practice* (Home Office Research Study No. 129, 1992); and C. Phillips and D. Brown, *Entry into the Criminal Justice System* (Home Office Research Study No. 185, 1998).

121 Choongh, above n. 45, p. 148.

The second common finding is that the request for legal advice does not necessarily translate into contact with a legal adviser. Sanders et al. discovered that a clear request for legal advice was not recorded on the custody record in 6% of cases; they also found that the police sometimes ignored a request or persuaded the suspect to cancel it.[122] It has been suggested that the main 'ploy' used by the police to avoid the exercise of the right to legal advice is rapid, incomplete or incomprehensible communication of a suspect's entitlements under PACE, with the result that 'in many cases – perhaps the majority – the police allow suspects who are unsure of their rights to remain unsure'.[123] The third and final common empirical finding is that the quality of legal advice is often well below the required standard. Several studies have highlighted the extent to which advisers (such as trainee solicitors, legal executives, clerks, secretaries or ex-police officers) were unqualified for their role, and the fact that the delivery and quality of legal advice was poor or inadequate for other reasons (for example, because it was given by telephone or because the pre-interview consultation was either too brief or never took place).[124] These studies also indicate that 'most legal advisers (nearly 78 per cent) did not intervene during the police interview, even if the questioning was obscure or overbearing, whilst . . . in 66 per cent of cases, the legal adviser said nothing at all. Where interventions did occur, they were more likely to assist the police than their client'.[125] Finally, the studies provide some evidence that legal advisers may be less than committed to due process values: for example, it has been reported that advisers 'rarely operate with a presumption of innocence and are loath to make the police prove their case, unless the client convinces them that he or she is innocent',[126] and also that they view police station work as 'unrewarding, unimportant and essentially non-adversarial'.[127]

---

122 Sanders et al., above n. 120, pp. 67-68.
123 Sanders and Bridges, above n. 117, p. 90. Even if the provisions of PACE are followed by the police (such as calling a solicitor when requested), the right can be subverted by practices such as 'informal' interviewing in cells or corridors: see A. Sanders, 'From Suspect to Trial' in Maguire, Morgan and Reiner, above n. 12, pp. 1051-1094, at pp. 1063-1064.
124 See J. Baldwin, *The Role of Legal Representatives at the Police Station* (Royal Commission on Criminal Justice Research Study No. 3, 1992); Brown, above n. 120; M. McConville and J. Hodgson, *Custodial Legal Advice and the Right to Silence* (Royal Commission on Criminal Justice Research Study No. 16, 1993); and Sanders and Bridges, above n. 117.
125 Lidstone and Palmer, above n. 34, p. 429. These sorts of findings prompted the Law Society and the Legal Aid Board to establish a scheme for the registration of solicitor representatives in order to improve the quality of legal advice to suspects. See generally, L. Bridges and J. Hodgson, 'Improving Custodial Legal Advice' [1995] Crim LR 101; A. Sanders, 'Access to Justice in the Police Station: An Elusive Dream?' in R. Young and D. Wall (eds.), *Access to Criminal Justice: Legal Aid, Lawyers and the Defence of Liberty* (Blackstone, 1996); and L. Bridges and S. Choongh, *Improving Police Station Legal Advice: The Impact of the Accreditation Scheme for Police Station Advisers* (Law Society and Legal Aid Board, 1998).
126 Sanders and Bridges, above n. 117, p. 97. See generally, M. McConville, J. Hodgson, L. Bridges and A. Pavlovic, *Standing Accused: The Organisation and Practices of Criminal Defence Lawyers in Britain* (Clarendon Press, 1994). It has also been highlighted that a suspect's gender affects his or her treatment by legal advisers (see, A. Worrall, *Offending Women: Female Lawbreakers and the Criminal Justice System* (Routledge, 1990), p. 21), and that women legal advisers are more likely to be patronised or marginalised by the police (McConville and Hodgson, above n. 124, p. 152).
127 J. Hodgson, 'No Defence for the Royal Commission' in McConville and Bridges, above n. 37, pp. 200-208, at p. 204. See generally, Sanders and Young, above n. 9, pp. 228-240.

Explaining the empirical findings: due process v crime control?

The empirical findings on the operation of section 58 and Code C of PACE make it clear that legally-secured due process values can be ignored or compromised by the actions and attitudes of police and legal advisers. Reforms have been suggested to remedy this and to improve the quality of legal advice available to detainees at police stations. The Royal Commission on Criminal Justice made several recommendations in this field, including a call for a 'thorough review' in 'the longer term' of 'the training, education, supervision and monitoring of all legal advisers who operate at police stations'.[128] The Law Society has pursued a range of initiatives in the field, including an accreditation scheme and the publication of a police station 'skills' package.[129] Whether one believes such measures can improve the situation of the detainee in police custody depends, in large part, on one's position within the broader academic debate about the role of the police in the criminal justice process. To date, two perspectives have tended to dominate the literature on this latter issue.

'The Case for the Prosecution' or '[A] critical, but guardedly positive, assessment of PACE'?

One of the most influential accounts of PACE, police culture and law reform strategies derives from the extensive body of research associated with Mike McConville and Andrew Sanders, in particular the text they wrote with Roger Leng, *The Case for the Prosecution*.[130] This research is generally pessimistic about the possibility of using law reform to achieve substantive change in criminal justice practices. It centres policing practices – the police are depicted as 'the key actors' in a criminal justice system which has 'case construction'[131] at its core – and characterises current policing, both on the street and in the police station, as dominated by 'crime control values'. The dominance of crime control ideology in the criminal justice system is attributed to 'capitalism's requirement of a strong state'.[132] They also argue that '[p]olice working rules are derived from a crime control ideology intended to keep the lid on a society structured on race, class, power and

---

128 See Recommendations 65-69 in Royal Commission on Criminal Justice, *Report* (Cm. 2263, 1993), pp. 193-194.
129 For further details, see the references cited above n. 120 and n. 51.
130 M. McConville, A. Sanders and R. Leng, *The Case for the Prosecution: Police Suspects and the Construction of Criminality* (Routledge, 1991). See also, A. Sanders and R. Young, *Criminal Justice* (Butterworths, 2000), pp. 733-760.
131 They argue that cases are socially constructed: 'It must be emphasized that at each point of the criminal justice process "what happened" is the subject of interpretation, addition, subtraction, selection and reformulation. This process is a *continuous* process, so that the meaning and status of "a case" are to be understood in terms of the particular time and context in which it is viewed, a meaning and status that it may not have possessed earlier or continued to possess thereafter. The construction of a case . . . infuses every action and activity of official actors from the initial selection of the suspect to final case disposition. Case construction implicates the actors in a discourse with legal rules and guidelines and involves them in using rules, manipulating rules and interpreting rules. . . . Evidence is not something "discovered" or "unearthed", but is produced by all the parties (victims, witnesses, suspect, lawyers and police) involved in the investigation of the case.' (ibid., pp. 12, 36).
132 McConville et al., above n. 130, p. 182.

privilege':[133] '[m]ost people who are stopped, searched, arrested, detained, and interrogated are young working-class men, especially in ethnic minorities' and, because '"we" [do not] bear the brunt of these powers', there is little concerted challenge to current practices.[134] PACE safeguards for suspects (including requirements for custody officers, record-keeping, legal advisers and tape-recording) are described as 'at best, due process ornaments on a crime control edifice'.[135] The Act is dismissed as a largely legitimating and bureaucratic legal framework for the continuance of oppressive policing and prosecution practices (such as stop and search or obtaining guilty pleas while in police detention). Their conclusion on its overall impact is that 'like any other new law, [it] has changed practices, but largely by *shifting* the unwanted behaviour instead of eradicating or even reducing it'.[136]

The most prominent, alternative academic perspective on PACE, police culture and reform strategies is provided by the work of David Dixon.[137] Dixon relies on, and agrees with, many of the empirical findings on the operation of PACE used by McConville, Sanders and others; however, he sets out to develop a more nuanced, context-based account of the Act and police practices thereunder. Dixon warns against the lure of a universal theory of law and policing: arguing that 'theoretical essentialism and empirical overgeneralization'[138] are to be avoided, he aims to counter claims that there has been a unitary state response to the regulation of policing; that police and judicial cultures are fixed and monolithic; and that reform strategies in the criminal justice field will inevitably fail.

Dixon, like McConville and Sanders, places significant emphasis on police culture and policing practices. He argues, however, that the former is not static, monolithic or inevitably dominated by crime control ideology, and that the latter are neither uniform nor motivated by identical reasons. He also chooses to locate PACE within a broader trend towards modernisation and codification of law, and approaches it as a complex legislative package of police powers *and* suspects' rights. On this account, the contingency of PACE is emphasised: it has different meanings and effects for different constituencies in different contexts. Dixon also argues that in this area, as in others, rights discourse must be used strategically: '[a]ppropriate targets and methods of reform must be chosen, e.g. not expecting legal regulation to have much success in controlling stop and search, but using it tactically where supervision can be more effective'.[139] At the same time, however, he emphasises that law is only one amongst a range of factors affecting criminal justice practices, that legal regulation has limits, and that accounts of policing need to engage with other theoretical perspectives in the social sciences.

---

133 Sanders, above n. 50, p. 193. A variant of this 'policing the dross' theme emphasises social disciplinary, rather than crime control, ideology. In this version, the aims of policing are described as 'maintaining authority, extracting deference, reproducing social control and inflicting summary punishment': Choongh, above n. 45, p. 41.

134 Sanders, above n. 123, p. 1068.

135 Sanders and Young, above n. 9, p. 130.

136 Sanders, above n. 123, p. 1067.

137 See Dixon, above n. 11.

138 Dixon, above n. 109, p. 522.

139 Ibid., pp. 535-536.

Changing police culture and practices

There appears to be substantial evidence to support Dixon's arguments about law reform, the diversity of policing practices, and the existence of competing police cultures. For example, it has been shown that policing practices vary according to a range of factors, including particular policing function (stop and search powers may be used more for social order maintenance on the street than for any other purpose[140]); geographical variations between police regions and forces (for example, the policy shift to 'zero-tolerance' policing in certain forces[141]); differences between police ranks and specialised units, between 'street' police and 'management' police; and the individual attitudes of officers to the perpetrators and victims of crime (in responding, for example, to racial attacks or white-collar crime, and in public order policing).[142] Feminist scholarship on policing has clearly demonstrated how gender operates as a significant variable in relation to police treatment of women as victims (for example, of sexual assault) and as offenders (for example, political protestors or prostitutes).[143] It has also shown how policy changes can lead to shifts in traditional policing practices, as in the move to mandatory arrest in domestic violence contexts;[144] the arrest of male kerb-crawlers rather than street prostitutes in Leeds;[145] or the introduction of 'community policing' in 'gay areas' in major cities such as London and Manchester.[146] Institutional changes, such as the creation of the Northern Ireland Parades Commission, can also have a transformative effect on aspects of policing.

There is also evidence to support Dixon's argument that police culture has changed in significant ways post-PACE. There have, for example, been fewer allegations of police assault in custody (excluding the situation in Northern Ireland[147]), even though the number of deaths in custody has risen and investigatory/inquest procedures remain flawed.[148] Research also suggests that

---

140 See Hillyard and Gordon, above n. 12; Choongh, above n. 45; and M. Brogden, T. Jefferson and S. Walklate, *Introducing Policework* (Unwin Hyman, 1988) (re age, race, gender and class bias in policing).

141 See generally, D. Dixon, 'Broken Windows, Zero Tolerance and the New York Miracle' (1998) 10 Current Issues in Crim J 96; and B. Campbell, *Goliath: Britain's Dangerous Places* (Methuen, 1993).

142 See Bowling, above n. 101; and Ch. 2.

143 F. Heidensohn, 'Gender and Crime' in Maguire, Morgan and Reiner, above n. 12, pp. 769-772. For an account of Birmingham policing, see B. Gwinnett, 'Policing Prostitution: Gender, The State and Community Politics' in V. Randall and G. Waylen (eds.), *Gender, Politics and the State* (Routledge, 1998), pp. 80-99. Cf. J. Phoenix, *Making Sense of Prostitution* (Macmillan, 1999) (police as a source of protection for some prostitutes).

144 See generally, C. Hoyle and A. Sanders, 'Police Response to Domestic Violence: From Victim Choice to Victim Empowerment' (2000) 40 BJ Crim 14.

145 The aim of the pilot Kerb Crawler Re-Education Scheme in West Yorkshire was to target male kerb crawling behaviour and reduce re-offending rates: see *The Guardian*, 17 Aug. 1999, p. 6.

146 See generally, A. Cherney, 'Gay and Lesbian Issues in Policing' (1999) 11 Current Issues in Crim J 35.

147 For a discussion of police abuse of suspects in Northern Ireland Holding Centres, see Ch. 3.

148 The total number of deaths in police custody in England and Wales between Apr. 1998 and Mar. 1999 was 67, of which a disproportionately high number (18%) were from ethnic minority groups. A Home Office study of 277 deaths between 1990-96 concluded that the majority of deaths resulted from self-harm, substance abuse and medical conditions; only 6% of these deaths may have been caused by police restraint: see *Deaths in Police Custody Statistics* (Home Office, 1999); and A. Leigh, G. Johnson and A. Ingram, *Deaths in Police Custody: Learning the Lessons* (Police Research Series Paper 26, 1998). Cf. R.W. Harding, 'Prisons are the Problem: A Re-Examination of Aboriginal and Non-Aboriginal Deaths in Custody' (1999) 32 ANZ J Crim 108.

some police officers perceive a 'professionalisation' of their roles post-PACE, that the environments of police stations have become more open to 'outsiders', including legal advisers and researchers, and that investigative methods have changed from the previously common practices of 'arresting on hunches' and fabricated confessions.[149] Rose's study of the London Metropolitan Police reinforces the idea of a decline in 'traditional' cop culture. He found contrasting examples of coercive, 'thin blue line' street policing alongside an awareness of the long-term futility of police confrontation with the local populace. He also found acceptance, and sometimes, approval of the new PACE regime, as well as an ability to work within its constraints. Other notable changes included the presence of better-educated, higher-paid officers with liberal political views who rejected the old masculinist 'canteen' culture,[150] a new generation of progressive, management-oriented senior police officers,[151] and an increase in the number of female, and (openly) lesbian and gay, police officers.[152]

Apart from such observational studies, television drama offers further evidence of the dynamic nature of police culture and of the impact of PACE. Police dramas reflect a significant shift in occupational culture – from the 1970s-style of *The Sweeney* to contemporary episodes of *The Bill* – while also acknowledging the continued existence of less savoury police cultures in *Between the Lines*, *Prime Suspect* and *Cops*. One police officer in Rose's study commented on the 'unreality' of US police drama in comparison with his own PACE-dominated working culture:

> One day I was watching the American TV series *NYPD Blue* with some police friends. They showed an interview where the cops threatened to beat up the suspect. And we all agreed, 'Couldn't we get some amazing results if we could do that here'. Because with a tape running, even if you wanted to, you can't.[153]

It has also been argued that police dramas such as *Prime Suspect* may play a valuable reforming role: the 'hegemonic masculinity' of canteen culture 'can be recognised as ultimately destructive not only of the moral well-being of men and women within the police but also of the processes of justice and accountability that should characterise the work of a police force within a

---

149 See generally, C. Walker, 'The Agenda of Miscarriages of Justice' in Walker and Starmer, above n. 5, pp. 3-30, at pp. 5-8; Dixon, above n. 33, pp. 156-169; T. Newton, 'The Place of Ethics in Investigative Interviewing by Police Officers' (1998) 37 Howard J 52; M. Innes, '"Professionalizing" the Role of the Police Informant: The British Experience' (2000) 9 Policing and Society 357; and M. Maguire, 'Policing by Risks and Targets: Some Dimensions and Implications of Intelligence-Led Crime Control' (2000) 9 Policing and Society 315.

150 For an argument that what occurs in the police canteen gives 'purpose and meaning to inherently problematic occupational experience', see P.A.J. Waddington, 'Police (Canteen) Sub-culture: An Appreciation' (1999) 39 BJ Crim 287.

151 See account provided by D. Rose, *In the Name of the Law: The Collapse of Criminal Justice* (Vintage, 1996); and R. Reiner, *The Politics of the Police* (OUP, 2000).

152 Discrimination and widespread harassment, however, continue to affect women officers' working conditions and careers: for discussion and references, see Heidensohn, above n. 143, pp. 769-772; and J.M. Brown, 'Aspects of Discriminatory Treatment of Women Police Officers Serving in Forces in England and Wales' (1998) 38 BJ Crim 265. See also, M. Burke, 'Homosexuality as Deviance: The Case of the Gay Police Officer' (1994) 34 BJ Crim 192.

153 Rose, above n. 151, p. 123.

democracy'.[154] Equally, however, contemporary police dramas illustrate how changes in police culture may also serve to mask discriminatory working practices – such as the incompetent and racist policing uncovered by the Stephen Lawrence Inquiry[155] – or make campaigns for increased police powers by intelligent, media-savvy Chief Constables appear more reasonable.

Such contradictions, however, prove the general thesis that police culture is rarely monolithic or static, and that a 'crime control' mentality does not necessarily determine all policing practices. In the context of police racism, Chan has argued that there is a need to re-examine the traditional meaning of police culture – 'a convenient label for a range of negative values, attitudes, and practice norms among police officers' – in order to better explain how and why reformist policies, rules and attitudes do succeed in certain arenas but are obstructed, or circumvented, in other arenas. She suggests a 'new framework for understanding police culture . . . which recognizes the interpretive and creative aspects of culture, allows for the existence of multiple cultures, and takes into account the political context and cognitive structures of police work.'[156] Thus, stock debates about whether changing the rules regulating police actions (such as PACE) or changing the police culture (such as promoting 'due process' values, 'professionalism' or anti-racism awareness) is the prime prerequisite for reform are inadequate. What is needed, instead, is a more theoretically sophisticated account of the relationships between the structural conditions of policing, police culture and police practice. The conclusion of her study of the New South Wales police force, and its efforts to counteract police racism, would appear to have obvious wider implications for UK debates on the effects of PACE, the HRA and institutional police reforms:

> [C]hanging police culture requires change not only in the cultural assumptions held by police officers but also in the political and organisational conditions of police work. In terms of improving police-minorities relations, this implies that strategies such as cross-cultural awareness training and community-based policing are ineffective on their own. They must be accompanied by appropriate structures of police accountability and legal regulation, as well as social reforms. However, change is difficult to achieve: it is traumatic and is therefore strongly resisted. Sustainable change can only be achieved through a combination of external pressure, organisational leadership and political commitment.[157]

Such a conclusion clearly leaves a role for law, legal institutions and civil liberties activism as tools for reforming policing (as, we have argued above, the evidence of the post-PACE era demonstrates). However, it also highlights that other factors

---

154 M. Eaton, 'A Fair Cop? Viewing the Effects of the Canteen Culture in *Prime Suspect* and *Between the Lines*' in D. Kidd-Hewitt and R. Osborne (eds.), *Crime and the Media: The Post-Modern Spectacle* (Pluto, 1995), p. 182. See generally, T. Newburn and E. Stanko (eds.), *Just Boys Doing Business: Men, Masculinities and Crime* (Routledge, 1994); and R. Collier, *Masculinities, Crime and Criminology* (Sage, 1998).

155 See W. Macpherson, *The Stephen Lawrence Inquiry* (Cm. 4262-I, 1999); and *Home Secretary's Action Plan: Second Annual Report on Progress* (2001) (www.homeoffice.gov.uk). For criticism of Macpherson's recommendations and the Labour government's commitment to 'anti-racism', see L. Bridges, 'The Lawrence Inquiry – Incompetence, Corruption, and Institutional Racism' (1999) 26 JLS 298. See also, Race Relations (Amendment) Act 2000 (police forces now subject to the Race Relations Act 1976).

156 J. Chan, 'Changing Police Culture' (1996) 36 BJ Crim 109, 110.

157 J. Chan, *Changing Police Culture: Policing in a Multicultural Society* (Cambridge UP, 1997), pp. 13-14. See M. Marks, 'Transforming Police Organisations From Within' (2000) 40 BJ Crim 557.

(particularly social and economic divisions, racism, media discourses, government policy, organisational autonomy, resourcing, operational officers' discretionary powers, etc) are equally/more important, and may not be susceptible to, or influenced by, legal regulation or human rights discourse.[158]

As the work of Dixon and Chan indicates, the challenge is 'to identify the limits and possibilities of change, and the potential for legal regulation to facilitate, encourage, and contribute to such change'.[159]

Towards an account of the right to legal advice in context

This section returns to our analysis of section 58 of PACE and the right to legal advice more generally. It isolates five ideas drawn from the work of McConville, Sanders, and Dixon in order to suggest how a more fully contextual account of the right to legal advice might be achieved.[160] More generally, of course, the aim of this case study is to encourage fresh critique of the entire package of 'fair trial' rights.

The first point to note is that scholarship like *The Case for the Prosecution* and *Law in Policing* suggests the need for civil liberties law and lawyers to refocus attention away from positivist accounts of PACE (and other legislation or case law) towards analysis of police powers as they actually operate within the criminal justice process. The empirical findings on section 58's guarantee of a right to legal advice cited earlier highlight how formal legal rights can be deprived of substantive effect. By acknowledging the importance of police culture to the impact of new legal rules, the civil liberties lawyer may avoid the temptation to equate 'rights-based' law reform (whether imposed by statute or case law) with progressive social change. This may be a particularly crucial insight given the temptation for predicting the far-reaching impact of the HRA in the criminal justice field, and the assumption that legal 'victories' in court automatically affect established practices and attitudes.

A second useful insight is provided by McConville et al. and others' emphasis on prosecution cases as socially constructed; that is, on criminal justice as a *process* not a system, and the impact of individual choices – to arrest, interview, release, charge, prosecute or dispose – on each and every case. 'Evidence is not something "discovered" or "unearthed", but is produced by all the parties (victims, witnesses, suspect, lawyers and police) involved in the investigation of the case.'[161] This reminds us that there is nothing inevitable about law enforcement; it is 'complicated social processes which transmute articulated criminal proscriptions into criminal justice enforcement'.[162] And importantly, it suggests that gaining access to legal advice when in custody may merely introduce another (albeit, sometimes vitally important) legal actor and narrative to the process of case construction; this factor alone is unlikely to determine the eventual outcome of a complex negotiated process. Knowledge of the *negotiated* processes of criminal justice also reveals the continued construction of defence solicitors as inevitably adversarial as an unhelpful caricature.

---

158 See generally, M. Brogden and C. Shearing, *Policing for a New South Africa* (Routledge, 1993); and the Patten Report, *A New Beginning: Policing in Northern Ireland* (1999) (www.belfast.org.uk).
159 Dixon, above n. 11, p. 317 (reference omitted).
160 For a fuller analysis of legal advisers, see Dixon, above n. 11, pp. 236-266.
161 Above n. 126, p. 36.
162 Lacey, above n. 8, p. 6.

Thirdly, claims to the effect that the police use 'ploys' to discourage suspects from exercising their right to legal advice under PACE are rendered problematic by the increasing recognition of diversity and variation in police practices and cultures. It is certainly true that 'ploys' are used,[163] but there is also evidence that police attitudes 'seem to be at least as much about routinization and the performance of familiar tasks without appreciating the suspect's dilemma, as of deliberate discouragement'.[164] Legal advisers may also see their role as routine and 'developing a reasonably comfortable, unstressful relationship with officers may be, at the level of everyday social interaction, as important as the . . . adviser's formal duties'.[165] Furthermore, 'custody officers are accurate when they warn suspects that a legal adviser is unlikely to be of much service in what are perceived to be trivial or straightforward cases'.[166] As Sanders points out, many suspects 'against whom there would often be plenty of evidence anyway' will confess guilt 'simply and speedily', or agree to '"deals" (confessions in exchange for favours or reduced charges)'.[167] The presence of a legal adviser may, in fact, be encouraged and welcomed by police if (as usually happens) the advice is to co-operate with the investigation.[168] These insights need to be added to the range of other factors listed above if the civil liberties lawyer is to achieve an understanding of how and why the right to legal advice is exercised.

Fourthly, research on the right to legal advice confirms broader critiques of rights discourse within capitalist societies, and foregrounds the importance of a civil liberties' focus on the funding and training of defence solicitors.[169] Economic power clearly affects the quality of legal advice in a police station: the middle-class suspect may have his or her own solicitor, but the more typical suspect, who has to avail of the public scheme, may be less well-served. Research suggests that financial considerations are the main concern of solicitors' firms; that is, they prioritise the 'efficient management and processing of . . . clients through the "machinery of justice" [rather] than . . . the delivery of justice itself'.[170] This fact received judicial recognition as far back as 1989 when Mann LJ accepted that 'there is an economic necessity to employ persons who will have no professional qualifications to attend at the interview of suspects'.[171] A controversial Criminal Defence Service has now been introduced, and a civil liberties perspective must remain alert to the difference that economic status and pressures will make to the day-to-day substance of formal legal rights.

Fifthly, public law scholarship on the judicial role in protecting human rights needs to be expand to include accounts of the judicial record in criminal law

163 See Choongh, above n. 45, pp. 148-165.
164 Dixon, above n. 109, pp. 524-525.
165 Dixon, above n. 11, p. 237.
166 Dixon, above n. 109, p. 525.
167 Sanders, above n. 123, p. 1063. In a 1993 study conducted for the Runciman Commission, it was found that 60% of a sample interviewed by the police made admissions and that there was already supporting evidence of guilt against 87% of those who confessed: see Royal Commission Research Study No. 13 (HMSO, 1993).
168 We discuss below the obvious relationship between the legal adviser's role and the restriction of the 'right to silence' debate. See generally, J.D. Jackson, 'Interpreting the Silence Provisions' [1995] Crim LR 587; K. Starmer and M. Woolf, 'The Right to Silence' in Walker and Starmer, above n. 5, pp. 100-118; and T. Bucke et al, *The Right of Silence* (Home Office, 2000).
169 See L. Bridges, 'The Royal Commission's Approach to Criminal Defence Services – A Case of Professional Incompetence' in McConville and Bridges, above n. 37, pp. 273-286.
170 M. McConville, et al, above n. 126, p. 295.
171 *R v Chief Constable of Avon and Somerset Constabulary, ex p Robinson* [1989] 2 All ER 15, 16.

cases. Equally, criminal law and criminal justice literature on this topic would benefit from closer engagement with critiques of human rights approaches.[172] Interpretation of PACE and its Codes provides judges with a clear opportunity to instil fair trial values and a discourse of rights into the criminal justice process; litigation under the Convention right to a fair trial should enhance this opportunity. Historically, however, the UK courts have not viewed their general role in terms of disciplining the police for wrongdoing, excluding evidence obtained illegally or unfairly, or developing a discourse of suspects' rights.[173] Indeed, judicial willingness to condone or overlook police illegality and brutality, and extend police powers, was a common feature of the pre-PACE era.[174] In recent years, particularly in the aftermath of the infamous miscarriages of justice cases, judicial attitudes have shifted somewhat – but not so much as to alter the pattern of accepting all 'relevant' evidence, downplaying police wrongdoing and emphasising the greater public interest in convicting suspects charged with serious offences.[175]

The power to exclude *confession* evidence under section 78 of PACE[176] has generated a body of case law which suggests that judges may, in certain contexts, be as concerned with punishing police disregard of PACE rules as with protecting the right to a fair trial for the accused.[177] While breaches of PACE and its Codes do not automatically mean that evidence will be rejected, improper denial of access to legal advice has been viewed as potentially serious and likely to adversely affect the fairness of proceedings. For example, the power to delay access to legal advice has been restrictively interpreted;[178] the police cannot avoid informing the detainee that a solicitor has arrived;[179] and police claims to suspects that 'we usually interview without a solicitor' have been declared impermissible.[180] The case law, however, does not point in one direction alone: where section 58 and Code C have been breached, the courts have clearly undermined fair trial values by accepting arguments that the presence of a solicitor would not have altered the conduct of the interview because the suspect was aware of, or waived, their rights[181] – the 'experienced criminal' proviso.

The courts have sometimes commented specifically on the actual role of the legal adviser.[182] The condemnation by the Court of Appeal of the passivity of

---

172 See Ashworth, above n. 10.
173 See *R v Sang* [1980] AC 402 (no discretion to exclude non-confession evidence on the ground that obtained improperly or unfairly); Mirfield, above n. 82; and Choongh, above n. 45, pp. 18-19.
174 *Dallison v Caffery* [1964] 2 All ER 610; and *Holgate-Mohammed v Duke* [1984] 1 All ER 1054.
175 See generally, K. Grevling, 'Fairness and the Exclusion of Evidence Under Section 78(1) of the Police and Criminal Evidence Act' (1997) 113 LQR 667.
176 But see A. Choo and S. Nash, 'What's the matter with Section 78?' [1999] Crim LR 929 (on continuing refusal of Court of Appeal to exclude other categories of 'improperly obtained but reliable' evidence).
177 See eg, *R v Canale* [1990] 2 All ER 187 (re the police's 'cynical disregard' of PACE rules on recording of interviews); *R v Weerdesteyn* [1995] 1 Cr App Rep 405 (re failure to observe PACE interview procedures); and *R v Ridley* (CA, 17 Dec. 1999).
178 *R v Samuel* [1988] 2 All ER 135. Cf. *R v Chief Constable of Avon, ex p Robinson* [1989] 2 All ER 15; and *R v Chief Constable of Northumbria, ex p Thompson*, The Times 20 Mar. 2001 (CA).
179 *R v Franklin* (CA), The Times, 16 Jun. 1994.
180 *R v Beycan* [1990] Crim LR 185.
181 *R v Alladice* (1988) 87 Cr App Rep 380; *R v Dunford* (1990) 91 Cr App Rep 150; *R v Oliphant* [1992] Crim LR 40; and *R v Anderson* [1993] Crim LR 447.
182 A significant consequence of PACE has been the availability of tape recordings of interviews, thus providing an insight into the behaviour of legal advisers during police questioning.

the solicitor in the *Cardiff Three* case – 'a travesty of an interview'[183] where one of the defendants denied involvement over 300 times – is a benchmark decision on the minimum duty of a legal adviser.[184] However, while judges may now recognise the oppressive and unreliable nature of interrogation *ex post facto*, they have shown no interest in contributing to the regulatory framework for the conduct of interviews; 'principles or detailed guidance to the police about what is expected of them'[185] remain absent from judicial discourse. Likewise, the function of the legal adviser still needs to be addressed in detail; the key question remains, 'what should defence lawyers do at police stations?'[186] Somewhat paradoxically, this issue has moved centre stage because of the effects of the restriction on the 'right to silence' in section 34 of the Criminal Justice and Public Order Act 1994. First introduced in Northern Ireland (in 1988) to combat the 'silent terrorist', and extended in 1994 to cope with the 'professional criminal' (and, arguably, because of police concern about assertive legal advisers) – despite the absence of evidence supporting such claims[187] – the courts have been forced to consider the implications of solicitors advising their clients to remain silent in custody (often for reasons, such as vulnerability and ignorance, which have little to do with the stereotypes of 'hardened' criminals).[188] Birch, in a review of the case law, has argued that section 34 should be repealed on the grounds of the complexity of the law, frequency of appeals, its relative evidential irrelevance and its questionable compatibility with Article 6 of the ECHR.[189] Its impact on the legal adviser in certain contexts is also a central cause for concern. Not only are most lawyers 'nowadays . . . aware that even private consultations at a police station may be bugged', but the solicitor has been:

> placed in a position of participant in the investigative process, and while it was, of course, always the case that the solicitor was a potential witness in the comparatively rare cases of misconduct by the police, he [sic] is now accountable for normal advice given in a routine case which may be explored in detail by strenuous cross-examination.[190]

As long as the 'right to silence' remains a key site of legal and political debate (and future litigation under Article 6), the purpose and role of the legal adviser will remain in the spotlight.

---

183 (1992) 97 Cr App Rep 99, 104. Cf. *R v Heaton* [1993] Crim LR 593 (no evidence in tape-recording of police bullying or hostility); and *Re M* [1999] 2 FLR 92 (re interviewing techniques in context of child sexual abuse allegations).

184 Choongh, above n. 45, p. 180, claims that 'tape-recordings are hardly ever used by defence lawyers, who rely almost exclusively on summaries prepared by the police which frequently omit details which would be of assistance to the defence'.

185 Dixon, above n. 11, p. 174. See also, J. Baldwin, 'Police Interview Techniques' (1993) 33 BJ Crim 325.

186 See E. Cape, 'Defence Services: What Should Defence Lawyers Do at Police Stations' in McConville and Bridges, above n. 37, pp. 186-199; and his 'Sidelining Defence Lawyers: Police Station Advice after *Condron*' (1997) 1 IJE&P 386.

187 See J. D. Jackson, 'Interpreting the Silence Provisions: The Northern Ireland Cases' [1995] Crim LR 587; and R. Munday, 'Inferences from Silence and European Human Rights Law' [1996] Crim LR 370. See also, s. 58 Youth Justice and Criminal Evidence Act 1999.

188 Dixon, above n. 11, pp. 258-266. See *R v Condron* [1997] 1 WLR 827 (re drawing inferences from 'no comment' interviews on legal advice); and *R v Argent* [1997] 2 Cr App Rep 27, 35 ('jury is not concerned with the correctness of the solicitor's advice . . . but with the reasonableness of the appellant's conduct'). The ECtHR in *Condron v UK* (2001) 31 EHRR 1 found a violation of Art. 6 because insufficient weight given to legal advice.

189 D. Birch, 'Suffering in Silence: A Cost-Benefit Analysis of Section 34 of the Criminal Justice and Public Order Act 1994' [1999] Crim LR 769.

190 D. Wright, 'The Solicitor in the Witness Box' [1998] Crim LR 44, 44, 47.

Finally, a focus on the position of defence lawyers in anti-terrorism contexts in Northern Ireland provides useful insights into the power relationship between police and legal advisers/suspects, an overly politicised context where suspects may adopt a tactic of silence, and the positive influence of international human rights discourse.[191] A person arrested or detained under anti-terrorism provisions in Northern Ireland was not covered by the equivalent to section 58 of PACE but had a right to consult privately with a solicitor.[192] In practice, access to a lawyer was often delayed on the alleged ground that the investigation would be prejudiced, and consultations could take place within the sight and hearing of a police officer. With regard to the presence of a solicitor during interviews, there was no express law or rule prohibiting it but a series of legal challenges demonstrated a firm judicial unwillingness to provide such a safeguard. The Northern Irish courts justified their stance by invoking Parliament's intention that legal advice should not be available in interview settings. The House of Lords, in *R v Chief Constable of the RUC, ex p Begley*, also firmly ruled that no relevant law – including Article 6 of the ECHR – afforded a right for terrorist detainees to have access to a solicitor in police interviews, and refused to consider extending the common law to provide such a right.[193] Despite the history of human rights abuses of detainees in police detention,[194] it was not until the European Court of Human Rights decision in *Murray (John) v UK* that a guaranteed right to legal advice (prior to any drawing of adverse inferences from silence in interviews) was eventually established.[195]

III.   THE TRIAL STAGE: RAPE AND THE CRIMINAL PROCESS

In this second case study, we shift attention to the trial stage. We aim to highlight how two key principles underpinning the right to a fair trial (disclosure and cross-examination) operate in practice and problematise assumptions about what constitutes 'fairness' or 'equality of arms' in the adversarial process. The case study focuses on one particular type of prosecution, the rape case. We have chosen this example because rape cases are both special and typical. Rape cases are special because they present a challenge to several standard accounts of policing and prosecution practices, as well as to assumptions about core 'fair trial' rights and typical outcomes within the criminal justice process. The

---

191 See Lawyers Committee for Human Rights, *Human Rights and Legal Defense in Northern Ireland* (New York, 1993); Human Rights Watch, *To Serve Without Favor: Policing, Human Rights and Accountability in Northern Ireland* (New York, 1997); and Ch. 3.

192 See Police and Criminal Evidence (NI) Order 1989, Art. 59 and Code C (re right to consult and have solicitor in interview); and EPA 1996, s. 47 (re right to only consult solicitor).

193 [1997] 4 All ER 833. Lord Browne-Wilkinson further justified his position by quoting from an official review of the EPA 1991: 'to allow solicitors to be present at interviews would be contradictory. Putting it another way, the regime of the holding centres contemplates that kind of [lengthy and persistent] questioning; but solicitors, quite legitimately, by advising their clients not to answer, would impair that regime'. In *Paton v Procurator Fiscal (Alloa)* (24 Nov. 1999), a non-terrorist case, the appellate High Court of Justiciary held that neither Scots law nor the Convention required that in all cases a detained person should be afforded the opportunity to have a solicitor present during a police interview.

194 See eg, C. Walker and B. Fitzpatrick, 'Holding Centres in Northern Ireland: the Independent Commissioner and the Rights of Detainees' [1999] EHRLR 27.

195 (1996) 22 EHRR 29. See Criminal Evidence (NI) Order 1999, s. 58; and TA 2000, s. 109 (re right to consult a solicitor prior to formal questioning). See also *Averill v UK* [2000] Crim LR 682.

defining characteristics of rape prosecutions – trial in the Crown Court, denial of criminal responsibility, and a defence strategy which suggests that no offence ever occurred as the complainant consented to sexual intercourse – are very different from the overwhelming majority of police investigations that proceed to prosecution: the latter, unlike the former, tend to result in guilty pleas, with over 90% of defendants in magistrates' courts and over 70% in the Crown Court pleading guilty. Accounts of policing which emphasise the dominance of a 'crime control' ethos, and the routine inevitability of conviction, also seem crude in the context of rape allegations. The conviction rate for rape fell from 24% in 1985 to 9% in 1996; that is, over 90% of defendants will be acquitted.[196] There is also evidence that police culture is particularly variable when dealing with rape, that hierarchial divisions exist between (female) chaperon officers and (male) detectives, and that the individual attitudes of police and doctors to issues of 'appropriate' gender behaviour differ markedly.[197]

Equally, however, rape cases can be said to be typical of other criminal prosecutions. For example, many of the 'problems' of the rape trial are simply an illustration of how criminal cases as a whole 'remain trapped in a body of rules which at times seem more apt to a game of snakes and ladders than to a system of justice', with the result that the adversarial process 'can obstruct rather than promote justice'.[198] Rape prosecutions also spotlight two of the most prominent of contemporary criminal justice narratives. The first of these narratives concerns 'victims' of crime and women's rights within the criminal justice system; the second emphasises the need to enhance the 'fair trial' rights of defendants in criminal cases. The first narrative is the outcome of an uneasy conjunction of interests between the agendas of government, victim-support groups and long-term feminist campaigns around the rape trial and violence against women. To date, it has generated multiple reform proposals, ranging from the officially approved emphasis on vulnerable witnesses (as evidenced in the 1998 Home Office report, *Speaking Up For Justice*, and the restrictions on cross-examination on previous sexual history introduced by the Youth Justice and Criminal Evidence Act 1999) to feminist recommendations for changing the criminal law[199] and improving police, CPS and forensic medical practices and attitudes in rape cases.

This first narrative also has increasing resonance on the international plane (amidst recognition of gender violence as a human rights issue[200]) and in

---

196 J. Harris and S. Grace, *A Question of Evidence? – Investigating and Prosecuting Rape in the 1990s* (Home Office Research Study No. 196, 1999), p. 153.

197 See eg, J. Temkin, 'Medical Evidence in Rape Cases: A Continuing Problem for Criminal Justice' (1998) 61 MLR 821; 'Reporting Rape in London: A Qualitative Study' (1999) 38 Howard J 17; and K. Cook, 'When is Rape a Real Crime?' 149 NLJ 1856 (10 Dec. 1999).

198 S. Sedley, 'How Laws Discriminate' *LRB*, 29 Apr. 1999, p. 27. See generally, J. Hunter and K. Cronin, *Evidence, Advocacy and Ethical Practice: A Criminal Trial Commentary* (Butterworths, 1995).

199 See eg, Lacey, above n. 93, pp. 98-124. See also, N. Lacey, 'Beset by Boundaries: The Home Office Review of Sex Offences' [2001] Crim LR 3.

200 *Aydin v Turkey* (1997) 25 EHRR 251 (rape and ill-treatment in police custody constitute torture under Art. 3, ECHR). See generally, S. Palmer, 'Rape in Marriage and the European Convention on Human Rights' (1997) 5 FLS 91; and D. Buss, 'Women at the Borders: Rape and Nationalism in International Law' (1998) 6 FLS 171; and her, 'Robes, Relics and Rights: The Vatican and the Beijing Conference on Women' (1998) 7 SLS 339. The Hague War Crimes Tribunal in Mar. 2000 commenced its first prosecutions for gender-related violence against women and girls during the conflict in the former Yugoslavia.

national constitutional courts. In early 1999,[201] for example, the (then) two women justices on the Canadian Supreme Court – L'Heureux-Dubé and McLachlin JJ – criticised an appeal court judge for relying on a defence of 'implied consent' in directing an acquittal in a sexual assault case, and for commenting that the 17-year-old female complainant did not 'enter [the accused's] trailer in a bonnet and crinolines'. Both justices also outlined a proactive role for judges in ridding legal culture of gender stereotyping:

> It is part of the role of this Court to denounce this kind of language, unfortunately still used today, which not only perpetuates archaic myths and stereotypes about the nature of sexual assaults but also ignores the law.[202] [. . .] [S]tereotypical assumptions find their roots in many cultures, including our own. They no longer, however, find a place in Canadian law.[203]

The HRA may strengthen the hold of this narrative of 'victims' of crime and women's rights within the criminal justice system. Yet, it is not clear that this would be an unambiguously positive outcome: as noted above, although the narrative has feminist resonance, it represents an uneasy conjunction of different interests and there is a substantial risk that the rising potency of contemporary, victim-oriented discourses might overwhelm other discourses of women's rights,[204] thereby intensifying the current appropriation of feminist ideas in furtherance of punitive, 'tough on crime' agendas.[205] What is clear, however, is that there can be no guarantee that this narrative – in any of its manifestations – will prevail in the post-HRA era. The doubt arises because a second narrative, more deeply entrenched than the first, will also compete for dominance in the coming years.

The second narrative is associated with the now commonplace prediction that arguments about the Convention right to a fair trial will be the 'most frequently invoked in our domestic courts when the Human Rights Act 1998 comes into force'.[206] It brings together an alliance of criminal law, evidence and criminal justice commentators who welcome the opportunity to re-orientate traditional legal doctrines – and, more broadly, the criminal justice process –

---

201   *R v Ewanchuk* [1999] 1 SCR 330. Canadian Supreme Court decisions are available at www.droit.umontreal.ca/doc/csc-scc/en/index.html.

202   Per L'Heureux-Dubé J, para. 95.

203   Per McLachlin J, para. 103. See similarly, *R v A* [2001] UKHL 25, [2001] 3 All ER 1, para. 124.

204   For concern about a similar phenomenon in the context of abortion, see T. Murphy, 'Health Confidentiality in the Age of Talk' in S. Sheldon and M. Thomson (eds.), *Feminist Perspectives on Health Care Law* (Cavendish, 1998), pp. 155-172, at p. 164.

205   J. Young, *The Exclusive Society: Social Exclusion, Crime and Difference in Late Modernity* (Sage, 1999) expresses similar concerns about the government appropriation of feminist ideas about 'zero tolerance' of domestic violence for populist 'law and order' initiatives, noting how '[t]he feminization of demands on law and order is a key factor in the transformation of public discourse' (pp. 136-140). See also, C. Smart, 'Law's Power, the Sexed Body, and Feminist Discourse' (1990) 70 JLS 194 (highlighting how the dominant 'victim-oriented conceptualization' of women in law reform proposals excludes other accounts, while also perpetuating the sexualisation of women's bodies within the rape trial process); D. Martin, 'Retribution Revisited: A Reconsideration of Feminist Criminal Law Reform Strategies' (1998) 36 Osg Hall LJ 151 (expressing concern about feminist involvement in 'the emergence of a rights-bearing and influential "victim"' within the criminal justice system); and K. Roach, *Due Process and Victims' Rights: The New Law and Politics of Criminal Justice* (Toronto UP, 1999) (identifying the 'criminalization of politics' in Canada).

206   Ashworth, above n. 66, p. 261. See also, A. Ashworth [2000] Crim LR 564.

on a foundation of substantive human rights.[207] In their accounts, the HRA is generally represented as a necessary corrective to the perceived domestic drift away from the historic 'fundamental principle'[208] of the criminal justice system: the duty to ensure a fair trial for the accused. To this end, the 'fair trial' narrative invokes the principles underpinning Article 6 of the ECHR, and the Strasbourg case law, in order to highlight how the rules of procedural fairness surrounding the criminal prosecution and trial should be strengthened in the post-HRA era. Moreover, while aware that the Act will not 'provide a panacea for all due process ills',[209] and that 'crime control philosophies may trump defendants' rights',[210] this narrative also urges an enhanced role for the UK judiciary in protecting the rights of suspects/defendants.

Advocating increased judicial intervention in the criminal trial – on the basis that it will augment 'fairness' – promises an uncertain future for rape prosecutions. The judicial record in sexual offences cases is highly controversial. It has long been argued that, in rape cases, traditional due process safeguards such as disclosure of 'relevant' evidence to defence lawyers and cross-examination of witnesses in court have operated, not to vindicate the innocence of the male accused, but to undermine and degrade the female complainant. Rights culture may intensify rather than ameliorate this phenomenon;[211] indeed, in the following sections, we shall highlight a series of Canadian Supreme Court decisions in sexual assault cases wherein the right to fair trial under the 1982 Canadian Charter of Rights has received controversial 'pro-defendant' interpretations. The Supreme Court's interpretation of 'fairness' (a) permitted the continuing use of the defence tactic of cross-examination on previous sexual history, and (b) was instrumental in legitimising a new legal strategy of seeking disclosure of the records of sexual-assault counselling centres in both civil and criminal proceedings. In addition, the Canadian courts' general concern with protecting the rights of defendants undercut statutory law reforms which were enacted, after successful feminist lobbying of the legislature, in reaction to judicial and defence lawyer tactics in sexual assault cases. However, in an apparent change of direction in 1999 the Supreme Court in *R v Mills* upheld the constitutionality of new legislation designed to restrict the disclosure of private records of complainants and acknowledged the importance of women's privacy and equality rights.[212] More recently, in *Darrach* the Court upheld (revised) statutory provisions limiting the scope of cross-examination on a complainant's sexual history.[213] The practical benefits of these judgments have, however, yet to be demonstrated at the lower level.

207 See eg, Cheney et al., above n. 66; and Walker and Starmer, above n. 5.
208 *R v Sang* [1979] 2 All ER 1222, 1248 (per Lord Scarman).
209 S.D. Sharpe, 'Article 6 and the Disclosure of Evidence in Criminal Trials' [1999] Crim LR 273, 277.
210 Sharpe, above n. 67, p. 849.
211 Note, however, the supportive comments of Lord Hoffmann in favour of an ongoing limitation on freedom of the press in the context of anonymity of rape complainants (above n. 83, p. 165).
212 [1999] 3 SCR 668. For background, see J. van Dieen, '*O'Connor* and Bill C-46: Differences in Approach' (1997) 23 Queen's LJ 1; and Gotell, below n. 253.
213 *R v Darrach* [2000] 2 SCR 443. See S.M. Chapman, 'Section 276 of the Criminal Code and the Admissibility of "Sexual Activity" Evidence' (1999) 25 Queen's LJ 121.

Rights culture, however, can also be beneficial. At the international level, the recognition of gender violence as a human rights issue, and the dramatic growth in rights consciousness and litigation strategies in many individual jurisdictions, suggest that myriad positive effects at institutional (legislative, judicial, police and prosecutorial) and local (rape crisis centre, social movement and individual) levels are possible. This indicates that human rights discourse could be used in the UK to challenge and redefine certain behaviour (as has been done, for example, in relation to the campaigns against domestic violence[214] and marital rape[215]), as well as providing a resource for mobilisation of different constituencies.[216]

Disclosure of evidence to the defence in rape cases

In this section, we focus on what is generally agreed to be a crucial stage in the prosecution process: the disclosure of evidence to defence lawyers in order to allow the accused to prepare for trial. We highlight the crucial importance of the right to disclosure, both in general 'fair trial' terms and more particularly in light of the history of miscarriages of justice in the UK. We also document the routine disclosure of doctors' notes prepared during forensic medical examination of women reporting sexual assault. Finally, we draw attention to some decisions of the Canadian Supreme Court wherein the accused's right to a fair trial was interpreted to permit court-sanctioned access to third-party, 'private' records held by rape counselling centres and other welfare agencies; the legislative response of the Canadian Parliament aimed at restricting this practice and protecting women's privacy and equality rights; and the subsequent decision in *R v Mills* accepting the constitutionality of this legislation. Important lessons for the UK are provided by this history of competing human rights discourses.

The disclosure principle

It is well-recognised that a 'fair trial' is impossible if a defendant is unaware of the charges against him or her, is unable to prepare a defence, or is prevented from presenting their case fully in court. To this end, Article 6 of the ECHR has been interpreted to ensure 'equality of arms' between state authorities and the accused in criminal proceedings; '[a] fair hearing requires that the prosecution disclose to the defence "all material evidence for or against the accused"'.[217] For the defence lawyer, the right of access to any material that undermines the prosecution case is fundamental to the meaning of 'fair trial'. The disclosure principle is a recognition of the power imbalance between state

---

214 See eg, D. Thomas and M. Beaseley, 'Domestic Violence as a Human Rights Issue' (1993) 15 HRQ 36.

215 See *CR v UK* (1995) 21 EHRR 363 (ECtHR rejected challenge to marital rape conviction on ground of retroactive law-making). For a commentary on this case, see Palmer, above n. 200.

216 See Buss, above n. 200; J. Roberts and R. Mohr (eds.), *Confronting Sexual Assault: A Decade of Legal and Social Change* (Toronto UP, 1994); and S. Engle Merry, 'Global Human Rights and Local Social Movements in a Legally Plural World' (1997) 12 CJLS 247.

217 Harris, O'Boyle and Warbrick, above n. 64, p. 213; *Edwards v UK* (1992) 15 EHRR 417; Lester and Pannick, above n. 64, p. 144; and Sharpe, above n. 209.

authorities and the accused, and it functions as a safeguard of fairness in the adversarial process.[218] It also acts as a deterrent against the over-zealous, careless or dishonest construction of the prosecution case by the police in the first place.[219]

The issue of non-disclosure of evidence has assumed particular significance in the UK as a result of the number and scale of miscarriages of justice directly attributable to prosecution concealment of exculpatory evidence. From 1989 onwards, a series of quashed convictions – in cases such as the *Guildford Four*, *Judith Ward* and the *Taylor Sisters*[220] – revealed how police, forensic experts and prosecution lawyers (deliberately or inadvertently) failed to disclose material that would have collapsed, or substantially weakened, the prosecution case. The Court of Appeal decision in *Ward* was seen as a watershed, providing judicial recognition that police malpractice was a constant risk, and also imposing a duty of full disclosure of all 'material' evidence on the prosecution in order to ensure a fair trial. However, the *Ward* decision also occasioned a police 'backlash' against alleged 'fishing expeditions' by defence lawyers. This proved successful in curtailing the judgment's implications[221] and, in a climate of populist 'law and order' and 'police efficiency' politics, led to the Criminal Procedure and Investigations Act 1996. The main purpose of the legislation was to re-entrench the discretion of the CPS and police as to the disclosure of evidence to the defence.[222]

Section 3(1) of the 1996 Act (and Code of Practice) obliges the prosecution to make primary disclosure of 'unused material' that, in its opinion, 'might undermine the case for the prosecution against the accused', or to issue a written statement that no such material exists. In light of past miscarriages of justice, the weakness of section 3 is that it 'vests an enormous discretion in the prosecutor both as to any assessment of relevance of the material concerned and also as to the impact that such material might have on the outcome of the case'.[223] In reality, of course, it is the police who retain ultimate influence. The prosecutor 'makes [the decision to disclose] based on the material generated by the attitudes and methodologies of others. . . . [T]he prosecutor cannot disclose what he or she does not know of';[224] thus, 'in most cases the issue of what material is to be disclosed . . . will be made by the police'.[225]

Aspects of the new law on disclosure have already been a target for criminal defence lawyers under Article 6 of the ECHR. Most significantly, the decision of the European Court of Human Rights in *Rowe and Davis* has established that

---

218 See Ashworth, above n. 10, Ch. 4.
219 See generally, S. Greer, 'Miscarriages of Justice Reconsidered' (1994) 57 MLR 58.
220 See respectively, *R v Hill, The Times*, 20 Oct. 1989; *R v Ward* [1993] 1 WLR 619; and *R v Taylor & Taylor* (1993) 98 Cr App Rep 361. A fuller list of cases is given in C. Walker, 'Miscarriages of Justice in Principle and Practice' in Walker and Starmer, above n. 5, pp. 45-52.
221 B. Fitzpatrick, 'Disclosure: Principles, Processes and Politics' in Walker and Starmer, above n. 5, pp. 151-169.
222 See N. Lacey, 'Missing the Wood . . . Pragmatism versus Theory in the Royal Commission' in McConville and Bridges, above n. 37, pp. 30-41; and D. Dixon, 'Police Investigative Procedures: Changing Legal and Political Context of Policing Practices' in Walker and Starmer, above n. 5, pp. 65-82. For an account of the provisions of the 1996 Act, see R. Leng and R. Taylor, *Blackstone's Guide to the Criminal Procedure and Investigations Act 1996* (Blackstone, 1996).
223 Sharpe, above n. 209, p. 275.
224 Fitzpatrick, above n. 221, p. 165.
225 Leng and Taylor, above n. 222, p. 15.

the prosecution must disclose all 'relevant' evidence to the defence or (in this instance, where evidence was secretly withheld on public interest immunity grounds) to the trial judge in order to guarantee a fair trial. It ruled:

> The right to an adversarial trial means, in a criminal case, that both prosecution and defence must be given the opportunity to have knowledge of and comment on the observations filed and the evidence adduced by the other party. . . . In some cases it may be necessary to withhold certain evidence from the defence so as to preserve the fundamental rights of another individual or to safeguard an important public interest. However, only such measures restricting the rights of the defence which are strictly necessary are permissible under Article 6(1) . . . [and] any difficulties caused to the defence by a limitation on its rights must be sufficiently counterbalanced by the procedures followed by the judicial authorities . . . .[226]

Many other challenges using Article 6 and the HRA seem likely to follow recent attempts to broaden prosecution/police disclosure.[227] A 1999 survey by the Criminal Bar Association, British Academy of Forensic Sciences and the Law Society revealed that prosecutors and police were failing to disclose relevant material, either because of incompetence, lack of understanding or blatant obstruction.[228] For many, the 1996 Act places too much trust in the integrity of a prosecution system that has produced numerous wrongful convictions in the past because of police malpractice;[229] a system which, up to March 2000, has generated 3,193 claims of miscarriages of justice to the Criminal Cases Review Commission.[230] The 1996 Act has also been criticised as an example of the 'new consensus' on criminal justice policies in British politics; a consensus that downplays the rights of the defendant and views 'fairness' of trials as predominantly about increasing conviction rates and deterrence through punishment.[231] The scale of such concerns prompted the Attorney-General to issue revised *Guidelines on Disclosure* in 2000, guidelines that bind all public prosecutors and are expected to 'have a persuasive effect on other participants in the criminal justice process'.[232]

The civil libertarian focus on a right to full disclosure of the prosecution case is crucial. Its weakness, however, is that it tends to conceive of the criminal prosecution in the stereotypical terms of powerful state pitted against individual accused. In addition, its emphasis on the risk of wrongful convictions has contributed to an under-developed conception of criminal *justice*, which loses

---

226 *Rowe & Davis v UK* (2000) 30 EHRR 1. The law on public interest immunity *(R v Davis, Rowe & Johnson* [1993] 1 WLR 613; *R v Keane* [1994] 1 WLR 746) was preserved by the 1996 Act but new procedures were created (ss. 14-16). In *Jasper v UK* (2000) 30 EHRR 97, the ECtHR (by 9:8) decided that where the prosecution had made an application to the trial judge to withhold the evidence in question, the defence had been notified that an application had been made, and the trial judge had been given the opportunity to monitor the need for assessment throughout the course of the trial, there was no violation of Art. 6.

227 See *R v Stratford Justices, ex p Imbert* [1999] 2 Cr App Rep 276; *R v DPP, ex p Lee* [1999] 2 All ER 737; and *R v Brushett*, 20 Dec. 2000 (CA).

228 B. Emmerson, 'Prosecution in the Dock', *The Guardian*, 15 Nov. 1999, p. 18.

229 See M. Maguire and C. Norris, 'Police Investigations: Practice and Malpractice' (1994) 21 JLS 72; and B. Woffinden, 'No, You Can't See. It Might Help Your Client', *The Guardian*, 4 May 1999, p. 8.

230 *Annual Report 1999-2000* (CCRC, 2000).

231 See Brownlee, above n. 14; and Young, above n. 205.

232 *Draft Attorney General's Guidelines on Disclosure* (Feb. 2000). See now *Disclosure of Information in Criminal Proceedings* (Nov. 2000) (www.lslo.gov.uk).

sight of other interests and rights involved in the pursuit of a fair trial. In particular, it downplays the expanding reach of the disclosure principle in relation to third parties, particularly in rape trials:

> It has become standard practice for defence lawyers in rape and indecency cases to seek to compel the production of any social services, education, psychiatric, medical or similar records concerning the complainant, in the hope that these will furnish material for cross-examination.[233]

We illustrate these points in the following paragraphs: first, by describing the history of routine disclosure of the notes of doctors involved in rape investigations in England; and secondly, by highlighting the negative impact of pre-1999 Canadian Supreme Court decisions authorising expansive disclosure of a range of records in sexual assault cases to defence lawyers. Our critique will centre on the 'fair trial' narrative that equates 'fairness' with full disclosure of any and all facts about the complainant in the rape prosecution; in other words, it will seek to challenge the assumption that the defence has a right to 'every scintilla of information which might possibly be useful . . .'.[234]

Disclosure of 'medical' evidence in rape cases

When the focus shifts to the rape prosecution, the issues of disclosure of 'relevant' evidence and the meaning of 'fair trial' appear in a new light. There are three key actors involved in the disclosure process in such prosecutions: first, the doctors involved in forensic examinations, who generally remain wedded to the routines and culture of ordinary medical practice; secondly, CPS lawyers who want the 'full facts' before deciding whether or not to prosecute; and finally, defence lawyers who view the written medical statement and doctors' notes as a treasure trove for cross-examination purposes.[235]

As many feminist critiques of the rape trial have highlighted, the dominant defence tactic is 'generally to undermine your confidence, confuse you about the sequence of events (so that you might contradict yourself), and cast a slur on your character', in particular by concentrating on personal lifestyle and sexual experiences.[236] The purpose of seeking full disclosure of notes in the possession of the prosecution (or forensic medical examiners) is recognised as going well beyond enabling the accused to prepare an adequate defence; the aim is strategically to undermine the prospect of the complainant receiving a

---

233 *R v H(L)* [1997] 1 Cr App Rep 176, 176-177 (per Sedley J) (re the seeking of documents under s. 2 of the Criminal Procedure (Attendance of Witnesses) Act 1965; now amended by s. 66, Criminal Procedure and Investigations Act 1996). See also, eg, *R v Reading Justices, ex p Berkshire CC* [1996] 1 Cr App Rep 239; *R v Azmy* (1996) 7 Med LR 415; *R v W(G)* (1997) 1 Cr App Rep 166 (CA); and *Re Pictons (Solicitors)* (unreported, 3 Dec. 1998, CA). The decision in *R v Brushett*, 20 Dec. 2000 (CA), demonstrates a much greater awareness (at least, in child abuse cases) of the need to limit disclosure of third party records when not 'material' to the defence case.

234 *R v O'Connor* [1995] 4 SCR 411, para. 194 (per McLachlin J).

235 J. Temkin, 'Medical Evidence in Rape Cases: A Continuing Problem for Criminal Justice' (1998) 61 MLR 821. Note *Z v Finland* (1997) 25 EHRR 371 re disclosure.

236 London Rape Crisis Centre, *Sexual Violence: The Reality for Women* (The Women's Press, 1999), p. 87. See generally, C. Smart, *Feminism and the Power of Law* (Routledge, 1989); and S. Lees, *Ruling Passions: Sexual Violence, Reputation and the Law* (Open UP, 1997).

fair trial by setting up a cross-examination on 'irrelevant' issues.[237] The Home Office report, *Speaking Up for Justice*, concedes that the detail of doctors' notes, alongside those of the police, provide the defence with 'ammunition in court'.[238] Moreover, some defence barristers freely admit to the critical adversarial advantages of obtaining such medical notes:

> Barrister 1 revealed that information gathering by doctors was regarded as a boon by the defence. She explained that when she was defending she would always call for the doctor's notes 'because you get lots of leads . . . they are a mine of useful information'. Conversely, Barrister 6 said: 'I don't believe it's part of the doctor's function to spend the first twenty minutes asking her about her medical history. This presents a difficulty for the prosecution and an advantage to the defence'.[239]

One of the main reasons for this focus on medical evidence is continuing police and CPS perceptions about the blameworthiness and veracity of individual women reporting rape, as well as CPS policy on the dropping of cases in the absence of 'expert' evidence.[240] CPS lawyers, however, also recognise the paradoxical nature of their emphasis on detailed doctors' notes:

> On the one hand, Crown Prosecutors are keen to have as much information as possible. They dread the prospect of evidence of which they were unaware emerging in court. As CPS SUS3 put it: 'I would much rather that far too much came out. It has to be disclosed anyway to the other side.' . . . On the other hand there is the view that too much information about previous sexual history is being collected by doctors. As CPS LON1 put it: '. . . We make it difficult for ourselves when your own doctor had gone down that road and has noted it in his notes. It's there. It's upfront. It's an issue in the case and it's very hard to resist'.[241]

Doctors also admit to confusion about their role, viewing the complainant as outside the 'normal' doctor/patient relationship[242] but also arguing that it is not for the medical expert 'to play the detective'.[243] For example, in Temkin's 1995 study of doctors performing forensic medical examinations in the south-

---

237 Some may argue that this is the whole point of the adversarial system, and rape prosecutions are no different than any other in terms of defence lawyer tactics. While there is some truth in this claim (which is why we suggest a rethink of the meaning of 'fair trial' generally), the distinctiveness of the rape trial seems clear because of its common law history and of the social construction of sexuality. See L. Ellison, 'Cross-Examination in Rape Trials' [1988] Crim LR 605 (tactical gains from embarrassing, intimidating and antagonising witnesses during cross-examination in all adversarial proceedings).

238 *Speaking Up for Justice* (Home Office, 1998), p. 169.

239 Temkin, above n. 235, p. 833.

240 See Rose, above n. 151; J. Temkin, 'Reporting Rape in London: A Qualitative Study' (1999) 38 Howard J 17; and J. Watson, 'Exclusion: The Victim's Point of View' NLJ, 16 Jul. 1999, p. 1085.

241 Temkin, above n. 235, p. 833.

242 See *N v Agrawal*, *The Times*, 9 Jun. 1999 (CA) (no duty of care owed to complainant that her forensic medical examiner attend court and give evidence). The Temkin study also highlights that the ethical issues of informed consent and confidentiality are rarely properly discussed with women prior to a doctor's physical examination and questioning. See GMC guidelines, *Seeking Patients' Consent: The Ethical Considerations* (1999) and *Confidentiality* (1995) (www.gmc-uk.org); and more generally, on the disregard of female patient autonomy by health care professionals, see S. Sheldon, '"A Responsible Body of Medical Men Skilled in that Particular Art . . .": Rethinking the Bolam Test' in S. Sheldon and M. Thomson (eds.), *Feminist Perspectives on Health Care Law* (Cavendish, 1998), pp. 15-32.

243 Temkin, above n. 235, p. 832. See also, S. Savage et al., 'Divided Loyalties?: The Police Surgeon and Criminal Justice' (1997) 7 Policing and Society 79.

east of England, there was considerable variation in the content of written statements, and the extent to which legally irrelevant but stigmatising views on a woman's past medical history, previous sexual experiences, clothing, family history and living circumstances were included. Those doctors who took detailed notes justified their actions in several ways, insisting for example that such records form part of a doctor's practice in getting a 'complete picture' of the patient, or finding out 'the truth'of what happened.[244]

The Canadian Supreme Court and disclosure in sexual assault cases

The role of the judiciary and rights discourse in determining the proper extent of disclosure in sexual assault cases has proved to be a particularly controversial issue in Canada.[245] In a series of majority decisions, the Canadian Supreme Court has interpreted the right to a fair trial in a way that appears to enhance due process values, yet has seriously undermined the prospect of women pursuing sexual assault prosecutions and reduced further the likelihood of convictions.[246] These decisions, and their consequences, are particularly important for a critique of 'fair trial' in that they highlight the limits of non-contextual, gender-neutral accounts of rules of procedural fairness. The Canadian experience also highlights how 'fair trial' litigation can be used by defence lawyers to legitimise new strategies in response to legislative reforms, in particular restrictions on the questioning of complainants about previous sexual history. Most seriously, these Supreme Court decisions have been directly responsible for disrupting the delivery of counselling services offered to women reporting sexual assault or abuse, and have contributed to the stigmatisation of therapeutic, non-legal accounts of rape.[247] The 1999 decision of the Supreme Court in *R v Mills* recognises, to some extent, the consequences of earlier rulings on the defence right to disclosure of 'relevant' evidence, and supports the Canadian Parliament's legislative attempt to limit the extent of such access; however, the wider consequences of the judicial undermining of sexual assault prosecutions over several years may remain largely unchanged.

Pre-*Mills*, the Canadian Supreme Court clearly demonstrated its commitment to fair trial principles by establishing that prosecution failure to make adequate disclosure infringes the accused's section 7 and 11(d) rights to fundamental justice and a fair hearing under the Charter. In *Stinchcombe*,[248] where

---

244 The current BMA guidelines, revised in response to the Criminal Procedure and Investigations Act 1996, emphasise that meaningful consent must first be obtained and that 'police surgeons should consciously attempt to separate out the forensic evidence, and any other information obtained which is likely to affect the outcome of the case, from information which is not germane to the case and was provided solely in the therapeutic context'. If the police or CPS request further information about the medical examination, which was omitted from the written report, the examining doctor should only divulge the information if the patient consents in writing, or when ordered to do so by a judge after a hearing. See BMA, *Confidentiality* (Oct. 1999) and *Revised Interim Guidelines on Confidentiality for Police Surgeons in England, Wales and Northern Ireland* (Feb. 1998) (www.bma.org.uk).

245 After feminist lobbying campaigns, the Canadian Criminal Code was amended in 1981 to replace the offence of rape with sexual assault of varying degrees of gravity.

246 K. Busby, 'Discriminatory Uses of Personal Records in Sexual Violence Cases' (1997) 9 CJWL 148.

247 K.D. Kelly, '"You Must Be Crazy If You Think You Were Raped"; Reflections on the Use of Complainants' Personal and Therapy Records in Sexual Assault Trials' (1997) 9 CJWL 178.

248 [1991] 3 SCR 326.

the prosecution refused to disclose witness statements favourable to the accused, it was held that the 'right to make full answer and defence is one of the pillars of criminal justice on which we heavily depend to ensure that the innocent are not convicted'. Thus, 'all relevant information' must be disclosed to the defence, and the prosecutor only has a discretion (reviewable by the court) to withhold 'clearly irrelevant' or privileged material and the identity of informers and vulnerable witnesses. The implications of this decision were made apparent in *O'Connor*[249] where the defence, for a Bishop charged with sexual offences committed 25 years earlier in a Catholic school, sought access to school records and an order for:

> all therapists, counsellors, psychologists and psychiatrists whom have treated any of [the complainants] with respect to allegations of sexual assault or sexual abuse to produce to the Crown copies of their complete file contents and any other related material including all documents, notes, records, reports, tape recordings and video tapes . . . .

On appeal, a 5:4 majority of the Supreme Court ruled that access to such confidential material, even though in the possession of third parties, could be relevant to an accused's right to a fair trial. A two-stage procedure was created requiring initial production of material 'useful to the defence' before a judge, who would then determine whether the material should be disclosed to defence lawyers to ensure a fair trial.

The negative impact of this 'fair trial' discourse on sexual assault prosecutions and the provision of counselling services in Canada is apparent from the *Carosella*[250] decision. The appellant, a teacher, was charged with sexual abuse committed in 1964 against the complainant, a former pupil. The sexual assault crisis centre which provided counselling to the complainant had adopted a policy of destroying files with police involvement *before* the serving of any court order. As a result, when the centre was ordered to disclose notes of its counselling session, the file was empty. On appeal, a 5:4 majority of the Supreme Court agreed that the trial judge had been correct to halt the prosecution as the accused's right to a fair trial was compromised by the destruction of the interview notes. In Sopinka J's opinion, the defence had a right to such material because it:

> could have assisted the defence in the preparation of cross-examination . . . [,] revealed the state of the complainant's perception and memory . . . [and] that some of the complainant's statements resulted from suggestions made by the interviewer. . . . The notes constituted the only written record of the alleged incidents which were not created as a result of an investigation.[251]

In May 1997, the Canadian government acted to amend provisions of the Criminal Code in order to establish a statutory scheme governing the production of personal records (referred to as Bill C-46).[252] The aim of the legislation was to impose stricter limits on the two-stage test developed by the Supreme Court

---

249 [1995] 4 SCR 411. See also, *LLA v Beharriell* [1995] 4 SCR 536 (application for access to counselling records relating to alleged sexual assault of complainant when six years old by former neighbour).

250 [1997] 1 SCR 80.

251 Ibid., para. 45.

252 An Act to Amend the Criminal Code (Production of Records in Sexual Offence Proceedings), SC 1997, c. 30.

in *O'Connor*, in particular by placing greater value on the complainant's privacy rights and acknowledging the general implications for women's equality rights in preventing such invasive legal procedures. Bill C-46, broadly welcomed by women's groups and condemned by criminal defence lawyers, quickly became 'the target of numerous Charter challenges'.[253] In October 1997 in *R v Mills*, following a defence application for access to the counselling, therapeutic and medical records of a 13-year old girl who alleged sexual assault, an Alberta court ruled that Bill C-46 substantially impaired the accused's fundamental right to a fair trial and was constitutionally invalid. The Canadian Supreme Court reversed the lower court decision in November 1999 and held that the 'dialogue between courts and legislatures' allowed Parliament to 'craft its own solution to the problem [of disclosure] consistent with the Charter [of Rights]'.

Towards fairness in disclosure in rape prosecutions

In the UK, the law relating to disclosure is an obvious litigation target under the HRA. The senior judiciary will face similar questions to their Canadian counterparts, not least because of the increasing concerns of defence lawyers and forensic scientists about 'the alarming rise in non-disclosure'.[254] Even the Director of Public Prosecutions has warned of 'the risk of a return to the sort of miscarriages of justice that were seen in the 1970s and 1980s'.[255] The choices that judges make in any such cases will have an impact not just on the 'prosecution' duty of disclosure under the Criminal Procedure and Investigations Act 1996 – that is, the material in the direct control of the police and CPS – but on the maintenance of a wider culture of confidentiality involving third parties such as doctors, counsellors and welfare agencies. The new *Attorney General's Guidelines on Disclosure* emphasise that primary disclosure must include 'any material that might go to the credibility of a prosecution witness' (paragraph 31), and that prosecution evidence includes information from liaison with local authorities, social service departments and similar agencies, and material that originates from, or has been produced by, third parties. While also emphasising that fairness must include the interests of 'victims and witnesses' (paragraph 3), the risk is that the current very fragile legal protection against 'fishing expeditions' for medical and counselling records in adult sexual offences cases will be swept further away, as happened in Canada, because of concerns about 'prosecution' non-disclosure, entrenched stereotypes about fabricated rape allegations, and the constantly evolving intimidatory tactics of defence lawyers. In some respects, this is already the reality:

> *Dispatches* found that many women had had their medical records called before the court – a concerning new variation on the enduring myth of the unreliable accuser: if she's not a slut, then she must be mad. In Sam's case, she'd had a termination.

---

253 One of these challenges, *Mills*, is discussed below, p. 204. For a critique of Canadian disclosure cases, see L. Gotell, 'Colonization Through Disclosure: Confidential Records, Sexual Assault Complainants and Canadian Law' (2001) 10 SLS (forthcoming).

254 G. Langdon-Down, 'The Alarming Rise in Non-Disclosure', *The Times*, 4 May 1999, p. 39; 'The Whole Truth and Nothing But', *The Independent*, 7 Dec. 1999.

255 M. Matthews, 'The Dangers of Leaving a Jury in the Dark', *The Times*, 11 Oct. 1999, p. 38.

'[The defence barrister] brought that up.' She also suffered from post-natal depression. 'He brought that up. He tried to prove that I didn't know my own mind.'[256]

As a starting point, therefore, we would suggest that both the minority decision of L'Heureux-Dubé J in *Carosella* and the majority decision in *Mills* provide the way forward for the UK courts when it comes to defining 'relevant' evidence, and the extent of the duty to disclose, in any litigation involving the provisions of the 1996 Act, the *Attorney General's Guidelines on Disclosure* and the HRA. These decisions provide a rights discourse that recognises both the importance of fairness in criminal trials and also, crucially, the social and legal contexts in which sexual violence occurs and is prosecuted in court.

For example, L'Heureux Dubé J disagrees with the majority's interpretation of 'fair trial' on several grounds. She argues that framing sexual assault prosecutions within a traditional 'state v. accused' dichotomy is inadequate; the central issue is *not* 'prosecution disclosure' as third parties, such as rape crisis centres, should not be treated as equivalent to state prosecution authorities. Secondly, she argues that a fair trial does not depend on the accused having access to every possible piece of evidence outside the immediate control of the prosecution; there is a limit to any system of criminal justice, and the interests and rights of complainants and third parties must be recognised. Thirdly, for a court to rule that an accused would not receive a fair trial requires evidence of prejudice; the records of third parties should not be available for a 'fishing expedition' for information. Finally, she emphasises that the 'virtually automatic' defence request for disclosure of any counselling records jeopardises effective therapeutic relationships: it undermines privacy, thereby dissuading many women from ever seeking counselling. Moreover, attempts to preserve the integrity of counselling by altering or destroying notes make it 'extremely likely that the therapeutical process . . . is being harmed in their absence'.[257]

Similarly, the majority decision in *Mills* acknowledges that all human rights must be interpreted in a contextual manner and that Parliament had acted as a 'significant ally for vulnerable groups' in light of their treatment by the legal system:

> The history of the treatment of sexual assault complainants by our society and by our legal system is an unfortunate one. Important change has occurred through legislation aimed at both recognizing the rights and interests of complainants in criminal proceedings, and debunking the stereotypes that have been so damaging to women and children, but the treatment of sexual assault complainants remains an ongoing problem. . . . Parliament . . . sought to recognize the prevalence of sexual violence against women and children and its disadvantageous impact on their rights, to encourage the reporting of incidents of sexual violence, to recognise the impact of the production of personal information on the efficacy of treatment, and to reconcile fairness to complainants with the rights of the accused. . . . Parliament may also be understood to be recognizing 'horizontal' equality concerns, where women's inequality results from the acts of other individuals and groups rather than the state, but which nonetheless may have many consequences for the criminal justice system.[258]

256 L. Brooks, 'Getting Away With It', *The Guardian*, 16 Mar. 2000 (re *Dispatches: Still Getting Away With Rape*, Channel 4 Television, Mar. 2000).
257 Above n. 250, para. 147.
258 Above n. 212, paras. 58-59.

While such judicial discourse from any Supreme Court is remarkably insightful and important, it must be borne in mind that it comes with caveats. Despite the importance attached to the privacy of medical, counselling and personal records in *Mills*, the Court also acknowledged that the 'accused's right must prevail where the lack of disclosure or production of the record would render him unable to make full answer and defence'. The avoidance of the conviction of an innocent individual is 'at the heart of the principles of fundamental justice'. Thus, despite the Canadian Parliament's detailed statement of the feminist goals of the legislation, the trial court will still have to 'strike a balance between . . . competing rights', with all the negative consequences that entails in terms of established legal practices and social norms. Not surprisingly, there is scepticism about the ability of this discourse to alter established practices and attitudes in the lower courts.

Since the early 1990s, the obvious injustice in the Charter of Rights being used not only to undermine individual sexual assault prosecutions, but also the entire culture and infrastructure created to support women in the aftermath of sexual violence has provoked much critical commentary.[259] Canadian women have had to choose 'to either seek counselling to deal with the aftermath of the violence or rely on the criminal justice system for protection and redress'.[260] Parallel legislative attempts to restrict cross-examination on previous sexual history have also been undercut by the widening of the duty to disclose 'relevant' material.[261] Indeed, the use of personal records (such as counselling notes and diaries) in legal proceedings appears to have entrenched much-criticised cross-examination tactics by allowing the re-introduction of 'rape myths' about the fabricated and unreliable testimony of women into legal defence strategies.[262]

Carosella and *Mills* also draw attention to the responsibility of other actors for downgrading the privacy of third-party records and, in effect, broadening the scope of cross-examination in sexual offences trials. In *Carosella*, the counselling centre's obvious awareness of the reality of defence disclosure tactics in sexual assault cases, and their commitment to safeguarding the interests of their clients, contrasts markedly with the diversity of attitudes amongst doctors involved in forensic medical examinations in the UK. The 'I just record information' or 'I'll fax notes to anybody' attitude of some doctors highlights the need for reconsideration of the currently blurred divide between the roles of 'prosecution expert' and 'doctor'.[263] It also indicates the need for a much

---

259 See eg, Gottell, above n. 253; and A. McColgan, *Women Under the Law: The False Promise of Human Rights* (Longman, 2000), pp. 218-252.
260 Busby, above n. 246, pp. 174-175.
261 See *R v Seaboyer; R v Gayme* [1991] 2 SCR 577 (s. 276 of the Criminal Code restricting the scope of cross-examination on past sexual history evidence declared unconstitutional as a violation of accused's right to a fair trial and right to be presumed innocent under Canadian Charter); and *R v Darrach* (1998) CRR LEXIS 403; [2000] 2 SCR 443 (amended s. 276 held to be constitutional by Ontario Court of Appeal and trial judge was correct to prevent cross-examination on the complainant's prior sexual relationship with appellant; decision upheld by Canadian Supreme Court in October 2000).
262 See also, *R v Osolin* [1993] 4 SCR 595 (trial judge's refusal to allow cross-examination on doctor-patient records reversed by Supreme Court on ground that privacy rights must be balanced against the right to a fair trial); and *M(A) v Ryan* [1997] 1 SCR 157 (current psychiatric records ordered to be disclosed in civil action for damages against former psychiatrist for sexual assault and gross indecency).
263 Temkin, above n. 235, pp. 838-839.

sharper understanding within the medical profession of the concepts of consent and confidentiality (as required by the revised GMC and BMA guidelines[264]). More fundamentally, the role of medical personnel and 'medical expertise' in the prosecution of rape raises difficult questions about the strategic worth of some medico-legal alliances,[265] especially in light of the gendered nature of doctor-patient relationships. In particular, although reform of the medical profession's treatment of assaulted women has been central to a broader reform of the process of rape trials, the emphasis on the 'scientific fact' of rape may also be part of the problem:

> [P]reliminary research suggests . . . that in Canada, as in the U.S., medical evidence obtained through specialized, expert examinations makes few positive contributions to the complainant's case. In many ways, that evidence represents an outmoded definition of the crime and has little relevance to key issues of consent. Cases and interviews further indicate that, for at least some assaulted women, the psychological consequences of sexual assault are more painful and enduring than the physical experience that is best captured in the medical evidence. Equally important, that evidence, though collected from the complainant, can sometimes do her case harm. It can be used to weigh the credibility of her case, determine whether she acted in accord with some norm of propriety, and provide knowledge of her past sexual history. In this sense, medical reform can work at cross purposes with legal reform.[266]

Much is at stake, therefore, in the future legal and political battles around 'prosecution disclosure' in the UK, and the competing versions of fairness and fair trial under the HRA.

Cross-examination on previous sexual history in the rape trial

In this section, we shall focus on the actual conduct of the rape trial, in particular the issue of defence cross-examination of the complainant about any previous sexual relationships. We highlight the importance of cross-examination as an aspect of the right to a fair trial. We also explore the reality of cross-examination tactics in the rape trial and the new attempts to restrict questioning about previous sexual history contained in the Youth Justice and Criminal Evidence Act 1999 (YJCEA). Finally, attention will be drawn to decisions of the Canadian Supreme Court wherein an accused's right to a fair trial under the Canadian Charter of Rights was interpreted in ways that undermined feminist-inspired legislative reforms aimed at curtailing defence tactics in sexual assault cases.

The right to cross-examination

Cross-examination is rightly celebrated as an important component of a defendant's right to a fair trial. It is represented as 'a powerful and valuable weapon for the purpose of testing the veracity of a witness and the accuracy

---

264 Above nn. 242 and 244.
265 See eg, R. Hunter, 'Gender in Evidence: Masculine Norms vs. Feminist Reforms' (1996) 19 Harv Women's LJ 12; and *R v Martin* [1999] Crim LR 97 (doctor giving medical evidence cannot give evidence as to the credibility of the patient).
266 G. Feldberg, 'Defining the Facts of Rape: The Uses of Medical Evidence in Sexual Assault Trials' (1997) 9 CJWL 89, 114. See D. Calvert-Smith (2000) 68 Med-Leg J 117.

and completeness of his [sic] story',[267] a representation central to literary and cinematic accounts of the (masculine) defence advocate. Under Article 6(3)(d) of the ECHR, the accused has a right 'to examine or have examined witnesses against him and to obtain the attendance and examination of witnesses on his behalf . . .'. The European Court of Human Rights, however, has provided little detail on the purpose or boundaries of cross-examination, bar generally requiring 'equality of arms' between both parties.[268] This approach is in line with the tradition of UK courts in their emphasis on overall fairness in criminal cases and on ensuring that an accused receives a fair trial by 'effective' legal representation. Thus, beyond celebrating the benefits of cross-examination in general terms, there is remarkably little judicial discussion as to its possible negative effects on witnesses or where the limits of cross-examination should lie. The 'paradox of advocacy' – 'it simultaneously espouses neutrality and partisanship'[269] – is not usually recognised in legal discourse. Instead, the dominant characterisation suggests a formal effectiveness:

> The limits of cross-examination are not susceptible of precise definition, for a connection between a fact elicited by cross-examination and a fact in issue may appear, if at all, only after other pieces of evidence are forthcoming. Nor is there any general test of relevance which a trial judge is able to apply in deciding, at the start of a cross-examination, whether a particular question should be allowed. Some of the most effective cross-examinations have begun by securing a witness' assent to a proposition of seeming irrelevance.[270]

Cross-examination tactics in rape trials

The Home Office report on the treatment of witnesses, *Speaking Up for Justice*, provides a very different account of the effects of cross-examination. While recognising the common law duty on judges to restrain 'unnecessary or improper or oppressive questions',[271] and the prohibition in the Bar's Code of Conduct on 'questions which are merely scandalous or intended or calculated only to vilify, insult or annoy', the report calls for more effective statutory measures to ensure that witnesses are treated with 'dignity and respect' when giving evidence in court. In particular, rape cases are recognised as the site of deliberately intimidatory cross-examination tactics. This perspective fits with an apparent willingness of the Court of Criminal Appeal to re-think the trial judge's traditional understanding of 'fairness' in rape prosecutions – that is, the perceived need to permit oppressive cross-examination by the defence for fear of a successful appeal. In *Brown*,[272] for example, the Court emphasised that

---

267 *Mechanical and General Inventions Co Ltd v Austin* [1935] AC 346, 359.
268 See Harris, O'Boyle and Warbrick, above n. 64, pp. 266-269. See *V and T v UK* (1999) 30 EHRR 121 (public trial in an adult court of a child was 'a severely intimidating procedure' and violated Art. 6 of the Convention); and *Doorson v Netherlands* (1996) 22 EHRR 330.
269 M. Thornton (ed.), *Public and Private: Feminist Legal Debates* (OUP, 1995), p. 195.
270 *Wakeley v R* (1990) 64 ALJR 321, 325 (Australian HC).
271 *R v Kalia* (1974) 60 Cr App Rep 200; *R v Morley* (1988) 87 Cr App Rep 218.
272 *R v Brown* (1988) 89 Cr App Rep 97 (unrepresented defendant cross-examining rape complainant). S. 34 of the YJCEA introduced a prohibition on defendants cross-examining complainants in sexual offence cases. But see *R v W* (CA, 13 Dec. 1999) (conviction for rape quashed because complainant's credibility not 'thoroughly pursued' by cross-examination of her father).

it was 'the clear duty of the trial judge . . . [to] do everything he can, consistently with giving the defendant a fair trial, to minimise the trauma suffered by other participants'.

One of the main proposals of *Speaking Up for Justice*, enacted as section 41 of the YJCEA, prohibits the cross-examination of complainants on their previous sexual history except in very limited circumstances. The Home Office rationale for the further narrowing of the previous restriction in section 2 of the Sexual Offences (Amendment) Act 1976 was because use of sexual history evidence had gone 'far beyond that demanded in the interests of relevance to the issues in the trial and suggests that it is [being] used, contrary to section 2, in an attempt to discredit the victim's character in the eyes of the jury'.[273] Much research confirms this conclusion; evidence of past sexual relationships is introduced as a defence tactic solely to argue that the complainant would not have refused consent to sexual intercourse with the defendant.[274] The rape trial thus takes the form of a 'pornographic vignette',[275] where 'patriarchal stories' dominate the culture of the courtroom. The new section 41 purported to prohibit the defence from cross-examining on any 'sexual behaviour' of a complainant, other than that relating to the event which was the subject-matter of the charge, without leave of the court. If the purpose of the cross-examination was solely to impugn the complainant's credibility as a witness, there was a blanket prohibition on questions.

The limitation on cross-examination in the YJCEA conformed with similar legislative attempts to introduce more restrictive 'rape shield' laws in Scotland, the US, Australia and Canada. However, the practical effect of such reforms remains limited, not least because of continuing judicial concern in each jurisdiction that excluding 'defence evidence of significant probative value . . . might rob the accused of a fair trial'[276] and the constant adaption of defence lawyer tactics. The long history of scepticism amongst judges and barristers that any problem exists with cross-examination on previous sexual history – 'the [English] Bar, so it seems, would not want there to be any further restrictions on the cross-examination of complainants';[277] 'Many, if not most judges think that the [section 2] restrictions . . . worked well' – indicates that a similar resistance will manifest itself in relation to the new statutory restrictions in the 1999 Act. Indeed, the decision of the House of Lords in *R v A* suggests that the opportunities for subverting statutory protections are substantial if deeply entrenched cultural assumptions about sexuality remain fixed.[278]

---

273 Above n. 238, p. 69.
274 See eg, Lees, above n. 236; and McColgan, above n. 259.
275 Smart, above n. 236, p. 39. See also A.E. Taslitz, *Rape and the Culture of the Courtroom* (New York UP, 1999).
276 Hunter and Cronin, above n. 198, p. 346.
277 Criminal Law Revision Committee, 15th Report, 1984, cited in Lacey and Wells, above n. 1, p. 396; and A. Geddes, 'The Exclusion of Evidence Relating to a Complainant's Sexual Behaviour in Sexual Offences Trials', NLJ, 16 Jul. 1999, p. 1086.
278 [2001] UKHL 25, [2001] 3 All ER 1. See generally, N. Kibble, 'The Sexual History Provisions: Charting a Course Between Inflexible Legislative Rules and Wholly Untrammelled Judicial Discretion?' [2000] Crim LR 274.

The Canadian Supreme Court and previous sexual history evidence

'Rape shield' provisions have been the focus of litigation in Canada on the ground that the right of the accused to a fair trial under the Charter of Rights is compromised. One of the most controversial rulings of the Canadian Supreme Court in this area was its 7:2 decision in the 1991 case of *Seaboyer*.[279] Seaboyer had been charged with sexual assault and was prevented from cross-examining the complainant as to other alleged acts of sexual intercourse which might have caused the bruises allegedly inflicted by force. Section 276 of the Criminal Code, enacted in response to the judicial perpetuation of 'myths' about the unreliability of rape allegations and defence lawyers' use of sexual history evidence to discredit the complainant, was declared unconstitutional on the grounds that it violated the accused's right to a fair trial under section 7, and the right to be presumed innocent under section 11(d), of the Charter. The majority ruled that, while the purpose of section 276 was laudable (eliminating prejudicial evidence, encouraging reporting of rape, protecting the complainant's privacy), its exclusion of past sexual history (except in limited circumstances[280]) was too narrow and rendered inadmissible evidence which might be essential to a fair trial. The majority believed that although evidence of sexual conduct and reputation in itself could not be regarded as indicative of either the complainant's credibility or consent, there had to be a judicial discretion to allow it where deemed to be relevant.

The Canadian government's reaction to the *Seaboyer* decision was to introduce amending legislation, which sought to respond to the majority's concerns but also placed clear statutory limits on trial judges' discretion.[281] The Ontario Court of Appeal ruled in *Darrach*,[282] where cross-examination on the complainant's prior sexual relationship with the appellant was disallowed, that the revised 'rape shield' provisions did not violate the Canadian Charter as the exclusion of evidence which is not relevant and probative cannot be considered a breach of constitutional rights. The Supreme Court upheld the constitutionality of the law in October 2000.

Towards fairness in cross examination on past sexual history

While the majority decision in *Seaboyer* claimed the high ground for an accused's right to a fair trial, another interpretation of the rights and values at stake in rape prosecutions was provided by the dissenting opinion of L'Heureux-Dubé J. Her judgment foregrounds the issues that are central to a deeper understanding of 'fairness' and the contexts in which the criminal justice system fails to respond to sexual violence. In *R v A*, when the House of Lords was asked to assess the compatibility of section 41 of the YJCEA with the right to fair trial under the HRA, a similar choice about the privileging of one particular conception of fair trial rights presented itself to the Law Lords.[283]

---

279 Above n. 261.
280 Where rebuttal evidence, evidence going to identity, and evidence relating to consent to sexual activity on the same occasion as the trial incident.
281 S. 276 of the Criminal Code (SC 1992, c. 38, s. 2); Chapman, above n. 213.
282 Above, n. 261.
283 See below, p. 214.

In Canada, as we noted above, the litigation against 'rape shield' provisions has been mirrored by litigation to gain disclosure of personal and medical records in sexual assault trials; in both contexts, the aim has been to increase the scope for cross-examination of the complainant on issues other than the alleged offence. The Supreme Court thus became an ally in defence lawyer tactics to undermine parliamentary efforts to make the trial process fairer for all victims of sexual violence, and to represent the *defendant* as the historically disadvantaged party in such criminal prosecutions. A starting point, therefore, would be the acknowledgement that these issues, as L'Heureux-Dubé J makes clear, 'must be examined in their broader political, social and historical context in order to attempt any kind of meaningful constitutional analysis'. Four key observations are contained within her judgment in *Seaboyer* with obvious relevance for the ongoing UK debate on cross-examination in rape trials.

First, the 'fear and constant reality of sexual assault affects how women conduct their lives and how they define their relationship with the larger society'. Secondly, a main cause for the under-reporting of sexual assault (and subsequent dropping of any charges) is women's 'perception that the institutions with which they would have to become involved will view their victimization in a stereotypical and biased fashion'. Thirdly, the responsibility of *judges* for the continuing perpetuation of myths about the culpability of rapists and the 'character' of assaulted women should be recognised and redressed. Fourthly, previous sexual history should be inadmissible (bar within very narrow statutory exceptions) because it should be seen as *irrelevant* to the question of consent to the alleged offence. Arguments that 'pattern' or 'similar fact' evidence is relevant and admissible are *only* persuasive if one accepts:

> the notion that women consent to sex based upon such extraneous considerations as the location of the act, the race, age or profession of the alleged assaulter and/or considerations of the nature of the sexual act engaged in. Though it feels somewhat odd to have to state this next proposition explicitly, consent is to a person and not to a circumstance.[284]

An alternative judicial discourse is, therefore, available to counter demands that the HRA should privilege the defendant's right to a fair trial in rape cases. While there can be no guarantee that this discourse will translate into changes in legal practices and attitudes (amongst police, doctors, prosecutors, defence lawyers and trial judges), it does at least hold out that potential. In contrast, commonplace cultural narratives and stereotypes about rape (and 'consent') tend to be reinforced where appellate courts undermine the aims of 'rape shield' laws by bolstering judicial discretion.

However, there still remains the task of highlighting how even full compliance with 'ideal' statutory provisions cannot remedy the faults of the rape trial. As Alison Young has argued, defence narratives are based on a 'strategy of insinuation':

> [I]f context and content were all that dictated the generation of narrative, then we could be sure that once certain procedures were agreed upon, once certain topics were accepted as permissible and other topics outlawed, then rape trials could proceed in ways that inflicted no further suffering on the part of the victim. However, I would argue that such suffering is produced as much through the process of law's

storytelling itself, as through the substantive detail of defence questioning. It is not enough for the victim to be villified through received ideas about dress or drink, she must also be made to rub up against the fantasy that informs the defence account, made to perform as a character in its narrative.[285]

It is also problematic that the 'ordeal' of cross-examination of the complainant has become the most commonly assumed 'reality' of the criminal justice system's response to rape. As we have highlighted above, most rape allegations will never ever reach the stage of a contested jury trial (because of non-reporting or police/CPS disbelief or case dropping). Thus, an over-emphasis on cross-examination deflects attention away from other equally problematic aspects of the criminal justice process, as well as leading to public expectations that 'law reform' will provide the necessary remedy.[286] The reality is that, while restrictions on cross-examination are practically and symbolically important, they are only a small step in the transformation of wider legal practices and attitudes in relation to rape prosecutions. As the Canadian experience demonstrates, the opportunities for subverting constraints on defence tactics are substantial; they will remain so as long as deeply entrenched, problematic cultural assumptions about women's and men's sexuality exist.

Rape prosecutions, rights discourse and the Human Rights Act

We agree with the feminist critiques of rape prosecutions. The doctrinal basis of rape law is based on patriarchal assumptions;[287] the adversarial nature of the trial intimidates witnesses and distorts testimony; the culture of barristers and the police is deeply gendered;[288] 'expert' evidence is often counter-productive; judicial narratives on 'rapists' and 'victims' can 'represent an unwitting eroticization of rape';[289] sentencing disparities legitimate myths about 'stranger rape';[290] the law on contempt does not recognise prejudicial media reporting of rape trials;[291] and the political agendas of governments and criminal justice

---

285 A. Young, 'The Waste Land of the Law, the Wordless Song of the Rape Victim' (1998) 22 Melbourne Univ LR 442, 456.

286 See D. Brereton, 'How Different are Rape Trials? A Comparison of the Cross-Examination of Complainants in Rape and Assault Trials' (1997) 37 BJ Crim 242.

287 See N. Naffine, 'Possession: Erotic Love in the Law of Rape' (1994) 57 MLR 10; and Lacey, above n. 93, pp. 98-124.

288 See eg, H. Kennedy, *Eve was Framed: Women and British Justice* (Vintage, 1992), p. 113 ('At legal dinners, rape jokes used to be constant, although there seems to be a bit more restraint now.'); and Rose, above n. 151, p. 307 (re the rape victim as a 'scrubber'). See also, J. Temkin, 'Prosecuting and Defending Rape: Perspectives from the Bar' (2000) 27 JLS 219.

289 L. Bender, '"With More Than Admiration He Admired": Images of Beauty and Defilement in Judicial Narratives of Rape' (1995) 18 Harv Women's LJ 265, 267.

290 K. Warner, 'Sentencing in Cases of Marital Rape: Towards Changing the Male Imagination' (2000) 20 LS 592.

291 On contempt laws generally, see G. Robertson and A. Nicol, *Media Law* (Penguin, 1992), pp. 261-304. Contrast with S. Lees, 'Media Reporting of Rape: The 1993 British "Date Rape" Controversy' in D. Kidd-Hewitt and R. Osborne (eds.), above n. 154, pp. 107-130; K. Soothill, S. Walby and P. Bagguley, 'Judges, the Media, and Rape' (1990) 17 JLS 211; and C. Carter, 'When the "Extraordinary" Becomes "Ordinary": Everyday News of Sexual Violence' in C. Carter, G. Branston and S. Allan (eds.), *News, Gender and Power* (Routledge, 1998), pp. 219–232. For an account of a similar phenomenon in relation to women killers, see C. Bell and M. Fox, 'Telling Stories of Women who Kill' (1996) 5 SLS 471.

agencies may be profoundly anti-feminist and counter-productive (as in the renewed focus on retribution and imprisonment). The only available conclusion is that law and legal discourses *are* a major problem – albeit not the only problem – adversely affecting the fairness of rape prosecutions.

In light of this, it would be unwise to predict a positive effect of the HRA in this area. In other rights cultures, 'reform' appears to be endlessly protracted, limited and, often, counter-productive. The more 'progressive' reforms in Canada and the US – such as redefinition of rape as sexual assault, the abolition of corroboration requirements, stricter restrictions on discussion of previous sexual history, introduction of rape trauma syndrome evidence, specialist prosecutor training – have not stopped judges and defence lawyers from circumventing the rules, and conviction rates for sexual assault have remained at low levels.[292] Carol Smart has provided an account of the rape trial that presents the most compelling argument about the limitations, if not impossibility, of law reform ever effecting substantive change within the courtroom and beyond. The trial is 'a process of disqualification (of women) and celebration (of phallocentrism)', and women's accounts of resistance are interpreted as 'consent' (in both social and legal terms) and inevitably become cast in the form of a 'pornographic vignette' during cross-examination.[293] US and Canadian research on the conduct of rape trials confirms the persistence of 'patriarchal stories' in the culture of the courtroom; despite the allegedly feminist influence on US and Canadian law reforms aimed at combating sexual violence.[294]

A further problem is that, for law reform even to be on offer, the legal system appears to require an account of rape that constructs a woman as 'the eternal victim because of her sex'.[295] Women complainants are expected to testify to rape as 'a humiliating, degrading, depersonalised, and terrifying ordeal', and all other accounts of rape which could perhaps 'become forms of resistance rather than sources of victimization',[296] and challenge the current problematic legal constructions of consent and sexual intimacy, tend to be silenced. This silencing is problematic on many levels. Women complainants may not be able to testify to the truth of their experience. Cases may be marked 'NFA' (no further action) by the police because women's accounts do not measure up to the preferred version. The capacity to acknowledge non-stranger rape – on current Home Office estimates, about 90% of all cases – is also compromised.[297] And accounts of male rapists are rendered reductionist and essentialist, which damages the potential for achieving a better understanding of the complex relationship between crime (including male and female rape) and masculinity.[298]

---

292 See Hunter, above n. 265. The Violence Against Women Act 1994 (see J. Goldscheid, 'Gender-Motivated Violence: Developing a Meaningful Paradigm for Civil Rights Enforcement' (1999) 22 Harv Women's LJ 123) was declared unconstitutional in *US v Morrison* 529 US 667 (2000).

293 Smart, above n. 236, p. 26.

294 See eg, Taslitz, above n. 275, pp. 7-10.

295 Smart, above n. 205, pp. 206, 208. See R. Jamieson, 'Genocide and the Social Production of Immorality' (1999) 3 Theor Crim 131 (re 'hegemonizing women as victims').

296 Ibid.

297 See eg, W. Holloway and T. Jefferson, '"A Kiss is Just a Kiss": Date Rape, Gender and Subjectivity' (1998) 1 Sexualities 405.

298 See eg, T. Jefferson, 'The Tyson Rape Trial: The Law, Feminism and Emotional "Truth"' (1997) 6 SLS 281. For an account of the representation of Thomas Hamilton who murdered 16 schoolchildren and their teacher in 1996, see R. Collier, 'After Dunblane: Crime, Corporeality, and the (Hetero)Sexing of the Bodies of Men' (1997) 24 JLS 177.

Progressive social change in combating sexual abuse and violence, therefore, is not easy to achieve. Yet pragmatism (if not a commitment to justice) requires that attention continues to be focused on (human rights) *law* reform: as Smart points out, rape 'is already in the legal domain, therefore it must be addressed on that terrain'.[299] Sometimes substantive change can follow even allegedly 'symbolic' legal victories: there is, for example, a recognition of a discourse of women's human rights in both majority and minority decisions from the Canadian Supreme Court, and within wider Canadian society. This could perhaps be attributed to distinctive features of the Canadian system, including the nature of the equality provisions of the Canadian Charter, the greater access of lobbying groups – such as the Aboriginal Women's Council, and the Women's Legal Education and Action Fund (LEAF) – to legislatures and courts, and the influence of law clerks on the culture of the Canadian Supreme Court. It may also, however, reflect feminist successes in politicising the issue of sexual violence using the language of women's rights, and a *judicial* desire to preserve the legitimacy of the criminal justice system by responding, occasionally, to socio-cultural shifts around 'acceptable' sexuality and gender roles. Sedley has highlighted a similar judicial responsiveness amongst English trial judges, noting that it is only because judges 'have listened to public concerns about the level of sentencing in rape cases that, with the support of the Court of Appeal, English trial judges now impose reasonably tough sentences on rapists'.[300] This suggests that, even though legal change is often incremental and painfully slow in this area, no legal culture is beyond reform. The best, albeit frustrating, conclusion remains that 'the criminal justice system and legal practice are still perhaps the most important and the most problematic sites for radical redefinitions to take root'.[301] It also means that human rights activism must not be confined to legal arenas; social, political and cultural strategies are equally important.[302]

CONCLUSION

The right to a fair trial is a fundamental principle of justice. This is reflected in both the common law tradition and in international human rights law. In this chapter, we have traced the tentative engagement of the civil liberties tradition with 'fair trial' questions and highlighted its historic tendency to focus on coercive state power, particularly the issues of police powers and wrongful convictions. We identified a series of catalysts which have broadened the interest in the right to a fair trial, in particular the influence of Article 6 of the ECHR. Our two case studies (on legal advice and the rape trial) focused on the need to contextualise the right to a fair trial and move beyond descriptive accounts of legal rules and human rights standards. In particular, we highlighted how

---

299 Smart, above n. 236, p. 49. See also, R. Graham, 'Deconstructing Reform: Exploring Oppositional Approaches to Research in Sexual Assault' (2001) 10 SLS 257 (emphasising the need 'to bring together practical reform with conceptual theorizing').
300 S. Sedley, 'A Bill of Rights for the United Kingdom: From London to Strasbourg by the Northwest Passage' (1998) 36 Osg Hall LJ 63, 79.
301 C. Smart, 'A History of Ambivalence and Conflict in the Discursive Construction of the "Child Victim" of Sexual Abuse' (1999) 8 SLS 391, 407.
302 See N. Puren and A. Young, 'Signifying Justice: Law, Culture and the Questions of Feminism' (1999) 13 Australian Feminist LJ 3; and T. Murphy and N. Whitty, 'What is a Fair Trial? Rape Prosecutions, Disclosure and the Human Rights Act' (2000) 8 FLS 143, pp. 157-163.

formal legal guarantees must be interpreted in the context of the complex relationships and processes that constitute the criminal justice system. Without an engagement with the critical scholarship on policing and criminalisation, the civil liberties tradition will fail to recognise the ideological and practical impact of the HRA, and to engage it for possible progressive ends. Indeed, we argued that understanding policing practices and police culture, and the *process* of criminal justice, is a key task for the creation of a human rights environment.

Our focus on the rape trial illustrated both the ordinary and extraordinary aspects of criminal prosecutions that eventually result in jury trial. We highlighted the substantial risks that legislative reforms, designed to address the failure of the legal system to respond to the incidence of sexual violence, are vulnerable to a civil liberties tradition that emphasises the priority of the defendant's right to a fair trial. A clear example of this is provided by the majority decision of the House of Lords in *R v A*, which rejected Parliament's policy decision (in section 41 of the Youth Justice and Criminal Evidence Act 1999) to further restrict cross-examination in rape trials on previous sexual behaviour. By insisting that trial judges must be free to determine the relevance of such evidence in order to ensure the 'fairness' of the rape trial, the majority not only ignored the problematic history of the *judicial* role, they also showed little interest in the expanded conception of a fair trial for which we have argued in this chapter – namely, a conception which incorporates respect for privacy and equality rights. In contrast, Lord Hope emphasised that the legislative response, 'in this highly sensitive and carefully researched field', achieved a proportionate 'balance': 'it was within the discretionary area of judgment for Parliament to decide not to follow [systems which relied on the exercise of a discretion by the trial judge]'; and the statute itself provided sufficient safeguards allowing the defendant to cross-examine where clearly relevant.[303]

Our overall argument is that there is a need to scrutinise and contextualise the meaning of 'fairness' in the criminal justice process and to challenge the rhetoric about (largely procedural) fair trial safeguards. We think that feminist law reform efforts may benefit from the creation of a women's human rights discourse in the UK, but gendered assumptions about the autonomy of women and sexuality are not going to be shifted by legal discourse alone.

The HRA, therefore, is likely to have some effect on some aspects of the criminal justice process, not least because of the volume of potential legal challenges in the criminal courts. As highlighted above, these outcomes may be very mixed, and sometimes symbolically important. Yet, while the promotion of fair trial values has the potential to positively transform some criminal justice practices and debates, it is also true that the range of actors and competing political, economic, bureaucratic and cultural forces within the criminal justice system means that the HRA may have little impact on established power relations and attitudes.[304]

303 *R v A* [2001] UKHL 25, [2001] 3 All ER 1, paras. 99 and 104.

304 See eg, Garland's account of the growth of punitive rhetoric and policies in the US and UK criminal justice systems, the inability of the sovereign nation state to deliver 'law and order', and the rise of order-maintenance and crime control through social organisations and community: *The Culture of Control: Crime and Social Order in Contemporary Society* (OUP, 2001).

Chapter Five

Prisoners' rights

INTRODUCTION

Prisoners' rights is often represented as one of the 'success stories' of the civil liberties tradition in the UK. In the third edition of their civil liberties casebook, Bailey, Harris and Jones observed that 'generally, and as a part of a process that is not yet complete, the courts have displayed a remarkable and quite unexpected willingness to involve themselves in the control of prison administration'.[1] By the time of the fourth edition in 1995, the authors felt comfortable deleting prisoners' rights from the topics covered in their book. In many respects, there is good reason for such optimism. Prisoners have won important legal victories in both domestic and European courts since the 1970s; these victories have, for example, significantly improved prisoners' rights to a fair hearing when faced with a disciplinary charge, to uncensored correspondence with their lawyer, and to be subject to adequate procedures in the determination of release dates.[2] New institutions such as the Prisons' Ombudsman[3] and the European Committee for the Prevention of Torture (CPT)[4] have also been created, offering new means of prison inspection and avenues of redress for prisoners. The significance of these developments cannot be underestimated: as recently as 1972, Lord Denning declared that the courts would not hear the claims of 'disgruntled prisoners'[5], and several judges equated prisons with the environment and ethos of a military institution.[6]

On another reading of the situation, however, equating increased legal regulation of prisoners with progress reflects a dangerous complacency.[7] While

---

1   S.H. Bailey, D.J. Harris and B.L. Jones, *Civil Liberties: Cases and Materials*, 3rd edn. (Butterworths, 1991), p. 684.
2   See generally, S. Livingstone and T. Owen, *Prison Law* (OUP, 1999).
3   The Prisons Ombudsman (currently Stephen Shaw) is appointed by the Home Secretary, is independent of the Prison Service and receives about 2,000 written complaints annually (mostly about adjudications): see *Prisons Ombudsman Annual Report 1999-00* (available at: www.homeoffice.gov.uk/prisons.htm). See also, P.E. Morris and R.J. Henham, 'The Scottish Prisons Complaints Commission: A Preliminary Study' (1999) 28 Anglo-Amer LR 365.
4   See generally, R. Morgan and M. Evans (eds.), *Protecting Prisoners: The Standards of the European Committee for the Prevention of Torture in Context* (OUP, 1999).
5   *Becker v Home Office* [1972] 2 All ER 676.
6   *R v Camphill Prison Deputy Governor, ex p King* [1984] 3 All ER 897, 901 (per Lawton LJ): 'In prisons, as in the armed services, those who have grievances can, and should, follow the way laid down for getting them dealt with.'
7   For an argument along these lines, see eg, M. Loughlin, 'The Underside of the Law: Judicial Review and the Prison Disciplinary System' (1993) 46 CLP 23.

the procedural rights of prisoners have improved, and supervisory mechanisms have been expanded, the substantive conditions of imprisonment are sometimes appalling and also differ markedly between prisons. For example, in 1991, the CPT concluded that conditions in three English prisons (Brixton, Leeds and Wandsworth) were of a standard that constituted 'inhuman and degrading treatment'.[8] In 1999, a Joint Prison Service/NHS Executive Report concluded that the standard of health care provided in British prisons breached Council of Europe guidelines. The Chief Inspector of Prisons for England and Wales (CIP) has produced regular reports condemning prison conditions as distinctly unhealthy and unsafe, and in 1995 his team walked out of Holloway Prison rather than continue an inspection – citing 'over-zealous security, prisoners being locked in their cells 23 hours a day, poor health care, bullying, low staff morale, inadequate education and activities, and very dirty conditions'.[9] The CIP also conducted thematic reviews, producing critical reports on issues such as life prisoners, suicide, women prisoners, young prisoners and prison health care. A small number of prisons have been singled out for especial criticism, including the following trenchant review of Wandsworth Prison's 'climate of fear':

> Never have I had to write about anything so inhuman and reprehensible as the way that prisoners, some of them seeking protection and some of them mentally disordered, were treated in the filthy and untidy segregation unit.[10]

The Wandsworth Prison report further listed allegations of staff assault on prisoners, routine intimidation, inadequate exercise and bathing facilities, and a culture of racism and sexism.[11] In 1999, following the largest police investigation into any prison, 24 officers at another London jail, Wormwood Scrubs, were charged with assaulting prisoners, a pattern of behaviour that was characterised in media reports as 'unprecedented brutality'. The CIP concluded that the 'rottenness' and 'evil' at Wormwood Scrubs Prison was so pervasive – in large part because of poor senior management/Prison Officer Association relations – that plausible remedial options included prison closure, the dismissal of most middle management, and prison privatisation.[12]

8 *Report to the United Kingdom Government on the Visit to the United Kingdom carried out by the European Committee for the Prevention of Torture and Inhuman or Degrading Treatment or Punishment from 29 July 1990 to 10 August 1990*, CPT/Inf (91) 15.

9 The last CIP was David Ramsbotham who visited around 50 prisons annually, either for full or short (unannounced) inspections. Most CIP reports are published at www.homeoffice.gov.uk. In May 2000, the Home Secretary announced that a new Chief Inspector of Prisons and Probation would replace the previous positions of Chief Inspector of Prisons and Chief Inspector of Probation. The move has been presented as part of a Home Office drive for greater accountability and co-operation between the prison and probation services; penal reformers, however, fear that it is an attempt to end highly critical CIP reports on prison conditions. The first holder of the new post is Anne Owers.

10 *Report on a Short Unannounced Inspection of HM Prison Wandsworth by HM Chief Inspector of Prisons 13-16 July 1999*, Preface.

11 A Howard League report in Mar. 2000 revealed that 35% of African-Caribbean and 34% of Asian suspects had bail requests refused compared with 26% of whites; and the rate of incarceration per 100,000 of the general population was 1,245 for black people, 185 for whites and 168 for Asians (available at: web.ukonline.co.uk/howard.league/). In Apr. 2000, the head of the Prison Service apologised to the family of an Asian teenager, Zahid Mubarek, who died after a suspected racial attack in his cell in Feltham Young Offenders' Institution, London.

12 *Report of an Unannounced Inspection of HM Prison Wormwood Scrubs by HM Chief Inspector of Prisons 8-12 March 1999*.

Prison conditions are not the only challenge to 'success story' accounts of prisoners' rights in the UK. It is surely worrying for example that the Prison Act, the key piece of legislation regulating prisons, is unchanged since 1952. The effects of the drift towards privatisation of prisons (currently seven out of 135 in England and Wales) also remain highly contested: while there is some evidence to suggest improvement in prison standards and more effective means of accountability in privately run institutions,[13] the economic incentives to increase prison populations and to cut costs are deeply worrying.[14] Overshadowing both of these concerns, and providing perhaps the most fundamental challenge to the 'success story', is the relentless growth in the number of people imprisoned.[15] Imprisonment tends now to be seen – both in the UK and elsewhere – as the answer to crime.[16] The consensus on this crosses party-political boundaries, as evidenced by the easy fit between the 'prison works' philosophy of the last Conservative administration and the 'tough on crime' stance of the current New Labour government. This 'punitive obsession',[17] or 'penal populism',[18] is also both fed and reflected by media discourses on crime and criminality, not least the normalisation of brutal and dehumanising 'chain-gang', 'super-max' and 'lock-down' prison cultures in US representations.[19]

Prisoners' rights, therefore, may not provide an unqualified 'success story'. It does, however, provide a further example of the limits of law and human rights discourse. As we highlighted in the discussion of policing in Chapter 4, increased legal regulation of institutions like the police – or prisons – cannot automatically be equated with progressive social change.[20] 'Rule breaking' and ineffective accountability mechanisms may be the norm in certain contexts (such as the discretion afforded to individuals in street policing or prison-wing supervision), and occupational cultures can legitimise values, attitudes and practice norms which are resistant to change even after apparently extensive law reform.

13 For example, in terms of contract termination and fines, Group 4 lost its contract to run Buckley Hall Prison in Rochdale in 1999 and Securicor was fined £800,000 for its operation of Parc Prison in Wales. The CIP inspected all private prisons and, generally, 'the reports have been reasonably favourable – more so, on balance, than reports relating to comparable public sector prisons': see R. Harding, 'Prison Privatisation: The Debate Starts to Mature' (1999) 11 Current Issues in Crim J 109, 113.

14 See generally, R. Harding, *Private Prisons and Public Accountability* (Open UP, 1997); and below, pp. 225-227. The former Prisons Minister, Paul Boateng, confirmed in Oct. 1999 that 'failing' public sector prisons will face privatisation bids as both 'public and prisoners benefit from such competitions as standards are raised and costs controlled': see www.homeoffice.gov.uk.

15 As of 30 April 2001, the prison population was 65,600: male adults (51,590) and young offenders (10,440); female adults (3,090) and young offenders (490). A total of 1,570 were under Home Detention Curfew. Assuming that custody rates continue to rise, the projected prison population by 2006 is 73,600 (for statistics see: www.hmprisonservice.gov.uk).

16 See generally, D. Garland, *Punishment and Modern Society: A Study in Social Theory* (OUP, 1990); and I. Brownlee, 'New Labour – New Penology? Punitive Rhetoric and the Limits of Managerialism in Criminal Justice Policy' (1998) 25 JLS 313.

17 R. Morgan, 'Imprisonment: Current Concerns and a Brief History since 1945' in M. Maguire, R. Morgan and R. Reiner (eds.), *The Oxford Handbook of Criminology* (Clarendon, 1997), pp. 1137-1194, at p. 1140. Se also, his 'New Labour "Law and Order" Politics and the House of Commons Home Affairs Committee Report on *Alternatives to Prison Sentences*' (1999) 1 Punishment & Society 109.

18 See A.E. Bottoms, 'The Philosophy and Politics of Punishment and Sentencing' in C. Clarkson and R. Morgan (eds.), *The Politics of Sentencing Reform* (OUP, 1995), pp. 17-49.

19 See generally, R.D. King, 'The Rise and Rise of Supermax' (1999) 1 Punishment & Society 163.

20 See pp. 183-188 More generally, see J. Chan, *Changing Police Culture: Policing in a Multicultural Society* (CUP, 1997).

Indifferent senior management, privatisation, poor industrial relations, a diverse and changing prison population and, especially, budgetary constraints have also been identified as further important variables affecting the implementation of law reform: in reporting on Wandsworth Prison, for example, the CIP noted that although 'its population . . . increased by 50% . . . it is still being required to make efficiency savings, which the Governor regards as cuts in his budget'.[21]

This is not to suggest that prison cultures are monolithic or unvarying; indeed, it is clear from the CIP reports that there are significant variations between prisons in terms of 'ethos', staff/prisoner relations and the oppressiveness of the regime.[22] Equally, however, it suggests that reformist policies, rules and attitudes will succeed only when and if certain conditions exist. Moreover, legal strategies alone may only ever result in improved procedural rights – which, as argued above, may not always be personally beneficial for the prisoner in the context of daily prison administration.[23] In the UK, for example, although the concept of 'prisoners' rights' can be traced to increased judicial intervention in an arena historically off-limits (prompted in large part by the European Court of Human Rights), judges remain largely concerned with the fairness of procedures rather than the substance of human rights. This can partly be blamed on the traditionally narrow parameters of judicial review (and the historic absence of a Bill of Rights in UK law), but it is also clear that prison administration is a site of power in respect of which judges have *deliberately* circumscribed their role. This, then, raises the larger question of whether civil liberties strategies can, and should, shift from their historic preoccupation with limiting the ways in which the state may interfere with individual liberty, towards the imposition of *positive obligations* to protect the human rights of prisoners.[24] There is, for example, a sharp contrast between the behaviour of the courts and that of the CIP; as noted above, the latter operates on an inspectorate model of regulation, and its role in promoting prison accountability and improving prison conditions has been widely commended:

> The UK Chief Inspectors have, over the years, shaken some prisons and often the Prison Service to the roots. Changes have followed – not always at a pace that the Chief Inspector finds acceptable, but at least they have occurred. The beauty of this is that the reports become a resource for interested parties: parliamentarians, the media, prisoners' action groups, prisoners themselves, families, NGOs, academics and so on.[25]

---

21   Above n. 10.

22   See eg, the CIP report on Wandsworth, above n. 10: 'Regrettably I have to report that, in no prison that I have inspected, has the "culture" that we found caused me greater concern than that in HMP Wandsworth. This is not just because of the grossly unsatisfactory nature of the regimes for many different types of prisoner that are described in the report, but because of the insidious nature of what the "Wandsworth way" – as the local "culture" was described to us – represents, in terms of the attitude of too many members of staff to prisoners and their duty of care for them'.

23   For an argument along these lines, see M. Loughlin, 'Review of Galligan, *Due Process and Fair Procedures* (Clarendon, 1996)' (1997) 17 LS 502.

24   There is some analogy here with the legal enforcement of performance standards in private prison contracts. However, our point here is the need to apply human rights norms across all public (and private) sector prisons.

25   Harding, above n. 13, pp. 112–113. Morgan, above n. 17, notes that '[t]he Chief Inspector's critiques have invariably attracted publicity, but they have sometimes lacked policy bite because it is not always clear by what standards he concludes that provisions are "impoverished", "degrading", "unacceptable", and so on. On the occasions when his criteria and solutions have been made precise, as in his unequivocal denunciation of "slopping out", the impact has been considerable' (p. 1172, references omitted). See further below, pp. 265-267.

In addition, the general approval for the CIP model reminds us of the ever-increasing need for civil libertarians to look beyond traditional accountability mechanisms and learn to operationalise the complex and overlapping web of accountability which surrounds prisons in the 'regulatory state'. This is not to suggest that there is no place for conventional human rights strategies – whether national or international – in achieving practical, or symbolically important, changes in prison administration. It is clear that human rights can act as an important catalyst in reforming prison cultures and highlighting the need for effective accountability mechanisms. Equally, however, as with law reform attempts in the context of policing, law is only one of a range of factors affecting prison practices and to limit oneself to seeking change by law reform would be to ignore the potential offered by the dense and overlapping nature of accountability in the modern UK prison structure.

This chapter aims to facilitate a deeper understanding of these issues. It will be divided into four sections. In Part I, we shall explore the changing character of imprisonment. Our objective will be to examine a range of influences that shape the modern prison environment, in particular the role of government policy, prison staff and prisoners themselves. We shall assess how these influences operate to facilitate, circumvent or resist the impact of legal regulation. Part II will examine the available strategies for the protection of prisoners' rights. In light of the relative novelty of this concept, we shall explore the types of claims typically made in respect of prisoners and how they relate to civil liberties strategies more generally. This discussion will also serve as a backdrop to Part III, where a number of key areas of tension, and the success or otherwise of the particular strategies adopted, will be examined. Finally, the Conclusion will assess the future directions of prison reform and, in light of the HRA, the likely influence of law and human rights discourse on the reform process.[26]

I.　THE CHANGING DYNAMICS OF IMPRISONMENT

Prisons often seem places of remarkable continuity. Many of the prisons still in use today were built over 100 years ago and the daily regime of most prisoners (unlock, wash, breakfast, work, lunch, work, dinner, evening association and lock-up) is often almost identical to that of their counterparts a century ago.[27] Yet, prisons have also undergone substantial changes: prisoners once worked in silence and engaged in pointless labour like breaking stones or walking on a treadmill, and, in the 1970s, prisons were wracked by frequent riots and industrial unrest by prison officers. Discontinuity is also evident in terms of space

---

26　The UK has three separate prison systems: England and Wales, Scotland and Northern Ireland. Most of the discussion in this chapter concentrates on the system in England and Wales, though reference is made at a number of points to the other systems, especially that in Northern Ireland.

27　For a seminal study of the emergence of the 'modern prison', an institution that is punitive rather than custodial-coercive and which operates systems of complete surveillance, see M. Foucault, *Discipline and Punish: The Birth of the Prison* (Allen Lane, 1977). See also, A. Howe, *Punish and Critique* (Routledge, 1994); M. Ignatieff, *A Just Measure of Pain* (Macmillan, 1978); S. McConville, *A History of English Prison Administration* (Routledge, 1981); and L. Radzinowicz and R. Hood, *The Emergence of Penal Policy in Victorian and Edwardian England* (Clarendon, 1990). For a history of the British transportation of convicts to Australia, see R. Hughes, *The Fatal Shore* (Harvill, 1996).

as well as time: some prisons are hives of activity, in others a permanent state of tension or apathy obtains.

The character of a prison system, or indeed any individual prison, can be traced to numerous factors. In the UK, for example, external catalysts such as managerialism and privatisation, and internal catalysts such as the 1990 Strangeways Prison riot, have had major effects on the prison system. Three other factors of particular importance, which we shall explore below, are government officials and policy, prison staff and prisoners. Understanding the influence of these factors is vital for an appreciation of the potential and limits of civil liberties strategies in relation to prisons. The inter-relationship between government policy, prison staff and prisoners, for example, often manifests itself in resistance to reform efforts; on occasions, however, it has provided opportunities for improving prison conditions. For example, release procedures for life sentence prisoners provoked little interest when the number of prisoners serving such sentences was less than 500. But, with the abolition of the death penalty and an increase in the number of offences for which a life sentence is available, the number of 'lifers' has grown to over 3,500,[28] and, as a result, concern over inconsistency in decisions has grown and more prisoners have been prepared to challenge perceived arbitrary treatment – challenges which the courts, both domestic and European, have been prepared to address.

Government officials and policy

It is well-recognised that there has been an increasing 'politicisation' of criminal justice since the mid-1970s in the UK.[29] Criminal justice issues have assumed a much higher political profile, and successive governments have competed to catch the populist vote in 'law and order' politics.[30] The rash of Criminal Justice Acts since the early 1980s is one obvious manifestation of this process; the increased political focus on prisons and prisoners is another. The latter may not seem that surprising given that prisons, unlike the police or courts, are under direct executive control. But government interest in the issue of imprisonment has been neither uniform nor consistent. At times, notably during the tenure of Michael Howard as Home Secretary in 1993-97, there has been very direct interest in the character of prisons. In other periods, Home Secretaries have appeared more willing to leave the development of prison policy and its execution to prison administrators, or to rely on officially commissioned reviews.[31] Whatever the individual approach of the Home Secretary, however, government policy can still impact on the conditions in prisons in significant ways. In what follows, we shall highlight particularly influential factors: first, the increase/decrease in prison populations; secondly, direct executive influence over prison regimes (especially where responding to official inquiries); and finally, the organisation of the prison system.

---

28   Of the current lifer population, over 80% are serving life for murder.

29   See Chs. 2 and 4.

30   For accounts of this phenomenon, see D. Downes and R. Morgan, 'Dumping the "Hostages to Fortune"? The Politics of Law and Order in Post-War Britain' and A. Ashworth, 'Sentencing' in Maguire, Morgan and Reiner, above n. 17, at pp. 87–134 and pp. 1095-1136 respectively.

31   See eg, the account by former Conservative Home Office Minister Lord Windelsham, *Responses to Crime Volume 2: Penal Policy in the Making* (OUP, 1993).

Increasing the prison population

The first factor influencing prison conditions is the number of people who go to prison. In the UK, government policy is, arguably, the most significant factor in determining prison numbers, although the courts, police and prosecution agencies also play an important part: as Morgan has noted, '[t]he size of our prison population is neither determined by, nor determines, the level of crime. It is very largely a symbolic gesture politically decided. It could be substantially smaller, as it is elsewhere in Europe in countries with crime patterns similar to our own'.[32] Governments' 'political choices' about prison numbers may take a number of different forms. Legislation, for example, can play an important role in reducing the prison population, as with the Criminal Justice Act 1991 (pursuing alternatives to imprisonment), or increasing it, as with the Crime and Disorder Act 1994 (promoting the centrality of imprisonment). Policy directives, such as former Home Secretary Leon Brittan's announcements on reduced parole at the 1983 Conservative Party conference, can lengthen prison sentences and hence increase numbers. The general commitment to building more prisons, evident since the late 1970s, has also created new opportunities to increase the prison population. One of the most profound catalysts for increased imprisonment and longer sentences has been the rhetoric of Home Secretaries: after Michael Howard's declaration at the 1993 Conservative Party conference that 'prison works', prison numbers rose by 7,000 in 12 months, despite the absence of any legislative initiatives which could account for a rise of such magnitude.[33]

Not surprisingly, the motivation for many such measures is electoral manoeuvring. Their impact, however, frequently causes resentment and despair among those responsible for running prisons. Recalling his frustration at the projected rise in the prison population flowing from amendment of proposed legislation, former Prison Service Director General Derek Lewis observed:

> I left the meeting depressed. It had rammed home how little control the Prison Service had over its own destiny. . . . A large part of the 1991 Criminal Justice Bill, carefully drafted by Home Office civil servants to correct major failures in the criminal justice system, was being cast aside on the basis of short-term backbench pressure and a few minutes superficial consideration.[34]

The same frustration is apparent in evidence given to the Woolf Inquiry, during which a former Director General pointed to the fact that 'the life and work of the Prison Service have, for the past 20 years, been distorted by the problem of overcrowding'.[35]

Executive influence on prison regimes

A second factor affecting prison conditions is direct executive influence over prison regimes and environments. As noted above, Home Secretaries have

---

32 Above n. 17, p. 1184.
33 This assertion was repeated in a 1996 White Paper: see *Protecting the Public: The Government's Strategy on Crime in England & Wales* (Cm. 3190, 1996).
34 D. Lewis, *Hidden Agendas: Politics, Law and Disorder* (Hamish Hamilton, 1997), p. 95.
35 See *Prison Disturbances April 1990: Report of an Inquiry by the Rt Hon Lord Justice Woolf (Part I and II) and His Honour Judge Stephen Tumim (Part II)* (Cm. 1456, 1991), paras. 11.135-136 (The Woolf Report).

sometimes been content to leave the development of prison policy and its execution to the Prison Service, prison governors and prison staff, or to rely on officially commissioned reports. Indeed the recent history of the development of prison regimes, at least in England and Wales, can be seen in terms of the latter: in particular, the May Report of 1979,[36] the Woolf Report of 1991,[37] and the Learmont Report of 1995.[38] Each of these reports had a very distinctive individual character and subsequent effect on the prison system. The May Report, produced in response to a pattern of industrial unrest, riots and demonstrations in prisons throughout the 1970s, signalled an end to the rehabilitative approach and advanced the notion of 'positive custody'. It was strongly criticised by academic commentators at the time for failing to provide a coherent philosophy to replace the outdated rhetoric of 'treatment and training', or even to offer a strategy to address overcrowding and deteriorating physical conditions, and it ultimately appeared to have little positive general impact on the prison system.[39] It did, however, recommend the creation of a Prisons Inspectorate (the CIP), which eventually became an important catalyst for prison reform.

By contrast, the Woolf Report, commissioned in the wake of the Strangeways Prison riot in 1990 (the worst in UK penal history), resulted in a major review of prison conditions. Woolf consulted widely (including with prisoners), and departed both from his narrow terms of reference and the traditional approach of conducting such inquiries. He produced what was 'in all but name the much needed and long overdue Royal Commission into prisons in England and Wales'.[40] The Report identified three themes of 'security, control and justice' as lying at the heart of the management of prisons and advocated a number of major changes to ensure that such values were promoted within the prison system.[41] These changes included reform of the prison discipline system, the creation of a Prisons Ombudsman, an end to 'slopping out' (whereby prisoners, lacking toilet facilities in cells, resort to buckets overnight), compacts between prisoners and staff, and a legally enforceable limit on prison numbers. Woolf argued that all of his recommendations needed to be included in an overall reform package; ultimately, however, they were 'cherry-picked' by successive Conservative Home Secretaries (Kenneth Baker and Kenneth Clarke) who were given responsibility for responding to the Report.[42] Thus, a Prisons Ombudsman

---

36 *Report of the Committee of Inquiry into the United Kingdom Prison Services* (Cmnd. 7673, 1979) (The May Report).

37 Above n. 35.

38 *Review of Prison Service Security in England and Wales and the Escape from Parkhurst Prison on Tuesday 3rd January 1995* (Cm. 3020, 1995) (The Learmont Report).

39 See eg, R. King and R. Morgan, *The Future of the Prison System* (Gower, 1980), who advance the notion of 'humane containment' which combines a commitment to reducing prison numbers with the advocacy of measures to improve the living conditions of prisoners and the basic delivery of services to them. Although not expressly referred to by Woolf, above n. 35, this approach seemed to underpin many of the recommendations of his inquiry, on which Rod Morgan served as an adviser.

40 V. Stern, *Bricks of Shame: Britain's Prisons* (Penguin, 1993), p. 253.

41 See the discussion of the problems with Woolf's preference for the concept of 'control' rather than 'order' in a prison context in Morgan, above n. 17, p. 1182; and his 'Following Woolf: The Prospects for Prisons Policy' (1992) 19 JLS 231, and 'An Awkward Anomaly: Remand Prisoners' in E. Player and M. Jenkins (eds.), *Prisons After Woolf: Reform through Riot* (Routledge, 1994), pp. 143-160.

42 See R. King and K. McDermott, *The State of our Prisons* (OUP, 1995), pp. 38-45.

was introduced and 'slopping out' ended (with substantial redesign of cells), but no legal limit was set on prison numbers. Furthermore, compacts, when they appeared, tended merely to acknowledge existing conditions rather than provide a benchmark for improvement.

The final key review, the Learmont Report of 1995, was published in a very different political climate to that of Woolf. By the time of the appointment of Michael Howard as Conservative Home Secretary in 1993, the general public and media concern about prison conditions and miscarriages of justice in a series of criminal cases (which had led to the establishment of a Royal Commission on Criminal Justice in 1991[43]) was evaporating – in the main, because of a right-wing shift in the criminal justice policies of both the Conservative and Labour Party. Howard himself was arguing for a 'prison works' agenda, including 'austere regimes' in prisons (eg, removing cell televisions) and a reduction in the number of home-leave arrangements for prisoners.[44] The major catalyst for the change in direction of penal policy, however, was the escape of a number of prisoners (including several convicted IRA terrorists) from the high-security Whitemoor and Parkhurst prisons in late 1994 and early 1995. The escapes prompted Howard to appoint a retired general, John Learmont, to conduct a review of security arrangements in British prisons. Learmont's report effectively undercut many of Woolf's recommendations, and emphasised security as the overriding concern, rather than one of a number of factors to be balanced. Moreover, unlike Woolf, it was implemented in full, and as a former prison governor noted, it (and the Woodcock Report into the Whitemoor escapes[45]) 'impacted on how the prison service operates at virtually every level'.[46] When the first New Labour Home Secretary, Jack Straw, took office in 1997, some of the 'austere regime' interventions, such as the ban on prisoner televisions, were rescinded; many others, however, including the limits on the amount of property prisoners can have in their cells, remain current government policy.

Organisation of the prison system

A third factor influencing prison conditions is government policy on the organisation of the prison system. Three particular aspects of the management of prisons have been to the forefront of penal policy in the UK since the early 1990s: first, the creation of the Prison Service as an executive agency with a Director General; secondly, the security classification of prisons; and finally, the introduction of the private sector into the management of prisons. In this section, we shall examine each of these in turn.

In 1991, in keeping with its drive to introduce greater efficiency in public services, and following concerns expressed in the Woolf Report that the prison

---

43   See M. McConville and L. Bridges (eds.), *Criminal Justice in Crisis* (Edward Elgar, 1994); and Ch. 4.

44   See R. Sparks, 'Penal "Austerity": The Doctrine of Less Eligibility Reborn' in R. Matthews and P. Francis (eds.), *Prisons 2000: An International Perspective on the Current State and Future of Imprisonment* (Macmillan, 1996), pp. 74-93.

45   *Report of the Inquiry into the Escape of Six Prisoners from the Special Secure Unit at Whitemoor Prison in Cambridgeshire on Friday 9 September 1994* (Cm. 2741, 1994) (The Woodcock Report).

46   D. Wilson and S. Bryans, *The Prison Governor: Theory and Practice* (1998) Prison Service Journal, p. 15.

system lacked direction, the Conservative government instituted a review into prison service management.[47] The resultant report recommended that the Prison Service cease to be an integral part of the Home Office and instead become an executive agency. The Director General of the new agency was to be given greater operational control of the service, while remaining accountable to the Home Secretary, who would continue to set the overall policy and budget of the service.[48] On 1 April 1993, these changes were implemented, although, in a manner characteristic of changes in the prison system, no fresh legislation was introduced to achieve them. The intention of the reforms was to give the Director General greater freedom as regards day-to-day management and the implementation of prison regimes, but the subsequent appointment of an openly 'interventionist' Home Secretary, Michael Howard, quickly revealed that political power still resided in the Home Office. Moreover, according to the then Director General, Derek Lewis, the Home Secretary was 'driven hither and thither by the breezes of media opinion and public mood. He [was] preoccupied with tactics to the exclusion of strategy'.[49] Thus, Howard regularly requested information on, and interfered with, minor operational decisions: one apparently typical intervention was against the decision of a governor at a Kent open prison to allow prisoners to play golf, which was felt to render the Prison Service vulnerable to media attack. The full scale of the Home Secretary's oversight was officially revealed by the Learmont Report: for example, between the period October 1994 to January 1995, government ministers sought 137 'full submissions' from the Prison Service.[50] The clear conflict in roles between the Home Secretary and the Director General came to a head in 1995 when, following the publication of the Learmont Report, Michael Howard dismissed Lewis, the first Director General of the Agency to have been brought in from the private sector. Howard's argument in his own defence – that the Report contained no criticism directed personally at him – did eventually generate a useful debate about ministerial responsibility over executive agencies,[51] but its immediate consequence was to further confuse the respective roles of Home Secretary and Director General. The election of the New Labour government in 1997 brought no clarification of this issue, although apparently better personal relations between government and the current Director General have resulted in the public appearance of a less antagonistic relationship. Of course, even if legislation or policy guidelines offering further detail on the role of the Director General were introduced, history indicates that a Home Secretary, if determined to do so, can have ultimate influence on the administration of prisons.[52]

A second important aspect of the organisation of the prison system is the security status and function of individual prisons. Since 1969, prisons have been divided into six different types: (1) dispersal prisons (housing those prisoners

---

47 *The Management of the Prison Service* (HMSO, 1991) (The Lygo Report).
48 On the issue of regulatory agencies more generally, see C. Harlow and R. Rawlings, *Law and Administration* (Butterworths, 1997), pp. 295-390.
49 Above n. 34, p. 119.
50 Above n. 38, para. 3.83.
51 See generally, D. Woodhouse, 'Ministerial Responsibility: Something Old, Something New' [1997] PL 262.
52 For a discussion of some of the challenges for administrative law raised by the creation of private prisons, see A.C. Aman, Jr., 'Administrative Law for a New Century' in M. Taggart (ed.), *The Province of Administrative Law* (Hart, 1997), pp. 90-117, at pp. 98-102.

considered to need a higher level of security); (2) training prisons (accommodating most sentenced prisoners); (3) local prisons (primarily responsible for those detained pending trial but also containing a significant number of sentenced prisoners); (4) women's prisons (the Prison Rules require that 'women prisoners shall normally be kept separate from male prisoners');[53] (5) open prisons (designed for low security offenders); and (6) young offender centres.[54] The distinctions are important in many respects, not least in the varying living conditions for prisoners. Furthermore, as we shall discuss below, strategies which may assist the protection of prisoners' rights at a dispersal prison (which are generally modern, well-resourced and limited in terms of population number, albeit with a higher level of security) may be of little help to remand prisoners in an overcrowded and decaying local prison. A significant change in prison classification was suggested by Learmont who argued for the option of a single high-security fortress, rather than the system of dispersal prisons. The likely cost of building such an establishment appears, however, to have weighed against it, although then Home Secretary, Michael Howard, was initially in favour, appearing impressed by the new generation of 'super-maximum' prisons in the US.[55] The increasing level of security at all prisons is perhaps the trade-off for this decision.[56]

The third aspect of prison organisation that needs to be highlighted, now a controversial feature of penal policy in several countries, is the privatisation of prisons. In the UK, the introduction by the Conservative government of the Criminal Justice Act 1991 ushered in the new era of involvement of the private sector in the running of prisons; as of 2000, seven institutions in England and Wales were 'contracted out' to one of four private companies.[57] At best, this development can be viewed as an attempt to provide modern facilities for prisoners and to introduce new management methods into the prison system. At worst, it can be classed as a move towards the 'prison-industrial complex', a

53 Rule 12(1). The Prison Rules 1999 (SI 1999/728) are available at: www.hmprisonservice.gov.uk. Given the relatively low number of women prisoners in the UK (although 'the number of women in prison has risen in most months since the beginning of 1993', leading to a 50% rise (see *Report of a Review of Principles, Policies and Procedures on Mothers and Babies/Children in Prison* (Prison Service, 1999), p. 7 (available at www.hmprisonservice.gov.uk)), it has not been seen as necessary to differentiate between the status of women's prisons. There are currently 16 prisons which hold women prisoners. More generally on the issue of women's prisons and women prisoners, see the references cited at n. 108 below.

54 See M. Leech and D. Cheney, *The Prisons Handbook 2000* (Waterside, 1999) for a comprehensive guide to the range of prisons. However, as Morgan, above n. 17, notes: '[i]t is increasingly common for institutions to have multiple functions (e.g. male prisons to have a small unit for females, adult prisons to have a wing for young prisoners, training prisons to include a small section for remand prisoners). This is an important development which, in the light of Woolf's recommendation that there be developed "community prisons", is likely to become more common. It has become more difficult, therefore, to delineate the numbers and characteristics of different types of institutions. Moreover, it is a feature of penal institutions that their titles and functions change rather more frequently than their facilities and culture' (p. 1166, references omitted).

55 See above n. 19.

56 Even before the Learmont Report, the Prison Service had already acquired a new high-security remand prison at Belmarsh in South London. See also, J.M. Schone, 'Legacy of a Conflict: Special Secure Units, Penal Policy and the Law' (1999) 27 Int JSL 207.

57 For background, see D.C. McDonald, 'Public Imprisonment by Private Means: The Re-Emergence of Private Prisons and Jails in the United States, the United Kingdom and Australia' (1994) 34 BJ Crim 29. See also, C. Parenti, *Lockdown America: Police and Prisons in the Age of Crisis* (Verso, 1999).

concept that has fuelled prison building and increases in the prison population in the US.[58] Harding, in a review of this privatisation debate, has argued that the reality is that 'contracted out' prisons are now 'a fact of penal life' and that, as a result, attention should now focus not on their existence per se but on issues such as prison standards, performance, comparability with the public sector, costs, access to key information and accountability.[59] He also warns against drawing conclusions from the somewhat unique experience of the US system, given the latter's high rate of imprisonment, weak regulatory controls, different types of contract ('design, construct, finance and manage' rather than management only), use of prison labour,[60] and influential 'penal lobby' of private corporations, politicians and media.[61]

Harding's advice is timely, and may be the only option for UK civil libertarians or human rights advocates given that the New Labour government appears to have abandoned its opposition policy of terminating existing private contracts and ceasing the building of new prisons. While the reasons for this political rethink are varied (albeit that it was probably predominantly electorally-minded), major influences appear to have been the financial costs of providing for a growing prison population, favourable reports on the quality of some aspects of the private prison sector,[62] and strategic utility of being able to threaten 'failing prisons' with privatisation. Private prisons, therefore, appear here to stay (although it is very unlikely that they will ever become more than a small part of the UK prison estate).[63] Serious questions remain, however, as to whether, when contrasted against a comparable public-sector prison, private prisons are actually more economical or, overall, offer prisoners better conditions. It is already clear that the ethos of a private prison may not remain fixed: one study, for example, has highlighted how the initial improved standards offered to remand prisoners in Wolds Prison deteriorated as management modified the prison regime in line with the regimes of public sector prisons.[64] There also

---

58   See N. Christie, *Crime Control as Industry: Towards GULAGS Western Style?* (Routledge, 1993).

59   Above n. 13, p. 109. This seems to be reinforced by a recent review of Australia's first privately managed prison which argues that '[i]n the final analysis, the status of the service provider may be less relevant than the pivotal role of the regulatory agency in establishing, monitoring and evaluating the implementation of correctional reform' (P. Moyle, *Profiting from Punishment: Private Prisons in Australia: Reform or Regression?* (Pluto, 2000)). For general discussions of the legitimacy of privatised prisons, see eg, R. Sparks, 'Can Prisons be Legitimate? Penal Politics, Privatization and the Timeliness of an Old Idea' (1994) 34 BJ Crim 14; and M. Ryan and T. Ward, 'Privatization and Penal Politics' in R. Matthews (ed.), *Privatizing Criminal Justice* (Sage, 1989), pp. 53–73.

60   'In one celebrated case, US Technologies sold its electronics plant in Austin, Texas, leaving its 150 workers unemployed. Six weeks later, the electronics plant re-opened – in a nearby prison': see R. White, 'On Prison Labour' (1999) 11 Current Issues in Crim J 243, 244. Two US companies, Corrections Corporation of America and Wackenhut, account for nearly 80% of the private prison market worldwide.

61   It should be noted that the Australian state of Victoria has the highest privatisation rate in the world, with 45% of its prisons in private sector control. In Oct. 1999, the state's newly elected Labour government announced that it intended to take its three private prisons back into public sector control: see Harding, above n. 13, p. 115.

62   See eg, A. James, K. Bottomley, A. Liebling and E. Clare, *Privatizing Prisons: Rhetoric and Reality* (Sage, 1997).

63   Interest in new private prisons has overshadowed the considerable public prison-building project that has occurred over the past decade. Moreover, even in the US, only 7% of nearly two million prisoners are in private prisons.

64   See A. James and K. Bottomley, 'Prison Privatisation and the Remand Population: Principle versus Pragmatism?' (1998) 37 Howard J 223.

appear to be major problems surrounding the use by the Immigration Service of private-sector detention centres to cope with especially marginalised and often traumatised groups of asylum-seekers.[65] Private prisons also pose important issues of legal regulation, which we shall discuss below in the section on accountability in prisons. What is beyond dispute, however, is that privatisation has acted as a major catalyst for change (whether positive or negative) in the public sector system, instituting significant shifts in management style with a corresponding effect on the lives of prisoners.[66]

Prison staff

Regardless of the government in power, the role of Home Office personnel, or the nature of penal policy, the task of running prisons falls to the approximately 44,000 staff employed within the prison system.[67] In terms of job description, around 1,000 are governor grade and 29,000 are prison officer grade, with civilian personnel, notably educational staff, making up the rest. Prison governors have the task of managing the prison. Section 7(1) of the Prison Act 1952 states that every prison must have a governor (and several of the larger prisons will have more than one).[68] Governors are subject to extensive direction from Prison Service headquarters as to how they deal with prisoners, both individually and collectively.[69] However, the very nature of prisons as complex institutions, often operating geographically far from headquarters and where circumstances on the ground change rapidly, means that, in practice, governors retain a significant level of operational discretion. Moreover, the Prison Act and Prison Rules reserve the power to make many significant decisions affecting a prisoner's life to the governor alone.

Despite this significant level of power, little is known about prison governors and their actions. Wilson and Bryans, former governors themselves, note that in 1997 just 13% were women and only 0.5% from ethnic minorities.[70] In addition, although the number rising through the ranks from officer grade is increasing, many of those at a senior level were recruited in the 1960s and 1970s at a time when the Prison Service advertised governing as appropriate to those with an interest in social work. This may indicate a reservoir of liberal political views amongst prison governors, in contrast to the earlier era of military-style figures, but no substantive research exists on the topic. Moreover, although individual governors may, therefore, not be totally in sympathy with increasingly punitive government policies on imprisonment, it is also likely that the effects of a 'managerialist' culture (emphasising targets, costs and audit) have impacted

---

65 See eg, the controversy over the Group 4-run 'processing centre' in a former RAF base (at Oakington, Cambridge) designed with the aim of deciding initial asylum applications within seven days and allegedly saving £30 million in housing and education costs: *The Guardian*, 20 Mar. 2000.

66 See Harding, above n. 14, pp. 134-149.

67 See Prisons Statistics at www.hmprisonservice.gov.uk.

68 The Director General, however, is a figure absent from the legislation.

69 A governor's level of control over a prisoner's individual fate declines as the latter's security level increases.

70 Above n. 46, p. 21. See P. Rock, *Reconstructing a Women's Prison: The Holloway Redevelopment Project 1968-88* (Clarendon, 1996) for an account of the impact of two women governors at Holloway Prison in the 1980s. The former head of Risley Women's Prison, Katie Dawson, took a sex discrimination action against the Prison Service.

on the prison sector in much the same way as they have on the health and education sectors.[71]

In addition, whatever their personal views on government policy, all prison governors face the need to manage their prison and to ensure both security (that prisoners do not escape) and order/control (that staff remain able to manage the prison). The ways in which these objectives are achieved will have significant consequences for the recognition and protection of prisoners' rights, and for prison cultures more generally.[72] In the early 1980s, Barak-Glantz identified four models or ideal types of prison management which continue to serve a useful analytical purpose.[73] These were the *authoritarian* model, the *bureaucratic-lawful* model, the *shared-powers* model, and the *inmate-control* model. The last two models have rarely been seen within the UK prison system. The Barlinnie Special Unit, which opened in 1973,[74] and the Grendon Underwood Prison, which operated from 1962,[75] perhaps come closest to the shared-powers model, where prisoners are given a degree of responsibility for organising their own lives. Elements of the Maze Prison in Northern Ireland (housing republican and loyalist paramilitary prisoners) have come close to the inmate-control experience, a factor of central significance to the political conflict in the 1970s (when special category status was abolished, leading to the 'dirty protest' followed by the 'hunger strikes'[76]). Women's prisons, with their historical emphasis on therapy and 'community creation', complicate Barak-Glantz's scheme because they do not exactly fit his 'shared-powers' or 'inmate-control' models, or either of the other two.[77] In 1971, for example, David Faulkner, Chair of the Holloway Redevelopment Group commented that '[Holloway Women's Prison] would be basically a secure general hospital: medical and psychiatric facilities would be its central feature and normal custodial facilities would comprise a relatively small part of the establishment'. He also characterised the three main themes of the intended redeveloped regime as follows:

---

71   See eg, J. Clarke and J. Newman, *The Manageral State* (Sage, 1997).

72   For example, Goodman, a probation officer in Holloway from 1981-84, argues that during that period 'close inter-personal working relationships within the prison were destroyed in an attempt to turn Holloway into a "proper prison"', and notes that 'the increasing repression in the regime, limiting movement of prisoners, restricting access to education, exercise and work' led to 'an immensely depressing situation for inmates and staff' ('Review of Rock, "Reconstructing a Women's Prison: The Holloway Redevelopment Project 1968-88"' (1999) 3 Theor Crim 498, 500).

73   I. Barak-Glantz, 'Towards a Conceptual Scheme of Prison Management' (1981) 61 Prison Service J 42.

74   See eg, J. Boyle, *A Sense of Freedom* (Pan, 1977).

75   For a discussion, see E. Genders and E. Player, *Grendon: A Study of a Therapeutic Prison* (OUP, 1994). For an account of the problems with the historical under-psychiatrisation of men's criminality, see H. Allen, *Justice Unbalanced* (Open UP, 1987). I.M. Young, *Intersecting Voices: Dilemmas of Gender, Political Philosophy, and Policy* (Princeton UP, 1997), pp. 75-94 discusses the disadvantages of an emphasis on 'group therapy' and 'talk' in the rehabilitation of drug offenders. Emerging tensions between law and psychiatry in the field of the treatment of sex offenders are discussed in C.B. Ramsey, 'California's Sexually Violent Predator Act: The Role of Psychiatrists, Courts, and Medical Determinations in Confining Sex Offenders' (1999) 26 Hastings Const LQ 469.

76   For accounts, see eg, D. Beresford, *Ten Men Dead* (Grafton, 1987); and B. Campbell, L. McKeown and F. O'Hagan, *Nor Meekly Serve My Time: The H Block Struggle 1976-81* (Beyond the Pale, 1994).

77   See eg, J. Camp, *Holloway Prison: The Place and the People* (David & Charles, 1974); Rock, above n. 70; A. Worrall, *Offending Women* (Routledge, 1989); and L. Zedner, *Women, Crime and Custody in Victorian England* (Clarendon, 1994).

One is what might be called immediate help and will include any medical treatment which the woman might need for her physical condition, and welfare work to help her arrange her personal affairs – for example someone to meet her children from school, to cook her husband's supper or to look after her domestic pets. The second theme is longer-term treatment, including psychiatric treatment . . . remedial treatment for those who are backward or illiterate, and group counselling or other forms of group therapy. Thirdly, there is community life – an attempt to construct a community with which she can identify herself.[78]

Interestingly, '[n]o-one came forward [at the time] to question the assumption that women required medical or psychiatric treatment. The only audible critical voice was that of the abolitionists . . . [who argued] imprisoning women was so ill-advised that there should be no plans for a new establishment at all'.[79]

Leaving women's prisons aside, however, it is arguable that prison management in the UK has hovered between the authoritarian and the bureaucratic-lawful, with the latter assuming greater prominence in recent years amidst the growth of a managerialist ideology which has impacted throughout the criminal justice system.[80] The managerialist emphasis on values, clear targets, ordered procedures and feedback mechanisms appears to fit with the bureaucratic-lawful model of accommodating prisoner grievances about basic entitlements;[81] by contrast, the authoritarian model, which displays an instinctive hostility to legal intervention and the assertion of prisoners' rights, is unable to cope with any process of external audit. One study of a prison in Illinois in the US in the 1970s highlighted a shift between the two models, and suggested that the bureaucratic-lawful approach may be adopted precisely because it is 'capable of handling the greatly increased demands for rationality and accountability coming from the courts and the political system'.[82]

The Prison Service has moved in a managerialist direction since the introduction of agency status and the increasing stress on priority areas, key performance indicators and targets for achieving them. In some respects, this may make it more receptive to the idea that prisoners have certain basic entitlements, and that prisons have an obligation to deliver them. With the introduction of private prison contracts, the amount of descriptive detail on standards and the attempts to compare prison performance have also increased. Acceptance of the desirability of having clear procedures to give substance to prisoners' rights may be overshadowed, however, by the perceived need for substantial managerial discretion at the Prison Service and governor level. Moreover, as several CIP reports have indicated, the overriding emphasis on 'efficiency' (in effect, cutting costs) has tended to dominate governors' ability to improve prison conditions or implement educational or health care programmes.[83] Other commentators have also pointed to the dangerous consequences of the emphasis on efficiency ushered in by the enthusiasm for 'managing prisoners', noting for example that:

---

78 D. Faulkner, 'The Redevelopment of Holloway Prison' (1971) Howard J 122, 122.
79 Rock, above n. 70, p. 107.
80 See eg, N. Lacey, 'Government as Manager, Citizen as Consumer: The Case of the Criminal Justice Act 1991' (1994) 75 MLR 534.
81 Bottoms, above n. 18, p. 31.
82 J. Jacobs, *Stateville: The Penitentiary in Mass Society* (Chicago UP, 1977), p. 209.
83 Above n. 9.

[it] makes austerity possible and the brutality of indifference to individual need and circumstance probable. . . . Prisoners [find] themselves not 'structurally redundant', as some argue, but structurally vital – as a means to political ends, as objects. . . . [They become] even more fully engaged in the management of their own incarceration.[84]

Prison officers, like prison governors, remain a seriously under-researched group in the UK prison system.[85] However, it is clear that, just as government policy may be frustrated by governors pursuing an independent agenda, prison officers can also undermine both of the historically dominant models of prison management: thus, an authoritarian approach may be compromised where prison officers reach agreements with groups of prisoners, and a bureaucratic approach will falter if officers deny prisoners stated entitlements. In the UK, conflicts between governors, often from a university graduate background, and prison officers, who historically have come directly into the service as school-leavers, have often seemed as much of a problem as those between prisoners and staff. Indeed, in 1978, prison governors gave evidence to the House of Commons Public Expenditure Committee that prison officers were the biggest concern in prison management.[86] The Conservative government's Fresh Start Initiative in 1987, which made it easier for prison officers to enter governor grades and abolished the post of Chief Officer, previously the highest that entry-level officers could aspire to, has gone some way towards ameliorating the conflict.[87] However, this historic tension – mirrored in several respects by the division between 'street police' and 'management police' – remains a significant influence on the delivery of even the most basic regimes in prisons, especially in times of policy change.

It has also been argued that 'all too often in the past, attempts to liberalise the prison systems have been obstructed and frustrated by the actions and prejudices of basic grade officers fearful of losing their "authority" and "control"'.[88] Certainly, in the 1970s, the Prison Officers Association (POA) did appear to be in effective control of many prisons and, although it was a powerful critic of overcrowding, it was also generally hostile to reforms designed to give greater autonomy to prisoners.[89] The unrestrained use of force by officers, notably when deployed as Minimum Use of Force Tactical Intervention (MUFTI)

---

84   A. Liebling, 'Doing Research in Prison: Breaking the Silence?' (1999) 3 Theor Crim 147, 165-166. The concept of 'managing prisoners' also contains other potential dangers, including the possibility that an increasing focus on risk will deepen pre-existing blindspots: see eg, K. Hannah-Moffat, 'Moral Agent or Actuarial Subject: Risk and Canadian Women's Imprisonment' (1999) 3 Theor Crim 71 for an argument that 'the concept of "risk" is gendered, ambiguous and flexible; that subjective disciplinary techniques of governing coexist and interrelate with actuarial techniques of risk management; and that actuarial techniques of assessing women prisoners' risks tend to redefine needs as risk factors' (p. 73).

85   The most extensive study was published over 25 years ago: see J. Thomas, *The English Prison Officer Since 1850: A Study in Conflict* (Routledge, 1972). For criticism of previous studies of prison staff as generally 'superficial and critical', see A. Liebling, D. Price and C. Elliott, 'Appreciative Inquiry and Relationships in Prison' (1999) 1 Punishment & Society 71.

86   See M. Fitzgerald and J. Sim, *British Prisons* (Blackwell, 1982), p. 14.

87   In addition, as Morgan, above n. 17, observes 'the simple world of the "gentleman" governors and prison "screws" of the 1940s and 1950s has been complicated by the employment of women in all institutions and at all levels . . .' (pp. 1179-1180).

88   M. Cavadino and J. Dignan, *The Penal System: An Introduction* (Sage, 1997), p. 129.

89   One of the CIP's criticisms of Wandsworth Prison concerned the amount of POA publicity material on display at the gate lodge: see above n. 10.

squads to deal with disturbances or during the prison protests in Northern Ireland, was a further matter of particular concern. During this period, control of working rotas by prison officers also led to a massive increase in overtime and, hence, the cost of prisons (of which staff costs have usually amounted to 70-80% of expenditure). This latter development was a major influence behind the pressure for the 1987 Fresh Start Initiative (which also dramatically decreased overtime), and it was also partly responsible for sparking government interest in privatisation.[90] Together, these developments, plus successful resort to the courts to seek injunctions against industrial action by the POA in 1993-94, led the former Director General, Derek Lewis, to the conclusion that '[o]f all the changes which have transformed the Prison Service in the 90s, none is more significant than the transformation of industrial relations'.[91]

It is important, however, not to become mired in stereotypes about officers. It has for example been suggested that 'prison officers are often less reactionary, and prison governors and administrators less progressive, than that caricature supposes'.[92] Moreover, even critics such as Fitzgerald and Sim seem to accept that much of the defensiveness exhibited by prison officers may stem from role confusion (whether they are mere 'turn-keys' or have a contribution to make in rehabilitating/training offenders) and uncertainty as to their employment future.[93] This suggests that although measures to ensure greater accountability of prison staff are vital, especially in respect of the unlawful use of force and extent of racism, effective protection of prisoners' rights is unlikely to occur unless officers as 'street-level bureaucrats'[94] also comprehend and endorse such developments. Moreover, as with certain policing functions and environments, prison officers are among those who retain 'situational' discretionary powers 'implicit within a particular operational or administrative context'; thus, no extension of regulatory mechanisms is likely to erase or fully control individual practices.[95]

Equally, however, there is no reason for despair or scepticism. As noted above, prison officer culture is not static; most recently, it has been influenced by a significant increase in the number of better-educated entrants, the growth in the number of female officers,[96] and increased managerialism. It should also be remembered that prison officers themselves have an interest in improving prison conditions, and not just because of personal pride in their growing professionalism:

90 Whereas UK governments appear to have identified overpaid officers as a threat to the efficient running of the prison system, in the US the report on the Santa Fe prison riot of 1980 (in which 33 prisoners were killed and five staff injured) noted that poorly paid and trained officers facilitated the breakdown in security and control: see R. Adams, *Prison Riots in Britain and the USA* (Macmillan, 1994), p. 95.

91 Lewis, above n. 34, p. 130.

92 R. Sparks, A. Bottoms and W. Hay, *Prisons and the Problem of Order* (Clarendon, 1996), p. 137.

93 Above n. 86, pp. 13-14.

94 S. Sturm, 'Resolving the Remedial Dilemma: Strategies of Judicial Intervention in Prisons' (1990) 138 U Penn LR 805.

95 N. Lacey, 'Introduction: Making Sense of Criminal Justice' in N. Lacey (ed.), *A Reader on Criminal Justice* (OUP, 1994), pp. 1-35, at p. 7. For a discussion of this phenomenon in relation to policing, see Chs. 2 and 4.

96 See eg, M. Cowburn, 'A Man's World: Gender Issues in Working with Male Sex Offenders in Prison' (1998) 37 Howard J 234 for a description of how prison culture affects male and female workers differently and a consideration of the implications for work with male sex offenders in prison.

> It should always be remembered that prison officers typically spend a far higher proportion of their lives in prison than do their charges. . . . The living conditions of prisoners are the working conditions of prison officers.[97]

Both prison officers and prisoners often feel, however, that they have little control over their environment. Researchers report on the 'extreme volatility of prison life – how quickly the atmosphere can change from "safe" to "unsafe"' for individuals who are at the whim of 'distinct and overlapping features of our social and political world' (including, most recently, the combination of emphasis on 'austerity', bureaucratic efficiency and security).[98] Liebling, for example, reports witnessing 'a dehumanizing moment, whereby new managerialism met popular punitiveness', and notes that 'prisoners (and staff) were on the receiving end of a rational choice model of human behaviour, a seemingly authoritarian era of prison management, and the concept of austerity'.[99] Researchers have also noted the tragic underestimation of both pain and fear in conventional approaches to prison life:[100] Rock has, for example, characterised life in the redesigned Holloway Prison in the late 1970s as 'suffering from a sense of anomie and danger, with staff and inmates trapped into two isolated worlds, and "both locked into temporal schedules quite different from those of civilian life"'.[101]

Prisoners

The third key influence on the character of the prison system and the dynamics of imprisonment, including the advancement of prisoners' rights, is obviously prisoners themselves. In this section, we shall begin by outlining the composition of the prison population before going on to discuss aspects of prisoners' culture. The former is particularly important given that public and media hostility to prisoners' rights is, in part, influenced by stereotypes about prisoners (which, even if true, would not constitute a justification for the state violation of human rights norms).[102]

It is clear that the imprisonment of a particular individual is the end result of a series of social, legal and political forces that cannot just be explained by the fact that a criminal offence was committed. As we highlighted in Chapter 4, criminal justice is first and foremost a *process*, whereby a combination of actors

---

97 Morgan, above n. 17, p. 1180.
98 Liebling, above n. 84, n. 5 and p. 165. The author provides an eloquent and thought-provoking account of the tensions experienced in doing prison research, in particular the question of using the feelings (of staff, prisoners and researchers themselves) as 'a significant guide to or even source of valuable data' (p. 147).
99 Ibid., p. 165.
100 See eg, J.R. Adler, 'Incidence of Fear in Prisons: Prisoner and Officer Assessments' (1998) 5 Web J CLI; and D. Garland, *Punishment and Modern Society* (OUP, 1990).
101 Goodman, above n. 72, p. 499 (quoting Rock, above n. 70, p. 252).
102 Not least because as Morgan, above n. 17, notes: '[p]risoners from socially privileged backgrounds attract disproportionate media attention largely because of their rarity. Prisons – their occupants, staff, and culture – are a feature and hazard of working-class or "underclass" life. Only governors have traditionally been "gentlemen", and invariably their reminiscences betray their identification with that strange animal, the "toff" prisoner thrust into an alien underclass world' (p. 1151, references omitted). See also, S. Morgan, 'Prison Lives: Critical Issues in Reading Prisoner Autobiography' (1999) 38 Howard J 328 (re key themes in prisoner autobiography and arguing that more attention should be paid to their role in prison research).

(including politicians, police, CPS, lawyers, courts and juries) and influences (including media, race, gender and resourcing considerations) determine which crimes are recognised, investigated, prosecuted, result in a conviction and receive a prison sentence.[103] Many people in prison have not actually been convicted of a criminal offence: out of a total prison population of 65,600 in England and Wales in April 2001, over 11,000 were prisoners held on remand awaiting trial.[104] In terms of length of sentence, the average prison sentence is less than 18 months, although over a third of prisoners are now serving sentences of four years plus and over 3,500 are imprisoned for life (a current average of 15/18 years).[105] In terms of type of crime, only about 25% of the prison population have been convicted of offences involving violence against the person: for example, in 2001, a total of 8,430 prisoners were imprisoned for drugs offences, 8,980 for burglary, 5,080 for sexual offences, and 4,840 for theft. It is also the case that for many sentenced offenders, prison is only one stage in the process of punishment. Before sentence, they may have spent a period in prison or remanded on bail; after prison, they may be on licence and subject to conditions including reporting to a probation officer. In addition, many of those who are convicted of criminal offences never end up in prison, but are sentenced to some other form of punishment, such as a fine, probation or community service; a fact that compromises the common argument that prisoners, because of the mere fact of *conviction*, should forfeit their human rights. It cannot be stressed too strongly, therefore, that the vagaries of the criminal justice process determine who does and does not become a prisoner.

A second obvious feature of prisoners is their vulnerability to a range of social problems both inside and outside prison; as many prison NGOs and successive Chief Inspectors of Prison have highlighted, the bulk of the prison population is composed of young males with little educational or employment background, and histories of alcohol/drug dependency, family breakdown and other social deprivation. Morgan's survey of the research evidence on the prison population demonstrates the extent of prisoner disadvantage:

> [P]risoners are disproportionately working-class (83 per cent of male prisoners are from manual, partly skilled, or unskilled groups, compared to 55 per cent of the population generally). . . . An implausibly high proportion, 23 per cent, reports having been in local authority care below the age of 16. For prisoners under 21 the figure is 38 per cent. . . . Many prisoners have generally precarious toeholds on life outside prison. 13 per cent had no permanent residence prior to their incarceration . . . [and] two-thirds were living in rented accommodation, nowadays very much a minority form of tenure . . . 43 per cent had no educational qualifications whatsoever (many of these prisoners are functionally illiterate) and only 8 per cent had qualifications beyond 'O' level. A third were unemployed before their imprisonment, two-fifths of those under 25: almost three times as many as one would expect to find in the population generally.[106]

103 See generally, N. Lacey, 'Criminology, Criminal Law and Criminalization' in Maguire, Morgan and Reiner, above n. 17, pp. 437-450; A. Sanders and R. Young, *Criminal Justice* (Butterworths, 2000); and Ch. 4.
104 *Prison Population Brief England and Wales: April 2001* (available at: www.homeoffice.gov.uk).
105 See below, pp. 268-270.
106 Above n. 17, pp. 1161-1162. For an account of the issues raised by mentally disordered offenders in the criminal justice system, see eg, J. Peay, 'Mentally Disordered Offenders' in Maguire, Morgan and Reiner, above n. 17, pp. 661-702; and P. Bartlett and R. Sandland, *Mental Health Law, Policy and Practice* (Blackstone, 1999).

These depressing statistics suggest that 'austere regimes' and denial of prisoners' rights are more likely to exacerbate than remedy the problems of many current prisoners. This is reinforced by the preponderance of concerns about prison suicides, bullying, drug use, racism, inadequate health care, disrupted family visits, limited education classes and reduced training workshops in surveys conducted by official (the CIP) and non-governmental (the Howard League) bodies.[107]

A focus on women prisoners further emphasises the pervasiveness of social and economic disadvantage, as well as raising other important issues about female criminal behaviour and the differential treatment of criminality within the criminal justice system.[108] A 1997 CIP survey[109] provides a detailed account of the characteristics of women prisoners: nearly two-thirds were mothers; only one-quarter of children were being cared for by the mother's partner;[110] 4% had their babies with them in prison;[111] 70% were living in rented accommodation and 10% were homeless; 70% had no previous employment and one-third were in debt; 70% were first-time prisoners, with a significant number of foreign nationals convicted of drug-trafficking; 36% had serious problems at school; 20% had spent time in care; 50% had suffered abuse, with one-third reporting physical and sexual abuse from a known adult male; 40% reported heavy drug use or addiction; and over 40% had harmed themselves intentionally and/or attempted suicide. In terms of offences committed, out of a total of 2,450 female prisoners, 890 were sentenced for drug offences, 420 for violence against the person, 430 for theft and 110 for fraud.

These findings are largely unremarkable and significantly belated given that since the 1970s feminist research has provided similar evidence. At the same time, however, central issues concerning gender, criminality and imprisonment remain under-explored and insufficiently theorised, including: why the use of imprisonment for women is increasing;[112] the continuing tendency to define criminal women as 'doubly deviant' and its impact on punishment;[113] the gender

---

107 For CIP reports, see above n. 9. The Howard League's reports are available at: web.ukonline.co.uk/howard.league/.

108 On the latter, see generally, F. Heidensohn, 'Gender and Crime' in Maguire, Morgan and Reiner, above n. 17, pp. 761-771; Howe, above n. 27; and S. Walklate, *Understanding Criminology* (Open UP, 1997), pp. 71-90.

109 See *Women in Prison: A Thematic Review by HM Chief Inspector of Prisons* (Home Office, 1997) (available at: www.homeoffice.gov.uk/hmipris). On the health care needs of women prisoners, see J. Kenney-Herbert, 'The Health Care of Women Prisoners in England and Wales: A Literature Review' (1999) 38 Howard J 54. More generally, see also *Justice for Women: The Need for Reform* (Prison Reform Trust, 2000); and S. Cook and S. Davies (eds.), *Harsh Punishment: International Experiences of Women's Imprisonment* (Northeastern UP, 1999).

110 The CIP's report, ibid., revealed that: '[n]early two-thirds of women interviewed were mothers with the majority having at least one child aged under 16. The average number of children which each of these women had was just under three. Approximately 4% had their child with them in prison, all these children were under 18 months old. Only a quarter of the children were being cared for by either their biological father or their mother's current partner. In contrast, a survey of male prisoners . . . found that over 90% of their children were being looked after by the mother or current partner. The main carers were the women's own mothers (27%) and/or family and friends (29%). More than one in ten of the women had children either in Local Authority care, fostered or adopted. Only a third claimed that the present caring arrangements for these children were permanent or likely to become so'.

111 The issue of mothers and babies/children in prison is discussed below at pp. 258-259. It was also the subject of a 1999 Prison Service report: see below n. 261.

112 See P. Carlen, *Alternatives to Women's Imprisonment* (Open UP, 1990) for an argument that women's prisons should be abolished or used only rarely.

113 Heidensohn, above n. 108, pp. 779-780.

implications of 'neo-liberal risk-based technologies';[114] the impact of gender on prisoner behaviour[115] and the intersection of a prisoner's gender with other aspects of identity such as race, religion or sexual orientation;[116] and the implications of reforming women's prisons (an aim rarely explicitly justified in terms of women's human rights discourse) for the wider experience of imprisonment.[117]

A further notable feature of prisoners in the UK has emerged in recent years: they are increasingly willing to resort to the courts as a means of establishing and asserting legal rights. In the 1980s, applications from prisoners began to make up a substantial number of judicial review applications in England and Wales[118] and, at one period, amounted for the majority of judicial review applications in Northern Ireland.[119] Some prisoners have developed an extensive experience of the use of law; for example, Leech (one of the authors of *The Prisons Handbook*) refers to 'more than thirty successful legal battles against the Home Office fought in every arena from the County Court to the House of Lords'.[120] However, prisoner litigation in the UK has never reached the scale of 'jailhouse-lawyering' prevalent in the US,[121] and prisoner claims for improved treatment have usually been pursued through other avenues. These have included varieties of collective protest such as the strikes co-ordinated by the Preservation of the Rights of Prisoners (PROP) in 1972[122] and the wave of paramilitary prisoner protests culminating in the 1981 'hunger strike' at the Maze Prison in Northern Ireland.[123] The most enduring form of protest, however, has been the prison riot, which routinely convulsed prisons in the UK from the early 1970s to the early 1990s, including the major disturbances at Hull Prison in 1976 and Strangeways Prison in 1990. The historic response of prison authorities to such riots has tended to be a punitive one in the short term, followed by a failure to examine the causes of a riot in the longer term.[124] The Woolf Report in 1991 marked a break with this traditional approach by acknowledging that a lack of justice in Strangeways Prison had made a fundamental contribution to the riot: 'If the Prison Service contains [the] prisoner in conditions which are inhumane or degrading . . . then a punishment of imprisonment which was justly imposed will result in injustice'.[125] However, as noted above, Woolf's recommendations were not implemented in full by

114 Hannah-Moffat, above n. 84, p. 74.
115 For a discussion of the significance of gender as a factor in prison organisation, and the significance of masculine identity in the 1990 Strangeways Prison riot, see E. Carrabine and B. Longhurst, 'Gender and Prison Organisation: Some Comments on Masculinities and Prison Management' (1998) 37 Howard J 161.
116 See generally, above n. 19.
117 The CIP called for a rethink of the design of women's prisons, not just in terms of location near major urban areas, but in terms of function; it has argued that, in light of the particular needs of this group, 'transitional prisons' providing for the re-integration of women into the community and appropriate social services are likely to be a more effective means of minimising the risk of re-offending for most prisoners: see *Women in Prison*, above n. 19.
118 See M. Sunkin et al., *Judicial Review in Perspective* (Cavendish, 1996).
119 See B. Hadfield and E. Weaver, 'Trends in Judicial Review in Northern Ireland' [1991] PL 12.
120 M. Leech, *A Product of the System* (Gollancz, 1992), p. 13.
121 See D. Milovanovic, 'Jailhouse Lawyers and Jailhouse Lawyering' (1988) 16 Int J Sociology of Law 455.
122 See M. Fitzgerald, *Prisoners in Revolt* (Penguin, 1977).
123 See above n. 76.
124 See Adams, above n. 90, pp. 170-192.
125 Above n. 35, para. 10.19.

government and, while riots may act as a catalyst in bringing prison conditions to public attention, history indicates that this does not mean that they will ultimately produce an improvement in prisoners' rights.

The concept of rights for prisoners may also have negative connotations within particular prison environments, and raise difficult strategic questions for human rights activists. For example, while many prisoners experience powerlessness in relation to many basic aspects of life within prisons, it is also true that some groups of prisoners can have significant power within an institution.[126] Prison staff may seek to co-opt any such influential groups in order to facilitate overall control, and these officer/group relationships may, in turn, lead to staff 'ignoring' inmate-group abuse of other prisoners. Such inmate subcultures are a prevalent feature of US male prisons, wherein divides along racial or ethnic lines (and also in accordance with sexual roles[127]) are common, but equivalent subcultures do not appear to exist in UK prisons. This cultural difference has been attributed to the presence in the US of sophisticated organised crime, street gang culture and maximum security prisons, as well as an endemic history of racial tension.[128] The 'lawlessness' of some US prisons, and the power of inmate groups to violate the rights of other prisoners (in particular via physical and sexual assaults), seems rather at odds with the perceived legalism of wider US culture. Some writers such as DiLulio have suggested that advances in terms of prisoners' rights (for example, in relation to discipline procedures) have actually demoralised prison staff and weakened control mechanisms, creating a vacuum into which gangs have stepped.[129] This perspective appears to suggest that earlier, more authoritarian, prison environments in the US may actually have offered better protection to a majority of prisoners, by ensuring prisoner safety and enabling basic services such as visits, work and education to be delivered without disruption. This view, however, has not gone unchallenged, both as to whether the past environment was so stable (and at what cost, in terms of repressive regimes) and the extent to which greater recognition of prisoners' rights has been a causal factor in the decline in prisoner safety in the US.[130] It has, for example, been argued that the massive growth in the US prison population, the increasing social and economic disparities within US society, the frequency of 'real life' sentences, as well as the factors identified above, are more likely causative influences on the brutalisation of US prison cultures.[131]

Researchers have found significant violence and harassment in UK prisons.[132] King and McDermott, for example, found that about 12% of prisoners reported

126 G. Sykes, *The Society of Captives* (Princeton UP, 1956).
127 See G.J. Knowles, 'Male Prison Rape: A Search for Causation and Prevention' (1999) 38 Howard J 267.
128 See eg, Morgan, above n. 17. A study of Scottish women prisoners also found little evidence of subcultures or of close inmate solidarity: see P. Carlen, *Women's Imprisonment* (Routledge, 1983).
129 J. DiLulio, 'The Old Regime and the Ruiz Revolution: The Impact of Federal Intervention on Texas Prisons' in J. DiLulio (ed.), *Courts, Corrections and the Constitution* (OUP, 1991), pp. 51-72, at p. 51.
130 See S. Ekland-Olson and S. Martin, '*Ruiz*: A Struggle over Legitimacy' in DiLulio, ibid., pp. 73-93.
131 What this debate may highlight for the UK context, however, is the extent to which security and control measures (such as prisoner searches or removal from association) need to be recognised as genuinely necessary to protect the rights of other vulnerable prisoners and to ensure effective prison administration.
132 See eg, Adler, above n. 100; and CIP reports, especially in respect of young offender institutions and bullying, above n. 9.

assaults by fellow prisoners, and that the rate rose as the security level increased.[133] They did not, however, find disproportionate levels of assaults on racial grounds, despite the fact that racial tension is a factor in UK prisons, especially given the over-representation of ethnic groups in the prison population.[134] The CIP's survey of women prisoners reported that one-third had been bullied, and the scale of violence and bullying (and the resulting self-harm) in young offender institutions has been highlighted as a particular concern by several CIP reports and also by the Howard League for Penal Reform.[135] There is also evidence that some groups of prisoners, notably sex-offenders, are especially vulnerable to violence from other prisoners and, as a result, may seek segregation for their own protection.[136]

II.   LEGAL STRATEGIES FOR PROTECTING PRISONERS' RIGHTS

The idea of asserting the civil liberties or legal/human rights of prisoners is a relatively new one in the UK. There has, however, been an abundant supply of prison *reformers* who have sought to improve conditions in prisons, dating back at least to the work of John Howard and Elizabeth Fry in the eighteenth century.[137] In the nineteenth century, individual reformers were supplemented by organisations such as the Howard League for Penal Reform, who urged politicians and prison officials to mitigate the harshness of prison conditions. Many of the demands of these prison reformers, such as a reduction in overcrowding and improved access to letters and visits, gave substance to the 'rights' of prisoners, but the discourse of rights was rarely used. This was not surprising given the historic absence of a human rights base to UK law. Moreover, even within the UK civil liberties tradition of emphasising state non-interference with 'liberties', the position of prisoners was considered unique: the fact of imprisonment, in effect, resulted in the near-total absence of legal regulation. The latter approach and its consequences was evident even up until the early 1980s, with judges stressing the internal autonomy of prisons:

> All prisons are likely to have within them a few prisoners intent on disrupting the administration. They are likely to have even more who delude themselves that they are the victims of injustice. To allow such men to have access to the High Court whenever they thought that the governor abused his powers, failed to give them a fair hearing or misconstrued the prison rules would undermine and weaken his authority and make management very difficult indeed. In prisons, as in the armed services, those who have grievances can, and should, follow the way laid down for getting them dealt with.[138]

---

133 Above n. 42, p. 122.

134 See eg, E. Genders and E. Player, *Race Relations in Prison* (OUP, 1989).

135 See eg, *Banged Up, Beaten Up, Cutting Up* (HLPR, 1995); and *Young Prisoners: A Thematic Review by HM Chief Inspector of Prisons for England and Wales* (1997) (available at: www.homeoffice.gov.uk).

136 For discussion of the 'victim's' contribution to assault in prison more generally, see K. Edgar and I. O'Donnell, 'Assault in Prison: The "Victim's" Contribution' (1998) 38 BJ Crim 635.

137 Above n. 27.

138 *R v Camphill Prison Deputy Governor, ex p King* [1984] 3 All ER 897, 901 (per Lawton LJ). See also, *Arbon v Anderson* [1943] KB 252, 255: 'it would be fatal to all discipline in prisons if governors and warders had to perform their duty with the fear of an action before their eyes if they in any way deviated from the rules' (per Lord Godard). A narrow negligence exception is *Ellis v Home Office* [1953] 2 QB 135 (prison authorities do owe a duty of care to prisoners).

A further explanation for the historical absence of a discourse of prisoners' rights in the UK can be found in the nature of pressure group practices: most often, these took non-legal forms, such as lobbying Parliament,[139] and charity-based campaigns for improved prison conditions tended to stress the likelihood of facilitating a prisoner's reform and rehabilitation back into society rather than the individual autonomy and integrity of prisoners.[140] The paternalism generated by the historic alliance between the professions of medicine, psychiatry and social services and the prison system, particularly in relation to female offenders (who were (and are) commonly characterised as 'ill' or 'deviant' and in need of treatment or therapy rather than punishment per se) may also have functioned as a further deterrent to the development of ideas of prisoners' rights.[141]

The prison reform lobby's predominant focus on issues such as prisoner access to work, education, family visits and early release – and the corresponding lack of discussion of the inhumanity of the prison system or the repressive methods by which control was maintained – persisted up until the late 1970s. A key shift occurred, however, with the publication in 1983 of JUSTICE's report, *Justice in Prisons*, and thereafter campaigning groups began to orientate their aims and documentation around the discourse of prisoners' rights. This shift mirrored broader patterns in the civil liberties tradition in the UK in the 1980s, amidst the deepening influence of European and international human rights discourse.[142] It is also arguable that the prominent role of Amnesty International, with its primary focus on the position of prisoners, was influential in drawing lawyers' attention to the importance of human rights standards in monitoring prison authorities (most obviously, of course, in the case of South Africa's treatment of the 'world's most famous prisoner', Nelson Mandela). It is even possible that the extent of the miscarriages of justice from 1989 onwards, with the release and testimony of the Guildford Four and Birmingham Six, concentrated public attention on the daily reality of life in UK prisons. Whatever the exact reasons, however, 'prisoners' rights', while still contested, are no longer a total misnomer in political and legal discourse in the UK.

In terms of the means of asserting, and seeking legal recognition of, prisoners' rights, three main legal strategies can be identified: a 'rule of law' strategy; a 'prison as public body' strategy; and a 'human rights of prisoners' strategy. There are obvious overlaps between these three strategies, particularly in terms of the initial need to satisfy the procedural rules of judicial review,[143] but as will be highlighted in what follows, there are also significant differences that merit attention. In Part III, we shall illustrate the use of these different legal strategies in a series of case studies on prisoner challenges to aspects of prison management or living conditions.

---

139 See C. Harlow and R. Rawlings, *Pressure Through Law* (Routledge, 1992).
140 More radical lobbying groups pursued an abolitionist line and also refused to engage in discussions as to what rights prisoners should have within prisons.
141 See generally, J. Sim, *Medical Power in Prisons: The Prison Medical Service in England 1774-1989* (Open UP, 1990).
142 See Ch. 1 generally.
143 Harlow and Rawlings, above n. 48.

The 'rule of law' strategy

The first legal strategy seeks simply to ensure that the prison authorities keep to the limits of their powers as set out in the relevant statute or rules. This may appear to be a very minimalist strategy and little more than an assertion of a narrow and classic version of the rule of law[144] – commonly subsumed under the 'ultra vires' or 'illegality' head of judicial review. However, it is remarkable how often prison authorities have failed to observe even minimal duties:

> According to their own rules we were entitled to one hour's exercise a day, yet they had never offered it to us. We asked about this and they said that the exercise was available to us but we weren't prepared to wear prison uniform to get it. Our argument was that this wasn't specified in the rules. This seemed to carry a bit of weight because the next day they came to us and offered us exercise – in the nude.[145]

This account may be extreme – it describes the circumstances of prisoners during the Northern Ireland Maze Prison protest in the 1970s – but the experience it documents is not unusual. As the Dutch writer Constantijn Kelk has observed, prisons are characterised by strictly defined duties for inmates, coupled with vaguely defined entitlements.[146] Thus, when prison authorities are forced to recognise the commitments contained in prison regulations, an important principle is established: prisoners have 'rights' (however weak) rather than mere privileges which can be withdrawn at any time and on any pretext. Not surprisingly, in their study of the maintenance of order in prisons, Sparks, Hay and Bottoms found that prisoners were especially concerned that the prison authorities 'deliver' on these written commitments, narrow as they might be: conformity with the 'letter of the law' was seen as key to the legitimacy and fairness of the internal order.[147]

The legal strategy of insisting on commitments being defined and honoured is especially threatening to authoritarian styles of prison management, which require the reproduction of deference to authority figures. Enabling prisoners to 'bring power to account'[148] within the environment of a prison is, therefore, much more radical than it may initially seem. Furthermore, as has been highlighted by several challenges on the issue of the legal accountability of the prison authorities, a 'rule of law' strategy can tease out what is and is not covered by existing rules, and thereby open up new debates as to the adequacy of the current legal regulation of prisons. Ultimately, however, this strategy exhibits the limitations of any approach that focuses only on the legal authority for actions, rather than the substantive merits of that action – the general criticism often levelled at the historic judicial review jurisdiction in the UK.[149] In practice, it means that prison authorities may remain free to define the limits of their

---

144 See eg, the accounts provided by A.V. Dicey, *Introduction to the Study of the Law of the Constitution* (Macmillan, 1939) (re the absolute supremacy of ordinary law over government officials) and J. Raz, 'The Rule of Law and its Virtue' (1977) 93 LQR 195.

145 See Campbell, McKeown and O'Hagan, above n. 76, p. 16.

146 Quoted in D. Van Zyl Smit, *South African Prison Law and Practice* (Durban: Butterworths, 1992), p. 45.

147 Sparks, Hay and Bottoms, above n. 92, p. 308.

148 See L. Taylor, 'Bringing Power to Particular Account: Peter Rajah and the Hull Board of Visitors' in P. Carlen and R. Collinson (eds.), *Radical Issues in Criminology* (Martin Robertson, 1980), pp. 25-39.

149 See generally, M. Hunt, *Using Human Rights Law in English Courts* (Hart, 1998).

own power and exercise of discretion. Furthermore, even when gaps or flaws in legal regulation have been identified, judges have historically considered themselves unable to provide rights or remedies via an emphasis on the 'rule of law'.

The 'prison as public body' strategy

The second legal strategy corresponds with the expansion of English administrative law in recent decades and focuses on the identification of the prison as equivalent to any other state/public body.[150] It rejects the historic notion of prison as an institution entirely separate from the rest of society and seeks to apply the legal norms governing other public institutions to the prison environment. The point of departure for this strategy is Lord Wilberforce's important observation that '[u]nder English law a prisoner retains all rights which are not taken away expressly or by necessary implication'.[151] In other words, once the loss of the right to liberty has been accepted, the onus is on the prison authorities to demonstrate the extent (if any) to which prisoners lose their rights to bodily integrity, privacy, or freedom of expression. They may do this by reference either to express legal justifications (for example, the Criminal Evidence (Amendment) Act 1997 permits compulsory drug testing) or to claims of operational necessity (for example, the need for staff surveillance of 'private' spaces to maintain order). The advantage of using this 'public law' strategy is that it offers an external critique of the prevailing prison regulations and practices, and reinforces the principle that people are sent to prison *as* punishment and not *for* punishment. Moreover, by introducing the judicial review standards of necessity and proportionality (even in the very weak version historically available in UK public law),[152] it may be possible to challenge the breadth of many prison regulations and their inappropriate application to low-risk and low-security prisoners.

This strategy, however, also has its limitations. One is the historical lack of a clear set of constitutional rights or values in UK law against which prison standards can be measured.[153] This absence has meant that judicial review has been hamstrung in its ability to hold public institutions to account and has remained primarily concerned with 'remedies and not rights'[154] – as is demonstrated by the judicial interpretation of the three contemporary review standards of 'illegality', 'unfair procedures' and 'irrationality'.[155] One of the major expectations of many public lawyers is that the HRA will transform judicial review from a procedural-based to a substantive rights-based jurisdiction (with obvious potential for more rigorous scrutiny of prison administration).[156]

---

150 See M. Hunt, 'Constitutionalism and the Contractualisation of Government' in Taggart, above n. 52, pp. 21-39.
151 *Raymond v Honey* [1983] 1 AC 1.
152 See generally, M. Supperstone and J. Coppel, 'Judicial Review After the Human Rights Act' (1999) 3 EHRLR 301; and G. Wong, 'Towards the Nutcracker Principle: Reconsidering the Objections to Proportionality' [2000] PL 92.
153 See S. Millns and N. Whitty, 'Public Law and Feminism' in S. Millns and N. Whitty (eds.), *Feminist Perspectives on Public Law* (Cavendish, 1999), pp. 1-17, at pp. 2-10.
154 *Davy v Spelthorne BC* [1984] AC 262, 272 (per Lord Wilberforce).
155 See generally, P.P. Craig, *Administrative Law* (Sweet & Maxwell, 1999).
156 See Supperstone and Coppel, above n. 152; and Ch. 1, pp. 27-29.

Unfortunately, however, this expectation may not be realised in practice. As several commentators have argued, the traditional procedural and substantive limitations of judicial review (including the public/private law divide, government contracts, rules of standing and issues of non-justiciability) remain manifest even in jurisdictions with Bills of Rights.[157] More generally, there continue to be significant questions about the merits of judicial review as a tool for promoting better public administration.[158] Apart from the question of whether court decisions will translate into progressive changes in attitudes and practices (especially in prison environments), the deflection of resources into litigation and the increased bureaucracy that 'legalised' procedures may entail raises doubts about the merits of some legal actions.[159]

It is, however, also the case that, in certain contexts, legal challenges based on the three judicial review standards of illegality, fairness and irrationality have proven very successful in bringing aspects of prison administration within a 'public law' framework. Obvious examples here include the court decisions imposing 'natural justice' standards on prison disciplinary hearings and those limiting the role of the Home Secretary in determining the length of sentences for certain categories of prisoners.[160] In some respects, it is evident that the ECHR has influenced individual judges in the general development of judicial review standards. For example, in non-prisoner contexts, certain judges – in cases such as *Coughlan*[160a] (allocation of resources and the 'right to a home'), *Smith*[160b] (sexual orientation and the 'right to privacy') and *Derbyshire County Council*[160c] (libel and the 'right to freedom of expression') – have incorporated human rights standards into the traditional common law discourse of judicial review. Equally, however, other senior judges have resisted such developments and insisted that the common law jurisdiction is equal to the ECHR, both in terms of analytical approach and outcome.[161] This difference of judicial approach towards developing a rights culture makes it unsurprising that the case law in prisoner contexts has varied in terms of its references to human rights. As we shall discuss further below, judges have sometimes been comfortable with recognising certain *rights* for prisoners (for example, the right of access to a lawyer[162]) and, in the process, they have sometimes drawn support from the ECHR. More usually, however, judges have steadfastly used the traditional parameters of judicial review to avoid wider discussion of the public law principles and human rights at stake in these cases: a notable (even notorious) example of this would be the curt and narrow judgment of the House of Lords in the *Hindley* case, which deferred to 'parliamentary intention' in relation to the Home Secretary's sentencing powers and contained no mention of the ECHR.[163]

---

157 See eg, the essays in Taggart, above n. 52.
158 Harlow and Rawlings, above n. 48.
159 See eg, Loughlin above n. 23, p. 505.
160 See below, pp. 268-277.
160a *R v North and East Devon HA, ex p Coughlan* [2000] 3 All ER 850 (CA).
160b *R v Ministry of Defence, ex p Smith* [1996] 1 All ER 257 (CA).
160c *Derbyshire County Council v Times Newspapers* [1993] 1 All ER 1011 (HL).
161 See discussion in *R v Secretary of State for the Home Department, ex p Daly* [2001] UKHL 26.
162 See *Raymond v Honey* [1983] 1 AC 1.
163 *R v Secretary of State for the Home Department, ex p Hindley* [2000] 2 All ER 385.

The 'human rights of prisoners' strategy

The third legal strategy seeks explicitly to go beyond the limitations of traditional judicial review by developing a *prisoners' human rights jurisdiction* in UK law. This approach has two main influences: first, the general list of rights included in the ECHR, which have been of growing importance since the 1970s and are now incorporated by the HRA; and secondly, the international instruments at the UN and European levels that are specifically aimed at improving the status of prisoners. In this section, we shall examine both of these influences in turn in more detail.

As noted above, there has been mixed judicial reaction to the general use of the ECHR as a catalyst for broadening the scope of judicial review to protect human rights. In litigation by prisoners, however, the Strasbourg jurisprudence has sometimes been unavoidable: most of the ECHR case law in this area has involved the UK government as a party, reflecting the long tradition of prisoners using the European Court of Human Rights as an avenue of 'final appeal'.[164] Domestic judges have also sometimes been willing to discover certain 'constitutional rights' of prisoners – primarily derived from a common law rather than an ECHR base – such as the right of access to a court and a solicitor,[165] and the freedom from retrospective sentencing flowing from the separation of powers doctrine.[166]

Where human rights arguments are explicitly acknowledged in prisoner litigation, a typical judicial response is to highlight the limitations on rights guarantees in prison environments. In early ECHR jurisprudence, it was argued that certain rights are *impliedly* limited by the very fact of imprisonment itself (and, as we have highlighted above, the dominant common law position was to deny the relevance of law to imprisonment). In addition, even if this hurdle can be overcome, the ECHR, like all Bills of Rights, allows for state interference with most protected human rights where it can be demonstrated that this is 'necessary in a democratic society'. In practice, this means that the context of imprisonment can be used to legitimate restrictions on fundamental rights. Prison authorities often assert one of the most compelling of state interests, namely public security, to justify typical restrictions on access to telecommunications or operational information, or the need for strip-searching or constant surveillance of prisoners. As we shall discuss below, judges show considerable deference to prison administrators' views on what is necessary to maintain security and control within the prison walls (especially in the contexts of high-risk prisoners or overcrowding) – and thus a weak test of reasonableness/ necessity appears to operate. It is also clear that even where the 'implied limitations' thesis is not explicitly invoked, it may continue to function as a

---

164 For a summary, see D.J. Harris, M. O'Boyle and C. Warbrick, *Law of the European Convention on Human Rights* (Butterworths, 1995); and S. Livingstone, 'The Impact of Judicial Review on Prisons' in B. Hadfield (ed.), *Judicial Review: A Thematic Approach* (Gill and Macmillan, 1995), pp. 167-185.

165 See eg, *R v Secretary of State for the Home Department, ex p Leech (No. 2)* [1993] 4 All ER 539 (a prison rule which allowed a governor to censor legal correspondence was ultra vires as the Prison Act 1952 did not confer a power to interfere with a fundamental right of access to court); and *Silver v UK* (1983) 5 EHRR 347.

166 See *R v Secretary of State for the Home Department, ex p Pierson* [1997] 3 All ER 577. But see the narrow interpretation of this principle in the *Hindley* litigation (below pp. 273-275).

subtext to many judicial pronouncements. Prison remains an institution whose very existence depends on the curtailment of certain rights, most notably those of liberty and privacy. It is therefore inevitable that general human rights standards, conceived primarily for free citizens, will clash head-on with the restrictions placed upon people detained in the repressive environment of prisons. Moreover, any such clashes may be exacerbated by judicial endorsement of public expectations about the ongoing punitive nature of imprisonment.

The second main influence on the legal strategy of promoting prisoners' human rights is the development of international standards on the treatment of prisoners. As Genevra Richardson, one of the main advocates of this approach, argues:

> [T]he claim to rights in prisoners should not end with the recognition of a significant residue. ... [P]risoners, by virtue of their exceptional and involuntary dependence, are in a special position and are therefore entitled to additional rights against the authorities; rights for example to adequate medical, educational and recreational facilities.[167]

This approach has a long pedigree at the UN level, stretching back to the 1955 UN Standard Minimum Rules on the Treatment of Prisoners.[168] In 1987, these Rules were largely reproduced in a regional version, the European Prison Rules.[169] The Rules are specifically designed for the reality of imprisonment, where deprivation of liberty and other 'pains of imprisonment' are presumed. Their minimum standards also move beyond a traditional civil and political rights focus and address the question of socio-economic rights; this is important given that the latter are often a greater need of prisoners in conditions of poor living standards and ill-health. The Rules may also help to direct attention towards the special needs of particular groups of prisoners, such as women, young offenders or drug addicts; a focus which is often lost in the interpretation of general human rights standards.

The expansiveness of this strategy, however, creates its own weaknesses. The first weakness derives from the difficulty of pointing to a legal basis for enforcing such standards in light of the content and ambit of domestic and international rights instruments. Not only is there a civil and political rights bias in such documents, but there is a strong tradition of non-enforceability of social and economic rights because of the implications for state funding.[170] Indeed, the stark reality is that minimum international standards can be ignored without fear of legal sanction, as is demonstrated by the UK's record of operating prisons in breach of some of the European Prison Rules.

The second weakness is that comparison with *minimum* standards of treatment carries the risk that the threshold for acceptable prison conditions will set a low level. The UN Standard Minimum Rules have, for example, been criticised as offering a low floor of protection, and it is surely significant that the UN itself

---

167 G. Richardson, 'From Rights to Expectations' in Player and Jenkins, above n. 41, pp. 78-97, at p. 79.

168 See generally, N. Rodley, *The Treatment of Prisoners Under International Law* (Clarendon, 1999).

169 For a discussion of the content of the European Rules and their implementation mechanisms, see K. Neale, 'The European Prison Rules: Contextual, Philosophical and Practical Aspects' in J. Muncie and R. Sparks (eds.), *Imprisonment: European Perspectives* (Sage, 1991), pp. 203-221.

170 For a discussion of social and economic rights, see eg, M. Craven, *The International Covenant on Economic, Social and Cultural Rights: A Perspective on Its Development* (Clarendon, 1998).

has felt the need to revisit the issue of standards on prisoners' treatment on more than one occasion.[171] In the UK, the saga of a Code of Minimum Living Standards also offers a cautionary tale. Long campaigned for by penal pressure groups and prison staff associations, and promised by governments from 1982 onwards, minimum standards were finally adopted by the Prison Service in 1994 as a set of *Operating Standards.* However, the standards were 'not prisoner entitlements' and they largely reproduced conditions that most prisons were *capable* of satisfying, rather than establishing the higher standards that they ought to satisfy.[172]

A third weakness is that although penal reformers have been unanimous in arguing for improved living conditions in all prisons, the political will that would be needed to give effect to such a policy has been lacking; indeed, the overriding factor in government policy-making seems to have been 'the dramatic growth in the prison population and the need to find places for them'.[173] Thus, the crucial recommendations of the Woolf Report on improving the quality of prison life – including reducing overcrowding, reviewing security classifications and limiting the transfer of prisoners from their home areas – were sidelined because of the commitment of successive Home Secretaries to increasing the number of prisoners and promoting the austerity/security of prisons. This expanding prison population – from 45,000 to over 65,000 in ten years – also means that even if the proposal to give legal effect to a code of minimum living standards via a new Prison Act managed to secure political support, achieving its objectives in all institutions (especially local prisons) would be extremely unlikely. Such difficulties do not, however, mean that the UK courts should not avail themselves of opportunities provided by the HRA to force government to provide a clearer statutory basis for the regulation of prisons and the interference with prisoners' rights (as happened in Canada after the Charter of Rights came into force[174]).

III.   SITES OF LEGAL CONFLICT

Reform efforts seeking to advance the cause of prisoners' rights in the UK have tended to pursue either the first or the second of the legal strategies outlined above. The third strategy has also been invoked in litigation, most notably in respect of UK prisons' cases brought before the Strasbourg Commission and Court. These latter cases have clearly had a significant impact on prison law and practice throughout the UK, but, overall, arguments couched in terms of prisoners' rights have perhaps been more prominent in reform campaigns directed at achieving administrative or legislative changes (for example, emphasising the human rights angle on deaths in custody, strip searching or Mother and Baby Units).

The focus on litigation is not unexpected; in part, at least, it can be attributed to the need to challenge historically unaccountable executive power and the

---

171 See eg, the Body of Principles for the Protection of All Persons Under and Form of Detention or Imprisonment (1988) and the Basic Principles for the Treatment of Prisoners (1990).
172 For a discussion of the process leading to the adoption of these standards, see King and McDermott, above n. 42, at pp. 53-55.
173 Morgan, above n. 17, p. 1170.
174 See eg, Hannah-Moffat, above n. 84; and S. Livingstone, 'Designing a New Framework for Prison Administration: The Experience of the Canadian Corrections and Conditional Release Act 1992' (1995) 24 Anglo-American LR 426.

absence of political interest in improving the conditions of prison life. One powerful indicator of the political disinterest is the fact that the UK rate of imprisonment is nearly the highest in Western Europe, reflecting what at least one commentator has described as 'a punitively British obsession'.[175] In addition, as we highlighted in Part I, serious government engagement with the systematic deficiencies in prison living conditions occurred only after prison rioting forced the issue into the public spotlight.

The *basic* quality of life in most UK prisons has improved in recent years, particularly in the post-Woolf Report era. Overcrowding continues to be a problem, but there have been positive changes to the physical environment, most notably through the introduction of sanitation in prison cells (though not always in private areas), daily rather than weekly showers and 'privileges' such as television sets in cells. The effects of the agency status of the Prison Service, a new managerialist ethos, increasing staff professionalism and the work of the Chief Inspector of Prisons have also contributed to the undermining of the authoritarian ethos of past prison cultures.

Individual prisoner grievances, however, remain an inevitable feature of prison life. Where a grievance exists, four main outcomes are likely: first, the prisoner will suffer in silence (a common response from vulnerable individuals and groups); secondly, a complaint will be made but ignored; thirdly, a complaint will be made and will then be accommodated within the prison system via the various responses of prison staff, governors, Boards of Visitors, the Prison Service, the Prisons Ombudsman, Prisons Minister or Home Secretary; or fourthly, a complaint will be articulated through a judicial review challenge. The *Prisons Ombudsman Annual Report 1999-2000* gives some indication of the principal subjects of complaint made by individual prisoners, albeit predominantly received from a category comprising male, long-term inmates.[176] In 1999, the bulk of grievances related to the conduct of adjudications (22%): a breakdown of these reveals that flawed procedures, inappropriate charges, use of witness and video evidence, levels of punishment and mandatory drug testing procedures[177] were the main areas of concern. Other complaints received by the Ombudsman in 1999 included: property/cash (17%), general conditions (10%), transfer/allocations (7%), letters/visits (7%), pre-release/release (6%), regime activities (6%), security/categorisation (6%), assaults (3%), medical (3%), food (1%), race (1%)[178] and segregation (1%).[179]

As the Ombudsman has highlighted, the nature of discretionary powers within the prison and the ineffectiveness of local accountability mechanisms are recurring concerns in these complaints:

---

175 Morgan, above n. 17, p. 1140.
176 Above n. 3, p. 15.
177 In 1998, 88,000 drug tests were conducted, of which about 15,600 resulted in adjudications. These adjudications constituted 40% of the total of complaints about adjudications received by the Prisons Ombudsman. There have been several judicial review challenges to drug-testing procedures: see eg, *R v Governor of Swaleside Prison, ex p Wynter* (1998) 10 Admin LR 597. See also, *Galloway v UK* [1999] EHRLR 119 (admissibility of complaint that random mandatory drug testing procedure in prisons and treatment of prisoner who had failed to comply with procedure breached rights under ECHR); and more generally on the political and legal background to policy of mandatory drug testing of prisoners, R. Hughes, 'Drug Injectors and Prison Mandatory Drug Testing' (2000) 39 Howard J 1.
178 The use of the word 'race' is undefined in the report.
179 Above n. 3.

The majority of complaints which reach me could, I believe, be resolved at the landing or wing level. However, this would require a cultural change throughout the Prison Service and a greater willingness of some staff to engage with prisoners about these issues at the outset and treat them more as individual human beings in their care. . . . [I]nformal resolution by the [Boards of Visitors] will not always be appropriate or possible. . . . I have [also] been concerned with the injustice inherent in the discretion of Prison Governors to decide unilaterally what items of property prisoners are allowed to retain in their possession. Although I fully appreciate the individual security circumstances of prisons, the inconsistent approach to facilities and privileges lists merely serves to cause needless confusion, frustration and expense for prisoners. This means items endorsed in one establishment can be banned when they move to another, often lower security, prison.[180]

The importance of this material is that it throws light on the type of complaints that do not proceed to litigation. While the banning of a prisoner's sound-system on the basis of its size in one prison and not another is a source of great concern and expense to the individual prisoner, a governor's claim that a ban was justified on security grounds (to enable thorough searches of each item) will insulate the decision against any possible legal challenge. Similarly, complaints about the use of security information (affecting decisions about transfer, closed visits, job allocation and drug testing) or the absence of non-smoking areas are unlikely to be successful. The risk of retaliation in prison also explains the low level of official complaints or litigation in relation to assaults or bullying. Where the Prison Service feels vulnerable to litigation, quashing 'the adjudication at the last minute, presumably in an attempt to render the legal proceedings unnecessary'[181] may be used as a preventive tactic. Finally, prison litigation can also be affected by factors such as access to proper legal advice, legal aid and the need to overcome the procedural hurdles of judicial review applications.

It is against this backdrop that we shall examine the points of tension which have resulted in legal challenges in the domestic and European courts. Such challenges have sometimes been the only mechanism available to individual prisoners; litigation has also been used as a companion strategy in prison reforms. In many instances, the European Court of Human Rights has acted as the catalyst for the UK courts' tentative interventions in the area of prison administration, thereby encouraging further recourse to the courts. As will become apparent, however, efforts to achieve legal recognition of rights for prisoners have met with limited success and, where rights have been established, the practical benefits have been mixed. At the same time, however, legal strategies can also be viewed as a considerable success given that prisons are no longer seen as the 'lawless agencies' of recent decades.[182]

Understanding this litigation history is crucial to an appreciation of the limits and potential of the HRA in improving the lives of prisoners and enhancing the accountability of the public and private institutions that serve a penal function. In some contexts, the judicial role will remain marginal and limited; in other contexts, however, there is scope for the explicit introduction of human rights norms into an arena where the reach of law once stopped at the prison perimeter. We shall explore five sites of legal tension: (1) establishing the

---

180 *Prisons Ombudsman Annual Report 1998-99*, p. 3.
181 Ibid., p. 24.
182 See eg, D. Greenberg and F. Stender, 'The Prison as a Lawless Agency' (1972) 21 Buffalo LR 799.

accountability of prison authorities; (2) maintaining prisoner contacts with the outside world, both legal and non-legal; (3) challenging discipline and control policies; (4) improving prison conditions; and (5) reforming prisoner release procedures.

(1) Establishing the accountability of prison authorities

The primary objective of many legal strategies has been to make prison authorities politically and legally accountable for their actions. If the exercise of executive power in a prison context is totally immune from, or can easily subvert, legal challenges, there may be little prospect of achieving more substantive reform objectives. Not surprisingly, therefore, much early prisoner litigation centered on basic questions such as questioning the source and parameters of executive powers.

The main basis for legal accountability of the prison system lies in the Prison Act 1952. This has remained essentially unchanged in scope since 1898,[183] indicating the extent of legislative disinterest in the legal character of imprisonment. It is also essentially an enabling statute, containing little detail on crucial issues such as the maximum number of prisoners in a cell, the frequency of personal searches or the number of family visits.[184] The key provision is, arguably, section 47 which provides that the Home Secretary may make rules for 'the regulation and management of prisons'. Section 47 means that the Prison Rules are effectively the 'law' governing the treatment of prisoners. However, these also avoid specific detail, and they contain many omissions and ambiguities:[185] as Morgan has argued, they are 'ungenerous in their provisions, are generally not specific and, even where specific, usually grant prison managers extensive discretion as to whether facilities will be provided and access assured'.[186] One example is the provision on searching which merely states that: 'Every prisoner shall be searched when taken into custody by an officer, on his reception into a prison and subsequently as the governor thinks necessary, or as the Secretary of State may direct'.[187] More guidance is provided to administrators via internal regulations, now titled Prison Service Orders (formerly, Standing Orders) and Instructions (formerly, Instructions to Governors and, thereafter, Circular Instructions).[188]

It might seem obvious that the Prison Rules should determine the legal accountability of prison authorities. The initial approach of the courts, however, was to suggest that while prisoners might be punished for violation of the Rules, prison staff could not be. In 1943, for example, the Court of Appeal ruled in *Arbon v Anderson*[189] that a prisoner could not take legal action for breach of the

---

183 For a history, see the references at n. 27 above.
184 For a discussion of the content of the Prison Act 1952, see Livingstone and Owen, above n. 2, pp. 5–15.
185 See generally, G. Richardson, *Law, Custody and Process: Prisons and Patients* (Hodder and Stoughton, 1993).
186 Above n. 17, p. 1164 (references omitted).
187 Prison Rules 1999, 41(1).
188 For more details, see: www.hmprisonservice.gov.uk.
189 [1943] KB 252. See also, *Hague v Deputy Governor of Parkhurst Prison* [1991] 3 All ER 733 (Prison Rules were regulatory in nature to govern prison regime, but not to protect prisoners against loss, injury, or damage nor to give them any right of action).

Prison Rules. This ruling was still upheld as late as 1972, although the courts were prepared to allow prisoners to pursue general negligence actions against the prison authorities.[190] In that 1972 case, *Becker v Home Office*, Lord Denning delivered a judgment that was replete with concerns about governors' autonomy, and insisted that 'if the courts were to entertain actions by disgruntled prisoners, the governor's life would be made intolerable'.[191] Within six years, however, the courts had moved away from this position and they began to call prison authorities to account for their actions. The reasons for this judicial change of position are not entirely clear, but two factors (which reappear frequently in the development of prisoners' rights law in the UK) may have exercised a major influence: first, the jurisprudence of the European Court of Human Rights, and secondly, the impact of the Hull Prison disturbances of 1976.

The European Court of Human Rights' influence derives from the 1975 decision in *Golder v UK*.[192] In upholding a prisoner's claim that refusal to forward a letter to his solicitor breached Articles 6 and 8 of the ECHR, the Court rejected the argument that prisoners were subject to any 'inherent limitations' on their rights by the fact of their imprisonment alone. Instead, the Court made it clear that restrictions on prisoners' rights had to be assessed by reference to standard ECHR criteria: in other words, restrictions had to be prescribed by law, fulfil a legitimate aim and satisfy the test of necessity in a democratic society.[193] Moreover, in contrast to the UK judiciary's approach of insulating prison authorities from legal action, the Court stressed the importance of allowing a prisoner access to legal advice in order to facilitate potential court challenges.

The second potential impetus for the UK judiciary's change of position on prison authorities' legal accountability was the Hull Prison disturbances of 1976. These lasted four days and were described by Paul Hill (one of the Guildford Four prisoners) as 'a spontaneous eruption of fury'.[194] Many of those accused of involvement in the disturbances were subsequently charged with disciplinary offences. However, as most had been transferred out to other prisons, an issue arose as to the mechanics of conducting disciplinary hearings. It was decided that a team of Hull Board of Visitors (BOV) members would travel around the country, holding hearings in different prisons and issuing penalties upon findings of guilt. Several prisoners received stiff penalties, sometimes lengthening their release dates by up to two years, and sought judicial review of the disciplinary adjudications. The Divisional Court declined jurisdiction, citing a number of precedents which suggested that prison disciplinary proceedings were beyond the scope of judicial intervention, but the Court of Appeal reversed. Their decision, *St Germain*,[195] may be seen as perhaps the landmark case of prison law in the UK. It clearly held prison authorities legally accountable for the operational conduct of a prison; indeed, the words of Shaw LJ, that 'the rights of a citizen, however circumscribed by a penal sentence or otherwise, must always be the concern of the Courts unless their jurisdiction

---

190   *Ellis v Home Office* [1953] 2 All ER 149 (re breach of duty of care to prisoners to take reasonable care for their safety). For a discussion of the limited scope of negligence actions for challenging poor prison conditions, see D. Feldman, *Civil Liberties and Human Rights in England and Wales* (OUP, 1993), pp. 289-291. See also, below pp. 266-267.
191   Above n. 5.
192   (1975) 1 EHRR 524.
193   See generally, Harris, O'Boyle and Warbrick, above n. 164.
194   P. Hill, *Stolen Years: Before and After Guildford* (Corgi, 1991), p. 172.
195   [1979] QB 425. See also, *R v DPP, ex p Manning* [2000] 3 WLR 463.

is clearly excluded by some statutory provision', marked the end of the era of judicial deference to a (self-imposed) principle of non-intervention in prison life.

The prison authorities, however, were unwilling to lose their immunity to judicial review without putting up a struggle and they sought to restrict the impact of *St Germain*. The decision in that case had concerned the 'quasi-judicial' procedure of Boards of Visitors hearing discipline charges brought by prison officers against prisoners. The Home Office subsequently sought to argue that it did not extend to the great majority of discipline hearings, which involved adjudications by governors, nor to the many other decisions (such as segregation within a prison, or transfer from it) which governors used to maintain order. This argument – in effect, that the courts were not qualified to second-guess such operational decisions – seems to have convinced the English judiciary given that the Court of Appeal refused to extend jurisdiction to cover governors' hearings in *King*.[196] However, the Court of Appeal in Northern Ireland took a different view,[197] and, when the House of Lords came to resolve this conflict in *Leech*,[198] it expressed a preference for broadening the scope of judicial review. Three years later, in *Hague*,[199] the Law Lords confirmed this stance by ruling that a governor's power to place a prisoner in solitary confinement 'for reasons of good order and discipline' (GOAD) could also be subject to judicial review.

The *Hague* decision marked the removal of the last barrier to judicial oversight of what happens in prisons. Prisoners are now entitled to bring any claim of 'unlawful' action by the prison authorities before the courts. Prison case law also indicates that judges are prepared to quash actions of the prison authorities which are based on the Prison Rules but are ultra vires the Prison Act,[200] or actions based on Orders or Instructions which do not comply with the Prison Rules.[201]

This evolution of the judicial approach to prisoners' complaints has been crucial in establishing that prisoners have certain rights which are enforceable in law. Equally, however, the importance of the victory in establishing the legal accountability of prison management, should not obscure the fact that the threshold is a de minimis one. The 'rights' of prisoners in this context are only the procedural rights familiar to all litigants in administrative law; that is, a right of access to court, and a right to challenge state action if it falls below the judicial review standards of illegality, unfairness and irrationality. This body of case law is clearly not rooted in a human rights discourse (which might be the distinguishing feature of litigation in the HRA era): on the contrary, it highlights the limitations of trying to 'fit' human rights claims within judicial review's narrow ideal of 'legality'.[202]

Further evidence of the minimal nature of the legal gain is provided by the fact that the House of Lords in *Hague* refused to overrule the *Arbon* position

---

196 *R v Deputy Governor Camphill Prison, ex p King* [1985] QB 735.
197 See *R v Governor Maze Prison, ex p McKiernan* (1985) 6 NIJB 6.
198 [1988] AC 533.
199 *Hague v Governor of Parkhurst Prison* [1991] 3 All ER 733.
200 See eg, *Raymond v Honey* [1983] 1 AC 1.
201 As in *Hague*, above n. 199, where an Instruction required governors receiving certain prisoners on transfer to place them immediately in solitary confinement. The relevant Prison Rule indicated that this was clearly a decision within the discretion of the receiving governor.
202 See generally, Supperstone and Coppel, above n. 156.

that damages are unavailable against the authorities for continuing to operate a regime in violation of the Prison Rules. The Law Lords emphasised that these were merely regulatory and provided for the management of prisons; Parliament had not intended them to be used to protect prisoners against loss or injury, or to provide any right of damages. This judicial deference to parliamentary intention means that prisoners, a group especially vulnerable to abuses of state power, continue to have access to a limited range of legal remedies.[203] It also provides a powerful manifestation of Hutchinson's claim that: '[f]or all the ballyhoo, the impact of the law on the administrative process is marginal.'[204] In other words, the substantive results flowing from the claimed 'revolution' in administrative law may be slight in some contexts. The *Hague* case also illustrates the inadequate nature of the Prison Rules as anything approaching a comprehensive code of protection for prisoners. Indeed, judicial discourse emphasising their primary purpose as a 'management tool' for prison administrators further undermines their usefulness as a legal resource for prisoners. The volume of litigation highlighting this deficiency has not, however, prompted government to consider the need for a new Prison Act.

Accountability to the courts is, of course, not the only way in which institutions can be rendered accountable or the cause of civil liberties advanced. One other possibility would be political accountability: however, as we have seen in our discussion of Michael Howard's response to the Learmont Report, the political accountability of the Home Secretary can be rather limited in this area. Moreover, even though the former Home Secretary, Jack Straw, restored the responsibility to answer parliamentary questions on the operation of the prison service, ministerial accountability remains too far removed from the daily environment of prisons to provide effective accountability. There is, however, a plethora of other oversight or 'accountability-forcing' mechanisms: indeed, one former prison governor has observed that 'from the inside one sometimes feels that prisons must be the most inspected, audited, overseen set of institutions in the country'.[205] The most important of these other mechanisms are Boards of Visitors (BOV), the Chief Inspector of Prisons (CIP) and the Prisons Ombudsman; in addition, the European Committee for the Prevention of Torture (CPT) is of increasing significance. Each of these mechanisms has limitations and none works to explicit standards of prisoners' rights (even the CPT does not limit itself to Article 3 of the ECHR), yet they have demonstrated a capacity to influence change which on occasions may be beyond the capacity of purely litigation-based strategies.

Section 6 of the Prison Act provides for every prison to have a BOV, made up of members of the public appointed by the Home Secretary, who have a duty to inspect the prison, receive prisoners complaints and make an annual report to the Home Secretary. Until 1992 in England and Wales they also had the task of adjudicating on more serious disciplinary offences,[206] and still retain a role

---

203 See Ch. 1 for a discussion of the remedies available under the HRA, including damages against public authorities. This is not to suggest that monetary compensation is always the ideal remedy; however, the *threat* of such litigation can often force changes in the attitudes and practices of public authorities (for example, police forces).

204 A. Hutchinson, 'The Rise and Ruse of Administrative Law and Scholarship' (1985) 48 MLR 293.

205 A. Coyle, *Prison Report No. 30* (Prison Reform Trust, 1995), p. 28. Coyle goes on to add: '[t]hat is as it should be, since we are the most abnormal institutions in the country, charged with depriving human beings of their liberty.'

206 This practice ceased earlier in Scotland, but continued in Northern Ireland to 2000.

in decisions to remove prisoners from association. In theory, Boards can play a very important role in protecting prisoners' rights and calling the authorities to account. In practice, however, they have tended to be marginalised by confusion between their disciplinary and inspection roles, the lack of clear standards by which to assess the conduct of the authorities, governors' control over their access to information and their own reluctance to establish their independence. A few Boards have departed from this trend and published their annual reports, but most are reluctant even to have their names published to the general public.[207]

In recent years, the other oversight mechanisms mentioned above have assumed greater importance than BOVs. As noted in the Introduction, the CIP, perhaps the most significant recommendation to emerge from the May Report, has issued a stream of reports on individual prisons and thematic issues which have often been sharply critical of government. These have often received extensive media coverage and have not been without influence in bringing about change: as Derek Lewis observed of former CIP, Stephen Tumim, 'although he had no formal powers to order changes, his criticisms were often enough to do the job'.[208] The CIP does not, however, receive complaints from individual prisoners and, for many years, prison reformers and civil liberties groups argued that this left a gap (especially as the internal grievance procedure was seen as slow and lacking independence, the BOVs too captured and powerless to perform this role, and judicial review was both too distant and limited to matters of procedure rather than substance). Woolf endorsed these concerns and proposed a Complaints Adjudicator, who would have the function of hearing the individual complaints of prisoners as to any matter affecting their treatment. Although the Prison Service initially opposed such a development, then Home Secretary Kenneth Clarke did approve the appointment of a Prison Ombudsman in 1993 (albeit on a non-statutory basis and with the power only to make recommendations rather than overrule the decisions of prison governors or Prison Service HQ). The current Ombudsman is receiving an increasing number of complaints, reports a high level of prison service compliance with his recommendations[209] and appears to play a particularly significant role in relation to matters such as transfer between prisons or the operation of adjudication systems, where arguably he can offer a quicker and more satisfactory resolution than is available by way of judicial review.[210]

A third mechanism of increasing significance is the CPT. This Committee is a product of the 1987 European Convention on the Prevention of Torture, Inhuman and Degrading Treatment or Punishment and is made up of independent experts from Member States. It visits places of detention throughout Convention states, backed-up by a power to conduct confidential meetings with both prisoners and staff, and publishes reports on those visited

---

207 See www.homeoffice.gov.uk/bov. Leech in *The Prisons Handbook 2000* (Waterside, 1999), pp. xiii–xiv, notes that he was denied access to the names of BOV chairs.

208 Above n. 34, pp. 27-28.

209 In 1999, 244 of the 248 recommendations made were accepted by the Prison Service: see Prisons Ombudsman, *Annual Report 1999-2000*, above n. 3, p. 13.

210 However, as Loughlin, above n. 23, has noted Ombudsmen as a group 'tend to view their role as being essentially mediative rather than adjudicatory [and] requiring them to develop principles of administrative conduct [for example, via codes of good practice] [would necessitate] a shift in their role' (p. 505).

(though only with the agreement of the governments concerned). It also publishes annual reports which often serve as statements of 'good practice' for imprisonment consistent with human rights standards.[211] The CPT's first report on a visit to the UK in 1990 described conditions at Brixton, Wandsworth and Leeds prisons as amounting to 'inhuman and degrading treatment'.[212] Subsequent follow-up visits have also been critical of things like the provision of medical care in prisons and the conditions of those held in immigration detention facilities. Importantly, there is some evidence that these CPT visits, and its oversight more generally, have not been without significance. Certainly, conditions in Brixton, Wandsworth and Leeds had improved by the time of the Committee's follow-up visit in 1994, and although other factors no doubt contributed to these changes, the CPT itself:

> undoubtedly contributed to a climate of opinion – and strengthened the hand of reforming officials and governors. British prisons needed kick-starting into the twentieth century. Through its 1990 visit, the CPT was one of the actors applying the boot.[213]

The issue of the accountability of the newest form of prison institutions, the privately managed facilities, also requires examination. As we noted above, these facilities are a relatively small, but growing, part of the prison estate. All have a BOV and come within the jurisdiction of the oversight and inspection bodies discussed above. Section 88 of the Criminal Justice Act 1991 provides that the Home Secretary retains the power to intervene when it appears to him that the Director has lost control of the prison, a power which has yet to be exercised. Since powers to discipline prisoners and to remove them from association remain with the Prison Service-appointed Controller, rather than the private sector Director, it is likely that many of the things prisoners are likely to become aggrieved about, and resort to law to challenge, remain the responsibility of the state. Perhaps because of this, there has been little opportunity for courts to rule on the legal responsibilities of private sector providers for the treatment of prisoners in their care. However, it seems likely that as institutions exercising a clearly public function they would be subject to judicial review and now to the HRA. In some ways, there is an opportunity to hold private prisons to even higher standards of accountability as their operators are required to conclude detailed contracts with the Home Office: on matters such as time out of cell or access to educational provision, these have on occasion proved more demanding than the targets set for public prisons. However, the extent to which such contracts can be used to advance accountability is hindered by the fact that the terms of several remain secret on grounds of commercial confidentiality (though where US companies are involved some have been disclosed under US regulatory requirements),[214] and that enforcement of such provisions remains at the discretion of the Home Office. Moreover, it seems unlikely that prisoners would be regarded as parties to the contract so as to give them direct rights to sue for enforcement of these contractual conditions. And, as *Hargeaves* reveals,

---

211 For a full discussion of the powers of the CPT, see R. Morgan and M. Evans, 'The CPT: An Introduction' in Morgan and Evans, above n. 4, pp. 3-30.
212 Above n. 8.
213 S. Shaw, 'The CPT and the United Kingdom' in Morgan and Evans, above n. 4, pp. 265-271, at p. 267.
214 For a discussion of the impact of commercial confidentiality in Victoria, Australia, see A. Freiberg, 'Commercial Confidentiality and Public Accountability for the Provision of Correctional Services' (1999) 11 Current Issues in Crim J 119.

even arguments that such conditions should give rise to legitimate expectations may run into clear judicial reluctance to convert policy guidance into legitimate expectations in the prison context.[215]

(2) Maintaining prisoner contacts with the outside world

The ability of prisoners to maintain contact with the outside world, whether by letter, visit or home leave has undergone a significant transformation in the past 30 years. Prior to the 1970s, extensive censorship was practised in UK prisons and letters to lawyers raising complaints about a prisoner's treatment were especially likely to be opened or stopped. The prison authorities operated what was known as the 'prior ventilation' rule, whereby all complaints had to be first raised via internal channels and decided upon, before a lawyer could be contacted. Given the (sometimes deliberate) slowness of such channels, many complaints simply got lost in the system. Prisoners also faced the possibility of being placed on a disciplinary charge of 'making false and malicious allegations' if their complaint was rejected. Moreover, even when a complaint had been prior ventilated, a prisoner still had to inform the prison authorities of the subject matter of their contact with a lawyer, a clear violation of lawyer-client confidentiality and a stark example of the unequal legal treatment of prisoners.

The contemporary position represents a substantial improvement on the earlier era of obstructing prisoner contacts with lawyers. Prisoners now have a general right, recognised in the Prison Rules, of confidential communication with their legal advisers and any court,[216] and routine censorship has ended for all but Category A prisoners. Prisoners' entitlement to visits has also increased, and all now have access to telephones. In addition, a steadily increasing number of prisoners participate in some form of temporary release.[217] As we shall explain below, litigation and lobbying have played a significant role in these reforms, but there has also been a shift in the views of the Home Office and Prison Service as to the value of contacts with the outside world. The mindset that regarded the maintenance of contact with the outside world as corrupting for the prisoner and dangerous for the institution has not entirely disappeared, but it has largely been replaced by one which recognises outside contact, especially with family members, as important for prisoners' well-being and as a factor in preventing re-offending.[218] Maintenance of such contacts is now seen as essential to achieving the goal of helping prisoners prepare to return to the community, and extra visits are offered to 'conforming' prisoners under the Incentives and Earned Privileges schemes (IEPS) that have operated in most prisons since 1995.[219]

The fact that extra visits have been included in IEPS is, however, rather telling; it demonstrates that visits are still seen as a 'privilege' for those displaying good

---

215   *R v Secretary of State for the Home Department, ex p Hargreaves* [1997] 1 All ER 397. See S. Foster, 'Legitimate Expectations and Prisoners' Rights: The Right to Get What You Are Given' (1997) 60 MLR 727.

216   Prison Rules 1999, 39(1).

217   For example, the *Prison Statistics: England and Wales 1999* indicate that the number of releases on temporary licence rose from 181,660 in 1996 to 256,179 in 1999.

218   See eg, the Woolf Report, above n. 35.

219   See Prison Rules 1999, 8. An IEPS will place prisoners on one of three privilege levels (basic, standard or enhanced) according to their behaviour in prison: the higher the level, the more privileges the prisoner is allowed.

behaviour rather than as a 'right' of prisoners and their families.[220] This in turn helps to explain why the 'rule of law' legal strategy outlined earlier has been the most successful of the available strategies in litigation on prisoner contact with the outside world. Judges have been the most receptive where prisoners have been able to construct contact claims in terms of the 'legality' of public authority action; a notable example is judicial legitimation of the need for unrestricted prisoner access to legal advice. In contrast, where claims have been constructed in terms of general rights to privacy or free expression, let alone claims about the specific individual needs of prisoners to maintain outside relationships, they have appeared far more vulnerable to restrictions on the grounds of internal security or the rights of victims. We shall explore these issues in more detail by looking at: (a) prisoners seeking legal advice; and (b) prisoners' entitlements to letters, visits and home leave.

(a)   Prisoners seeking legal advice

The major breakthrough on legal advice was the 1975 decision of the European Court of Human Rights in *Golder v UK*.[221] Golder's letters to his solicitor concerning a proposed defamation action against a prison officer were stopped because he had not gone through the 'prior ventilation' system. His subsequent challenge in Strasbourg established that the operation of this ventilation rule infringed the Article 6(1) right to a fair trial, in particular the right of access to a court: the European Court of Human Rights reasoned that this right would not be effective if it did not also include a corollary right of access to a lawyer.

This principle endorsed the notion of equal treatment of prisoners and non-prisoners in relation to the right to confidential communication with a legal adviser. Unfortunately, however, it took until the 1990s before the principle was fully recognised in the UK prison systems. The prison system initially sought to replace its 'prior ventilation' rule with one requiring 'simultaneous ventilation', that is, complaints had to be raised internally at the same time as they were forwarded to lawyers if censorship of the correspondence was to be avoided. This new rule was declared unlawful in cases such as *Anderson*[222] and *Raymond v Honey*[223] on the ground that it infringed the 'constitutional right' of access to the courts – which could only be removed by explicit statutory authority[224] – but, despite this, the prison authorities clung to a narrow reading of the Prison Rules to stop such correspondence where a writ had not been issued.[225] It eventually took a further ruling of the European Court of Human Rights in *Campbell v UK*,[226]

---

220 The Prison Ombudsman's *Annual Report 1998-1999*, above n. 180, notes that 'there are dangers that the schemes are used more as a sanction than an incentive to good behaviour and that the criteria are applied inconsistently', but goes on to emphasise that the schemes 'may be settling down' given that 'relatively few complaints' about them were received during the reporting period. He does, however, note ongoing concerns over complaints received about some prison schemes' adverse treatment of prisoners who maintain their innocence (p. 31).

221 (1975) 1 EHRR 524.

222 *R v Secretary of State for the Home Department, ex p Anderson* [1984] QB 778.

223 [1983] 1 AC 1.

224 As the Prison Act 1952 was silent on the matter, a Prison Rule was found to be incapable of offering such authority.

225 See *Guilfoyle v Home Office* [1981] QB 309, where Lord Denning observed that the relevant Prison Rule authorised such confidential communication only where legal proceedings had been commenced.

226 *Campbell v UK* (1992) 15 EHRR 137.

quickly followed by a decision of the Court of Appeal in *Leech (No. 2)*,[227] to establish that whenever a prisoner wishes to correspond with their lawyer they have the right to do so in confidence. The current position is that letters which are marked as legal correspondence should not be opened, read or stopped unless the governor has reasonable cause to believe that they contain an illicit enclosure, or that their contents would endanger prison security, the safety of other prisoners or are otherwise of a criminal nature.[228] Moreover, even in the latter situations, the governor must offer a prisoner the opportunity to be present when a letter is opened.[229]

The Court of Appeal's decision in *Leech (No. 2)* was especially noteworthy in that Steyn LJ took the view that access to the courts was such a fundamental constitutional right, that an impediment to it could be justified only if it was shown to be the 'minimum necessary interference' to achieve some other legitimate objective. This is a more exacting test than the 'reasonableness/ irrationality' standard of judicial review (which judges have often found to be satisfied in the prison context) and means that it is no longer lawful to interfere with legal correspondence because of a *general* concern about weapons or drugs being smuggled into prison – especially as the alternative of opening the letter in the prisoner's presence is available.[230] It seems, however, that the courts' clarification of the position on prisoners' correspondence with legal advisers has not, as yet, filtered through to prison practices; the Prison Ombudsman continues to receive a 'relatively consistent number of complaints' about interference with outside communications:

> Mr X complained that his outgoing letters to his solicitors were being opened, despite the prohibition on this practice. In response, the prison said that such letters had to be sealed in front of an officer and that, in any event, the prison was not aware that the solicitors in question represented Mr X. On investigation I established that Prison Service Headquarters took the view that, if the credentials of a representative were in question, the prisoner should be questioned and only as a last resort should outgoing mail be opened in the presence of the prisoner. . . . I was satisfied that prisoners should be allowed to hand in legal correspondence in sealed envelopes and the policy the prison was operating was contrary to central guidance.[231]

It should also be noted that the courts have taken a different position on prisoner/legal adviser communications where security considerations are viewed as genuine and overwhelming: in such circumstances, they have been willing to sanction a reduced guarantee of confidential legal communication. In *O'Dhuibhir*,[232] for example, the use of closed legal visits for prisoners categorised as exceptional security risks (in this instance, the prisoner applicants were IRA members who had been involved in the Whitemoor Prison escape of 1994) was upheld, even though it was clear that this made lawyer-client communication substantially more difficult.[233] Security considerations were also allowed to limit

227 *R v Secretary of State for the Home Department, ex p Leech (No. 2)* [1994] QB 198.
228 Prison Rules 1999, 39(1)-(3).
229 Ibid., 39(4).
230 This had already been sanctioned by the (former) European Commission of Human Rights in the friendly settlement of *McComb v UK* (1986) 50 D & R 81.
231 *Annual Report 1998-99*, above n. 3, p. 35.
232 *R v Secretary of State for the Home Department, ex p O'Dhuibhir* [1997] COD 315 (CA).
233 Closed visits require the placing of a glass screen between the prisoner and the visitor. Lawyers argued that this created particular difficulties for consulting with clients about the contents of documents, which had to be passed through a slit at the bottom of the screen. Closed legal visits to exceptional risk Category A prisoners were discontinued from Jul. 1997.

the confidentiality of legal correspondence in *Simms and Main*.[234] The prisoners argued that the Learmont Report's recommendation that cell searches be conducted with no inmates present (lest they intimidate the officers involved), meant that there was a risk that legal papers would be read. The Court of Appeal insisted that the policy was the minimum necessary to satisfy security and control concerns but the House of Lords has subsequently ruled that such a blanket policy is unlawful.[235]

These limitations aside, the case law on legal correspondence represents an important extension of a fundamental legal right to prisoners as a group, and opens up the practical possibility of other aspects of imprisonment being subjected to public scrutiny. Such scrutiny, however, is primarily *legal* scrutiny and in that sense these cases can be seen as an adjunct to the case law establishing the principle of legal jurisdiction over prison administration. Together, they indicate that the emphasis is more on legitimation of law's role in establishing the boundaries of legal authority within the prison environment than on developing a jurisprudence of prisoners' rights. This reflects a broader trend at the domestic level whereby progressive judicial rhetoric regarding prisoners emerges only in cases where fundamental principles of legality (such as source of legal authority or access to legal advice or the court) are in question. Such an approach fits comfortably within the existing parameters of judicial review and generally involves little substantive change in the social relations between prisoners and the state. A notable recent example of the approach is *Simms and O'Brien*, a case involving a challenge to limits on prisoners' access to journalists. The House of Lords could easily have upheld the prisoner's claim on a general right to freedom of expression basis but, while acknowledging the importance of this right in a democracy, they proceeded to emphasise the specific ground of the need for media access to prisoners to highlight miscarriage of justice claims:

> My Lords, my judgment does not involve tearing up the rule book governing prisons. On the contrary I have taken full account of the essential public interest in maintaining order and discipline in prisons. But, I am satisfied that consistently with order and discipline in prisons it is administratively workable to allow prisoners to be interviewed for the narrow purposes here at stake notably if a proper foundation is laid in correspondence for the requested interview or interviews. One has to recognise that oral interviews with journalists are not in the same category as visits by relatives and friends and require more careful control and regulation. That is achievable. This view is supported by the favourable judgment of past experience. Moreover, in reality an oral interview is simply a necessary and practical extension of the right of a prisoner to correspond to journalists about his conviction. ... The criminal justice system has been shown to be fallible. Yet the effect of the judgment of the Court of Appeal is to outlaw the safety valve of effective investigative journalism.[236]

234 *R v Secretary of State for the Home Department, ex p Simms and Main* [1998] 2 All ER 491 (CA).
235 *R v Secretary of State for the Home Department, ex p Daly* [2001] UKHL 26, [2001] 3 All ER 433. Following allegations that conversations between lawyers and IRA prisoners at Belmarsh Prison in 1992 were bugged, the solicitor involved, Gareth Peirce, argued that 'all lawyers must proceed on the basis that this [practice] still continues': *The Guardian*, 5 Mar. 2000.
236 *R v Secretary of State for the Home Department, ex p Simms and O'Brien* [1999] 3 All ER 400, 412 (per Lord Steyn).

(b)   Prisoners maintaining non-legal contacts

Non-legal contacts by prisoners generally fall into one of two categories: first, contacts with 'family' members and secondly, contacts with other members of the public. Imprisonment obviously involves interference with family life, both for the (convicted) prisoner and for other family members. In US prison litigation, courts have on occasions alluded to the 'innocence' of family members as a factor to be considered when reviewing restrictions placed on contact by way of letter or visit.[237] This idea has not, however, been directly invoked in either UK or ECHR litigation. In the UK, the Prison Rules make no distinction between family and non-family members, allowing all convicted prisoners at least two visits per month (normally of 30 minutes duration) and the right to send at least one letter weekly at public expense.[238] It is only family members, however, who have access to public financial assistance from the Assisted Prison Visits Unit, and the Prison Service Order on visits and letters emphasises that contact with family members should be refused only in exceptional circumstances.

Research indicates that most prisoners look forward to visits and see them as crucial to maintaining family contact. Prisoners maintain this stance in spite of the fact that 'visits often created as much anxiety as they solved'.[239] Many governors exercise their discretion to offer more than the statutory minimum of family visits. Some prisons have also adopted creative approaches in responding to the needs of particular groups of prisoners.[240] Holloway Prison, for example, has an all-day visit scheme which allows women prisoners who are parents to have increased contact with children for whom they are normally the primary, if not sole, parent. The importance of such measures is highlighted by the fact that the CIP's report on *Women in Prison* heard repeatedly from women prisoners and staff working with them that 'continued contact with the outside and particularly with family is central to their lives'.[241] The Report notes that '[t]his is a logical outcome of most women's role as primary carers or mainstays of the home and of their sense of identity based in relation to others'.[242]

Interestingly, however, legal attempts to invoke the need to maintain family contact as a strategy for improving prisoners' rights have been largely unsuccessful. Applications under the ECHR system challenging the Home Office's refusal to allow conjugal visits,[243] or to permit transfer to a prison closer

---

237 US cases upholding a higher level of restrictions on correspondence with non-family members include: *Procunier v Martinez* (1974) 416 US 396; *Thornburgh v Abbott* (1989) 490 US 401; and *Turner v Safely* (1987) 482 US 78.

238 Unconvicted prisoners are entitled to unlimited visits (though most prisons limit this to three per week in addition to legal visits).

239 See King and McDermott, above n. 42, p. 262.

240 Visitors' needs also need to be met, particularly given that most visitors are women with children who may have travelled significant distances via public transport: see the CIP's report, *Women in Prison*, above n. 109, paras. 8.09-8.19. For a discussion of the situation of the families of politically motivated prisoners in Northern Ireland, see K. McEvoy et al., 'The Home Front: The Families of Politically Motivated Prisoners in Northern Ireland' (1999) 39 BJ Crim 175.

241 Ibid., para. 8.02.

242 Ibid.

243 *X v UK* (1975) 2 D & R 105. See also *ELH v UK* [1998] EHRLR 231 (admissibility of claim that refusal of conjugal visits for Catholic married prisoners who wished to procreate breached rights under ECHR).

to family members, have been rejected as 'manifestly ill-founded'.[244] Moreover, although the European Court of Human Rights has recognised that restrictions on correspondence with family members require strong justification by the state authorities,[245] it has also made it clear that such correspondence may be examined by the authorities.[246] Domestic courts have likewise been prepared to allow the invocation of the grounds of security and administrative convenience to defeat arguments for increased information concerning prisoner classification[247] and to deny open visits with high-security prisoners.[248] As regards conjugal visits,[249] the Home Office has always insisted that it prefers to afford such family contact by way of temporary release schemes.[250] In *Hargreaves*, the Court of Appeal, rejected a prisoner's claim of a legitimate expectation of release based on the policy and an inmate compact at the start of his sentence.[251] It also argued that Article 8 of the ECHR had not been breached given that the interference with the convicted prisoner's family life had occurred at the time of imposition of a lawful sentence, and that provision for prison visits meant that prisoners were not totally cut off from their families.

Research on prisoners' contact with their families and prisoners' families themselves may be helpful in encouraging more positive approaches from the courts and the prison authorities. This literature is 'increasingly moving beyond the notion of treating [families] as if they belonged to a homogeneous group subjected to identical experiences', and has begun to explore '[t]he diverse experiences of black and Asian families, non-nuclear families or families where relationships had broken down, families of women prisoners and the families of older prisoners'.[252] This is an important development, not least because the implications of traditional notions of 'family' need to examined if *all* prisoners

---

244   *Wakefield v UK* (1990) 66 D & R 251.

245   *Silver v UK* (1983) 5 EHRR 347.

246   See *Boyle and Rice v UK* (1988) 10 EHRR 425.

247   See *R v Secretary of State for the Home Department, ex p McAvoy* [1998] 1 WLR 790 (CA).

248   See O'Dhuibhir, above n. 232.

249   The issue of sexual practices in prison is characterised by official avoidance and under-research. In *R v Secretary of State for the Home Department, ex p Fielding*, *The Times*, 21 Jul. 1999, the policy of the Prison Service that condoms should be available to inmates only on prescription, and not on demand, was upheld as lawful. The Prison Service's policy was that it did not wish to be seen in any way to encourage homosexual sex in prison, and that as a result condoms were not freely available for purchase; however, recognising that sex did take place, its policy also permitted prison medical officers to prescribe condoms when they perceived a health risk (particularly of HIV) to exist. The CIP's report on *Women in Prison* noted that: '[h]ealth promotion information and advice should be given in culturally sensitive ways; for example, it is pointless to discuss safer sex with all new prisoners as though this has the same meaning in all cultures. . . . There is a serious problem of HIV infection in many African countries and information about this sensitive matter is crucial, both from an individual and a public health viewpoint' (above n. 109, para. 7.15).

250   See *R v Secretary of State for the Home Department, ex p Mellor*, *The Times*, 4 April, 2001 (CA) (no right to IVF facilities under HRA).

251   Above n. 214. The Court of Appeal took the view that the Home Secretary was free to change the policy, that the doctrine of legitimate expectation only required that each case be examined individually, and that the policy did not violate the reasonableness standard of judicial review. The case was heard at a time when there were substantial concerns about prisoners committing offences whilst on licence.

252   McEvoy et al., above n. 241, p. 176 citing R. Light, 'Black and Asian Prisoners' Families' (1995) 34 Howard J 209; I. Paylor and D. Smith, 'Who are Prisoners' Families?' (1994) 2 JSWFL 131; and D. Caddle and D. Crisp, *Imprisoned Women and Mothers* (Home Office Research Study No. 162, 1997).

are to benefit from the emphasis on contact with the outside world. Prisoners who do not wish to have any such contacts will also require consideration, and the creative approaches adopted by some prisons in relation to foreign national prisoners, who have particular problems in maintaining contact with home and may be disadvantaged by an emphasis on visits as the key mechanism for contact, need to publicised and encouraged.[253]

The impact of the HRA on judicial scrutiny of justifications for restrictions on family contacts remains unclear. To date, domestic judges have generally appeared satisfied that UK law accords with Convention standards. There is, however, some evidence of a judicial rethink on Mother and Baby Units, influenced in part by the growing acceptance of the child-centred approach of the Children Act 1989 and the development of a discourse of children's human rights.[254] In 1998, the Divisional Court indicated that the 'best interests of the child' test in the Children Act, and in the UN Convention on the Rights of the Child 1989, may require searching examination of the justifications advanced by governors for removal of children from such units.[255] There is also evidence of an increasing awareness of the problems presented by life in Mother and Baby Units, not least the risk of women harming their own or other children and the resulting need to adopt child protection procedures.[256] In 1999, a Prison Service Working Group reported on this area, and its recommendations now form the basis of a new Prison Service Order which emphasises that the overriding principle must be the best interests of the child (and not, as in the past, a concern with prison discipline).[257] One particularly notable feature of this Report was its emphasis on the need to satisfy international human rights standards: 'Prison Service policy will reflect the ECHR, Article 8, save where it is necessary to restrict the prisoner's rights for a legitimate reason, such as good order and discipline, or the safety of others including babies'.[258] However, while judges may be willing to examine the lawfulness of individual governors' decisions, the current policy that children may only stay in units until the age of 18 months has been found to be lawful and reasonable. As Lord Woolf argued in *P and Q*: 'It is not for the courts to run the prisons'.[259]

---

253 For more detail on such approaches, see above n. 109, paras. 8.06-8.07.
254 See generally, G. Van Bueren, *The International Law on the Rights of the Child* (Martinus Nijhoff, 1998).
255 See 'Inmate's Baby Unit Ban Reviewed', *The Guardian*, 17 Nov. 1998. Generally, children may remain with their mothers in such units up to the age of 18 months. Previously, in cases such as *R v Secretary of State for the Home Department, ex p Hickling* [1986] Fam Law 140 (CA) and *R v Secretary of State for the Home Department, ex p Togher* (unreported, 1 Feb. 1995), the courts had rejected challenges to the removal of children from such units where the governors had based removal decisions, at least in part, on the mother's allegedly disruptive behaviour. See also, *R v Secretary of State for the Home Department, ex p Sullivan*, *The Independent*, 21 Jul. 1997 (re removal of pregnant woman from a unit and judicial emphasis on application of ordinary prison discipline in such units).
256 Above n. 109, paras. 3.42-3.43.
257 See Prison Service, 'New Procedures for Prison Mother and Baby Units' (21 Dec. 1999, 77N/99).
258 *Report of a Review of Principles, Policies and Procedures on Mothers and Babies/Children in Prison*, p. 27 (available at: www.hmprisonservice.gov.uk). The case of Roisin McAliskey, whose extradition to Germany was halted on health grounds after her transfer to a specialist Mother and Baby Unit, also helped to focus media and public attention on this area.
259 See *R v Secretary of State for the Home Department, ex p P and Q*, *The Times*, 17 May 2001 (policy did not contravene Children Act 1989 or Art. 8 ECHR).

Judicial deference has historically been even more pronounced as regards prisoner contact with non-family members. The European Court of Human Rights' decision in *Silver* did prompt substantial revision of the Order regulating correspondence, moving it towards more narrowly drawn restrictions,[260] but prisoners continue to have only a limited right to freedom of expression and a high degree of state interference is permitted. In *Simms and O'Brien*, for example, a restriction on access to journalists was overturned by the House of Lords only on the narrow ground that it inhibited the highlighting of possible miscarriages of justice, and the stance of the Court of Appeal that a prisoner loses the right to freedom of expression on entering prison was left undisturbed.[261] This leaves open the possibility that media restrictions may be lawful where a prisoner seeks to highlight other concerns, such as prison conditions or other matters of clear public interest. Similarly, in *Bamber*,[262] the Court of Appeal refused leave to challenge a blanket ban on prisoners contacting phone-in radio programmes, justifying its ruling on the grounds that prison authorities would be unable to monitor in advance the content of a prisoner's conversation and its conformity with existing prison regulations. The (former) European Commission of Human Rights endorsed the Court of Appeal's view, although it did stress that prisoners retained a right of freedom of expression and rejected the UK government's argument that restrictions were justified to protect the interests of crime victims.[263]

This latter factor – which may be described as an 'offence to victims' justification – and public distaste at prisoners profiting from publicisation of their criminal activities[264] appear to lie at the heart of ongoing contact restrictions.[265] It is, for example, difficult to understand how order within a prison might be jeopardised by prisoners' contributions to public debate outside it.[266] Civil, criminal and disciplinary penalties already operate so as to discourage prisoners from making public statements that go beyond the bounds of free expression in a democracy, making blanket forms of prior restraint seem somewhat disproportionate. The latter forms of restraint also ignore the reality of media organisations' vetting of 'suitable' contributions from members of the public. Overall, therefore, it seems that there is a deep reluctance to recognise that imprisonment should not amount to a deprivation of the rights of citizenship.[267]

260 For the current position on Standing Order 5, see Livingstone and Owen, above n. 2, pp. 225-226.

261 Above n. 236.

262 *R v Secretary of State for the Home Department, ex p Bamber* (unreported, 15 Feb. 1996).

263 *Bamber v UK* [1998] 2 EHRLR 110. The Commission noted that prisoners had other means of communicating with the media, including seeking permission to do so, and considered the restriction justified on the grounds of preserving order and protecting the interests of others.

264 The fear of potential media payouts to former defendants, such as Louise Woodward, may have bolstered the social distaste for hearing 'the voice of the prisoner'. The Press Code contains a prohibition on payments to former criminals, but it has been selectively interpreted (see eg, the serialisation of former IRA prisoner Sean O'Callaghan's memoirs).

265 The growing influence of 'victims' rights' may also be relevant: see further Ch. 4.

266 The authorities may take the view that normal safeguards against 'offensive' expression, for example libel laws, may be less effective in respect of those in prison. However, this is true in respect of many individuals who have no financial resources to lose or are undeterred by possible legal sanction.

267 Re the prohibition on voting by prisoners, see *R v Secretary of State for the Home Department, ex p Pearson*, 4 April 2001 (Div Ct) (disenfranchisement compatible with HRA).

(3) Challenging discipline and control policies

Prison authorities have a wide range of techniques at their disposal to maintain discipline and control within prisons. These include the architecture of the prison, the mix of prisoners (governors may prefer to have more short-term or long-term prisoners depending on the objectives being pursued) and the level of available resources.[268] These are supplemented by a wide range of formal powers; for example, to grant or remove privileges, transfer prisoners to another institution, remove them from association within the prison, place them on formal disciplinary charges or even resort to the use of physical force. There have also been concerns, perhaps less prevalent now than in the past, as to the use of drugs to control prisoners.[269]

The approach taken to control will largely be determined by the individual institution, although security requirements will be dictated from Prison Service headquarters. This can produce considerable variations: Sparks, Hay and Bottoms found significant differences with respect to issues such as the use of disciplinary charges or removal from association, even amongst dispersal prisons,[270] and studies of women's prisons have also generally found intrusive environments where formal and informal disciplinary powers are used to enforce ideas of 'proper women' [271] or even to treat women prisoners as children.[272]

Reform strategies, including legal challenges, have tended to identify disciplinary powers as a particular target, a trend which intensified following Woolf (which, as noted above, sought to shift the aim of the prison system towards balancing the needs of security, control and *justice for prisoners*[273]). In some respects, it appears to have been a successful strategy: considerable changes to the formal disciplinary system have been implemented since the early 1990s. In other respects, however, it is clear that there is still a need for further improvements, not least because the level of disciplinary charges and punishments has continued to rise.[274]

The springboard for judicial examination of the formal prison disciplinary system was provided by the Court of Appeal in 1978 in *St Germain*, a decision which appears to have been influenced, at least in part, by the unsatisfactory

---

268 See generally, Foucault, above n. 27. The redesign of Holloway Prison in the 1970s threw up a number of problems: '[a]mazingly all the windows were made of glass and were made up of sections that were tall and narrow, but still wide enough for women to squeeze through. Over 200 panes of glass were demolished in the first four months after opening' (Goodman, above n. 72, p. 499).

269 Sim, above n. 141. In *Freeman v Home Office* [1984] 1 All ER 1036 a prisoner unsuccessfully claimed that he could not be said to have given voluntary consent to being given drugs in prison in light of the coercive character of the environment.

270 See Sparks, Hay and Bottoms, above n. 92, pp. 151-153.

271 See eg, R. Dobash, R. Dobash and S. Gutteridge, *The Imprisonment of Women* (OUP, 1986), p. 146, noting that women are more likely than men to be charged with offences involving swearing or even self-mutilation. See more generally, Hannah-Moffat, above n. 84 (analysing a proposed model of risk assessment for Canadian women prisoners and arguing that 'seemingly neutral actuarial categories like risk are shaped by wider factors like gender' (p. 74)); and M. Bertrand, 'Incarceration as a Gendering Strategy' (1999) 14 CJLS 45.

272 See eg, P. Carlen, 'Papa's Discipline: Disciplinary Modes in the Scottish Women's Prison' in N. Lacey (ed.), *A Reader on Criminal Justice* (OUP, 1994), pp. 331-352.

273 Above n. 35.

274 See J. Ditchfield and M. Lock, 'The Prison Disciplinary System: Effects of the 1 April 1992 Changes' in *Prisons and Prisoners* (Home Office, 1994), pp. 54-59. Interestingly, they note that figures were stable between 1982-89 but rose thereafter.

quality of justice offered by the Hull BOV in hearing cases arising out of the Hull Prison Riot.[275] Certainly, a year later, in *St Germain (No. 2)*,[276] the Divisional Court quashed many of the Board's adjudications for basic procedural flaws (such as failure to allow the defence to call witnesses or to cross-examine). This trend continued throughout the 1980s as courts began to impose a growing list of procedural requirements on Board adjudications, including an entitlement for prisoners to have legal representations in certain hearings.[277] Similar dissatisfaction with Board adjudications emerged outside the courts: in 1983, an amendment to the Prison Rules deprived Boards of the right to award unlimited loss of remission,[278] and later, in 1992, on the recommendation of the Woolf Report, the then Conservative government concluded that Boards should no longer be involved in disciplinary adjudications and that governors should either refer incidents to the police (if they regarded them as sufficiently serious) or hear the disciplinary charge themselves.

These changes to the disciplinary power of BOVs have been important; as noted above, however, there are still many outstanding problems and questions, not least the merits of focusing on judicial oversight in dealing with a closed world that is replete with discretionary power. This idea of a closed world, where individuals may meet in different capacities, is apparent in several judicial decisions. In *Lewis*,[279] for example, Lord Woolf was not prepared to find that there might be bias where a BOV member who also sat on the local Parole Board heard a discipline charge involving a prisoner, and similar reasoning has been applied to governors' adjudications.[280] A further example of how ordinary, 'outside' legal standards on evidence and procedure do not apply in the prison context is provided by *Hibbert*, wherein a court refused to grant legal representation before a governor because the facts revealed only a 'simple case' of alleged assault.[281] Moreover, the interest in external scrutiny of adjudications by BOVs has not been paralleled in respect of adjudications by governors, in spite of the fact that governors hear over 90% of all disciplinary charges and are subject to pressures which are not conducive to impartial processes or results:

> [T]he inter-personal relationships between staff and staff, and staff and governor, may all have their influence on the hearing. Governors may find themselves subject to formal protest raised by the Prison Officers Association over the manner in which

---

275 *R v Board of Visitors of Hull Prison, ex p St Germain* [1979] 1 QB 425.

276 *R v Board of Visitors of Hull Prison, ex p St Germain (No. 2)* [1979] 3 All ER 545.

277 See eg, on the issue of prisoners' rights to legal advice, assistance and representation, *R v Secretary of State for the Home Department, ex p Tarrant* [1984] 1 All ER 799; *R v Board of Governors of the Maze Prison, ex p Hone* [1988] 1 All ER 321 (HL) (natural justice does not provide a universal right to legal representation and every case is to be considered on its merits); and *Campbell & Fell v UK* (1984) 7 EHRR 165. For a summary of developments in this period, see S. Livingstone, 'The Changing Face of Prison Discipline' in Player and Jenkins, above n. 41, pp. 97-111.

278 Prior to the Criminal Justice Act 1991, all sentenced prisoners were entitled to remission of one-third on their sentence, and loss of remission operated effectively as a further sentence. Further Prison Rules changes in 1992 reduced the number of offences prisoners could be disciplined for, but left broad prohibitions such as 'disobeying any lawful order' (an offence which has in the past been found to have been committed by 'making cat-like noises in the presence of the prison dog': see P. Quinn, 'Reflexivity Run Riot: The Survival of the Prison Catch-all' (1995) 34 Howard J 354).

279 *R v Board of Visitors Frankland Prison, ex p Lewis* [1986] 1 WLR 130.

280 *R v HM Prison Service, ex p Hibbert* (unreported, 16 Jan. 1997).

281 Legal representation in governors' adjudications is very rare: in 1994, the CPT revealed that it had only been granted in four instances in the previous two years (above n. 8).

they have adjudicated. A governor may be swayed by the exigencies of the regime to order a particular punishment in the hope that it may have some general deterrent effect or because of some more mundane institutional reason such as that the segregation unit is full.[282]

It is not that there is no point whatsoever to legal challenges in respect of prison discipline and control. It is clear, for example, that the revised 1995 Prison Discipline Manual was heavily influenced by the judicial review experience of the previous two decades.[283] It is also the case that the Prisons Ombudsman has been able to use his power to inquire into errors of fact as well as procedure with regard to discipline proceedings to force greater transparency and proceduralism.[284] It also needs to be recognised, however, that discretion is fundamental to the discipline and control system of prison, and that although 'the scope of the rules is in principle so wide that they may be seen as being violated *all the time*', formal disciplinary action is not taken at 'every opportunity that presents itself'; indeed, to do so, would be to jeopardise 'what [the prison staff] are also trying to cultivate'.[285] Moreover, it is not inevitable that a focus on prisoners' rights will automatically enhance the fair treatment of prisoners. Loughlin, for example, has cast doubt on the merits of adopting a general rule whereby prisoners as of right would be entitled to legal representation before governors' disciplinary hearings, noting that:

> Prison governors determine more than 100,000 disciplinary actions each year, many of which deal with relatively minor infractions against the disciplinary code and result in fairly small penalties being imposed. Further, in respect of the 100,000 or so findings of guilt each year, only 2,500 appeals are made. Whilst this statistic is scarcely determinative of the issue of fair treatment, it does place into some context the question of whether universal representation – with its attendant technicalities, adversarial style, inevitable delays, and increased costs – will automatically enhance the fair treatment of prisoners.[286]

All of this provides the backdrop against which the debate about the role of the HRA in this area will take place. The standards of Article 6 of the ECHR will provide the courts with an opportunity to revisit the issue of prison discipline, including, for example, the question of whether adjudications by governors can be described as proceedings before 'an independent and impartial tribunal'. To date, however, both UK and Strasbourg courts appear to take the view that the levels of punishment available at such adjudications (currently a maximum of 42 added days) are insufficient to regard them as the hearing of 'criminal charges' which might attract the protections of Article 6.[287]

There is also, of course, the issue of 'oblique discipline';[288] that is, 'informal' systems of discipline and control, such as prisoner removal from association,

---

282 P. Quinn, 'Adjudications in Prison: Custody, Care and a Little Less Justice' in M. Leech (ed.), *The Prisoners' Handbook* (OUP, 1995), pp. 320-328, at p. 322.

283 In part, however, this may have been an attempt at 'judge-proofing' a form of administrative decision-making: for discussion of this phenomenon, see eg, Harlow and Rawlings, above n. 48.

284 In a ruling with potentially far-reaching consequences for high-security prisons, the Prison Ombudsman found that the conditions in which Michael Sams, a convicted murderer, was being held at a high-security Close Supervision Centre (CSC) were too harsh and directed that he should be moved to a more moderate jail: see *The Independent*, 22 Feb. 2000.

285 See Sparks, Bottoms and Hay, above n. 92, p. 151.

286 Above n. 23, p. 505.

287 See eg, *Pelle v France* (1986) 50 D & R 263 (18 days insufficient); and *Greenfield v Secretary of State for the Home Department*, *The Times*, 6 March 2001 (additional 21 days was a disciplinary sanction).

288 M. Loughlin and P.M. Quinn, 'Prisons, Rules and Courts: A Study in Administrative Law' (1993) 56 MLR 497, 521 (quoting McKenna, *Justice in Prison* (Justice, 1983), p. 67).

transfer or withdrawal of earned privileges. The 'culture of privileges', and its centrality to the authorities' daily control of prisoners, is at the core of prison life. Monitoring these forms of control is, however, extremely difficult: the Prison Ombudsman, for example, has 'investigated several cases which revealed that some adjudicators are still awarding punishments which are outside their powers' but notes that '[un]fortunately, where the punishment has already been served, there is little [he] can do to benefit the prisoner'.[289] The courts have, not surprisingly, been reluctant even to impose procedural restrictions on the use of such administrative powers;[290] a recognition, perhaps, of the practical limitations on their ability effectively to monitor this aspect of prison life. In *Hague*, for example, the House of Lords rejected arguments that prisoners subject to Rule 43 (now Rule 45) removal from association should be entitled to a hearing before the decision was taken and/or reasons thereafter.[291] This was despite the fact that solitary confinement resulting from the use of Rule 45 could last much longer than that ordered after conviction of a disciplinary offence. A similar approach is evident in respect of the authorities' use of inter-prison transfers and, although the courts have ruled that such powers must be exercised reasonably,[292] it seems highly unlikely that judges will be prepared to find any actions of the prison authorities in this context to be unreasonable/irrational. Judicial enthusiasm for injecting procedural safeguards into the operation of IEPS[293] also appears to be negligible, if not non-existent, despite the fact that the Prisons Ombudsman has indicated concern that this could become a form of unreviewable 'back door' disciplinary system.[294]

This is not to suggest, however, that legalism has no role to play in relation to the informal justice system. Procedures for prison transfer were, for example, re-written even before the *Hague* case so as to provide that prisoners would normally be given reasons for decisions. The HRA also provides a mechanism for increased challenges to discipline and control policies, even if only to reduce their arbitrary exercise. Article 3, for example, provides a means to scrutinise the use of lengthy periods of solitary confinement and to question whether such practices amount to punishment.[295] It needs to be recognised, however, that there are practical limitations on the ability of outside

---

289 Above n. 180, pp. 20-21. Part of the problem is the use of immediate sanctions where there has been a violation of Prison Rule 51 (the offence of disobeying any lawful order (formerly Rule 47)).

290 It should be noted, however, that in *Leech v Deputy Governor of Parkhurst Prison* [1988] 1 AC 533, 566 the House of Lords 'refused to draw a strict distinction between a governor's disciplinary and managerial functions for the purpose of holding the latter to be beyond the scope of judicial review; Lord Bridge simply stated that it was wrong to draw jurisdictional lines on a purely defensive basis': see Loughlin and Quinn, above n. 288, p. 521.

291 *Hague v Deputy Governor of Parkhurst Prison* [1991] 3 All ER 733.

292 See eg, *R v Secretary of State for the Home Department, ex p McAvoy* [1998] 1 WLR 790.

293 See *R v Secretary of State for the Home Department, ex p Hepworth* [1998] COD 146.

294 See above n. 180.

295 The right to family life in Art. 8 might be used to challenge certain forms of disciplinary action taken against 'disruptive mother' prisoners. It should be noted, however, that past decisions of the (former) European Commission of Human Rights are not particularly helpful: see eg, *X v UK* (1981) 21 D & R 95 where 760 days under Prison Rule 43 was considered not to breach Art. 3. More generally, on the Art. 3 standard of 'inhuman or degrading treatment or punishment', see Harris, O'Boyle and Warbrick, above n. 192, pp. 55-89; and *Selmouni v France* (1999) 29 EHRR 403 (concept of torture extended to include serious physical and mental suffering caused by police assault on person in detention).

bodies effectively to supervise disciplinary and control powers in prisons, and also that outcomes which increase the clarity of rules may do little to curb managerial prerogatives or assuage the discontent of prisoners subject to perceived arbitrary action.[296] This does not mean that we should give up on the possibility of change in this area – the Woolf Report, for example, noted the damage caused by the pervasiveness of prisoner grievances about 'a lack of justice' within the prison system[297] – but simply that we may need to be more imaginative about the means of achieving it. If we are not, 'justice in prisons secured through the exercise of responsibility and respect'[298] will most likely remain elusive.

(4) Improving prison conditions

Prison conditions are a matter for celebration in few societies; in the UK, during the early 1980s, they became a matter of significant concern. Overcrowding, especially in respect of remand prisoners, was the key problem, in particular because of its knock-on effect on other aspects of prison conditions. Overcrowding brings curtailment of visits, education, work and association as prison staff struggle to maintain normal security and control procedures in the face of increased numbers. It can mean that food takes longer to deliver and arrives cold. Such knock-on effects bring not only significant physical deprivations for prisoners but also a loss of legitimacy for the prison authorities: prisoners tend to place a high stress on the regular delivery of services such as food or visits and failure to deliver them can be the cause of a flashpoint and longer-term resentment.

Living conditions in UK adult prisons have, however, improved in the past decade. Slopping out ended in 1996, no prisoners are now held three to a cell designed for one and prisoners spend an average of 11 hours out of cell. Ongoing rises in the prison population have meant that many prisons are now operating at well over 100% capacity, but few have reached the 170% plus rates of occupancy which were common in the 1980s. These improvements in living conditions are due, at least in part, to a major programme of new prison building and the refurbishment of existing institutions. Efforts to translate such improvements into legal form have, however, largely been unsuccessful: Woolf's recommendation of a legal ceiling on the number of people a prison could take was rejected, and the Code of Operating Standards, launched in 1994, remains for guidance alone. This means that there is a risk that the gains made in recent years may be reversed in more difficult times. It also exposes the limits of law and litigation in this area. The minimalist 'rule of law' approach, for example, lacks detailed standards on matters such as cell occupancy, food or visits, in respect of which the authorities might be called to account. Equally, the approach which applies general human rights norms to public institutions such as prisons has struggled to identify which particular right(s) might be infringed here. The outcomes of rights-based interventionist prison litigation in the US also provide further evidence of

296 See Sparks, Bottoms and Hay, above n. 92, p. 270.
297 Above n. 35, para. 9.24.
298 Ibid.

the need for caution.[299] The US prison experience is, of course, entirely different to that which prevails elsewhere; at the same time, however, its prison conditions' case law is a powerful reminder both of the limitations of judicial oversight of autonomous institutions and the extent to which prison conditions are dependent upon the vicissitudes of popular will. Currently, US political opinion, and a significant section of judicial opinion, seems hostile to extensive judicial intervention in response to prison conditions (although many court orders from an early interventionist phase in the 1970s and 1980s remain in place and a number of new cases continue to be brought[300]). Dispute also continues to rage as to whether an earlier phase of judicial intervention in prison conditions, spearheaded by the lower federal courts using the Eighth Amendment's prohibition on 'cruel and unusual punishment', was entirely beneficial. What cannot be disputed, however, is that this prison litigation has done little, if anything, to stem the rising tide of the US prison population, which is now over two million and involves imprisoning nearly six times as many people as are imprisoned in the UK. Indeed, some commentators have suggested that, by making prison conditions more tolerable, this litigation may paradoxically have contributed to the rise.

Whatever its merits, there was, however, little chance of US-style conditions' litigation prevailing in the UK. For one thing, the UK courts faced the difficulty of finding an appropriate legal vehicle for such claims. Attempts to revive the 1689 Bill of Rights prohibition on 'cruel and unusual punishment' were rejected in the case of *Williams v Home Office (No 2)*.[301] At one time, there appeared to be some judicial support for the idea that intolerable conditions could be the foundation for a false imprisonment claim (on the ground that they were making the punishment much worse than the courts had ordered), but this was roundly rejected by the House of Lords in *Hague*.[302] This decision also indicated that negligence claims based on poor conditions would need to show clear evidence of injury. More recently, the courts have extended the liability of prison

---

299 From the early 1970s, lower federal courts, who had previously maintained a 'hands off' approach to prisons similar to the UK, upheld challenges to the 'totality of prison conditions' based on the Eighth Amendment prohibition on 'cruel and unusual punishment'. Many of these cases arose from appalling circumstances of neglect and brutality, on a scale that no contemporary UK prison has seen. For details on this case law, see eg, S. Sturm, 'The Legacy and Future of Corrections Litigation' (1994) 143 U Penn LR 638; and L. Yackle, *Reform and Regret: The Story of Federal Judicial Involvement in the Alabama Prison System* (OUP, 1989). The US Supreme Court was never prepared to go as far as lower courts in declaring conditions to be unconstitutional and, by the early 1990s, it had made it substantially more difficult to engage in litigation in this area. This stance was reinforced by the US Congress in 1995 in the Prison Litigation Reform Act. See Amnesty International reports on US prison conditions at: www.amnestyusa.org/rightsforall/.

300 Contemporary cases tend to focus on inter-prison violence and the oppressive environment of maximum security prisons: see eg, *Madrid v Gomez* 889 F Supp 1146 (1995).

301 [1981] 1 All ER 1211. The case concerned the use of 'control units' for prisoners seen as disruptive and who were held in very restrictive solitary confinement for long periods. Tudor Evans J felt that such conditions would have to be cruel and unusual: he was not convinced they were cruel, given that there was access to recreation, nor were they unusual as similar units existed in the US and Canada. Six years later, in *R v Secretary of State for the Home Department, ex p Herbage (No. 2)* [1987] QB 1077, the Court of Appeal demonstrated greater sympathy to such arguments (although the facts were somewhat peculiar and the case concerned only a discovery application). The Prison Service eventually subsequently abandoned the challenged conditions on the grounds that they were too oppressive.

302 [1992] 1 AC 58.

authorities in relation to the prevention of attacks on both prison staff and fellow prisoners. In *Connor*, the Scottish Court of Session held that there was a duty on the prison authorities to advise a prison officer about the risk of violent behaviour if two brothers were allowed to work together.[303] In *Hartshorn*, the defendant prisoner who required 100 stitches after a razor attack, successfully sued the Home Office for failing to take security measures to prevent prisoners from different blocks from leaving a common area in order to minimise the risk of violence.[304] In the health care context, there appears to be a shift in the legal guarantee of an equal standard of health care between a prison hospital and those outside: in *Brooks*, it was held that a prisoner in a prison hospital was entitled to the same standard of obstetric care as she would have received if she had been at liberty.[305]

The European judiciary has been as unwilling as its UK counterpart to become involved in setting or enforcing standards for conditions of detention.[306] It has been slow to find breaches of Article 3 in respect of conditions for remand or sentenced prisoners, and this has been true both of cases challenging high security isolation units[307] and those raising more general conditions matters.[308] The eastward expansion of the Convention may, of course, bring more challenging conditions into Strasbourg's ambit in the future and lead to a more interventionist jurisprudence. Equally, judges in the UK may be prepared to go further than their Strasbourg counterparts when asked to interpret Convention guarantees under the HRA. It seems unlikely, however, that domestic judges will overcome their reluctance to finding living conditions produced by crowding or neglect as amounting to even degrading treatment. Moreover, even if they do change tack, they lack the broad remedial powers to bring real or immediate change to prisons. Past experience indicates that demands for specific improvements in the circumstances of prisoners, pursued through institutions specific to the prison environment, may be more effective in producing change. This suggests that civil liberties campaigners would do better to focus on such demands, rather than looking to the generalised standards provided by judicial discourse. One useful task as regards the former might be to look in detail at how the specific circumstances of prison conditions affect different groups of prisoners in different ways. The CIP has, for example, argued that the prison service has systematically failed to consider the specific circumstances of women prisoners: 'in the prison system equality is everywhere conflated with uniformity: women are treated as if they are men'.[309]

---

303   *Connor v Secretary of State for Scotland, The Times*, 22 Mar. 2000.

304   *Hartshorn v Home Office* (unreported, 21 Jan. 1999, CA). Cf. *Egerton v Home Office* [1978] Crim LR 494 (no compensation in respect of attack on a prisoner who had just come off (former) Rule 43); and *Thompson v Home Office* 8 Mar. 2001 (CA).

305   *Brooks v Home Office* [1999] 2 FLR 33 (prison is required to provide same standard of care as a psychiatric hospital), casting doubt on *Knight v Home Office* [1990] 3 All ER 237.

306   The Privy Council has generally shown little interest in finding the duration for, and conditions in, which prisoners facing the death penalty are held as breaching human rights standards: see *Higgs and Mitchell v Minister of National Security* [2000] 2 AC 228; and *Chadee v Comr of Prisons* (unreported, 30 Jun. 1999). Cf. *Guerra v Baptiste* [1995] 4 All ER 583 (delay of four-and-a-half years, and 17 hours' notice of impending execution, held to violate constitutional rights).

307   See eg, *Krocher and Muller v Switzerland* (1982) 34 D & R 24.

308   See the findings of violation of Art. 3 in *Dougoz v Greece* (ECtHR, 6 Mar. 2001); and *Keenan v UK* (ECtHR, 3 April 2001).

309   Above n. 109, para. 3.46.

(5) Reforming prisoner release procedures

The issue of prisoner release procedures, especially in relation to indeterminate sentences, has been the most heavily litigated aspect of prison law in the last decade. It could, of course, be argued that there is little significance in this fact as the issue has more to do with the pre-eminent judicial function of sentencing than prison law per se; release procedures, on this perspective, are a form of 'external' prison law, relating more to the length rather than the conditions of detention.[310] There are several reasons, however, why release procedures *should* be viewed as central to a prisoners' rights analysis. First, the right to liberty is, by definition, restricted by the fact of imprisonment and the length of sentences increases the interference with this fundamental right of a democratic society.[311] Secondly, the peculiar UK history of politicians effectively determining the punishment of certain categories of prisoners raises basic constitutional questions about the separation of powers in a democracy, the accountability of Ministers and the underlying political values of the legal and political systems.[312] The issue also indicates the shifting nature of institutional power struggles as prison reformers, who, throughout the twentieth century, campaigned for 'liberal' politicians rather than judges to determine prisoner release dates, now seek to return the function to judges in place of 'punitive' Ministers.[313] Thirdly, both the general policy and individual decisions on release may dramatically affect the internal prison environment, in particular in terms of the 'greying' (or ageing) of the prison population and the likelihood of grievances leading to increased tension.[314] Finally, many decisions within prisons are either taken with a view to a prisoner's impending release, such as the granting of home leave, or themselves affect the chances of release.[315]

Indeterminate sentences have been one of the most controversial areas of prison litigation in the UK. Much of the focus has been on the various types of potential 'life' sentence imposed for serious crimes; that is, mandatory and discretionary life imprisonment for adults, and detention 'during Her Majesty's pleasure' for offenders under the age of 18. Indeterminate sentences generally are a creation of the twentieth century when liberal reformers, swayed by a belief in 'expert' scientific ability to identify and treat the causes of crime, advocated them as a preferable alternative to fixed sentences of penal servitude, especially for young offenders.[316] The discretionary life sentence was developed in the 1950s amidst growing concern about fixed-term sentences providing

---

310 Van Zyl Smit, above n. 146, pp. 53-54.

311 See generally, Feldman above n. 190, for extensive coverage of the right to liberty.

312 The Law Lord, Lord Steyn, has argued: 'The function of determining the tariff in the case of mandatory life sentence prisoners ought to be performed in public by neutral judges. That function ought not to be performed by the Home Secretary': 'The Weakest and Least Dangerous Department of Government' [1997] PL 83, 93.

313 This is more in line with what happens in other European states: see eg, D. Van Zyl Smit, 'Is Life Imprisonment Unconstitutional: The German Experience' [1992] PL 263.

314 See eg, A. Rutherford, 'The Greying of America's Prisons', NLJ 24 Sep. 1999, p. 1396. For an account of the reactions of long-term prisoners to the changes in policy on release procedures in the 1990s, see Liebling, above n. 84, pp. 161-162.

315 See eg, *R v Secretary of State for the Home Department, ex p Duggan* [1994] 3 All ER 277 (reasons must be given for allocation to security Category A because such an allocation significantly lessens the prospect of release).

316 D. Garland, *Punishment and Welfare: A History of Penal Strategies* (Gower, 1985).

inadequate protection against 'dangerous offenders'.[317] It allowed judges a discretion to pass a term of life as opposed to a fixed term of years, and the decision on release was left to the Home Secretary (and Secretaries of State in Scotland and Northern Ireland). The mandatory life sentence was introduced in the Murder (Abolition of Death Penalty) Act 1965 to coincide with the abolition of the death penalty for all categories of murder. The Act also provided that judges should be able to specify a minimum period that someone sentenced to 'life' should serve and that, before releasing a convicted murderer, the Home Secretary should consult the trial judge (if available) and the Lord Chief Justice.[318]

Although the decision ultimately remained for the Home Secretary, from 1967 he was required to consult with the Parole Board (an appointed body) as well as the judiciary. The practice evolved whereby the Home Secretary divided the sentence into two parts, the 'tariff' stage (the minimum period which the prisoner will serve to satisfy the requirements of retribution and deterrence) and the 'risk' stage (where the concern was whether the prisoner was now safe to release).[319] None of this was set down in statute and, in practice, it seems the tariff was the more important element. Prisoners had no input into this process.[320]

The introduction of mandatory life sentences for murder increased both the number of life prisoners and the time they spent in prison: whereas 76 people were sentenced to life in 1965, this had risen to 396 in 1999 and the overall 'lifer' population in the same year stood at more than 4,200, of whom 714 had served more than 15 years.[321] These rises created their own tensions. The rise in length of time served, for example, gave more prisoners a reason to feel aggrieved at the procedure for deciding on their release. The rise in the number of life prisoners exposed more inconsistencies in the informal and secretive way in which decisions were reached. Tension increased in the early 1980s when politicians visibly used the issue of release of life prisoners to display their 'law and order' credentials. The most notable public manifestation of this was then Home Secretary Leon Brittan's statement at the 1983 Conservative Party conference that those convicted of certain classes of murder, including terrorist murders and child murders, could expect to serve at least 20 years before release. A less visible manifestation was the increase in the number of

---

317 See eg, *R v Wilkinson* (1983) 5 Cr App Rep (S) 105, wherein Lord Lane CJ observed that such a sentence was appropriate for those who could not be dealt with under the Mental Health Act but who posed a significant danger to the public: 'It is sometimes impossible to say when the danger will subside, therefore an indeterminate sentence is required so that the prisoner's progress can be monitored.'

318 See generally, L. Blom-Cooper and T. Morris, '"Life" Until Death: Interpretations of Section 1(1) of the Murder (Abolition of the Death Penalty) Act 1965' [1999] Crim LR 899. Even before mandatory and discretionary life sentences were introduced, a significant number of prisoners had their death sentences commuted to life imprisonment. Research for the 1953 Royal Commission on Capital Punishment found that 45% of all those sentenced to death from 1900-49 had their sentences commuted; many of them ended up serving relatively short sentences of 8-10 years and few served more than 15 years.

319 Increasingly the Parole Board's main role has been to advise on the risk phase: see the Parole Board's website at: www.paroleboard.gov.uk.

320 This position was upheld by the Court of Appeal in *Payne v Lord Harris of Greenwich* [1981] 1 WLR 754, where a life prisoner was not given any opportunity to make representations to the Parole Board as to why it should recommend his release, nor any account of the reasons for its refusal.

321 See *Prison Statistics: England and Wales 1999* (Cm. 4805, 2000).

cases where the Home Secretary lengthened the tariff period beyond that recommended by the trial judge.[322]

The combination of these historical and political factors means that litigation on prisoner release procedures has taken on heightened constitutional significance. As senior judges have belatedly recognised, the issues involved go to the heart of the principle of separation of powers,[323] and the potential role of the courts in instilling deeper constitutional values into UK public law. Furthermore, if the litmus test of a democracy is a citizen's right to liberty, the judicial reaction to a politician effectively determining the length of prison sentences can be taken as indicative of the judiciary's perception of their role in engendering a human rights culture. The issue of executive influence over prisoner release has also generated debate within civil liberties, with 'abolitionists' arguing that the Home Secretary's role is fundamentally inconsistent with concepts of due process,[324] while 'reformers' insist on the ultimate democratic legitimacy of Parliament and its legislative backing for ministerial discretion. This latter argument pays little attention, however, to the reality of executive dominance of Parliament and the legislative process, and the absence of meaningful constraints on Home Office autonomy in such a highly politicised area of party politics.[325] A further often unacknowledged factor is the judicial instinct for safeguarding its own reputation; there may be little desire for appropriating jurisdiction over the contentious issue of prisoner release – a factor seen in the Privy Council's apparent reluctance to become involved in restricting the use of the death penalty in Caribbean jurisdictions.[326]

Developing case law on prisoner release procedures

Until the late 1980s, there was little judicial enthusiasm for challenging the autonomy of the Home Secretary in setting general policy on prisoner releases or for questioning decisions and procedures in individual cases. *Payne*, for example, inhibited any meaningful scrutiny of the operation of the life prisoner release scheme.[327] Its authority was further reinforced by the House of Lords' decision in *Findlay*, where former Conservative Home Secretary Leon Brittan's 1983 policy announcement was unsuccessfully challenged by four prisoners who had been scheduled for release at the time it was made, but who continued to be detained as they had served less than 20 years as required by the new policy.[328] Such judicial deference suggested that the courts were happy to tolerate

---

322 See *Sentenced for Life: Reform of the Law and Procedure for those Sentenced to Life Imprisonment* (JUSTICE, 1996), p. 16.

323 See eg, *R v Secretary of State for the Home Department, ex p Doody* [1994] 1 AC 531 (per Lord Mustill); *R v Secretary of State for the Home Department, ex p Venables and Thompson* [1997] 3 All ER 97 (per Lord Steyn); and *R v Secretary of State for the Home Department, ex p Pierson* [1997] 3 All ER 577 (per Lords Steyn and Hope).

324 *Report of the Committee on the Penalty for Homicide* (Prison Reform Trust, 1993).

325 The extent of the politicisation is slowly being revealed; for example, the Criminal Cases Review Commission has been petitioned to re-examine the conviction and hanging of Ruth Ellis in 1955, following recently discovered Home Office correspondence suggesting that her sentence was not commuted by the then Home Secretary because it would have intensified the political campaign for abolition of the death penalty: see *The Guardian*, 28 Nov. 1999.

326 See interview with Lord Browne-Wilkinson, *The Lawyer*, 17 May 1999.

327 Above n. 321.

328 *Findlay v Secretary of State for the Home Department* [1985] 1 AC 318.

an essentially secret, unaccountable and politically motivated process, despite the implications for the lives of many prisoners.

The catalyst for a domestic judicial shift was again the European Court of Human Rights. In a series of cases, the Court found prisoner release procedures to be inconsistent with the ECHR. First, in decisions on discretionary life sentences, the Court made it clear that the operation of these sentences was inconsistent with Article 5's guarantee of a right to liberty.[329] It reasoned that as such sentences were imposed for a specific reason, prisoners serving them should only be detained after the expiry of the tariff phase of the sentence if the reason for detention persisted (for example, if a convicted arsonist was likely to commit the same crime upon release). However, just as the initial imprisonment was under judicial control, continuing detention and the examination of the reasons for it also had to be under judicial authority in order to satisfy the requirements of Article 5. The Parole Board, which could only make recommendations to the Home Secretary, did not satisfy this requirement; it also could not satisfy the Article 5(4) requirement that anyone subject to detention has a right to seek review of its continuation by a 'court'. As a result of these decisions, Parliament was forced to radically revise the procedures for the release of discretionary life prisoners in the 1991 Criminal Justice Act. Decisions have now effectively been removed from the discretion of the Home Secretary: the two-phase approach has been retained, but the tariff is now set in open court by the judge (subject to appeal), and the 'risk' phase is decided upon by Discretionary Lifer Panels, chaired by a judge. Prisoners now have a right to see all relevant information and to be legally represented, and must be released if it is considered unnecessary to detain them for the protection of the public.

As the same release procedures were used for both mandatory and discretionary life prisoners, it was expected that the European Court of Human Rights would also find the approach in respect of the former (numerically, the much larger group) to be in violation of Article 5. However, in *Wynne v UK*, the Court distinguished them on the basis that, as the life sentence for murder was a mandatory sentence, it must be expected that those sentenced to it would remain in prison for life, subject to the executive deciding to release them earlier.[330] In effect, the whole of the life sentence was regarded as flowing from the initial judicial decision at trial and, hence, as consistent with Article 5(1).

Shifting domestic judicial attitudes have, however, led to some reform of the release procedure for mandatory lifers. The chief concern has been with the setting of the tariff phase and the extent to which this can depart from judicially controlled sentencing decisions. In *Doody*, the House of Lords held that the Home Secretary must inform prisoners who are serving mandatory life sentences of the term of imprisonment recommended for them by the judiciary, and allow them to make representations regarding it, before the final term is set.[331] Pierson, one of the applicants in the *Doody* case, subsequently sought to take

---

329 On Art. 5 see generally, Harris, O'Boyle and Warbrick, above n. 164, pp. 97-162. See eg, *Weeks v United Kingdom* (1987) 10 EHRR 293; and *Thynne, Wilson and Gunnell v United Kingdom* (1990) 13 EHRR 666. Peay, above n. 106, draws attention to the fact that the ECtHR decisions on discretionary life prisoners have been central to improving the legal position on release of mentally disordered offenders.

330 *Wynne v UK* (1994) 19 EHRR 333.

331 *R v Secretary of State for the Home Department, ex p Doody* [1994] 1 AC 531.

advantage of this new emphasis on transparency by challenging the arrangements for setting his own tariff. He had been convicted of the double murder of his parents and the Home Secretary decided to increase the tariff from the judicial recommendation of 15 to 20 years purely on the grounds of retribution and deterrence. The House of Lords held that the Home Secretary was not entitled, bar in 'exceptional circumstances', to increase the tariff previously set as a minimum term for a life sentence prisoner; to increase a tariff so fixed was contrary to the fundamental principle of not retrospectively increasing lawful sentences.[332]

Two recent cases – *Venables and Thompson*[333] and *Hindley*[334] – have served as notable flashpoints, in particular on the issue of whether sentencing is essentially a judicial or executive function, the commitment of the courts to curbing executive power, and the dramatic contrast between the common law and ECHR approaches to prisoners' rights. In both cases, successive Home Secretaries, with clear political motivations, increased the prisoners' tariffs beyond that recommended by the judiciary. The first case, *Venables and Thompson*, involved two child defendants (aged ten at the time of the offence) who had abducted and killed a two-year-old, James Bulger, in 1992. Their actions provoked a major media and political outcry about the alleged societal collapse in moral values, the rise in child criminality and the need for punitive criminal justice policies.[335] At trial, the judge recommended eight years imprisonment, which was subsequently increased to ten years by the Lord Chief Justice. It was then increased to 15 years by the then Home Secretary, Michael Howard, in response to a petition signed by 278,000 people (organised by relatives of James Bulger) and 21,000 coupons forwarded by readers of *The Sun* newspaper.

The defendants successfully challenged the Home Secretary's decision on the ground that to fix a minimum 15-year period of detention for those detained 'during Her Majesty's pleasure' failed to take account of changing circumstances of child prisoners, who required a review of their progress at regular intervals and the possibility of varying the tariff.[336] Furthermore, taking account of media

332 *R v Secretary of State for the Home Department, ex p Pierson* [1997] 3 All ER 577. However, there was no clear majority in the case and it remained unclear what exactly it decided. Lords Steyn and Hope took the view that in decisions affecting sentencing the Home Secretary was bound by a common law principle of non-aggravation of penalties (that is, no retrospective sentencing). Lord Goff, who made up the third of the majority, based his decision on the narrow ground that at the time of making the decision the Home Secretary was acting on the basis of policy statements which did not allow retrospective tariff increases. Lords Browne-Wilkinson and Lloyd denied the existence of any such principle. The House of Lords in *Hindley* (see below, pp. 274–275), refused to resolve the confusion and distinguished *Hindley* 'on the facts'.

333 *R v Secretary of State for the Home Department, ex p Venables and Thompson* [1998] AC 407.

334 *R v Secretary of State for the Home Department, ex p Hindley* [1998] QB 751 (DC); [2000] 1 QB 152 (CA); [2000] 2 All ER 385 (HL).

335 See generally, B. Morrison, *As If* (Granta Books, 1998); and R Collier, *Masculinities, Crime and Criminology* (Sage, 1998).

336 By the time the House of Lords came to decide on the *Venables and Thompson* case, the ECtHR had ruled in *Hussain and Singh v UK* (1996) 22 EHRR 1 that the failure to allow continuing judicial oversight of prisoners sentenced to detention 'during Her Majesty's pleasure' was in breach of Art. 5 of the ECHR. At the time of *Hussain*, the procedures for making decisions on release of such prisoners were identical to those for 'lifers'. However, this was criticised by the Strasbourg court which took the view that in the case of such young prisoners more regular review of progress was required. See generally, D. Haydon and P. Scraton, '"Condemn a Little More, Understand a Little Less": The Political Context and Rights' Implications of the Domestic and European Rulings in the Venables-Thompson Case' (2000) 27 JLS 416.

and public demands for a higher tariff was held to be unlawful, as the Home Secretary's role was equivalent to a sentencing exercise. The European Court of Human Rights went much further, however, in assessing the trial and sentencing procedures for young offenders in the UK against the standards of international human rights norms.[337] As discussed in Chapter 4, the Court found that the suffering caused to the children by the formal and intimidatory nature of the Crown Court proceedings violated the right to a fair trial under Article 6. The Court also ruled that the fixing of a tariff by the Home Secretary amounted to a sentencing exercise and, as a politician was clearly not independent of the executive, there had been a breach of Article 6(1) in respect of the determination of the defendants' sentences. In addition, the absence of any periodic review by a judicial body of their dangerousness to the public and thus the continuing lawfulness of their detention was found to violate Article 5(4). The consequence of this decision, highlighting the bias inherent in a political actor determining prison sentences, was the transfer of the power to set tariffs in children's cases to the Lord Chief Justice in March 2000.[338]

The second case concerned Myra Hindley, whose involvement with a co-accused, Ian Brady, in the abduction and murder of five children in the early 1960s led to her subsequent demonisation as 'uniquely evil' in legal, media and political discourses.[339] The length of Hindley's sentence has varied depending on the era and the decision-makers involved: the trial judge in 1965 did not fix a tariff but envisaged that the defendant would be released from prison; a former Lord Chief Justice recommended 25 years; a former Home Secretary in 1985 set the tariff at 30 years; and, since 1990, successive Home Secretaries have set the tariff at 'whole life'.[340] The alleged justification for the latter increases was Hindley's revelations in 1987 to the police of her greater knowledge and involvement in the five murders committed by Brady and herself. The impetus for these revelations is disputed but appears to have been three-fold: first, 'confession' is generally required as a sign of prisoner rehabilitation prior to any release; secondly, they were disclosed in order to illustrate the dominance of her co-accused;[341] and thirdly, they were intended to help relatives to locate the remaining bodies.

Media campaigns against Hindley's release, as well as the views of victims' and police organisations, have, however, made Home Secretaries treat the case as an issue of pure politics, a point alluded to but left undiscussed by then Lord Chief Justice in hearing Hindley's judicial review application at first instance:

> The applicant clearly feels that she is held hostage to public opinion, condemned to pass the rest of her life in prison, although no longer judged a danger to anyone, because of her notoriety and the public obloquy which would fall on any Home Secretary who ordered her release.[342]

337 *V and T v UK* (1999) 30 EHRR 121.

338 *Practice Note (Crown Court: trial of children and young persons)* [2000] 2 All ER 284; and Ch. 6.

339 See generally, H. Kennedy, *Eve Was Framed: Women and British Justice* (Vintage, 1993), pp. 240-262; and J. Smith, *Different for Girls* (Chatto & Windus, 1997), pp. 133-147.

340 The whole life tariff was introduced in 1988 and, as of Mar. 2001, there were 23 prisoners subject to this sentence.

341 In a television documentary in Mar. 2000, made with Hindley's co-operation, new evidence of the rape and abuse of Hindley by Brady during the course of their relationship was revealed.

342 [1998] 2 WLR 505, 528 (per Lord Bingham).

The judgments in the *Hindley* litigation are remarkable, not just because some of the most senior judicial figures involved have argued in other contexts for a human rights basis to UK law,[343] but also because of the inescapable impression that the judiciary were content to avoid engaging with human rights values in favour of deference to executive power (at least in 'controversial' cases). There is an emphasis both on distinguishing *Hindley* 'on the facts' and justifying increasingly punitive responses by successive Home Secretaries in light of information disclosed over 20 years after the original trial. For example, in the Divisional Court, Lord Bingham found a majority in *Pierson* for the proposition that a so-called 'provisional' tariff could be increased provided that the prisoner had no legitimate expectation otherwise. Furthermore, as Lord Woolf in the Court of Appeal emphasised, Hindley was never told about her tariff of 30 years (despite her repeated written requests to the Home Office). Thus, unlike in *Pierson*, the subsequent increase from 30 years to a whole life tariff interfered with no legitimate expectation (as Hindley was kept deliberately ignorant of her case details[344]) and, furthermore, there had been no legal obligation to allow her an opportunity to make representations before changing a 'provisional' tariff.

Most remarkably, the leading House of Lords judgment, effectively determining whether an inmate of 34 years should now die in prison,[345] is a mere five pages, makes no mention of ECHR case law and refuses to engage with the principled argument as to why a Home Secretary can engage in a 'sentencing' exercise without the constraints under which a judge operates.[346] As Lord Steyn, who gave the leading judgment, argued:

> For my part it is unnecessary in this case to resolve the conflict which emerged in *Pierson*. The argument fails on the facts. The decision made by the Secretary of State in March 1985 was expressed to be 'provisional' and was not either directly or indirectly communicated to Hindley. She was unaware of it until 1994 when she was told of the provisional decision and was also told that in 1990 the Secretary of State ... reconsidered the tariff in her case and decided that it should be on whole life tariff. ... [Hindley's counsel further] argued that the principle stated ... in *Pierson* can be broadened to apply to a provisional and uncommunicated decision. There is no principled basis for this argument and I would reject it.[347]

343 For eg, two of the judges have used extra-judicial writing to argue for the incorporation of the ECHR: see T. Bingham, 'The European Convention on Human Rights: Time to Incorporate' (1993) 109 LQR 390 and 'The Way We Live Now: Human Rights in the New Millennium' (1998) 1 Web J CLI; and Woolf, 'Droit Public – English Style' [1995] PL 57.

344 *Doody*, above n. 324, established that it was unlawful not to tell a prisoner about the judicial recommendation of their tariff.

345 The circumstances in which the Moors Murderers may die in prison has also been the subject of legal regulation. In *R v Collins, ex p Brady* (2001) 58 BMLR 173, the High Court ruled that Ian Brady was not entitled to starve himself to death but could lawfully be force-fed by hospital staff on the grounds of mental incompetence.

346 In part, perhaps, this can be explained by the Law Lords' attitude to the HRA in *R v DPP, ex p Kebilene* [1999] 4 All ER 801 (the HL indicated that it would not entertain arguments directly based on the HRA until Oct. 2000). This does not, however, explain the complete absence of discussion of the possible relevance of the ECHR and Strasbourg case law.

347 In *Venables and Thompson*, above n. 333, Lord Steyn stated: 'The comparison between the position of the Home Secretary, when he fixes a tariff representing the punitive element of the sentence, and the position of the sentencing judge is correct. In fixing a tariff the Home Secretary is carrying out, contrary to the constitutional principle of the separation of powers between the executive and the judiciary, a classic judicial function' (p. 526). If this is so, the refusal to fully engage with its implications in *Hindley* is all the more stark.

Lord Steyn went on to emphasise that, even if Hindley had been successful on this ground, the Home Secretary's previous 'incomplete knowledge' of her exact involvement in the five murders justified the subsequent increase in the tariff: '[I]n deciding what was proper retribution and deterrence for murders of which she had been convicted he was entitled to take into account that she committed them knowing the fate of Brady's earlier victims'. The punitive flavour of judicial rhetoric is particularly stark in response to arguments that a whole life sentence was disproportionate in light of the personal circumstances of the applicant:

> Counsel for Hindley argued that in the light of her age at the time of the murders (22 to 23 years), the dominance of Brady over her and that she has now spent 34 years in prison, there is now no justifiable basis for maintaining a whole life tariff in her case. On the other hand, even in the sordid history of crimes against children the murders committed by Hindley, jointly with Ian Brady, were uniquely evil. . . . They abducted, terrified, tortured and killed their victims before burying their bodies on Saddleworth Moor. . . . The pitiless and depraved ordeal of the victims, and the torment of their families, place these crimes in terms of comparative wickedness in an exceptional category.

Hindley has now applied to the final avenue of legal appeal, the European Court of Human Rights. Bar the death of the applicant (in light of her deteriorating health), or a change in the Home Secretary's attitude (which seems unlikely), that Court may eventually determine whether retrospective punishment is a lawful feature of UK public law and whether the Home Secretary is a sufficiently unbiased actor for such a task. A decision in favour of Hindley would most likely provoke a now-familiar bout of 'Euro scepticism' in popular discourse; which increasingly views defendant and prisoner rights in the criminal justice field as an undesirable 'foreign' influence:

> [T]he Eurocrats . . . have used the European Courts, as in the recent Bulger case, to confront and marginalise our own common-law system, whose proven ability to bring peace and prosperity over centuries is no longer considered to be an argument for retaining it . . . .[348]

In light of the obvious historic reluctance by senior judges to acknowledge a central role for the ECHR in remedying the deficits in this area of law, judges must also bear some responsibility for popular downgrading of international human rights discourse in the UK. On the other hand, increased domestic judicial oversight of release procedures, through the emphasis on procedural fairness, has had some positive impact. For example, Home Secretaries have significantly reduced the number of cases in which they raise tariffs above judicial recommendations: in 1988, the judicial recommendation on tariffs was exceeded in 59% of cases; in 1994, this proportion had dropped to 4%.[349]

Nevertheless, the Crime (Sentences) Act 1997 retains the discretion of the Home Secretary with respect to the entire release procedure and successive Home Secretaries have confirmed the policy whereby they are entitled to increase tariffs and to do so retrospectively.

It is likely that one area of future debate will be the growing centrality of 'risk' in discourses about offending and public safety. To date, the courts have

---

348 R. Scruton, *The Spectator*, 1 Apr. 2000, pp. 35-36. See *Ex p Anderson*, below p. 277.
349 *Sentenced for Life: Reform of the Law and Procedure for those Sentenced to Life Imprisonment* (JUSTICE, 1996), p. 31.

demonstrated a much greater deference to the executive in relation to the assessment of the risk phase of the tariff. For example, in *Stafford* the House of Lords upheld the claim that 'risk to the public' could include the risk of serious non-violent offences unconnected with the murder which led to the original life sentence.[350] Thus, it was lawful to refuse to release on licence a mandatory life sentence prisoner who had served the tariff term on the ground that he might commit another offence (even, as in this case, where the original offence was murder and the subsequent offence one of forgery).

It remains to be seen whether judges (who are familiar with setting tariffs) will be comfortable with second-guessing the views of politicians, the Parole Board and psychiatric experts as to potential risk.[351] To date, it has been the case that as regards criminal justice more generally:

> jurisprudential notions of free will and responsibility [have not been displaced] by genetic essentialism in the courtroom, where the tendency is for an increased emphasis upon moral responsibility of all offenders for their actions. However, in other areas of the criminal justice system, we are seeing the emergence of new conceptions of the individual 'genetically at risk' of offending, and the development of crime prevention strategies based upon a rationale of public health.[352]

Such ideas may eventually spill over into the courtroom, but thus far the case law on prisoners merely indicates that procedures for risk assessment need to be more transparent.[353] Since 1993, successive Home Secretaries have declared that, in deciding whether to sanction release, they are entitled to consider not only whether a prisoner poses a risk to the public but also whether their release might undermine public confidence in the administration of the justice. This clear bow in a populist direction, a trend familiar from criminal justice policy in the US and Canada, marks a sharp move away from an individualised approach to sentencing towards an idea of general public protection.

As we noted at the start of this section, the civil liberties position in relation to prisoner releases has almost come full circle. At the beginning of the twentieth century, the progressive position was to encourage indeterminate sentences, in the hope that enlightened politicians and bureaucrats would mitigate the harshness of judicial decisions. At its end, groups such as Justice and the Prison

---

350 *R v Secretary of State for the Home Department, ex p Stafford* [1998] 4 All ER 7.

351 The Scottish Parliament's enactment of 'emergency' legislation in the form of the Mental Health (Public Safety and Appeals) Scotland Act 1999, following the release of a convicted killer from hospital, was upheld by the Scottish courts.

352 N. Rose, 'The Biology of Culpability: Pathological Identity and Crime Control in a Biological Culture' (2000) 4 Theor Crim 5, 5.

353 See eg, *R v Secretary of State for the Home Department, ex p Follen* [1996] COD 169 (prisoners should see much of the information which goes to the Board and reasons must be given for refusal). In an interesting decision, the Court of Appeal rejected the idea that anyone who protests their innocence can per se be regarded as an unacceptable risk but did indicate that a failure to participate in pre-release programmes to address offending behaviour can be taken into account: see *R v Home Secretary for the Home Department, ex p Zulfikar, The Times,* 26 Jul. 1995. See also, *R v Parole Board and Secretary of State for the Home Department, ex p Oyston* (unreported, 1 Mar. 2000, CA) (primary task of the Parole Board is to consider the risk to the public if parole is granted and denial of guilt not necessarily conclusive against recommending parole); and *R v Secretary of State for the Home Department and Governor of HM Prison Whatton, ex p Willis* (unreported, 18 Feb. 2000, QB) (policy of Home Secretary with regard to offering sex offenders' home detention curfew was not unlawful as entitled to differentiate between the risk posed by sex offenders and other offenders).

Reform Trust advocate a move in the direction of determinate sentences even for murder, reserving the life sentence for the most exceptional case. The judiciary in the UK have gone a long way towards curbing the discretion of politicians to disregard their views in the area of life sentence release. The crucial issue for the senior judiciary in the HRA era is whether they will remove this discretion entirely. The case of *R v Secretary of State for the Home Department, ex p Anderson and Taylor* may provide an answer.[354] The Divisional Court made it clear that it felt itself bound by European case law to hold that Articles 5 and 6 of the ECHR did not prevent the Home Secretary from setting the tariff element of a mandatory life sentence for murder. It also felt itself bound by successive House of Lords decisions (such as *Hindley*) to hold that Parliament could lawfully confer such a power on the Home Secretary by primary legislation. Yet, Sullivan and Penry-Davey JJ expressed clear unease with this conclusion and, on appeal, the senior judiciary may feel that the HRA now also provides them with the opportunity to reconsider long-held positions.

CONCLUSION

The development of prisoners' rights has clearly moved a long way from the early 1970s. Legal recognition of prisoners' rights to due process in the domestic and European courts has led to major changes in areas like prison adjudications and prisoner release procedures. Legal changes have also opened up contact between prison and the outside world, ensuring that prison is no longer so closed a world. Above all, the legal accountability of prison authorities for their actions has been clearly recognised, with the result that prisons are no longer the lawless agencies of the past and seem less likely – despite the declining faith in the rehabilitative ideal – to retreat into 'austere regimes' in the future.

It is also wise, however, to express caution about how far the development of prisoners' rights has gone. Litigation for prisoners' rights has not been uniformly influential. In areas such as the informal disciplinary system, rights claims have been brushed aside by arguments based on security or the demands of internal prison management. They have made little impact on the issue of living conditions and, overall, might be said to be of greater use to some groups of prisoners (notably long-term male prisoners[355]) than others (including women prisoners or those awaiting trial). In these areas, other institutions such as the Inspectorate or Ombudsman, have arguably proved more influential, and they have tended to frame their claims in terms of pragmatism as much as rights.

The vulnerability of general rights claims to arguments based on security or the needs of internal management suggests that caution is also appropriate when it comes to the likely impact of the HRA on prisons. Prison law and practice in the UK has already been the focus of considerable examination for Convention-compatibility via an extensive Strasbourg jurisprudence. Although this has proved very influential in some areas, there are also many cases where the European Court has displayed reluctance to intervene and domestic courts may well choose to follow much of this jurisprudence. However, there is one way in which the Act could have a major impact on prisons. This lies in the requirement that many restrictions on Convention rights must be 'prescribed

---

354 Div Ct, 22 Feb. 2001.
355 Women comprise only 4% of life sentence prisoners.

by law'. As we have seen, many restrictions on prisoners' rights, for example in respect of searches or censorship, are based not on the Prison Act but merely on the Prison Rules or, more commonly, on Standing Orders or Instructions to Governors. Courts could take the view that restrictions on fundamental rights like privacy or free expression should be clearly stated by Parliament rather than being left to the dictates of the Home Secretary or the Prison Service. Certainly, this was the position of the Canadian courts after the Charter of Rights was introduced in 1982.

If the UK courts were to take a similar view, there might be a need for a new Prison Act. This could provide the opportunity for a more extensive debate on how imprisonment might be reconciled with human rights, whether prisoners should have specific rights and how the needs of different groups of prisoners might be recognised. It might be an opportunity for further reflection on whether recognising the role of rights in imprisonment has any implications for the objectives of imprisonment. It might also pose a danger, however, in that politicians might decide that a more austere regime was more in keeping with the tough approach they have espoused in recent years and seek to limit the discretion which the present legal structure allows to managers and governors.

A further reason for caution about the development and future of prisoners' rights is that if such strategies are narrowly law-centred they run the risk of stunting the potential for civil libertarians to harness the 'extended accountability'[356] mechanisms that are characteristic of the modern UK prison system. The civil libertarian will need to range wider than Parliament and the courts, even if the latter eventually work to secure a role for public law principles in relation to all exercises of power. The challenge will be to define and map the dense and overlapping accountability mechanisms (ranging from litigation, the CIP, the Ombudsman and the CPT, to voluntary organisations, the media and the standards developed as a result of the contracting-out process) and then 'to know when, where and how to make appropriate strategic interventions in complex accountability networks to secure appropriate normative structures and outcomes'.[357]

And finally it should not be forgotten that prisoners' rights – whether manifested in improved complaints procedures or some other way – may be of little value to prisoners who find themselves crammed into small cells with little opportunity for exercise or association or rehabilitation. Ultimately, therefore, there is a need to connect strategies of prisoners' rights with strategies of rights protection in the criminal justice system more generally.

356 C. Scott, 'Accountability in the Regulatory State' (2000) 27 JLS 38, 38.
357 Ibid., at p. 57.

Chapter Six

Democratising privacy

INTRODUCTION

Concern about invasion of privacy has been commonplace in the UK in recent decades. The subject's ubiquity, even notoriety, should not, however, be taken as evidence of agreement on the social value of privacy, the scope of the interests which merit protection under a right to privacy, or the grounds for legitimate interference with such a right. On the contrary, lack of agreement about such matters is endemic. This is not at all surprising: privacy means different things to different people, and is valued differently, because '[a]t the heart of the concern to protect "privacy" lies a conception of the individual and his or her relationship with society'[1] and individuals, and cultures, have always disagreed about this relationship.

Disagreement about the value of privacy is very much in evidence in academic commentaries, where scepticism about privacy tends to be promoted by communitarians who fear privacy's capacity to foil the common good.[2] Scepticism about the value of privacy is also evident in some feminist scholarship, primarily because of the gender inequality that has been shored up by the historic lifeline between property and privacy – which privileged the idea of 'one's home as one's castle' in ways that grounded and secured the power of a patriarchal family model.[3] Lack of agreement about privacy is also fuelled by privacy advocates, who agree that privacy has value but disagree about what that value is and about which interests merit legal protection as privacy-related. One prominent example is provided by international human rights law, wherein the European Convention on Human Rights, the International Covenant on Civil and Political Rights, and the Universal Declaration of Human Rights protect privacy but differ in terms of the scope of the protection offered.[4] Of late, privacy advocates and sceptics alike have been stirred up by a sharpening of fear induced by threats to privacy via technology,[5] and by governmental responses

1 R. Wacks, *Personal Information: Privacy and the Law* (Clarendon, 1993), p. 7.
2 See eg, A. Etzioni, *The Limits of Privacy* (Basic Books, 2000).
3 See eg, C.A. MacKinnon, *Towards a Feminist Theory of the State* (Harvard UP, 1989).
4 The ICCPR and the UNDHR recognise a right to legal protection against arbitrary interference with privacy, family, home or correspondence and against attacks on honour and reputation; Art. 8(1), ECHR provides only for a right to 'respect for' private life, family life, home and correspondence.
5 See eg, S. Davis, *Big Brother: Britain's Web of Surveillance and the New Technological Order* (Pan, 1996).

to technology, such as the Regulation of Investigatory Powers Act 2000 (RIPA). Sceptics have also sought to emphasise the threat to 'traditional values' inherent in privacy's burgeoning protection for 'non-traditional' families and other intimate associations. The controversial decisions in *Douglas v Hello! Ltd* and *Venables and Thompson v News Group Newspapers* have pushed privacy rights further into the spotlight.

This chapter will be structured around these disagreements and developments. It will begin, however, with a history of the protection for 'the right to privacy' in this jurisdiction. Part II will then outline the approach of the European Court of Human Rights to Article 8 claims for respect for private life, family life, home and correspondence. In Parts III and IV we shall engage with a perennial theme in commentaries on the right to privacy: the question of the purpose, or value, of privacy, and in particular whether there is a common feature linking together the various and disparate interests which are commonly protected by a right to privacy. Part III will focus solely on whether property might fulfil this role, whereas Part IV will range more widely. Finally, in Parts V and VI, we shall engage with questions of application or classification. By this we mean, questions relating, first, to the acts, decisions, relationships, spaces and information that merit inclusion under a right to privacy; and, secondly, to the issue of what constitutes a legitimate ground for limiting or interfering with the right. Part V is intended to provide a sense of the context in which these questions of application will be decided. It outlines media, corporate and governmental practices in what has been described as 'information society'. Part VI will then engage directly with questions of application, focusing on circumstances where it is argued that privacy must give way (for example, because of the public interest in the information) or has no relevance.

I.　AN OVERVIEW OF PRIVACY LAW

Parliament, the press and privacy

In the UK, in recent decades, privacy has generated a great deal of commentary, a mixed bag of case law, and a meagre amount of legislation. In part, this is because of the historic preoccupation with two themes: first, that the law did not recognise a right to privacy, although it did offer 'some protection to privacy'[6] (albeit 'under-theorized',[7] 'indirect'[8] and 'patchy and inadequate'[9]); and secondly, that privacy legislation would be nightmarishly difficult to draft. Parliament (or, more accurately, Conservative and Labour governments alike) was the most robust champion of the latter theme: despite a clutch of increasingly anxious official reports and a number of private members' bills,[10]

6　T. Bingham, 'The Way We Live Now: Human Rights in the New Millennium' (1998) 1 Web JCLI 1.

7　D. Feldman, 'Secrecy, Dignity, or Autonomy? Views of Privacy as Civil Liberty' (1994) CLP 41, 42.

8　S.H. Bailey, B.L. Jones and D.J. Harris, *Civil Liberties: Cases and Materials* (Butterworths, 1995), p. 517.

9　Bingham, above n. 6.

10　Successive governments failed to act on the proposals for limiting press intrusion into private life put forward by: the Younger Committee (1972); the Calcutt Committee (1990 and 1993); the National Heritage Select Committee (1993); and the Lord Chancellor's Department (1993). For more details on these proposals, see Bailey, Harris and Jones, above n. 8, pp. 516-527.

it never showed serious inclination towards legislating on privacy, in particular on the issue of a civil remedy for a breach of privacy.[11] Rather, its preferred formula for privacy debates centred on 'a seemingly endless argument about whether or not it [would be] possible to "define" privacy in a legally meaningful manner'.[12]

Parliament's preoccupation with alleged definitional difficulties is somewhat suspect: the fact that other jurisdictions have managed to enact comprehensive privacy legislation, and that a range of constitutional courts have developed sophisticated privacy jurisprudence,[13] suggests that governments' primary motivation may have been to stall, or blunt calls for, privacy legislation. Support for this suggestion can be found in the 'pitch and toss of [the] remarkable contest between Parliament and the press' in the UK:

> The pattern is familiar. Private lives are made public spectacle by the tabloids. A general sense of unease ensues. Politicians appear to fret. Judges lament the incapacity of the common law to help. Committees are established. 'Privacy' legislation is proposed. Alarms are sounded by the quality press about the onslaught against freedom of speech. Inertia settles on politicians, reluctant to offend newspaper editors. The debate subsides until the next series of sensationalist disclosures.[14]

Politicians' desire to court the media, rather than definitional difficulties surrounding privacy, may therefore be the principal reason for the poor parliamentary showing on privacy in recent decades. Media practices, in particular tabloid intrusion into the 'private life' of 'public figures', have also had the further damaging effect of colonising privacy. That is, they have been allowed to dominate debate on privacy, thereby excluding other privacy-related interests; moreover, their dominance has done nothing to stop key 'privacy and the press' concepts, such as 'public interest' and 'press freedom', becoming encrusted in further layers of cliché.[15]

Media practices may continue to garner excessive attention in privacy debates in the HRA era. In this respect, it is noteworthy that much of the critical press comment during the parliamentary stages of the Human Rights Bill was directed towards the possibility of judges creating a right of privacy against newspapers. Academics' focus on the future 'horizontal effect' of the HRA also seems to have been driven by this issue,[16] as was the general debate over whether the Press Complaints Commission (PCC), a self-regulatory body established by the

---

11 Parliament has, however, provided regimes for protecting certain privacy interests against unjustified intrusion: see eg, the Interception of Communications Act 1985 (enacted after the ECtHR decision in *Malone* (see below p. 284)); the Protection from Harassment Act 1997 (prompted by the CA's decision in *Khorasandjian v Bush* (see below p. 287)); and the Data Protection Act 1998 (required by Council Directive 95/46/EC on the processing of information, including CCTV tapes, about individuals).

12 J.D.R. Craig, 'Privacy in the Workplace and the Impact of European Convention Incorporation on United Kingdom Labour Law' (1998) 19 Comp Lab L&P J 373, 382.

13 For comparative material on privacy, see eg, the essays in B.S. Markesinis (ed.), *Protecting Privacy* (OUP, 1999).

14 R. Wacks, *Privacy and Press Freedom* (Blackstone, 1995), p. 1.

15 The 'ambivalent attitude to the blessings of the media' (J.G. Fleming, *The American Tort Process* (Clarendon, 1988), p. 93) manifested in defamation law – which until the 1990s privileged reputation rights over freedom of speech – was a further aggravating factor.

16 See the discussion of this matter in Ch. 1. On its relevance to the specific issue of privacy and the press, see B.S. Markesinis, 'Privacy, Freedom of Expression, and the Horizontality of the Human Rights Bill: Lessons from Germany' (1999) 115 LQR 47.

press themselves, came within the definition of 'public authority' in section 6 of the HRA. Clear evidence of the ongoing power of the media to influence government policy in this area emerged with the late addition of section 12 to the HRA.[17] This section obliges the courts to pay 'particular regard' to the Article 10 right to freedom of expression and offers increased procedural safeguards in relation to the granting of ex parte injunctions.[18]

The HRA does, of course, list the ECHR's Article 8 right to respect for private and family life, home, and correspondence amongst its 'Convention rights', thereby providing plenty of scope for development of privacy law over the coming years. Indeed, the clamour over 'privacy and the press' during the parliamentary debates on the Act, is merely one manifestation of what appears to be a consensus that the HRA will perhaps have its 'greatest impact' in the field of privacy:

> It will make it unlawful for any public authority . . . to breach the right to respect for private life in Article 8 of the ECHR. It may go further and be at least indirectly applicable against private individuals and companies. It is likely, in the light of recent authority from the Commission of Human Rights and extra-judicial comments of judges in the United Kingdom, to be used as the springboard for the development of existing causes of action so as to fill the gaps in the patchy protection of privacy in English law.[19]

The HRA aside, however, it would be an exaggeration to describe the parliamentary record on privacy as anything other than slim pickings. Moreover, the historic undervaluing of privacy in UK law was recently reinforced by Parliament's enactment of the Regulation of Investigatory Powers Act 2000, in the face of an extraordinarily wide spectrum of opposition and outrage.[20] In part, the Act was a response to concerns about inadequate legal authority for certain investigatory practices and telephone interceptions (as highlighted by several European Court of Human Rights decisions[21]). It introduces full statutory backing for a range of covert surveillance and interception practices performed by public authorities (such as tapping phones, bugging property, using informants, tracking devices and

---

17   For details of the intervention by Lord Wakeham, Chair of the PCC, which led to the addition of s. 12 to the HRA, see R. Singh, 'Privacy and the Media: The Human Rights Bill' in Markesinis, above n. 13, pp. 169-190, at pp. 184-189.

18   S. Grosz, J. Beatson and P. Duffy, *Human Rights: The 1998 Act and the European Convention* (Sweet & Maxwell, 1999), pp. 98-104 argue that s. 12 is 'unlikely to make any practical difference. [The ECHR] itself requires any right to privacy to be balanced against the right to freedom of expression'.

19   Singh, above n. 17, p. 190. See further the comments of Lord Irvine, the Lord Chancellor, during debates on the HRA: 'as I have often said, the judges are pen-poised regardless of incorporation of the Convention to develop a right of privacy to be protected by the common law. This is not me saying so; they have said so. . . . [Using the HRA], the courts will be able to adapt and develop the common law by relying on existing domestic principles in the law of trespass, nuisance, copyright, confidence and the like, to fashion a common law right to privacy . . . .' (583 HL 784 (24 Nov. 1997)).

20   The text of the RIPA is available at: www.hmso.gov.uk. The Foundation for Information Policy Research (FIPR) website has an excellent collection of parliamentary and media responses to the legislation: see www.fipr.org. Opposition to the RIPA encompassed a wide range of media, commercial, professional, NGO and civil liberties organisations, as well as the Data Protection Commissioner.

21   See below, pp. 295-296. See also S. Uglow, 'Covert Surveillance and the European Convention on Human Rights' [1999] Crim LR 287; and the Telecommunications (Lawful Business Practice) (Interception of Communications) Regulations 2000 (determining the effect of the Telecommunications Data Protection Directive 1997 on the confidentiality of public and private telecoms networks and the permitted grounds for interceptions).

undercover agents); preserves the established pattern of non-judicial (that is, ministerial and police) issuing of warrants; and creates a new tort of unlawful interception of a private telecommunications system. Conventional 'oversight' mechanisms are included: the Act provides for Commissioners[22] and a complaints Tribunal, but the decisions of the latter are explicitly said not to be 'subject to appeal or be liable to be questioned in any court'.[23]

It was the government's tailoring of the Act to target Internet use, however, which generated all the controversy. On the basis of unsubstantiated allegations that hacking and use of encryption present serious threats to law enforcement, the Act introduces powers, first, to compel Internet Service Providers (ISPs) to install 'black boxes' on their networks which will re-route Internet traffic to MI5 premises, and, secondly, to require the handover of 'keys' for any suspect encrypted data.[24] Critics dismiss these powers as 'technically inept', easily circumvented and counter to IT industry-moves towards universal encryption.[25] However, it is the sheer scale of privacy invasions permitted that has drawn the most opposition; the Act effectively sanctions 'state snooping' – by GCHQ and MI6, as well as MI5, due to the international nature of on-line communications – on millions of Internet users (including journalists and NGOs) without the need for specific warrants, or provision of effective judicial oversight.[26] Taken as a whole, the Act outraged a unique coalition of critics, from the e-commerce world to civil libertarians, which perhaps helps to explain why the Act has been labelled 'the worst UK legislation ever'.[27]

The judiciary and the 'right to privacy': a special relationship?

The judicial record on privacy is far more interesting than the parliamentary one. Privacy-related claims have provoked a range of responses from the senior judiciary and, pre the HRA, provided the occasion for considerable development of the common law. Historically, however, the most common judicial response to privacy violations was to issue an explicit request (latterly accompanied by a threat of recrimination) for reform via legislation.[28] *Kaye*

---

22 See eg, *Annual Report of the Interception of Communications Commissioner for 1998* (Cm. 4364, 1999) (available at: www.homeoffice.gov.uk).

23 RIPA, s. 67(8). See H. Fenwick, *Civil Rights* (Longman, 2000), pp. 295-416.

24 For further information on encryption, see Cyber-Rights & Cyber-Liberties (UK) (at: www.cyber-rights.org) and Privacy International (at: www.privacyinternational.org). The American Civil Liberties Union (ACLU) is also conducting a similar campaign against the FBI use of 'Carnivore', a 'black box' attached to an ISP network which can scan millions of on-line communications per second: see www.aclu.org.

25 See I. Brown and B. Gladman, 'The Regulation of Investigatory Powers Bill' (Jul. 2000) at www.fipr.org.

26 Cf. *R v Duarte* [1990] 1 SCR 30 (Canadian SCt held that electronic surveillance of private communications by state authorities, without prior judicial authorisation, infringed the right to privacy under the Canadian Charter of Rights).

27 613 HL 906 (25 May 2000) (Earl of Northesk, citing *The Observer*).

28 The same theme was pursued in extra-judicial writing: see eg, Lord Bingham, 'Should There Be a Law to Protect Rights of Personal Privacy?' [1996] EHRLR 450, 461-462 ('[m]y preference would be for legislation, which would mean that the rules which the courts applied would carry the imprimatur of democratic approval. But if, for whatever reason, legislation is not forthcoming, I think it almost inevitable that cases will arise in the courts in which the need to give relief is obvious and pressing; and when such cases do arise, I do not think the courts will be found wanting').

v Robertson, wherein the Court of Appeal chorused for parliamentary action, provides a classic example of this response.[29] The Court held that it had no power to grant a remedy for infringement of privacy where a reporter and a photographer employed by a Sunday tabloid newspaper intruded on Gordon Kaye, a well-known television actor, taking photographs of him for publication, without his consent whilst he was recovering in hospital after a serious road accident.[30] It also expressed its dismay at this outcome and famously every member of the Court called upon Parliament to remedy matters – Leggatt LJ was perhaps the most emphatic of the three, arguing that the right to privacy 'has so long been disregarded . . . that it can be recognised now only by the legislature' and expressing the hope 'that the making good of this signal shortcoming in our law will not long be delayed'.[31]

More recently, the senior judiciary have shown interest in drawing other actors into the circle of privacy regulators. In *Ex p BBC*[32] and *Ex p Granada*,[33] they embraced the role of bodies such as the Independent Television Commission, the Press Complaints Commission and the Broadcasting Standards Commission in devising codes on media responsibilities and responding to complaints.[34] They have, as we shall see below, also shaken off 'judge as lawmaker' controversy and begun to make what appear to be moves towards shaping a right to privacy. However, we need first to examine a second set of traditional judicial responses to privacy claims, one where judges either denied that a privacy interest was implicated or accorded it little weight. Examples of cases in this second group include *Malone*[35] and *Brown*.[36] The first of these cases, *Malone*, concerned telephone tapping by the police. It established the lack of a right to privacy as against the state, as well as demonstrating the general inclination of the courts towards deference to the executive on matters of 'national security' or 'serious crime' and their willingness to maintain a 'jurisprudence of the Cold War'.[37] In *Malone*, Megarry VC declared that English law did not entertain actions for invasion of privacy unless the invasion

---

29   [1991] FSR 62.
30   The CA did uphold the grant of an interlocutory injunction against the newspaper using the tort of malicious falsehood.
31   Above n. 29, p. 71. Feldman notes that the case 'illustrates an attitude characteristic of English civil liberties law. The judges were clearly of the view that the absence of a right to privacy in English law was so well established that it could be remedied only by Parliament': *Human Rights and Civil Liberties in England and Wales* (Clarendon, 1993), p. 388. Cl. 9 of the PCC's *Code of Practice* now sets benchmarks for journalists and photographers making inquiries at hospitals or other similar institutions.
32   *R v Broadcasting Complaints Commission, ex p British Broadcasting Corpn* [2000] 3 All ER 989 (CA). The case also raises the important question of the privacy rights of corporations: see also *Service Corpn International v Channel 4 Television Corpn* [1999] EMLR 83 (application for injunction preventing the broadcast of documentary showing 'disrespectful and abusive treatment of corpses' in funeral home refused on public interest grounds).
33   *R v Broadcasting Complaints Commission, ex p Granada Television Ltd* [1995] EMLR 163.
34   Privacy codes received a further boost from the HRA, wherein s. 12(4)(b) directs courts to have regard to 'any relevant privacy code' in considering whether to grant any relief which, if granted, might affect the exercise of the Convention right to freedom of expression. See eg, PCC *Code of Practice* (1999) (available at: www.pcc.org.uk).
35   *Malone v Metropolitan Police Comr* [1979] 2 All ER 620.
36   *R v Brown* [1993] 2 All ER 75.
37   L. Lustgarten and I. Leigh, *In From the Cold: National Security and Parliamentary Democracy* (Clarendon, 1994), p. 329. The revelations of the 'Spycatcher' era, namely Peter Wright's confirmation that MI5 'bugged and burgled' across London without fear of sanction, provoked little judicial concern about systematic state violations of privacy: see further Ch. 7.

amounted to one of the established tortious or equitable causes of action (for example, trespass or breach of confidence).[38] He noted Article 8 of the ECHR but held it incapable of creating directly enforceable rights in English law; he also acknowledged the US courts' development of English common law into a broader privacy law but said that the very nature of English law (whereby anything that was not prohibited by law was lawful) meant that he could not follow such a lead.[39] *Malone's* case, however, ultimately led to the enactment of the (now repealed) Interception of Communications Act 1985 following a successful application to the European Court of Human Rights which held that the legal regulation of the circumstances of telephone interceptions was not expressed with sufficient clarity as required under Article 8(2) of the ECHR.[40]

More recently, in *R v Khan (Sultan)*,[41] where the police placed a listening device on a private premises as part of a drug-dealing investigation, the House of Lords faced the question of whether evidence obtained by methods which violated privacy ought to have been excluded from a criminal trial. The Law Lords concluded that there was no rule requiring automatic exclusion of illegally obtained evidence. Crucially, they saw no need to discuss the privacy implications of the case: under English law, there was, they said, nothing unlawful about a breach of privacy and, in any event, the common law (and section 78 of PACE) permitted illegally obtained prosecution evidence to be admitted in criminal proceedings at the discretion of the judge. The absence of statutory authority (as distinct from Home Office guidelines) for the police action, and the fact that the evidence could only be attained 'by means of a civil trespass and, on the face of it, criminal damage to property', proved insufficient triggers for judicial examination of what Lord Nicholls described as the question of whether the traditional 'piecemeal protection of privacy law' had developed to the extent that 'a more comprehensive principle [could] be seen to exist'.[42] Moreover, Lord Nolan declared his relief at the court's conclusion, emphasising that he would deem it 'a strange reflection on our law if a man who has admitted his participation in the illegal importation of a large quantity of heroin should

---

38 Malone failed in both of these causes of action as it was held that the telephone tapping had not involved a trespass (it occurred in the Post Office) and the public telephone system could not be considered a confidential network.

39 In addition, and establishing a precedent for judges in subsequent cases, he described what he saw as the clear need for legislation to protect privacy: see [1979] 2 All ER 620, 649.

40 *Malone v UK* (1984) 7 EHRR 14 (law must adequately indicate circumstances in which, and the conditions on which, public authorities are empowered to resort to interceptions). See also, *R v Secretary of State for the Home Department, ex p Ruddock* [1987] 2 All ER 518 (re telephone intercepts of member of Campaign for Nuclear Disarmament); *Harman and Hewitt v UK* (1992) 14 EHRR 657 (EComHR holding that MI5 surveillance of officers of the National Council for Civil Liberties breached Arts. 8 and 13; led to friendly settlement and to the enactment of the Security Service Act 1989); *Morgans v DPP* [2000] 2 All ER 522 (HL) (evidence obtained by telephone intercepts strictly limited to purposes outlined in Interception of Communications Act 1985); and *R v X, The Times*, 23 May 2000 (CA) (use of fruits of foreign telephone intercepts admissible in criminal proceedings and justified under Art. 8). For the current statutory framework on telephone interceptions, see RIPA.

41 [1996] 3 All ER 289. The ECtHR in *Khan v UK* [2000] Crim LR 684 found breaches of Arts. 8 and 13 on the basis that Home Office and police guidelines were not 'in accordance with law' as required by Art. 8(2). See also, *Govell v UK* (EComHR) App. No. 27237/95, 14 Jan. 1998; and RIPA.

42 Ibid., p. 302.

have his conviction set aside on the grounds that his privacy has been invaded'.[43] *Halford,* where a police authority recorded private telephone conversations between a police officer (who was suing them for alleged sex discrimination) and her lawyer when using an internal office telephone system, yielded a similarly impoverished view on privacy. The applicant took her case to the European Court of Human Rights after unsuccessfully petitioning the Interception of Communications Tribunal (and the Home Office). The Court held that the absence of any legal regulation in UK law of intrusion on such internal telephone systems did not comply with the requirement in Article 8(2) that interferences with the right to respect for privacy be 'in accordance with law'. It also found a breach of the Article 13 right to an effective remedy because, in the absence of legal regulation, the applicant had no legal remedy.[44]

Privacy-related claims faltered in a different context – the policing of gay communities – in *R v Brown.*[45] In this case, a majority of the House of Lords skirted the privacy implications of their ruling upholding convictions under the Offences Against the Person Act 1861 of adult men who had participated in consensual, private sado-masochistic sex. Moreover, although in a later assault case involving a heterosexual couple, the Court of Appeal allowed a defence of the woman's consent to branding of initials on her body,[46] it was decided in *Emmett* that consent is not a defence where there is a risk of permanent injury.[47] The issue of consent must always be problematised, yet the majority decision in *Brown* can only be viewed as 'a worrying development in terms of privacy law'.[48] It disrespects people's autonomy, and the alleged public interest in preventing such private sexual activity between consenting adults appears little more than a veneer for homophobia.[49] The precedent is made more worrying by the fact that the European Court of Human Rights decided that the *Brown* decision was justifiable under Article 8(2) on the ground of protecting health

43   Ibid. For a similar deferential attitude to police use of the breach of peace power to enter private property, see *McLeod v Metropolitan Police Comr* [1994] 4 All ER 553 (CA) (sufficient excuse to enter home). By contrast, the ECtHR in *McLeod v UK* (1998) 27 EHRR 493 found a violation of Art. 8 on the grounds that the police did not take sufficient steps to verify the legal basis for their entry into the private home.

44   See *Halford v UK* (1997) 24 EHRR 523. For discussion of privacy in the employment context, see eg, Craig above n. 12 and his *Privacy and Employment Law* (Hart, 1999); and S. Palmer, 'Human Rights: Implications for Labour Law' (2000) 59 CLJ 168, 186-190.

45   [1993] 2 All ER 75. An example of the weakness of public law in recognising the right to privacy (in the context of sexual orientation discrimination) is *R v Ministry of Defence, ex p Smith* [1996] 1 All ER 257, wherein the CA refused to consider Art. 8 in reviewing a policy of dismissal of lesbians and gays from the armed services. The ECtHR subsequently found violations of Arts. 8 and 13 because of the 'exceptional intrusion' into private life and the absence of any effective remedy: *Smith v UK* (1999) 29 EHRR 493.

46   *R v Wilson* [1997] QB 47. Furthermore, as Feldman points out 'it would be interesting to know whether the result of *Wilson* would have been the same had either party admitted to deriving any sexual satisfaction from the procedure': see 'Human Dignity as a Legal Value – Part II' [2000] PL 61, 73-74.

47   *R v Emmett, The Times,* 15 Oct. 1999 (consensual heterosexual sado-masochistic acts, involving asphyxiation and the igniting of lighter fuel poured on body, held to be unlawful).

48   Feldman, above n. 46, p. 73.

49   See C.F. Stychin, *Law's Desire* (Routledge, 1995), Ch. 7; and L.J. Moran, 'Violence and the Law: The Case of Sado-Masochism' (1995) 4 SLS 225. See also, N. Dearden, 'The Queen and the "Bolton Seven"' (1999) 7 FLS 317; and T. Butt and J. Hearn, 'The Sexualization of Corporal Punishment: The Construction of Sexual Meaning' (1998) 1 Sexualities 203.

and morals (and went on to question whether the activities were covered by Article 8(1)'s respect for private life).[50]

A *developing right to privacy*?

We move now to the third group of cases relevant to the development of a right to privacy. These cases suggest a 'more accommodating'[51] approach to privacy interests. In particular, they dangle the possibility of a more expansive approach towards certain causes of action (most notably, breach of confidence), and evidence a willingness to engage with the array of difficult balances between 'rights' and 'public interests' (such as that between privacy, or more narrowly, reputation, and press freedom) which envelope this area. Equally, however, identification of privacy values or interests remains haphazard and largely underdeveloped in these cases; for the most part, the senior judiciary persist with a policy of 'hint and defer' on such matters – as for example in *Khan* where Lord Nicholls expressed his preference for leaving open 'for another occasion' the 'important question' of whether the piecemeal protection of privacy could be moulded into a more comprehensive legal principle.[52] Furthermore, on at least one occasion in recent years, plaudits for judicial creativity in the privacy field have been shown to be premature. The praise followed *Khorasandjian v Bush*,[53] wherein the Court of Appeal developed the law of private nuisance so as to create a tort of harassment in order to provide a remedy where a person was subject to persistent and unwanted telephone calls. But, four years later, in 1997, the House of Lords in *Hunter v Canary Wharf*[54] overruled *Khorasandjian* in part, reinstating the traditional principle that an interest in land is required before a person can sue for private nuisance; indeed, in Lord Goff's view, the Court of Appeal in *Khorasandjian* had 'exploit[ed] the law of private nuisance in order to create by the back door a tort of harassment'.

We would argue that this final group of cases can best be understood if it is approached by focusing on three matters: first, the creeping influence of concepts such as autonomy and dignity; secondly, the courts' increasingly explicit engagement with proportionality and the weighting of interests more generally; and finally, the debate over developing the breach of confidence action. Judges' increasing concern with concepts such as autonomy, respect and dignity can be glimpsed across a spectrum of cases; '[b]roadly, some of them are concerned with the protection of personal information and image, others with control over access to, or use of, the individual's person or body, while a third group

---

50   *Laskey v UK* (1997) 24 EHRR 39. See, however, *ADT v UK* [2000] 2 FLR 697 (gross indecency prosecution of man involved in consensual oral sex and masturbation with other men held to violate Art. 8).

51   Feldman, above n. 7, at p. 45.

52   Above n. 41, p. 176. Contrast the varied judicial understandings of 'privacy' interests in: *R v Brentwood BC, ex p Peck* [1998] EMLR 697 (re provision of CCTV footage to media depicting events surrounding an attempted suicide); *Ex p BBC*, above n. 32 (re privacy rights of individuals and companies); *Charleston v News Group Newspapers Ltd* [1995] 2 All ER 313 (HL) (re control of personal image); and *Nottingham CC v October Films Ltd* [1999] 2 FLR 347 (re restrictions on media filming of homeless children).

53   [1993] 3 All ER 669.

54   [1997] 2 All ER 426.

involves the freedom to take fundamental decisions about sexual conduct and patterns of life'.[55] Thus, for example, victims of harassment acquired common law protection as a result of *Khorasandjian v Bush*, prior to legislative backing for a tort of harassment in 1997. The law on medical treatment has also been broadened, providing greater recognition of patient autonomy and dignity.[56]

The second pertinent issue is the courts' increasing engagement in privacy cases with concepts such as proportionality. It has, for example, been argued that *Ex p Thorpe*[57] is evidence that 'the judiciary are already adjudicating in a manner consonant with the European Convention'[58] – that is, they are embracing the proportionality principle underlying Article 8. *Thorpe* concerned the justifiability of police disclosure of information about the criminal record and whereabouts of two individuals who had been released after serving sentences for sex offences. Bingham LCJ in the Divisional Court (in a judgment endorsed by the Court of Appeal) approached the case by outlining the general presumption in favour of non-disclosure in such circumstances based on the value of privacy to ex-offenders, before highlighting the justifiability of the police action on the ground that 'there is a strong public interest in ensuring that the police are able to disclose information about offenders where that is necessary for the prevention or the detection of crime, or for the protection of young or other vulnerable people'.[59]

The cases of *Re L*[60] and *Ex p LM*,[61] concerning police and local authority disclosure of information about past *allegations* of suspected sexual abuse, highlight the commitment of judges to applying the 'pressing need' test for disclosure via the balancing of the right of an individual to a private life against the public interest in protecting children from abuse.[62] Explicit engagement with assessment of competing rights and interests is also evident in the areas of

---

55   E. Barendt, 'Privacy as a Constitutional Value' in P. Birks (ed.), *Privacy and Loyalty* (Clarendon, 1997), pp. 1-14, at p. 5. For an explanation of the relationship between autonomy, dignity and respect, and an account of the protection of dignity in English law, see D. Feldman, 'Human Dignity as a Legal Value – Parts I and II' [1999] PL 682 and [2000] PL 61.

56   See eg, *Re A (Mental Patient: Sterilisation)* [2000] Lloyd's Rep Med 87 (CA) (sterilisation not in best interests of patient and ECHR protected rights of those unable to speak for themselves); and *St George's Healthcare NHS Trust v S* [1998] 3 All ER 673 (CA) (upholding general rule re competent adults that administering medical treatment is a battery unless patient has consented thereto in context of forced obstetric intervention). See also, *Reeves v Metropolitan Police Comr* [1999] 3 All ER 897 (HL) (re principle of human autonomy).

57   [1997] 4 All ER 691 (DC); affd [1999] QB 396 (CA).

58   R. Mullender, 'Privacy, Paedophilia and the European Convention on Human Rights: A Deontological Approach [1998] PL 384, 387. On the DC decision, see N.W. Barber, 'Privacy and the Police: Private Right, Public Rights or Human Right? *R v Chief Constable of North Wales Police, ex p AB*' [1997] PL 19.

59   Above n. 57, p. 732. See also, *Preston BC v McGrath, The Times*, 19 May, 2000 (CA) and *Woolgar v Chief Constable of the Sussex Police* [1999] 3 All ER 604 (CA) (police permitted to disclose confidential material to appropriate bodies when in public interest, but person affected entitled to be informed in advance to allow possible court challenge); and *Marcel v Metropolitan Police Comr* [1992] Ch 225 (powers to seize and retain property are conferred for the performance of public functions and cannot be used to make information available to private individuals for private purposes). For a discussion of the legal protection for journalists' sources, see Ch. 7.

60   *Re L (Minors) (Sexual Abuse: Disclosure)* [1999] 1 WLR 299 (CA).

61   *R v Local Authority in the Midlands, ex p LM* [2000] 1 FLR 612.

62   Cf. *R v Secretary of State for Health, ex p C* [2000] 1 FLR 627 (CA) (Department of Health's maintenance of an index of names (the Consultancy Service Index) of people considered unsuitable for employment in child care field justified under prerogative powers of Crown).

health care[63] and deportation,[64] and especially in family law proceedings where increasing reference is made to the Article 8 jurisprudence on the need to respect for private and family life in Children Act 1989 cases.[65]

A second illustration of the courts' greater ease with reconciling privacy claims with other interests is provided by the recent reorientation of libel law. In 1993, in *Derbyshire County Council v Times Newspapers*, the House of Lords removed the right to sue for defamation from government bodies, declaring that the public interest required openness to uninhibited criticism.[66] Lord Keith insisted that it was 'of the highest public importance that a democratically elected governmental body, or indeed any governmental body, should be open to uninhibited public criticism', and that the threat of a defamation action 'must inevitably have an inhibiting effect on freedom of speech' given the difficulty of proving the truth of facts which would justify publication.[67] More recently, in *Reynolds v Times Newspapers*, the Law Lords tackled the question of whether individuals involved in governmental or public affairs should have limitations placed on their rights to sue for libel.[68] Their ruling rejected the creation of a new category of qualified privilege relating to political information given the interest in protecting individual reputations and promoting accurate reporting, but accepted that the media should be free to publish inaccurate information on matters of public interest provided it acts fairly and reasonably and follows professional journalistic standards.[69]

Pre- HRA judges came closest to developing a privacy jurisprudence in breach of confidence actions; indeed, one Law Lord argued that this action 'involves no more than an invasion of privacy'.[70] In many respects, however, the breach of confidence action seemed an unlikely vehicle for privacy developments. The parameters of the remedy have traditionally been narrow: the information must not be public knowledge; it must have been imparted in circumstances where an obligation of confidence exists; and there must have been an unauthorised use of the information.[71] Most cases have arisen in the context of commercial and government secrets, but the category of 'personal information' has, in recent years, provided the greatest impetus to revising the doctrinal basis of the action. Cases such as *Francome v Mirror Group Newspapers*,[72] *Stephens v Avery*,[73]

63　See eg, *R v North and East Devon HA, ex p Coughlan* [2000] 3 All ER 850 (CA) (closure of home for severely disabled unlawful and a violation of Art. 8, ECHR's right to respect for home).

64　See eg, *B v Secretary of State for the Home Department* [2000] 2 CMLR 1086 (CA) (power to deport had to be balanced against B's right to free movement under EU law and right to family life under Art. 8, ECHR and must be proportionate response).

65　See eg, *Re L (A Child)* [2000] 2 FCR 404 (CA); and *Re F (Adult Patient)* [2000] 3 WLR 1740 (CA).

66　[1993] AC 534. See also *Goldsmith v Bhoyrul* [1997] 4 All ER 268 (political party, allegedly defamed during general election campaigning, held incapable of suing).

67　Ibid., at pp. 547-548.

68　[1999] 4 All ER 609 (HL).

69　The court would take account of factors such as: (1) the level of seriousness of the allegation; (2) the type of information; (3) the source; (4) verification attempts; (5) status of the information; (6) urgency; (7) whether any attempt to obtain comment from the claimant had been made; (8) whether both sides of the story were included in the publication; (9) the tone of the published material; and (10) the background to, and timing of, the publication.

70　*A-G v Guardian Newspapers Ltd (No. 2)* [1990] 1 AC 109, 255 (per Lord Keith).

71　*Coco v AN Clark (Engineers) Ltd* [1969] RPC 41.

72　[1984] 1 WLR 892 (CA) (interlocutory injunction upheld preventing publication of unlawfully intercepted telephone conversations between leading jockey and wife about alleged gambling activities).

73　[1988] Ch 449 (details of sexual relationship subject to duty of confidence).

and *X and Y* [74] indicated the judicial willingness to protect information exchanged in confidential relationships or settings, and/or to prevent 'unconscionable' profiting from the disclosure of that private information. The traditional requirement that some prior relationship must exist between the parties before an obligation of confidence arises has been gradually relaxed;[75] indeed, in many respects, the *Francome* decision ran contrary to the *Malone* case by providing an injunction in the context of telephone tapping.[76]

Overall, commentators on breach of confidence have been divided about the cause of action. Wilson argued that 'discrete areas of law which enjoy no obvious thematic unity have been united and organised by a new moral principle – privacy';[77] Wacks disagreed, however, arguing that at best the cases point to 'a growing recognition of the principle of unconscionability'.[78] Such disagreements are inevitable given the case law. Judicial dicta differ in their emphases, focusing on the protection of 'confidential information' as a property right;[79] on the need to maintain 'trust' in certain relationships (marital, sexual, doctor-patient, employer-employee);[80] and on the need to prevent 'unconscionable' behaviour (in particular, achieving unfair advantage or monetary gain, or acting unlawfully). Case law also reflects a tension between the preservation of confidentiality in different contexts and the 'public interest' in disclosing certain types of information.[81] The understanding of when information reaches the 'public domain' has also varied, as evidenced by the grant of an injunction to Cherie Booth restraining further publication of the revelations of the 'Downing Street nanny'.[82] And, as we highlight in Chapter 7, the lines are even more blurred where the state purports to use the breach of confidence action as a

---

74   [1988] 2 All ER 648 (public interest in protecting confidentiality of hospital records identifying AIDS patients outweighed public interest in press freedom, particularly as records procured unlawfully).

75   See *A-G v Guardian Newspapers Ltd (No. 2)* [1990] 1 AC 109, 281 (per Lord Goff) ('a duty of confidence arises when confidential information comes to the knowledge of a person (the confidant) in circumstances, where he has notice, or is held to have agreed, that the information is confidential, with the effect that it would be just in all the circumstances that he should be precluded from disclosing the information to others').

76   The RIPA makes it unlawful to intercept communications on public and private telecommunications systems.

77   W. Wilson, 'Privacy, Confidence and Press Freedom: A Study in Judicial Activism' (1990) 53 MLR 43, 54.

78   R. Wacks, *Privacy and Press Freedom* (Blackstone, 1995), p. 79. Other authors also argue that 'conceptual uncertainty has led to confusion in the case law' and that the 'true foundation' of the action is 'an obligation of conscience': R.G. Toulson and C.M. Phipps, *Confidentiality* (Sweet & Maxwell, 1996), p. 37.

79   See *Murray v Yorkshire Fund Managers Ltd* [1998] 2 All ER 1015 (re group business plan); *Creation Records Ltd v News Group Newspapers Ltd* [1997] EMLR 444 (publication of unauthorised photograph of Oasis album cover shoot obtained surreptitiously was breach of confidence); and *Shelley Films Ltd v Rex Features Ltd* [1994] EMLR 134 (re photograph of film costume obtained surreptitiously).

80   See *Cornelius v De Taranto* [2001] EMLR 12 (damages awarded for breach of confidence in relation to disclosure of medico-legal report by doctor); and *Barrymore v News Group Newspapers Ltd* [1997] FSR 600 (re intimate gay relationship).

81   See eg, *Woodward v Hutchins* [1977] 1 WLR 760 (re public interest in knowing the truth); *Schering Chemicals Ltd v Falkman Ltd* [1982] QB 1 (restricting 'bad publicity' for company); *W v Egdell* [1990] Ch 359 (disclosure of confidential medical report to authorities justified on public safety grounds); and *Ashworth Hospital Authority v MGN Ltd* [2001] 1 All ER 991 (CA).

82   See M. Stephens, 'Downing Street Confidential', *The Times*, 14 Mar. 2000 (arguing that 'confidential' material already in public domain as published in over 1 million copies of *The Mail on Sunday* newspaper). See discussion of *Douglas* below pp. 327-328.

'national security' tool to prevent public interest 'whistle-blowing' by public servants and to stifle investigative journalism.

The basis and scope of the breach of confidence action, and its inter-relationship with Article 8 of the ECHR, thus remain unclear. Most recently, conflicting indicators of judicial conceptualisations of privacy interests under this heading have been provided by the cases of *Ex p Source Informatics*, *Hellewell* and *Douglas v Hello! Ltd*. The first case, *Ex p Source Informatics*, represents an attempt to confine the breach of confidence action within narrow parameters in the health information context; namely, the protection of patient details pertaining to *personal identity* only. It arose as a result of a practice whereby general practitioners and pharmacists provided anonymised drug prescription details to a private company, which sold the information to the pharmaceutical industry for use in 'targeted marketing'. The Department of Health objected to the practice on the grounds that a duty of confidence was owed by the professions, that prior patient consent was needed for such a scheme, and that such targeted marketing had the effect of unnecessarily inflating the NHS drugs bill. The Court of Appeal was unimpressed by the Department's arguments, and overturned the lower court's finding that the scheme was a clear breach of confidence in the absence of patient consent. Rejecting a broad patient-centred analysis of privacy,[83] and omitting consideration of the issue of commercial exploitation, Simon Brown LJ argued that the main question to be answered was: 'would a reasonable pharmacist's conscience be troubled by the proposed use to be made of patients' prescriptions?':

> The concern of the law here is to protect the confider's personal privacy. . . . The patient has no proprietorial claim to the prescription form or to the information it contains. . . . If, as I conclude, his only legitimate interest is in the protection of his privacy and, if that is safeguarded, I fail to see how his will could be thought thwarted or his personal integrity undermined.[84]

The Court did concede that, 'for certain limited purposes' such as research, patients were in fact being identified by the use of health information; it reasoned, however, that if 'such identifiable data is very strictly controlled', the scope of the duty of confidentiality was either circumscribed or there was a public interest defence. Consequently, if the Department of Health wanted to stop such schemes, it would have to look to legislation; breach of confidence 'cannot be distorted for the purpose'.[85]

By contrast, the second case cited above, *Hellewell*, wherein the plaintiff sued in relation to police use of his 'mugshot' photograph taken while in police custody, suggests the possibility of expansive use of the breach of confidence action. The suggestion can be found in the oft-quoted obiter comments of (then) Laws J:

---

83 Indeed, the CA invoked the spectre of 'problems' such as 'the well recognised reluctance of certain people to accept the views of those in authority as to just what is or is not good for them, and let us postulate, the occasional patient who expressly purports to refuse permission for his prescription form to be used for any purpose save only the dispensing of the prescribed drug': [2000] 2 WLR 953, 956.

84 Ibid.

85 The Court also suggested that the aim of the Data Protection Act 1998 (based on Council Directive 95/46/EC) was to protect the 'right to privacy', but 'commonsense and justice' indicated that this should not cover the collection of health data where a person's identity was concealed.

If someone with a telephoto lens were to take from a distance and with no authority a picture of another engaged in some private act, his subsequent disclosure of the photograph would, in my judgment, as surely amount to a breach of confidence as if he had found or stolen a letter or diary in which the act was recounted and proceeded to publish it. In such a case, the law would protect what might reasonably be called a right of privacy, although the name accorded to the cause of action would be breach of confidence.[86]

A range of commentators drew attention to Laws J's position. Arden suggested that the courts could 'use the [ECHR] as a catalyst' to develop the law in this direction;[87] a view endorsed by Singh, who also pointed out that the European Commission's decision in *Spencer v UK* 'could be seen as a "green light" to those judges who would like to develop the common law (in particular breach of confidence) so as to recognise a right to privacy'.[88] The Commission dismissed the Spencers' application on the ground that they had failed to exhaust domestic remedies, emphasising that it considered that:

the remedy of breach of confidence (against the newspapers and their sources) was available to applicants and that the applicants have not demonstrated that it was insufficient or ineffective in the circumstances of their cases. It considers that, insofar as relevant doubts remain concerning the financial awards to be made following a finding of a breach of confidence, they are not such as to warrant a conclusion that the breach of confidence action is ineffective or insufficient but rather a conclusion that *the matter should be put to the domestic courts for consideration in order to allow those courts, through the common law system in the United Kingdom, the opportunity to develop existing rights by way of interpretation.*[89]

As we shall see below, in *Douglas v Hello! Ltd*, the Court of Appeal finally created a right to privacy.[90]

II.   THE EUROPEAN CONVENTION ON HUMAN RIGHTS AND PRIVACY

Article 8 of the ECHR states:

(1) Everyone has the right to respect for his private and family life, his home and his correspondence.
(2) There shall be no interference by a public authority with the exercise of this right except such as is in accordance with the law and is necessary in a democratic society in the interests of national security, public safety or the economic well-being of the country, for the prevention of disorder or crime, for the protection of health or morals, or for the protection of the rights and freedoms of others.

The jurisprudence of the European Court of Human Rights on privacy is more complex than that on other Convention rights. There are several reasons for this. First, Article 8's range is such that it 'offers opportunities for creative advocacy to bring within [its ambit] interests which are otherwise inadequately

---

86   [1995] 1 WLR 804. Cf. *Law Debenture Trust Group v Malley*, *The Independent*, 25 Oct. 1999 (covert surveillance a legitimate course to pursue on appropriate occasions in the investigations of pension claims).
87   M. Arden, 'The Future of the Law of Privacy' (1999) 9 KCLJ 1, 12.
88   Singh, above n. 17, p. 179.
89   (1997) 25 EHRR 105 (emphasis added).
90   [2001] 2 All ER 289. See below pp. 327-328.

protected'; furthermore, such opportunities tend to be widely availed of because 'people disagree about the values which privacy-related rights protect'.[91] Secondly, there is the paradox of privacy: while privacy rights are an important mechanism for protecting individuals' interests, protecting one person's privacy sometimes involves violating another person's, and may also expose individuals to increased state regulation:

> On the one hand, there is the concern to control the state's capacity to interfere in central matters of inter-personal relationships: consensual sexual activities, parent and child relations, conversation and correspondence, where the principal concern of the right-holder is keeping the state out. On the other hand, the state's assistance is called for to protect persons from harm inflicted by others: exploitative sexual conduct, children damaged by parents, communications which harass the recipient.[92]

Thirdly, the reference to 'respect' for the interests in Article 8(1) has been interpreted as creating both positive and negative obligations on state authorities.[93] Fourthly, there are many overlaps between the interests protected by Article 8 and other provisions of the ECHR, such as Article 3 (for example, in relation to physical and emotional integrity or dignity[94]), Article 6 (for example, in relation to the confidentiality of legal correspondence,[95] the fairness of evidence-gathering methods by state authorities,[96] or the impact of legal proceedings on family life[97]) and Article 12 (for example, in relation to marriage[98]). Lastly, the 'absence of a theoretical conspectus' in the interpretation of Article 8 has led to 'inevitably descriptive' accounts of the jurisprudence and made predicting future trends a 'hazardous' exercise.[99]

Commentators have, however, drawn some general conclusions about Article 8 jurisprudence.[100] First, many emphasise the generous definitional approach towards private life, family life, home and correspondence – the four interests listed in Article 8(1). In cases concerning the meaning of 'private life', the Court has embraced a definition that goes beyond the protection of an intimate sphere of personal autonomy. Interests and activities, central both to one's sense of self and well-being and one's relationships with wider society, have been considered worthy of respect: for example, personal identity[101] and

---

91 D. Feldman, 'The Developing Scope of Article 8 of the European Convention on Human Rights' [1997] EHRLR 266, 266-267. Feldman praises the ECtHR's response, in particular because it avoids 'trying to define artificially distinct private and public categories or arenas' and looks instead to 'a range of underlying values', such as personal autonomy, human dignity, physical and moral integrity, personal identity, and the social importance of family life: see 'Privacy-related Rights and their Social Value' in Birks, above n. 55, pp. 15-50, at p. 31.

92 D.J. Harris, M. O'Boyle and C. Warbrick, *Law of the European Convention* (Butterworths, 1995), p. 353.

93 See Ch. 1, pp. 35-39 for discussion of the extent of general duty on the courts to protect Convention rights in the private sphere and the possible 'horizontal effect' of the HRA.

94 *Costello-Roberts v UK* (1993) 19 EHRR 112 (re corporal punishment of children).

95 *Niemietz v Germany* (1992) 16 EHRR 97.

96 *Khan v UK* [2000] Crim LR 684.

97 *W v UK* (1987) 10 EHRR 29.

98 See eg, *Rees v UK* (1986) 9 EHRR 56; and *Cossey v UK* (1990) 13 EHRR 622.

99 Harris, O'Boyle and Warbrick, above n. 92, p. 303.

100 See eg, Feldman, above n. 91; Harris, O'Boyle and Warbrick, above n. 92; and A. Lester and D. Pannick, *Human Rights Law and Practice* (Butterworths, 1999), pp. 165-190. See www.beagle.org.uk/hra/website for updates on Art. 8 case law.

101 See *Stgerna v Finland* (1994) 24 EHRR 195 (change of surname); and *Gaskin v UK* (1989) 12 EHRR 36 (access to care records).

sexual autonomy;[102] bodily integrity and well-being;[103] private zones;[104] and personal information.[105] In cases concerning the protection of 'family life', the Court has gradually widened the range of relationships within the institution of the family[106] and increasingly given substance to the concept of children's rights.[107] Cases on the protection of 'home' have dealt with rights to access and occupation,[108] peaceful enjoyment of residence,[109] and non-intrusion by state authorities.[110] Finally, there is the case law on the right to respect for 'correspondence' (a term covering letter and telephone communications),[111] which has been of particular significance for lawyer-client communications, especially where the client is imprisoned.[112]

In some contexts, the Court has emphasised that the obligation on state authorities to 'respect' the interests listed in Article 8(1) goes further than a mere negative obligation not to interfere with privacy: *positive* state action may be required, albeit the choice of action remains largely at the discretion of the state.[113] As the Court pointed out in *Sheffield and Horsham*, 'the notion of "respect" is not clear-cut, especially as far as the positive obligations inherent in that concept are concerned . . . [and] regard must be had to the fair balance that has to be struck between the general interests of the community and the interests of the individual . . .'.[114] The imposition of a positive obligation to take legal steps to prevent interference with Article 8 has been most marked in the sphere of family life. It has been held that states must act to prevent discrimination against children on the grounds of a parent's marital status;[115] to ensure proper procedural safeguards in relation to adoption;[116] to ensure access to family law

---

102 See *CR v UK* (1995) 21 EHRR 363 (no marital exemption for rape); and *Dudgeon v UK* (1981) 4 EHRR 149 (criminalisation of private adult gay sexual relations).

103 *Lopez Ostra v Spain* (1994) 20 EHRR 277 (pollution from waste-treatment plant); and *X and Y v Netherlands* (1985) 8 EHRR 235 (sexual assault of minor with mental disability).

104 *Niemietz v Germany*, above n. 95; and *Friedl v Austria* (1995) 21 EHRR 83 (photographing demonstrators on public street).

105 See *Amann v Switzerland* (2000) 30 EHRR 843 (card index); *Z v Finland* (1997) 25 EHRR 371 (medical records); and *Murray v UK* (1994) 19 EHRR 193 (police fingerprinting).

106 *X, Y and Z v UK* (1997) 24 EHRR 143 (woman, transsexual partner and child conceived by AI constitute a family); *Kroon v Netherlands* (1994) 19 EHRR 263 ('family life' includes de facto family ties); and *Johnston v Ireland* (1986) 9 EHRR 203 ('illegitimate' children included).

107 *Stubbings v UK* (1996) 23 EHRR 213 (child sex abuse complaints).

108 *Akdivar v Turkey* (1996) 23 EHRR 143; and *Cyprus v Turkey* (1983) 15 EHRR 509.

109 *Lopez Ostra v Spain*, above n. 103 (pollution forced residents to evacuate homes).

110 *Murray v UK* (1994) 19 EHRR 193 (anti-terrorism powers); and *Chappell v UK* (1989) 12 EHRR 1 (Anton Piller orders).

111 *Halford v UK* (1997) 24 EHRR 523 (internal telephone system); *A v France* (1993) 17 EHRR 462 (telephone); *Hewitt and Harman v UK* (1992) 14 EHRR 657 (mail); and *Malone v UK* (1984) 7 EHRR 14 (telephone).

112 *Campbell v UK* (1992) 15 EHRR 137; *Silver v UK* (1983) 5 EHRR 347; and *Golder v UK* (1975) 1 EHRR 524.

113 *Kroon v Netherlands*, above n. 106; and *Airey v Ireland* (1979) 2 EHRR 305. See Ch. 1, pp. 35-39 for discussion of the extent of general duty on the courts to protect Convention rights in the private sphere and the possible 'horizontal effect' of the HRA.

114 *Sheffield and Horsham v UK* (1998) 27 EHRR 163, para. 52 (no obligation to recognise post-operative sexual identity in birth register); and *B v France* (1992) 16 EHRR 1 (obligation to amend official identity documents given impact on social and professional life). See generally, *Gustavfsson v Sweden* (1996) 22 EHRR 409; *Platform 'Ärtzte fur das Leben' v Austria* (1988) 13 EHRR 204; and *X and Y v Netherlands* (1985) 8 EHRR 235.

115 *Marckx v Belgium* (1979) 2 EHRR 330; and *Johnston v Ireland* (1986) 9 EHRR 203.

116 *Keegan v Ireland* (1994) 18 EHRR 342 (re failure to consult father prior to adoption of child).

proceedings;[117] and to provide information about personal history when in care.[118] More generally, in *X and Y v The Netherlands*, in finding a violation of Article 8 because of the absence of the possibility of criminal prosecution of an adult male for the sexual assault of a mentally disabled female minor, the Court emphasised that the obligation to respect private life may 'involve the adoption of measures . . . even in the sphere of the relations of individuals themselves'.[119] Overall, however, the general trend in the Court's case law is that 'any duty of positive intervention laid upon the state is quite restricted in its scope, and second, that its substantive content is largely within the state's discretion'.[120]

In many cases, it will be obvious that an interference with the rights protected by Article 8(1) has occurred (for example, police intrusion on property); however, complaints have been accepted where actual interference cannot easily be proven,[121] or where there is only a risk of interference.[122] The Court will then proceed to assess whether the interference can be justified under Article 8(2). State authorities will seek to justify the interference by pointing to a legitimate aim (for example, interference with prisoners' correspondence to prevent crime[123]). As a consequence of this, the determination of the case will hinge on two criteria: whether the interference can be said to be 'in accordance with the law'; and whether it meets the 'necessary in a democratic society' test.

The first of these criteria has 'been a prominent issue in three kinds of cases: secret surveillance, especially telephone-tapping; taking children into care; and interfering with detained persons' correspondence'.[124] To take one illustration: the historical absence of a statutory basis for police and security service surveillance, or for the interception of communications, has been found to breach Article 8(2) in a series of UK cases – including *Malone*,[125] *Hewitt and Harman*,[126] *Halford*,[127] *Govell*[128] and *Khan*.[129] Reliance on Home Office and police guidelines instead of legislation, and the traditional absence of oversight and complaints mechanisms, have been considered insufficient to meet the requirements of legality: as the European Court of Human Rights said in *Khan*, 'the law must be sufficiently clear in its terms to give individuals an adequate indication as to the circumstances in which and the conditions on which public authorities are entitled to resort to such covert measures'.[130] But, while the Court has insisted on the need for statutory frameworks to regulate police and

---

117 *Airey v Ireland* (1979) 2 EHRR 305 (re legal aid provision for judicial separation).
118 *Gaskin v UK* (1989) 12 EHRR 36.
119 See also *Guerra v Italy* (1998) 26 EHRR 357 (positive obligation to provide information to occupants of area at high risk of environmental pollution).
120 G. Phillipson, 'The Human Rights Act, "Horizontal Effect" and the Common Law: A Bang or a Whimper?' (1999) 62 MLR 824, 841. See eg, *Osman v UK* (1998) 29 EHRR 245.
121 *Klass v Germany* (1978) 2 EHRR 214 (re wire-tapping).
122 *Dudgeon v UK*, above n. 102; and *Norris v Ireland* (1988) 13 EHRR 186 (mere existence of legislation criminalising same-sex conduct affected private life of adult gay men).
123 *Campbell and Fell v UK* (1984) 7 EHRR 165.
124 Harris, O'Boyle and Warbrick, above n. 92, p. 338. See further Ch. 5 on the impact of the ECHR on prisoners' rights.
125 *Malone v UK*, above n. 111.
126 *Hewitt and Harman*, above n. 111.
127 *Halford v UK*, above n. 111.
128 *Govell v UK* [1997] EHRLR 438.
129 *Khan v UK* [2000] Crim LR 684 (violation of Arts. 8 and 13).
130 Ibid., para. 26.

security service activities, it has left the actual content of the legislation (for example, the continuing role of the Home Secretary in issuing warrants), and the depth of independent scrutiny of alleged privacy violations, to the discretion of state authorities.[131] This means that once a detailed statutory framework, providing for some judicial oversight, is in place, applicants are unlikely to succeed in establishing an absence of legal protection against 'arbitrary' exercise of state power.[132] Thus, for example, the Court's condemnation of the lack of legal precision and safeguards in *Kopp v Switzerland* appears to have been motivated primarily by the violation of legal professional privilege in the case, and by the 'astonishing' practice of an official in the Post Office's legal department making determinations on lawyer-client communications without supervision by an independent judge.[133]

The Article 8(2) criterion 'necessary in a democratic society' requires states to demonstrate that there is 'a pressing social need' for the interference with privacy rights and that the means employed are proportionate to the legitimate aim pursued. In applying this test, the Court has emphasised the need for a contextual assessment of the privacy interests at stake, the intrusiveness of the privacy violation, and the nature and weight of the competing public interests. It has also emphasised that the margin of appreciation afforded to national authorities may be generous in some contexts. In cases on children's welfare, and in particular on removal of children from families and imposition of access conditions on parents, it has tended to defer to the national authorities, provided legally-based procedural safeguards are in place.[134] By contrast, the Court has shown willingness to review decisions of states on deportation (in particular where deporting an individual will interfere with (if not destroy) family life).[135]

It has also shown a willingness to challenge state claims about the appropriate limits of sexual autonomy in the private sphere. In *Dudgeon, Norris* and *Modinos* the Court marked out a legally-protected private sphere for consensual sexual activities between adult men on the basis of the importance of the privacy context. It rejected state claims that criminalisation was necessary either for the protection of public morals or the rights of others, appealing to European

---

131 *Christie v UK* 78-A DR 119 (1994) EComHR (framework of Interception of Communications Act 1985 satisfied Art. 8(2)); *Esbester v UK* (1993) 18 EHRR CD 72 (EComHR) (framework of Security Services Act 1989 satisfied Art. 8) ; and *Leander v Sweden* (1987) 9 EHRR 433 (security vetting of employees). Cf. *Kruslin v France* (1990) 12 EHRR 547.

132 See *Kruslin*, ibid., where the ECtHR did find French legislation and case law on telephone surveillance defective because it did not provide sufficient guarantees against arbitrary use of surveillance powers.

133 *Kopp v Switzerland* (1998) 27 EHRR 91.

134 See for violations of Art. 8, *Johansen v Norway* (1996) 23 EHRR 33; *McMichael v UK* (1995) 20 EHRR 205; *Boyle v UK* (1994) 19 EHRR 179; *Olsson v Sweden (No. 2)* (1992) 17 EHRR 134; and *W v UK* (1987) 10 EHRR 29. See *TP v UK* EComHR (10 Sep. 1999) (delay in providing daughter's video interview to mother in case of suspected child abuse violated Art. 8's guarantee of parental participation in decision-making procedures).

135 See *Ciliz v Netherlands* [2000] 2 FLR 469 (deportation of alien violated Art. 8 given relationship between father and son); and *Beldjoudi v France* (1992) 14 EHRR 801 (disproportionate to deport alien with family ties because of criminal record). Cf. *Bouchelikia v France* (1997) 25 EHRR 696 (serious criminal activity); *Gull v Switzerland* (1996) 22 EHRR 93 (no failure to respect family life as fair balance achieved between interests of family and national authorities); and *Abdulaziz, Cabalas and Balkandali v UK* (1985) 7 EHRR 471 (no right to enter a country to found a new family).

democratic traditions of pluralism, tolerance and broadmindedness.[136] The Court has reinforced the narrow margin of appreciation afforded to national authorities in this area in two further cases, *Lustig-Prean and Beckett v UK* and *ADT v UK*. In the former case, it held that a blanket ban on lesbians and gays in the UK armed services was not justified as necessary in a democratic society. It rejected government claims of decreased operational effectiveness and – because of the exceptionally intrusive surveillance, and automatic discharge, of suspected gays and lesbians – found the policy in breach of Article 8's protection for 'a most intimate aspect of private life'.[137] More recently, in *ADT v UK*, it condemned the prosecution of a group of gay men under the law of gross indecency. The legal action was initiated after police seizure of a video from the applicant's home depicting him and other men engaged in consensual oral sex and masturbation. The Court held that neither the legislation nor the prosecution were justified under Article 8, pointing to the narrow margin of appreciation, the absence of any public health considerations and the 'purely private nature of the behaviour'.[138] This ruling must, however, be contrasted with the earlier decision of the Court in *Laskey, Jaggard and Brown v UK* where a prosecution of men engaged in consensual sexual practices, involving the infliction of pain, was held to be compatible with Article 8.[139]

A tendency towards uncritical acceptance of states' claims of national security and crime prevention justifications for their actions is, arguably, evident in the Court's jurisprudence on interception of telephone communications[140] and the collection of personal data in employment vetting.[141] In particular, as highlighted in *Amann v Switzerland*, although state surveillance constitutes a serious interference with privacy, once there is a legal framework indicating 'with sufficient clarity the scope and conditions of exercise of the authorities' discretionary power', the Court tends to take the view that it is for national courts to interpret and apply such provisions.[142] The Court's approach to interference with prisoner correspondence, and the confidentiality of lawyer-client communications, has been much more robust:[143] in *Foxley*, for example, Article 8 was interpreted as requiring a high level of respect for 'the principles of confidentiality and professional privilege attaching to relations between a lawyer and . . . client'.[144] Protection of private premises against intrusion by

---

136 See respectively, *Dudgeon v UK*, above n. 102; *Norris v Ireland*, above n. 122; and *Modinos v Cyprus* (1993) 16 EHRR 485. See also *Sutherland v UK* [1998] EHRLR 117, EComHR (distinction between gay and heterosexual age of consent not justified). Cf. *Bowers v Hardwick* 478 US 186 (1986) (wherein majority of US SCt refused to declare Georgia's anti-sodomy statute unconstitutional under the right to privacy).

137 (1999) 29 EHRR 548. See also *Smith and Grady v UK* (1999) 29 EHRR 493.

138 [2000] 2 FLR 697, para. 38.

139 (1997) 24 EHRR 39. See L.J. Moran, '*Laskey v The United Kingdom*: Learning the Limits of Privacy' (1998) 61 MLR 77.

140 *Klass v Germany*, above n. 121.

141 *Leander v Sweden*, above n. 131.

142 (2000) 30 EHRR 843 (interception of telephone calls, and creation and storage of card index, violated Art. 8(2) 'in accordance with the law' criterion). See also *Kopp v Switzerland*, above n. 133 (lack of supervision of telephone interceptions violated Art. 8). For a similarly deferential attitude in a different context, see *MS v Sweden* (1997) 28 EHRR 313; and *Z v Finland*, above n. 105.

143 *Campbell v UK*, above n. 112; and *Golder v UK*, above n.112.

144 [2000] 8 BHRC 571.

state authorities has also generated robust case law[145] – although not in every context as evidenced by the Court's failure to find a breach of Article 8 in *Laskey, Jaggard and Brown*.[146]

III.   PROPERTY AND PRIVACY

In this Part, we shall begin consideration of a perennial theme of privacy commentaries: that is, whether there is a common feature which links together the range of interests which are protected by privacy? Our focus here will be on property; in Part IV, we shall widen the search to consider other contenders. Starting with property is deliberate: there is a considerable amount of evidence pointing to a link between property and privacy. Consider, for example, that trespass, private nuisance and breach of confidence – traditionally used as the starting point in descriptions or assessments of the indirect protection of privacy in UK law – are all proprietary in character. This in turn points us towards the classic view of property as 'a set of entitlements delimiting the bounds of legitimate state power and thus providing a sphere of freedom for the individual'.[147] Can it be said, then, that privacy is 'quite literally, pulled from the hat of property'?[148] That the 'old property rhetoric has been simply transferred to this area', as evidenced for example by the fact that 'privacy, like the old right of property, has been imagined . . . generally as marking off a protected sphere surrounding the individual'?[149]

We would argue that property is both insufficient and undesirable as the core feature of privacy. To begin with, it tends today to be seen as a 'bundle of rights', wherein no individual right – bar perhaps excludability[150] – is essential; a view which has even caused a debate about whether 'property' is a distinct

---

145 *McLeod v UK* (1998) 27 EHRR 493 (police entry onto private property disproportionate) *Niemietz v Germany*, above n. 95 (search of lawyer's office not justified); and *Funke v France* (1993) 16 EHRR 297 (search warrants for customs authorities to enter and seize property disproportionate in the absence of prior judicial authorisation).

146 *Laskey*, above n. 139; and *Chappell v UK*, above n. 110 (execution of Anton Piller order justified to protect copyright).

147 C. Rotherham, 'Conceptions of Property in Common Law Discourse' (1998) 18 LS 43, 51-52. See eg, *Entick v Carrington* (1765) 19 St Tr 1029 (holding that the King's Secretary had no authority to issue a warrant to search the home of John Entick for seditious papers, and emphasising that '[t]he great end for which men entered society was to secure their property. That right is preserved sacred and incommunicable in all instances where it has not been abridged by some public law for the good of the whole': per Camden LCJ at p. 1060). This understanding also provided the ideological foundation for the US SCt's original vision of substantive due process. Its foundational capacity was, however, compromised by the New Deal. Substantive due process was reborn in *Griswold v Connecticut* using a right to privacy, rather than a right to property and contract: for more detail, see B. Ackerman, *We The People* (Harvard UP, 1993).

148 M.A. Glendon, *Rights Talk* (Harvard UP, 1991), p. 40.

149 Ibid., p. 51. Property's historic centrality to individual autonomy and limited government is readily understandable: 'In some ways property is the ideal symbol for the limits to governmental authority because of its concrete character. Physical invasion of private property is a particularly obvious kind of public violation of private rights; one's property can form a literal material boundary to the legitimate scope of state power. . . . [Moreover,] virtually everyone talks about . . . property ownership as freestanding, as a source of independence from the state, not as a condition requiring the state to give it its meaning' (J. Nedelsky, *Private Property and the Limits of American Constitutionalism* (Chicago UP, 1990), pp. 247-248).

150 K. Gray, 'Property in Thin Air' [1991] CLJ 252.

legal category at all.[151] Furthermore, despite property's lasting allure, as manifested most recently in increased efforts to promote the idea of 'the body as property' so as to enhance autonomy, it is surely not an effective shield for rights: as Nedelsky reminds us property 'has become more than ever an economic concept, while it is less and less a source of autonomy for most people'.[152] Of course, property was, in fact, never an effective shield for rights. Rather, it protected only some people's rights against state interference, reinforcing inequality and injustice by facilitating their trampling of other people's rights and limiting the reach of any state efforts at redistributive justice. Secondly, linking property and privacy may provide ammunition for critics of modern privacy developments. In the US, for example, communitarian critics of privacy-based Supreme Court decisions such as *Roe v Wade* have sought to damn privacy 'by association': they point to what they see as the negative legacy of property – in particular its promotion of an isolated, individualist conception of the self and its rhetoric of absoluteness – made manifest in modern privacy rights and seek to detail its damaging effects on the 'common good'.[153] Finally, as Cohen has argued, to see property as the core feature of privacy may be to undermine the potential of privacy. Invoking the privacy jurisprudence of the US Supreme Court, she suggests that it is:

> precisely in the differentiation of personal rights from the paradigm of property, and their elevation to a higher status, that we are witnessing one of the most important normative developments in contemporary constitutional jurisprudence ... an attempt to give the constitutional values once associated with property and freedom of contract a primacy now unencumbered by inegalitarian tradition or by the possessive individualist model of the self, and to protect them in their own right.[154]

The symbolic power of property language does, however, make it extremely difficult to dismiss it entirely. To illustrate this point, consider the upsurge in property language around the human body, deployed with the aim of protecting what appear to be privacy interests, in the face of bewildering and ever-expanding opportunities presented by scientific technology (in areas such as organ transplantation, cloning and genetic engineering more generally).[155] The question is: do these arguments present a challenge to dismissals of property's relevance to privacy? Might the concept of the body as property protect key privacy interests – such as autonomy, dignity and bodily integrity – and foreground individual privacy rights as 'an important corrective'[156] to the traditional pre-eminence (and flaws) of entity privacy? Could it challenge the increasing tendency to think of genetic information primarily as information, submerging the individuals and cultures from which it is taken?[157]

151 See eg, J.E. Penner, *The Idea of Property in Law* (OUP, 1997).
152 Above n. 149, p. 250.
153 For effective rebuttals of such arguments, see eg, Feldman, above n. 91; or F.D. Schoeman, *Privacy and Social Freedom* (CUP, 1992).
154 J.L. Cohen, 'Resdescribing Privacy: Identity, Difference, and the Abortion Controversy' (1992) 3 Col J Gender & Law 43, 109-110.
155 For an excellent overview of this development – on which our discussion is based – see C.F. Stychin, 'Body Talk: Rethinking Autonomy, Commodification and the Embodied Legal Self' in S. Sheldon and M. Thomson (eds.), *Feminist Perspectives on Health Care Law* (Cavendish, 1998), pp. 211-236. See more generally, A. Hyde, *Bodies of Law* (Princeton UP, 1997).
156 Cohen, above n. 154, p. 62.
157 See in particular, the patenting of cell lines from indigenous populations: V. Shiva, *Biopiracy: The Plunder of Nature and Knowledge* (South End Press, 1997).

Inquiries into this question have been undertaken in a number of fields – including health care law, criminal law and intellectual property law[158] – yielding a range of answers (and providing a salutary reminder that individuals can also be the 'objects of property'[159] (for example, under conditions of slavery)). Harris and Munzer, for example, conclude that property concepts are neither necessary nor particularly helpful in the context of bodies.[160] They insist that the concept of ownership as applied to the body 'potentially proves too much';[161] thus, although Harris agrees that there may be a place for a 'bodily use freedom principle', and Munzer posits some limited property rights in bodies (such as the 'right to publicity' recognised in US privacy law[162]), both stick firm on the matter of people not owning their bodies in the traditional property law sense. Others, starting from a position less concerned with property law doctrine, have however singled out the potential for emancipation in property rhetoric, emphasising for example that:

> women's autonomy, power and control vis à vis the medical establishment, might be enhanced not only by the general claim that a woman's body is her property, but by the position that all stages of potential life issuing from her body are her property – and remain so even when they are no longer within her body. Similarly, this position might be seen to aid women in struggles over power and oppression with their male sexual partners – both in regard to struggles specifically around reproduction and more generally.[163]

But is the question of the body as property this cut and dried? Stychin suggests that it is not. He shows how claims that we do not 'own' our bodies often 'rely upon a very specific and particular conception of ownership' – absolute dominion – 'which is something of a legal fiction, and always subject to exceptions', and he reminds us that although 'courts will sometimes find a property interest in the body, and sometimes not . . . those results are reached on the basis of ethical and political considerations, and not legal doctrine'.[164] He also cautions against the conclusions of those who embrace property as essentially feminist, and those who argue that the body as property leads *necessarily* to commodification of bodies and body parts, and associated ills.[165]

---

158 See respectively, J. Nedelsky, 'Property in Potential Life: A Relational Approach to Choosing Legal Categories' (1993) 6 CJ Law & Jur 343; N. Naffine, 'The Body Bag' in N. Naffine and R. Owens (eds.), *Sexing the Subject of Law* (Law Book Company, 1997), pp. 79-93; and A. Pottage, 'The Inscription of Life in Law: Genes, Patents, and Bio-Politics' (1998) 61 MLR 740. The increasing commercial value of 'character merchandising' is also impacting on intellectual property law, providing additional evidence that 'the lines between the person and property are beginning to blur in the law' (M. Davies, 'Queer Property, Queer Persons: Self-Ownership and Beyond' (1999) 8 SLS 327, 337): see eg, Julia Roberts' and Jeanette Winterson's successful battles to prevent 'cybersquatters' using their names as internet domain names.

159 P. Williams, *The Alchemy of Race and Rights* (Harvard UP, 1991), p. 216. See also, C. Harris, 'Whiteness as Property' (1993) 106 Harv LR 1707 for an argument that property's capacity for oppression does not simply reside in legal relationships.

160 See respectively, J.W. Harris, 'Who Owns My Body?' (1996) 16 OJLS 55 and S.R. Munzer, *A Theory of Property* (CUP, 1990).

161 Harris, ibid., p. 65.

162 See below, pp. 315-317.

163 Above n. 158, p. 347. Nedelsky herself does not support this view of property: see below, p. 301. Cf. B. Brown, 'Reconciling Property Law with Advances in Reproductive Science' (1995) 6 Stan L&Pol'y R 73.

164 Above n. 155, p. 216. See *R v B* [2001] 1 All ER 577 (HL).

165 For such arguments, see eg, E.R. Gold, *Body Parts: Property Rights and the Ownership of Human Biological Materials* (Georgetown UP, 1996); and S.R. Munzer, 'An Uneasy Case Against Property Rights in Body Parts' (1994) 11 Social Phil & Policy 259. Cf. R.P. Petchesky, 'The Body as Property: A Feminist Re-Vision' in F.D. Ginsburg and R. Rapp (eds.), *Conceiving the New World Order* (California UP, 1995), pp. 387-405.

Stychin offers an alternative to these positions on the body as property.[166] He proposes that as a starting point we need 'a better set of questions concerning bodies and their "owners"'.[167] This might be achieved, he says, by working from an exposé of the submerged connections between property rhetoric and a particular view of autonomy (one rooted in market-driven and individualistic ideas) towards a 'reinvigorated notion of autonomy'[168] (one grounded in a different conception of individuals, foregrounding their 'embeddedness in relations'[169] with others rather than their isolation and boundedness). This proposal suggests that the project of the 'body as property' could enhance the standing of bodily integrity in privacy analysis, without either reviving a damaging property paradigm or positing an absolute right to do with one's body as one pleases. It offers a springboard from which to argue that 'bodily integrity is central to an individual's identity and should be protected by privacy rights as fundamental, only to be overruled if a truly compelling state interest is at stake, and only on neutral grounds'.[170]

We suspect that arguments for the body as property will become more intense over the coming years, not least because notions of privacy, still based largely on 'the revelation of intimate social facts',[171] may not adequately protect individuals' interests in genetic information. To illustrate this point, consider what happened to John Moore, a man who underwent treatment for leukaemia at the University of California Medical Centre and found subsequently that his genetic material had been used without his consent to develop a new cell line, which had immense commercial value.[172] On discovering what had happened, Moore, not surprisingly, brought a range of actions, including violation of his right to privacy – after all, 'the market had taken from him the most "private" information of all, information about his own genetic structure'.[173] Moore's only successful cause of action was for breach of fiduciary duty by the doctors at the Medical Centre; he failed to convince the court that his privacy had been violated. Boyle suggests that this latter outcome was entirely predictable given dominant understandings of privacy, and in particular understandings of what constitutes 'private information':

166 As Stychin explains, this alternative is based on the work of Jennifer Nedelsky: see her work cited in nn. 158, 169. For similar ideas of revisioned autonomy in the specific context of abortion, see eg, D. Cornell, *The Imaginary Domain* (Routledge, 1995); and I. Karpin, 'Reimagining Maternal Selfhood: Transgressing Body Boundaries and the Law' (1994) 2 AFLJ 36.
167 Above n. 155, p. 236.
168 Ibid.
169 J. Nedelsky, 'Reconceiving Autonomy: Sources, Thoughts and Possibilities' (1989) 1 Yale J Law & Feminism 7, 10.
170 Cohen, above n. 154, p. 115. Cohen uses the language of US constitutional law but it can readily be translated to that of Arts. 8 and 14. The proposal also has some resonance with the recent interest in developing positive rights approaches to property: Rotherham, above n. 147, pp. 56-58 ('Most would argue that a need exists for a legally delineated sphere of freedom for the individual and that property has traditionally served this purpose. However, it is an error to seek this aspiration in a pre-political and pre-existing space, the boundaries of which are demarcated by the understanding of property as exclusive and absolute. An alternative lies in the elaboration of a functional understanding of property – the construction of a conception of property that can serve to create a place for the individual in the modern world without completely ignoring broader societal interests.').
171 J. Boyle, *Shamans, Software and Spleens: Law and the Construction of the Information Society* (Harvard UP, 1996), p. 105.
172 *Moore v The Regents of the University of California* 793 P2d 479 (1990) (California SCt).
173 Boyle, above n. 171, p. 105.

There is something in the way that our culture has constructed the notion of [private information] that makes it more hospitable to the protection of '*social*' facts than '*natural*' facts. Even with the obvious borderline cases – hereditary diseases, for example – revelations are thought to be violative of a person's privacy only when some particular social significance has been given to the genetic coding. The difficulty with Moore's case is, first, that no one would think worse of him for having a genetic make-up that could be mined for a socially valuable drug and, second, that specialized knowledge would be necessary to make the connection between the 'facts revealed' and the 'inner life'.[174]

IV.   THE VALUE OF PRIVACY: SEARCHING FOR A COMMON FEATURE

In the preceding Part, we suggested that it may not be helpful to see property as grounding or securing privacy, and more specifically that the historic lifeline between property and privacy may limit understandings of privacy and provide an easy target for privacy critics. Furthermore, although we believe that privacy analysis might be enhanced by promoting bodily integrity as central to an individual's identity, privacy cannot be understood via a focus on the body alone.[175] In this Part, we shall pursue the theme of how best to conceive of the *value* of privacy. This will require extending the search for an answer to the question of whether there is a common feature linking together the various and disparate interests which merit protection under a right to privacy.

The material discussed below is not new, yet the difficulties it describes persist as both fundamental and seemingly interminable.[176] These difficulties appear to fall into two categories: primary and secondary. Examples of the latter include the question of whether there can be said to be privacy in public places or in respect of 'public facts'? Is privacy in public a total non-starter, or merely somewhat compromised (depending on the degree of publicness or some other factor(s))? Alternatively, should 'publicness' be accorded no trump-value? A second difficulty arises from privacy's imbrication in contentious matters. In the US, for example, debate on the right to privacy occurs in the shadow of doctrinal and political concerns about judicial activism;[177] furthermore, since

---

174 Ibid.

175 Cf. K. Thomas, 'Beyond the Privacy Principle' (1992) 92 Col LR 1431.

176 See eg, Feldman, above n. 7, 50 (noting that '[p]rivacy, as a weapon in the protection of civil liberties, is like a shotgun spraying pellets somewhat indiscriminately over a wide area of human endeavour, rather than a rifle delivering a powerful blow at a well-defined target'); and R. Wacks, 'The Poverty of Privacy' (1980) 96 LQR 73 (emphasising the weaknesses of a multi-purpose use of privacy).

177 In *Griswold v Connecticut* 381 US 479 (1965) the SCt 'discovered' a right to privacy derived from the 'penumbras' of a range of rights explicit in the first Nine Amendments of the US Constitution. The scope of this right has subsequently been highly contested: see *Roe v Wade* 410 US 113 (1973), *Bowers v Hardwick* 478 US 186 (1986) and *Washington v Glucksberg* 521 US 702 (1997). US law also recognises four 'privacy' torts: (i) intrusion upon the plaintiff's seclusion or solitude, or into their private affairs; (ii) public disclosure of embarrassing private facts about the plaintiff; (iii) publicity which places the plaintiff in a false light in the public eye; and (iv) appropriation, for the defendant's advantage, of the plaintiff's name or likeness. For a brief outline of both aspects of US privacy law, see R. Wacks, *Privacy and Press Freedom* (Blackstone, 1995), pp. 10-17. Privacy interests are also protected by Fourth Amendment rules on search and seizure.

the US Supreme Court's 1973 opinion in *Roe v Wade*,[178] the right to privacy also tends to be viewed through the prism of the debate over the privacy justification for abortion rights. A further complication in discussing privacy – currently playing out very strongly in the US – is created by the 'right to one's image': is it appropriate that this 'right to publicity' (involving the explicit linkage of personality and personal enterprise) is a thriving aspect of current US privacy law?[179] Alternatively, is its strength a useful reminder that publicity (or 'voice') – the corollary concept of privacy – ought not to be treated as a residual category? In other words, that in providing a description of the interests served by a right to privacy, we ought to invoke '*both* voice and privacy as crucial to any project for democratization that seeks to avoid exclusion, levelling, and homogenization'.[180] The question of whether privacy protects reputation and honour has also been contentious.[181] In particular, is defamation law an offspring of privacy protection, should it be 'constitutionalised' so as to bolster media freedom and reduce abuse by public figures or officials,[182] and is there a need for an additional remedy for the publication of 'true' but 'private' facts?

These secondary difficulties – raising specific issues about privacy in public, bodily autonomy, image, reputation, and honour – stem from deeper difficulties and, frequently, lead privacy commentators back to the general question laid out at the start of this Part: that is, is there a common feature which links together the various and disparate interests which are (or seek to be) protected by a right to privacy? Or is the concept of a privacy right confused and 'at best a misnomer for some other right or set of rights'?[183] We have already noted that both autonomy and property have been used as justifications for privacy protection; Wacks prefers a focus on information;[184] while other commentaries and case law on privacy contain references to human dignity and to the interest in honour and reputation, in bodily and moral integrity, in one's name and identity, and of course, most famously of all, to the interest in 'the right to be

---

178 Ibid. The holding in *Roe* was almost entirely gutted (although not actually overturned) by the SCt's majority opinion in *Planned Parenthood of South East Pennsylvania v Casey* 112 SCt 2791 (1992). Interestingly, the latter opinion makes no mention of privacy nor does it explain this omission, rather it invokes the idea of a 'realm of personal liberty'. On the US right to privacy and abortion, see eg, Cohen, above n. 154.

179 D.A. Anderson, 'The Failure of American Privacy Law' in Markesinis, above n. 13, pp. 139-168. English law has occasionally offered indirect protection to this right via an action in defamation: see eg, *Tolley v JS Fry & Sons Ltd* [1931] AC 333.

180 J.L. Cohen, 'Democracy, Difference, and the Right of Privacy' in S. Benhabib (ed.), *Democracy and Difference: Contesting the Boundaries of the Political* (Princeton UP, 1996), pp. 187-217, at p. 189.

181 Feldman, above n. 91, p. 56 has argued that '[t]he importance of dignity to autonomy also explains why [Art.17, ICCPR] lumps rights to honour and reputation together with privacy, family, home or correspondence . . . honour and reputation together are akin to dignity in allowing one to develop a flourishing social and business life, and honour is a particularly important contributor to the self-respect and dignity which form a major part of one's view of oneself'.

182 On this issue, see eg, I. Loveland, 'Privacy and Political Speech: An Agenda for the "Constitutionalisation" of the Law of Libel' in Birks, above n. 55, pp. 51-92; and I. Loveland, *Political Libels* (Hart, 2000).

183 Cohen, above n. 154, p. 1, n. 1 (describing the views of J.J. Thomson, 'The Right to Privacy' (1975) 4 Philosophy and Public Aff 295 (reprinted in F.D. Schoeman (ed.), *Philosophical Dimensions of Privacy: An Anthology* (CUP, 1984), pp. 272-289)).

184 See R. Wacks, *The Protection of Privacy* (Sweet & Maxwell, 1980); 'The Poverty of Privacy' (1980) 96 LQR 73; *Personal Information: Privacy and the Law* (Clarendon, 1993); and *Privacy and Press Freedom* (Blackstone, 1995).

let alone'.[185] Even more broadly, privacy protection has occasionally been characterised as an aspect of the protection of liberty[186] – although this would appear to run the risk of entirely collapsing privacy and providing powerful ammunition for privacy sceptics. The possibility that there is simply no common feature which could link together the interests protected by a right to privacy has also been given serious consideration.

The aim of this Part is to clear away some of the confusion about the sorts of values that are protected by privacy. We shall begin by examining the distorting effect of the 'organising principle'[187] of the public-private divide on discussions of the right to privacy. This will be followed by direct engagement with a range of the values which commentators and case law claim are served by a right to privacy.

The public-private divide

The public-private divide is commonly presented as a linch-pin of 'the liberal way of thinking about the social world'.[188] For some time now, however, it has just as commonly been the target of critique and reconstructive projects. Critique of the divide is, however, no easy matter; numerous attempts have themselves been criticised for reifying the divide, suppressing interrelationships between public and private, and exaggerating sovereign power and the role of the state. The basic problem seems to be that in critiquing the divide 'one gets sucked into the very categorisation one is attempting to undermine'.[189] The difficulties often start with the question of what is meant by the public-private divide. Is it a descriptive claim, a normative argument or both? Is there a divide, or a dichotomy which privileges one sphere over the other? And what is the relationship between the divide and privacy?

Critique of the public-private divide is perhaps most closely associated with feminist theory and politics. Laws, practices and stereotypes excluding women from the public sphere of work and politics (and discriminating against them when they gain access) have been core themes of feminist work. Exposing the injustices perpetuated by inappropriate protection of the private sphere has been an equally prominent commitment (as captured most famously in the phrase 'the personal is political'):

---

185 This idea is most often associated with S.D. Warren and L.D. Brandeis, 'The Right to Privacy' (1890) 4 Harv LR 193 (reprinted in R. Wacks (ed.), *Privacy: Volume II* (Dartmouth, 1993), pp. 3-30). In this article, Warren and Brandeis drew support for their conclusion that US law protected a right to privacy from a range of English precedents on defamation, copyright, property and breach of confidence.

186 As emphasised, eg, by the US SCt in its case law on the right to privacy.

187 '[T]he conceptual/material matrices that articulate norms, relations, institutions, resources, and practices in particular, socially meaningful ways': see D. Cooper, '"And You Can't Find Me Nowhere": Relocating Identity and Structure within Equality Jurisprudence' (2000) 27 JLS 249, 261 (explaining it as different to ideology (ie 'more than [a framework] of ideas and beliefs') and identifying two types – social and normative-epistemological – and citing public/private as an example of the latter).

188 D. Kennedy, 'The Stages of the Decline of the Public/Private Distinction' (1982) 130 U Penn LR 1349, 1349.

189 N. Lacey, *Unspeakable Subjects: Feminist Essays in Legal and Social Theory* (Hart, 1998), p. 83. See N. Rose, 'Beyond the Public/Private Division: Law, Power and the Family' (1987) 14 JLS 61 for an argument that the problem lies with the privileging of critique over genealogy in radical theory.

[B]y now we should all be familiar with the charges. . . . [T]he public/private dichotomy has . . . served to reinforce and perpetuate social hierarchies and inequity between the sexes in all spheres of life. . . . [It] has played a key role in ideologies justifying both the exclusion of women from full membership in the political community and the denial of equality of opportunity to them in economic life. It has also helped to reinforce cultural stereotypes about gender, to perpetuate the ascription of status on this basis, to screen out so-called private issues from public discussion and debate, and to shield the asymmetrical power relations governing the gendered division of labor and other aspects of 'intimate relationships' in the home from the demands of justice.[190]

The feminist idea that 'the personal is political' has triggered deep and sustained critique of the public-private divide. Ironically, today, this success is also a problem: '"the personal is political" . . . defies ownership and is potentially and promiscuously compatible with every sphere and every social group', such that now '[t]here are few institutional spaces which do not derive their power relations from a personal that has become politicized or a particular that operates as a universal'.[191] In short, although the personal may still need to be rendered political in the feminist sense, unpacking the public-private divide is made increasingly complicated by myriad features of everyday life which undermine or rework the divide – and do so, most often, by centring the personal. Consider, for example, the popularity of mobile phones and 'kiss-and-tell' chat shows; the rise of autobiography and docu-drama; the 'privatising impulse'[192] of many governments; and the proliferation of viewing technology – from CCTV to ultrasound and web-cams. Legal scholarship reflects this burgeoning sense of complication, referring for example to ideas of different publics and different privates, as well as a range of hybrids, in assessing the 'province of administrative law',[193] as well as striving more generally for a new sophistication on the public-private divide.[194]

Privacy explained?

It is clear then that the public-private divide has made it difficult to focus on describing the good that privacy rights protect. In fact, in certain quarters, critique of the divide has been thought 'to entail, further, the rather startling view that there is in fact no such thing as a legitimate sphere of privacy at all'.[195] For some feminists, for example, privacy is 'a site which depoliticizes many of the constituent activities and injuries of women – reproduction, domestic assault, incest, unremunerated household labor, and compulsory emotional and sexual service to men'.[196] This, however, is not an unanimous feminist view; in particular,

---

190 Cohen, above n. 180, p. 189.
191 L. McLaughlin, 'Gender, Privacy and Publicity in "Media Event Space"' in C. Carter et al. (eds.), *News, Gender and Power* (Routledge, 1998), pp. 71-90, at p. 81.
192 M. Thornton, 'Introduction' in M. Thornton (ed.), *Public and Private: Feminist Legal Debates* (OUP, 1995), pp. xiii-xviii, at p. xvi.
193 See the essays in M. Taggart (ed.), *The Province of Administrative Law* (Hart, 1997).
194 See eg, S.B. Boyd (ed.), *Challenging the Public/Private Divide: Feminism, Law and Public Policy* (Toronto UP, 1997); and Cooper, above n. 187.
195 P.J. Steinberger, 'Public and Private' (1999) XLVII Political Studies 292, 298 (citing as an example the views of Catharine MacKinnon in *Towards a Feminist Theory of the State* (Harvard UP, 1989), pp. 188, 191).
196 W. Brown, 'Suffering Rights as Paradoxes' (2000) 7 Constellations 230, 236.

'for those concerned with sexual freedom, with welfare rights for the poor, and with the rights to bodily integrity of historically denied, racially subjugated peoples, privacy generally appears as unambiguously valuable'.[197] What we see here, according to Brown, is one of the paradoxes of privacy:

> [D]epending on the function of privacy in the powers that make the subject, and depending on the particular dimension of marked identity that is at issue, privacy will be seen variously to advance or deter emancipation, to cloak inequality or procure equality. [In short,] concern with securing certain legal terrain does not simply differ, but often works at cross purposes for differently marked identities.[198]

Further privacy paradoxes have been identified by other commentators. For example, it has been argued that historically there was a 'fertile and complex polarity between secrecy and privacy . . . [such that] secrecy was seen as both the greatest defence and principal enemy of privacy'.[199] Similarly, a range of commentators on contemporary trends have noted the paradox that today 'just as we seek more privacy for ourselves, we all seek more transparency from others'.[200] For the US communitarian writer, Amitai Etzioni, the privacy paradox centres on the fact that, contrary to privacy-advocates' frequent depiction of the state as 'Big Brother', the greatest threat to privacy may come not from the state but from companies and 'privacy merchants' who 'sell off our privacy for profit', and moreover that we may need to lean on the state to protect privacy from 'Big Bucks'.[201] This latter point leads directly to a privacy paradox identified by Cohen: 'while privacy rights purport to be the means for protecting individuals from state power . . . such rights seem to expose people to increased regulation by state agencies, thereby destroying both the solidarity of family community and the autonomy of the individual'.[202]

It may be useful to recap at this point. Two propositions have been put forward: first, that it may not be helpful to see property as the sole interest grounding or secured by the right to privacy; and secondly, that the grip of the ideology of the public-private divide has compromised appreciation of the value of privacy. We need now to 'take the next step, move beyond the hermeneutics of suspicion [of both property and the public-private divide], and attempt to redescribe the good that privacy rights protect'.[203] As Cohen reminds us:

> Precisely because the issues, relations, and arrangements once construed to be private, natural, and thus beyond justice, have become matters of public debate and political struggle, precisely when boundaries are being redrawn, and when

---

197 Ibid.
198 Ibid. See also Moran, above n. 139, on how the right to privacy is mediated by a range of factors and on the need to recognise that 'human rights are not necessarily about inclusion and recognition of difference'.
199 D. Vincent, *The Culture of Secrecy: Britain, 1832-1998* (OUP, 1998), pp. 18, 20. This issue will be examined in Ch. 7. More generally on the links between privacy and secrecy, see S. Bok, *Secrets: On the Ethics of Concealment and Revelation* (Vintage, 1983); and K.L. Scheppele, *Legal Secrets* (Chicago UP, 1988).
200 G. Laurie, Review of Markesinis, above n. 13, (2000) 116 LQR 173, 175 (referring to the chapters by Picard and Anderson).
201 Etzioni, above n. 2.
202 Above n. 154, p. 46.
203 Cohen, above n. 180, p. 191.

meanings have become destabilized, it is time to enter the fray and rethink privacy rights in ways that enhance, rather than restrict, freedom *and* equality.[204]

This, however, is not an easy thing to do. Privacy rhetoric is as closely associated with negative discourses (such as domination, selfishness and inappropriate secrecy) as with positive ones. Its challengers – including freedom of the press and 'the common good' – are capable of deploying equally powerful rhetoric. Defences of privacy are also radically disparate, and privacy, as a general theme, has been worked to an extent suggestive of panic or desperation. In short, Lord Woolf may not have been guilty of exaggeration when he said that:

> we are here in an area involving open textured concepts. An interference with privacy is not even like the elephant, of which it can be said it is at least easy to recognise if not define. The meaning of privacy can be influenced by the context in which it appears.[205]

We shall begin with the argument that control over personal information lies at the core of privacy. In the UK, this view has been most closely associated with Raymond Wacks' writings.[206] Wacks acknowledges the myriad ways in which we cleave to privacy, but insists that 'at the core of the preoccupation with the "right to privacy" is the protection against the misuse of personal, sensitive information'.[207] He defines personal information as 'those facts, communications, or opinions which relate to the individual and which it would be reasonable to expect him to regard as intimate or sensitive and therefore to want to withhold or at least to restrict their collection, use, or circulation'.[208] His claim is that protecting such information would meet much of the public concern about interference with privacy and avoid the problems thrown up by dependence on privacy itself.

Is Wacks correct about privacy? His proposal has considerable immediate appeal because it captures the attraction of thinking of privacy in terms of control.[209] It is also undeniable that control over personal information is relevant to supporting privacy interests; as Feldman has pointed out, such control:

> helps us to forge and conduct personal and social relationships which form an important part of the construction of social life. It also protects individual choice, preventing people from being diverted from their chosen path by the knowledge that others will be offended by it or might try to bring pressure to bear on them to abandon it.[210]

Nevertheless, we are not convinced that a focus on personal information alone is desirable. Recall first the case of John Moore, the patient whose cell-line was

---

204 Ibid.

205 *Ex p BBC*, above n. 32, p. 994.

206 See above n. 184 for some of his work in this field. See similarly, W.A. Parent, 'A New Definition of Privacy for the Law' (1983) 2 Law & Phil 305 (reprinted in R. Wacks (ed.), *Privacy: Volume I* (Dartmouth, 1993), pp. 23-56).

207 Wacks, above n. 1, p. 10.

208 Ibid., p. 26.

209 The idea of control, and in particular of privacy as a condition of 'limited accessibility', is a perennial theme in privacy theorising: see eg, R. Gavison, 'Privacy and the Limits of Law' (1980) 89 Yale LJ 421; and T. Gerety, 'Redefining Privacy' (1977) 12 Harv CR-CL L Rev 233 (reprinted in *Privacy: Volume I*, above n. 206, at pp. 129-180 and 199-262 respectively).

210 Above n. 7, pp. 53-54.

exploited for commercial gain without his knowledge. We saw that Moore failed to convince the California Supreme Court that his privacy had been violated, and that some commentators have predicted similar problems in the future unless we broaden the current understanding of 'personal information', or take a more expansive approach to the purpose of privacy.

Secondly, and more importantly, Wacks' proposal runs the risk of undervaluing other aspects of privacy protection – such as autonomy and dignity – which are far more contested. As Cohen puts it, the principle of informational privacy, 'if not its applications, is widely accepted today. The debates are over the extent, rather than the very idea, of our right to informational privacy'.[211] By comparison, where privacy is seen as being concerned with securing autonomy and/or dignity vis-à-vis sexual relations, child rearing or reproductive matters, 'the very principle, rather than the reach, of an individual right to privacy, is . . . contested'.[212] This contestation pervades commentaries on the value of privacy, and has had the effect of producing layers of debate on whether dignity or autonomy is the true interest served by privacy. Bloustein's suggestion that the violation of human dignity is the feature common to all invasions of privacy has met with particular criticism.[213] Gavison's response, which is accommodating towards dignity's relevance to privacy whilst disagreeing that it represents privacy's true purpose, is fairly typical:

> We may well be concerned with invasions of privacy, at least in part, because they are violations of dignity. But there are ways to offend dignity and personality that have nothing to do with privacy. Having to beg or sell one's body in order to survive are serious affronts to dignity, but do not appear to involve loss of privacy.[214]

Arguments that privacy is, at core, about 'autonomy, identity, and intimacy',[215] or 'respect, love, friendship and trust',[216] have fared little better. The result is that there is *no* agreement on the value of privacy; rather, '[t]here is a theory explaining the value of privacy which should be palatable to each political taste'.[217] We suspect that the search for privacy's core value, or purpose, has been, is – and probably can only ever be – an unsatisfying pursuit. As Feldman has said, in answering the question 'what is distinctive about, or at the core of, privacy?':

> One interest is autonomy, and other contenders include moral integrity, personal dignity, honour, reputation, a degree of solitude, family life, intimacy, and control over one's home and business environments. Any attempt to identify a single interest at the core of privacy is doomed to failure, because privacy derives its weight and importance from its capacity to foster the conditions for a wide range of other aspects

---

211 Above n. 154, p. 48.
212 Ibid.
213 E.J. Bloustein, 'Privacy as an Aspect of Human Dignity: An Answer to Dean Prosser' (1964) 39 NYULR 962, 1003 (arguing that one 'who is compelled to live every minute of [his/her] life among others and whose every need, thought, desire, fancy, or gratification is subject to public scrutiny, has been deprived of . . . individuality and human dignity'). Support for dignity as the core feature of privacy can also be found in: E. Picard, 'The Right to Privacy in French Law' in Markesinis, above n. 13, pp. 49-104. For discussion of dignity with reference to the ECHR and English law, see Feldman, above n. 55.
214 Above n. 209, p. 438.
215 Gerety, above n. 209, p. 236.
216 C. Fried, 'Privacy' (1968) 77 Yale LJ 475, 477 (reprinted in *Privacy: Volume I*, above n. 206, pp. 57-76).
217 R. Bagshaw, 'Obstacles on the Path to Privacy Torts' in Birks, above n. 55, pp. 133-144, at p. 135.

of human flourishing. The core of privacy therefore depends on one's idea of humanity and human flourishing, which is in part culturally conditioned.[218]

Emphasising one of the following – protected places, protected information, intimate associations, autonomous choice or bodily integrity – in discussing privacy would be equally misleading: privacy has not just one or two but *all* of these dimensions. This is not to deny that at certain junctures it may be necessary to prioritise the defence or redescription of one particular dimension. Present-day conditions, for example, suggest the need to show why 'privacy for intimate associations should and need not involve bias towards "normal" relationships while constituting others as deviant'.[219] Similarly, respect for individual privacy must be made to fit with respect for family, or other intimate associations, and home – as Cohen has pointed out, 'one needs privacy *within*, as well as for, intimate relationships, the home, and communicative interaction'.[220]

By way of conclusion, then, we would suggest the following four points. First, normative debate and insight can be of tremendous value, especially when the pace of change seems overwhelming. Thus, there is considerable merit in engaging with moves to rethink property, autonomy and the organising principle of public-private, and to understand dignity. Equally however – and this is the second point – normative insight on the value of privacy, even a definition of privacy, cannot of itself provide answers to the questions of application: that is, what acts, decisions, relationships, spaces and information should be protected by the right to privacy, and when is interference justifiable after a prima facie right has been established? As Feldman reminds us '[d]eciding on the proper scope of such rights and any limits on them is a matter of practical politics'.[221] Cohen echoes this view when she says that answers to the question of application 'ultimately depend on the cultural self-understanding of the members of a society and on the outcome of political contestation over cultural norms, codes, and social relations that constitute the practices of privacy and which shift over time'.[222] Thirdly, we would suggest that privacy as a cause of action should not be overworked; in particular, there is a constant need to guard against treating privacy as co-extensive with the far more expansive notion of liberty,[223] which is a perennial risk because of privacy's association with the idea of right to be let

---

218 Above n. 91, p. 21. Feldman uses this essay, and another, above n. 7, to outline privacy-related rights (rather than a right to privacy) and an idea of privacy with both individualistic and communitarian aspects, although principally relating to 'relating to the control over access to various dimensions [space, time, action and information] of social spheres shared with other people' wherein '[t]he interaction of the spheres and the various dimensions of privacy affect the weight which different values will have in influencing the development of the law'.

219 Cohen, above n. 154, p. 116.

220 Ibid.

221 Above n. 91, p. 27.

222 Feldman, above n. 7, pp. 50-51 pursues a similar inquiry in order to answer the question of when law should protect privacy interests. He posits a three-stage test: 'First, is the interest really related to privacy? Secondly, how significant is the interest to the maintenance of a justifiable claim to privacy, both generally and in the particular circumstances of the case? Thirdly, how serious is the infringment of the interest?' He also emphasises that '[t]he first question must be capable of being answered "yes" before the other two questions can arise', and that '[q]uestions two and three, by contrast, are matters of degree, requiring courts and legislators to balance the weight of privacy interests against, other, competing, claims of a private- or public-interest nature' (eg, freedom of the press).

223 As DeCew points out, however, this is not to deny that in some cases there can be both an invasion of privacy and a violation of liberty: J.W. DeCew, 'The Scope of Privacy in Law and Ethics' (1986) 5 Law & Phil 145, 165 (reprinted in *Privacy: Volume I*, above n. 206, pp. 99-126).

alone or to be free of state interference. Finally, we would suggest that law should not be overworked; technology may yield solutions to technologically created privacy problems,[224] and self-regulation (whether by corporations, employers, the media or Internet communities) is not inevitably ineffectual.[225]

V.   'THE WAY WE LIVE NOW':[226] THE INFORMATION SOCIETY AND PRIVACY

'The future is almost here.'[227] This future is often represented as threatening to privacy, echoing concerns which stretch back at least until 1890 when Warren and Brandeis, authors of the article credited with giving rise to the torts of privacy in US law, characterised the need for 'the right to be let alone' in the following terms:

> The intensity and complexity of life, *attendant upon advancing civilisation*, have rendered necessary some retreat from the world, and man, under the refining influence of culture, has become more sensitive to publicity, so that solitude and privacy have become more essential to the individual; but *modern enterprise and invention* have, through invasions upon his privacy, subjected him to mental pain and distress, far greater than could be inflicted by mere bodily injury.[228]

There are, however, discontinuities as well as continuities with the past, and the discontinuities point to 'a new landscape'[229] for privacy law and policy – one shaped by trends in governance and media culture, and facilitated by technological advances. The emerging landscape is commonly referred to as 'surveillance' or 'information society'.[230] It will be the subject of this Part of the chapter. The final section, Part VI, will then look at circumstances where it is argued that privacy must give way or has no relevance.

Technology, commerce and governance in information society

Technologically, things are very different from what they were even a few decades ago, and the pace of change shows no sign of slowing down. Today's technology

224 For a range of perspectives on the efficacy of such solutions, see the essays by Goldman, Cavoukian and Gellman in C.J. Bennett and R. Grant (eds.), *Visions of Privacy: Policy Choices for a Digital Age* (Toronto UP, 1999), pp. 97-148; and R. Wacks, 'Privacy in Cyberspace: Personal Information, Free Speech, and the Internet' in Birks, above n. 55, pp. 93-112. Presently, however, it seems undeniable that 'using technology to protect privacy often calls for significant effort on the part of the individual who seeks the privacy. Low privacy protection remains the default condition in much modern technology': see C.J. Bennett and R. Grant, 'Conclusion' in Bennett and Grant, pp. 263-267, at p. 264.

225 For an argument predicting market-based privacy solutions as the corporate norm, see M.J. Culnan and R.J. Bies, 'Managing Privacy Concerns Strategically: The Implications of Fair Information Practices for Marketing in the Twenty-first Century' in Bennett and Grant, ibid., pp. 149-167. Internet communities have also developed various forms of 'netiquette' to respect users' personal safety and privacy.

226 We take this phrase from Bingham, above n. 6.

227 Wacks, above n. 224, p. 94.

228 Above n. 185, p. 196 (emphasis added). Similarly, in 1928, in *Olmstead v US* 277 US 438 (1928), Brandeis J, a justice of the US SCt, noted that 'discovery and invention have made it possible for the government, by means far more effective than stretching upon the rack to obtain disclosure in court of what is whispered in the closet. The progress of science in furnishing the government with means of espionage is not likely to stop with wire-tapping'.

229 C.J. Bennett and R. Grant, 'Introduction' in Bennett and Grant, above n. 224, pp. 3-16.

230 For an attempt to formulate a systematic theory of information society, see M. Castells, *The Rise of Network Society* (Blackwell, 2000).

provides smart cards; call management services; satellite-tracking systems which can pinpoint the exact location of vehicles and individuals; surveillance cameras, sometimes invisible to the human eye, which can monitor any space; telephone and email communications which can be intercepted and traced to their source worldwide;[231] databases, containing vast reservoirs of personal information (sometimes including DNA profiles[232]), which criss-cross 'public' and 'private' sectors, and transcend national borders;[233] and an 'information superhighway' which makes it possible to send instantaneous transmissions to audiences of unparalleled size. Tomorrow's technology promises even more – it promises to be able to predict and modify individual futures using genetic science.

Technology is not, however, the driving force behind the changing landscape of privacy: rather, it facilitates trends in governing domains, such as deregulation.[234] Increasingly, governments, businesses and a range of other actors apply technology to personal information in pursuit of their individual goals – whether those be more effective 'targeted marketing', law enforcement or delivery of services.[235] Hence, the now familiar mixture of 'crime control', 'national security' and 'commercial interests' justifications for a proliferation of practices such as electronic surveillance,[236] economic espionage,[237] employment vetting,[238] and 'customer profiling'. In this environment, personal information has become something to be 'collected, matched, traded, and profiled as part of the routine engagement with both public and private institutions. It moves openly across borders. It knows fewer national or organizational attachments'.[239]

Boyle suggests that '[t]he best way to understand the change might be to see it as a shift from administration by *actuarial statistics* to administration by *personal biography*'.[240] His view receives support from others, including Marx who argues that:

> We are becoming a transparent society of record such that documentation of our history, current identity, location, and physiological and psychological states and

---

231 Alleged systematic tapping of telephone communications between Ireland and Britain from 1990-97 is being challenged under the ECHR by an alliance of UK and Irish civil liberties organisations after Channel 4 News revealed the former use of a disused tower in Cheshire in Jul. 1999.

232 See eg, the Inspectorate of Constabulary report, *Under the Microscope* (HMSO, 2000), detailing concerns about illegal retention of DNA samples in thousands of cases (available at www.homeoffice.gov.uk/hmic).

233 The storage of data 'offshore' is an increasing practice of global corporations.

234 Bennett and Grant, above n. 229, p. 3.

235 A notable feature of the opposition to the RIPA was the extent to which state powers to monitor email communications were characterised as damaging to the UK's economic standing and the future of e-commerce, especially after the enactment of the Electronic Communications Act 2000.

236 See eg, S.A. Sundstrom, 'You've Got Mail (And the Government Knows It): Applying the Fourth Amendment to Workplace E-Mail Monitoring' (1998) NYULR 2064.

237 A French public prosecutor, and a European Parliament committee, are currently conducting investigations into the activities of the US-controlled Echelon spying network, because of allegations of worldwide economic espionage. It is estimated that over 30 countries have satellite spy stations.

238 Palmer, above n. 44, pp. 187-188 has argued that 'the recent phenomena in employment practices of video surveillance, drug testing, intercepting employees email and monitoring use of the internet might all be in breach of Article 8'.

239 Bennett and Grant, above n. 229, p. 3.

240 Boyle, above n. 171, p. 15.

behaviour is increasingly possible. With predictive profiles there are even claims to be able to know individual futures.[241]

By way of illustration, consider the issue of centralised accumulation of information acquired from the ubiquitous surveillance camera.[242] Very often, the collection of information 'occurs invisibly, automatically, and remotely – being built into routine activities'.[243] The information accumulated by such cameras is also often in the public domain: motorway CCTV, for example, can hardly be said to be intruding into a private realm, given that '[w]herever we drive, we drive in the public world, and thus normally subject to unobjectionable public observation'.[244] Thus, one might ask: why be concerned about CCTV's impact on privacy? We would argue that concern is appropriate for several reasons,[245] including the fact that the ubiquity of surveillance will affect the way we think about privacy, and that information, whether it is private or uncontroversially public, acquires a different value when it is centrally accumulated:

> as readers of detective fiction well know – by accumulating a lot of disparate pieces of public information, you can construct a fairly detailed picture of a person's private life. You can find out who her friends are, what she does for fun or profit, and from such facts others can be inferred, whether she is punctual, whether she is faithful, and so on . . . .[246]

This, then, is part of the potential of modern technology, and, as Boyle and others have pointed out, it comes with risks as well as benefits[247] — which perhaps helps to explain why people report increasing concern about the 'erosion of personal privacy even as they volunteer extensive information about themselves

---

241 G.T. Marx, 'Ethics for the New Surveillance' in Bennett and Grant, above n. 224, pp. 39-67, at p. 40.

242 The related phenomenon of 'dataveillance' (the ability to track people's on-line activities (such as email, websites, e-commerce)) provides another collection of 'user profiles' which may be of considerable interest to employers, marketing organisations, government agencies, the media and individual 'hackers'.

243 Marx, above n. 241, p. 40.

244 J.H. Reiman, 'Driving to the Panopticon: A Philosophical Exploration of the Risks to Privacy Posed by the Highway Technology of the Future' (1995) 11 Computer & High Tech LJ 27, 28-29 (cited in E. Paton Simpson, 'Private Circles and Public Squares: Invasion of Privacy by the Publication of "Private Facts"' (1998) 61 MLR 318). On the UK's new Specs system of digital cameras, see 'Digital Trap is End of the Road for Speedsters', *The Times*, 29 Jul. 2000.

245 Claims that expansive usage of CCTV prevents crime, reduces fear of crime or increases conviction rates are unproven and hotly disputed in the UK: see eg, E. Short and J. Ditton, 'Seen and Now Heard: Talking to the Targets of Open Street CCTV' (1998) 38 BJ Crim 404. For analyses of CCTV, see: C. Norris and G. Armstrong, *The Maximum Surveillance Society: The Rise of CCTV* (Berg, 1999); C. Norris, J. Morgan and G. Armstrong (eds.), *Surveillance, Closed Circuit Television and Social Control* (Ashgate, 1998); S. Davies, *Big Brother: Britain's Web of Surveillance and the New Technological Order* (Pan, 1996); and J. Fiske, 'Surveilling the City: Whiteness, the Black Man and Democratic Totalitarianism' (1998) 15 Theory, Culture & Society 67.

246 Above n. 244.

247 In *Marcel v Metropolitan Police Comr*, Browne-Wilkinson VC described 'a dossier of private information' as 'the badge of the totalitarian state'. Paton Simpson, above n. 244, p. 334 highlights a different 'compilation threat: the proliferation of media outlets – and their tendency to concentrate on the same stories – increases the likelihood of scattered disclosure of different facts and thus the likelihood of "jigsaw identification" (of, for example, a victim in criminal proceedings)'. On this issue, see further *Committee on Privacy and Related Matters* (Cm. 1102, 1990), paras. 10.16-10.19 (the Calcutt Report); and the PCC *Code of Practice*, cl. 7 (children in sexual offences cases).

in exchange for coupons, catalogues, and credit'.[248] It is after all hard to avoid the sense that something is awry when 'the exercise of freedom requires incessant proof of legitimate identity',[249] when a host of databases which store our personal details must give appropriate accounts of us if we hope to access the privileges of modern living, including mortgages, a telephone, gas, electricity or employment. It is already clear that some have more to fear from this use of technology than others. Access to welfare is now conditional on 'agreeing' to the state being the superintendent of one's daily life.[250] One illustration of this is provided by the Child Support Agency, an awkward hybrid of state-corporate norms and methods, which achieved notoriety in the late 1990s when its practices provoked thousands of claimant-mothers to incur penalties, or opt to come off benefit, rather than agree to revealing the identity of their child's 'absent father'.[251] Generally, however, loss of privacy for welfare claimants occasions little public controversy, with apparently high levels of acceptance of government arguments that surveillance networks are essential in the 'war' against the allegedly 'work shy', 'welfare scroungers' and 'bogus immigrants'. Similarly, there has been little concern about equivalent practices at the European level, where the advent of 'open borders' has been paralleled by the construction of a racialised 'Fortress Europe' at the perimeters, with increased monitoring and centralisation of records on suspected 'non-Europeans'.[252]

There is no single cause of privacy problems in this evolving landscape of deregulation, globalisation, and mass data-processing. Rather, problems arise 'when technologies work perfectly and when they fail. They arise when administrative, political, and economic elites have worthy motives and when they do not. They arise through human fallibility and infallibility.'[253] Even identifying privacy problems is difficult. To illustrate this point, we can return to the issue of CCTV. Satisfactory characterisation of CCTV is immensely difficult. CCTV is commonly installed for 'our safety', or for some other sensible-sounding good.[254] Motorway CCTV, for example, supplies 'useful information for management purposes';[255] invading privacy is not its stated purpose and it

---

248 Bennett and Grant, above n. 224, p. 264. A report from Demos, a UK-based think-tank, concludes that there is public acceptance of the new uses of personal information provided that the information is used appropriately and confidentiality is preserved, and that the public make little distinction between the obligations of the public and private sectors in this regard: see Perri 6, *The Future of Privacy* (Demos, 1998).

249 N. Rose, 'Government and Control' (2000) 40 BJ Crim 321.

250 W. Brown, *States of Injury: Power and Freedom in Late Modernity* (Princeton UP, 1995), p. 168. On the construction of dependency, see N. Fraser, *Justice Interruptus: Reflections on the 'Postsocialist' Condition* (Routledge, 1997), pp. 121-150. This can be seen as the latest example of 'the deep vein of class discrimination which informs the conception of legitimate secrecy': a home-visitors' movement was developed in the nineteenth century as part of 'a strategy of urban development which sought maximum privacy for the civilized, and complete publicity for the unwashed': Vincent, above n. 199, p. 23.

251 See C. Harlow, 'Accountability, New Public Management and the Problems of the Child Support Agency' (1999) 26 JLS 150, 158 and 163 (re the CSA's 'regular breaches of confidentiality').

252 The UK joined the Schengen Information System in May 2000, a database of over 14 million records. Cf. P.A. Thomas, 'Identity Cards' (1995) 58 MLR 702.

253 Bennett and Grant, above n. 229, p. 4.

254 See eg, *Re DH (A Minor) (Child Abuse)* [1994] 1 FLR 679 (covert video surveillance of parents suspected of child abuse permitted and resulting evidence generally admissible).

255 M. Lianos with M. Douglas, 'Dangerization and the End of Deviance: The Institutional Environment' (2000) 40 BJ Crim 261, 271.

seems to have no interest in distinguishing between information on traffic congestion and weather conditions as opposed to joy-riding:

> all three situations belong to the category 'must be dealt with', the images are not being gathered as part of an attempt to exert general control upon human beings but as a detailed map which can supply answers to elaborate inquiries directed at improving institutional operationality.[256]

This makes characterisation of the spread of CCTV as evidence of a 'maximum security society' or an 'electronic Panopticon' seem outlandish.[257] Equally however, CCTV *can* invade privacy, even if that is not its primary purpose. Moreover, it is but one example of a range of practices, grounded in surveillance networks, which are spread across everyday life in information society, and which require further analysis precisely because of the way in which they blur the boundary between service and control, and thereby change our conception of freedom.[258]

There will be no single solution to the privacy problems of information society. As Bennett and Grant have noted, the 1980s' focus on a privacy protection policy encompassing legislative action on fair information principles – which would apply to every organisation that processed personal data and be overseen and enforced by an independent agency – has now given way to more complex discussions which focus on issues such as the merits of privacy-enhancing technology, market-based privacy solutions, property rights over the commercial exploitation of personal information, and the prospects for globalisation of privacy standards.[259] We are less interested here in solutions than in emphasising the prior point that questions about privacy 'are changing before our eyes'[260] – that the evolving landscape has the capacity, 'if not to end privacy, then to redefine what we mean by the term'.[261] Indeed, as Boyle has pointed out, '[a] significant but unexamined process of rhetorical and *interpretive* construction' is already underway: '[c]onsciously and unconsciously, we are already developing the language of entitlement for a world in which information – genetic, electronic, proprietary – is one of the main sources and forms of wealth'.[262] Matters are further complicated by the fact that this new language is layered on top of a liberal tradition which has traditionally prized 'free access to and transmission of information as the lifeblood of the public sphere', and which itself is already in conflict with 'our strong idea of intellectual property rights on the one hand, and our vision of individual privacy on the other'.[263]

It also has to be acknowledged, however, that technology has often furthered the liberal goal of free access and transmission of information. For example, it has been argued that technology has forged a new public sphere, allowing an international on-line citizenry to expose the secret workings of governments and corporations.[264] There is also evidence that international human rights activism has benefited from harnessing the Internet as a campaigning and

---

256 Ibid.
257 For criticism of such characterisations, see Rose, above n. 249.
258 See generally, Rose, ibid., and Lianos with Douglas, above n. 255.
259 Bennett and Grant, above n. 229, pp. 5-14.
260 Wacks, above n. 224, p. 93.
261 Boyle, above n. 171, p. xii.
262 Ibid.
263 Ibid.
264 See C.P. Walker and Y. Akdeniz, 'Virtual Democracy' [1998] PL 489.

communication tool,[265] and human rights NGOs and monitors have been using video technology to record public protest and expose criminal behaviour on the part of police and security forces. The installation of cameras in police stations (and interrogation rooms) also provides an important new safeguard for suspects in detention.

Media culture and practices in information society

We need to turn now to another aspect of information society which is reshaping how we think about privacy: media culture and practices. This topic has long dominated debates on privacy but has become more pressing amidst changing media characteristics in information society. The first of these characteristics is the huge demand for stories created by the multiplication of media outlets. All sorts of stories can be deemed 'newsworthy' but 'human-interest' ones are amongst the most highly prized – not just stories of tragedy or celebration, but stories pertaining to every scrap of everyday life.[266] In telling these stories, media outlets 'strive to get an ever more "direct" grasp on the "raw material" of people's experience'.[267] As a result, reporting of facts is not enough, and increasingly seems less of a priority than being 'at the scene' or otherwise accessing aural or visual recordings.[268]

A second characteristic of media culture in information society is higher levels of manufactured publicity, a phenomenon which seems certain to expand in the future given the commercial incentives involved. Manufactured publicity manifests itself in a range of ways. It pervades television programming, where more and more scheduling is dedicated to fly-on-the-wall documentaries about the everyday lives of ordinary people, and kiss-and-tell-style chatshows which place 'a premium on the emotional and visceral rather than the rational and thoughtful, [and which prefer] personalised story to questions of collective good'.[269] In information society, one can be celebrated for being a celebrity: '[e]ntire publications . . . are dedicated to this kind of journalism, a surprisingly large number of column inches in the quality press are also filled in this way' and the coincidence of media and celebrity interests has also spawned a literary sub-genre, 'the celebrity interview'.[270] Moreover, as we saw above, the media's

---

265 See eg, S. Davies, 'Spanners in the Works: How the Privacy Movement is Adapting to the Challenge of Big Brother' in Bennett and Grant, above n. 224, pp. 244-262. On states' efforts to censor the Internet, see Human Rights Watch, '"Silencing the Net": The Threat to Freedom of Expression Online' (1996) (available at: www.cwrl.utexas.edu/~monitors/).

266 See eg, *Big Brother*, a hit Channel 4 series, in which ten volunteers spend more than two months locked in a house – with their every activity followed by camera, screened on the web and television, and avidly reported by the tabloids – culminating in a weekly 'finale' in which one volunteer is ejected following an audience vote.

267 M. Hansen, 'Foreword' in O. Negt et al., *Public Sphere and Experience: Toward an Analysis of the Bourgeois and Proletarian Public Sphere* (Minnesota UP, 1993), pp. ix-xix, at p. xii.

268 In *French Estate v A-G of Ontario* (1996) 134 DLR (4th) 587, a Canadian criminal trial for the murders of two teenage girls by a heterosexual couple, Paul Bernardo and Karla Homolka, the judge used common law privacy interests to exclude public access to the visual portion of video recordings which the accused had made of the girls' ordeal and which were admitted in evidence. The girls' families criticised the judge for releasing the audio from the tapes.

269 J. Gamson, 'Taking the Talk Show Challenge: Television, Emotion, and Public Sphere' (1999) 6 Constellations 190, 191.

270 D. Lodge, 'Public Property', *The Times*, 7 Jul. 2000.

constant need for stories is such that 'the modern scale of celebrity goes a long way down':

> it is now possible for people who are living ordinary private lives to become famous, for at least a short time, through the media – by, for instance, volunteering or agreeing to be the subject of a fly-on-the-wall TV documentary.[271]

The fact that there is a never-ending supply of people ready to sign up for these stories or programmes – willing to allow the media into their homes, furnish intimate details, and be photographed or filmed in compromising situations – and that these stories and programmes are then consumed by ever larger audiences, must surely cause us to question the impact that information society is having on conceptions of privacy.[272]

Manufactured publicity also arises from the coincidence of media outlets' and celebrities' interests in maximising revenue.[273] Today, many public figures construct not just a public persona for public consumption but also a 'private life'. Should such figures, then, determine the occasions when the media may publish 'private facts'? And how do we determine what constitutes a 'private fact' in such circumstances?[274] A hard line was taken by the Court of Appeal in the 1977 case, *Woodward v Hutchins*, wherein a pop group unsuccessfully sued for breach of confidence against their former manager when he threatened to reveal matters about their private lives. The Court pointed to the myriad ways in which the group had courted publicity and insisted that 'those who seek and welcome publicity of every kind bearing on their private lives so long as it shows them in a favourable light are in no position to complain of an invasion of their privacy by publicity which shows them in an unfavourable light'.[275]

Further questions arise if one takes account of state actors' practices of manufactured publicity. Consider, for example, that in the UK, as elsewhere, there is increasing concern about the use of 'spin' and tactical 'leaking' by political parties,[276] and about the relationship between the media and the criminal justice system, amidst stories of police leaking of prejudicial information in attempts to influence the public perception of policing and criminal investigations.[277] The most dominant example is, arguably, the extraordinary symbiotic relationship between the British Royal Family and the media. The monarchy has always been dependent on, and has actively sought, popular legitimacy through its mass representation, yet – as examples from the Queen

---

271 Ibid.

272 Details may also be revealed without one's knowledge or consent: Feldman, above n. 91, pp. 48-49 describes the problems thrown up by a commercial video, *Caught in the Act!*, which was made up of a compilation of extracts from thousands of hours of tapes recorded on CCTV by private security firms. The firms sold the tapes – which 'included shots of people making love in lifts, getting undressed in changing rooms, and indulging in self-flagellation in shop doorways by night' – to a film-maker, who subsequently launched the video.

273 This is a notoriously fragile relationship, and as Sedley has predicted Art. 8 claims 'may quite rapidly establish a rich jurisprudence of privacy claims for the famous': see his, *Freedom, Law and Justice* (Sweet & Maxwell, 1999), p. 46.

274 See further below, pp. 317-324.

275 [1977] 1 WLR 760.

276 For discussion, see eg, I. Crewe and B. Gosschalk, *Political Communication: The General Election Campaign of 1992* (CUP, 1995). 'Spin' and 'tactical leaking' are, however, unpredictable and are prone to ricochet at their originators in unwanted, unexpected ways.

277 See eg, *Wilson v Layne* 526 US 603 (1999) (US SCt held that media 'ride-alongs' with police into homes of suspects during the execution of warrants violated the Fourth Amendment rights of homeowners).

Victoria era up to the Prince William era testify – it has much to lose when the 'private lives' contradict the public façade.[278]

The final issue we wish to raise in this section on information society concerns the rise of abstract intimacy. Today, '[m]any of our most intense feelings of connection are abstract', relying 'heavily on memory and psychology and occasional meetings, at best, rather than on routine flesh and blood interaction'.[279] We use resources such as 'history, literature, poetry, art, music, photography, film and television' to nourish 'connections with absent people and to make meaningful connections quickly, if imperfectly, with the people around us who tomorrow may be gone'.[280] Moreover, this is a process which needs to stretch 'only a little to encompass people whom we have never met, but whose lives we have been exposed to at the breakfast table, [or] on the evening news'.[281]

As with much else in information society, the rise of the phenomenon of 'abstract intimacy' brings both good and bad. On the one hand, increased openness to this type of intimacy may engender a wider spectrum of empathy and engagement; a sort of 'reflective solidarity of strangers'.[282] Equally, however, it may feed generalised indifference, cynical interest and greed for detail about the lives of others we have never met nor are ever likely to meet.[283] Moreover, abstract intimacy seems to intensify 'the politics of exposure and judgment'[284] of contemporary media cultures. Within these cultures (which encompass 'satellite television, twenty-four hour cable news, and the Internet, not to mention print journalism'), 'it's all news, all of the time [and] we "know" things instantly, before they are reported, when they are only hints, possibilities, suspicions'.[285] This culture, combined with abstract intimacy, multiplies the opportunities to demonise (or to sanctify) individuals within the blink of an eye. In recent years, for example, it has been at least partly responsible both for a British nation in mourning for its 'Queen of Hearts' (Diana, Princess of Wales), and a US public who opted for jaded resignation towards the sexual choices of their President.[286] Abstract intimacy is thus a volatile phenomenon and, if its progressive possibilities are to be realised and its downside kept in check, it will be necessary to expend further thought on the value of privacy and of publicity.

VI.   TRUMPING PRIVACY

This final Part looks at circumstances where it is argued that privacy should give way or has no application. It focuses on two such circumstances: first, the

---

278 See B. Pimlott, 'Monarchy and the Message' (1998) 69 Pol Q 91.
279 The phrase 'abstract intimacy', and the explanation of the phenomenon, are taken from R. Stones, 'Abstract Intimacies: The Princess and the President' (1999) 2 Sexualities 255.
280 Ibid., p. 256.
281 Ibid.
282 This phrase is taken from J. Dean, *Solidarity of Strangers: Feminism After Identity Politics* (California UP, 1996).
283 For discussion of this point in the context of TV audience-participation chatshows, see J. Gamson, *Freaks Talk Back: Tabloid Talk Shows and Sexual Nonconformity* (Chicago UP, 1998).
284 J. Dean, 'Making (It) Public' (1999) 6 Constellations 157, 158.
285 Ibid., p. 160.
286 For analyses of the Clinton-Lewinsky affair see eg, L. Chancer, 'The Clinton Affair: Rethinking Personal as Political' (1998) 7 New Politics 8; Dean, above n. 284; or the special issue of Sexualities, above n. 279.

question of whether one can argue for privacy in public, or the privacy of public facts; and secondly, the merits of contemporary 'common good' justifications for reducing or removing the privacy rights of particular groups (for example, the trend towards 'naming and shaming' of suspected paedophiles).

Privacy, power and democratic publicity

In part, these issues direct our attention to questions of power; in particular, to ask *who* has the power to draw the line between public and private, and, where privacy is violated, to ask whether the resulting publicity actually enhances public-sphere deliberation or other democratic values? Fraser has centred these questions in her work and argued for the development of what she terms 'democratic publicity'[287] – a concept which, she believes, might provide part of the solution to the 'ongoing struggle to achieve a more equitable balance in the social relations of privacy and publicity'.[288] Fraser's specific focus is the early 1990s' senate hearings on the appointment of Clarence Thomas to the US Supreme Court – an event which raised the nature of contemporary publicity, especially its gendered asymmetry, in a particularly gripping way.[289] During the hearings, law professor Anita Hill – a former colleague of Thomas – raised an allegation of sexual harassment against him, generating a debate which drew worldwide attention. Ostensibly, the debate was about who was 'telling the truth' about alleged sexual harassment in the workplace (and more fundamentally, of course, about whether Thomas was a suitable judicial candidate). However, Fraser delves beneath this layer of the debate so as to focus attention on the way that Thomas succeeded in ring-fencing his 'private life', whereas Hill, despite her best efforts, could not. Indeed, Hill found that although she 'sought to keep the focus on her complaint and on the evidence that corroborated it, the principal focus soon became her character'.[290]

Fraser uses the Hill-Thomas case study to highlight the lack of parity vis-à-vis the power to draw a line between public and private, and more generally as a starting point for an investigation into the commonplace assumption that publicity necessarily enhances democracy. Her conclusion makes the case for moving beyond current understandings of publicity and public interest towards a concept of 'democratic publicity', which would require us to centre questions of *power* and revisit ideas about public and private.[291] This concept of democratic publicity echoes an idea put forward by Schauer in an article in the early 1990s.[292]

---

287 N. Fraser, *Justice Interruptus: Critical Reflections on the 'Postsocialist' Condition* (Routledge, 1997), pp. 99-120.
288 Ibid.
289 More details on the Senate hearings are available from Fraser, ibid. or T. Morrison (ed.), *Race-ing Justice, En-Gendering Race: Essays on Anita Hill, Clarence Thomas and the Construction of Social Reality* (Pantheon, 1992).
290 Ibid., p. 106.
291 One might also use the idea of 'democratic publicity' to assess claims about the emergence of information as 'a new form of capital', in particular its 'elevation into the first division of key resources and commodities' and the fact that it is increasingly managed within a system of private ownership with access regulated by payment, rather than being deposited in open 'library' systems with minimal entry requirements: see G. Locksley, 'Information Technology and Capitalist Development' (1986) 27 Capital and Class 89.
292 F. Schauer, 'Reflections on the Value of Truth' (1991) 41 Case Western L Rev 699 (reproduced in *Privacy: Volume II*, above n. 185, pp. 407-432).

Schauer's proposal develops out of drawing a distinction between the truth of a proposition and the social value of its propagation, and promotes the utility of thinking of privacy, like power, in terms of control:

> we should examine privacy law by looking at the class of individuals or institutions empowered by an increase in the information brought about by a relaxation of the current standard and at whose expense it occurs. Conversely, we should examine the class comparatively empowered, and at whose expense, when information transfer is constricted by making invasion of privacy actions more available.[293]

Schauer draws an analogy between loss of privacy and conscription; while not denying that the 'power over the facts of one's life, just like power over one's body . . . might have to be sacrificed to the public good', he warns that 'we ought to be most wary of any system . . . that disproportionately selects the weak and those who are already socially or politically powerless'.[294] His focus on power rather than truth prompts a different approach to weighing the competing interests of publicity (or, free speech) and privacy: it suggests that rather than asking merely 'whether the result was a victory or a defeat for the media', we should expand our inquiries to include assessment of 'the costs of public deliberation as . . . [well as] the possibility of its constriction', and consideration of 'who will have that knowledge, at whose expense that knowledge is gained, and what, if any, are the social benefits or costs of that shift in power'.[295]

A different perspective on this issue is provided by Dean's investigation of publicity. She analyses the President Clinton-Monica Lewinsky affair and her conclusions suggest that democratic publicity is a difficult – and possibly misguided – goal. In particular, she warns against assuming that democratic publicity merely requires effective differentiation between 'consumer-oriented' publicity and 'critical' publicity.[296] Dean insists that this dichotomy 'makes no sense' because the 'media are both at once':

> Media repeatedly criticize themselves and use this self-criticism to sell copy and generate an audience. Reporters interview each other and newspapers report information available on the Net. Talking heads attack the polarizing emotion and spectacle of television shows featuring talking heads. In an 800-channel satellite TV universe, it is necessary to feed the pundit. [In short,] critical commentary on the failures of publicity . . . feeds the very media machine it criticizes, motivating the talking heads, generating Web copy, feeding the pundits.[297]

---

293 Ibid., p. 718.
294 Ibid., p. 724.
295 Ibid.
296 Here, Dean is engaging with a distinction drawn in some of Habermas' work: see J. Habermas, *The Structural Transformation of the Public Sphere: An Inquiry Into a Category of Bourgeois Society*, trans. T. Burger (Polity, 1989) and 'Further Reflections on the Public Sphere' in C. Calhoun (ed.), *Habermas and the Public Sphere* (MIT, 1992), pp. 421-479.
297 Above n. 284, p. 164. For a similar analysis of the O.J. Simpson trial, see McLaughlin, above n. 191, pp. 81-82 ('[T]he Simpson case offers an extraordinary opportunity to analyze how media events may open up a forum for the public discussion of formerly "private" concerns, such as domestic violence while, at the same time, they allow the spectacular representation of celebrity power and murder to act as a shield and a substitute for public debate of the issues. . . . The case unfolded as an exposé; it was itself an exposé of the public of late capitalist society.')

Privacy in public

These three proposals seem an appropriate, if daunting, starting point from which to consider the questions set out at the start of this section.[298] The first of those questions concerns privacy in public, and the application of privacy arguments to public facts.[299] Earlier in this chapter we noted the harm done by dichotomisation of public and private spheres. The view that 'public facts' merit no protection under privacy law perpetuates the notion of a clear divide between public and private, in particular because it suggests that 'any given piece of information belongs in either one category or the other'.[300] To take this view, would be to ignore the fact that descriptively 'it can make an enormous difference whether a fact is know by a few people or broadcast to thousands', and also that 'as normative concepts, "public" and "private" are not absolute but matters of degree . . . .'.[301] The inappropriateness of taking an absolutist approach to public facts versus private facts is made very clear by the US case of *Florida Star v BJF*.[302] Here, a reporter copied information on a rape from a full police report which had been left inadvertently in a pressroom. The information, which included the complainant's name, was subsequently published in a newspaper. Thereafter, the complainant received threatening phone calls and unwanted publicity, and during a subsequent civil action against the newspaper for invasion of privacy, she testified that she had felt compelled to move house, change her telephone number and seek police protection. The reporter admitted to having taken down the details from the police report with full knowledge that she was not allowed to do so, and to having seen the signs in the pressroom which made it clear that names of rape victims were not matters of public record and were not to be published.

The US Supreme Court, however, chose to overturn a jury's award of civil damages against the newspaper, in part because it took the view that 'punishing the press for its dissemination of information which is already publicly available is relatively unlikely to advance the interests in the service of which the State seeks to act'.[303] We disagree with this reasoning, and take the view that rigid public-private demarcations should not be determinative of cases on 'public facts'; the test of public interest justification seems preferable in such circumstances. So, for example, the European Court of Human Rights in *Spycatcher* was right to condemn as disproportionate the continuance of an injunction against UK newspapers, given the widespread importation of copies of the book published overseas and the public interest in revealing the information.[304] Equally, however, it seems appropriate that the judge in the

---

298 The idea of 'democratic publicity' might also be used as a starting point for considering disclosure of material in legal proceedings, such as rape trials: see T. Murphy and N. Whitty, 'What is a Fair Trial? Rape Prosecutions, Disclosure and the Human Rights Act' (2000) 8 FLS 1.

299 In *Katz v New York* 389 US 347 (1967), for example, the US SCt condemned the interception of conversations from *public* telephone boxes on the ground that the Fourth Amendment 'is about people, not places'.

300 Paton-Simpson, above n. 244, p. 325.

301 Ibid., pp. 324, 325.

302 491 US 524 (1989). In this jurisdiction, the Sexual Offences (Amendment) Act 1976 (as amended) protects the anonymity of rape complainants; the reporting of legal proceedings is also affected by other legislation (such as the Contempt of Court Act 1981).

303 Ibid., p. 537.

304 *Observer and Guardian Newspapers v UK* (1991) 14 EHRR 153.

'Downing Street Nanny' case upheld an injunction against the publication of the former nanny's memoirs in *The Mail on Sunday*, and refused to equate publication in a newspaper already on the street (and in an Internet edition) with the memoirs being in the 'public domain'.[305] There is something unsatisfactory about the claim that Cherie Booth should merely have had access to 'damages from the betrayer . . . once the confidentiality genie was free of its bottle'.[306] The monetary sums involved in such damages claims do not appear to deter media conglomerates; furthermore, in this case, even newspaper editors were agreed that *The Mail on Sunday* could not avail itself of a public interest argument: '[m]ost journalists agree[d], for once, with *The Sun*, which . . . stated: "Nobody should have the spotlight shone on everything they do in their own home. This kitchen-table tittle-tattle had no public interest justification".'[307]

It is not enough, therefore, to base the scope of privacy protection on bald concepts of public and private. As more and more personal facts, often of the most intimate kind, circulate in a range of 'public' arenas,[308] we need to move beyond the idea of a public-private divide, no matter how appealing it may seem.[309] Developing a framework for privacy in public will also require us to move beyond an 'information' focus on the right to privacy. This, as Paton-Simpson explains, is because 'there are cases where a publication is invasive of privacy, and yet the communication of information is not really the essence of the complaint'.[310] Consider, for example, the increasingly pervasive media practice of being 'live at the scene', ready to transmit 'the full story' via compelling images and the rawness of breaking news. Here, '[t]he objection is not the amount of knowledge gained by the audience but something which is harder to pin down',[311] and which has to do with the fact that today's aural and visual recordings 'have a qualitatively different impact on privacy . . . [, they] do not merely convey information about a person, but also give the audience experience of that person'.[312] Paton-Simpson illustrates these points for us by analysing the nature of a complaint about the broadcast of close-up pictures of mourners at a funeral:

> One aspect of the complaint is that the gaze of the television camera inhibits the free expression of grief; mourners are usually protected by social norms which prohibit such close 'staring'. Another aspect, even if mourners are unaware they are

---

305 M. Stephens, 'Downing Street Confidential', *The Times*, 14 Mar. 2000.
306 Ibid.
307 R. Greenslade, 'Dangerous Liaisons', *The Guardian*, 13 Mar. 2000.
308 The profusion of free Internet sites devoted to voyeurism and exhibitionism has meant that (anonymous) private individuals, by submitting personal photographs/video clips of their relatives or members of the public (for example, beach photos), may be responsible for serious invasions of privacy – of which the subjects of the visual representation (who are overwhelmingly female) may remain ignorant. One individual voyeur can generate worldwide Internet distribution, exploding the distinction traditionally drawn between the taking of unauthorised photographs/footage and the subsequent decision to publish or broadcast which was based on the operation of third-party editorial control.
309 S. 12(4) HRA requires an assessment of the extent to which 'the material has, or is about to, become available to the public', or 'it is, or would be, in the public interest for the material to be published'. In *Venables and Thompson* [2001] 1 All ER 908, the HCt issued a life-time injunction under Art 2, ECHR in order to preserve the anonymity of V and T upon their release from detention.
310 Paton-Simpson, above n. 244, p. 337.
311 Ibid.
312 Ibid. See also, Paton-Simpson, 'Privacy and the Reasonable Paranoid' (2000) 50 UTLJ 305.

being filmed, is that a private tragedy has been turned into public entertainment, showing a lack of respect for public dignity.[313]

Privacy codes generally warn against overly-intrusive and distressing media coverage of events such as funerals, yet the boundaries of the 'public interest' justification are constantly tested by the clamour for ever more 'dramatic', 'real-life' representations.

Other jurisdictions have recently made some headway in untangling the issues at the core of 'privacy in public' cases. In what follows, we shall outline three examples, each one from a different jurisdiction. The first case is *Les Éditions Vice-Versa Inc v Aubry*.[314] It is a decision of the Canadian Supreme Court upholding the award of $2,000 civil damages against a photographer and magazine publisher for printing a photograph of a 17-year-old, taken without consent while she was sitting on the step of a public building in Montreal. The majority decided that the right to control one's image was an element of the right to privacy under the Quebec Charter of Rights, and that, in this context, it outweighed the right to freedom of expression because of the absence of consent and the nature of the information. The Court distinguished the facts before it from the case of an individual[315] who was photographed in a crowd at a sporting event or a demonstration, or who appeared 'in an incidental manner in a photograph in a public place':

> the artistic expression of the photograph, which was alleged to have illustrated contemporary urban life, cannot justify the infringement of the right to privacy it entails. It has not been shown that the public's interest in seeing this photograph is predominant. . . . [T]he [subject's] right to protection of her image is more important than the . . . right to publish the photograph . . . without first obtaining her permission.[316]

Our second example is drawn from California which has enacted 'anti-paparazzi' legislation to restrain the activities of journalists and photographers who go 'to any lengths and use the latest technology to obtain . . . pictures or soundbites'.[317] The legislation mounts a two-pronged attack on the paparazzi. First, it creates a new tort of 'constructive invasion of privacy', which addresses 'the capturing of visual or audio images through the use of sensory enhancing technology if these images could not have been captured without a trespass and without the enhanced technology'. The idea behind the tort is to stretch the protection provided by physical space: 'not only does [it] prevent people from walking on

---

313 Ibid., p. 337. The prime case study is the television coverage of the Northern Ireland conflict which, arguably, reflected the uneasy balance between protecting the privacy of close relatives of the deceased and representing the highly political nature of Republican/Catholic funerals.

314 [1998] 1 SCR 591.

315 The SCt's decision distinguishes private individuals from public figures, and emphasises that: 'certain aspects of the private life of a person who is engaged in a public activity or has acquired a certain notoriety can become matters of public interest. This is true, in particular, of artists and politicians, but also, more generally, of all those whose professional success depends on public opinion. There are also cases where a previously unknown individual is called on to play a high-profile role in a matter within the public domain, such as an important trial. . .' (para. 58).

316 Paras. 62-65. The SCt also noted that 'the photograph was used for commercial purposes, in particular to sell the magazine'.

317 Statement of actor, Michael J. Fox, to Congressional hearings on federal privacy legislation. See generally, 'Privacy, Technology and the California "Anti-Paparazzi" Statute' (1999) 112 Harv LR 1367.

to the physical space around a person's property; it also prevents them from using technology to "shrink" that space and thereby to "trespass" by non-physical means'.[318] Secondly, the legislation seeks to regulate the market for intrusively obtained information: a defendant is potentially liable for increased damages, for any commercial proceeds flowing from the privacy violation, and for any inducement of a third party to invade a person's privacy.

Doubts remain as to how influential the California statute will be in practice – in light of the requirements that a plaintiff must have a 'reasonable expectation of privacy', be engaged in 'a personal or familial activity', and that the use of technology must be 'offensive to a reasonable person'[319] – but it marks a significant attempt to challenge dominant media practices in a First Amendment culture. Not surprisingly, the US 'anti-paparazzi' debate has generated fierce controversy and division. Some have welcomed the opportunity to challenge the claim that paparazzi can shield behind the concept of freedom of the press, and reject the claim that celebrities have no right to privacy in public, arguing that when a person 'trespasses upon another's private life in a ruthless manner and with a greedy motive, an assault upon universal notions of decency and propriety has been committed'.[320] Other commentators denounce the creation of sweeping curbs on the press based merely on the 'insensitivity of a few prying photographers',[321] and argue that the expressive and informational value of photography must be recognised and protected:

> A picture of a celebrity entering a restaurant or vacationing on a beach hardly appears to be of the same societal importance as a photograph of a political protest, or of a politician accepting a bribe. However, the problem with [the new laws] is that they would also discourage the aggressive pursuit of information of legitimate concern to the public. There is simply no easy way to distinguish between legitimate newsgathering and the gathering of news that is purely sensational.[322]

The final example we want to highlight is the decision of the German Federal Court in the *Princess Caroline of Monaco* case.[323] The Princess, who was photographed whilst dining with a male friend in a garden restaurant in France,

---

318 Ibid., p. 1379.
319 See discussion of 'reasonable' expectations of privacy in the *Princess Caroline* case below. See also, *Wolfson v Lewis* 924 F Supp 1413 (E.D. Pa.1996) (injunction issued where intrusion upon seclusion by *Inside Edition* reporters who persistently followed the plaintiffs, filmed their home and child, and used a 'shotgun' microphone to record conversations conducted within the home).
320 S.A. Madere, 'Paparazzi Legislation: Policy Arguments and Legal Analysis in Support of their Constitutionality' (1999) 46 UCLA LR 1633, 1670 (arguing that paparazzi engage in dangerous and intimidating tactics; are motivated solely by financial motives; and do not fulfil the traditional role of the press because of the value of the information gathered).
321 'Privacy, Photography and the Press' (1998) 111 Harv LR 1086, 1103.
322 Ibid., p. 1102. For the classic account of British tabloid journalism, see P. Chippindale and C. Horrie, *Stick It Up Your Punter!: The Uncut Story of The Sun Newspaper* (Pocket, 1998). More recently, the media identified 'Mary Bell', convicted in 1968 for killing two children, following the serialisation of *Cries Unheard* by Gitta Sereny in 1998 – despite the existence of a court order protecting her identity. The media actions revealed Bell's past to her 14-year-old daughter.
323 BGH 19 Dec. 1995, BGHZ 131 pp. 332-346. The case is discussed by Arden, above n. 87; Bingham, above n. 6; and B.S. Markesinis and N. Nolte, 'Some Comparative Reflections on the Right to Privacy of Public Figures in Public Places' in Birks, above n. 55, pp. 113-131, as a useful example for UK courts to consider in developing privacy law. Cl. 3 of the PCC *Code of Practice* states that the 'use of long lens photography to take pictures of people in private places without their consent is unacceptable' and that private places are 'public or private property where there is a reasonable expectation of privacy'.

claimed a breach of privacy under German law (which protects personality, dignity and the general right to control one's image).[324] Her claim for an injunction against further publication of the photos in Germany was denied in the lower courts on the ground that her privacy rights were not violated because she was in a public space and non-consensual publication of images of 'figures of contemporary history' was generally lawful. The Federal Court reversed this decision, rejecting the argument that privacy 'stopped at [one's] doorstep'. The Court defined a 'place of seclusion' as any place where a person took obvious steps to withdraw from the general public (for example, being in a secluded restaurant, a hotel room, a sports centre); by contrast, dining or shopping where a person did not 'retreat' from the public gaze would not generate a similar expectation of privacy. It also assessed the public interest in publication of the 'information':

> When weighing up the various interests involved, the information value of the events depicted plays a significant role. The greater the interest of the public in being informed, the more the protected interests of the person of contemporary history must recede in favour of the public's need for information. Conversely, the need to protect the depicted person's privacy gains in weight as the value of the information which the public obtains from the photographs decreases. Here . . . pictures of totally private events of the plaintiff's life cannot be recognised as worthy of protection.[325]

German law has thus managed to extend 'the spatial zone of legal protection of privacy of public figures to public places',[326] and put down a marker that 'the public are not entitled to know every detail of the life of a public figure'.[327] It seems only fair that public figures should have a measure of privacy, even when they are in public; at the same time, however, the difficulties of applying the tests set down by the court in an environment characterised by increasing amounts of manufactured publicity should not be underestimated.

Privacy violations and the common good

We conclude this chapter by highlighting a troubling new dimension of public interest-based violations of privacy: the proliferating claims that certain groups should forfeit aspects of their privacy in the interests of the common good. These claims have been most pronounced in relation to those convicted of sex offences against children, and in the US they have already led to federal and state 'naming and shaming' laws – commonly referred to as 'Megan's Law', following a campaign fronted by the parents of a seven-year-old, Megan Kanka, who was killed by a convicted sex offender in New Jersey in 1991.[328] The federal

---

324 See generally, B.S. Markesinis, *The German Law of Torts* (OUP, 1994).

325 In doing so, it used an approach similar to that of the Canadian SCt in *Aubry*, above n. 314.

326 Markesinis and Nolte, above n. 323, p. 121.

327 Arden, above n. 87, p. 15.

328 See eg, M.L. Skoglund, 'Private Threats, Public Stigma? Avoiding False Dichotomies in the Application of Megan's Law to the Juvenile Justice System' (2000) 84 Minnesota LR 1805. The US legislation has proven counter-productive in several respects, leading for example to: increased vigilante attacks; constant relocation of high-risk individuals; an increased likelihood of child-abuse networks; the hindering of rehabilitation efforts for ex-prisoners; and the distortion of the extent and nature of child sexual abuse (which is predominantly intra-family). The fact that sex offenders' registers may include all those convicted of 'sex offences', including, eg, gay men convicted of sexual offences, raises further problems of discrimination and stigmatisation.

law requires individual states to release 'relevant' information about certain groups of sex offenders to the public, but leaves the decision on how this should be done to the states themselves. This has led to a range of different state practices: in Louisiana, for example, 'sex offenders can be made to wear special clothes or carry sandwich boards listing their crimes'; in Oregon, 'molesters can be forced to post a sign – a scarlet M – in their windows'; and elsewhere 'prison service officials knock on the doors of every house neighbouring a released paedophile or rapist'.[329] In the summer of 2000, a UK newspaper, *The News of the World*, began a campaign for similar laws in the UK following the killing of an eight-year-old, Sarah Payne. At first, the campaign called for the public to have an automatic right to know the names and addresses of convicted sex offenders living in their area, via open access to the sex offenders' register, currently under the control of the police;[330] it was later amended to a demand for controlled access to such information.[331]

These developments are one example of a wider trend towards 'naming and shaming' of individuals who have committed criminal offences, or are considered in breach of certain norms of social behaviour. Other examples include the publication of a 'rogues' gallery of suspected football hooligans';[332] proposals to create a 'most wanted' list of 'drug lords' on the Internet;[333] and the discharging of orders under the Children and Young Persons Act 1933 to permit the media identification of juvenile defendants.[334] Together, they raise complex questions about 'the culture of high crime societies'[335] – most notably, about emerging practices of inclusion and exclusion.[336] They also present a fundamental challenge to thinking about privacy. In the US, the challenge has been made explicit by communitarian writers, such as Etzioni, who argue that

---

329 E. Vulliamy and N. Paton Walsh, 'Can Megan Give Us An Answer?', *The Observer*, 6 Aug. 2000.
330 See the Sex Offenders Act 1997; Home Office, *The Crime and Disorder Act 1998: Sex Offender Orders Guidance* (1998) (available at: www.homeoffice.gov.uk); and the Protection of Children Act 1999. The 1997 Act requires sex offenders convicted or cautioned on or after 1 Sep. 1997, or who were serving custodial or community sentences or were under post-release supervision at that date, to notify the police of their names and addresses and of any subsequent changes. For anyone imprisoned for 30 months or more, this is a lifetime requirement.
331 *The News of the World's* 'naming and shaming' campaign was condemned by police representatives, NACRO and children's charities, such as the NSPCC. The existing private register has a high rate of compliance and is viewed, by the agencies involved, as potentially more effective in monitoring high-risk offenders: see J. Plotnikoff and R. Woolfson, *Where Are They Now?: An Evaluation of Sex Offender Registration in England and Wales* (Police Research Series Paper No. 126, Aug. 2000).
332 In Jul. 2000, 29 high-resolution stills of Leeds United supporters (copied from security videos and police photographs) were published by the police after an outbreak of violence at a Leeds-Galatasaray football match.
333 See 'Drug Lords May Be "Named and Shamed" on Net', *The Times*, 29 Jul. 2000.
334 See eg, *R v Central Criminal Court, ex p West, Blankson and Copeland* (unreported, Div Ct, 24 Jul. 2000) (upholding trial judge's balancing of public interest in open justice against welfare of juvenile applicants, who were convicted of murder and attempted murder); and *McKerry v Teesdale and Wear Valley Justices* [2000] Crim LR 594 (anonymity could be dispensed with when in public interest such as juvenile being 'serious danger to public').
335 D. Garland, 'The Culture of High Crime Societies: Some Preconditions of Recent "Law and Order" Policies' (2000) 40 BJ Crim 347. It should also be noted that the emphasis on exposing the *individual* who is a 'danger to the public' deflects attention from the institutional history of child abuse – in residential homes, schools, the Catholic Church – and ignores the historical practice of disbelieving the 'victim': see C. Smart, 'A History of Ambivalence and Conflict in the Discursive Construction of the "Child Victim" of Sexual Abuse' (1999) 8 SLS 391.
336 See generally, Rose, above n. 249.

the aggrandisement of privacy rights, which they see as part and parcel of the radical individualism which has run rampant in recent decades, needs to be ousted in favour of a 'new privacy equation' manifesting higher levels of respect for the common good – in particular, for interests such as child welfare and community safety.[337] This sort of argument has an ageless allure, but it is especially potent at present in both the UK and the US amidst widespread interest in the politics of the 'Third Way' and electoral competition on issues of crime control. It is crucial, however, that neither its potency, nor the fact that privacy can sometimes legitimately be interfered with, should blind us to the problems with this proposed new privacy equation.

The first problem is that its juxtapositioning of privacy and the common good disregards the social value of privacy rights.[338] The second problem is that its trumpeting of the common good glosses over the fact that there is no 'single overarching conception of the good, or a single substantive collective identity' upon which all are agreed in either the US or the UK: it fails to acknowledge 'difference and potential conflict between individual and group identity, and among group identities'.[339] Its most troublesome aspect, however, is its promotion of exclusion: as Rose explains, stripping paedophiles of privacy rights is but one instance of 'a whole variety of paralegal forms of confinement [which] are being devised, including pre-emptive or preventive detention prior to a crime being committed or after a determinate sentence has been served, not so much in the name of law and order, but in the name of the community that they threaten, the name of the actual or potential victims they violate'.[340] The communitarians' new equation of privacy must be challenged: by promoting the idea that 'the conventions of "rule of law" must be waived for the protection of the community against a growing number of "predators" . . . and the incorrigibly anti-social',[341] it constitutes a new and, we would argue, objectionable take on the concept of what is 'necessary in a democratic society'. In other words, 'naming and shaming' is not only about privacy violations – it is about the limits of freedom in late modern societies.

CONCLUSION

'Anyone who studies the law of privacy today may well feel a sense of uneasiness.'[342] Scholarly articles mull over the essence of privacy, disagreeing about whether it is an individual right or not, and whether it has, or needs to have, a core feature. Recently, however, domestic judges, with a history of cajoling and threatening Parliament, have finally carved out new territory

---

337 See Etzioni, above n. 2. In Canada, *R v Sharpe* [2001] 1 SCR 45 concerning a prosecution for possession of 'child pornography' has generated a somewhat similar debate. The controversy arose because the trial judge declared the relevant provision of the Criminal Code incompatible with the Canadian Charter of Rights on the ground that 'the invasion of freedom of expression and personal privacy [was] profound', and that the provision failed the proportionality test because of its overbroad nature. The BC Court of Appeal upheld the lower court decision; the Supreme Court reversed it.

338 See eg, Feldman, above n. 55, for a defence of privacy rights along these lines.

339 Cohen, above n. 154, pp. 98-99.

340 Above n. 249, p. 334.

341 Ibid. See Z. Bauman, *In Search of Politics* (Polity, 1999), pp. 9-57.

342 Gavison, above n. 209, p. 421.

for privacy rights in the UK. The landmark cases in which this took place are, first, *Douglas and Zeta-Jones v Hello! Ltd* [343] and, secondly, *Venables and Thompson v News Group Newspapers Ltd.*[344] In *Douglas*, the Court of Appeal had to determine which of two rival magazines, *Hello!* or *OK!*, had the right to publish exclusive pictures of the wedding of the celebrities, Michael Douglas and Catherine Zeta-Jones. The couple had signed a £1 million deal with *OK!* but, despite security measures at the wedding event, *Hello!* had been able to obtain some secretly-taken photographs. An interim injunction was issued to restrain publication by *Hello!* but, on appeal, the Court of Appeal ruled that the injunction should be discharged on the balance of convenience test and in the interests of media freedom. The crucial finding, however, was that Douglas and Zeta-Jones had a right to privacy in English law, grounded in an extension of the breach of confidence action, which could be the subject of a future claim for damages against *Hello!* magazine.

While not rejecting the possibility that the 'horizontal effect' of the HRA 1998 might not also ground a discrete (Article 8 right to privacy) action between two *private* parties, the Court opted for 'filling the gap' in the common law using the existing breach of confidence action. It argued that, under the section 6 HRA duty to apply Convention rights, the court was entitled to cure the long-standing deficiencies in the law in respect of a right to privacy. Sedley LJ emphasised that a concept of privacy accords recognition:

> to the fact that the law has to protect not only those people whose trust has been abused but those who simply find themselves subjected to an unwanted intrusion into their personal lives. The law no longer needs to construct an artificial relationship of confidentiality between intruder and victim: it can recognise privacy itself as a legal principle drawn from the fundamental value of personal autonomy.[345]

In the second case, *Venables and Thompson*, Butler-Sloss P also extended the law of confidence to grant a life-long injunction against the disclosure of the identity or whereabouts of either Jon Venables or Robert Thompson (the defendants in the James Bulger case) upon their release from secure detention. She acknowledged that the grant of such an injunction was exceptional, but was 'entirely satisfied that there is a real and serious risk to the rights of [Venables and Thompson] under Articles 2 and 3'[346] [of the ECHR] – namely, that there was a real possibility that the media or members of the public would seek them out and cause them serious or fatal harm.

The media are vehemently divided in their response to these cases. The government's views on burgeoning privacy rights are also unclear. During the Parliamentary debates on the Human Rights Bill, members of the government spoke in terms which suggested that they welcomed the judicially-created right to privacy that was waiting around the HRA-corner. But the government went on to enact the Regulation of Investigatory Powers Act 2000, a piece of legislation which provoked an outpouring of concern about privacy violations paralleled

---

343 [2001] 2 All ER 289 (CA).
344 [2001] 1 All ER 908 (HCt).
345 Above n. 343, para. 126.
346 Above n. 344, para. 86. Art. 2, ECHR protects the right to life; Art. 3, ECHR protects against torture or inhuman or degrading treatment.

only by that seen at the time of the death of Diana, Princess of Wales.[347] Meanwhile, the 'information age' marches on, and ever larger numbers of us are subjects of CCTV and hand over personal details in exchange for the media promise of '15 minutes of fame' or for consumer items – from medicines and mortgages to mobiles and make-up. In short, then, privacy paradoxes appear to be ever on the increase.

The uneasiness surrounding privacy may, in part, explain why this chapter has answered very few questions definitively, and also why it has raised far more questions than it has answered. At the same time, however, no amount of uneasiness can detract from privacy's enduring appeal or importance. It should not be forgotten, for example, that in recent years privacy rights have been a key site for politicising discrimination and procuring greater equality, especially in the fields of sexual and reproductive freedom. All the signs are that privacy will retain its central position in the HRA era – indeed, the social and legal value placed on privacy may well be a major force in determining the wider culture of freedom in 'information society'.

---

347 The then Home Secretary, Jack Straw, claimed that 'the RIPA powers, simply put, are essential to help keep the UK a safe place for everyone to live and work': Home Office Press Release, 28 Aug. 2000. Several commentators have predicted that provisions of the Act – especially in relation to the potential interception of journalist or lawyer-client communications, and the reversal of the burden of proof in relation to disclosing encryption keys – may be found in violation of Arts. 6 or 8 of the Convention. The RIPA may provide the opportunity for UK judges to insist on the requirement of prior judicial authorisation before interference with privacy rights.

Chapter Seven

Beyond the Secret State

INTRODUCTION

The 'Secret State' is classic civil liberties terrain.[1] In large part this is because, historically, it had everything to attract the faithful. It offered, for example, opportunities for serious challenge to supremacist accounts of 'British liberty'. It also provided ammunition for intra-civil liberties feuds on the question of where power ought to reside: thus, it confirmed prejudices about 'Establishment judges' yet it also upset chronicles of Parliament's allegedly superior role in defending civil liberties (not least because no list of 'spectacular [parliamentary] failures'[2] could omit the notorious Official Secrets Act 1911). Overall, the law and culture of official secrecy offered up such extensive evidence of the state as Leviathan that Geoffrey Robertson, a prominent civil libertarian, was prompted to claim that '[n]o other Western democracy is so obsessed with keeping from the public information about its public servants, or so relentless in plumbing new legal depths to staunch leaks from its bureaucracy'.[3]

The alleged raison d'être for some of the law and culture of secrecy – 'national security' – also provided an ideal bogey for the civil liberties tradition, as did national security's historic guardians, MI5 and MI6.[4] It is generally agreed now that national security is an 'essentially contested concept'.[5] In the UK, however, it was historically so under-contested that, in 1977, Lord Denning could

---

1   A major early civil liberties work on this theme is D. Williams, *Not in the Public Interest: The Problem of Security in Democracy* (Hutchinson, 1965).

2   K.D. Ewing and C.A. Gearty, *The Struggle for Civil Liberties: Political Freedom and the Rule of Law in Britain 1914-1945* (OUP, 2000), p. 25.

3   G. Robertson, *Freedom, The Individual and The Law* (Penguin, 1993), p. 129. See also, Liberty, *Censored: Freedom of Expression and Human Rights* (NCCL, 1994); and C. Harlow and R. Rawlings, *Pressure Through Law* (Routledge, 1992), p. 172 ('official secrecy is a starred item on the agenda of civil liberties campaigners').

4   MI5, also known as the Security Service, is the agency responsible for internal security. MI6, also known as the Secret Intelligence Service (SIS), is responsible for external security. The 'third secret service' is Government Communications Headquarters (GCHQ), which is responsible for communications surveillance centres at Cheltenham and elsewhere.

5   As pointed out by L. Lustgarten and I. Leigh, *In From the Cold: National Security and Parliamentary Democracy* (Clarendon, 1994), p. 4, the term can be traced back to a mid-twentieth century article by W.B. Gallie. They explain its meaning as follows: 'This means not only that it contains an ineradicable ideological or moral element which makes any empirical refutation impossible, but equally that the contest for acceptance of any particular definition is itself a highly political one, in the sense that a competition for power at an ideological level is involved.'

announce with apparent ease that, in national security cases, 'even natural justice must take a back seat'.[6] In later decades, other judges made similar pronouncements, emphasising for example that the 'interest of the State [was] synonymous with the policies of the Government of the day',[7] and that 'the maintenance of national security' provided the underpinning for, and foundation of, 'all our civil liberties'.[8]

National security's alleged nemesis – variously, freedom of expression, freedom of information, open government or a vibrant 'Fourth Estate' – provided a failsafe civil liberties rallying cry.[9] It was, moreover, rarely out of use for long. Each decade brought its own shocking flashpoints. In the 1970s, for example, the 'ABC trial' brought evidence of crass use of the Official Secrets Act 1911 against journalists who had revealed Britain's spy network.[10] The late 1980s were scarred by *Spycatcher*: the Thatcher government, notoriously, piled legal action upon legal action in an attempt to prevent the UK publication of the memoirs of former MI5 agent, Peter Wright. More recently, in 1992, the Matrix Churchill 'Arms to Iraq' trial, exposed cavalier politicians, infighting amongst government departments, shady security service activities and private arms deals: in effect, it unblocked 'a vast dam of mendacity, releasing a torrent which eventually drowned the prosecution and almost capsized the [Conservative] government'.[11]

All of this provides the backdrop against which this chapter broaches the question of civil liberties engagement with secrecy and national security in the Human Rights Act era. In Part I we provide an overview of the contemporary scene and we suggest that the pre-eminent question arising from developments over recent decades is: are we now beyond the 'Secret State'? That question will permeate the entire chapter. Part II addresses it by looking, not at the law, but at the *culture* of secrecy: law was, of course, relevant to the culture of secrecy but, as was suggested by the 1972 Franks Report on *Section 2 of the Official Secrets Act 1911*, 'constitutional arrangements, political tradition, and national character, habit and ways of thought'[12] were far more important.[13] The law on

---

6   *R v Secretary of State for the Home Department, ex p Hosenball* [1977] 3 All ER 452 (CA).
7   *R v Ponting* [1985] Crim LR 318 (CCC) (per McCowan J).
8   *R v Secretary of State for the Home Department, ex p Cheblak* [1991] 2 All ER 319, 334 (CA) (per Lord Donaldson MR). The case concerned a challenge to the internment of Iraqis and Palestinians during the Gulf War. The full quote reads: 'although they give rise to tensions at the interface, "national security" and "civil liberties" are on the same side. In accepting as we must, that to some extent the needs of national security must displace civil liberties, albeit to the least possible extent, it is not irrelevant to remember that the maintenance of national security underpins and is the foundation of all our civil liberties'.
9   P. Birkinshaw, *Freedom of Information: The Law, the Practice and the Ideal* (Butterworths, 1996), p. 1 says that '"Freedom of Information" has become a rallying cry of libertarians, if not quite the contemporary equivalent of "Wilkes and Liberty" in eighteenth-century London or "Reform" in nineteenth-century England'.
10 *R v Aubrey, Berry and Campbell* [1979] Crim LR 284.
11 G. Robertson, *The Justice Game* (Vintage, 1999), p. 316.
12 *Departmental Committee on Section 2 of the Official Secrets Act 1911* (Cmnd 5104, 1972), p. 34 (the Franks Report). S. 2 of the 1911 Act made it an offence for any person to communicate certain classes of information 'other than to a person to whom he is authorised to communicate it, or a person to whom it is in the interest of the State his duty to communicate it'. It applied to information about a 'prohibited place', confidential information and any information obtained by an accused 'owing to his position as a person who holds or has held office under His Majesty, or as a person who holds or has held a contract made on behalf of His Majesty, or as a person who is or has been employed under a person who holds or has held such an office or contract'.
13 The history of the security services in the UK provides further support for an emphasis on matters additional to the law: it is a history characterised by the intentional *absence* of law.

official secrecy and national security, in particular the Official Secrets Acts of 1889, 1911 and 1989, will be the subject of Parts III and IV. In Part V, we move to an overview of the 'Secret State' post-1989. This period is marked by complex, apparently-contradictory developments, including the falling-away of communism; the ascent of neo-liberalism as the epitome of 'modern' government; the 'statutory baptism' of the security services, MI5 and MI6,[14] and the subsequent embrace of public relations by a range of spies and spymasters; escalating distrust of government; and a groundswell in favour of freedom of information and open government. Finally, in Part VI, we make some preliminary suggestions with respect to a fundamental question: namely, what ought to be the scope and nature of the civil liberties critique of national security and official secrecy in the 'new world order' given that some acclaim the 'demise of Leviathan', others ponder whether Leviathan is merely 'in repose',[15] and a further grouping warns of a newly minted Leviathan?

I.   BEYOND THE SECRET STATE

Of late, the classic civil liberties terrain outlined in the Introduction to this chapter appears to have shifted considerably. In large part, this can be attributed to the fact that initiatives by government, and others, over recent decades have redrawn the map of governing arrangements: the new map leaves many once-familiar ideas about the 'Secret State' reeking of obsolescence. Consider for example how, increasingly, classifications such as 'Parliament versus Government versus Judiciary, checks and balances, and so on'[16] seem somewhat quaint. References to an 'over-mighty executive' also generate unease; they, too, seem like a throwback to an earlier era. In similar vein, the idea of a monolithic civil service centred in Whitehall is, at best, a subject for amusing but dated comedy series. Perhaps most crucially of all, Northern Ireland – so often the alleged justification for repressive legislation and practices, and for a quiescent Westminster Parliament – has a sophisticated peace process. Moreover, the cataclysmic event of 'Bloody Sunday' in 1972 is the subject of a new official inquiry, which is slowly prising open secrets and re-examining military events that were never expected to be revisited.[17] The nation, it could be argued, is in the process of re-imagining itself and, as part of this, it has accepted the need to face its own (secret) history.[18]

---

14   'Statutory baptism' was given to MI5 in 1989 (the Security Service Act 1989) and to MI6 in 1994 (The Intelligence Services Act 1994). The term 'statutory baptism' is taken from N. Walker, *Policing in a Changing Constitutional Order* (Sweet & Maxwell, 2000), p. 221.

15   B. Wright, 'Quiescent Leviathan: Citizenship and National Security Measures in Late Modernity' (1998) 25 JLS 213, 236. Wright himself concludes that 'while there are new discourses of political rationality around national security, an altered mix between international co-operation and national self-interest and an increasing anxiety about refugees and economic espionage, intellectual property and private technology interests, the nation state continues to orchestrate repressive responses. These powers respond to pressures from above and below but they, and the state's underlying anxiety about disorder, are hardly being abandoned'.

16   I. Leigh, 'Secrets of the Political Constitution' (1999) 62 MLR 298, 309.

17   See www.bloody-Sunday-inquiry.org.uk. See also, the legal action before the ECtHR by a combination of Irish and UK civil liberties organisations alleging systematic surveillance by UK security and intelligence services of all telephone calls between Ireland and the UK.

18   This point is discussed further below pp. 375-376. More generally on the theme of facing history in order to face the UK's future, see the Parekh Report, *The Future of Multi-Ethnic Britain* (Profile Books, 2000).

The national re-imagining is, of course, also grounded in constitutional reform. As part of this reform package, freedom of information has been given a new prominence, having acquired statutory backing in 1998 and 2000.[19] The New Labour government responsible for that legislation also insists that it is committed to both open government and data protection; it has promised that it 'will govern with a new spirit of openness . . . [in] partnership with the people'.[20] For the first time, a Prime Minister has acknowledged that '[t]he traditional culture of secrecy will only be broken down by giving people in the United Kingdom the legal right to know'.[21]

For many, however, it is the centrepiece of New Labour's constitutional reform programme – the Human Rights Act 1998 – which provides the best evidence that we may be beyond the 'Secret State'. The Act, it is said, signals the potential demise of that most potent of civil liberties targets: the Official Secrets Act 1989 (OSA). It provides explicit statutory protection for the right to freedom of expression in Article 10. Furthermore, national security's capacity to operate as a limiting principle under Article 10(2) is tempered explicitly by the requirement that restrictions be 'necessary in a democratic society'.[22] The sense that there has been change is given a further boost by an apparent shift in the approach of the European Court of Human Rights towards weighing 'national security' interests: it seems that the traditionally generous 'margin of appreciation' afforded to member states is being replaced by a more searching analysis.[23]

The array of new legal weapons for challenging the OSA 1989 was embraced almost immediately by what appears to be a new breed of 'whistleblower' in the security services. David Shayler, for example, a one-time 'political exile in Paris' returned voluntarily to the UK in 2000 to face a criminal prosecution.[24] Senior judges responded in dramatic fashion to the initial rounds of the Shayler litigation involving the media, emphasising that the familiar *Spycatcher*-style injunctions

---

19 See the Public Interest Disclosure Act 1998; and the Freedom of Information Act 2000. For analysis of the 1998 Act, see eg, Y. Cripps, 'The Public Interest Disclosure Act 1998' in J. Beatson and Y. Cripps (eds.), *Freedom of Expression and Freedom of Information: Essays in Honour of Sir David Williams* (OUP, 2000), pp. 275-288; J. Gobert and M. Punch, 'Whistleblowers, the Public Interest and the Public Interest Disclosure Act' (2000) 63 MLR 25; and L. Vickers, 'Whistling in the Wind? The Public Interest Disclosure Act 1998' (2000) 20 LS 428.

20 Lord Irvine, 'Constitutional Reform and a Bill of Rights' [1997] EHRLR 483.

21 *Your Right To Know: Freedom of Information* (Cm. 3818, 1997), Preface. See below, pp. 363-365.

22 Art. 10(1) provides, in part, that 'Everyone has the right to freedom of expression. This right shall include freedom to hold opinions and to receive and impart information and ideas without interference by public authority and regardless of frontiers. . . .'. Art. 10(2) provides that: 'The exercise of these freedoms, since it carries with it duties and responsibilities, may be subject to such formalities, conditions, restrictions or penalties as are prescribed by law and are necessary in a democratic society, in the interests of national security, territorial integrity or public safety, for the prevention of disorder or crime, for the protection of health or morals, for the protection of the reputation or rights of others, for preventing the disclosure of information received in confidence, or for maintaining the authority and impartiality of the judiciary.'

23 The most significant recent examples involving the UK are: *McCann* (1995) 21 EHRR 97; *Chahal* (1996) 23 EHRR 413; *Tinnelly* (1998) 27 EHRR 249; and *Jordan* (4 May 2001).

24 See M. Hollingsworth and N. Fielding, *Defending the Realm: MI5 and the Shayler Affair* (Andre Deutsch, 2000). In Apr. 2001, the Shayler defence team commenced an HRA-challenge to the OSA 1989 – invoking Art. 10 (re the absence of a harm test or public interest defence) – amidst media speculation that the criminal trial might eventually be abandoned. Significantly, Shayler's allegations about MI6 involvement in an assassination attempt plot to kill Libyan leader, Colonel Gadaffi, in 1995 were not included in the criminal charges, and are the subject of a Crown Prosecution Service investigation. See below, n. 226.

can no longer be used to subject 'the press to the censorship of the Attorney General'.[25] In particular, they departed from 'Cold War' precedents to proclaim the importance of press freedom in relation to matters of national security:

> Inconvenient or embarrassing revelations, whether for the security services or for public authorities should not be suppressed. Legal proceedings directed towards the working papers of an individual journalist or the premises of a newspaper or television programme publishing his or her reports, or the threat of such proceedings tends to inhibit discussion. . . . [T]he public is entitled to know the facts and, as the eyes and ears of the public, journalists are entitled to investigate and report the facts. [26]

In discussing the status of the 'Secret State' it would be misleading, however, to emphasise only post-1997 constitutional reform and its flagship, the HRA: there was also talk predating, and independent of, the Act of a new 'spirit of constitutional discipline'.[27] For example, episodes of sleaze and scandal in the early 1990s and, more importantly, the official reports thereon[28] foregrounded the need for a new governing etiquette; that is, for 'an outline of standards for how the political and administrative élite which governs the nation ought to behave'.[29] The judiciary were also jolted out of complacency as regards accepting ministerial assurances as to the content and bona fides of Public Interest Immunity (PII) certificates, the traditional device for keeping government information out of public forums.[30] Further evidence of an emergent new spirit was provided when, shortly after a sweeping general-election victory in 1997, New Labour announced that it would add an 'ethical' dimension to foreign policy. This addition never materialised fully but its brief appearance suggested that human rights considerations might eventually be made a relevant criterion in matters such as the granting of export licences to arms exporters.[31]

The immediate pre-HRA era also brought other notable developments. The Bank of England, a famously secretive institution, was cast free of government control and it proceeded immediately to publish the minutes of its meetings.

---

25 See *A-G v Punch Ltd* [2001] EWCA Civ 403, [2001] 2 All ER 655 (CA) (per Phillips MR) (condemning A-G's use of broadly-worded injunctions to prevent media reporting of the Shayler litigation); and *A-G v Times Newspapers* [2001] EWCA Civ 97, [2001] 1 WLR 885 (CA) (rejection of A-G's argument that, as regards the revelations of the former MI6 agent, Richard Tomlinson, the newspaper must demonstrate that the material was in public domain before publication).

26 *R v Central Criminal Court, ex p Bright* [2001] 2 All ER 244 (DC) (PACE 1984 does not oblige media to hand over to prosecution authorities information relating to Shayler allegations of an MI6 plot to assassinate the Libyan leader, Colonel Gadaffi).

27 L. Lustgarten, 'The Arms Trade and the Constitution: Beyond the Scott Report' (1998) 61 MLR 499, 499.

28 See the Scott Report on 'Arms to Iraq' (*Report of the Inquiry into the Export of Defence Equipment and Dual-Use Goods to Iraq and Related Prosecutions* (1996)) and the Nolan Report on 'Sleaze in Government' (*Report of the Committee on Standards in Public Life* (Cm. 2850-I, 1995)).

29 Lustgarten, above n. 27, p. 499.

30 For more details, see eg, I. Leigh and L. Lustgarten, 'Five Volumes in Search of Accountability: The Scott Report' (1996) 59 MLR 695; Leigh, above n. 16; and A. Tomkins, *The Constitution After Scott: Government Unwrapped* (Clarendon, 1998). The Saville Inquiry in Northern Ireland is taking a more robust approach to PII certificates, demanding and examining the full text of documents before agreeing to PII applications.

31 As yet, the promised legislation on regulating the arms trade has not materialised. UK arms sales to military regimes are continuing as before. For an argument that human rights considerations ought to be a factor in the granting of export licences, see L. Lustgarten, 'Constitutional Discipline and the Arms Trade: The Scott Report and Beyond' (1998) 69 Pol Q 422.

The once-secret recent exploits of the Special Air Service (SAS) also began to be aired to the public: first, through the officially-approved memoirs of the British Commander in the Gulf War, General Peter de la Billiere[32] and, later, through a string of bestsellers written by former SAS soldiers.[33] The biggest shift of the pre-HRA era, however, was the sweeping away of 'the particular British tradition of clothing secrecy in secrecy'.[34] Over the last decade, the secret services – MI5 and MI6 – have been rendered unrecognisably recognisable. '[They] . . . have a statutory existence. We know who heads them and where they operate from'.[35] Moreover, the services themselves appear to revel in their modernisation. They have, for example, displayed an impressive talent for public relations in almost everything they have done in recent years – from their choice of working environment (MI6's 'extraordinary gold pyramid at Vauxhall: surely a decoy?') to the 'glossy booklets' they shell out 'telling us about themselves'.[36] MI5, the agency concerned with internal security, has also been affected profoundly by developments in policing, in particular the increasing involvement of a 'multiplicity of institutional forms'[37] in the delivery of policing and security services and technologies.[38] The organisation is now bound within what Neil Walker describes as 'a powerful incrementalist dynamic'[39] of ever-greater national and supra-national policing strategies and operations: increasingly, therefore, the once-secret MI5 co-operates both domestically (with the National Criminal Intelligence Service (NCIS) and the National Crime Squad (NCS)) and at EU level (in Schengen and Europol).[40] In the HRA era, there are also some 'signs of an evolving oversight and a strengthening accountability'[41] as a result of the Regulation of Investigatory Powers Act 2000 (RIPA); a statute which has brought further 'legalisation' to all security service and policing agencies, but has also widened surveillance powers (for example, monitoring of electronic communications by the Government Technical Assistance Centre, a new body located in the premises of MI5) and adopted a strikingly minimalist approach to the promotion and protection of human rights.

32 P. de la Billiere, *Storm Command* (Harper Collins, 1995).
33 See eg, A. McNab, *Bravo Two Zero* (Corgi, 1994). For an analysis of recent discourses on the 'SAS soldier', see J. Newsinger, *Dangerous Men: Myth, Masculinity and the SAS* (Pluto, 1997).
34 D. Vincent, *The Culture of Secrecy: Britain, 1832-1998* (OUP, 1998), p. ix.
35 B. Porter, 'Boarder or Day Boy?', *LRB*, 15 Jul. 1999, 13, at pp. 14-15. As noted above, MI5 was put on a statutory footing in 1989 (the Security Service Act 1989); MI6 followed suit in 1994 (the Intelligence Services Act 1994). For commentary on the statutes, see respectively, I. Leigh and L. Lustgarten, 'The Security Service Act 1989' (1989) 52 MLR 801 and J. Wadham, 'The Intelligence Services Act 1994' (1994) 57 MLR 916.
36 Porter, ibid. See also the 'glossy' MI5 website at: www.mi5.gov.uk.
37 I. Loader, 'Plural Policing and Democratic Governance' (2000) 9 SLS 323, 323.
38 See eg, the Security Service Act 1996, ss. 1(1), 1(2) and 2, amending earlier legislation to provide MI5 with new duties in relation to the prevention and detection of serious crime. Walker, above n. 14, p. 222 argues that: '[a] combination of the Service's post-Cold War excess capacity . . . its experience of collaborating with the police against terrorism, and the determination of Government to mount a multi-strategic offensive against organised crime, produced a climate of policy which favoured the progressive encroachment of the Security Service upon the traditional domain of policing.'
39 Above n. 14, p. 223.
40 For more detail, see eg, L. Johnston, *Policing Britain: Risk, Security and Governance* (Longman, 2000); and Walker, ibid.
41 H. Fenwick, *Civil Rights: New Labour, Freedom and the Human Rights Act* (Longman, 2000), p. 336. See also, Y. Akdeniz et al., 'RIPA (1): BigBrother.gov.uk: State Surveillance in the Age of Information and Rights' [2001] Crim LR 73; and P. Mirfield, 'RIPA (2): Evidential Aspects' [2001] Crim LR 91.

Other recent trends also evidence a new pattern of governing arrangements and thereby further compound the sense that the 'Secret State' may have gone the way of the dinosaur. The national context has become 'more fragmented and less deferential'[42] as individuals have responded to their re-branding as clients, consumers and citizens. To take one obvious example, the culture of paternalism and secrecy in the NHS has been rocked by patient outrage at medical cover-ups, as evidenced by the Redfern and Kennedy Inquiries into events surrounding children's deaths in hospital.[43] More generally, it is increasingly clear that a newly-bullish public is alert to sleaze in government and is 'less and less willing to doff its cap to a monarchical state'.[44]

The global context, too, has altered. Historic friends and enemies of the UK state have moved on. The Commonwealth is long fragmented, the Cold War is over and the Berlin Wall has become a newsreel memory. Neo-liberalism has been acclaimed as triumphant and state after state has signed up for liberal capitalist credentials, provoking grandiose claims that the 'end of history' is nigh.[45] A further seismic shift was confirmed when NATO intervened in the Kosovo War: by deploying 'protection of human rights' as its legitimation for intervening in the 'internal affairs' of a foreign state, NATO fractured the historic relationship between human rights and international law and threw down a fundamental challenge to conventional thinking about the authority of 'the sovereign state'.[46] The UK also appears to be at a crucial crossroads in determining its own future national security agenda. Will it commit fully to a 'European' defence strategy, or will it pursue a 'special relationship' with the US (which has a Bush-administration that is committed to developing a 'missile shield' against new 'global enemies')? Less controversially, a range of democracies (including Australia, Canada, New Zealand and Ireland) have turned their attention in recent years to improving freedom of information. The EU is pursuing a similar course: in addressing its own 'democratic deficit', it seems intent on prioritising rights of access to EU information.[47] A range of individual states have also revised the ways in which they regulate their security services.[48] Finally, in an arguably connected development, numerous scholars worldwide have turned away from analysis of the state as Leviathan, and the repressive uses of law, and opted instead for themes such as state formation, governmentality and citizenship.[49]

---

42 Vincent, above n. 34, p. 308.
43 See respectively, *Royal Liverpool Children's Inquiry Report* (available at: www.rlcinquiry.org.uk) (re taking, storage and use of organs without consent) and *Bristol Royal Infirmary Inquiry: Interim Report* (available at: www.bristol-inquiry.org.uk/bristol.htm) (re deaths following surgery).
44 D. Marquand, 'Democracy in Britain' (2000) 71 Pol Q 268, 273.
45 See F. Fukuyama, *The End of History and the Last Man* (Free Press, 1992).
46 For discussion, see below pp. 372-374.
47 In May 2001, the European Parliament voted to bind EU institutions to a new code of public access to EU documents. For background see eg, D. Curtin, 'Citizens' Fundamental Right of Access to EU Information: An Evolving Digital Passepartout' (2000) 37 CMLR 7. The promise of greater transparency can be traced back to the 1997 Amsterdam Treaty; one trigger was *Carvel v EU Council*, Case T-194/94, [1996] All ER (EC) 53 (CFI) (a case concerning a *Guardian* journalist wherein the ECJ ruled that the Council has broken its own rules on access).
48 For details, see eg, Birkinshaw, above n. 9, pp. 50-81; and I. Leigh, 'Secret Proceedings in Canada' (1996) 34 Osg Hall LJ 113.
49 For an argument to this effect, see Wright, above n. 15.

Are we then beyond the 'Secret State'? The question is a difficult one. The developments outlined above ought not to be belittled. At the same time, however, old ways linger on and, paradoxically, in some respects they appear to have been entrenched by the general trend for 'openness'. New developments also appear to be spawning new configurations of security and secrecy. In what follows, we deal first with the tenacity of the old ways and then, more briefly, with emerging challenges. We shall return to the latter issue, and address it in more detail, in Part VI.

The evidence that old ways subsist is not inconsiderable. First, there is ongoing use of criminal and civil sanctions against investigative journalists and former members of the security services and army personnel.[50] A common feature of the collapsed prosecutions against journalists has been the attempt to criminalise disclosure of information that is already in the public domain. This would seem to indicate that reports that the OSA 1989 is officially considered 'unworkable' and is destined for sweeping reform in the HRA era[51] may be excessively optimistic.

Secondly, double standards are still operating as regards both the granting of 'authorisation' to former security-services' personnel to write memoirs and the granting of access to 'national security' records. There is, for example, an interesting contrast between the treatment of Richard Tomlinson, an ex-MI6 agent, who sought official co-operation in relation to his memoirs and that of Stella Rimmington, the former Director General of MI5. Tomlinson was refused authorisation and served a prison sentence in 1997 after pleading guilty to breaching the OSA 1989 while attempting to find a publisher.[52] Rimmington, by contrast, obtained approval for her memoirs, *Open Secret*, and the book's pre-publication publicity, which describes it as an account of the 'difficult task of balancing openness and secrecy in [her] professional and private life', promises that Rimmington will promote it via the 'chat-show circuit'.[53]

The question of access to 'national security' files is also troubling. The trend for 'official histories' of MI5 and MI6 has been criticised as 'reeking of hypocrisy'. In effect, the security and intelligence services are providing 'notionally classified

---

50   Tony Geraghty and Nigel Wylde were charged under the OSA 1989 following the publication of the book, *The Irish War* (Harper Collins, 1998). Wylde was a computer consultant who had worked for the MoD in Northern Ireland; Geraghty was a journalist (he was the first journalist to be prosecuted under the 1989 Act). The charges against both were dropped in 2000 on the advice of the A-G. In 2000, a former undercover soldier, known as 'Martin Ingram', was arrested on suspicion of breaching the OSA 1989 following the publication in *The Sunday Times* in 1999 of articles written by the journalist Liam Clarke, based on interviews with 'Ingram', detailing undercover operations in Northern Ireland. In Apr. 2001, the MoD obtained an injunction preventing Ulster Television from showing a documentary alleging that soldiers committed serious criminal acts, with official knowledge, while working as double agents within the IRA.

51   See M. Bright, 'Former Spies To Be Given a Licence to Tell', *The Observer*, 31 Dec. 2000 (claiming that spy memoirs will be permitted if vetted in advance, and that a narrower definition of national security risk – 'grave threat to the state' – is to be introduced).

52   In Jan. 2001, his memoirs were published in Russia and other countries under the title, *The Big Breach: From Top Security to Maximum Security*. See D. Campbell, 'Reading This Open Book of British Spies', *The Guardian*, 14 May 1999 (alleging that Tomlinson had placed the names of 124 MI6 members, including agents serving in the Balkans, on the Internet).

53   Contrast *A-G v Blake* [2000] 4 All ER 385 (HL) (wherein the HL, as a 'punishment', extended the private law claim to restitutionary damages against profits made by George Blake, a former MI6 agent who escaped to the Soviet Union in the 1966, from his memoirs, *No Other Choice*).

information to selected writers for mutual reward':[54] much of this information is already in the public domain but the idea of 'behind-the-scenes' access generates both an aura of respectability and the prospect of higher sales.[55] Those who are not officially approved for access are treated very differently, however. In 1997, whilst researching their book, *The Struggle for Civil Liberties: Political Freedom and the Rule of Law in Britain 1914-1945*, Keith Ewing and Conor Gearty wrote to the Home Office requesting access to files relating to the period 1908 to 1945. They asked that 101 pieces be opened: they were informed that '[a]ll but one are closed for 100 years'.[56] Relatedly, new mechanisms of oversight and accountability do not appear to have ended the practice of keeping information about the activities of the security services from the Home Secretary.[57] Evidence of this is provided by what became known as the 'KGB Granny' affair, which brought to light how MI5 and MI6 had kept the identity of former KGB agents living in the UK from government ministers for over six years. The affair also illustrated that the decision on whether or not to investigate and prosecute 87-year-old Melita Norwood, the 'KGB Granny', was taken by MI5 alone – that is, without consulting or informing ministers.[58] Finally, to the dismay of historians, MI5 continues to destroy evidence of its own past activities; thousands of files have been shredded. Two prompts towards recent shredding appear to have been, first, curbing embarrassment following leaks by former agents and, second, (and paradoxically,) the trend towards open government. In effect, MI5 seems to have destroyed files in an attempt to avoid potential compulsory disclosure.[59]

Official secrecy is also alive and kicking outside the realm of 'national security'. The final version of the Freedom of Information Act 2000 induced 'a vehement sense of betrayal'[60] at the watering-down of the initial proposals and

---

54 R. Norton-Taylor, 'Hot Air and Humbug', *The Guardian*, 2 Oct. 1999. Examples of books written with the 'co-operation' of MI6 include C. Andrew and V. Mitrokhin, *The Mitrokhin Archive* (Penguin, 2000); and A. Judd, *The Quest for C* (Harper Collins, 2000) (focusing on the life of MI6's first director, Cumming).

55 Norton-Taylor, ibid., points to the following example of how the services are seeking to control the release of information: 'MI6 . . . provided special access to the makers of the BBC television series, *The Spying Game*, which included an interview with Sir Gerald Warner, former MI6 deputy chief, who not so long ago complained that his safety had been put at risk by being named in the *Guardian*.'

56 Ewing and Gearty, above n. 2, p. 419.

57 In 2000, MI5 agreed to unprecedented scrutiny of its files by the parliamentary committee established under the Intelligence Services Act 1994, the Intelligence and Security Committee, in order to defuse criticism of its handling of the 'Vasili Mitrokhin Archive'. MI5 and MI6 liaised directly and indirectly with the media to release information from the archive, which contains papers on the KGB's infiltration of security services (including those of the US and the UK). For details on the use of secret services' intelligence in government decision-making, see eg, Tomkins, above n. 30, Ch. 4.

58 See the statement made by Prime Minister Tony Blair: 351 HC Debs 576 (13 Jun. 2000).

59 No opposition appears to have come from the Labour politicians targeted, despite the fact that a large number – eg, Peter Hain, Clare Short, Harriet Harman, Joan Ruddock, Jack Straw and Peter Mandelson – allegedly were placed under surveillance by security services and military intelligence in relation to alleged subversive activities in the 1970s and 1980s. In a statement to the House of Commons in 1998, the Home Secretary, Jack Straw, revealed that, of 725,000 files opened by MI5 since 1909, 285,000 have been destroyed (110,000 of these destructions occurred in the early 1990s): 317 HC Debs 251-254 (29 Jul. 1998).

60 P. Birkinshaw and N. Parry, 'The End of the Beginning? The Freedom of Information Bill 1991' (1999) 26 JLS 538, 553.

the defiant consolidation of executive power over official information. Political parties and others continue to seek to influence media agendas by making officially-tailored disclosures or, more often, by pre-emptive leaking.[61] Historians still make an annual pilgrimage to the Public Records Office in Kew in the hope of accessing 30-year-old secrets about the UK's past. Their hopes are sometimes dashed: further restrictions have, for example, recently been placed on the disclosure of records dealing with Edward VIII's abdication in 1936. A sense of dejà-vu also suffuses the Phillips Report into BSE, published in October 2000: the Report peels back the layers of official secrecy that protected bungled decision-making for over a decade and generated ongoing crises in both public health and public trust. This and other recent scandals may invoke more than a sense of dejà-vu, however. They may also feed a worrying disaffection: as Stephen Sedley has pointed out, 'repeated revelations over recent years that people in whom the public put its trust have been lying not only to the media but to Parliament and the courts have *shaken our confidence in our own scepticism*'.[62]

Finally, mention needs to be made of some of the ways in which new developments – such as the altered remit of the security services or the emergence within NATO of what Orford has called 'muscular humanitarianism'[63] – may be generating new problems. The increasing involvement of MI5 in the prevention and detection of 'serious crime' – tasks it shares with other agencies – means that 'spy masters' (and policing) have become a much more complex target for the civil libertarian. The grip of capitalism on liberal democracies also points to emerging problems. Commercial espionage appears to have become a priority for countries who desire a decisive advantage, but what are we to make of 'friendly' governments spying on one another?[64] Similarly, will powerful transnational companies, and public-private partnerships, hide behind 'commercial confidentiality' to counter the trend towards 'openness' and 'disclosure'? Relatedly, are discourses on 'freedom of information' focused too exclusively on individuals' needs for information to be 'effective citizens'? That is, do they assume 'a rather bright line between what is public and private', and approach 'issues involving information as primarily a governmental issue', at a time when 'the real-world basis' of such a distinction between government and the private sector is 'fast becoming a part of the past'?[65] More generally, will the lever provided by the emerging culture of freedom of information be used most often in company-on-company litigation, as competitors seek to gain a commercial advantage or to stymie the advantage of others?[66]

These are the sorts of questions to which we shall return in Part VI. In addition, Part V will provide further details on the post-1990 'glasnost'. In the

---

61   See eg, P. Oborne, *Alastair Campbell: New Labour and the Rise of the Media Class* (Aurum, 1999).
62   S. Sedley, 'Information as a Human Right' in Beatson and Cripps (eds.), above n. 19, pp. 239-248, at p. 239.
63   A. Orford, 'Muscular Humanitarianism: Reading the Narratives of the New Interventionism' (1999) 10 EJIL 679.
64   France, and members of the European Parliament, are investigating the US-led Echelon spying network (which includes the Cheltenham-based GCHQ), after allegations of economic espionage in relation to the award of military and aviation contracts.
65   A.C. Aman, Jr., 'Information, Privacy and Technology' in Beatson and Cripps (eds.), above n. 19, pp. 325-348, at p. 328.
66   This has been the pattern in the US: see Aman, Jr., ibid., p. 332. It has, however, had the further effect of opening up to the public some of what goes on inside companies.

intervening Parts, we shall look, first, at the traditional 'culture of secrecy' in the UK and, secondly, at the Official Secrets Acts of 1889, 1911 and 1989.

II.   SECRECY: THE BRITISH WAY

Secrecy, spies and spying are inextricably linked in British popular culture. Good evidence of this is provided, for example, by the world of Ian Fleming's James Bond. Therein, a code of blanket but 'honourable' secrecy is promoted as fundamental to effective 'Defence of the Realm'.[67] The '00s' were the (quintessentially English[68]) gentlemen servants of 'Her Majesty's Secret Services': as is well-known, they were bound by total, life-long allegiance to the Crown; trusted with a 'licence to kill'; and were rarely distant from activities that appeared the very stuff of espionage. They traversed an exceptionally shadowy world wherein personal identities had to be masked by initials such as 'Q' and the locations of central London buildings were non-facts. In their world, it was entirely plausible that *any* disclosure of 'insider' information potentially could lead to the demise of good and the triumph of evil: '007' may have had a maverick streak but he never failed to understand this core truth about his world. In addition, in his environment, secrecy blended perfectly with the gentlemanly virtues of reserve and reticence. That is, the secrecy of Her Majesty's Secret Services was never the secrecy of 'foreign despotism' or of 'dirty tricks'.

But what, if anything, is the relationship between the world of the '00s' and that of British secrecy itself? The relationship seems to be a complex one. There are parallels, but only some of them run deep: others, by contrast, have been pumped up by the security services themselves, with the assistance of consecutive governments and the civil service in Whitehall. One deep parallel concerns the paramount principle of 'vigilance'. In the British 'Secret State', threats to 'British lives and interests' (and to those of 'our allies') were both always-present and potentially fatal. Two World Wars helped to keep the principle of 'war-readiness' at the forefront of everyone's mind. Threats were, however, never seen as merely external to national borders: the 'enemy within' was deemed to co-exist with (and, sometimes, to act as agent or agitator for) the more deadly external forces. Germany and the Soviet Union featured prominently in the latter category for much of the twentieth century: the former was the source of concern about the 'spy scare in Edwardian England, "hidden hand" in the First World War [and] Nazism in the 1930s and 1940s';[69] the latter was an enduring preoccupation because 'the Red Menace [was] orchestrated from Moscow'.[70] At the same time, however, the slow decline of the 'British Empire', as well as the flow of social and economic change in British society, fomented the sense

---

67   The titles are classic: eg, *On Her Majesty's Secret Service; Live And Let Die;* and *The Man With The Golden Gun.*

68   As many of the references throughout this chapter will indicate, description and analysis of what has become known as the '*British* culture of secrecy' tends generally to elide '*Englishness*' with 'Britishness'. Of course, the most successful 007 was a Scot: Sean Connery.

69   R. Thurlow, *The Secret State: British Internal Security in the Twentieth Century* (Blackwell, 1994), p. 396.

70   Ibid. For other discussions of these points, see C. Pincher, *Their Trade is Treachery* (Sidgwick & Jackson, 1982); C. Andrew, *Secret Service: The Making of the British Intelligence Community* (Sceptre, 1986); and S. Dorril, *MI6: Fifty Years of Special Operations* (Fourth Estate, 2000).

of shadowy enemies *on all fronts*.[71] Furthermore, the backgrounds and closed working worlds of security services' members, their civil service 'handlers' at Whitehall and members of Parliament fed this general sense that 'the enemy' was (not far) out there.[72]

A second deep parallel between fact and fiction on secrecy, spies and spying concerns what has variously been described as the 'passion for secrecy' or 'the British disease [of secrecy]' as regards national security. If one leaves to one side the 'off-the-record' lobby briefings that were provided by a series of governments to a largely deferential press, it is clear that, in the UK, secrecy – or in Porter's more apposite phrase 'secret secrecy' – prevailed as regards the activities and culture of the security services (and all other intelligence and defence organisations, such as GCHQ).[73] The UK, in a move that set it apart from many other countries, adopted a position of official denial in respect of the existence of the secret services:

> Questions about them in Parliament were ignored; writing to them was like sending messages to Father Christmas; they operated from invisible headquarters: shoddy office blocks in London, blanks on the Ordinance Survey map.[74]

Most of the time, this position appeared to suit both governments and the security services themselves. Both appreciated the flexibility that 'secret secrecy' offered to them: it allowed both to be 'prepared' – that is, largely unconstrained – as regards any future threats. 'Secret secrecy' also suited their individual purposes. It suited the security services because, on occasion, it protected them from embarrassment over genuine gaffs and, more importantly, from 'the suspicions that [attached] to better-known [foreign] secret agencies, and the dangers of wing-clipping that [followed]'.[75] It suited many governments because it protected them from what might called the paradox of the 'British way': that is, from the distaste for secret plans and dirty tricks as 'un-British' which featured alongside the 'passion for secrecy' in Establishment thinking. In connection with this, Thurlow directs attention to the 'instructive atmosphere' of John le Carre's spy novels wherein:

> the seedy secret world of Smiley's people is kept at arms length from the work of government by the administrative intermediary from Whitehall . . . Not only does such an arrangement remove responsibility for dubious activities from politicians in the fictional world, but it also enables them to pretend that they are not aware of what is allegedly going on, that if it is illegal it will be dealt with, for such behaviour is not the British way.[76]

---

71 Scotland Yard's Special Branch was created in 1883 to counter the threat posed by militant Irish nationalism.

72 Porter, above n. 35, p. 14 notes that former Prime Minister 'Edward Heath describes MI5 operatives as the sort of men who would follow people on the Underground because they were reading the *Daily Mirror*' and that other Establishment figures have characterised the secret service personnel with whom they have had encounters as 'limited, obsessed and politically prejudiced'.

73 Porter, ibid., explains the concept of 'secret secrecy' as follows: '[n]ot only are we secretive, we are secretive about how secretive we are. We aren't allowed to know, and don't on the whole seem to care, what is being kept from us'.

74 Ibid., p. 13.

75 Ibid.

76 Thurlow, above n. 69, p. 395. See also Porter, ibid., commenting that '[i]f this had been a less liberal country, it might well have become a less secretive one'.

In his book, *Spycatcher*, former MI5 agent Peter Wright supplements the le Carre account by pointing out that the 'administrative intermediary from Whitehall' also deliberately asked no questions: 'we did have fun. For five years we bugged and burgled our way across London at the State's behest, while pompous bowler-hatted civil servants in Whitehall pretended to look the other way.'[77] As we shall see below, however, this blanketing of the activities of the security services contributed to an elision of 'national security' with secrecy, which caused deep and enduring problems.[78] In particular, the elision provided cover historically for gross violations of civil liberties. It also stymied critical thinking – or perhaps it would be better to say any thinking whatsoever – on what Lustgarten and Leigh call 'a democratic conception of national security'.[79]

A third parallel between the real and fictional worlds of secrecy, spies and spying concerns the resourcefulness and bravery of some members of the intelligence and security services. It was these virtues, for example, which helped to crack the German Enigma code during the Second World War.[80] The belief that British lives were saved and democracy depended on the security services ingrained absolute secrecy as a 'price worth paying', and bolstered the notion that the 'people in the field' had to be defended against attack. In 1998 then Foreign Secretary, Robin Cook, appeared to reflect this sentiment when he emphasised that MI6 cannot speak for themselves because 'the nature of what they do means that we cannot shout about their achievements if we want them to remain effective. But let me say I have been struck by the range and quality of the work'.[81]

As noted earlier, however, parallels between fiction and fact were also played up by the security services, with the assistance of ministers and Whitehall. MI5, for example, 'actively promoted its own image and frequently encouraged myths about its power and influence. . . . All communications with MI5 headquarters were to be sent by telegram in code, however prosaic the contents'.[82] More generally, the 'gloss' of the '007 factor' provided cover for the culture of 'botched amateurism and eccentricity'[83] that operated alongside the services' 'public' reputation for efficiency and effectiveness. Very often, MI5 and MI6 were preoccupied with their own competition for individual dominance. They sought, for example, to blame one another for mistakes: a stance which does not tend to lead to critical reflection on how and why things went wrong, and

---

77 P. Wright, *Spycatcher* (Heinemann, 1987), p. 54.

78 For the same emphasis, see in particular, Lustgarten and Leigh, above n. 5, p. 30 noting that '[i]n the minds of many people, and particularly in discussions in the media, national security and secrecy are so entangled that they seem to be identical. This is a mistaken equation and an unfortunate confusion, for although there is some overlap, they are for the most part unconnected'.

79 See Lustgarten and Leigh, above n. 5, pp. 3-38 for proposals as to how such a conception of national security might be created. The proposals are also outlined below pp. 371-372.

80 For more details on the breaking of the code, see eg, H. Sebag-Montefiore, *Enigma* (Phoenix, 2001). A. Hodges, *Alan Turing: The Enigma* (Vintage, 1992) provides a biography of a key figure involved in the breaking of the code.

81 *The Observer*, 26 Mar. 2000.

82 N. West, *MI5: British Security Service Operations 1909-1945* (Grafton, 1981), p. 19. See also the MI5 website, above n. 36, for a webpage explicitly rebutting the notion that both the colour of the carpet in the MI5 building and the canteen menu are 'official secrets'.

83 Birkinshaw, above n. 9, p. 27. See also, B. Levin, *The Pendulum Years: Britain and the Sixties* (Pan Books, 1977), p. 51: '[John Profumo, Secretary of State for War] assumed that the security services had discovered his liaison with [Christine Keeler in 1961] . . . In this he was greatly over-estimating the ability of the security services as, alas, others frequently have, to the great peril of the realm, for in fact the security services knew nothing of the affair.'

how similar mistakes might be prevented in the future.[84] Notoriously, there were instances where the services made the mistake of failing to notice the double-agent treachery of their own colleagues.[85] Taking stock of all of this, the historian David Vincent urges the need for a measured and thoughtful approach to the history of the security services:

> On some occasions the spies and spymasters held the fate of nations in their hands, on others they represented little more than a pioneering form of care in the community for distressed former public-school boys. It is not clear at times whether their obscurity was a defence against ridicule, or their eccentricity a constructed distraction from their more deliberate purpose.[86]

Vincent, however, also insists rightly that no sensible approach to the British 'Secret State' would look at the security services alone. Secrecy, as he, numerous other historians and some lawyers have emphasised, was '*the British way*', not merely the security services' way.[87] Historians, and some lawyers, have also been steadfast in their insistence that the 'British way of secrecy' was more cultural than institutional. In particular, that it was the product of an 'unwritten ethos'. To see the 'Secret State' in this way, they emphasise, is to understand:

> both . . . its success, which can be credited very largely to the culturally-bolstered probity of those who exercised it; and . . . its resilience – cultures are able to adapt to changes in circumstances more subtly than institutions can. Hence the hold gentlemanly reticence still has on certain areas of British public life, including the secret services, despite the relative scarcity of English gentlemen.[88]

---

84 See eg, P. Knightley, *The Second Oldest Profession: The Spy as Bureaucrat, Patriot, Fantasist and Whore* (Pan, 1987), arguing that the security services are essentially bureaucracies, with the same interest in empire-building, and blame-avoidance in the event of failure and scandals, as other government departments.

85 See eg, West, above n. 82, p. 425 on Anthony Blunt 'who volunteered his services to the War Office in 1938. In reply he received by the same post, but in two separate envelopes, an official refusal of his offer and acceptance. Ignoring the refusal, Blunt took a posting in 1939 . . . and began a Staff Officer's intelligence course'.

86 Vincent, above n. 34, pp. 16-17. See also, C. Hitchens, 'The Spy Who Went Out in the Cold', *Vanity Fair* Oct. 2000, p. 36 at p. 44: 'At Oxford, one could always spot the potential recruit. He was the baying foxhunting enthusiast with muttonchop side-whiskers and a sporty waistcoat, as thick as two bricks but fond of guzzling sherry with the more depraved dons. I personally spotted the one in my class, only wavering when I thought it was too obvious, but later reading contentedly of his calamitous exposure as a failed gunrunner for MI6.' See also, Wright, above n. 77, p. 36: 'Every year the Office virtually closed to attend the Lord's Test Match, where MI5 had an unofficial patch in the Lord's Tavern. And every morning senior officers, almost without exception, spent the first half hour of the day on *The Times* crossword.'

87 For similar points, see eg, P. Hennessy, *Whitehall* (Secker & Warburg, 1989), p. 347 (arguing that secrecy was not only the civil service's way but 'as much a part of the English landscape as the Cotswolds. It goes with the grain of our society'); L. Lustgarten, 'Review of K.D. Ewing and C.A. Gearty, *The Struggle for Civil Liberties* (OUP, 2000)' [2000] PL 739, 740 (arguing that surveillance 'has been, and remains, a key issue for the political Left, particularly where the use of informers serves to spread distrust and obsessive secrecy among activists'); C. Ponting, *Secrecy in Britain* (Basil Blackwell, 1990); and D. Wilson (ed.), *The Secrets File: The Case for Freedom of Information in Britain Today* (Heinemann, 1984), p. 1 (arguing that secrecy is 'more entrenched in the psyche of the governing and managerial elite than is the case in any comparable country').

88 Porter, above n. 35, p. 14. For an insight into the changing worlds of 'gentlemen', compare R. McKibbin, *Classes and Cultures: England 1918-1951* (OUP, 1998); A. Sampson, *The Anatomy of Britain* (Hodder & Stoughton, 1962); and J. Paxman, *Friends in High Places: Who Runs Britain?* (Penguin, 1991). For the flipside of the 'British culture of secrecy' – that is, extensive violations, at various periods, of the privacy of those individuals and groups who were deemed to have lost the 'right' to keep secrets (eg, social welfare claimants, trade unionists, student activists and homosexuals) – see generally, Ch. 6.

To see the 'Secret State' in this way, however, does not amount to saying that law was irrelevant to the phenomenon. Law *did* play a role, most notably via successive Official Secrets Acts. We shall discuss that legislation in the next two parts of the chapter. The point, however, is that law played *a supporting role*. Thus, the 'Secret State' was not the product of law or other institutional measures alone; it was also, and pre-eminently, a cultural phenomenon and, as we emphasise in the remainder of this section, it can in large part be traced back to fears that were generated and sustained by the UK's class system. Similarly, the challenge to the 'Secret State' in the late-twentieth century was also prompted in large part by cultural change: here, too, law played a supporting role. In particular, crass attempts to enforce the Official Secrets Act 1911 eventually helped to bring it into disrepute, and the burgeoning emphasis on human rights provided a lever against the 'culture of secrecy', specifically, the latter's elision of 'national security' with secrecy.[89]

Several commentators have traced the emergence of the 'Secret State' to the fears that rocked governing culture in the nineteenth century when it became clear that, with expanded governmental functions, came a corresponding expansion in government employees. Government, in other words, could no longer be 'a semi-private matter for the élite'.[90] As a consequence of fears about the impact of expansion of government – in particular, about the impact of expansion on the civil service's ethos of 'gentlemanly secrecy' – emphasis began to be placed on *control* of 'official information'.[91]

The civil service's ethos of 'gentlemanly secrecy' was much prized; correspondingly, its loss was greatly feared. Its 'protected status' is evident for example in the resistance to the 1854 Northcote-Trevelyan Report's recommendation of competitive entry into the civil service based on examination. Outraged opponents of the recommendation insisted that 'honourable secrecy' depended on qualities which could never be made 'the subject of examination'.[92] Its 'protected status' also contributed to 'the peculiar combination of integrity and invisibility'[93] that came to characterise the British civil service and thus to the (not entirely implausible) description of the service as 'the best civil service in the world'.

Fear became almost rampant when, from the late-nineteenth century onwards, growth in central administration made civil service expansion unavoidable. That expansion introduced a new 'lower-class' of employee to the civil service, one who could not be trusted to share the code of 'honourable secrecy' of his or her 'gentlemanly' superiors and who, therefore, threatened the entire 'unwritten ethos'. The spectre of the 'disloyal Crown servant' emerged at around this time and began its long haunt of officialdom.[94] It invoked the

---

89   See further below, pp. 354-359.
90   C. Ponting, 'Review of D. Vincent, *The Culture of Secrecy: Britain 1832-1998* (OUP, 1998)' (2000) 27 JLS 335, 336.
91   Vincent documents a parallel growth in professional secrecy at the same period, as doctors, social workers and others sought to mark out and protect individual spheres of competence.
92   George Cornewall Lewis, cited in Birkinshaw, above n. 9, p. 93.
93   Vincent, above n. 34, p. 123.
94   Birkinshaw, above n. 9, p. 96 notes the issuance in 1873 of a Treasury minute on *The Premature Disclosure of Official Documents*. The minute expressed 'concern at what today we would refer to as civil service "leaks" to the press'. It castigated the unauthorised use of official information as 'the worst fault a civil servant can commit. It is on the same footing as cowardice by a soldier. It is unprofessional': see D. Hooper, *Official Secrets: The Use and Abuse of the Act* (Secker & Warburg, 1987), p. 21.

idea of ever-increasing numbers of government employees who could not be *trusted* to keep information secret.[95] This spectre was the catalyst for the Official Secrets Act 1911, which purported to institutionalise the 'unwritten ethos' by requiring employees to 'sign the Official Secrets Act'.[96]

But the new law on 'signing the Act' never quite dampened down fears associated with the ever-increasing number of 'non-gentleman', civil service employees. Moreover, as was made clear by evidence given to the 1972 Franks Committee on *Section 2 of the Official Secrets Act 1911*, many senior civil servants felt that the 'dangers multiplied in proportion to the distance from the centre' because '[e]xplicit trust, let alone implicit authorization, had no abode at the penumbra of the system' where one found 'troublesome but indispensable staff [who] were beyond the reach of convention or regulation':

> junior clerks who arrived without a history, the 'girls who get married, go off to have babies and then come back', the tens of thousands of employees who viewed the civil service as not a vocation but a perch in a varied or truncated career. So little was known about the past or future of the typists that those employed on sensitive work were having to be re-vetted every year.[97]

The law was also no match for the exponential growth of information technology, which had a dramatic effect on the culture of 'leaking'. As Vincent points out, the 'growing presence in government offices of the photocopier and then the FAX machine meant that illicit communication was no longer dependent on theft or memory as in the time of the prototype leaker . . .'.[98]

Parallel trends can be found in the history of the security services over the course of the twentieth century. Thus, Peter Wright's book, *Spycatcher*, reveals that MI5 was pushed, 'belatedly, into accepting a computerized Registry' but only when the problem of staffing and vetting became insurmountable – that is when, despite the fact that 'more than three hundred girls' were employed, 'the surge of file collection' was such that 'the pressure for more recruits was never-ending'.[99] More recently, traces of the premium placed historically on 'honourable secrecy' can be found in the tut-tutting over David Shayler's 'inappropriate' background and the related general rumblings about the dangers of introducing 'diversity' into the ranks of MI5.[100]

The final decades of the twentieth century brought particularly seismic changes in governing culture, which affected both the civil service and the security services in a far-reaching way. Many, although by no means all, of these changes can be traced to the clash between the ethos of Thatcherism and that of 'honourable secrecy'. In the immediate post-1979 era, civil service mandarins

---

95 Early drafts of the 1889 legislation were titled the 'Breach of Official Trust Bill' and 'The Public Documents Act'.

96 It institutionalised the ethos in other ways too: as Ponting, above n. 90, p. 336 points out: 'the Franks committee found out in the early 1970s [that] nobody in Whitehall could explain how authorization [to release information] was obtained except that those at the top "knew" when it could and could not be done.'

97 Vincent, above n. 34, p. 251.

98 Ibid., p. 263.

99 Above n. 77, p. 39. Wright also revealed that, up until the early 1970s, MI5 had been using a manual system of card files wherein 'needles were placed through the holes in the master card to locate any other cards which fitted the same constellation'.

100 See below pp. 366-368.

initially attempted to cling onto the service's traditional ethos.[101] Their attempts, however, were destined for failure amidst the transformation of media practices by a new breed of government press officers and politicians, who prioritised selective leaking to (select) journalists as a way by which to both control news agendas and deflect blame onto others.[102] The leak was elevated to 'an instrument of [Mrs Thatcher's] personal power'.[103]

The Thatcher era was not 'against secrecy, but it was deeply hostile to the forces which had maintained official secrecy'.[104] Moreover, the law on secrecy appears to have been a trifling consideration for some of its key figures. Bernard Ingham, Mrs Thatcher's rumbustious press officer, famously declared that he 'never regarded the Official Secrets Act as a constraint on operations':

> Indeed, I regard myself as licensed to break that law as and when I judge necessary.[105]

Thatcherism also brought a series of radical reforms to the civil service and thereby further compromised residual traces of the tradition of 'honourable secrecy'. Efficiency drives, outside contractors, new procedures and agencies left the old civil service traditions in tatters. Some individual civil servants reacted in a 'non-traditional' way to these developments: they 'blew the whistle' on 'unconstitutional' behaviour on the part of ministers. Two dramatic examples of this phenomenon were Sarah Tisdall and Clive Ponting. In 1983, Tisdall, who worked in the Foreign Office, blew the whistle on the secret deployment of nuclear Cruise missiles in Britain. A year later, in 1984, Ponting, who worked in the Ministry of Defence, blew the whistle on misleading accounts of the torpedoing of the *General Belgrano* during the Falklands War.[106]

In effect, then, by the twilight of the twentieth century, traditional political conventions had disappeared and tensions were pervasive: civil servants 'no longer trusted Ministers . . . ; politicians no longer trusted their advisers to observe their traditions of discrete reserve'.[107] Structural and personnel reforms, modelled on private sector norms, vied with the remnants of the civil service ethos that had been established a century earlier. Thatcherism's effects on British society more generally caused further ripples in the 'culture of secrecy'. In particular, Thatcherism's appeal to individualism and its attacks on consensus, privilege and bureaucracy, encouraged more self-assurance and less deference amongst the middle classes.

---

101 Hennessy, above n. 87, pp. 664-665 notes that, in 1983, after a series of leaks, the head of the Civil Service appealed to Permanent Secretaries to reassert 'the values and the sense of professional obligation and loyalty which will make . . . leaks unacceptable and unthinkable at any time'.

102 The 'other' who took the blame was often the civil service.

103 P. Jenkins, *Mrs Thatcher's Revolution: The Ending of the Socialist Era* (Jonathan Cape, 1987), p. 184.

104 Porter, above n. 35, p. 14. Some of the forces of official secrecy appeared to escape cost-cutting: 'MI5 earned [Prime Minister Thatcher's] undying gratitude. Thames House is a measure of the effectiveness of MI5's strategy. Nigel Lawson, the former Chancellor of the Exchequer, remarked acidly of Thatcher's attitude: ". . . Margaret, an avid reader of the works of Frederick Forsyth, was positively besotted by [the security services]"': see S. Milne, *The Enemy Within: The Secret War Against the Miners* (Verso, 1994), p. 249.

105 Cited in C. Hitchens, 'What is This Bernard', *LRB*, 10 Jan. 1991, p. 13.

106 Tisdall was sentenced to six months' imprisonment under the OSA 1911; the Ponting case delivered the death-knell to the OSA 1911 when the jury defied the judge's direction effectively to convict. See C. Ponting, *The Right to Know: The Inside Story of the Belgrano Affair* (Sphere Books, 1985); and K.D. Ewing and C.A. Gearty, *Freedom Under Thatcher: Civil Liberties in Modern Britain* (OUP, 1990), pp. 129-169.

107 Vincent, above n. 34, p. 264.

As we shall see below, 1989 brought a new and much-opposed Official Secrets Act. Yet as Vincent points out, the Act's dependence on 'a conception of a monolithic civil service',[108] at a time when such an entity no longer existed, was rather telling. Without that entity, the traditional 'delicate' relationship between the law and culture of official secrecy could not be sustained, and the future promised further unavoidable change.

III.   A SUPPORTING ROLE: THE OFFICIAL SECRETS ACTS OF 1889 AND 1911

In Part II, following numerous historians, we emphasised that the 'British way of secrecy' was more cultural than institutional. Law, we said, played only a supporting role. In that role, however, it was rarely less than effective. In particular, as we show in this Part, it propped up the 'culture of secrecy' within government. Our particular interest here, however, is to show how law facilitated the elision of 'national security' with 'official secrecy' and helped, thus, to stymie the development of 'a democratic conception' of national security.

The 1889 and 1911 Acts: second time lucky?

The Official Secrets Act 1889 was seldom used.[109] It is of interest, however, because it established key precedents. First, it set a pattern for governmental 'tactics' on handling Parliament and the public. That pattern involved nurturing passive acquiescence via a combination of appeals to protecting the 'national interest', non-partisanship and curtailed debate. Thus, scare stories about the dangers of foreign espionage were used to lever the 1889 Act into place when, in fact, government's principal impetus was a desire to control the leaking of information by civil servants. Secondly, the 1889 Act set a pattern for legislative design in its attempt at catch-all provisions designed to prevent any disclosure that was not 'authorised', irrespective of the nature of the information or the purpose of the disclosure.

The infamous Official Secrets Act 1911 was a much more effective piece of legislation than its 1889 predecessor.[110] It, too, was sold to Parliament and the public by means of anti-espionage rhetoric (especially anti-German rhetoric – indeed, it became common currency at that time that Britain was 'swarming with German spies disguised as waiters, barbers and tourists'[111]). But, as was made clear by the Franks Report in 1972, the glossing of the 1911 Act as 'crisis legislation, aimed mainly at espionage'[112] was almost pure pretext. The Report points out that, although 'the Government elected not to volunteer complete explanations of their Bill in Parliament. And Parliament, in the special circumstances of that summer, did not look behind the explanations offered', the truth behind the legislation was 'clear enough from the text of the Bill alone':

---

108 Ibid., p. 309.
109 Hooper, above n. 94, p. 23 argues that, in part, this was because of legal difficulties concerning its application: eg, the state had to prove that the communication caused harm.
110 For statistics on the use of the 1911 Act, see Birkinshaw, above n. 9, p. 100.
111 For details of the writings of William Le Queux, such as *The Invasion of 1910* (1906) and *Spies of the Kaiser* (1909), see R.M. Thomas, *Espionage and Secrecy: The Official Secrets Acts 1911-1989 of the United Kingdom* (Routledge, 1991), pp. 4-5.
112 The Franks Report, above n. 12, para. 50.

This legislation had long been desired by governments. It has been carefully prepared over a period of years. One of its objects was to give greater protection against leakages of any kind of official information whether or not connected with defence or national security. . . . Although s 2 of the Act was much wider in a number of respects than s 2 of the 1889 Act, the files suggest that the Government in 1911 honestly believed that it introduced no new principle, but merely put into practice more effectually the principle of using criminal sanctions to protect official information.[113]

Section 2 was the core of the 1911 Act: in comparison to section 2, section 1, which was directed at preventing disclosure of information 'useful to an enemy' or concerning a 'prohibited place', was pure espionage law.[114] Section 2's target, not surprisingly, was the 'disloyal' civil servant.[115] The section effectively made it an offence for any civil servant to disclose any information that came into their possession as a result of their employment, unless 'authorised' to communicate it. Its intended effect was not only to prevent all 'official' information from reaching the public domain, but also that all information generated by government should be classified as 'official secrets' – irrespective of content or the impact of public disclosure. The crux, of course, was in the proviso: unless 'authorised' to communicate the information. In other words, those with power and influence had little to fear; they were trusted with the discretion to continue authorising themselves to release information.

The key to understanding the 1911 Act is to focus on its intended role in maintaining authority and deference within the government apparatus. 'Signing the Official Secrets Act' emerged thereafter as a mantra about demonstrating absolute allegiance to one's employer. The logic of prosecutions under the Act, rather than the number thereof, also emerged as key.[116] That logic is captured perfectly by Vincent: 'deploy it against the lesser figures in order to intimidate the larger.'[117] Compton Mackenzie, novelist and Lord Rector of Glasgow University, fell victim to this policy in 1932 after writing an account of his time as head of counter-intelligence in Greece during World War I. Pursuing 'such Draconian action over so minor an aspect of the hostilities [of WWI] so long after so much else had been published was at first sight puzzling', yet it made total sense once one understood that Mackenzie was being scapegoated:

[t]he issue, as it most always had been since the first Official Secrets Act of 1889, was the maintenance not of security but of authority.[118]

---

113 Ibid.
114 S.1 of the OSA 1911, which is still in force, aims to prevent access to 'prohibited places' (such as military installations) and the disclosure of information 'useful to an enemy'. It has been used mainly against individuals engaged in spying for foreign governments: see eg, *R v Prime* (1983) 5 Cr App Rep 127 (re GCHQ employee passing information to Soviet intelligence service).
115 Other important provisions were: s. 6 (police power to arrest without warrant); s. 8 (consent of the A-G required for prosecution); and s. 9 (new police powers of entry and search). For more detail, see eg, S.H. Bailey, D.J. Harris and B.L. Jones, *Civil Liberties: Cases and Materials* (Butterworths, 1995), pp. 452-465.
116 Hooper, above n. 94, pp. 345-385 provides the following 'numbers': an average of one prosecution under the OSA every two years, until the Thatcher era when, in an attempt to curb the growing practices of whistleblowing and leaking, prosecutions multiplied to an average of three per year.
117 Vincent, above n. 34, p. 170.
118 Ibid., p. 171.

Clive Ponting, the civil servant who was prosecuted unsuccessfully several decades later after he had 'gone public' on the torpedoing of the *General Belgrano* during the Falkands War, confirms this point. The 1911 Act was used 'almost entirely when unimportant information was released by people lower down the state hierarchy or when information was released that was judged damaging to the government rather than "the state"'.[119]

Offical secrets and national security: creating the link

At the start of this Part, we emphasised that law, in its supporting role in propping up the British 'culture of secrecy', facilitated an enduring linkage of the concepts of 'national security' (or, to use the traditional terminology, the 'Defence of the Realm'[120]) and secret government. This linkage helped to ring-fence the 'culture of secrecy'; as we show in this section, however, it also both gave rise to an exaggerated conception of the requirements of 'national security' and protected that conception from challenge.

The linkage between the concepts of national security and secret government was forged in two ways. First, threats to national security – both internal and external, both genuine and bogus – were used to shore up the 'culture of secrecy'. For example, as we pointed out in the last section, although the principal impetus behind the OSA 1911 was a desire to maintain control amidst expansion of central government, the Act was sold to Parliament and the public as a measure essential to effective defence of national security against foreign espionage. The notion of 'threats to national security' also helped to smooth the passage of other 'crisis legislation' (such as the Emergency Powers Act 1920, which was used to crush the General Strike in 1926),[121] leading Ewing and Gearty to argue that:

> the series of crises of law and order that unfolded during [the period between 1914 and 1945] bridged the gap between the old order and the new democratic society that was emerging, enabling the former to deploy the law in a rearguard, pre-emptive action against the changes that it was thought democracy was likely to bring.[122]

In addition, as in the US (albeit to a much lesser degree than happened with the McCarthyite purges), homophobia was constructed and sustained through appeals to national security.[123] In the 1950s, following the introduction of a

---

119 Ponting, above n. 90, p. 336.

120 See eg, Defence of the Realm Acts 1914-1915.

121 'Threats to national security' also legitimated developments such as the creation of the secret services (and their non-statutory existence up until the late 1980s and early 1990s) and the introduction of vetting for government employees.

122 Above n. 2, p. 416. Their detailed historical account of the suppression of Irish republicanism in the first decades of the twentieth century provides a backdrop to our account of post-1970s anti-terrorism policy in Ch. 3.

123 See R.J. Corber, *In the Name of National Security: Hitchcock, Homophobia, and the Political Construction of Gender in Postwar America* (Duke UP, 1993). For similar associations drawn between political/religious identities and national security risk, see K. McEvoy and C. White, 'Security Vetting in Northern Ireland: Loyalty, Redress and Citizenship' (1992) 61 MLR 341. See also, *Tinnelly and McElduff v UK* (1998) 27 EHRR 249 (ECtHR) (re violation of Art. 6, ECHR arising from the operation of security vetting procedures in Northern Ireland). C. White, 'Security Vetting: Discrimination and the Right to a Fair Trial' [1999] PL 406 discusses post-*Tinnelly* reforms to anti-discrimination legislation in Northern Ireland.

system of 'positive vetting', homosexuality became equated with potential disloyalty, thereby creating a new category of 'dangerous' person deemed a risk to national security.[124] The homosexual civil servant was an 'enemy within': that is, a public servant with access to 'sensitive' information who was deemed susceptible to the influence of other governments. The intention was that positive vetting would expose the personal secrets of the individual and thus safeguard the official secrets of the nation.

The second aspect of the linkage between the concepts of national security and secret government was that the 'culture of secrecy' made exposure and reform of inappropriate 'national security' mandates and methods very unlikely.[125] The novelist Compton Mackenzie, who as noted earlier was one of the victims of the 1911 Act, reinforces this point, by emphasising the chilling effect of the idea of 'official secrets':

> [It] has become a bogy for the whole country and is used with extreme skills always to suggest in the mind of the general public that an act approaching espionage has been committed, an act against the safety of the realm. Any man accused of violating the Official Secrets Act in whatever ridiculous way runs the risk of creating in the public mind a prejudice against himself, so much has the sinister aspect been forced upon people.[126]

What is particularly intriguing about the British 'Secret State's' linkage of national security and secrecy is that it endured for so long – long after other democracies had re-organised their security services into public buildings and identified senior personnel, and long after major changes in both British society and international relations. Commentators have singled out an array of political and economic reasons for this peculiarity of 'the British way'. Lustgarten, for example, has suggested that 'habits of mind engendered by the [First World] War – secrecy, executive authoritarianism and the abandonment of Victorian notions of individual liberty – remained dominant' for a long time thereafter.[127] In his book with Leigh, *In From the Cold: National Security and Parliamentary Democracy*, he has also highlighted the fall-out from the 'loss of Empire', and the search for 'a role in the post-imperial world', as key influences:

> Britain . . . persisted in trying to maintain its status as a world power long after it lacked the wherewithal to do so. . . . Britain [for example] continued to commit a

---

124 See L.J. Moran, 'The Uses of Homosexuality: Homosexuality for National Security' (1991) 19 Int J Sociology of Law 149. Moran highlights, however, that homosexuals were hired and remained within the UK government at high levels, and could avoid dismissal if their homosexuality remained 'invisible' and did transgress class boundaries. See *R v Director of GCHQ, ex p Hodges, The Times,* 26 Jul. 1988 (re GCHQ employee losing his positive-vetting clearance because of 'the frequency and nature of his homosexual relationships and the social circles which he frequented in consequence of his homosexual inclinations').

125 The US, which has had far more extensive regulatory structures than the UK, also struggles with the linkage between national security and secrecy. See eg, D.P. Moynihan, *Secrecy* (Yale UP, 1998), pp. 211-212 noting in relation to the Iran-Contra scandal that: '[s]ecrecy almost ruined yet another [US] presidency. Off it went to buy arms abroad, with the National Security Council now opting for covert action of its own, all hidden by secrecy. . . . Had it not been possible for those involved with Iran-Contra to act under a vast umbrella of secrets, they would have been told to stop. Recall that most of what they were doing was kept from the rest of the government. (It is still not clear what the CIA knew, outside the director himself.)'

126 Quoted in Vincent, above n. 34, p. 183. See also, A. Rogers, *Secrecy and Power in the British State: A History of the Official Secrets Act, 1911-1989* (Pluto, 1997).

127 Lustgarten, above n. 87, p. 740.

substantially higher proportion of GNP to military spending than any other western European state.[128]

Others point additionally to the obsessions of the Cold War period, and the 'unhealed wound'[129] in the intelligence community following the revelation of Burgess and Maclean (Foreign Office), Philby and Blake (MI6), and Blunt (MI5) as Soviet spies. The UK's 'special relationship' with the US, which became the new global power in the world, may have been a further influence given the exclusive sharing of intelligence between US and British security services.[130] Whatever the reasons, 'the dominant . . . cast of mind – cast in the mould of "national security" – paradoxically insisted upon and propagated the notion of a basic *insecurity* that grew directly out of the expansiveness of its conception of security. Britain, though a strong state, acted in many ways as though it were a weak one'.[131] In what follows, we focus on the damaging impact of the exaggerated understanding of national security in the period between 1911 and 1989. We look, first, at the mass violations of civil liberties to which it gave rise and, secondly, at the extended failure on the part of the media to challenge 'the national security mindset'. We also look closely at the role played by the judiciary in giving backing to measures that were alleged to be essential to national security (most notoriously, in recent years, during the *Spycatcher* litigation).

The enemy within

The security services were a key force of oppressive state action in the British 'Secret State'. They acted both 'under orders' (that is, where they were used as a political tool by individual governments to further partisan policies and attack those deemed to be 'enemies') and as autonomous empires.[132] Ewing and Gearty's historical study of civil liberties in the period 1914-1945 provides evidence of consistent state repression of, for example, the Communist Party

---

128 Lustgarten and Leigh, above n. 5, p. 25-26. They go on to note that '[i]n most accounts, the Suez fiasco [of 1956] is treated as a turning-point, after which the realities of diminished capability began to be respected'. On Suez, see eg, S. Lucas, *Britain and Suez: The Lion's Last Roar* (Manchester UP, 1996). See also, more generally, B. Porter, *Britain, Europe and the World 1850-1986: Delusions of Grandeur* (Allen & Unwin, 1987).

129 S. McCabe, 'National Security and Freedom of Information' in L. Gostin (ed.), *Civil Liberties in Conflict* (Routledge, 1988), pp. 185-207, at p. 205.

130 But members of the British security services remained confused about their role. See eg, Wright, above n. 77, p. 75: 'The principal problem in postwar British Intelligence was the lack of clear thinking about the relative role of the various Intelligence Services. In the post-imperial era Britain required, above all, an efficient domestic Intelligence organisation. MI6, particularly after the emergence of GCHQ, was quite simply of less importance.'

131 Lustgarten and Leigh, above n. 5, p. 25 (references omitted).

132 See generally, P. Gill, *Policing Politics: Security Intelligence and the Liberal Democratic State* (Frank Cass, 1994). In both instances, the methods by which the security services achieved their objectives were often objectionable or illegal; in the former case, however, government ministers and civil servants were directly complicit, even though (as was usually the case) the exact details of operations were kept from them: see generally, Lustgarten and Leigh, above n. 5, pp. 363-373. Parallels can be found in other jurisdictions: see eg, D. Porch, *The French Secret Services* (OUP, 1997), pp. 455-467 (re the sinking of the Greenpeace ship, *The Rainbow Warrior*, in New Zealand in 1985 by French secret services); J. Joyce and P. Murtagh, *The Boss: Charles J. Haughey in Government* (Poolbeg Press, 1983) (re the telephone-tapping of journalists by the Irish police on the orders of government ministers); and A. Summers, *Official and Confidential: The Secret Life of J. Edgar Hoover* (Corgi, 1994) (re the targeting of US civil rights groups, Vietnam War protesters, actors and politicians by the FBI).

in the 1920s and the National Unemployed Workers Movement in the 1930s; in effect, evidence of how 'activities of suspect citizens, immigrants and aliens were kept under constant watch by means of physical surveillance, the use of paid informers, and the interception of mail and telegraphic communication'.[133] This study helps to place in context MI5's notorious involvement in the forgery of a letter, urging members of the Communist Party and the Labour Party to foment a revolution, which appeared in the *Daily Mail* three days before the 1924 General Election (which, the Labour Party lost).[134]

It should not be assumed that the targeting of individuals and organisations on 'national security' grounds was confined to particular decades or 'flashpoints':[135] examples of targeting are peppered throughout the history of the British 'Secret State', including the internment of tens of thousands of British citizens and refugees during the 1940s;[136] and the surveillance of members of the National Council for Civil Liberties (NCCL),[137] the Campaign for Nuclear Disarmament (CND)[138] and the environmental organisation, Greenpeace. Milne, in his book, *The Enemy Within: The Secret War Against the Miners*, gives details of what (allegedly) was done during what became known as the 'get-Scargill' affair.[139] 'Scargill' is Arthur Scargill, who was the leader of the National Union of Miners (NUM) during the massive industrial stoppages of the 1980s, and had long been an alleged target of the security services. Relatedly, cabinet papers from 1971, released in January 2001, provide official confirmation of what has long been suspected – that in the 1970s, MI5 engaged in routine spying on trade unionists and Communist Party officials.

There is also evidence suggesting that, throughout the period between 1911 and 1989, MI5 acted 'quite consciously to frustrate rather than to serve the democratic process'.[140] Such behaviour is, of course, in no way exclusive to the British security services. What made the British services different, however, was that the British 'culture of secrecy' made oversight or exposure – by the executive, Parliament, the judiciary or the media – an unlikely prospect. Indeed, as noted earlier, that culture left the security services without statutory backing until the late 1980s and early 1990s. In effect, the 'culture of secrecy', in particular

---

133 McCabe, above n. 129, p. 189.

134 Ewing and Gearty, above n. 2, p. 153.

135 See Ch. 3 for a critique of anti-terrorism law and policy in relation to Northern Ireland-related terrorism.

136 N. Stammers, *Civil Liberties in Britain During the Second World War: A Political Study* (Croom Helm, 1983); and A.W. Simpson, *In the Highest Degree Odious: Detention Without Trial in Wartime Britain* (Clarendon, 1992).

137 Robertson, above n. 11, p. 53 (re the bugging of NCCL executive members).

138 The association of the issue of nuclear power with national security and total secrecy has been especially damaging. Consider, eg, the cover-up about the nuclear accident at Windscale (now Sellafield) in 1957, or the UK's secret role in the 1962 Cuban Missile Crisis. See also the comment of R.W. Johnson, 'Bugger Everyone': Review of P. Hennessy, *The Prime Minister: The Office and Its Holders Since 1945* (Allen Lane, 2000)', *LRB*, 19 Oct. 2000, p. 10 at p. 11: 'It is intriguing to read of the great nuclear shelters for VIPs under the Cotswolds, to learn that the royal yacht Britannia was a fully fledged command and control centre with washdown facilities to deal with nuclear fallout, but the most striking thing is that neither the public nor Parliament was ever told how close the country was to nuclear war'.

139 Above n. 104.

140 Ewing and Gearty, above n. 2, p. 153. See also, M. Hollingsworth and R. Norton-Taylor, *Blacklist: The Inside Story of Political Vetting* (Hogarth, 1988) on the historic links between MI5 and the Economic League, an organisation created to provide employers with information on potentially 'subversive' employees.

its linkage of (an expansive concept of) national security with absolute secrecy, provided the security services with ideal cover for creating and preserving monopolies of power, warding-off public exposure of wrongdoing or incompetence, and avoiding externally-driven reform.[141] The mandate and the methods of the security services were as broad as ministers, or the services themselves, wished them to be. Moreover, exactly how broad they were, and what actions were taken, is still unclear because the tradition of keeping 'national security' information secret is still with us.

National security, official secrecy and the media

The linkage between national security and secrecy received additional support from a surprising quarter: the media. The 'D-Notice Committee' (a system of voluntary media regulation on issues of national security) can, in fact, be used as a case study in media self-censorship.[142] The committee, which comprises senior civil servants, members of the armed forces and representatives of the media, was established in 1912 (although, in line with the British 'culture of secrecy', its existence was undisclosed for 40 years[143]). Its aim was to achieve consensus between government and the press on the publication of certain information.[144] In practice, the Committee issued D-Notices advising the media of information which had to be kept secret on grounds of national security,[145] and the entire enterprise was founded on an appeal to honourable relations and trust between government and journalists (or, more importantly, newspaper proprietors). Thus, the Committee would:

> put the press to their honour in the schoolboy sense of the term, prior to any experiments which the board may wish to keep secret, by issuing a communiqué to the press association stating what is going to be carried out and asking them to co-operate in the publication of information likely to be of value to foreign countries.[146]

Lustgarten and Leigh provide further support for the view that the entire system was grounded in a 'chaps together' mentality, emphasising that '[w]ithin this structure editors and politicians know each other on social terms and frequently meet informally. They share the same social background and outlook, which produces a consensual, implicit understanding and permits substantial voluntary agreement about what is and is not fit to become public knowledge'.[147] This

---

141 See eg, Porch, above n. 132, p. 475 arguing that '[p]olitical favoritism, rivalry and distrust among [French] intelligence organizations, the military control of foreign intelligence, the priority accorded domestic spying, has meant that competence, information and analytical resources are unevenly distributed among the various intelligence services'.

142 Its full name is the Defence, Press and Broadcasting Advisory Committee. Its secretary has always been a senior armed forces' officer. On occasion, broadcasting laws have operated so as to give some backing to the Committee's D-Notices (see G. Robertson and A. Nicol, *Media Law* (Penguin, 1992), pp. 436-437); the threat of prosecution under the OSA may also have operated as an indirect back-up to the 'voluntariness' of the system.

143 Williams, above n. 1, p. 85. For more on the system, see eg, D. Fairley, 'D Notices, Official Secrets and the Law' (1990) 10 OJLS 430; and J. Jaconelli, 'The "D" Notice System' [1982] PL 37.

144 See generally, Birkinshaw, above n. 9, pp. 171-172.

145 Such notices are also known as DA-Notices.

146 Suggestion of a Director of Naval Intelligence in 1912, cited in Vincent, above n. 34, p. 127.

147 Lustgarten and Leigh, above n. 5, p. 260.

shared sense of what was in the national interest was, of course, supplemented by the fact that both parties benefited from the arrangement.

The consequences of this 'cosy co-operation'[148] between media and the government were far-reaching. For example, no details about the early development of atomic weapons ever leaked out:

> Journalists found themselves thrust back into the pre-1914 world of security paranoia. . . . The gentleman's agreement [of the D Notice system] was deployed in 1947 and 1948 to forbid stories on the location or progress of work on the bomb.[149]

The media's docility also had considerable longevity. For example, 'until 1977 a D-notice covered the revelation of the very existence of GCHQ and other SIGINT [signals-intercept] bases'.[150] Ironically, as Robertson and Nicol point out, 'these were secrets to be kept from the British public and not from the Russians, whose spy satellites had long been able to identify any communications intercept aerials'.[151] Similarly, in 1986, during litigation in the Australian courts which was part of the extended *Spycatcher* saga, a D-Notice was issued to prevent UK journalists 'from giving the name of the legal adviser to MI5, although it had already been revealed in the Australian press'.[152]

From the mid-1970s onwards, however, there was evidence of a fracturing in the historic deference of the media. Key influences included: more leaking; mass television; and the growth of hard-hitting investigative journalism by individuals such as Duncan Campbell, 'one of a new breed of post-Watergate journalists who did not accept the unilateral right of the State to define national security'.[153] His exposé of the role of the communications surveillance centre, GCHQ, in *Time Out* in May 1976 was something of watershed in media-government relations on information relating to national security. That article led to the prosecution of Campbell and two other British journalists under section 1 of the Official Secrets Act 1911 in the *ABC* trial,[154] and the deportation of a US journalist on the ground of threat to national security in *Hosenball*.[155] Its opening words were as follows:

> Britain's largest spy network organisation is not MI5 or MI6 but an electronic intelligence network controlled from a country town in the Cotswolds. With the huge US National Security Agency as partner, it intercepts and decodes communications throughout the world. Freelance writer *Duncan Campbell* and *Mark Hosenball* trace the rise to power of the electronic eavesdroppers.[156]

Yet as Geoffrey Robertson (a member of the defence team in the *ABC* trial) explains, the legal actions against Campbell and the others did not generate

---

148 Robertson and Nicol, above n. 142, p. 436.
149 Vincent, above n. 34, p. 200.
150 Robertson and Nicol, above n. 142, p. 437.
151 Ibid.
152 McCabe, above n. 129, p. 206.
153 Robertson, above n. 11, p. 111-112. He continues '[w]hat made [Campbell] especially irritating was that, unlike others of this ilk, he had the technical expertise (first-class honours in physics, a Master of Science) to see through official press releases'.
154 *R v Aubrey, Berry and Campbell* [1979] Crim LR 284 (the defendants were eventually found guilty on s. 2, OSA charges). See also *R v Aitken* (1971, unreported) (prosecution of journalists under s. 2, OSA 1911 for publishing in the *Sunday Telegraph* confidential information about the Nigerian civil war).
155 *R v Secretary of State for Home Affairs, ex p Hosenball* [1977] 1 WLR 766 (CA).
156 Cited in Robertson, above n. 11, p. 107.

media-wide outrage. The government had, it seems, chosen its target with a degree of care:

> Campbell . . . was young and left-wing. He [must have appeared a] suitable candidate . . . for an exercise designed to prove that such critical journalism was as inimical to the safety of the State as the treason of those who collaborated with the enemy. . . . The government's action went uncondemned and virtually unreported in the national press, which appeared entirely unconcerned by this unprecedented attack on its own freedom. This was thanks to a 'whispering campaign' by MI5 through its editorial contacts on Fleet Street and in the BBC.[157]

The judiciary

Law, as we have emphasised, has always played a supporting role as regards the British 'culture of secrecy'.[158] Further support for this is provided by the fact that for much of the twentieth century, despite several 'infamous cases' involving national security matters, the judicial presence in this field was largely a background one. National security cases, as Lustgarten and Leigh have pointed out, 'directly or merely as an undertone, do not bulk large in the judicial calendar'.[159] There were few criminal prosecutions under the Official Secrets Act 1911. Moreover, when national security matters were raised in judicial review proceedings (especially, when the country was 'at war'), the judiciary made it absolutely clear that they saw their role as a non-interventionist one; they would not be the ones to lift the veil of secrecy covering government actions.

The consequences of this judicial abstention were extremely harmful in terms of increased human rights violations. Moreover, it appears that the executive took great ideological comfort from the 'green light' given to them by the courts.[160] Ewing and Gearty's 1914-45 survey of civil liberties quite rightly damns the judiciary for not using the (albeit limited) tools available to them. It is inexcusable that judges did not insist that executive actions had to be backed by legal authority, and that the (minimal) procedural requirements of (mostly emergency) statutes and regulations had to be followed. Yet, while the judiciary did prove 'utterly useless as a bulwark against oppressive executive action, when ostensibly undertaken in defence of the state or public order' and did 'spinelessly [ratify] the exercise of executive power against political dissent', it would be wrong to give the judiciary more than 'a secondary role'[161] in the British 'culture of secrecy'. Moreover, the secondary role they adopted tallies with what was expected of them within the British constitutional tradition. That tradition, with its fantasy of common law liberty, was grounded in Parliament giving the executive the powers for which it asked when it was alleged that 'Defence of the Realm' was at stake. If members of Parliament were not prepared to force some accountability on ministers, the traditional conception of the judicial

---

157 Ibid., pp. 111-112.
158 Consider, eg, the historic 'secrets' of the British medical profession in relation to the refusal to disclose medical records to patients, and the widespread practice of retaining organs after post-mortem examinations.
159 Lustgarten and Leigh, above n. 5, p. 320.
160 See eg, the detailed histories in Ewing and Gearty, above n. 2; and Simpson, above n. 136, on the thousands needlessly interned during 1940-45.
161 Lustgarten, above n. 87, pp. 740-741.

role would not have involved filling the ensuing void.[162] In addition, bonds of trust and loyalty between the 'gentleman class' most likely compounded judicial disinclination to countenance a bucking of constitutional tradition. Similarly, claims about the needs of national security made by government ministers and 'military men' may have had special status where judges themselves (or their relatives) had experienced military service.[163]

A reasonably contemporary example of the judiciary's 'secondary role' in national security cases is provided by the judicial record in post-1970 cases relating to the Northern Ireland conflict. That record shows that, irrespective of whether judges saw their task as to identify with executive interests, or were motivated by broader patriotic instincts, or were engaged actively in adjudicating upon legal outcomes, the end result was overwhelmingly helpful in sanctioning state policy at a time of perceived 'crisis'.[164] Moreover, judges also always had the option of falling back on the tactic of making the 'practicalities' of disclosing information to the court appear insurmountable – as evidenced, for example, in the unwavering acceptance of Public Interest Immunity certificates signed by ministers.[165]

In the remainder of this section we provide a sample of historic cases, drawn from the period 1911-89, which indicates the judicial approach to national security and its constant companion, official secrecy.[166] Our starting point is an *obiter dictum* in *The Zamora*, the World War I case that set the tone for decisions over future decades:

> those who are responsible for the national security must be the sole judges of what the national security requires. It would be obviously undesirable that such matters should be made the subject of evidence in a Court of law or otherwise discussed in public.[167]

---

162 One obvious contemporary example of this constitutional deference, in a case involving traditional executive powers in the field of national security, was the judicial refusal to question any of the justifications put forward for the (former) blanket ban on lesbians and gays in the armed forces: see *R v Ministry of Defence, ex p Smith* [1996] 1 All ER 257 (CA). Cf. the approach of the ECtHR: see *Smith & Grady v UK* (1999) 29 EHRR 493.

163 Lustgarten and Leigh, above n. 5, p. 179 note that 'Lord Atkin suffered remarkable ostracism at the hands of his judicial brethren following his dissent in *Liversedge v Anderson* [[1942] AC 206 (HL) re internment powers], although this may have been partly because of the tone of his speech'. The use of senior judges to inquire into national security matters, such as Lord Denning in the Profumo Affair in 1963, complicated the arena further as judges were allowed 'secret access' to some information and personnel. Once the 'legalisation' of this area began in the 1980s, in fear of increasing ECtHR litigation, the trend was for senior judges to sit in 'oversight' roles in relation to interception of communications, police surveillance and security service activities: see Interception of Communications Act 1985; Security Service Act 1989; Intelligence Services Act 1994; and Police Act 1997. See now RIPA 2000; for commentaries, see above n. 41.

164 See generally, Ch. 3.

165 See the wartime decision, *Duncan v Cammell Laird & Co Ltd* [1942] AC 624 (HL) (suppression of evidence, on the authority of ministerial affidavit, relating to submarine accident in civil litigation could not be questioned by courts as minister was the sole judge of 'the public interest'). The decision in *Conway v Rimmer* [1968] AC 910 (HL) established that the courts could inspect the suppressed evidence and form its own view as to the merits of using PII certificates. On the consequences of the historic deference, see the discussion of the Matrix Churchill trial and Scott Inquiry below, pp. 362-363.

166 See B. Dickson, 'Judicial Review and National Security' in B. Hadfield (ed.), *Judicial Review: A Thematic Approach* (Gill & Macmillan, 1995), pp. 187-227; and G. Carne, 'Thawing The Big Chill: Reform, Rhetoric and Regression in the Security Intelligence Mandate' (1996) 22 Monash Univ LR 379, 387-401.

167 [1916] 2 AC 77, 107 (PC) (per Lord Parker). The Privy Council ruled that the UK government's requisitioning of a neutral ship's cargo of copper was unlawful as the Crown evidence did not indicate the reason for its action.

We move from here directly to the 1960s, a period when CND activism threw down a challenge to UK defence policy. In *Chandler*, which concerned a prosecution under section 1 of the OSA 1911[168] of demonstrators who had planned to enter an RAF base in order to lie in front of aircraft, the House of Lords indicated its approval of the convictions by emphasising that 'the disposition and armament of the armed forces are and for centuries have been within the exclusive discretion of the Crown'. It also insisted that the statutory wording 'interests of the state' ought generally to be seen as synonymous with the government's own conception of national security.[169]

In the 1970s, amidst a surge in investigative journalism, the Home Secretary used deportation powers to expel the US journalist, Mark Hosenball, for reporting the existence of the GCHQ spying network. In the Court of Appeal, Lord Denning articulated a vision of the UK under permanent threat:

> [T]imes of peace hold their dangers too. Spies, subverters and saboteurs may be mingling amongst us, putting on a most innocent exterior. They may be endangering the lives of the men in our secret service, as Mr Hosenball is said to do.[170]

In the 1980s, the Thatcher government acted without prior consultation to ban trade unions at GCHQ on the ground of alleged risk to national security. The Law Lords, in dismissing the challenge to this action, bolstered their 'jurisprudence of the Cold War'[171] by stating limply that 'the Government alone has access to the necessary information, and in any event the judicial process is unsuitable for reaching decisions on national security'.[172] Moreover, in those 1980s cases, such as *Ruddock*[173] (involving telephone surveillance) and *Stitt*[174] (exclusion order under the (former) Prevention of Terrorism Act) – where judges started to insist that claims of national security required some evidence and could not simply be accepted without question – satisfying this

---

168 Most notoriously, s. 1 was used in the prosecution of journalists in the 'ABC' trial, above n. 10. The OSA 1911 search power was also used in 1987 – in an attempt to stop the journalist Duncan Campbell, from revealing that the MoD had secretly spent £500m on a spy satellite (Zircon) without the knowledge of Parliament – when the police raided the offices of BBC Scotland (and Campbell's London home and the offices of the *New Statesman* under PACE powers).

169 *Chandler v DPP* [1964] AC 763, 791 (HL) (per Lord Reid).

170 *R v Secretary of State for Home Affairs, ex p Hosenball* [1977] 1 WLR 766, 778 (CA). The *Crossman Diaries* case, *A-G v Jonathan Cape Ltd* [1975] 3 All ER 484, provided one chink of light on government information. The action for breach of confidence was extended so as to place Cabinet ministers and civil servants under a duty of confidentiality in relation to official information. However, it was also held that the granting of an injunction depended on the competing public interests at stake and any prior publication of the information. Here, the fact that time had elapsed since the events described in the diaries meant that the balance favoured publication of Cabinet discussions.

171 Lustgarten and Leigh, above n. 5, p. 329.

172 *CCSU v Minister for the Civil Service* [1985] AC 374, 402 (HL) (per Lord Fraser).

173 *R v Secretary of State for Home Affairs, ex p Ruddock* [1987] 2 All ER 518 (HCt) (re surveillance of leader of CND).

174 *The Times*, 2 Feb. 1987. Up until the late 1980s, the ECtHR engaged in deferential scrutiny of cases alleging human rights violations on the ground of national security, usually granting a liberal 'margin of appreciation' to member states. The most significant counter-examples involving the UK are *Brogan* (1988); *Spycatcher* (1991); *McCann* (1995); *Chahal* (1996); *Tinnelly* (1998); and *Jordan* (2001).

standard was never onerous. It also never resulted in the compelled disclosure of any 'national security' information to the persons affected.[175]

The two most notorious encounters between official secrecy and national security in the 1980s were, first, the Clive Ponting trial and, secondly, the manic pursuit through the courts of former MI5 agent, Peter Wright, who sought to publish *Spycatcher: The Candid Memoirs of an Intelligence Officer*.[176] In *Ponting*, the defendant was a former senior civil servant in the Ministry of Defence who leaked documents concerning the sinking of the *General Begrano* during the Falklands War to Tam Dalyell MP, who had asked parliamentary questions about the circumstances surrounding the order to torpedo the ship.[177] Ignoring the direction of the trial judge, McCowan J, that section 2 of the Official Secrets Act 1911 permitted no public interest defence, the jury acquitted Ponting and, thereby, provided a catalyst for reform – the eventual outcome of which was the Official Secrets Act 1989.

In *Spycatcher*, a criminal prosecution of Peter Wright was made impossible because of his Australian residence, and the government sought instead to obtain injunctions in Australia (and several other countries including the UK) in an attempt to prevent publication of Wright's book, extracts therefrom, and news reports containing allegations made in the book. The government's argument was that Wright, as a former member of MI5, was bound by a lifelong duty of confidentiality, and that *any* breach of this duty ought to be restrained by injunction given the public interest in maintaining national security.[178] In effect, however, the government was seeking to deploy law in a frenzied attempt to stop (former) security service personnel speaking out openly.[179]

The litigation saga was complex. In 1985, the government obtained an interlocutory injunction in New South Wales restraining Wright and his publishers from publishing *Spycatcher* in Australia. The full hearing was scheduled for June 1986. Prior to that hearing, however, two UK newspapers, the *Observer* and the *Guardian*, published articles containing details of Wright's allegations. The government then sought and obtained interlocutory injunctions against both newspapers in the UK courts, preventing them from making any further disclosures in the UK. The next development was the

---

175 See the hostility towards the protection of journalistic sources when interpreting s. 10 of the Contempt of Court Act 1981: *Secretary of State for Defence v Guardian Newspapers* [1985] AC 339 (HL) (re return of documents relating to the secret deployment of Cruise missiles at Greenham Common, leading to the identification and imprisonment of whistleblower Sarah Tisdall); and *DPP v Channel 4 Television* [1993] 2 All ER 517 (CA) (re refusal to reveal source behind documentary alleging collusion between Northern Ireland security forces and Loyalist paramilitaries). Cf. *Goodwin v UK* (1996) 22 EHRR 123 (court order to disclose source in order to enable a company to identify a 'disloyal' employee was not justifiable).

176 A chronology of the *Spycatcher* litigation is provided in Bailey, Harris and Jones, above n. 115, pp. 474-477.

177 *R v Ponting* [1985] Crim LR 318. See also, Ponting, above n. 106; and 'R v Ponting' (1987) 14 JLS 366. Cf. R.M. Thomas, 'The British Official Secrets Acts 1911-1939 and the Ponting Case' [1986] Crim LR 491, 507 (arguing that the 'principles underlying the [OSA] remain sound' and that 'care must be taken, if removing the existing obscurity, not to open up a clear *public interest* defence').

178 See *Crossman Diaries* case, above n. 170.

179 Wright's allegations of criminal and unconstitutional conduct on the part of MI5 officers (for example, the bugging of diplomats and the plot to assassinate President Nasser of Egypt during the Suez crisis) had previously been published: see discussion in *A-G v Guardian Newspapers Ltd (No 2)* [1988] 3 All ER 545, 559-564 (per Scott J).

government's failure to obtain a permanent injunction in Australia,[180] following which *Spycatcher* went on sale throughout the world and thousands of copies were imported into the UK. Then, prior to the publication of the US version of the book, a UK newspaper, *The Sunday Times*, published the first extract of an intended serialisation of *Spycatcher*. The government sought and obtained an interlocutory injunction against the newspaper preventing any further publication.

The House of Lords, in *Spycatcher (No 1)*, upheld the interlocutory injunctions against the three UK newspapers, *The Observer*, *The Guardian* and *The Sunday Times*. Wright was condemned for his 'treachery', and the majority seemed unconcerned about the fact that they were upholding injunctions so as to protect the 'confidentiality' of information (including reports of the Australian proceedings in open court) which, by this point, was public knowledge worldwide.[181]

The action for permanent injunctions against the three newspapers was heard in 1987. At first instance, Scott J discharged the injunctions against each newspaper, but held the publishers of *The Sunday Times* accountable for the profits obtained from the serialisation. His decision was upheld by a majority of the House of Lords in *Spycatcher (No 2)*.[182] The Law Lords concluded that all possible damage to the public interest had occurred given the publication of *Spycatcher* abroad and the ready availability of copies in the UK.[183]

The effect of *Spycatcher (No 2)* is that the government can obtain an injunction preventing publication once it is shown that 'the disclosure is likely to damage or has damaged the public interest'.[184] However, because the House of Lords held that it was always in the public interest for members and former members of the security services to owe a lifelong duty of confidence, disclosure by such individuals of any information relating to the activities of MI5, MI6 or GCHQ was said to be harmful to national security:

> The work of a member of MI5 and the information which he acquires in the course of that work must necessarily be secret and confidential and be kept secret and confidential by him. There is no room for discrimination between secrets of greater or lesser importance, nor any room for close examination of the precise manner in which revelation of any particular matter may prejudice the national interest. Any attempt to do so would lead to further damage.[185]

180 *A-G (UK) v Heinemann Publishers Australian Pty Ltd* (1987) 75 ALR 353 (NSW CA); and (1988) 78 ALR 449 (HCt of Australia).

181 *A-G v Guardian Newspapers* [1987] All ER 316 (HL). Lord Bridge, in dissent, wrote that he now was convinced of need for the incorporation of the ECHR into UK law.

182 *A-G v Guardian Newspapers Ltd (No 2)* [1988] 3 All ER 545 (HL).

183 For an early application of *Spycatcher (No 2)*, see *Lord Advocate v Scotsman Publications Ltd* [1990] 1 AC 812 (HL) (re refusal of injunction to prevent publication of extracts from memoirs of former MI6 employee, on the basis that the information did not damage national security and had already been disclosed by the circulation of copies of the book).

184 [1988] 3 All ER 545, 640 (per Lord Keith).

185 Ibid., 642 (per Lord Keith). This explains why Scott J's recognition of some national security contexts where 'the public interest required disclosure' (eg, allegations of assassination plots or interference with the democratic process) was not echoed with any conviction in the HL. Some of the judgments appear to suggest that only publication of very specific (corroborated) allegations of wrongdoing, in the absence of all other background information, might override the duty of confidentiality, but the legal position remains fuzzy. Similarly, Scott J's identification of the media (and thus the public) as the appropriate recipient of the information, because of its 'legitimate role in disclosing scandals by government', was downplayed in the House of Lords. In an illuminating ranking of alternative recipients of evidence of wrongdoing, Lord Griffiths listed 'any senior member of his service or any member of the establishment, or the police' before 'fellow citizens'. See the extra-judicial comments by (now) Lord Scott, 'Confidentiality' in Beatson and Cripps (eds.), above n. 19, pp. 267-274.

The House of Lords in *Spycatcher (No 2)* did recognise that the position was different where injunctions were sought against the media or a member of the public. In respect of this category, it was held that communicating information 'about some aspect of government activity which does no harm to the interests of the nation cannot, even where the original disclosure has been made in breach of confidence, be restrained on the ground of a nebulous equitable duty of conscience serving no useful practical purpose'.[186]

A further aspect of the *Spycatcher* litigation saga that merits attention concerns the interaction between the law on breach of confidence and the law on contempt of court. This interaction was made manifest when, following the publication of further material from *Spycatcher* by three newspapers who were *not* parties to the original interlocutory injunctions, the government succeeded in convincing the courts of the need to impose yet another legal restraint on media freedom in the interests of national security.[187] Invoking the offence of intentional contempt of court, the House of Lords held that the newspapers did not have to be party to the original proceedings in order to interfere with the administration of justice in the ongoing litigation. Moreover, instead of imposing a requirement that the Attorney-General should seek a specific injunction against each newspaper – which would have obliged the government to prove the necessity of interfering with freedom of expression and that the information was not in the public domain – the House of Lords appeared to place the onus on newspaper editors to go to court (or to contact the Attorney-General) before publishing any material which might subvert an existing court order. In effect, an injunction against one newspaper preventing the publication of 'national security' information could bind all other newspapers in the jurisdiction.[188]

186 [1988] 3 All ER 545, 640 (per Lord Keith). In *Observer & Guardian v UK*, the ECtHR (1991) 14 EHRR 153 (by a majority of 14 to 10) ruled that the injunctions were not in breach of Art. 10, ECHR in the period prior to publication of *Spycatcher* in the US. However, after publication abroad, the ECtHR held unanimously that the confidentiality of the information was destroyed and injunctions thereafter could not be justified. The limitation of the judgment lies in the ECtHR's ready acceptance of both the need to preserve the absolute confidentiality of Wright's allegations and the claim that national security was at risk. Questions as to the compatibility of a lifelong duty of confidentiality with a guarantee of freedom of expression; the fact that similar memoirs had been published in other countries without similar government prohibitions; the attempts to impose territorial restrictions on such information in the era of satellite communications; and the imposition of the burden on the defendant newspapers to prove that disclosure was in the public interest were raised in several dissenting opinions but ignored by the majority of the ECtHR. These latter questions will feature prominently in the *Shayler* litigation.

187 *A-G v Times Newspapers Ltd* [1991] 2 All ER 398 (HL). Cf. Lord Donaldson MR in *A-G v Newspaper Publishing plc* [1988] Ch 333, 361 (CA): 'this case is not primarily about national security or official secrets. It is about the right of private citizens and public authorities to seek and obtain the protection of the courts for confidential information which they claim to be their property'.

188 The CA in January and March 2001, in light of Art. 10, ECHR and s. 12 of the HRA 1998, significantly 're-interpreted' *Spycatcher (No 2)* in relation to the publication of the Tomlinson (MI6) and Shayler (MI5) allegations by the media: see *A-G v Times Newspapers Ltd* [2001] 1 WLR 885 (CA); and *A-G v Punch Ltd* [2001] 2 All ER 655 (CA); and below pp. 366-368.

IV.   THE OFFICIAL SECRETS 1989: 'LEGISLATION TO LAST A GENERATION'?[189]

1989 had the appearance of being a turning-point for government: it was the year in which MI5 was given a statutory mandate, and it marked the passage of new official secrets legislation, the Official Secrets Act 1989.[190] The direction in which government intended to turn, however, was less clear: as Vincent points out, despite government claims that the new OSA was a liberalising measure because it repealed the notorious 'catch-all' section 2 of the 1911 Act, '[e]verything about the Act suggested that it was an error of timing . . . In practice, [it] opened more windows on the past than on the future'.[191]

The 1989 Act purported to reduce the prohibition on disclosure of 'official information' to four main categories: security and intelligence (section 1); defence (section 2); international relations (section 3); and criminal investigations (section 4).[192] Disclosure of information in the latter three categories has to be 'damaging' before an offence is committed.[193] In relation to information involving the security and intelligence services, however, the 1989 Act bolstered the 'culture of secrecy'. The most important provision, section 1, states:

> A person who is or has been—
> (a) a member of the security and intelligence services; or
> (b) a person notified that he is subject to the provisions of this subsection,
> is guilty of an offence if without lawful authority he discloses any information, document or other article relating to security and intelligence which is or has been in his possession by virtue of his position as a member of any of those services or in the course of his work while the notification is or was in force.

The intention behind section 1(1)(a) is to use criminal sanctions to impose a lifelong ban on any member, or former member, of the security services revealing *any* information relating to their work – irrespective of the nature, or the impact, of that disclosure, or the fact of any prior publication. All disclosures, without lawful authorisation, are deemed to be damaging to national security: communications revealing illegality are in the same category as those revealing trivial facts.[194]

To further ensure secrecy, section 1(1)(b) provides that 'notified' individuals with access to national security information – civil servants, armed forces personnel, police officers, secretarial staff – are also subject to the same blanket prohibition on disclosure.[195] In effect, therefore, the individuals who are often best placed to reveal evidence of unlawful, or undemocratic, behaviour by

---

189 'We are legislating for a generation: we are not legislating for the next five years': Nicholas Budgen MP, Jun. 1989.

190 As noted earlier, s. 1 of OSA 1911 remains in force and is directed at espionage.

191 Vincent, above n. 34, p. 307.

192 For more information, see D. Feldman, *Civil Liberties and Human Rights in England and Wales* (Clarendon, 1993), pp. 668-673; or Robertson and Nicol, above n. 142, pp. 418-428.

193 The Act provides a definition of 'damaging' for each category of information.

194 For a recent formulation of this idea, see eg, *A-G v Blake* [2000] 4 All ER 385, 399-400 (HL) (per Lord Nicholls): 'Secret information is the lifeblood of these services . . . An absolute rule against disclosure, visible to all, makes good sense.'

195 There is a third grouping: Crown servants and government contractors who are *not* notified commit an offence under s. 1(3) if they make a *damaging* disclosure (widely defined in s. 1(4)) of any information relating to security or intelligence.

'national security' agencies are stopped in their tracks: the 1989 Act provides neither a public interest nor a prior publication defence for the 'insider' who wishes to speak out.[196]

V.   GLASNOST

Armed with the OSA 1989, the UK government 'entered the last decade of the [twentieth] century with its defences against subversion newly entrenched'.[197] The early years of that decade also brought evidence that, so far as the senior judiciary were concerned, the national security-official secrecy nexus remained rock solid. In *Cheblak*, for example, a case concerning an order made by the Home Secretary following the outbreak of the Gulf War, for the deportation of a long-term British resident, the Court of Appeal emphasised that 'in the case of national security, the responsibility is exclusively that of the government of the day'.[198] It noted that 'Mr Cheblak's record . . . [made] the Home Secretary's decision [to order deportation] surprising' but went on to insist that it could not investigate the evidence. One member of the court, Lord Donaldson, added that he was confident that the Home Secretary was 'fully accountable to Parliament'. He also emphasised that 'to some extent the needs of national security must displace civil liberties . . .'.[199]

Elsewhere, however, the early years of the 1990s brought evidence of a new order. As emphasised in Part I, a re-imagining of 'the British way' had taken hold; deference was less common, and information and consultation were emerging as priorities for individuals and groups in their dealings with all sorts of different entities. 'The external enemy was [also] in a state of advanced

---

196 S. 5 of the 1989 Act deals with 'outsiders' (third parties who come into possession of information or material which has been disclosed by others) and makes it an offence to further disclose the information, if it causes damage, and they know or have reasonable cause to know that it does so. This means that newspapers facing prosecution can rely on a prior publication defence to prove that no further damage could occur from publishing the security and intelligence information.

197 Vincent, above n. 34, p. 309.

198 The applicant was a Palestinian academic who had campaigned publicly for Iraqi withdrawal from Kuwait. After recommendations made by the 'Three Wise Men' panel to the Home Secretary, he was not deported. Following *Chahal v UK* (1996) 23 EHRR 413, wherein the ECtHR examined the adequacy of the review system, and assessed how rights could be protected even in national security contexts, the government introduced the Special Immigration Appeals Commission Act 1997 which provides for the appointment of 'special counsel' in such cases. For discussion of this area, see eg, I. Leigh, 'The Gulf War Deportations and the Courts' [1991] PL 331 (arguing, first, that the accuracy and bias of intelligence information could be tested in cross-examination without questioning national security policy and, secondly, that the confidentiality of sources could be preserved by the introduction of procedures involving security-cleared lawyers, as in Canada). See Leigh, above n. 48, for details on the Canadian procedures.

199 *R v Secretary of State for the Home Department, ex p Cheblak* [1991] 2 All ER 319, 330 and 334 (CA). See also, *R v Secretary of State for the Home Department, ex p Brind* [1991] 1 AC 696 (HL) (re 'broadcasting ban' on alleged terrorists and supporters of terrorism); and *Balfour v Foreign Commonwealth Office* [1994] 2 All ER 588 (CA) (re upholding a PII certificate without inspecting MI6 documents relating to the dismissal of Balfour from the diplomatic service). Cf. Simon Brown LJ, writing extra-judicially in 1994: 'The very words "national security" have acquired . . . an almost mystical significance . . . [which] instantly discourages the court from satisfactorily fulfilling its normal role of deciding where the balance of public interest lies.' ('Public Interest Immunity' [1994] PL 579, 589)

dissolution':[200] 'the Wall' had come down, and the archives of the East German Stasi and the Soviet KGB had been thrown open to all-comers. We outlined these and other developments earlier in the chapter. In this Part, we aim therefore to deepen that outline by providing more information on four of the catalysts that brought the UK to its current position, namely, 'beyond the Secret State'.

Inside the belly of government: sleaze and secrets

The first catalyst we examine is Matrix Churchill. This is a scandal that stretched across the first half of the 1990s; indeed, it has been said of it that, '[o]n the Richter scale of scandals, . . . [it deserves] to be classified as causing serious structural damage to the foundations of the state'.[201] It concerned 'the borderland where foreign policy, defence policy and considerations of supposed "national security" converge'.[202] Specifically, it was about the issuing of licences, in apparent contravention of government guidelines on the arms trade and, apparently, without the knowledge of Parliament, for the export of military and related 'dual-use' equipment (that is, equipment which had legitimate civilian uses but which was easily adaptable for military purposes). Following an investigation into the activities of one exporter, Matrix Churchill, its directors were charged with knowingly exporting goods with intent to evade export restrictions. They, however, argued that they had obtained licences from the Department of Trade and Industry (DTI) who had known all about – and, in fact, encouraged – their trade with Iraq.

It transpired that one the directors of the firm, Paul Henderson, was an agent for MI6; 'a real-life James Bond',[203] who had openly visited Iraqi arms factories on business trips and provided valuable intelligence information to his MI6 'handlers'. Prior to the directors' trial, however, Public Interest Immunity (PII) certificates were signed by ministers in four government departments – DTI, Ministry of Defence, Home Office and Foreign Office – on the grounds of both the contents and class of the governmental papers which the defence sought access to. Various claims were made about the need to protect 'national security', 'commercial confidentiality' and the 'public interest' in promoting candour within the civil service. After several days of argument, the trial judge ordered the disclosure of crucial policy documents (containing civil service advice to ministers) and heavily-censored intelligence documents, containing MI5 and MI6 briefings.[204] Using this information, defence lawyers obtained an admission from former minister Alan Clark, during cross-examination, of an official cover-up of the UK-Iraqi arms trade. The Attorney-General was forced to withdraw the prosecution and the trial collapsed.

The fall-out from the Matrix Churchill trial forced the government to set up an official inquiry, under (now) Lord Scott. The public hearings and final report spotlighted the government and revealed that, despite the apparent ban on

---

200 Vincent, above n. 34, p. 309.
201 I. Leigh, 'Matrix Churchill, Supergun and the Scott Inquiry' [1993] PL 630, 647.
202 Lustgarten, above n. 27, p. 500.
203 J. Sweeney, *Trading With The Enemy: Britain's Arming of Iraq* (Pan, 1993), p. 15.
204 See A. Tomkins, 'Public Interest Immunity After Matrix Churchill' [1993] PL 650; and 'Intelligence and Government' (1997) 50 Parl Affairs 109.

arms trade with Iraq, ministers and civil servants had secretly encouraged and approved such trade. There was a good deal of evidence of this approval. In the margin of a memo dated 1989, William Waldegrave, a Foreign Office Minister, had written '[s]crewdrivers can be required to make hydrogen bombs'. DTI officials endorsed the export of guns to an Iraqi arms factory and then claimed that the weapons had no military purpose because they were for 'sporting use' only.[205] Foreign Office documents revealed that civil servants had secretly advised arms exporters that, in order to avoid 'presentational difficulties', they should 'produce and ship as fast as [possible]'.[206]

The civil libertarian verdict on Matrix Churchill was damning. Robertson, the defence lawyer for Paul Henderson, concluded that, although it was 'no conspiracy, in the sense that there was no grand design, or grand designer', government '(its mandarins as much as its ministers)' had behaved as it always had done – namely, when it sensed a threat of exposure, its motive was 'self-protection: damage to others [was] incidental'.[207] For Robertson and other civil liberties commentators, Matrix Churchill was yet another example of the corrosiveness of the British 'culture of secrecy'; it was also evidence of the tattered framework of governing:

> Was this the final outrage on democracy by a *fin de siecle* government intoxicated from four successive electoral victories, long past shocking press, media and the public in its short cuts or back-doubling through constitutional conventions, and apparently long past caring?[208]

The civil libertarian verdict on the Scott Report into Matrix Churchill which was published in February 1996 was not damning, but it was less than effusive.[209] The general sense seemed to be that the 1,800-page report was insufficiently forceful: that there was a gap between its criticisms (of individuals, of departments and of the toolkit of government secrecy (especially PII certificates)) and its recommendations, and that as a result a prime opportunity for prising reform from a badly-bruised government was wasted. There was also a sense, however, that even the toughest of recommendations from Scott might not have secured change given the depth and breadth of the problems.[210]

Freedom of information: from principle to practice

The second, albeit related, catalyst was provided by the move of the campaign for freedom of information from the periphery of non-governmental activism to the core of party politics. This move was evident, for example, in New Labour's 1997 General Election manifesto commitment to a Freedom of Information

---

205 Cited in Robertson, above n. 11, p. 332.
206 Ibid., p. 324.
207 Ibid., pp. 325-326.
208 P. Birkinshaw, 'Government and the End of its Tether: Matrix Churchill and the Scott Report' (1996) 23 JLS 406, 406 (reference omitted).
209 See eg, Leigh and Lustgarten, above n. 30, pp. 723-724 arguing that '[i]t was as though [Scott] could not bring himself to believe that men of this eminence – "respectability", the Victorians would have said – could really behave badly'.
210 See eg, Birkinshaw, above n. 208, asking '. . . does the episode reveal systemic weaknesses in the British constitutional apparatus now in desperate need of a complete overhaul? And, behind it all, there is the relationship between government and the arms trade and the promotion of British industry in one of its few world-wide success stories'.

Act (FoI).[211] The subsequent White Paper, *Your Right To Know*, suggested that New Labour intended to make good on this commitment.[212] More importantly, it also suggested that any such legislation would have far-reaching effects on the traditional 'culture of secrecy'. In particular, the detailed proposals indicated that there would not be a ministerial veto on disclosure of information. Instead, there would be an independent Information Commissioner with the power (backed by the courts) to override public authorities after weighing the public interest in disclosure against the need for secrecy. Most significantly, the test for non-disclosure would be the prevention of 'substantial harm'. Furthermore, information relating to the formulation or development of government policy (such as Cabinet Committee papers) would be one of the categories of material open to disclosure under the FoI regime.

The Freedom of Information Act 2000 does not tally, however, with the White Paper.[213] It seems that in the period which elapsed between the two, the New Labour government although still committed to *the principle* of freedom of information, became 'increasingly aware of the political realities of introducing freedom of information *in practice*'.[214] Moreover, neither the five backbench revolts in the House of Commons during the parliamentary debates on the legislation, nor the fact that there was a coalition of interests ranged against the new Act,[215] prevented the government from abdicating on the promises made in its own White Paper.[216]

The principal contrast between the White Paper and the final version of the Act is that the latter replaces promised freedom of information with what is, in effect, 'a discretionary scheme of official control of public information in statutory form'.[217] The contrast is evidenced by the following features of the new legislation. First, the traditional ministerial veto over disclosure remains firmly in place; the Information Commissioner can indicate that it is in the 'public interest' to disclose information, but has no power to compel disclosure. As Birkinshaw and Parry have pointed out, '[t]he Home Secretary made plain he was not going to give away political power to a non-elected official'.[218] Secondly, the range of exemptions from disclosure is now so wide that the

---

211 See generally, Birkinshaw, above n. 9, pp. 50-81.

212 For more details, see eg, P. Birkinshaw, 'An "All Singin' and All Dancin'" Affair: The New Labour Government's Proposals for Freedom of Information' [1998] PL 176; or S. Palmer, 'Freedom of Information: The New Proposals' in Beatson and Cripps, above n. 19, pp. 249-266.

213 Several commentators trace the 'gap' between the promise of the White Paper and the actual legislation to the fact that, in 1998, the Home Office took over responsibility for freedom of information.

214 M. Flinders, 'The Politics of Accountability: A Case Study of Freedom of Information Legislation in the United Kingdom' (2000) Pol Q 422, 433 (emphasis added). For a similar argument, see eg, Birkinshaw and Parry, above n. 60, p. 554.

215 Birkinshaw and Parry, ibid., p. 546. Note that in the period between the White Paper and the final statute there were 'rumours of enormous lobbying by commercial and utility interests'.

216 Clive Ponting, the civil servant who blew the whistle on the Belgrano Affair, has criticised the Act in strong terms. See above n. 90, p. 337: 'Cynics had long argued that it was perfectly possible to pass a toothless Freedom of Information Act that provided no enforceable rights to obtain more information. However, only a few in this group would have believed that a reactionary Home Secretary, in alliance with vested interests in Whitehall, would have the chutzpah to introduce such legislation and actually widen the scope of official secrecy at the same time. . . . There is little doubt that the last opportunity for a generation to reform the culture of secrecy has been lost.'

217 Flinders, above n. 214, p. 433.

218 Birkinshaw and Parry, above n. 60, p. 554.

majority of government information could potentially be exempt under the various headings (for example, policy advice, security and intelligence services, private or commercial confidences, etc). Thirdly, the Act changes the test for non-disclosure from 'substantial harm' to 'causing prejudice', a much lower threshold for authorities to meet.

The contrast between the Act and the White Paper was also made crystal clear in the evidence given by then Home Secretary, Jack Straw, to the Public Administration Committee. His evidence indicated that a rather worrying strain of nostalgia may permeate the government's preferred approach to official secrecy:

> the Home Secretary repeatedly sought to recreate the idea of '*honourable secrecy*'. Implicit in the government's rationale is the principle that decisions on disclosure rightly belong in the hands of ministers (and their officials) who could be trusted to use their discretion in the public interest.[219]

Changing media practices

The third catalyst is the burgeoning diversity of media practices. Relationships between media and government are now much more complex than before: established patterns (such as the D-Notice Committee[220] and ruthless government control of media agendas in wartime[221]) co-exist with a new post-*Spycatcher* mindset whereby assertions that publication is 'in the public interest' are increasingly prevalent, if not rampant.

The latter is a particularly confusing development, which encompasses both positive and negative trends. On the one hand, it brings with it evidence of a new independence of mind on the part of journalists covering defence and security issues. In particular, there is evidence that the Official Secrets Act 1989 is 'universally discounted'.[222] This was the conclusion drawn, for example, by Lustgarten and Leigh following interviews they conducted with journalists for their 1994 book, *In From the Cold: National Security and Parliamentary Democracy*. In those interviews, journalists expressed the view that the 1989 Act was not 'aimed at them but at civil servants, in order to prevent leaks' and, interestingly, when the journalists were:

> [a]sked what sort of material they would themselves refuse to publish if it came their way, their examples would all have come within the 1989 Act, but that was not the reason for their reticence. Very striking was the fact that they were guided by their own sense of what should be suppressed.[223]

---

219 Flinders, above n. 214, p. 433 (emphasis added).
220 Eg, in Aug. 1997, the Committee contacted *The Observer* with a request that it not publish the name of the new deputy director of MI5. The newspaper went ahead with its planned report ('[o]ur report does not simply name Ms Manningham-Buller, it also reveals the poisonous office politics inside MI5 and the service's failure to pass a management audit. These are matters of public interest'), and also informed its readers of MI5's request that it remove the name from its story.
221 2,700 media representatives accompanied NATO forces when they entered Kosovo. On this issue, see eg, P. Knightley, *The First Casualty: The War Correspondent as Hero and Myth Maker From The Crimea to Kosovo* (Prion Books, 2000); P. Taylor, *War and the Media: Propaganda and Persuasion in the Gulf War* (Manchester UP, 1998); and R Harris, *Gotcha! The Media, the Government and the Falklands Crisis* (Faber, 1983).
222 Lustgarten and Leigh, above n. 5, p. 262.
223 Ibid.

On the other hand, however, as news organisations work with 'their own sense of what should be suppressed', it appears that many of them operate commercially-driven criteria as the basis of their determinations of 'newsworthiness'. There is also increasing dependence on official sources for information, and privileged access to 'battle arenas' for exclusive pictures or footage, with the result that news reports can resemble official press releases.

Certain 'national security' stories will emerge under these criteria; others will not. This is evident in the contrast between the extensive coverage of David Shayler and the under-reporting of the Saville Inquiry into Bloody Sunday. It is also evident, as Robertson has pointed out, in the fact that the large sections of the media chose not to cover the *Matrix Churchill* trial in 1992:

> For all the ministers and civil servants and government lawyers these proceedings would ultimately draw into the lashing coils of its post-mortem, the media would go scot-free. It neither covered nor comprehended the case, after its combined investigative talents had failed to discover how 'UK Ltd' had been arming Iraq in contravention of stated government policy ever since that policy was first stated by Geoffrey Howe back in 1985. The BBC did not attend at all until the very last day.[224]

'The name is Shayler, David Shayler'

The last and ongoing catalyst – one that may yet rupture the traditional national security-official secrecy nexus (and do so in more dramatic fashion than Clive Ponting's trial under section 2 of the 1911 OSA) – is the David Shayler affair. Shayler joined MI5 in November 1991, as a successful entrant in its new 'outreach' recruitment drive. He alleges, however, that he became disillusioned with the service after his complaints and warnings about 'incompetence' were ignored (leading, he claims, to some botched MI5 operations in London). He also alleges that he discovered information about MI6 involvement in an assassination plot against the Libyan leader, Colonel Gadaffi, and about MI5 surveillance of Labour politicians, including Jack Straw and Peter Mandelson, and of defence lawyers while they conducted confidential interviews with suspected (IRA) terrorist inmates in Belmarsh high-security prison.

Shayler resigned from MI5 in October 1996 and later approached a newspaper with his revelations, including alleged copies of official MI5 documents. Articles appeared in *The Mail on Sunday* and *The Evening Standard* in late August 1997. Prior to further intended publication in the former newspaper on 31 August 1997, the Attorney-General obtained injunctions against Shayler and Associated Newspapers prohibiting both from disclosing any further information obtained by Shayler 'in the course of or by virtue of his employment' in MI5.[225]

In August 1998, Shayler was arrested by French police while living in Paris. He was imprisoned for several months whilst awaiting extradition proceedings in relation to charges under the OSA 1989 in England. The extradition attempt failed: the French court ruled that his 'whistleblowing' was politically motivated. On 21 August 2000, Shayler returned voluntarily to England, He was arrested

---

224 Robertson, above n. 11, p. 328.
225 See facts outlined in *A-G v Punch Ltd* [2001] 2 All ER 655 (CA). See also, *UN Special Rappoteur Report on Freedom of Expression: United Kingdom* (E/CN.4/2000/63/Add.3, 11 Feb. 2000), para. 60.

and charged under section 1 of the OSA 1989. The charges are limited to the allegations made to *The Mail on Sunday* in 1997 (which, significantly, do *not* include the Gadaffi plot details or other revelations) and the alleged theft of MI5 documents. In April 2001, a preliminary hearing on the compatibility of section 1 of the OSA 1989 with the Human Rights Act 1998 commenced – with the main emphasis being on whether a life-long, blanket ban on disclosure of 'national security' information was compatible with the right to freedom of expression under Article 10 of the ECHR, and whether a fair trial under Article 6 of the ECHR was possible if no 'public interest' defence was available. It coincided with a well-orchestrated media campaign by Shayler's legal and media advisers (including the civil liberties organisation, Liberty). Shayler himself told the waiting media that his case would 'put the British state on trial'.[226]

To date, the most remarkable aspect of the Shayler litigation is that, what is in many respects a twenty-first century re-run of *Spycatcher*, has resulted in very different legal outcomes and judicial commentary. The HRA is obviously a key influence, but there is also a novel boldness in the celebration of common law constitutionalism in the historically 'no-go' area of national security. For example, in July 2000, the Divisional Court ruled that blanket production orders under PACE 1984 did not oblige journalists to disclose information, which Shayler had provided to them, relating to the alleged Gadaffi plot. Judge LJ insisted that '[i]nconvenient or embarrassing revelations, whether for the security services or for public authorities should not be suppressed',[227] and he emphasised that the common law – he considered that there was no need to refer to the ECHR – provided the necessary protection for journalists to pursue their role of informing the public. Compelling evidence would, he said, normally be required to demonstrate that the public interest was served by the seizure of the working papers of a journalist or media outlet.

More significantly, in March 2001, a majority of the Court of Appeal held that where a court had ordered that specified facts in the Shayler litigation were not to be published, a third party who, with knowledge of the injunction, published them would only commit contempt if that third party thereby *knowingly* defeated *the purpose* for which the injunction was made. Thus, the former editor of *Punch* magazine was held not to be guilty of contempt for publishing an article by Shayler which the Attorney-General alleged damaged national security. Lord Phillips MR scrutinised the *Spycatcher No (2)* jurisprudence on the relationship between breach of confidence and contempt of court,[228] and concluded that the media could not be subject to 'censorship of the Attorney General' through a legal requirement that they must seek prior approval before every publication. The purpose of the injunction – to preserve until trial the confidentiality of information whose disclosure arguably posed a risk to national security – *was* defeated when

---

226 On 16 May, 2001, Moses J ruled that there was no conflict between the OSA 1989 and the HRA 1998 (on appeal to CA).

227 *R v Central Criminal Court, ex p Bright* [2001] 2 All ER 244 (DC) (PACE 1984 does not oblige media to hand over to prosecution authorities information relating to Shayler allegations of an MI6 plot to assassinate the Libyan leader, Colonel Gadaffi).

228 See above, pp. 358-359.

Punch magazine published new details about MI5 operations. However, there was no evidence to prove that the editor had *intentionally* committed a contempt; he did not believe that he was damaging national security by publishing and thought that the government lawyers were delaying their approval in order to stifle the article.[229]

In effect, the Shayler litigation has generated a state of flux as regards the OSA 1989 and the *Spycatcher (No 2)* jurisprudence. More broadly, it indicates a potential 'constitutional moment', one which may bring the activities of MI5 and MI6 under unparalleled public scrutiny and may, perhaps, fracture the national security-official security nexus. Media reports suggest that both MI5 and ministers would like to 'draw a line under the case' and move on; as is evidenced, however, by *Ponting* and *Matrix Churchill* and, of course, by the initial stages of *Shayler* itself, criminal prosecutions offer potentially far-reaching catalysts for reform – 'moving on' may not be an option.

VI.   'MISSION IMPOSSIBLE'?: NEW DIRECTIONS FOR CIVIL LIBERTIES LAW IN THE HRA ERA

We return now to the question that suffuses this chapter: are we 'beyond the "Secret State"'? Earlier, in Part I, we suggested that the traditional 'culture of secrecy' lingers on. We also highlighted the Janus face of recent trends. That is, the ways in which they bolster the traditional culture and generate new problems at the same time as they create new opportunities. One example, raised earlier, should serve to reinforce this point: namely, that as their old missions have faded, the security services have sought and acquired new 'policing' roles, thereby creating not just new concerns but also a much more complex target for civil liberties law.[230]

In short, the current position is complex. We agree, therefore, with those who have said that '[i]t is time for a new way of thinking about secrecy'.[231] It is also time to look at new ways of securing national security. In what follows, we address these themes in a preliminary way by looking briefly at some emergent configurations of secrecy and national security. Specifically, we look in turn at two key issues: first, the lingering presence in the UK of what David Marquand calls a 'constitutional vacuum'.[232] Secondly, the challenging constellations emerging from the new world order – in particular, the questions that arise from NATO's armed human rights policy during the Kosovo War and from the

---

229 Simon LJ dissented on this point: 'True it may well be, as Mr Steen protests, that he had no *intention* of endangering national security and did not think he was doing so. That, however, is not the point. As he himself candidly admitted, he was not qualified to make that judgment. . . . [H]e intended to take upon himself the responsibility for determining whether national security was risked and thereby he thwarted the court's intention' (para. 138). Note that all three judges believed that the A-G could have proceeded against *Punch* on the basis that they had aided and abetted a breach by Shayler of the injunction.

230 As evidenced, eg, by the UK's involvement in the European Schengen information system (a Strasbourg-based database which, at the end of 1997, held over 14 million records on fugitives, firearms and stolen vehicles), and in the US-led economic espionage network.

231 Commission on Protecting and Reducing Government Secrecy, *Secrecy: Report of the Commission on Protecting and Reducing Government Secrecy* (Washington, DC: Government Printing Office, 1997), p. xxi.

232 Above n. 44, p. 268.

burgeoning influence of a 'culture of secrecy' grounded in the practices of transnational corporations (such as securing 'company loyalty', protecting 'commercial confidentiality', and 'security vetting' of potential customers[233]).

Constitutional vacuum?

As we have seen throughout this book, the New Labour government have what seems like a deep commitment to refreshed democracy. Yet, as Marquand and others have pointed out, they are struggling to answer the 'obvious consequential questions: What sort of modern society? What kind of reconstruction, informed by what vision of democracy?'[234] In part, as evidenced by the disappointing hybridity of the Freedom of Information Act 2000, these questions are a problem for the government because:

> [although] the old constitution is broke: partly by social change, partly by Thatcher and partly by Blair . . . irrespective of party, [politicians] are still in thrall to it. So are the functionaries of Millbank and Smith Square and what is left of the mandarinate of Whitehall. As for ministers, they half-want to disperse power in the interests of modernisation from below, and half-want to concentrate it in the interests of modernisation from above.[235]

In effect, modernisation is in vogue but the old ways linger on. In addition, new 'New Labour' ways have emerged which are a cause for further concern: here we are thinking in particular of, first, the leadership's apparent sidelining of Westminster and Cabinet decision-making and, secondly, its embrace of a philosophy of *'un partito, una voce'* as it has set about 'establishing a degree of control within its own party without precedent in modern British political history'.[236] Of course, neither of these developments is all-encompassing: factors such as empire-building by individual ministers and incompetence generate obvious obstacles.[237] Yet the fact that both developments appear to be justified by notions of democratisation of party politics and of 'government for, and of, the people'[238] makes them particularly worrying.

It seems likely that the tensions which give rise to this constitutional vacuum will play out with particular force vis-à-vis the future of the 'Secret State'. As we have seen, for the UK, official secrecy has been 'a belief system, a way of life'.[239] It has often been 'all consuming'.[240] There can be no doubt that judgment has been damaged. Ministers and mandarins have been and, in some cases, continue

---

233 Porter, above n. 14, p. 15.
234 Marquand, above n. 44, p. 273.
235 Ibid., p. 274. R.A.W. Rhodes, 'New Labour's Civil Service: Summing-Up Joining-Up' (2000) 71 Pol Q 151, 163, makes a similar point in his analysis of New Labour's 1999 White Paper on civil service reform, *Modernising Government*: 'There is much to welcome in New Labour's modernising programme for central, local and devolved government. But the government lacks the trust it seeks to inspire. It fears the independence it bestows. . . . Hands-off is the hardest lesson of all for British central government to learn.'
236 P. Mair, 'Partyless Democracy: Solving the Paradox of New Labour?' (2000) NLR (II) 21, 23.
237 For development of this idea, see A. Barnett's response to Mair's article 'New Labour at Sea' (2000) NLR (II) 80.
238 On New Labour's style of government, see eg, Mair, above n. 236; and D. Marquand, *Progressive Dilemma: From Lloyd George to Blair* (Phoenix Grant, 1999), pp. 225-246.
239 Moynihan, above n. 125, p. 206.
240 Ibid.

to be prime victims of the culture of secrecy.[241] The public has also been affected; distrust is not endemic (as it appears to be, for example, in the US where conspiracy theories seem part-and-parcel of how the nation imagines itself[242]) but, in the wake of the 'drain of legitimacy'[243] that displaced Conservative rule, it has been articulated with increasing regularity. It is also fed by a near-constant outpouring of scandals.

The ebbing away of public trust in government stretches back through several decades but it appears to have crystallised during the period of Conservative government from 1979-97, when the 'institutional iconoclasm'[244] of Thatcherism had the (surely unforeseen) effect of creating a less deferential polity. This ebbing away was then exacerbated by the response of central government, which became:

> ever more aggressive and ever more determined to concentrate power in its own hands. For its pains, [however,] it became ever more isolated from, and ever more suspect to, the society for which it claimed to speak. The more vigorously the Thatcherites' capitalist renaissance roared ahead, the less legitimate became the institutions through which they had procured it.[245]

The process of constitutional reform and democratic renewal instituted by New Labour is clearly intended to stem this drain of legitimation. Yet there is already evidence that the government's publicly favoured mix of constitutionalism and plebiscitarianism is problematic. In particular, 'the myth of popular sovereignty' is open to manipulation: it offers 'a handy substitute for the equally mythical parliamentary sovereignty of the past, offering a way to disguise our old friend, *autonomous executive power*, in new clothes'.[246] In addition, it needs to be remembered that neither the 'hollowing out' of the UK state, nor the New Labour 'democratic renewal' package, have had much impact on the panoply of 'national security' measures available to government.[247] The breadth of these measures is made more worrying by the fact that New Labour, as evidenced by the Freedom of Information Act 2000, has chosen to champion ministerial

---

241 See eg, MI5's lack of disclosure re the Mitrokhin Archive, above n. 57. Moynihan, ibid., p. 202 recounts the lasting thrall of the Cold War culture of secrecy in the US: 'The Cold War ended; secrecy as a mode of governance continued as if nothing had changed . . . [For example,] early in 1993, the Senate Committee on Foreign Relations asked to be briefed on the conflict that had broken out in Bosnia and adjacent countries. A sizeable contingent of generals arrived, accompanied by civilians. In the manner of President Ford's briefings decades earlier, the man from the agency began. But first the question: is everybody here cleared? One asked oneself: cleared for what? Premature Chetnik sympathies? Latent Titoist tendencies? We *had* no secrets about the Balkans. But this was now government routine.'

242 Moynihan, ibid., p. 219 notes that '[t]he most notorious conspiracy theories, of course, play upon the unwillingness of the vast majority of the American public to accept that President Kennedy was assassinated in 1963 by Lee Harvey Oswald'. On the US' conspiracy culture, see generally J. Dean, *Aliens in America: Conspiracy Cultures from Outerspace to Cyberspace* (Cornell UP, 1998).

243 Marquand, above n. 44, p. 273.

244 Vincent, above n. 34, p. 309.

245 Marquand, above n. 44, p. 273.

246 Ibid., p. 275 (emphasis added).

247 Wright, above n. 15, p. 214 arguing that '[a] huge array of national security laws continues to be found in jurisdictions such as the United Kingdom . . . despite the appearances of the dispersal of central state power . . . There are dangers in assuming that our most repressive laws are moribund historical remnants, administered in highly particular circumstances, when they remain the state's final resource, short of military force, in perceived crisis'.

responsibility to Parliament as the ongoing centrepiece of the national security framework.

The upshot is that, post-constitutional reform, a rethinking of 'national security' in a manner befitting the new governing order has yet to take place. This is a crucial yet immensely complex project. A decent starting point has been provided, however, by Lustgarten and Leigh in their 1994 book, *In From the Cold: National Security and Parliamentary Democracy*. Therein they outlined a 'democratic conception' of national security which, in essence, proposes that protection of human rights and the health of democratic institutions should be at the core of what is regarded as national security.[248] On this account, rights become 'major constituents of national security *itself*',[249] such that where they are interfered with by an action taken in the name of national security:

> justification cannot be established merely by 'weighing' the needs of national security against the loss of individual liberty. The loss of liberty must be counted on *both* sides of the scale and thus deducted from any assessed gain in national security, as well as recognized as a loss to the individuals or groups specifically affected.[250]

Lustgarten and Leigh's proposal also provides that 'national security powers' should exist only where government can meet a democratic standard of proof; that is to say, where it can marshal 'a comprehensive elaboration of the character of the danger, its degree of seriousness and immediacy, the interests and range of persons affected, the reasonably anticipated duration of the proposed measure, and a credible explanation of why it is likely to achieve results beyond the capability of existing repressive powers'.[251]

This proposal is given a clear window of opportunity by the Human Rights Act 1998, which foregrounds proportionality and compels a spelling-out of the different interests traditionally cloaked by the heading 'national security'.[252] However, as Lustgarten and Leigh have emphasised since setting down their initial proposal in 1994, a 'democratic conception' of national security cannot be centred on the Act alone or, indeed, on the broader accountability debate that focuses on questions of Parliamentary reform and judicial role. We need also to think more laterally. We need, for example, to take account of the influence that the fragmentation of governing power has had, and may have, on government attempts to operate as 'an over-mighty Executive'.[253] Questions of institutional culture in the security services may also need to be addressed more seriously.[254] A more fundamental rethinking

---

248 See generally, Lustgarten and Leigh, above n. 5, pp. 3-35.

249 Ibid., p. 5.

250 Ibid., p. 9.

251 Ibid., p. 15 (footnote omitted).

252 See similarly R. Atkey, 'Reconciling Freedom of Expression and National Security' (1991) 41 UTLJ 38, 53: arguing that '[o]ne cannot overemphasize the importance of the role that the proportionality test should play in such an exercise. Not only does it force one to spell out different interests that have traditionally been grouped under the heading national security or that should now be viewed as warranting special protection given the realities of our modern-day political economy, but it also forces one to craft governmental powers to ensure that they do not infringe rights any more than is absolutely necessary in order to secure a given interest'.

253 See Leigh, above n. 16, pp. 308-309 for this suggestion.

254 See the suggestion along these lines in R.A. Watt, 'Review of L. Lustgarten and I. Leigh, *In From the Cold: National Security and Parliamentary Democracy* (Clarendon, 1994)' (1996) 112 LQR 165, 169. For an argument in favour of addressing institutional culture in the broader context of policing, see Ch. 4 above.

has recently been proposed by Lustgarten who nominates a 'fourth way' for New Labour – namely, withdrawal from the arms trade:

> not as a calculation of long-term diplomatic or political advantage, or in light of reassessment of economic benefits, nor even as a matter of moral scruple about others, but to protect our national security in the truest sense ... Conversion of the arms industry to civilian uses is not, as it is normally seen, a matter of economic or foreign policy: it is a constitutional imperative.[255]

None of this can be addressed in an adequate way, however, until the culture of 'official secrecy' is pierced. Recognising this, Lustgarten and Leigh's democratic conception of national security also proposes, first, that 'decisions as to secrecy should be based on the nature of the material, not on the official position held or formerly held by any person'[256] and, secondly, that where secrecy is justified, it cannot be maintained indefinitely – a time limit on concealment must apply (for example, five years) in order that 'the public may become aware of activities that might, even indirectly and inadvertently, have effected the conduct of domestic politics'.[257]

It is particularly disappointing, therefore, that the Freedom of Information Act 2000 generally excludes 'security and intelligence services', 'commercial confidences', 'national security', and 'defence' information from its statutory rights of access. Indeed, as Leigh has pointed out, '[a] large proportion of the information disclosed by the government to the Scott Inquiry, but previously withheld from Parliament and the public, about export licence applications, defence procurement and Iraqi attempts at proliferation would fall into [exempted] categories'[258] under the 2000 Act. A similar problem is manifest in the Public Interest Disclosure Act 1998, which excludes both employees involved in intelligence and security activities and those who breach the Official Secrets Act 1989 when they whistleblow. Articles 8 and 10 of the Human Rights Act may, however, provide some room for manoeuvre here: whether they actually do depends on the general approach adopted by the courts to the definition of 'national security' and the proportionality test.[259] In line with this, Cripps has emphasised that the impact of the HRA (and the Public Interest Disclosure Act) 'in protecting workers from public, and potentially private, sector employers who retaliate against them for disclosing or attempting to disclose information which the public has an interest in receiving' will depend on both 'liberal interpretation and a protective spirit on the part of the judiciary'.[260]

War and Privatisation

We turn now to a second key challenge confronting civil liberties in future engagements with 'national security' and 'secrecy': the Janus face of the new world order of 'global interconnectedness'. We begin by looking at the challenge this presents for constructing a democratic conception of national security.

---

255 Lustgarten, above n. 31, p. 430.
256 Lustgarten and Leigh, above n. 5, p. 30.
257 Ibid., p. 32.
258 Leigh, above n. 16, p. 301.
259 See Vickers, above n. 19, pp. 442-443.
260 Cripps, above n. 19, p. 287. See also, Sedley, above n. 62, pp. 239-248.

Thereafter, we deal with the question of emerging cultures of (non-official) secrecy, an issue that links with our discussion of privacy in Chapter 6.

'Muscular humanitarianism'[261]

Recent years have brought a novel and greatly troubling conjunction of national security and human rights – namely, that protecting national security can entail 'defending' human rights on foreign territory. This idea is, for example, inherent in (former) US Secretary of State Madeleine Albright's explanation of the US' involvement in the NATO bombing of Serbia in the spring of 1999 during the Kosovo War. Her explanation depicts '[t]he promotion of human rights [as] not just a kind of international social work [but as] indispensable for *our* safety and well being.'[262] The question is: what are we to make of this conjunction of national security and human rights? It cuts through traditional distinctions between war and peace (and, relatedly, between war and police violence[263]), and between domestic and foreign policy. It has thrown up difficult questions about the duty imposed by the UN Charter to collectivise the use of force, deepening the 'restlessness' about multilateral action as the basis of modern public international law.[264] It points also, Beck has argued, to the perpetuation of old ways under the glossy cloak of human rights:

> Put very cautiously: the military humanism which the West has taken up by embracing human rights fills the [post Cold War] vacuum perfectly by providing institutions, which have been deprived of an enemy, with a cosmopolitan mission. . . . Precisely because the worldwide demand for fundamental human rights is entirely legitimate and the resulting interventions are regarded as disinterested, it often remains unnoticed how neatly they can be dovetailed with old-fashioned aims of imperialist world politics . . . while internally they simultaneously encourage the creation of stage roles which give 'lame ducks' – politicians and military men – the opportunity to bathe in the glamour of renewed activity and legitimacy.[265]

The post-Kosovo conjunction of national security and human rights may thus represent a mixed advance.[266] The growing US impulse towards unilateral action complicates the picture yet further.[267] Similarly, claims made in connection with global citizenship, and the vogue for mobility, are compromised by the increasing identification of international migration as a 'national security' threat.

---

261 We take this section heading from Orford, above n. 63.
262 M. Albright, quoted in U. Beck, 'The Cosmopolitan Perspective: Sociology of the Second Age of Modernity' (2000) 51 BJ Soc 79, 82 (emphasis added).
263 For development of this point, see H. Caygill, 'Perpetual Police? Kosovo and the Elision of Police and Military Violence' (2001) 4 EJST 73, 74 suggesting that the conflict in Kosovo 'can plausibly be regarded as a struggle between two rival police forces and concepts of police, the Serbian "police" operating to restore order within their sovereign territory and the international "police" of NATO's new strategic concept'.
264 J.C. Hathaway, 'America, Defender of Democratic Legitimacy?' (2000) 11 EJIL 121, 121. See also, C. Chinkin, 'The State That Acts Alone: Bully, Good Samaritan or Iconoclast?' (2000) 11 EJIL 31.
265 Beck, above n. 262, p. 86.
266 See also G. Delanty et al., 'War and Social Theory: Reflections after Kosovo' (2001) 4 EJST 5, 5 arguing that 'the time [is] right to bring the issues raised in these interventions back into social theory that retains an inclination to see peace and order as the significant normality and war and violence as the negligible exception'.
267 See Hathaway, above n. 264.

The rampancy of 'security vetting'[268] in everyday life in countries like the UK and the US, which was discussed in Chapter 6, also contains the potential, in its premise of constant internal and external threats, to aggravate the difficulty of constructing a democratic conception of national security.

Privatisation

The challenge of constructing a democratic conception of national security should not be underestimated. Nor should the related challenge of juggling secrecy, privacy and freedom of information in ways appropriate to a world order characterised by rampant distrust, and prioritisation of the market. Furthermore, as outlined in Chapter 6, there is also the hazard of a less than sophisticated approach both to questions of when publicity can legitimately be given to private facts, and to questions of when public record information should receive privacy protection.[269]

Earlier in this Part we outlined Lustgarten and Leigh's suggestions for alleviating the impact of the culture of *official secrecy* on questions of national security. Here we address the issue of the broader 'culture of secrecy'. Historically, that culture was not concerned only with the Defence of the Realm; nor was it the prerogative of government alone.[270] As Vincent has pointed out, the 'culture of secrecy' was so pervasive that it provides a gateway to the 'social history of trust' in the UK. More importantly, as he goes on say, that history surely merits close study in our current climate given that 'the probity of all sources of authority is under attack'.[271]

This social history of trust reveals layers of blocked communication. It reminds us – and this is the point we want to emphasise here – that the state was not the only one keeping secrets, and that 'non-official secrecy' on matters (such as reproductive control) which may not have ranked highly on accepted 'scales of significance'[272] caused lasting damage to both societal and individual health and well-being in myriad ways. The reason for emphasising this is that, as Porter reminds us, 'secrecy has a way of developing new strains'. In particular, '[f]ree-market capitalism has a dozen associated values it could put in place' of the traditional culture of official secrecy:

> Company loyalty is one. The notion of sensitive market intelligence is another.[273]

The point we are driving at is that the attitude of transnational corporations towards the control and dissemination of information merits scrutiny in any project that seeks to achieve a better balance between secrecy, privacy and freedom of information.[274] There are at least two reasons for this. First, as

---

268 See eg, N. Rose, 'Government and Control' (2000) 40 BJ Crim 321, 340 ('Does this person have sufficient funds to make this purchase; is this citizen entitled to enter this national territory; is this person creditworthy; is this individual a potential suspect in this criminal case; is this person a good insurance risk?').
269 See Ch. 6, pp. 317-326.
270 In developing this point, we follow Vincent, above n. 34.
271 Ibid., p. ix.
272 Ibid.
273 Porter, above n. 35, p. 15.
274 See more generally, G. Monbiot, *Captive State: The Corporate Takeover of Britain* (Macmillan, 2000).

Birkinshaw reminds us, these companies 'may wield economic power to rival that of governments'.[275] Searching questions need therefore to be asked:

> Is there likely to be information held by these bodies which in the public interest should be publicly available and which should not be protected by claims to commercial confidentiality? What are the legitimate claims of commercial confidentiality? Too often the feeling is present that if a matter is commercial, it is confidential, even when it is an activity for, or of, government.[276]

The second reason for critical examination of commercial confidentiality is that New Labour's model of a 'new Britain' borrows heavily from the language of business and entrepreneurship. Its own style of governing, for example, looks openly to 'modern business management to teach it how to deliver'.[277] One can interpret this trend in both optimistic and pessimistic fashion. On the one hand, businesses' emergent focus on obligations of customer satisfaction perhaps contains ideas whereby 'open communication might spread from commerce to government'. On the other hand, however, there is 'the possibility of a mutual reinforcement of devices for closure'[278] via their individual emphases on maintaining confidentiality.

CONCLUSION

This chapter spans a period from circa 1889 to 2001. In that period, British society clearly has experienced tremendous social and political changes. We have argued, however, that changes to the 'Secret State' have been painfully slow in coming; the traditional 'culture of secrecy' provided the foundation for the creation of the Secret State, and has continued to exert a tenacious grip. We highlighted a particularly corrosive nexus of 'national security' and 'official secrecy' throughout the twentieth century, a nexus which permitted every form of exaggeration, obfuscation, denial and paranoia to take hold, and provided the cover for anti-democratic forces and often systematic violations of human rights. Secrecy became a 'way of life' because it suited so many, particularly in government, but also in other circles of power. Looking back from our vantage point today, it should be seen as truly extraordinary, for example, that the security services could exist in a 'phantom space' for so long; that respect for a 'right to privacy' was almost fatally undermined because of a near-obsession with spies and spying in British culture (witness the judicial hopelessness at condemning the 'bugging and burgling' of state actors); and that 'official secrets' have provided the cover for a self-willed collective amnesia about the UK's past.

This chapter, however, has also argued that we have moved 'Beyond the Secret State' due to a complex combination of (social, economic, political, legal) forces operating at individual, group, local, national, supranational and global levels. Information flows, and communication channels, have been transformed by these changes, providing the opportunity to unlearn the ways of the past, but also throwing up new dilemmas and challenges. The 'crisis' in

---

275 Birkinshaw, above n. 212, p. 187.
276 Ibid.
277 Barnett, above n. 237, pp. 87-88.
278 Vincent, above n. 34, p. 310.

the medical profession, for example, is as much about patients challenging hierarchies of power and notions of expertise as it is about the scarcity of NHS resources. The relationship between citizen and government is different to the earlier era of deference and cultural acceptance of 'never knowing what happened': locking away the public records of public events for 100 years should become increasingly unsustainable. Yet, as is obvious throughout the chapter, we have given law only a supporting role on the wider stage of secrecy. This was true for the Official Secrets Act 1911 and may still be true for the future, despite the potential contained within the Human Rights Act 1998, Freedom of Information Act 2000, Public Interest Disclosure Act 1998 and other legal resources and actors. The 'right to know' will need a much stronger basis than just legal foundations: it requires a cultural shift towards openness and the casting off of the, often reassuring, cloak of secrecy.

It may, therefore, be appropriate to close the chapter with a cautious note of optimism on this latter point. The example we have in mind is the opportunity provided for 'facing history' that is inherent in the Saville Inquiry into the events in Northern Ireland in 1972 known as 'Bloody Sunday'.[279] The term 'facing history' is of course associated most closely with South Africa's Truth and Reconciliation Commission.[280] The idea is also evident in the recent Parekh Report, which argues that 'some of the dominant stories in Britain need to be changed – stories about the past, the present and the future'.[281] 'Facing history' invokes the idea that a country needs to work towards a more open and inclusive account of its own past, before it is able to work towards a more democratic future. It suggests that greater attention should be paid to the wide-ranging societal interest in inquiring into memory and acknowledging different forms of truth, in particular the fact that as we become 'more aware that there are alternative ways of truth telling . . . we are therefore more responsible for the forms we use to tell our truths'.[282]

The Saville Inquiry can be seen as both an important component of a more inclusive 'Northern Ireland constitutionalism' and ongoing peace process, and as a response to the interest in creating new spaces for hearing and debating narratives about past events. Its subject matter is of obvious relevance to some of the content of this chapter – the daily discussions of 'national security' considerations, PII certificates, MI5's 'role in Northern Ireland', 'shoot to kill' policies, Ministry of Defence documents, the 'culture of secrecy' in Whitehall – and it reflects the most genuine attempt yet to place a public spotlight on the (sometimes necessarily) shadowy activities and beliefs that were one component of the 'Secret State'. Much more importantly, the Saville Inquiry demonstrates the importance of the past: it re-affirms the significance of historical inquiry and preserving historical records; and it provides a space for evaluating our changing relationship to history and the 'politics of memory'.[283]

---

279 See www.bloody-Sunday-inquiry.org.uk.
280 See eg, D. Dyzenhaus, *Judging the Judges, Judging Ourselves: Truth, Reconciliation and the Apartheid Legal Order* (Hart Publishing, 1998); and M. Minow, *Between Vengeance and Forgiveness: Facing History after Genocide and Mass Violence* (Beacon Press, 1998).
281 The Parekh Report, above n. 18, p. 103.
282 M. Osiel, *Mass Atrocity, Collective Memory and the Law* (Transaction, 1997), p. 251.
283 T. Garton-Ash, 'The Truth About Dictatorship', *New York Review of Books* (19 Feb. 1998) 35, 35.

Chapter Eight

The stuff of legend: freedom of expression and equality

INTRODUCTION

This chapter is about freedom of expression and equality. In effect, this means that it is about the things that help make liberalism 'that which we cannot not want'.[1] It also means that it is about two difficult goods, and the even more difficult relationship between them. Of late, that relationship has become the subject of intense and protracted scrutiny. In part, this may be an effect of the increasing turn towards law by a range of groups who seek to challenge disrespect, exclusion and oppression by compelling recognition (for example, through state regulation of hate speech and harassment or exemptions from generally applicable rules).[2] In any event, 'sunny formulations'[3] of freedom and equality seem to have become rather unfashionable and the question of how best to trade-off between these 'transcendent commitments'[4] is more and more central. In line with this, empowerment and resistance have begun to displace freedom as the language of choice amongst activists and critical theorists. Enthusiastic discourses of freedom have, in fact, largely been abandoned by all but some postmodernists and those whom Wendy Brown calls the 'relentlessly self-interested'.[5] Similarly, straightforward discourses of equality as sameness, or identical treatment, have largely been abandoned. The emphasis instead is on either the 'hard questions' of equality in a context of difference or the pros and cons of focusing solely on social exclusion. In short, then, a grammar of paradox, tension and complexity, rather than 'sunny formulations' of freedom and equality, appears to be on the ascent.

The disorienting choice between freedom of expression and equality is but one part of a larger and more vexed range of choices associated with late-

---

1 G. Spivak, *Outside in the Teaching Machine* (Routledge, 1993), pp. 45-46 (cited in W. Brown, 'Suffering Rights as Paradoxes' (2000) 7 Constellations 230, 230).
2 Throughout this chapter, we use the term 'recognition' to describe group-based claims for justice and equality through difference. Specifically, unlike C. Taylor, 'Multiculturalism and the Politics of Recognition' in A. Gutmann (ed.), *Multiculturalism* (Princeton UP, 1992), we do not understand recognition as merely limited claims for justice in terms of cultural respect and preservation.
3 Brown, ibid., p. 230.
4 O. Fiss, *The Irony of Free Speech* (Harvard UP, 1996), pp. 12-13.
5 W. Brown, *States of Injury: Power and Freedom in Late Modernity* (Princeton UP, 1995), p. 25.

modern currents of difference and diversity. These choices reach from the apparently superficial to the self-evidently complicated. For example, the very language (both legal and non-legal) that is used to describe and define discrimination creates difficulties. Thus, does the prohibition on sex discrimination cover sexual orientation discrimination? Does the dominant understanding of 'racism' equate it with colour racism, thereby excluding cultural racism?[6] Is 'ethnic' used as a 'synonym for not-white or not-Western'?[7] Do the terms 'minority' and 'majority' both denigrate those assigned to the former category and obscure differences within each category? Does emphasis on 'equality' inhibit recognition of difference?

An example of a self-evident complication can be found in the relationship between liberalism and multiculturalism. The UK, as the Parekh Report notes, is 'both a community of citizens *and* a community of communities, both a liberal and a multicultural society, and needs to reconcile their sometimes conflicting requirements'.[8] One reason for the endless complications is that both liberalism and multiculturalism are the subject of independent contestation. Both, for example, have to contend with the 'new liberalism' of Third-Way government, and with the potent seam of conservative nationalism. Both also face contestation from within. Thus, for example, on the one hand, multiculturalism has helped us to see that the withholding of recognition can be a form of oppression and, on the other hand, it is criticised for reifying, or essentialising, differences between groups. Moreover, the way forward is not immediately obvious, given that deconstructive approaches to identity have faced searing criticism for promoting a 'fetish of identity'[9] and, thereby, swamping questions of power.

The turn towards difference and diversity is, however, not just endlessly complicated. It is also compromised by reverse currents of various kinds.[10] Aggressive nationalisms and other violent hatreds represent an extreme example of a reverse current. But apparently well-intentioned measures and policies can also serve to construct or reinforce reverse currents. The grammar of social inclusion and exclusion provides a good example of this latter type of reverse current. That grammar is New Labour's '"preferred term" to summarise its policy and programme as a whole';[11] it is also reasonably voguish in certain academic circles. It presents a potential reverse current because, in tandem with other forces, it may serve to mothball equality: it may, in effect, dislodge equality as a core objective of democracy.[12]

---

6 In the UK context, cultural racism refers primarily to racism directed against Muslims. For discussion of cultural racism, see eg, T. Modood, 'Introduction' in T. Modood and P. Werbner (eds.), *The Politics of Multiculturalism in the New Europe: Racism, Identity and Community* (Zed Books, 1997), at p. 4.

7 *The Future of Multi-Ethnic Britain: The Parekh Report* (Runnymede Trust, 2000), p. xxiii (hereinafter, the Parekh Report).

8 Ibid., p. ix (emphasis added).

9 Spivak, above n. 1, p. 14.

10 For this point, see generally J. Young, 'Cannibalism and Bulimia: Patterns of Social Control in Late Modernity' (1999) 3 Theor Crim 387.

11 Above n. 7, p. 76.

12 This concern has been expressed, eg, by D. Cooper, '"And You Can't Find Me Nowhere": Relocating Identity and Structure within Equality Jurisprudence' (2000) 27 JLS 249, 250; and R. Dworkin, *Sovereign Equality* (Harvard UP, 2000), p. 1.

The most useful advice, it seems to us, comes from those who call for critical pragmatism.[13] By critical pragmatism we mean the stance to rights that we have sought to endorse throughout this book, a stance which is captured perfectly by Didi Herman in the following passage:

> Rights claims are neither inherently radical rearticulations nor dangerous and diversionary. More often than not they are neither, occasionally they may be both. To say that rights are difficult, complicated tools for social change does not mean that the struggle for their acquisition is doomed or that 'real issues' are being obscured. At the same time, an unreflexive seeking of rights and yet more rights may not bring about the changes to social relations many of us would like to see.[14]

Critical pragmatism is, however, an elusive state. Moreover, even working towards it can be exhausting when faced with the rapidly proliferating opportunities for engagement with issues of freedom of expression and equality which are opened up by multi-level governance: each opportunity may have progressive potential, yet, simultaneously, each may be problematic.

We believe, therefore, that critical pragmatism needs to be complemented by a second virtue – imagination. Like critical pragmatism, imagination is an under-explored and elusive virtue. The cultural theorist Stuart Hall, for example, has observed recently that imagination has not been contemporary social theory's 'strongest suit'. Things do seem, however, to be changing: so much so, in fact, that the project of imagination has become almost voguish in law circles.[15] For lawyers, the project is associated primarily with legal theory, and in particular with the work of Boaventura de Sousa Santos[16] and, more recently, William Twining.[17] For example, Twining's latest book, *Globalisation and Legal Theory*, calls for an injection of imagination in jurisprudence. We need, he says, to nurture an understanding of legal theory and legal orders as maps, impressions or metaphors given that otherwise we cannot hope to 'come

---

13 See eg, D. Herman, 'Beyond the Rights Debate' (1993) 2 SLS 25; D. Herman, 'The Good, the Bad, and the Smugly: Perspectives on the Canadian Charter of Rights and Freedoms' (1994) 14 OJLS 589; C.F. Stychin, *A Nation by Rights: National Cultures, Sexual Identity Politics, and the Discourse of Rights* (Temple, UP, 1998); C.F. Stychin, '*Grant*-ing Rights: The Politics of Rights, Sexuality and European Union' (2000a) 51 NILQ 281; and C.F. Stychin, '"A Stranger to its Laws": Sovereign Bodies, Global Sexualities, and Transnational Citizens' (2000b) 27 JLS 601.

14 Above n. 13, (1993), p. 40.

15 Imagination has also acquired enhanced status in other scholarship: see eg, M. Barrett, *Imagination in Theory: Essays on Writing and Culture* (Polity, 1999); L. McNay, *Gender and Agency: Reconfiguring the Subject in Feminist and Social Theory* (Polity, 2000) (arguing that theoretical work on identity formation or subjectification has privileged a negative paradigm – 'subjectification as subjection' – and that this should be paired with a 'generative' approach which would admit of a '*creative or imaginative* substrate to action' (emphasis added)); and R. Rorty, *Contingency, Irony, and Solidarity* (CUP, 1989) and his 'Human Rights, Rationality and Sentimentality' in S. Shute and S. Hurley (eds.), *On Human Rights: The Oxford Amnesty Lectures 1993* (Basic Books, 1993), pp. 111-134 (arguing that in place of the illusory 'truths' of liberalism, twenty-first century politics will embrace our imaginative capacity).

16 B. de Sousa Santos, *Towards a New Common Sense* (Routledge, 1995).

17 See also, eg, D. Cooper, *Governing Out of Order: Space, Law and the Politics of Belonging* (Rivers Oram, 1998); R. Unger, 'Legal Analysis as Institutional Imagination' (1996) 59 MLR 1; and A. Hutchinson, 'In Other Words: Putting Sex and Pornography in Context' (1995) 8 Can J of Law & Juris 107, 133 (arguing that '[t]here is no outside to the world of words and no final escape from the finitude of politics. Rather than continue as an abstract practice of intellectual deep-sea diving in which the ambition is to touch bottom and drop social anchor once-and-for-all, philosophizing must become more self-consciously an active practice of learning to swim with the turtles').

anywhere near to catching in today's world the complexity, elusiveness and variety of phenomena of law which it is the task of [jurisprudence] to try to understand, describe and explain'.[18] For Twining, and for de Sousa Santos too, what is crucial is 'the complexities and elusiveness of reality, the difficulties of grasping it, and the value of imagination and multiple perspectives in facing these difficulties'.[19]

Ranging more broadly, one finds that imagination suffuses the recent Parekh Report on *The Future of Multi-Ethnic Britain*; its mark is evident, for example, in the Report's use of novelist Ben Okri's account of nations as types of 'imagined communities'[20] and its identification of the urgent need to re-imagine Britain's 'past story and present identity'.[21] It has also been suggested that, because '[a]ll over the world, more and more people look at their own lives through the optic of possible ways of life offered in every conceivable way by the mass media':

> imagination is now *a social praxis*: [that is], for many people in many societies, and in innumerable different variants, [imagination] has become the engine for the fashioning of public life.[22]

This chapter engages with the challenges of critical pragmatism and imagination in the following way. Parts I and II present an overview of the standing of freedom of expression and the principles of non-discrimination and equality within the civil liberties tradition. Together, these Parts provide the backdrop to the chapter. In Part III, we reach our principal concern: the vexed question of the relationship between freedom of expression and equality in a society which is turning itself towards the language of rights and which needs actively to synergise liberalism and multiculturalism and to create a sense of belonging. We seek to address this question by focusing on two recent attempts to use the law to compel recognition of group-based harm and the criticisms raised against these attempts. The final Part provides the chapter's conclusion. In particular, it fleshes out the case for critical pragmatism and imagination as core virtues of a civil liberties law for the Human Rights Act era.

I.   FREEDOM OF EXPRESSION IN THE CIVIL LIBERTIES TRADITION

Freedom of expression is often regarded as iconic for civil liberties. Defence of this freedom is associated with fire and brimstone, and absolutism, of an unparalleled quantity and quality. This is certainly one's sense of US civil libertarian commentators and activists, and it is arguably also the case in respect of some of their UK counterparts. The UK civil liberties tradition has

---

18 W. Twining, *Globalisation and Legal Theory* (Butterworths, 2000), p. 63.
19 Ibid., p. 243.
20 The idea of 'imagined communities' comes from B. Anderson, *Imagined Communities* (Verso, 1991). The Parekh Report, above n. 7, p. 103, cites the following passage from B. Okri, *Birds of Heaven* (Phoenix, 1996): "'Stories . . . are the secret reservoir of values: change the stories individuals and nations live by and tell themselves and you change the individuals and nations . . . Nations and people are largely the stories they feed themselves. If they tell themselves stories that are lies, they will suffer the future consequences of those lies. If they tell themselves stories that face their own truths, they will free their histories for future flowerings.'"
21 Parekh Report, ibid., p. 105.
22 A. Appadurai, cited in U. Beck, *The Brave New World of Work* (Polity, 2000), p. 157.

represented 'freedom of speech'[23] as fragile, if not under almost constant threat, throughout the twentieth century. Readers of civil liberties texts must be left reeling by the accounts of Official Secrets legislation, obscenity and indecency prosecutions, defamation restrictions, contempt of court threats, breach of confidence actions, restraints on public protest, and the patchwork of regulatory bodies and codes devoted to controlling imports, the press, broadcasting, advertising and cinema/video classifications.[24]

A stance of anti-censorship shapes much of the civil liberties literature. This position has its roots, as in other western democracies, in the rich history of political and legal battles fought against various forms of religious and political authoritarianism and elitism.[25] As Robertson explains:

> 'If liberty means anything at all, it means the right to tell people what they do not want to hear,' said George Orwell – ironically, in an introduction to *Animal Farm* which Gollancz, his left-wing publishers, declined to publish lest it give offence to Stalin.[26]

In many of these historic contexts, there appeared little need for elaborate theorisation of 'free speech'; the 'enemy' was obvious and censorship was one of the dragons that had to be slayed. The civil liberties response to several contemporary free speech flashpoints, for example, the use of the Official Secrets Act against genuine 'whistleblowers' and investigative journalists has marked parallels with this stance. Other flashpoints, however, highlight more diverse and nuanced responses from different civil liberties constituencies and other actors. Thus, while classic free speech arguments appear to predominate in relation to government attempts to regulate the novel medium of the Internet,[27] the questions raised, for example, by regulation of media conglomerates,[28] the David Irving ('Holocaust-denier') libel trial,[29] the construction of reproductive health information,[30] and the stigmatisation of racist speech[31] are characterised by a search for more sophisticated analyses of freedom of expression.

23 The seventeenth century origins of 'freedom of speech' and 'freedom of the press' in English law are distinct: the former phrase was first associated with immunity for *parliamentarians* and given recognition in the Bill of Rights 1689; the latter was associated with the removal of Crown licensing controls over the printing and publication of books and pamphlets: see G. Marshall, 'Press Freedom and Free Speech Theory' [1992] PL 40.

24 See eg, G. Robertson, *Freedom, the Individual and the Law* (Penguin, 1993); and G. Robertson and A. Nicol, *Media Law* (Penguin, 1992). For a detailed account of 100 years of British film censorship, and the range of political, legal and bureaucratic factors that influenced individual film bans/cuts, see T. Dewe Mathews, *Censored* (Chatto & Windus, 1994). For critical discussion of representation, see eg, S. Hall (ed.), *Representation: Cultural Representations and Signifying Practices* (Sage, 1996); and M. Humm, *Feminism and Film Theory* (Edinburgh UP, 1997).

25 See eg, the references in K.D. Ewing and C.A. Gearty, *The Struggle for Civil Liberties: Political Freedom and the Rule of Law in Britain 1914-1945* (OUP, 2000); S. Walker, *In Defence of American Liberties: A History of the ACLU* (OUP, 1990); and J. Curran and J. Seaton, *Power Without Responsibility: The Press and Broadcasting in Britain* (Routledge, 1997). See generally, the journal 'Index on Censorship'; and ARTICLE 19 publications (www.article19.org).

26 G. Robertson, *The Justice Game* (Vintage, 1999), p. 381.

27 See Y. Akdeniz et al., *The Internet, Law and Society* (Longman Pearson, 2000); L. Lessig, *Code and Other Laws of Cyberspace* (Basic, 1999); and Liberty (ed.), *Liberating Cyberspace: Civil Liberties, Human Rights and the Internet* (Pluto, 1998).

28 See generally, T. Gibbons, *Regulating the Media* (Sweet & Maxwell, 1998).

29 See *Irving v Lipstadt and Penguin Books Ltd* (HCt, 11 April, 2000).

30 See eg, S. Coliver (ed.), *The Right To Know: Human Rights and Access to Reproductive Health Information* (ARTICLE 19, 1995).

31 See eg, S. Coliver (ed.), *Striking A Balance: Hate Speech, Freedom of Expression and Non-Discrimination* (ARTICLE 19, 1992).

Civil liberties commentators and activists have not been the only ones moved
to defend freedom of expression. In the US, judges too have proved susceptible
to the allure of 'free speech' and have provided a bank of quotable quotes on
this freedom's virtues. Consider, for example, how often one encounters citation
of the words of former US Supreme Court justice, Holmes J, in dissent in the
1919 case of *Abrams v US*, wherein he echoed John Stuart Mill's defence of
speech that 'the best test of truth is the power of the thought to get itself
accepted in the competition of the market'.[32] UK judges, in contrast to their
US counterparts, have not provided a similar bank of quotable quotes on the
importance of freedom of expression. Indeed, until recently, they were most
often castigated in civil liberties circles for their defence of absurdities and
their pandering to executive and class interests. Complaints about the judiciary's
treatment of this freedom stretch to a very, very long list, although a sample of
the choicest listings would probably include the following: the judicial attempts
to regulate 'obscene' publications;[33] the banning of Peter Wright's book,
Spycatcher;[34] the 'terror to authorship' which was nurtured by the historical
emphasis on strict liability for defamation;[35] and the House of Lords' refusal in
Brind – involving a challenge by journalists to a 'Broadcasting Ban' on hearing
the voices of members of Northern Irish terrorist/political organisations – to
give any weight to a legal principle of freedom of expression.[36] The common
complaint that the UK judiciary paid only 'lip-service to [freedom of
expression's] importance'[37] has also been given credence by the fact that, on
occasion, the Strasbourg Court has reached directly opposite conclusions under
Article 10 of the ECHR.[38]

Of late, however, there have been 'important indications that the [UK] courts
are loosening up'.[39] McCrudden, for example, picks up on the trend amongst
the higher courts for paying heed to Article 10 'even before incorporation of the
Convention had been politically likely'.[40] The recent turn towards common law
constitutionalism has also improved the standing of freedom of expression as
part of the core protectorate of the common law: indeed, according to Judge LJ
free speech is 'bred in the bone of the common law'.[41] Ironically, however, this
principle, and more generally the enthusiasm for 'recovering' an indigenous
rights tradition, may also boost parochial tendencies and an exasperating
approach towards 'non-domestic' rights case law.[42] We shall return to this latter

32   250 US 616, 630 (1919).
33   *R v Hicklin* (1868) LR 3 QB 360 (re 'tendency to deprave and corrupt' test); and the Obscene
     Publications Act 1959, discussed below, pp. 417-421.
34   *A-G v Guardian Newspapers Ltd (No 2)* [1988] 3 All ER 545, discussed in Ch. 7.
35   *Knupffer v London Express Newspaper Ltd* [1942] 2 All ER 555, 561 (per Goddard LJ).
36   *R v Secretary of State for the Home Department, ex p Brind* [1991] AC 696 (HL).
37   E. Barendt, *Freedom of Speech* (Clarendon, 1987), p. 332.
38   See eg, *Sunday Times v UK* (1979) 2 EHRR 245; *Observer and Guardian v UK* (1991) 14 EHRR
     153; and *Goodwin v UK* (1996) 22 EHRR 123. Cf. *Handyside v UK* (1976) 1 EHRR 737 (states
     have a margin of appreciation to determine the protection of morals re censorship laws).
39   K.D. Ewing, 'The Politics of the British Constitution' [2000] PL 405, 407.
40   C. McCrudden, 'The Impact on Freedom of Speech' in B.S. Markesinis (ed.), *The Impact of
     the Human Rights Bill on English Law* (OUP, 1998), pp. 85-109.
41   *R v Central Criminal Court, ex p Bright* [2001] 2 All ER 244.
42   For detail on the vogue for common law constitutionalism, see Ch. 1. For commentary
     specifically on freedom of expression within this tradition, see M. Hunt, *Using Human Rights
     in English Courts* (Hart, 1997); and J. Laws, 'Law and Democracy' [1995] PL 72.

point below. For now, we want to emphasise what appear to be positive aspects of recent trends. First, certain individual areas of law which are all about limiting freedom of expression, and which had been relatively lifeless, have become sites of renewed interest, debate and fresh thinking. In defamation cases, for example, the courts have dealt more decisively in recent years with the problem of excessive jury awards,[43] and they have begun also to broach the deep problems with strict liability (albeit with a pronounced enthusiasm for turning inwards towards common-law constitutionalism rather than outwards to comparative rights jurisprudence).[44]

Secondly, and more generally, individual judges have begun to speak with considerable flourish on the merits of protecting freedom of expression. One example of this is Lord Steyn's crisp explanation of the intrinsic and instrumental importance of freedom of expression in *Simms*. Notably, Lord Steyn also emphasised the importance of context:

> The value of free speech in a particular case must be measured in specifics. Not all types of speech have an equal value. For example, no prisoner would ever be permitted to have interviews with a journalist to publish pornographic material or to give vent to so-called hate speech. . . . But the free speech at stake in the present cases is qualitatively of a very different order. . . . They wish to challenge the safety of their convictions. In principle it is not easy to conceive of a more important function which free speech might fulfil.[45]

A second example is provided by Sedley LJ's eloquent defence of the street-corner speaker in *Redmond-Bate v DPP*, wherein it was emphasised that the right to freedom of expression covers the 'irritating, the contentious, the heretical, the unwelcome and the provocative provided it did not tend to provoke violence'.[46] Writing extra-judicially, Lord Scott has provided a third example by putting a liberal spin on case law on confidentiality and claiming that the principle of open disclosure of government information, where no 'sufficient public interest' is at stake, is now 'self-evidently necessary in a mature democracy'.[47] And, a fourth and final example would be the Privy Council's recent emphatic rejection of state interference with broadcasting freedom.[48]

---

43   See eg, *Rantzen v Mirror Group Newspapers* [1993] 4 All ER 975 (CA); and *John v Mirror Group Newspapers* [1996] 2 All ER 35 (CA). The ECtHR's decision in *Tolstoy Miloslavksy v UK* (1995) 20 EHRR 442 influenced this development (award of £1.5m in libel damages amounted to infringement of Art. 10, ECHR).

44   See the recent easing of this in the context of political libel in *Derbyshire County Council v Times Newspapers Ltd* [1993] 1 All ER 1011 (HL) and *Reynolds v Times Newspapers* [1999] 4 All ER 609 (HL). On libel, see eg, E. Barendt et al., *Libel and the Media: The Chilling Effect* (Clarendon, 1997); and I. Loveland, *Political Libels* (Hart, 2000).

45   *R v Secretary of State for the Home Department, ex p Simms* [1999] 3 All ER 400, 408 (HL) (per Lord Steyn). Cf. Lord Hoffmann's remark in the same case that 'the adoption of the [ECHR] as part of domestic law is unlikely to involve radical change in our notions of fundamental human rights' (at 413). For an overview and discussion of theories of freedom of expression, see eg, the essays in T. Campbell and W. Sadurski (eds.), *Freedom of Communication* (Dartmouth, 1994).

46   [1999] Crim LR 998. See also *R v Video Appeals Committee of the BBFC, ex p BBFC* [2000] EMLR 850 (VAC had struck reasonable balance between freedom of expression and the potential harm to child viewers).

47   R. Scott, 'Confidentiality' in J. Beatson and Y. Cripps (eds.), *Freedom of Expression and Freedom of Information: Essays in Honour of Sir David Williams* (OUP, 2000), pp. 267-274, at p. 267.

48   *Observer Publications Ltd v Matthew* [2001] UKPC 11.

The vogue for arguments based on freedom of expression is not limited to the senior judiciary, however. Such arguments are now commonplace in all sorts of debates in the UK and, in the HRA-era, they will doubtless become even more prevalent. The press was fastest off the mark in seeking to wield freedom of expression as 'an ace of trumps',[49] using it as the basis of arguments that led to the inclusion of section 12 in the HRA. That section, which purports to bolster Article 10 by reminding courts of the importance of freedom of expression (and gives extra procedural safeguards to the media in 'prior restraint' litigation), was conceived following concerns raised by Lord Wakeham (in his capacity as chairperson of the Press Complaints Commission, the self-regulatory body of the press) and others that, without an explicit brake in the statute itself, the HRA could lead to a law of privacy that would restrict legitimate press reporting and overly threaten media freedom. However, as predicted by several commentators,[50] and confirmed by Sedley LJ in *Douglas and Zeta-Jones v Hello! Ltd*, section 12 cannot be interpreted so as to give *precedence* to Article 10 of the ECHR:

> The European Court of Human Rights has always recognised the high importance of free media of communication in a democracy, but its jurisprudence does not – and could not consistently with the Convention itself – give Article 10(1) the presumptive priority which is given, for example, to the First Amendment in the jurisprudence of the United States' courts. Everything will ultimately depend on the proper balance between privacy and publicity in the situation facing the court. . . . Neither element is a trump card. They will be articulated by the principles of legality and proportionality which, as always, constitute the mechanism by which the court reaches its conclusion on countervailing or qualified rights.[51]

Similarly, the decision of Butler-Sloss LJ in *Venables and Thompson v News Group Newspapers*, safeguarding the anonymity of the plaintiffs upon their eventual release from prison, resulted from the need to weigh the media's right to freedom of expression under Article 10 of the ECHR against the court's greater duty to protect the plaintiffs' right to life and well-being under Article 2 of the ECHR.[52] Not surprisingly, media reaction to these two cases has been a mixture of shock and hostility towards what is seen as a 'gradual erosion of press freedom in this country'. As Rusbridger, the editor of *The Guardian* acknowledges:

> The reality is dawning on newspaper lawyers and editors that the courts are – with some degree of relish – about to embark on a process of establishing and developing a right to privacy. . . . Recent judgments in a variety of courts since the introduction of the Human Rights Act have tended to show a keen appreciation of the importance of Article 10, which protects freedom of expression. But . . . judges are also determined to carve out a concept of responsible reporting which shows due recognition of other, sometimes conflicting rights.[53]

---

49   Cf. F. Schauer, *Free Speech: A Philosophical Inquiry* (CUP, 1982), p. 9 arguing that '[i]f there is a free speech principle, it means that free speech is a good card to hold. It does not mean that free speech is the ace of trumps'.
50   See eg, A. Lester and D. Pannick, *Human Rights Law and Practice* (Butterworths, 1999), p. 47.
51   [2001] 2 All ER 289, paras. 135-136 (per Sedley LJ).
52   [2001] 1 All ER 908. See also *A-G v Punch Ltd* [2001] 2 All ER 655, discussed in Ch. 7.
53   A. Rusbridger, 'Courting Disaster', *Guardian*, 19 Mar. 2001 (calling for a united approach by tabloid and broadsheet editors and proprietors to the new challenges posed to the press by the HRA).

Of course, the press is only one of a string of 'repeat players' from previous freedom of expression debates expected to feature prominently in the early years of the HRA era – challenges to the common law offence of blasphemous libel; to the content and policing of the Obscene Publications Act and customs legislation; and to a range of broadcasting and advertising regulations are also anticipated. New players, and those who were sidelined in earlier freedom of expression debates, may also garner attention and provoke controversy. One prominent example from the latter category is the EU, a long-time[54] but (at least in UK civil liberties circles) little-discussed player in freedom of expression debates, which has obvious ambitions in the field: it has, for example, recently sought to extend its influence on issues such as workplace harassment,[55] and to colonise fresh ground via its Directive on Tobacco Advertising.[56]

It would appear, therefore, that rosy times lie ahead for the civil liberties tradition's alleged favourite freedom. This is not to suggest that freedom of expression rights will predominate over other rights – the ECHR jurisprudence depends on context[57] – but that the freedom will be ever-present in arguments in courtrooms, in legislatures and elsewhere. This presence may be Janus-faced, however. Three general points arise for consideration here. The first was made several years ago by Gardner in a review of freedom of expression in English law. Drawing attention to the ease with which higher courts were accommodating Article 10 of the Convention, Gardner warned of the danger of becoming caught up in a race to the bottom – albeit one clothed with 'an aura of [international human rights] respectability' and replete with 'impressive references to grand ideals':

> [T]o present it as a virtue [that the common law of England already accepts the standards of Article 10] is to trade on the widespread but mistaken view that accommodating international human rights jurisprudence is the same thing as respecting human rights. There could come a point, indeed, where it would be better to have no Convention on Human Rights at all than one that can be used to legitimate and congratulate any decision under the sun.[58]

The second problem also arises from the UK courts' flaunting of the parallels between the common law principle of free speech and the standards set by Article 10 jurisprudence. It is not concerned with the vacuity of ECHR case law, however, but with the turning inwards that may result from inappropriate celebration of the common law's rights tradition.[59] If this phenomenon deepens

---

54 See eg, *Conegate Ltd v Customs and Excise Comrs*, Case 121/85, [1986] 2 All ER 688 (ECJ); and *Society for the Protection of Unborn Children (Ireland) Ltd v Grogan*, Case 159/90, [1991] 3 CMLR 849 (ECJ).

55 Below p. 417.

56 Directive 98/43/EC on the approximation of the laws, regulations and administrative provisions of the member states relating to the advertising and sponsorship of tobacco products. OJ 1998 L213/9. See the successful challenge to this Directive in *Germany v European Parliament and Council*, C-376/98 [2000] All ER (EC) 769 (ECJ).

57 See eg, the ECtHR decisions on racist expression: *Kuhnen v Germany* (1988) 56 DR 205 (re publication of racist pamphlets); *Jersild v Denmark* (1994) 19 EHRR 1 (re television documentary on racists); and *Sander v UK* [2000] Crim LR 767 (re racist remarks of jurors).

58 J. Gardner, 'Freedom of Expression' in C. McCrudden and G. Chambers (eds.), *Individual Rights and the Law in Britain* (OUP, 1994), pp. 209-238, at p. 236.

59 See *R v Secretary of State for the Home Department, ex p Simms* [1999] 3 All ER 400, 413 (HL) (per Lord Hoffmann): 'the adoption of the [ECHR] as part of domestic law is unlikely to involve radical change in our notions of fundamental human rights'.

in the HRA era – and remember the fanfare surrounding the statute's enactment spoke of 'rights brought *home*' and 'a *British* Bill of Rights' – we may acquire only a 'domesticated' right to freedom of expression. In other words, the HRA may become the justification for less, as opposed to more, engagement with rights thinking in other national and supranational regimes.[60]

The third point arises from criticism of the US civil libertarian free speech tradition. It is associated most closely with the work of Richard Abel and Stanley Fish, and it presents US civil liberties scholars and activists in a most unflattering light.[61] Abel and Fish aim to illustrate the vacuity of 'phrases such as free speech as they are used now', and to describe the harm that is done when such a 'procedural shibboleth' or 'meaningless abstraction' is deemed to be talismanic. There is, Fish says, 'little free speech about free speech' in the US: beneath its buffed surface, this alleged 'orthodoxy of tolerance' is, in fact, deeply intolerant of dissent, criticism or scrutiny of any sort whatsoever. Abel's criticism of what he describes as 'civil libertarianism' is even more scathing than Fish's. He singles out the 'poverty' of civil libertarianism, a condition founded upon obsession with state abstention from speech regulation, naïve optimism about the capacity of a 'marketplace of ideas' to generate debate, knowledge and pluralism, and refusal to endorse anything other than ethical relativism. Why, Abel asks, does civil libertarianism refuse to consider the costs of certain types of speech – hate speech, for example? Why, too, does it delude itself, first, that the state is, or could ever be, neutral on expression and, second, that state neutrality is the alpha and omega when private power and money can function as such powerful censors?

Abel's work is controversial.[62] He has been accused of caricaturing the US civil liberties tradition and has worried activists by his apparent downgrading of freedom of expression as an independent political or moral principle. Yet, as Fish points out, US legal culture does seem to offer ongoing instances of individuals and groups who act as if a winning argument involves merely 'running the First Amendment up the nearest flagpole and rushing to salute it'.[63] Thus, Abel's criticism may provide a salutary warning for UK civil libertarians. We may, for example, need to develop a better understanding of US legal and cultural norms on free speech if the 'special relationship' – whereunder UK courts and academics look to US First Amendment case law – is not to end up as a deeply damaging relationship.[64] It needs to be appreciated, for example, that First Amendment jurisprudence springs from a culture of neo-liberalism which has no European parallel. It would be a retrograde step for freedom of expression analysis in the UK to parallel the US focus on state

---

60   As suggested by C.F. Stychin, 'New Labor, New "Britain?" Constitutionalism, Sovereignty and Nation/State in Transition' (1999) 19 Studies in Law, Politics and Society 139.

61   See respectively, R. Abel, *Speech and Respect* (Sweet & Maxwell, 1994) (and the epilogue in 'Public Freedom, Private Constraint' (1994) 21 JLS 374) and S. Fish, *There's No Such Thing as Free Speech* (OUP, 1994). Abel also considers the clashes in the UK which followed the publication of Salman Rushdie's novel, *The Satanic Verses*.

62   See eg, E. Paton, 'Respecting Freedom Speech' (1995) 15 OJLS 597.

63   Fish, above n. 61, p. 113.

64   See McCrudden, above n. 40, commenting upon the different approaches of the US SCt and the ECtHR to the 'free market place of ideas'. More generally, see I. Loveland (ed.), *A Special Relationship? American Influences on Public Law in the United Kingdom* (Clarendon, 1995); and I. Loveland (ed.), *Importing the First Amendment* (Hart Publishing, 1998).

action. As we explained in Chapter 1, the civil liberties tradition must move beyond the historical paradigm of sovereign state versus the individual, and engage with the shifts in governance over the last two decades, as well as the complexity and blurring of private and public spheres.[65] A sophisticated understanding of state power will be essential to the imminent debate on the appropriate reach of the HRA – its 'horizontal effect' – in the regulation of private power and actors.[66]

II. EQUALITY AND NON-DISCRIMINATION IN THE CIVIL LIBERTIES TRADITION

In this Part, we turn from freedom of expression to the principles of non-discrimination and equality.[67] The principles are a linchpin of law- and policy-making in late-modern democracies. Indeed, they have all but 'gained an almost unique status among legal doctrines', becoming 'almost a first principle of civic virtue'.[68] Increasingly, therefore, '[n]o one opposes equality'.[69] As Phillips says, we no longer have to defend the idea of citizens being of intrinsically equal worth 'by reference to divine injunction or by evidence that all humans are the same':

> Equality has become the default position, the principle to which we return when arguments for inequality have failed. Even the most vigorous defence of inequality typically starts from some statement of egalitarianism, employing equality before the law to defend the inequalities of private property, or equality of opportunity to defend inequalities in income and wealth. Where people continue to promote institutions premised on social inequality, they usually do so in terms that pretend the inequality away.[70]

Of course, this may have come to pass because equality contrives to be 'simultaneously obvious and amorphous'.[71] All the same, there has been an

---

65 See Ch. 1, pp. 35-39.

66 See eg, *Douglas and Zeta-Jones v Hello! Ltd*, above n. 51: 'Since the coming into force of the Human Rights Act 1998, the courts as a public authority cannot act in a way which is incompatible with a Convention right: section 6(1). That arguably includes their activity in interpreting and developing the common law, even where no public authority is a party to the litigation. Whether this extends to creating a new cause of action between private persons and bodies is more controversial, since to do so would appear to circumvent the restrictions on proceedings contained in section 7(1) of the Act and on remedies in section 8(1). But it is unnecessary to determine that issue in these proceedings . . .' (per Keene LJ).

67 These principles are sometimes used interchangeably. They are also sometimes linked to one another by an emphasis on justification: that is, unequal treatment of equal situations, which is not objectively and reasonably justifiable, constitutes discrimination. For the most part, references to equality in this chapter invoke the idea of moving beyond non-discrimination towards measures aimed at recognising difference and diversity.

68 W.E. Parmet, 'Aids and the Limits of Discrimination Law' (1987) 15 Law, Medicine and Health Care 61, 62.

69 R. Silberman Abella, 'Equality, Human Rights, Women and the Justice System' (1994) 39 McGill LJ 489, 490.

70 A. Phillips, *Which Equalities Matter?* (Polity, 1999), p. 2. More recently, the journalist Andrew Rawnsley has argued that, within the Conservative Party, '[w]hen the ghost of Enoch Powell foams with blood, these days even he deploys euphemisms': see A. Rawnsley, 'Tories May Stoop But They Won't Conquer' *Observer*, 1 Apr. 2001, p. 29.

71 W.E. Parmet, 'Discrimination and Disability: The Challenges of the ADA' (1990) 18 Law, Medicine & Health Care 331.

undeniable shift towards thinking of equality *through* difference rather than as identical treatment or assimilation of certain differences. This, in turn, has meant that 'tricky questions are more widely acknowledged'.[72] It has led also to a questioning of tolerance as a vehicle for equality. In particular, the notion that an extensive realm of private freedom ought to be sufficient to guarantee equal respect has been challenged by recognition strategies which attach 'as much weight to public activities and contestations as to the protections of the private sphere'.[73] So, for example, lesbians and gays in challenging a range of legal rules (including section 28 which provides that local authorities shall not 'intentionally promote homosexuality' or 'promote the teaching . . . of the acceptability of homosexuality as a pretended family relationship'[74]) have argued that decriminalisation of homosexuality is not enough. This is because the 'tolerance that depends on keeping one's head down can be viewed as inequitable (why are some groups allowed to flaunt their practices in public while others have to keep them to themselves?), and does not do much to address the basis on which a group has found itself disparaged or despised'.[75]

A further layer of welcome complexity was added to debates on equality by the Stephen Lawrence Inquiry. The Inquiry centred the concept of institutional racism in its report on the police investigation into the murder of Stephen Lawrence in South London in 1993. In using this concept, the Inquiry insisted that it should not be taken to have 'produce[d] a definition cast in stone, or a final answer . . .'. Rather, emphasising that 'we must do our best to express what we mean by those words', and pointing to the continuity between its approach and that of the Scarman Report of 1981,[76] it described what it saw as:

> the collective failure of an organisation to provide an appropriate and professional service to people because of their colour, culture or ethnic origin. It can be seen or detected in processes, attitudes and behaviour which amount to discrimination through unwitting prejudice, ignorance, thoughtlessness, and racist stereotyping . . . .[77]

Following the Inquiry's report, the concept of institutional racism was elevated at a quite incredible pace within a range of official discourses. The elevation of

72   Phillips, above n. 70, p. 27.
73   Ibid., p. 28.
74   Local Government Act 1986, s. 2A, inserted by Local Government Act 1988, s. 28, amended by Local Government Act 2000, s. 104. See also, the Sex and Relationship Guidance issued under the Learning and Skills Act 2000 which says that '[t]here should be no direct promotion of sexual orientation'. The Scottish Parliament has repealed s. 28 for Scotland: see Ethical Standards in Public Life (Scotland) Act 2000, ss. 25-26.
75   Phillips, above n. 70. Indeed, it has been argued that '[a]fter the Sexual Offences Act 1967, [s. 28] was a major regression. Most jurisdictions move from decriminalisation to an equal age of consent to anti-discrimination legislation. Very few have adopted the minimally tolerant, "not a crime but no promotion" position that Britain did in 1988': see R. Wintemute, 'Lesbian and Gay Inequality 2000: The Potential of the Human Rights Act 1998 and the Need for an Equality Act 2002' (2000) 6 EHRLR 603, 606. See also, A.M. Smith, *New Right Discourses on Race and Sexuality* (Cambridge UP, 1994) on the construction of the 'good homosexual' in Parliamentary debates on s. 28, ie, 'a law-abiding, disease-free, self-closeting homosexual figure who knew her or his proper place on the secret fringes of mainstream society' (p. 18).
76   *The Brixton Disorders 10-12 April 1981* (Cmnd. 8427, 1981), paras. 2.22, 4.62-4.63 (the Scarman Report).
77   *Report of an Inquiry by Sir William MacPherson of Cluny* (Cm. 4262-I, 1999), paras. 6.34 (the Stephen Lawrence Inquiry). Four years after Stephen Lawrence's death, the Home Secretary established an inquiry into the police investigation of the murder. The inquiry was conducted by William MacPherson, a HCt judge, and its report was published in early 1999.

the concept was all the more remarkable given that '[f]or 30 years British officialdom had consistently denied that [institutional racism] had any meaning when applied to Britain'.[78] 'Now, however, [institutional racism] has become part of the conceptual vocabulary of substantial numbers of people',[79] and this opens up the possibility of a more nuanced approach to law and social change, and also places a welcome focus on the ways in which social and cultural processes regulate conduct. Two other recent reports – the Parekh Report on *The Future of Multi-Ethnic Britain* and *The Independent Review of UK Anti-Discrimination Legislation*[80] – contain yet more sophisticated understandings of equality and non-discrimination. Both reports are characterised by a direct and vigorous engagement with difficult themes. Both also broach the fundamental questions of how best to achieve a synergy between equality and diversity, and between liberty and solidarity or cohesion. And, importantly, both acknowledge the role, and the limits, of law.

Parts III and IV of this chapter will pursue the twists and turns of recent equality debates. The purpose of this Part, however, is different. It seeks to explain why non-discrimination and equality have been less well-represented in the civil liberties tradition than might have been expected.[81] Each of the following three sections will proffer a different explanation for this apparent anomaly. We wish to be clear that the goal is not to berate the civil liberties tradition, but rather to establish a backdrop against which Parts III and IV can make a case for exploring means by which to bridge the chasm between, on the one hand, the richness of freedom and equality debates in theoretical work and (many) political practices and, on the other hand, the approach adopted to freedom of expression and equality in the civil liberties tradition and, more recently, in the literature of HRA euphoria. We should also say that, as has been the case throughout this book, we are using the label 'civil liberties tradition' in an attempt to capture broad trends. This means, in particular, that in most of what follows we adopt the dominant pattern of suppressing Northern Ireland's civil liberties tradition.[82] Hence, we spend no time exploring the rich seam of equality thinking contained, for example, within the reports of the (former) Standing Advisory Committee on Human Rights (SACHR).

Anti-discrimination law: a late starter

One possible way to account for the comparatively poor showing of equality and non-discrimination issues within the civil liberties law tradition is to argue that anti-discrimination law itself is 'a relatively recent phenomenon'.[83] Indeed,

---

78 Parekh Report, above n. 7, p. 71.
79 Ibid.
80 B. Hepple, M. Coussey and T. Choudhury, *Equality: A New Framework. Report of the Independent Review of UK Anti-Discrimination Legislation* (Hart, 2000) (hereinafter, the Hepple Review).
81 Notable exceptions include D. Feldman, *Civil Liberties and Human Rights in England and Wales* (OUP, 1993), pp 845-908; F. Klug, K. Starmer and S. Weir, *The Three Pillars of Liberty – Political Rights in the United Kingdom* (Routledge, 1995); L. Lustgarten, 'Racial Inequality and the Limits of Law' (1986) 49 MLR 68; and C. McCrudden and G. Chambers, above n. 58.
82 For criticism of this phenomenon within public law, see J. Morison and S. Livingstone, *Reshaping Public Power* (Sweet & Maxwell, 1995).
83 C. McCrudden, 'Introduction' in C. McCrudden (ed.), *Anti-Discrimination Law* (Dartmouth, 1991), pp. xi-xxxi, at p. xi. For an overview of developments, see eg, A. Lester, 'Equality and UK Law: Past, Present and Future' [2001] PL 77.

for most of the twentieth century, the legislature made only limited interventions to curb discrimination,[84] and judicial commitment to the principles of non-discrimination and equality was negligible.[85] There was a turning point in 1975, however, and we take that year as our start date in the following section, which outlines the main features of anti-discrimination law in the UK.

Overview of anti-discrimination law

ANTI-DISCRIMINATION LEGISLATION

The Equal Pay Act (EPA), enacted in 1970, came into force in 1975: the delay was due to the fact that employers were deemed to need several years to prepare for the legislation's demands. The statute covers sex discrimination in pay. 1975 was also the year in which the Sex Discrimination Act (SDA)[86] was enacted and came into force. The SDA outlaws discrimination on the grounds of sex in education, employment, recruitment and training, the provision of goods, services and facilities, and in the disposal and management of premises.[87] It also prohibits discrimination against married persons and, since 1999, it has prohibited direct discrimination on the ground of gender reassignment.[88] It is also clear now that discrimination on grounds of pregnancy will generally amount to unlawful sex discrimination.[89]

In 1976, one year after the SDA, Parliament enacted the Race Relations Act (RRA), outlawing discrimination on grounds of colour, race, nationality, or ethnic or national origins in spheres akin to those under the SDA. The RRA also prohibits discrimination by planning authorities, and in relation to membership of private clubs and other associations over a certain size.[90] Two notable amendments, prompted in part by the Stephen Lawrence Inquiry's finding of institutionalised racism both in the Metropolitan Police Service and in other police services and institutions countrywide,[91] were made to the RRA in 2000: first, to prohibit race discrimination by public authorities and, secondly, to impose a duty on such authorities to eliminate unlawful racial discrimination and promote equality of opportunity and good relations between persons of different racial groups.[92]

---

84 See eg, the Race Relations Acts of 1965 and 1968, described in Hepple et al., above n. 80, p. 6, as 'first-' and 'second-generation' legislation.

85 See below, pp. 393-395.

86 For Northern Ireland, see the Sex Discrimination (NI) Order 1976, SI 1976/1042 (NI 15), as amended.

87 It does, however, contain a series of exemptions and exceptions, some of which are controversial.

88 See respectively, SDA, ss. 3(1) and 2A. Both sections are limited to the employment sphere, and s. 2A prohibits only direct discrimination. S. 2A(1) provides that '[a] person ("A") discriminates against another person ("B") . . . if he treats B less favourably than he treats or would treat other persons, and does so on the ground that B intends to undergo, is undergoing or has undergone gender reassignment'. It was prompted by the ECJ's ruling in *P v S and Cornwall County Council* Case C-13/94 [1996] ECR I-2143 that the Equal Treatment Directive applied to discrimination arising from gender reassignment.

89 See eg, *Webb v EMO Air Cargo (UK) Ltd (No 2)* [1994] 4 All ER 115 (ECJ).

90 See respectively, ss. 19A, 25 and 26.

91 Above n. 77, para. 6.54.

92 See RRA 1976 (as amended by the Race Relations (Amendment) Act 2000), ss. 19B and 71.

Northern Ireland was not covered by the RRA and, indeed, was left without race relations legislation until 1997.[93] It has, however, had legislation dating back to 1976 prohibiting discrimination on grounds of religious belief or political opinion in employment.[94] The evolution of that legislation merits detailed study by all those who claim an interest in using law to achieve equality and combat discrimination: the legislation's burgeoning emphasis on tackling structural inequality, whether caused by discrimination or not, and its gradually widening embrace of positive action are particularly notable.[95] Northern Ireland has also broken the mould more recently in imposing relatively unambiguous duties upon public authorities in respect of non-discrimination and equality. These duties are contained within sections 75 and 76 of the Northern Ireland Act 1998 (NIA). The latter section imposes the duty of non-discrimination: it makes it unlawful for a public authority to 'discriminate, or to aid or incite another person to discriminate, against a person or class of person on the grounds of religious belief or political opinion'. Section 75, by contrast, deals with the duty to promote equality. It provides that each 'public authority' is required, in carrying out its functions relating to Northern Ireland, to have 'due regard to the need to promote equality of opportunity'.[96] In effect, section 75 centres the concept of 'equality mainstreaming' – that is, the integration of equality into all aspects of law- and policy-making:

> [I]t concentrates on government proactively taking equality into account. It does not concentrate primarily on discrimination as the problem to be resolved. Mainstreaming approaches are intended to be anticipatory, rather than essentially retrospective, to be extensively participatory, rather than limited to small groups of the knowledgeable and to be integrated into the activities of those primarily involved in policy-making.[97]

Crucially, section 75 is not limited to consideration of persons of different religious beliefs or political opinions: it also applies in respect of persons of different racial groups, ages, marital status or sexual orientation; between women and men generally; between individuals with a disability and those without, and between individuals with dependants and those without. Moreover,

---

93 See the Race Relations (NI) Order 1997, SI 1997/869 (NI 6), hereinafter RR(NI)O.

94 See the Fair Employment and Treatment (NI) Order 1998, SI 1998/3162 (NI 21), hereinafter FETO. This legislation amends and consolidates the Fair Employment Acts 1976 and 1989: eg it extends the prohibition on discrimination beyond the employment sphere to further and higher education, the provision of goods, services and facilities, and the disposal and management of premises.

95 See FETO, esp. Art. 4 (allowing action designed to 'secure fair participation in employment by members of the Protestant or Catholic community'); Art. 50 (re workplace monitoring); and Art. 55 (re workplace review). A campaign in the US on what were known as the 'MacBride Principles' also paid dividends throughout the 1980s. Its objective was to bring pressure to bear on US organisations to ensure fair employment practices in their Northern Ireland subsidiaries. For more detail on this campaign, see C. McCrudden, 'Human Rights Codes for Transnational Corporations: What Can the Sullivan and MacBride Principles Tell Us' (1999) 19 OJLS 167.

96 Without prejudice to this obligation, s. 75 also requires public authorities to have regard to the desirability of promoting good relations between persons of different religious belief, political opinion or racial group.

97 C. McCrudden, 'Mainstreaming Equality in the Governance of Northern Ireland' (1999) 22 Fordham Int LJ 1696, p. 1769. S. 2 of the Race Relations (Amendment) Act 2000 appears to draw on the Northern Ireland experience in introducing a duty on British public authorities to promote equality of opportunity.

the Act seeks also to provide a robust mechanism for the enforcement of the section 75 duty, specifically, by requiring public authorities to draw up, and undertake periodic review of, equality schemes.[98]

Finally, mention needs also to be made of two other recent enactments: the Human Rights Act 1998 (HRA) and the Disability Discrimination Act 1995 (DDA). The former statute is of course the vehicle by which the UK partially incorporated the European Convention on Human Rights (ECHR).[99] At present, the ECHR does not contain a free-standing equality guarantee.[100] It has only Article 14, which is parasitic upon other Convention rights – in other words, Article 14 requires that the discrimination must relate to another Convention right:

> *The enjoyment of the rights and freedoms set forth in this Convention shall be secured without discrimination* on any ground such as sex, race, colour, language, religion, political or other opinion, national or social origin, association with a national minority, property, birth or other status.[101]

It would be misleading, however, to suggest that the absence of a free-standing equality guarantee means that the HRA will have little impact on equality and non-discrimination issues in the UK, or that the Strasbourg authorities have no means by which to influence such issues. The latter have been deeply cautious to date; the Strasbourg Court, for example, has repeatedly chosen to avoid Article 14 in gay rights cases.[102] Yet, as has been pointed out by others, this need not stop UK courts from using the HRA in a more generous manner.[103] The courts could, for example, use it as the means by which to broach long-term domestic concerns about religious discrimination within the blasphemy law, and in the funding of religious schools and the largely Christian orientation of working hours.[104] There are also areas outside the scope of current anti-discrimination law – immigration, for example – which could benefit significantly from the Article 14 guarantee. It needs to be remembered, however,

---

98 NIA 1998, Sch. 9.

99 For discussion of the potential impact of other recent 'constitutional change' legislation (specifically, the Scotland Act 1998, the Government of Wales Act 1998 and the NIA 1998, all of which deal with devolution and allow some scope for the respective legislative bodies to develop equality policies), see Hepple et al., above n. 80, pp. 7-9. Specifically on Northern Ireland, see *Equal Rights and Human Rights – Their Role in Peace Building: The Equality Provisions of the Good Friday Agreement and the NI Act* (Committee on the Administration of Justice, 1999).

100 See below pp. 403-405 for further discussion of the ECHR, including Protocol 12, a development designed to create a free-standing non-discrimination guarantee.

101 For a particularly restrictive approach to this requirement, see *Choudhury v UK*, Application No. 17439/90 (EComHR) (challenge under Arts. 9 and 14 to finding of the Div Ct that the offence of blasphemy protected only the Christian religion).

102 See Wintemute, above n. 75, citing *Dudgeon v UK* (1981) 4 EHRR 149; *Smith and Grady v UK* (1999) 29 EHRR 493; *Lustig-Prean and Beckett v UK* (1999) 29 EHRR 548 and *ADT v UK* [2000] Crim LR 1009, but noting that the cases were decided in this way 'because the Court was convinced that the treatment would violate the [ECHR] even if it were applied to heterosexual persons'. In *Salguerio da Silva Mouta v Portugal* [2001] 1 FCR 653, the ECtHR found a violation of Art. 14, holding that a Portuguese court in a child custody case had made 'a distinction dictated by considerations relating to sexual orientation of the father, a distinction which cannot be tolerated under the Convention'. See *Macdonald v Ministry of Defence* (2001) IRLR 431 (EAT).

103 See eg, S. Fredman, 'Equality Issues' in Markesinis, above n. 40, pp. 111-132.

104 The *Guardian* newspaper's campaign against the Treason Felony Act 1848, which threatens those who advocate abolition of the monarchy with imprisonment, provides a further opportunity to challenge the Established Church of England.

that 'the impact of Article 14 depends to a large extent on the way in which the domestic courts interpret the concept of equality'.[105]

The Disability Discrimination Act 1995 is the final recent statutory development that deserves specific mention.[106] This Act applies throughout the UK, prohibiting discrimination against disabled people in the fields of employment, provision of services and sale or rental of property. It is both similar to and different from previous anti-discrimination statutes. In particular, it differs from previous legislation by allowing for a general defence of justification of direct discrimination, by omitting a prohibition on indirect discrimination, and by introducing a positive duty to make reasonable adjustments for disabled individuals.[107]

In 2000, after several years of wrangling, a Disability Rights Commission charged with enforcing the Disability Discrimination Act came into being.[108] This commission is the latest addition to a lengthening list of such bodies. In Britain, there are other separate commissions under the SDA and the RRA – respectively, the Equal Opportunities Commission (EOC) and the Commission for Racial Equality (CRE). In Northern Ireland, by contrast, three formerly separate commissions (dealing respectively with race, sex and religion) were merged in 1999 to create the Equality Commission Northern Ireland (ECNI). The new body also has responsibilities for monitoring the positive duties imposed on public authorities under the Northern Ireland Act 1998, and for disability discrimination. It is complemented by the Northern Ireland Human Rights Commission, which has a remit that extends to equality issues.[109]

THE COURTS, ANTI-DISCRIMINATION AND EQUALITY

Parliament's slow start on equality and non-discrimination was not an isolated phenomenon. The courts were also late developers in this sphere and, even in recent years, their commitment to the principles of non-discrimination and equality has sometimes been lukewarm.[110] The common law, for example, has been almost equality-averse: 'personal freedom; property (and with it contractual freedom); reputation; and fair procedure in matters effecting the individual' have been its top-ranking concerns and, in protecting these 'basic interests', judges have endorsed both capricious exercises of the freedom to contract and a notoriously limited view of equality before the law.[111]

The interpretation of legislation aimed specifically at promoting non-discrimination has also been criticised.[112] In a series of judicial review cases, for

---

105 Fredman, ibid., p. 111.
106 See generally, C. Gooding, *Blackstone's Guide to the Disability Discrimination Act 1995* (Blackstone, 1995); and her, 'Disability Discrimination Act: From Statute to Practice' (2000) 20 CSP 533. Disability receives no explicit mention in Art. 14, ECHR, but the ECtHR has held that 'other status' covers individuals with disabilities: see *Botta v Italy* (1998) 26 EHRR 241.
107 The s. 6 positive duty was argued to make prohibition of indirect discrimination irrelevant.
108 See the Disability Rights Commission Act 1999.
109 The Northern Ireland model has been commended by the Parekh Report, above n. 7.
110 Cf. eg, *Ahmad v ILEA* [1978] QB 36 (CA) (per Scarman LJ (dissenting)).
111 Klug, Starmer and Weir, above n. 81, p. 116.
112 See eg, C. McCrudden, 'Racial Discrimination' in McCrudden and Chambers, above n. 58, pp. 409-455, at p. 447 arguing that the dominant approach adopted by the HL to the Race Relations Act 1968 was that 'the legislation should be restrictively interpreted because it interfered with common law liberties'.

example, the courts have been less than committed – if not hostile to – applying principles of non-discrimination and equality. The former section 71 of the RRA proved a particular sticking-point in this respect.[113] That section imposed a duty on local authorities 'to make appropriate arrangements with a view to securing that their various functions are carried out with due regard to the need (a) to eliminate unlawful racial discrimination; and (b) to promote equality of opportunity, and good relations, between persons of different racial groups'. The House of Lords' attitude to the section was made clear in *Wheeler v Leicester City Council*.[114] The case involved a judicial review challenge by members of a rugby club against the Leicester City Council's decision to refuse them entry to their regular training ground because of their failure to seek to dissuade fellow club members not to tour South Africa in contravention of an international anti-apartheid ban on sporting links. The Council sought to rely on section 71, placing particular emphasis on the fact that approximately one-quarter of the city's population was African-Caribbean and Asian. The House of Lords, however, ruled in favour of the rugby club. The Law Lords insisted that '[t]he club could not be punished because the club had done nothing wrong' and issued a warning that, although persuasion – even 'powerful persuasion' – was acceptable, 'in a field where other views can equally legitimately be held, persuasion, however powerful, must not be allowed to cross that line where it moves into the field of illegitimate pressure coupled with the threat of sanctions'.[115]

Eleven years after *Wheeler*, the Court of Appeal handed down a decision in *R v Ministry of Defence, ex p Smith*[116] which suggested that little had changed in the higher courts' attitude towards the relationship between non-discrimination, equality and judicial review. *Smith* concerned a judicial review challenge brought by a group of servicewomen and men who had been dismissed from their employment in pursuance of the (then) blanket ban on lesbians and gays in the military.[117] The Court of Appeal upheld the decision of the Divisional Court that the ban could not be said to be beyond the range of responses open to a reasonable decision-maker and, accordingly, could not be considered to be 'irrational'.[118] The European Court of Human Rights saw the matter differently, however. It ruled that the armed forces' ban clearly violated the right to privacy in Article 8 of the Convention, and that the applicants' right to judicial review could not be said to constitute an effective remedy as required by Article 13, ECHR given that the threshold at which the irrationality test was set:

> effectively excluded any consideration by the domestic courts of the question of whether the interference with the applicants' rights answered a pressing social need or was proportionate to the national security and public order aims pursued,

---

113 For Northern Ireland, see RR(NI)O, Art. 67 and also NIA, s. 75 (imposing a duty on all public authorities in Northern Ireland).

114 [1985] 2 All ER 1106 (HL).

115 See respectively, ibid., p. 1112 (per Lord Templeman) and p. 1111 (per Lord Roskill). See A. Hutchinson and M. Jones, '*Wheeler*-Dealing: An Essay on Law, Politics and Speech' (1988) 15 JLS 263.

116 [1996] 1 All ER 257 (CA).

117 During the proceedings, the Ministry of Defence justified its policy on the grounds of 'morale and unit effectiveness, the . . . role of the services as guardian of recruits under the age of 18, and . . . the requirement of communal living in many service situations'.

118 In justification, the CA (especially Bingham MR) placed particular emphasis on: the need to defer to Parliament's view on the policy; the fact that sexual orientation was not a prohibited ground in domestic or EC employment law; the fact that no right to privacy existed in UK law; and the narrow parameters of the judicial review jurisdiction.

principles which lie at the heart of the Court's analysis of complaints under Article 8 of the Convention.[119]

THE INFLUENCE OF THE EU

The rather mean-spirited approach of the UK courts – and Parliament – towards the principles of non-discrimination and equality becomes even clearer if one examines the impact of EC law on UK anti-discrimination norms. EC law has had a far-reaching influence on UK sex-discrimination law, ushering in significant developments in respect of equal pay for equal work and prohibitions on discrimination against pregnant workers, part-time workers and transgendered workers.[120] Admittedly, however, concepts *from* the UK have influenced EC law in recent years, and this trend may deepen over coming years.[121] But the EU's influence over UK discrimination law should also expand quite considerably in the near future. The EC Burden of Proof Directive, for example, requires amendment of the Sex Discrimination Act's definition of indirect discrimination by July 2001.[122] More important, however, is Article 13 EC, which was added by the Amsterdam Treaty. This Article has the potential to bring deep and pervasive change to member states' approaches to equality. It provides that:

> Without prejudice to the other provisions of this Treaty and *within the limits of the powers conferred by it upon the Community*, the Council, acting unanimously, on a proposal from the Commission and after consulting the European Parliament, may take appropriate action to combat discrimination based on sex, racial or ethnic origin, religion or belief, disability, age or sexual orientation (emphasis added).

The text of Article 13 was a disappointment to some commentators. Specifically, the expectation that EC law-making on discrimination would be confined to spheres in which the EC already had powers granted to it by the EC Treaty was seen as an unfortunate limitation.[123] Why allow the EC to adopt anti-discrimination laws, but not *general* anti-discrimination laws? Interestingly, however, the first legislative measure to have been adopted under Article 13 – the Race Directive, adopted in June 2000 – seems to have side-stepped the expectation allegedly imposed by the text of the Article.[124] In particular, the

---

119 *Smith and Grady v UK* (1999) 29 EHRR 493, para. 138. See also *Lustig-Prean and Beckett v UK* (1999) 29 EHRR 548.

120 See eg, Art. 141 (ex Art. 119) EC Treaty and the Equal Treatment Directive 76/207/EC.

121 For eg, use may be made of the Northern Ireland experience with mainstreaming, and of the UK's experience with anti-discrimination enforcement bodies such as the CRE.

122 Council Directive 97/80/EC. OJ 1998 L 14/6. Hepple et al., above n. 80, p. 31 proposes that *all* UK anti-discrimination legislation should adopt this Directive's approach to indirect discrimination.

123 See eg, M. Bell, 'The New Article 13 EC Treaty: A Sound Basis for European Anti-Discrimination Law?' (1999) 6 Maastricht J of European & Comp Law 5.

124 Council Directive 2000/43/EC. OJ L 180/22. Its full title is Council Directive Implementing the Principle of Equal Treatment between Persons Irrespective of Racial or Ethnic Origin. It came into force on 19 Jul. 2000 and member states have until 19 Jul. 2003 to bring their national laws, regulations and administrative provisions into line with it. Its blanket exclusion of racially discriminatory provisions governing the entry, residence and treatment of third-country nationals and stateless persons has been criticised as inconsistent with human rights: see eg, A. Lester, 'New European Equality Measures' [2000] PL 562, 565. More generally on the Directive, see E. Guild, 'The EC Directive on Race Discrimination: Surprises, Possibilities and Limitations' (2000) 29 ILJ 416.

Directive's scope appears to extend beyond a prohibition on discrimination on grounds of race and ethnic origin in employment to discrimination in relation to education, housing, healthcare and social protection.[125]

A second directive under Article 13 EC is under consideration. It is generally referred to as the Equal Treatment, or Framework, Directive.[126] Crucially, however, agreement on this Directive may be far less easy to achieve than on the Race Directive. In the first place, agreement on the latter acquired an unexpected urgency following political events in Austria in the summer of 2000 – specifically, the entry into government of Jörg Haider's Freedom Party – and the response of other EU member states thereto. More fundamentally, however, agreement on the Equal Treatment Directive may prove elusive because of the subject-matter of the Directive itself: the Directive broaches the question of equal opportunities in employment – in particular, it seeks to prohibit discrimination on grounds of 'racial or ethnic origin, religion or belief, disability, age or sexual orientation'. This subject-matter makes it almost inevitable that arguments of economic inefficiency and inappropriate liberalisation will delay agreement and also encourage potentially deep compromises. It also raises questions about the desirability of carving up the grounds of discrimination, and the applicable fields, between a range of legal instruments.

Finally, mention must be made of the EU Charter of Fundamental Rights, an initiative aimed at nurturing a more effective human rights culture and policy as part of the core of the evolving EU project.[127] EU heads of state committed themselves to this initiative in 1999. Thereafter progress on a draft charter was swift – incredibly so given the political sensitivity of the project and the obviously extensive ambitions of its proponents. In December 2000, however, the member states, meeting at Nice, chose neither to incorporate nor otherwise to recognise the Charter within the body of the Treaty. Instead, they promulgated it as a declaration of the European institutions – in other words, post-Nice, the Charter is 'soft law'.[128] The member states' choice certainly does not preclude subsequent integration of the Charter within the Treaty framework; indeed, the remarkably-high public profile of the entire Charter drafting process – generated in part by the process' emphasis on participation and debate[129] – would appear to single out both the Charter itself and the process by which it was created as potential flagship projects within the evolving EU.[130]

---

125 Ibid., Art. 3.

126 Its full title is Council Directive establishing a General Framework for Equal Treatment in Employment on the grounds of Race, Ethnic Origin, Religion or Belief, Disability, Age or Sexual Orientation.

127 For the background to the Charter, see the reports from the following three independent committees: *For a Europe of Civic and Social Rights*, Report by the Comité des Sages (1996); *Leading by Example: A Human Rights Agenda for the EU for the Year 2000*, Agenda of the Comité des Sages and Final Project Report (1998); and *Affirming Fundamental Human Rights in the EU*, Report of the Expert Group on Fundamental Rights (1999). See also, P. Alston (ed.), *The EU and Human Rights* (OUP, 1999); and J.H.H. Weiler, 'Editorial: Does the European Union Truly Need a Charter of Rights?' (2000) 6 ELJ 95.

128 Solemn Proclamation of the European Parliament, the Commission and the Council of December 7 2000, OJ C 346/1.

129 For discussion, see G. de Búrca, 'The Drafting of the European Union Charter of Fundamental Rights' (2001) 26 ELR 126.

130 For a similar argument using the example of equality provisions of the NIA 1998 as a model for evolving constitutionalism, see C. Harvey, 'Governing After the Rights Revolution' (2000) 27 JLS 61.

Law, law and more law

A second way to account for the comparatively poor showing of equality and non-discrimination within the civil liberties tradition is to focus on the question of what is necessary in order to see and treat each other as equals. This question, which would seem to be central to any engagement with equality, has received only limited attention from civil liberties lawyers. In dedicated equality coverage, it has been submerged by the detail of anti-discrimination law – that is, priority has been given to exposition of the provisions of the EPA, SDA, RRA, DDA and (albeit less commonly) FETO. Similarly, in the coverage of issues such as freedom of religion or immigration, the consideration of equality has remained largely in the shadows or had a rather watery feel.

Explaining the detail of anti-discrimination law *is* a gargantuan task. Indeed, the recent Independent Review of UK Anti-Discrimination Legislation (the Hepple Review) builds its argument for a new anti-discrimination framework, involving the harmonisation of legislation, in part on the fact that the present framework suffers from *too much law*.[131] The Review goes on to emphasise that the excess of law is rendered more problematic by the fact that:

> the statutes are written in a language and style that renders them largely inaccessible to those whose actions they are intended to influence. Human resource managers, trade union officials, officers of public authorities, and those who represent victims of discrimination find difficulty in picking their way through it all. Specialist lawyers can also be mystified . . . Many examples could be given of the difficulties which courts and tribunals have had in interpreting the obscure wording of [the statutes].[132]

The civil liberties lawyer who has sought to go beyond description of the current law towards evaluation thereof has faced an even more difficult task. Here the problem arises not just from the fact that there is too much law, but also from the fact that the law is '*inconsistent* and inherently unsatisfactory'.[133] The Review team pointed, for example, to myriad indefensible differences between the SDA, RRA, DDA and FETO, and to gaps and anomalies between the EPA and the SDA. It also questioned whether current legislation, specifically the SDA and EPA, meets the standards expected by EC law.

Towards evaluation: the example of 'justification' of discrimination

It is understandable, therefore, that a civil liberties lawyer could easily become so entangled with explaining the inconsistencies in current anti-discrimination law that broader themes would be left untouched. Consider, for example, the problems which arise even if this civil liberties lawyer limits evaluation to one issue alone – take, for example, the task of evaluating the concept of 'justification' of discrimination under the current law. To begin with, the civil liberties lawyer would need to look at the relevance of justification in the context

---

131 Hepple et al., above n. 80, pp. 21-23. The Review argues that a new framework is needed for three reasons: first, because of challenges to the present framework; secondly, because of the changing face of disadvantage and discrimination; and thirdly, because of changed social and employment practices.
132 Ibid. But see P. Fitzpatrick, 'Racism and the Innocence of Law' (1988) 14 JLS 119; and L. Lustgarten, 'Racial Inequality and the Limits of Law' (1986) 49 MLR 68.
133 Above n. 80, pp. 22-23.

of direct discrimination. Prohibition of direct discrimination lies at the core of current anti-discrimination law, where it serves to entrench the most basic notion of equality – namely, that likes should be treated alike.[134] In upholding this idea of equality as 'consistent treatment',[135] the SDA, RRA and FETO do not permit justification as a defence to direct discrimination.[136] They do, however, provide for specific exemptions from their general prohibitions on direct discrimination, and these exemptions could be seen as indirect instances of 'justified', or permissible, discrimination. Several of these exemptions are increasingly controversial. There is, for example, a deepening sense that the lists of 'genuine occupational qualifications' in the SDA and RRA are unhelpful and ought to be replaced by a general defence which would require it to be shown that the essential functions of a job demand that it be performed by a person of a particular ethnic origin, sex, etc. There is discontent also with the SDA's exemptions for private members' clubs[137] and for insurance policies.[138] The exemption for discrimination on the ground of protecting national security, which features across the spectrum of UK anti-discrimination legislation, has also provoked concern, although recent amendments – which, in part, were prompted by an adverse ruling from the European Court of Human Rights in the case of *Tinnelly and McElduff v UK*[139] – may blunt some of the criticism.[140]

The DDA, in contrast to the SDA, RRA and FETO, does allow for justification of direct discrimination.[141] Section 5 of the Act defines discrimination in two ways: first, less favourable treatment for a reason related to disability; and secondly, a failure to comply with a duty to make reasonable adjustments. It also provides that both types of discrimination can be justified, and the threshold for such justification has been described as 'very low'.[142] The question arises as to why disability discrimination should be singled out in this manner. Those seeking to argue for a singling-out tend to answer by emphasising that disability, unlike race and sex, requires difference to be taken into account. What their arguments often ignore, however, is that there are both more inclusive and less inclusive ways of dealing with difference.[143] The general defence of justification

---

134 Another problematic aspect of direct discrimination – namely, the need to find an appropriate comparator – is discussed below, pp. 414-417, in the context of sexual harassment.

135 S. Fredman, *A Critical Review of the Concept of Equality in UK Anti-Discrimination Law*, Working Paper No. 3 for the Independent Review of the Enforcement of UK Anti-Discrimination Legislation (Centre for Public Law, 1999), pp. 3-5.

136 See respectively, SDA, s. 1(1)(a) and SD(NI)O, Art. 3(1)(a); RRA, s. 1(1)(a) and RR(NI)O, Art. 3(1)(a); and FETO, Art. 3(2)(a).

137 Similar exemptions appear in the DDA and FETO. For discussion, see eg, J. Gardner, 'Private Activities and Personal Autonomy: At the Margins of Anti-discrimination Law' in B. Hepple and E. Szyszczak (eds.), *Discrimination: The Limits of Law* (Mansell, 1992), pp. 148-171; and D. Rhode, *Justice and Gender* (Harvard UP, 1991).

138 SDA, s. 45; SD(NI)O, s. 46. For criticism of this exemption as reinforcing gendered assumptions, see eg, D. Pannick, *Sex Discrimination Law* (OUP, 1985), pp. 189-195; and *Equality in the 21st Century: A New Sex Law for Britain* (EOC, 1998), p. 8.

139 (1998) 27 EHRR 249.

140 See C. White, 'Security Vetting, Discrimination and the Right to a Fair Trial' [1999] PL 406.

141 As does the EPA.

142 *HJ Heinz Co v Kenrick* [2000] IRLR 144, 146 (EAT).

143 On difference and disability discrimination, see A. Silvers, D. Wasserman and M.B. Mahowald (eds.), *Disability, Difference, Discrimination: Perspectives on Justice in Bioethics and Public Policy* (Rowman and Littlefield, 1999) (arguing that the focus should not be on the needs of 'disabled' people but on structural questions).

in the DDA falls conclusively into the latter category.[144] The Hepple Review, by contrast, aims for the former approach by advocating for a provision that would allow justification 'only on specified rational grounds' – for example, on the ground that 'an individual would not be able to perform the essential functions of the job, with or without reasonable adjustments'.[145]

The second stage of a civil liberties lawyer's evaluation of the concept of 'justification' of discrimination under the current law would centre on the prohibition on indirect discrimination in the SDA, RRA and FETO.[146] There is considerable dispute about the best way of defining indirect discrimination. For present purposes, however, we can work with the definition provided by Article 2(2) of the Burden of Proof Directive, a definition which has to be incorporated into UK law on sex discrimination by July 2001:

> For the purposes of the principle of equal treatment . . . indirect discrimination shall exist where an apparently neutral provision, criterion or practice disadvantages a substantially higher proportion of the members of one sex unless that provision, criterion or practice is appropriate and necessary and can be justified by objective factors unrelated to sex.[147]

Prohibition of this form of discrimination is commonly seen as an essential component of an overall anti-discrimination package: it is considered to offer an acceptable means by which to incorporate a more substantive, less formal approach to equality, and to provide a sophisticated mechanism for responding to the problem that equal treatment does not always produce equal results. In particular, with indirect discrimination 'it is not the equality of treatment meted out to the individual that ultimately matters, but the fact that it has a disparate impact on an individual because of his or her membership of the disadvantaged group'.[148]

Currently, the SDA, RRA and FETO allow for a defence of justification of indirect discrimination. In fact, the operation of the defence has been one of the defining influences on the development of indirect discrimination law; many would argue that its operation has also been inherently problematic. That there have been problems is, however, not surprising. The defence compels courts and tribunals to grapple with competing policy values: on the one hand, the employer's interest in efficiency and profit and, on the other, the removal of unacceptable barriers to the advancement of protected groups. It requires 'complex and sensitive decisions as to the ways in which employment policies operate in practice, and as to the cost society is prepared to impose on employers to eliminate practices with an adverse impact', and it is understandable, therefore, that such decisions can easily prove unsatisfactory if they are taken without 'awareness of the causes and impact of discriminatory practices'.[149]

---

144 This is characteristic of the overall tenor of the DDA: see B. Doyle, *Reform of the Disability Discrimination Act*, Working Paper No. 4 for the Independent Review of the Enforcement of UK Anti-Discrimination Legislation (Centre for Public Law, 1999), p. 1 (describing the DDA as 'reluctant law reform . . . [containing] a number of deliberately designed hoops and hurdles which are creating barriers to effective anti-discrimination law in the field of disability').

145 Hepple et al., above n. 80, pp. 36-37.

146 See respectively, SDA, s. 1(1)(b) and SD(NI)O, Art. 3(1)(b); RRA, s. 1(1)(b) and RR(NI)O, Art. 3(1)(b); and FETO, Art. 3(2)(b).

147 97/80/EC.

148 Fredman, above n. 135, p. 6. The concept of indirect discrimination is generally traced back to the US SCt's opinion in *Griggs v Duke Power* 401 US 424 (1971).

149 R.J. Townshend-Smith, *Discrimination Law: Text, Cases and Materials* (Cavendish, 1998), p. 291.

The Hepple Review commends the approach towards indirect discrimination adopted by the Burden of Proof Directive, and suggests that it should be used as a template for change across the spectrum of UK legislation.[150] It also argues for the concept of 'reasonable accommodation' as the best means by which to combat arguments against the extension of the prohibition on indirect discrimination to discrimination against disabled persons or persons of a religious group. Thus, it recommends that

> a provision, criterion or practice should not be regarded as appropriate or necessary in the case of indirect discrimination which disadvantages disabled persons or persons of a religious group, unless the needs of that group cannot be reasonably accommodated without causing undue hardship on the person responsible for accommodating those needs, having regard to factors such as financial and other costs and health and safety requirements.[151]

This approach, it suggests, would assist us in working towards equality *through* difference or diversity.

The final element in an evaluation of the concept of 'justification' in discrimination law is consideration of positive action. Here, the central question is: does the law's centring of equal treatment mean that positive action is 'unjustifiable'? Fredman argues that, to answer this question, we need to decide whether equality is symmetric or asymmetric:

> A symmetric approach regards equality as an absolute principle, to which all individuals have a right. An asymmetric approach, by contrast, perceives of equality as part of a wider social project, namely the alleviation of disadvantage. From this perspective there is indeed a morally significant difference between a general . . . classification that causes further disadvantage to those who have suffered from prejudice, and a classification framed to help them.[152]

In the UK, however, this question has received minimal attention. Not surprisingly, therefore, the role and justification of positive action also remain under-addressed. The exception to this is Northern Ireland, where fair employment legislation has gone beyond prohibiting discrimination and promoting equality of opportunity, and has moved towards special measures designed to overcome disadvantage.[153] Northern Ireland's current fair employment legislation – FETO 1998 – adopts what Fredman describes as an asymmetric approach towards equality. But, as she goes on to point out, it does so in a cautious manner by opting for positive action[154] as an explicit derogation

---

150 Cf. Art. 2 (3) of the Race Directive, above n. 124, which defines indirect discrimination as occurring where 'an apparently neutral provision, criterion or practice would put persons of a racial or ethnic origin at a particular disadvantage compared with other persons, unless that provision, criterion or practice is objectively justified by a legitimate aim and the means of achieving that aim are appropriate and necessary'. This definition was chosen in order explicitly to remove the need for statistical evidence.

151 Hepple et al., above n. 80, p. 32.

152 Fredman, above n. 135, p. 9.

153 Cf. SDA, ss. 47-48; SD(NI)O, Arts. 48-49; RRA, ss. 35-38; and RR(NI)O, Art. 37 as examples of the extremely limited provision for positive measures to provide training for employees from under-represented groups and to encourage potential employees.

154 Art. 4(1) defines this as 'action designed to secure fair participation in employment of the Protestant, or members of the Roman Catholic, community in [Northern Ireland] by means including – (a) the adoption of practices encouraging such participation; and (b) the modification or abandonment of practices that have or may have the effect of restricting or discouraging such participation'.

from an essentially symmetrical approach to equality. Thus, FETO contains specific provisions protecting certain types of positive action from the direct and indirect discrimination prohibitions elsewhere in the legislation.

Positive action may, however, be a concept on the brink of discovery *across* the UK. Ideas of 'fair participation' and 'fair access' appear to have increasing legitimacy. The need for debate on positive action is also highlighted by developments such as the DDA's duty to make reasonable adjustments and the new positive duties for public authorities. Moreover, EC law has also rallied recently towards allowing positive action. In particular, Article 141 EC now provides that:

> With a view to ensuring full equality in practice between men and women in working life, the principle of equal treatment shall not prevent any Member State from maintaining or adopting measures providing for specific advantages in order to make it easier for the under-represented sex to pursue a vocational activity or to prevent or compensate for disadvantages in professional careers.

A lesser engagement?

Having examined positive action, the civil liberties lawyer could draw to a close the evaluation of the concept of 'justification' of discrimination under UK law. It will be remembered that the purpose of including such an account here was to highlight how evaluation of even a small slice of current anti-discrimination law can require a civil liberties lawyer to pursue a study of quite considerable scope. It should be clear, then, that this lawyer might very easily never get to the broader, deeper themes of equality – to the issue, for example, of trying to determine what is necessary to see and treat each other as equals and whether this requires active recognition of difference and diversity. Description and doctrinal analysis of existing anti-discrimination law might also seem more appealing to a civil liberties lawyer than broader themes, given their better fit with the positivist tradition in legal research and writing. Description and analysis of existing anti-discrimination law probably also appeal as more manageable topics: non-discrimination and, more especially, equality raise innumerable hard questions, and equality's 'everywhere'-capacity can also be overwhelming. Textbook writers, faced with the constraints of their medium, may gravitate towards material that is more easily packaged. Furthermore, in an era of recognition of anti-democratic injuries – that is, a period when individuals and groups have sought state redress against harms such as harassment and hate speech – these textbook writers may have decided that by talking about free speech they were also addressing the hard questions of equality. Support for this idea could, for example, have been found in the work of Catharine MacKinnon, probably the best-known anti-pornography feminist within legal circles, who is on record as describing '[t]he law of equality and the law of freedom of speech [as] on a collision course [in the US]'.[155] In similar fashion, following the 1992 Canadian Supreme Court opinion in *R v Butler*,[156] wherein the concept of obscenity was reformulated, another US feminist law professor, Ann Scales, commented that '[o]bscenity law in Canada is now about equality'.[157]

---

155 C. MacKinnon, *Only Words* (Harvard UP, 1993), p. 71.
156 [1992] 1 SCR 452. *Butler* is discussed below pp. 420–421.
157 A. Scales, 'Avoiding Constitutional Depression: Bad Attitudes and the Fate of *Butler*' (1994) 7 Can J of Women and the Law 349, 358.

The sense that others have engaged more fully than civil liberties lawyers with equality is not easily shifted, however. Consider, for example, the extent to which European lawyers have addressed the principle of equal treatment or non-discrimination in EC law. Moreover, much of their scholarship on this subject exhibits not only a strong critical edge but also, crucially, a capacity for contextualising critical theory on equality and on the politics of rights more generally in the circumstances of the EU.[158] In recent years, the scholarship's long-time focus on sex discrimination has also expanded explicitly to encompass other grounds of discrimination, largely as a result of Article 13 of the EC Treaty and of the European Court of Justice's ruling in *Grant v South-West Trains*[159] (which implied that EC law's prohibition on discrimination based directly on the sex of a worker did not include discrimination on the basis of sexual orientation).

It is worth reflecting on why reference to this scholarship, and to EU debates and developments more generally, is almost entirely absent from the civil liberties tradition. The tradition has had a long-time European focus, but it has been concentrated almost exclusively on the European Convention of Human Rights. This exclusive focus is regrettable. In recent years, it has also become even less understandable: why is it that, amidst commentary after commentary espousing HRA-scepticism, cynicism or euphoria, one rarely finds any attention being paid to the EU's obvious ambitions in the fields of non-discrimination and equality, or to the impact that an EU Charter of Rights could have on rights protection in the UK?

Those working in the field of international human rights have also turned their attention to the non-discrimination and equality guarantees in international agreements. The issue of gender mainstreaming, for example, was placed at centre-stage by the Fourth United Nations World Conference on Women, which took place in Beijing in 1995.[160] The UN Human Rights Committee, which monitors the International Covenant on Civil and Political Rights, also provoked interest in equality and non-discrimination following its view in *Toonen v Australia*,[161] wherein it concluded that laws in the state of Tasmania criminalising same-sex sexual acts violated Australia's obligations under the Covenant. More generally, there has been an increase in interest in the range of guarantees of non-discrimination contained within international human rights instruments. General guarantees of non-discrimination can be found in the UN Declaration of Human Rights (Article 7), the International Covenant on Civil and Political Rights (Articles 2(1), 3 and 26), and the International Covenant on Economic, Social and Cultural Rights (Articles 2(2) and 3). By contrast, issues of discrimination on specific grounds are addressed by the Convention on the Elimination of All Forms of Racial Discrimination, the Convention on the Elimination of Discrimination Against Women, the

---

158 See eg, A. Dashwood and S. O'Leary (eds.), *The Principle of Equal Treatment in EC Law* (Sweet & Maxwell, 1997); T.K. Hervey and D. O'Keefe (eds.), *Sex Equality Law in the European Union* (Wiley, 1996); and G. More, 'The Principle of Equal Treatment: From Market Unifier to Fundamental Right?' in P. Craig and G. de Búrca (eds.), *The Evolution of EU Law* (OUP, 1999), pp. 517-554.

159 Case C-249/96 [1998] ECR I-621. For discussion, see below p. 411.

160 *Report of the Fourth World Conference on Women*, UN Doc A/Conf 177/20 (1995).

161 Communication No. 488/1992, 31 Mar. 1994. For commentary, see eg, C.F. Stychin, *A Nation by Rights: National Cultures, Sexual Identity Politics, and the Discourse of Rights* (Temple UP, 1998), pp. 145-193.

Convention on the Rights of the Child and the Declaration on the Elimination of All Forms of Intolerance and of Discrimination Based on Religion or Belief.

A third group with a record of interest in equality issues is labour lawyers.[162] This grouping has engaged with International Labour Organisation Conventions[163] and the European Social Charter,[164] as well as with domestic law.[165] Moreover, as with EC and international human rights scholarship, the literature associated with this grouping generally gives the impression of being interested in the question of the broad values informing interpretation of an equality principle. This latter issue is, of course, also the theme of a diverse range of quality theoretical work: in 1991, an anthology on equality and non-discrimination characterised the theoretical literature as 'remarkably rich and diverse in its approach',[166] and these trends have deepened considerably over the intervening years. In particular, long-term, high-profile commentators, such as Ronald Dworkin, have sought to build on earlier work,[167] whilst new commentators, associated principally with the fields of social and critical theory, and in particular with feminism and lesbian and gay theory, have shed light on old questions and raised new issues.[168] Against this backdrop, the approach adopted within the civil liberties tradition to the principles of equality and non-discrimination might be deemed disappointingly limited.

Article 14, ECHR

We move finally to a third possible reason for the civil liberties tradition's relative neglect of equality: the ECHR's promulgation of a traditional liberal approach to non-discrimination and equality. The Convention, it has been said, 'recreates [the] liberal "cultural contract" by adopting a dual approach to minority protection':

> Its predominant concern is with the toleration of minorities. . . . A framework of individual rights (Articles 2-11) ensures that citizens are free to express their particular identity in the private sphere, either individually or in association with others, without state interference . . . [T]oleration [is supplemented] with a second strategy guaranteeing an individual right to non-discrimination, which the ECHR secures . . . Article 14.[169]

In effect, then, the ECHR seeks to foreground toleration and non-discrimination rather than equality. Essentially, it 'reflects the main features of the liberal approach by sustaining a neutral public sphere, which avoids references to issues of private identity such as sexuality, culture, race, religion, or language'.[170] Moreover, this liberal approach is only lightly leavened by multiculturalism.

---

162 Two of whom – Keith Ewing and Paul O'Higgins – are also prominent civil liberties scholars.
163 In 1999, the UK ratified ILO Convention 111 concerning discrimination in respect of employment and occupation.
164 The ESC is the counterpart to the ECHR. It dates from 1961 and, as its title indicates, it addresses economic and social rights. It was revised in 1996, and entered into force on 1 Jul. 1999. The UK has yet to ratify the revised version. For further details, see eg, K.D. Ewing, 'Social Rights and Human Rights: Britain and the Social Charter – the Conservative Legacy' (2000) 2 EHRLR 91.
165 See eg, S. Palmer, 'Human Rights: Implications for Labour Law' (2000) 59 CLJ 168.
166 See McCrudden, above n. 83, p. xi (introducing a collection of 'classic' equality articles).
167 See Dworkin, above n. 12.
168 See eg, Cooper, above n. 12; and Stychin, above n. 13.
169 M. Malik, 'Governing After the Human Rights Act' (2000) 63 MLR 281, 290-291.
170 Ibid., p. 291.

The dominance of the liberal approach can be seen, for example, in the Strasbourg authorities' cleavage to the Article 8 right to privacy, rather than to Article 14, in cases such as *ADT v UK* and *Dudgeon v UK*. It is also evident in the nature of the Article 14 ECHR prohibition on discrimination[171] and in the Strasbourg authorities approach thereto. Several features of Article 14 merit singling out in this regard. First, the Article is parasitic; that is, Article 14 does not provide a free-standing prohibition of discrimination in general[172] – only the 'rights and freedoms set forth in [the] Convention' must be secured without discrimination. There is, however, a new Protocol – Protocol 12 – which purports to extend the equality guarantee to all rights 'set forth by law'. The Protocol has been signed by almost a dozen governments of Council of Europe states. The UK government, however, has not yet signed.

Secondly, the European Court of Human Rights remains annoyingly aloof from the concept of indirect discrimination. As noted above, indirect discrimination arises where a criterion which is applied equally to different designated groups is such that a considerably smaller proportion of one designated group can comply. A prohibition on indirect discrimination has been a core feature of UK anti-discrimination legislation since the Sex Discrimination Act 1975. The Strasbourg court, however, has not yet embraced the notion. In *Abdulaziz*, for example, the Court implicitly rejected the concept of indirect discrimination in declaring that the UK's immigration rules were not unlawful simply because 'the mass immigration against which [they] were directed consisted mainly of would-be immigrants from the New Commonwealth and Pakistan, and that as a result they affected at the material time fewer white people than others'.[173]

The third problematic feature of Article 14 is that *all* discrimination is capable of being justified. The Strasbourg authorities have signalled, however, that they require 'very weighty reasons to be advanced' to justify discrimination based on sex, nationality or race, or against children born outside marriage. They appear also to be adopting a stricter position in cases involving discrimination in the area of religious freedom.[174]

The three above-listed limitations on Article 14's capacity to act as a lever against discrimination are not the only shortcomings of the ECHR as an equality tool. The margin of appreciation has had considerable hold over the Strasbourg authorities in equality cases. Furthermore, the (former) European Commission on Human Rights positioned itself as less than employee-friendly in its treatment

---

171 On Art. 14 case law, see eg, R. Clayton et al., *The Law of Human Rights* (OUP, 2000), Ch. 17; D.J. Harris, M. O'Boyle and C. Warbrick, *Law of the European Convention on Human Rights* (Butterworths, 1995), pp. 462-488; S. Grosz, J. Beatson and P. Duffy, *Human Rights: The 1998 Act and the European Convention* (Sweet & Maxwell, 1999), pp. 324-332; and A. Lester and D. Pannick (eds.), *Human Rights Law and Practice* (Butterworths, 1999), pp. 225-232.

172 Three qualifications should be noted, however: (1) an tenuous link with another provision in the ECHR may be sufficient to activate Art. 14 (*Schmidt and Dahlström v Sweden* (1976) 1 EHRR 632); (2) the ECtHR has held that there can be a violation of Art. 14, in conjunction with another Article, even if there is no violation of that other Article taken alone (see *Belgian Linguistics Case (No 2)* (1968) 1 EHRR 252 at 283, para. 9; and *Abdulaziz, Cabales and Balkandali v UK* (1985) 7 EHRR 471); and (3) discrimination unrelated to the enjoyment of a Convention right might still violate the ECHR (see *Belgian Linguistics*).

173 See eg, *Abdulaziz*, ibid. Grosz, Beatson and Duffy, above n. 171, p. 326 emphasise that *Abudulaziz* may be a special case, ie the political sensitivity of immigration may have inhibited the ECtHR.

174 See *Belgian Linguistics*, above n. 172, for an outline of the ECtHR's general approach to reviewing Art. 14 compliance.

of several applications under the Convention. Two Article 9 cases – *Ahmad v UK* and *Stedman v UK* – should serve to illustrate what appears to have been a tendency towards rigid formalism on the part of the Commission.

In *Ahmad*, in holding that there had been no violation of the applicant's right to freedom of religion, the Commission emphasised that the content of the Article 9 right could 'as regards the modality of a particular manifestation, be influenced by the situation of the person claiming that freedom', including any employment contract to which the person was a party.[175] It also disposed of the applicant's Article 14 claim in a summary fashion, comparing the applicant's treatment with that of members of other minority religions and holding that since both had to comply with the norms of the majority religion, there had been no less favourable treatment. In the second case, *Stedman*, the Commission examined an application by a woman who had been dismissed from her employment 'for refusing on religious grounds to accept a contract which meant that she would have to work on Sundays'. In a deeply formalistic decision, the Commission disposed of her application using the argument that she had been dismissed 'for failing to agree to work certain hours rather than for her religious belief as such and was free to resign and did in effect resign from her employment'.[176]

III. EXPRESSION AND EQUALITY IN THE AGE OF RECOGNITION

Having sketched the status of freedom of expression, non-discrimination and equality in the civil liberties tradition, we turn, in the remainder of the chapter, to our principal concern. That is, the vexed question of the relationship between freedom of expression and equality in a society which is shifting actively towards the language of rights. This shift makes it even more urgent to address the complex task of synergising liberalism and multiculturalism, and of forging a sense of identification or belonging.

We shall begin by outlining the changed attitude to difference and diversity in the UK. Then, the focus will be narrowed to the role of law in facilitating equality through difference. We aim to concretise relevant issues by looking at two attempts to use law to compel recognition: first, sexual harassment law; and second, pornography as an equality wrong rather than a cause of offence or protected free speech. The Part concludes with a summary of the most prominent of the critical responses to these two attempts to use law as a tool for recognition.

The late-modern way: injury, identity and law reform

The shift from modernity to the present day (or late modernity) has been described in many different ways. One fairly common theme, however, concerns

---

175 (1981) 4 EHRR 126 (EComHR). Ahmad, a schoolteacher, claimed that he was forced to resign his post when his employer (a local education authority) insisted that his attendance at a mosque for Friday prayers (which made him 45 minutes late for afternoon classes) was incompatible with his full-time contract. For the CA's rejection of his claim of unfair dismissal, with a powerful dissent from Scarman LJ, see [1978] QB 36.

176 (1997) 23 EHRR 168 (EComHR). See *Dahlab v Switzerland* ECtHR, 15 Feb. 2001.

what the criminologist, Jock Young, has described as a change in attitude towards difference and diversity. So, for example, one often encounters the idea that difference and diversity are 'staples of late modernity'.[177] But what is meant by this? It may refer to the consumption practices of late-modern societies; today, many of us consume diversity, and we 'do not recoil at difference but recast it as a commodity and sell it in the local supermarket or magazine'.[178] The food we eat, the chatshows we watch, the music to which we listen, the clothes we wear and the ways in which we are encouraged to decorate our homes – all of these things illustrate the embrace of difference and diversity within consumption practices. But late-modern societies do not only consume difference and diversity; they are also open to, and work towards, transforming themselves so that difference and diversity can be respected. This latter aspect of the changed attitude to difference and diversity is sometimes described in terms of a shift from a modern to a late-modern approach towards equality – that is, from an approach which at best admitted of, and worked towards, equality as identical treatment to the present-day preoccupation with equality *through* difference.

Mixophilia and mixophobia

Late-modern societies also exhibit opposite or reverse currents, however. Thus, as Zygmunt Bauman has suggested, our apparent 'taste for mixophilia is constantly buffeted by the opposite tendency mixophobia'.[179] This is evidenced, for example, by the violent nationalisms, racisms and homophobia which ripple through late-modern societies. Reverse currents are also not always about intentional hatred and exclusion: they can be traced, for example, to institutional racism, and to a liberal 'live and let live' strategy which allows those who have agreed to tolerate 'minorities' to wear their tolerance as 'a badge of superiority'.[180] Reverse currents also stem from reasonable anxieties and concerns about how a society can be both cohesive and respectful of difference. In the UK, this particular current has taken on a sharper edge following recent devolutions of power. Reverse currents also tend to gather speed and strength where there is inaction, or insufficiently purposeful action, on the 'hard questions' of difference and diversity. Thus, the Hepple Review, for example, points out that '[t]oday there is growing emphasis on cultural diversity and, *at the same time*, the need to bind together the constituent groups on the basis of shared values such as human rights and equality'.[181] The Parekh Report pursues a similar theme, urging a 'move from "multicultural drift" to a purposeful process of change' which would centre solidarity *and* liberty, cohesion *and* difference.[182]

---

177 Young, above n. 10, p. 389. E. Probyn, *Carnal Appetites* (Routledge, 2000) also uses food as a lens through which to examine a range of contemporary debates.
178 Young, ibid.
179 Z. Bauman, *Life in Fragments* (Blackwells, 1995), p. 221 (cited in Young, ibid., wherein late-modernity's 'criminology of intolerance' – namely its increasing unwillingness to accept 'difficult people' and 'dangerous classes' – is identified as the second component of the shift from modernity to late-modernity).
180 Phillips, above n. 70, p. 28.
181 Hepple et al., above n. 80, p. 11.
182 Parekh Report, above n. 7, p. 11.

The emphasis on these themes in the Hepple Review and the Parekh Report is both timely and necessary. It coincides with similar emphases in Northern Ireland's constitutional settlement and with a vogue amongst politicians, policy-makers and an assortment of commentators for rebranding 'Britishness'. The question of 'British national identity' is nothing new: it has been 'a subject of agonised debate in Britain since the early 1960s, triggered off initially by the loss of empire, then by the rise of the welfare state, postwar black and Asian migration and entry into the European Community . . .'.[183] It has also been the subject of a protracted argument between conservative nationalists and liberals (many of whom see any talk of 'belonging' or 'national identity' as raising 'the spectre of an assimilationist nationalism'[184] which might oppress minorities). Recently, however, a range of triggers seem to have propelled the issue from the margins to the centre of interest and debate. Devolution is one such trigger: it has provoked palpable fear about the alleged excesses of Scottish nationalism, as well as a crisis around Englishness.[185] Another trigger is provided by the violence associated with English football supporters abroad: this has led, for example, to reflection on the racism of versions of national identity (which is complemented by the debate about institutional racism generated by the Lawrence Inquiry).[186] A rather more positive trigger has been provided by the recent upsurge of interest within constitutional theory in versions of 'republican thinking' which emphasise the value of shared identity in a plural polity. Northern Ireland's ongoing project of constitutional settlement provides yet another important influence, as does the belief, held it would seem by some parts of the Conservative Party, that there are 'votes to be grubbed up in the gutter' if one can combine 'Europhobia together with immigration-bashing into a rave about Britain becoming "a foreign land"'.[187]

These triggers have prompted a renewed and complex debate about how best to generate a 'politics of belonging' in the present-day UK wherein liberalism, devolution and multiculturalism are also 'official' virtues. In some circles, identification via citizenship is promoted as a possible binding agent or glue; as a force for cohesion and solidarity to counter any fragmentation of the polity which might be a side-effect of increased claims for different treatment in the wake of both devolution and the incorporation of the ECHR. Tony Blair, for example, turned to the language of national citizenship in condemning those who planted the nail bombs that exploded in Brixton, Brick Lane and Soho in late April and early May 1999. The bombs were targeted respectively at London's African-Caribbean, Asian and gay communities: three people were killed by the Soho bomb, and many were injured during the attacks. Far-right

---

183 B. Parekh, 'Defining British National Identity' (2000) 71 Pol Q 4, 4.
184 Malik, above n. 169, p. 284.
185 E. Darian-Smith, *Bridging Divides: The Channel Tunnel and English Legal Identity in the New Europe* (California UP, 1999) (distinguishing Englishness from Britishness, and arguing that 'modern English identity is, above all, about inclusion and exclusion, which was intricately mapped onto the British state's spatial expression as an isolated island-nation' (p. 89)).
186 In the summer of 2000, the Home Secretary, Jack Straw, said that football hooliganism and racism were largely caused by English people with a distorted and racist view of their nationality: see *Guardian*, 17 Jul. 2000. Cf. A. King, 'Football Fandom and Post-national Identity in the New Europe' (2000) 51 BJ Soc 419 (emphasising the post-national loyalties of English fans of Manchester United Football Club).
187 Rawnsley, above n. 70.

organisations claimed responsibility for the bombs; ultimately, however, 'the perpetrator turned out to be a lone young man, consumed by . . . hatred'.[188] When Blair condemned the planting of the bombs and detailed the police action to find the perpetrator, he insisted that his government was 'doing more than bringing the killers to justice. [It was] defending what it means to be British':

> The true outcasts today, the true minorities, those truly excluded are not the different races and religions of Britain, but the racists, the bombers, the violent criminals who hate that vision of Britain and wish to destroy it.[189]

On some accounts, however, citizenship emerges somewhat disturbingly as a master political identity, ranking above other identities or rendering them irrelevant. This is a particular problem, for example, with conservative nationalist accounts of citizenship. Other accounts of citizenship are resolutely unattractive for different reasons: New Labour's cleavage to 'active citizenship' is characterised, for example, by preoccupations with paid work and with 'supporting families', which at times appear primarily to be cost-saving measures for the state.[190] It appears, therefore, that we are confronted with the paradox of citizenship: it is a force for both inclusion and exclusion, for both unity and division. The most obviously problematic use of citizenship discourse occurs in the areas of migration and mobility,[191] where 'citizenship' can provide states with 'an internationally acceptable rationale for regulating the movements of those who appear (or threaten to appear) on or within their borders as refugees from war and other forms of institutionalised violence, or simply in search of what they believe will be a better life':

> [Citizenship] . . . helps to keep the poor in their place and, by promoting discrimination against the foreigner, it appears to offer some benefits even to the poorest of citizens who remain at home.[192]

It is worrying, therefore, that in the summer of 2000, the UN Committee on the Elimination of Racial Discrimination, in its critical response to the UK government's report on measures taken in recent years to tackle racism, emphasised the need for the government to 'take leadership in sending out positive messages about asylum seekers'. In particular, the Committee reminded the government that 'racism is indivisible; there cannot be a trade-off between fair treatment of minority groups already here and those that newly arrive'.[193]

Problematic use of 'citizenship' in the context of mobility and migration is not the sole prerogative of states, however; it can also be found in the law and politics of migration and mobility in the EU. Thus, aspects of the project of EU citizenship, as well as of the law on immigration and asylum and on free movement of persons, have drawn stinging criticism in recent years for their

---

188 R. Hansen, 'British Citizenship after Empire: A Defence' (2000) 71 Pol Q 42, 42.
189 Quoted in ibid., p. 42.
190 For discussion, see eg, N. Rose, *Powers of Freedom: Reframing Political Thought* (Cambridge UP, 1999), p. 166ff.
191 For extended discussion, see eg, C. Harvey, *Seeking Asylum in the UK: Problems and Prospects* (Butterworths, 2000).
192 B. Hindess, 'Divide and Rule: The International Character of Modern Citizenship' (1998) 1 EJST 57, 68.
193 A. Owers, *Guardian*, 25 Aug. 2000.

creation and perpetuation of an exclusionary European identity.[194] The very fact, for example, that asylum and immigration issues were dealt with initially under the same legal framework as police co-operation, international crime and terrorism lent credence to depictions of asylum-seekers and immigrants as a threat to security.[195] Commentators have also documented the ways in which the history of 'free movement of persons' both created and reinforced inequality.[196] Carole Lyons, for example, has argued that '[f]ree movement of persons . . . developed around the notion [of] "insider" privilege'. She has also warned that the evolving project of EU citizenship contains the possibility of both opening up a post-national citizenship *and* exacerbating, or 'constitutionalizing', the inequalities inherent in free movement provisions.[197]

Law, theory and the turn to recognition

Law and law-makers – at both state and supra-state level – are mired within the late-modern currents of difference and diversity. This is the case even when all the protagonists profess commitment to a similar goal. In recent decades, for example, the UK Parliament and the courts have faced an increasing number of calls for laws to be abandoned in order that difference and diversity can be better respected. But the same argument has been used to ground calls for laws to be extended, and for new laws to be introduced. There are, in short, rather divergent views on how (and indeed whether) to use law to achieve equality through difference.

The ongoing dispute over the future of the common law offence of blasphemy provides an illustration of this phenomenon. The last 15 years have thrown up arguments that the offence should be abandoned, that it should be extended to cover other religions, and that it should be replaced by a law criminalising incitement to religious hatred, and *all* of these arguments make a claim to being grounded in a commitment to enhancing respect for difference and diversity, and redressing or preventing harm.[198] A huge part of the problem in

194 For an argument that this is the historic pattern of European identity, see P. Fitzpatrick, 'New Europe, Old Stories: Myths of Identity and Legality in the European Union' in P. Fitzpatrick and J.H. Bergeron (eds.), *Europe's Other: European Law Between Modernity and Postmodernity* (Ashgate, 1998), pp. 27-45.

195 See Art. K. 1, 1993 TEU. For commentaries on the current law and politics of asylum in Europe, see eg, M. Bell, 'Mainstreaming Equality Norms into European Union Asylum Law' (2001) 26 EL Rev 20; and C.J. Harvey, 'Dissident Voices: Refugees, Human Rights and Asylum in Europe' (2000) 9 SLS 367.

196 See eg, R. Cholewinski, 'The Rights of Non-EC Immigrant Workers and their Families in EC Countries of Employment' in J. Dine and B. Watt (eds.), *Discrimination Law: Concepts, Limitations and Justifications* (Longman, 1996); and T. Hervey, 'Migrant Workers and their Families in the European Union: The Pervasive Market Ideology of Community Law' in J. Shaw and G. More (eds.), *New Legal Dynamics of the European Union* (OUP, 1996), pp. 91-110.

197 C. Lyons, 'The Politics of Alterity and Exclusion in the European Union' in Fitzpatrick and Bergeron (eds.), above n. 194, pp. 157-174 at p. 160.

198 Art. 10 is unlikely to be a vehicle of change on this issue unless UK courts unshackle themselves from Strasbourg jurisprudence (as they are entitled to do). The ECtHR, faced with what it deems to be a lack of European consensus, has shown an exasperating degree of restraint in its treatment of cases involving clashes between religious sensibilities and freedom of expression: see eg, *Otto-Preminger Institute v Austria* (1994) 19 EHRR 34; and *Wingrove v UK* (1996) 24 EHRR 1.

the blasphemy, and other similar, debates is that there are different views amongst the protagonists on what constitutes 'harm'. Moreover, the different groups often seem to operate with no knowledge of, or interest in, other groups' views. This, alongside other issues, creates fertile terrain for interminable juxtapositionings of freedom and equality, heated arguments over allegedly 'unrecognisable' differences, and deep disagreements about whether liberalism can, or should, accommodate 'group-differentiated' citizenship.[199] It seems likely that this terrain will become even more contested now that 'rights have been brought home'. Hard questions may be met with unhelpful assertions of the priority of particular rights. They may also become excessively bound up with the language of human rights alone, which would undermine attempts to move us towards a model of rights conflict wherein '[t]he logic of multiculturalism qualifies and informs the logic of human rights, just as the logic of human rights qualifies the logic of multiculturalism'.[200] The latter 'dialogic' model of conflict resolution *is* an attainable ideal: for example, it has already produced constructive thinking on what is described as a 'right of exit', that is, the right of individuals to move away from their community, which is an important companion to rights of communities.[201]

Questions of recognition do not preoccupy only law-makers, however: they also worry their way through a great deal of recent critical theory. In what follows, we seek therefore to provide a basic map of this vast field before moving on to focus specifically on two case-studies of recognition-based law reform. Our map identifies three broad groupings within recent critical theory, all of which are disturbed by the turn towards recognition. The first grouping to which we wish to draw attention deliberates at length on the displacement of economic questions of inequality involved in the turn towards recognition.[202] That is, on the shift from the material to what are seen as primarily political and cultural questions, from 'the economics of equality' to 'the politics of constitutional reform'[203] or, in Nancy Fraser's well-known description, from questions of redistribution to ones of recognition.[204] The argument here is not that we would do well to return to the 'class' politics of the 1970s; rather, it is that, in redressing the 'injustices' of an exclusive focus on socio-economic transformation, there has been not merely a dislodgement but a wholescale displacement of economic questions of inequality.

---

199 The phrase comes from Will Kymlicka: see his, *Multicultural Citizenship: A Liberal Theory of Minority Rights* (Clarendon, 1995) which argues that liberalism has been at best ambiguous about group rights, and its future as a credible philosophy of government will depend on its ability to accommodate such rights. For another influential argument in this area, see I.M. Young, *Justice and the Politics of Difference* (Princeton UP, 1990) and her more recent book, *Inclusion and Democracy* (OUP, 2000).

200 Parekh Report, above n. 7, p. 91.

201 See eg, Parekh Report, ibid., p. 37 and J. Weeks, *Invented Moralities* (Polity, 1995).

202 This can perhaps be attributed, at least in part, to the ongoing influence of Charles Taylor's 1992 essay, above n. 2, wherein groups' calls for recognition are characterised as claims for a limited form of justice which has no explicit connection with issues of political inclusion or structural equality.

203 A. Phillips, 'From Inequality to Difference: A Severe Case of Displacement?' (1998) NLR 143, 143.

204 See N. Fraser, *Justice Interruptus: Critical Reflections on the 'Postsocialist' Condition* (Routledge, 1997), 11-40 and *Adding Insult to Injury* (Verso, 2000). See also, N. Klein, *No Logo* (Flamingo, 2001). But see C. Calhoun, '"New Social Movements" of the Early Nineteenth Century' (1993) 17 Social Science History 385 for an argument that 'identity concerns' have long been part of the agenda of social movements.

Carl Stychin has explored the apparent paradox of recognition/redistribution in the specific context of lesbian and gay citizenship strategies within Europe.[205] His chosen case-studies are, first, the European Court of Justice's decision in *Grant v South-West Trains*[206] and, secondly, the 1997 UK immigration guidelines allowing for unification of same-sex partners.[207] His aim is to highlight the paradox of same-sex partnership recognition. That is, the ways in which this example of legal recognition, which is grounded in the language of citizenship and human rights, can both enable *and* constrain.

Grant actually provides an example of an unsuccessful recognition claim: it was the case in which the European Court of Justice held that an employer's refusal to grant travel concessions to a person with whom a worker has a same-sex 'stable relationship' did not amount to prohibited discrimination based on sex, even where such concessions are granted to a person with whom a worker has a heterosexual stable relationship, whether married or unmarried. Stychin, however, uses this 'failure' of recognition as a prompt for critical reflection on what he describes as 'the sometimes taken-for-granted politics of European sexual citizenship rights'.[208] Thus, building on the work of EC sex-equality lawyers, which problematises the focus on the 'market citizen', mobility of workers and facilitation of transnational capitalism within EC rights discourse, he makes a case for greater alertness to the limitations of recognition achieved through this rights discourse as 'a vehicle for challenging underlying structural barriers to full citizenship':

> The argument . . . is that rights do little, if anything to alter underlying structures which produce . . . inequality, such as the role of unpaid labour in the private sphere, and barriers to entry in the workplace . . . Activists and academics should pay greater attention to whether that gendered economy is challenged by lesbian and gay legal struggles, or alternatively, whether the lesbian or gay subject is naturalised within the political economy through the (eventually successful) claiming of rights.[209]

Stychin's second case study – the immigration guidelines allowing same-sex couple reunification which were introduced by the New Labour government in 1997 – also evidences the 'double-edgedness' of recognition via 'citizenship rights'. In other words, it brings out again the way in which recognition may serve both to enable and to constrain. Stychin shows, for example, that while the immigration guidelines may allow for reunification of same-sex couples across national frontiers – and, as he says, this *is* an important development, both symbolically and for individual couples – they are also a tool for the 'responsibilisation' of citizenship.[210] The guidelines, he reminds us, place particular emphasis on 'stable', past (and intended post-unification) cohabitation, and on the parties' interdependent and, thus, privatised financial

---

205 Stychin (2000a) and (2000b), above n. 13. See also S. Boyd, 'Family, Law and Sexuality: Feminist Engagements' (1999) 8 SLS 369 (using the recognition/redistribution debate to analyse the Canadian SCt's decision in *M v H* [1999] 2 SCR 3).

206 Case C-249/96 [1998] ECR I-621.

207 See now Common Law and Same Sex Relationships (Unmarried Partners) Requirements of the Immigration Rules (2001) (available at: www.ind.homeoffice.gov.uk).

208 Above n. 13, (2000a) p. 282.

209 Ibid., p. 293.

210 See also, R.A. Elman, 'The Limits of Citizenship: Migration, Sex Discrimination and Same-Sex Partners in EU Law' (2000) 38 JCMS 729 (arguing against the recognition strategy in *Grant*, above n. 206, because it presumes that '*relationships*' (whether spousal, cohabitational, sexual or familial) provide justifiable criteria for citizenship and the privileges associated with it').

responsibility. The government thereby is placed in what it may well see as a 'win-win' situation: it can explicitly justify this 'recognition' of same-sex couples 'on the basis of conformity with human rights' and at the same time it can follow through on New Labour ideology 'by further entrenching the principle of privatization of the financial costs of migration onto "stable" relationships based on in(ter)dependence'. Thus:

> [l]iberal law reform occurs, but only within a strict set of constraints as to the requirements which are imposed as the price of recognition for the good homosexual. Recognition rights, as opposed to redistributive politics, are inexpensive for the neo-liberal state.[211]

Other commentators have been more condemnatory than Stychin about various European governments' embrace of recognition claims. Slavoj Zizek, for example, has pointed to what he sees as the 'zombification of the social democratic project' inherent in the embrace of 'Third Way-style' social democracy, which is underway in a number of European states:

> Expelling the material realities of sweated labour, collective production and anomic licence from its visions of the East, the official imaginary naturally has no time for traces of the working class in the West. In today's political discourse, the very term 'worker' tends to have disappeared from sight, substituted or obliterated by 'immigrants' – Algerians in France, Turks in Germany, Mexicans in the USA, etc. In the new vocabulary, the class problematic of exploitation is transformed into the multiculturalist problematic of 'intolerance of the Other', and the investment of liberals in the particular rights of ethnic minorities draws much of its energy from the repression of the general category of the collective labourer. The 'disappearance' of the working class then fatally unleashes its reappearance in the guise of aggressive nativism. Liberals and populists meet on common ground: all they talk about is identity . . . .[212]

We move now to a second, rather more eclectic, grouping which is critical of the turn towards recognition. The members of this second grouping have different political orientations, but they also have a common concern about what they perceive to be a carving-up of the polity into selfish individuals and interest-groups. 'Identity politics', they argue, leads to 'enclaving' and ends up impoverishing, rather than enriching, democracy. This politics is also accused of 'over-politicization – and its sidekick, depoliticization'; in other words, of promoting a form of politicisation 'that empties political action of its real meaning'.[213] Communitarian-leaning members of this grouping tend, in particular, to emphasis that 'recognition' can destroy any concept of the 'common good'.[214] By contrast, other members, whose political orientation is liberal nationalist, allege that 'identity politics' weakens national identification (which, it is argued, is the best option for a 'politics of belonging' in a plural society).[215]

---

211 Above n. 13, (2000b) p. 618.
212 S. Zizek, 'Why We All Love to Hate Haider?' (2000) NLR 37, 37, 44-45.
213 Phillips, above n. 70, p. 99.
214 See eg, J.B. Elshtain, *Democracy on Trial* (Basic Books, 1995).
215 See eg, D. Miller, *On Nationality* (OUP, 1995). Cf. Young, above n. 19, pp. 81-120 and, in a UK context, the Parekh Report, above n. 7, and P. Werbner, 'Divided Loyalties, Empowered Citizenship? Muslims in Britain' (2000) 4 Citizenship Studies 307 (arguing that 'far from revealing ambiguous loyalties or unbridgeable cultural chasms, British Muslim transnational loyalties have challenged the national polity to explore new forms of multiculturalism and to work for new global human rights causes').

There has been a further batch of high-profile disagreements around the question of whether recognition claims, particularly 'successful' ones, distort identity, and also whether they install practices of unfreedom or, what Wendy Brown calls, a 'plastic cage'.[216] We shall return to the latter argument below: in essence, it proposes that the turn towards the state (and also, presumably, towards other governing entities such as the ECJ) compromises freedom and boosts sovereign power.[217] The former argument – that recognition claims distort identity – tends to take multiculturalism, which is much-vaunted in other circles, as a key target. For some (mainly liberal) critics, multiculturalism's apparent prioritisation of groups over individuals – its 'encouragement of a "groupiness" that is at odds with individualism'[218] – creates severe problems. For other (mainly postmodern) critics, the problem lies in the way in which (versions of) multiculturalism, by representing difference as a series of essential attributes or authenticities, paradoxically end up facilitating, and perhaps even nurturing, prejudice and exclusion.[219] This latter criticism remains controversial, but it has had a powerful influence. It has, for example, helped to raise the question of whether individuals within 'equalised' groups can be left with unequal power.[220] It has also led to an increasing insistence on non-essential, or historicised, identity politics. This latter insistence, in turn, has led to a proliferation of interest in concepts such as hybridity, fragmentation and diaspora.[221] Thus, the cultural theorist Stuart Hall has argued recently that the category of 'the black subject' can no longer serve as a basis for identity politics in the UK; that there is 'no guarantee, from nature or from experience, to justify it'.[222] Similarly, the Parekh Report emphasises that although '[d]ifference now matters profoundly':

> differences are not necessarily either/or – many people are learning to live 'in between', it has been said, or with more than one identity. The famous Tebbit cricket test is not only racially demeaning but is also out of date. People today are constantly juggling different, not always wholly compatible, identities.[223]

All of these debates feed into a further, more general debate about what constitutes 'progress'. In the next three sections, we look at this latter debate via a case-study of two recent attempts to use the law to compel 'recognition'. The first attempt concerns the recognition of sexual harassment as sex discrimination; the second concerns calls for a 'modern' pornography law, one based on harm rather than offensiveness and situated alongside prohibitions

---

216 W. Brown, *States of Injury* (Princeton UP, 1995), p. 28.

217 Below pp. 424-427.

218 Phillips, above n. 70, p. 35.

219 Note, however, that as I.M. Young, *Inclusion and Democracy* (OUP, 2000), p. 87 points out '[g]roup-differentiated political movements themselves, along with their theoreticians, have developed sophisticated critiques of such tendencies'. In other words, it was not simply a case of waiting for critics to point out the problems with certain identity claims.

220 See eg, the texts cited above n. 201 which discuss 'rights of exit' from groups.

221 See eg, R. Braidotti, *Nomadic Subjects: Embodiment and Sexual Difference in Contemporary Feminist Theory* (Columbia UP, 1994); P. Gilroy, *The Black Atlantic: Modernity and Double Consciousness* (Harvard UP, 1993); and D. Haraway, *Simians, Cyborgs and Women: The Reinvention of Nature* (Routledge, 1991).

222 Barrett, above n. 15, p. 166 (describing S. Hall, 'What is this "Black" in Black Popular Culture?' in D. Morley and K.H. Chen (eds.), *Stuart Hall: Critical Dialogues in Cultural Studies* (Routledge, 1996).

223 Above n. 7, p. 36.

on hate speech. We have chosen to focus on sex harassment and pornography because they are pre-eminent examples of '[recognition] wars without end', and because they illustrate very clearly how freedom of expression and equality often get turned into a zero-sum game. We shall begin by outlining the 'progress' that has been made in both areas. This will be followed by a description of an array of the arguments that have been raised against these developments; arguments that may become all too familiar in the HRA era.

Case study 1: sexual harassment

Sexual harassment has been front-page news over the last decade. In large part, this has been because of the US' fascination with the sexual practices of a former President (Bill Clinton) and a current Supreme Court Justice (Clarence Thomas).[224] Amidst this saturation coverage, it would be easy to forget that sexual harassment is still relatively new to law and, moreover, that the concept of sexual harassment itself has no more than a brief history. Credit for bridging the gap between sexual harassment as an embryonic moral wrong and sexual harassment as a harm requiring specific legal redress tends to go to Catharine MacKinnon's 1979 book, *Sexual Harassment of Working Women*.[225] In the book, MacKinnon defined sexual harassment as 'the unwanted imposition of sexual requirements in the context of a relationship of unequal power'.[226] More importantly, she provided a detailed argument as to why sexual harassment should be treated as a legal harm and, crucially, why it should be a harm of *gender inequality*[227] rather than 'a gender generic issue of obscenity, assault or labor relations'.[228]

MacKinnon's emphasis on harassment as sex discrimination was entirely intentional. Every possible trace of doubt about this was eliminated upon the publication of later work, such as *Feminism Unmodified* and *Toward a Feminist Theory of the State*, which details her theory of gender and her project to use law to achieve substantive equality.[229] Initially, however, MacKinnon's emphasis on

---

224 For sophisticated analyses, see eg, J.L. Cohen, 'The Hijacking of Sexual Harassment' (1999) 6 Constellations 142 (using the impeachment of former US President Bill Clinton as a springboard to argue that conceptualisations of sex harassment which are dominant in the US 'play into the hands of social conservatives whose interests are not gender equality, but the reinscription of traditional gender norms at work and at home'); and T. Morrison (ed.), *Race-ing Justice, En-gendering Power: Essays on Anita Hill, Clarence Thomas, and the Construction of Social Reality* (Pantheon, 1992).

225 C. MacKinnon, *Sexual Harassment of Working Women* (Yale UP, 1979). In *Only Words* (Harvard UP, 1993), MacKinnon seeks to enhance the original argument by emphasising the illocutionary and silencing effects of sexually harassing speech so as to armour-plate harassment law against the criticism that it interferes excessively with personal or expressive freedom.

226 Ibid., (1979) pp. 1-2.

227 Sex discrimination had been made an actionable wrong by Title VII of the Civil Rights Act 1964, which declared it unlawful for an employer 'to discriminate against any individual with respect to . . . compensation, terms, conditions or privileges of employment, because of such individual's . . . sex . . .'.

228 Brown, above n. 216, p. 130.

229 C. MacKinnon, *Feminism Unmodified* (Harvard UP, 1987) and *Toward a Feminist Theory of the State* (Harvard UP, 1989). For appraisals of MacKinnon's version of feminist jurisprudence, see eg, Brown above n. 216; or E. Jackson, 'Catharine MacKinnon and Feminist Jurisprudence' (1992) 19 JLS 195. See below pp. 419-421 for details of MacKinnon's interventions on pornography.

harassment as discrimination was perceived mainly as an attempt to decommission the discourse of workplace harassment as grounded in natural desire, as a private, intimate matter between a woman and a man. By focusing on sex discrimination law, sexual harassment could be seen as an 'institutionalised practice' and this, in turn, allowed the harm of harassment to be understood 'in terms of group-based inequality and discrimination, not as a dignity harm, a moral injury, or an offense to a code of good conduct'.[230]

MacKinnon's argument on harassment as discrimination found favour with the US courts. By 1986, the US Supreme Court had acknowledged both *quid pro quo* harassment ('this for that' – in other words, the conditioning of employment benefits on submission to sexual advances) and, more controversially, hostile working environment harassment (which arises where an employee's working conditions are discriminatorily affected by the workplace's contamination by ridicule and insult).[231] In recent years, the Court has sought to expand employer liability for workplace sexual harassment, and has upheld a complaint of same-sex harassment as unlawful sex discrimination.[232]

Harassment law in the UK, like its US counterpart, is largely a 'judicial gloss'[233] on anti-discrimination legislation; existing anti-discrimination statutes contain no *express* prohibition on harassment.[234] Consider, for example, the approach to sexual harassment. Sexual harassment at work does not *per se* constitute unlawful sex discrimination under the SDA. But the Act makes it unlawful for an employer to discriminate against employees on the grounds of sex by subjecting them to any detriment, and the courts have used this to allow sex harassment (whether *quid pro quo* or hostile working environment) to be treated as direct discrimination.[235] For the most part, this has meant that 'the same questions have to be asked as in a direct discrimination claim based on, for example, non-appointment or non-promotion. The plaintiff has to show less favourable treatment on the ground of sex which is sufficient to constitute a detriment'.[236] Employer liability for harassment under the SDA can be either

---

230 J.L. Cohen, 'Personal Autonomy and the Law: Sexual Harassment and the Dilemma of Regulating "Intimacy"' (1999) 6 Constellations 443, 449. See B. Bowling, *Violent Racism: Victimization, Policing and Social Context* (Clarendon, 1999) for an argument that the conception of racial violence in terms of 'incidents' tears such violence from its context and treats it as a discrete event.

231 *Meritor Savings Bank FSB v Vinson* 477 US 57 (1986).

232 See *Burlington Industries v Ellerth* 524 US 742 (1998) and *Faragher v City of Boca Raton* 524 US 575 (1998) (employer liability); and *Oncale v Sundowner Offshore Services* 523 US 75 (1998) (same-sex harassment). Cf. *Smith v Gardner Merchant Ltd* [1998] IRLR 510 (CA) (same-sex harassment not actionable under SDA) but, note also, the EAT decision in *MacDonald v Ministry of Defence* (2001) IRLR 431 (EAT) (sexual orientation discrimination is sex discrimination within the SDA).

233 Hepple et al., above n. 80, p. 39.

234 Other possible remedies for workplace harassment include the law of contract; the law on constructive unfair dismissal; the Protection from Harassment Act 1997, below p. 416; trespass torts (see J. Conaghan, 'Gendered Harms and the Law of Tort: Remedying (Sexual) Harassment Law' (1996) 16 OJLS 407); and the criminal law (see provisions on telephone harassment (*R v Ireland* [1997] 4 All ER 225 (HL); Telecommunications Act 1984, s. 43(1)); obscene letters and parcels (Malicious Communications Act 1988, s. 1(1)); and harassing words or behaviour (Public Order Act 1986, as amended, ss. 4-5)).

235 *Strathclyde Regional Council v Porcelli* [1986] IRLR 134 (CS). The CA acknowledged hostile working environment harassment as falling within the law in a case under the RRA: see *De Souza v Automobile Association* [1986] IRLR 103.

236 Townshend-Smith, above n. 149, p. 237.

vicarious (that is, liability for 'anything done by a person in the course of his employment . . . whether or not it was done with the employer's knowledge or approval')[237] or direct (where the employer either is the harasser or has subjected the harassed employee to a detriment by failing to act reasonably to prevent harassment of which s/he had, or should have had, knowledge).[238] Section 42, which makes it unlawful to assist the discriminatory act of another, allows for harassers themselves to be found liable where vicarious liability on the part of the employer has been established.[239]

The courts' development of harassment as discrimination has been far from trouble-free, and there is now considerable dispute about how best to interpret the language of the statutes on issues such as whether a comparator is needed in harassment cases, the meaning of 'detriment', and vicarious liability. The extent of the problems was made manifest by the decision of the Hepple Review to avoid discrimination law when making recommendations on how best to deal with workplace harassment. The Review team call for a new statutory tort of harassment and bullying at work, dismissing harassment's placement within anti-discrimination law as problematic because of the focus on 'less favourable treatment', (which frequently leads courts and tribunals to invoke an unhelpful comparative approach[240]) and on showing a 'detriment'.[241] The advent of the Protection from Harassment Act 1997 – a statute, enacted principally to deal with stalking, which introduces both criminal and civil liability for harassment – adds a further layer of difficulty to the consideration of harassment as discrimination.[242] The Act could potentially be used by harassed employees. But, should this possibility be embraced? It has been argued that the legislation's 'perpetrator focus and emphasis on criminal redress . . . with a civil action thrown in almost for good measure' could circumscribe its usefulness to harassed employees. Furthermore, the fact that, prior to its enactment, this legislation was packaged as a component part of the (then) Conservative government's commitment to 'law and order' provides an additional reason for caution.[243]

---

237 S. 41, SDA. See *Jones v Tower Boot Co Ltd* [1997] IRLR 168 (CA) (taking a broad approach to 'course of employment' under the vicarious liability provision in the RRA (s. 32)). The legislation does contain an often-used defence which allows employers to argue that they could not reasonably have done anything more (s. 41(3) SDA; s. 32(3) RRA).

238 S. 42, SDA. See *Burton and Rhule v De Vere Hotels* [1996] IRLR 596 (EAT) (discussing direct liability under the corresponding provision of the RRA).

239 See R. Mullender, 'Racial Harassment, Sexual Harassment, and the Expressive Function of Law' (1998) 61 MLR 236 arguing that harassers should be held liable at common law rather than relying solely on employers' liability, given that under the latter route 'the [harasser's] expression of a pernicious prejudice is, at once, identified as conduct that calls forth a legal response and yet is not, itself, the direct object of a legal sanction'.

240 See eg, *Stewart v Cleveland Guest (Engineering) Ltd* [1994] IRLR 440 (EAT) (a workplace display of pictures of nude women deemed gender-neutral because a hypothetical man might also have complained about it). The comparator approach is not all-pervasive: see *British Telecommunications plc v Williams* [1997] IRLR 668 (EAT) (under the SDA) and *Sidhu v Aerospace Composite Technology Ltd* [1999] IRLR 683 (EAT) (under the RRA).

241 It has been accepted that a single, serious act can amount to a detriment: *Bracebridge Engineering Ltd v Darby* [1990] IRLR 3 (EAT).

242 S. 1 requires a 'course of conduct' before liability can arise but it avoids the need to prove any intention to harass – defendants are liable if they know or ought to know that the conduct amounts to harassment.

243 See J. Conaghan, 'Enhancing Civil Remedies for (Sexual) Harassment: S. 3 of the Protection from Harassment Act 1997' (1999) 7 FLS 203.

At various junctures in the past, EC law and policy on sexual harassment has acted as a beacon for flailing domestic courts and tribunals. The European Commission, for example, had a notable influence on the development of sexual harassment law, in particular via a *Recommendation* and a *Code of Practice on the Protection of the Dignity of Women and Men at Work*. Both documents date from the early 1990s, and both offer definitions of sexual harassment. The Recommendation provides that conduct of a sexual nature, or other conduct based on sex affecting the dignity of women and men at work is unacceptable if:

(a) such conduct is unwanted, unreasonable and offensive to the recipient;
(b) is used . . . as a basis for an [employment] decision; and/or
(c) such conduct creates an intimidating, hostile or humiliating work environment for the recipient.[244]

The *Code of Practice* complements this, defining sexual harassment as 'unwanted conduct of a sexual nature, or other conduct based on sex affecting the dignity of women and men at work . . . [It] can include unwanted physical, verbal or non-verbal conduct'.[245]

The EU has signalled recently that it intends to deal rather more aggressively with harassment. It has used the Race Directive, for example, to provide that harassment is prohibited discrimination. More interestingly, it has defined harassment as unwanted conduct 'with the purpose or effect of violating the dignity of a person and of creating an intimidating, hostile, degrading, humiliating or offensive environment'.[246] A similar approach is used in the proposed Equal Treatment Directive. This development, as others have pointed out, purports to be harassment as discrimination but it certainly is not harassment as discrimination 'as we know it':

> The prohibited 'discrimination' in fact is not discrimination in any way which one would ordinarily use the term. It is something rather different. It is not dependent on the intentions of the perpetrator; the effect on the victim is sufficient for the prohibited activity to have taken place. It requires both a violation of dignity and the creation of an environment which fulfils one of the five descriptions.[247]

Case study 2: Beyond obscenity

Obscenity law, like sex harassment law, has been the subject of considerable speculation and impassioned proposals for repackaging. Unlike sex harassment law, however, 'obscenity' as a legal wrong is not new to law. The Obscene Publications Act 1959 (along with customs legislation[248]) is the principal legal mechanism for the control of 'obscene' material. The Act, which originates in the common law offence of 'obscene libel',[249] has several distinctive features. First, a literary or pictorial representation must 'tend to deprave and corrupt'

244 Commission Recommendation 91/131/EC. OJ 1991 L 49/1.
245 Issued in accordance with the Resolution of the Council of Ministers, OJ 1990 C 157.
246 Art. 2(3).
247 Guild, above n. 124, p. 421.
248 See eg, *Conegate Ltd v Customs and Excise Comrs*, Case 121/85, [1986] 2 All ER 688 (ECJ); and *R v Bow St Magistrates, ex p Noncyp* [1990] 1 QB 123 (CA).
249 See B. Brown, 'Symbolic Politics and Pornography' (1992) 21 Economy and Society 45, 55-56 for an argument that 'the more "archaic" libels capture the symbolic harm of pornography far better than modern obscenity law'.

its audience (section 1); historically, moral vulnerability was seen as linked to harmful social consequences, but the present-day meaning of the test remains ambiguous. Secondly, the 1959 Act requires that the publication be assessed as a whole as to its effect on its likely audience, and it allows for a 'public good' defence for material with literary, scientific, or other merits (section 4).

Changing social mores have been a powerful influence on both the meaning of 'obscenity' and the extent of regulation. That this is the case can be seen, for example, in the pattern of acquittals of the publishers of books such *as Lady Chatterley's Lover* (1960) and *Last Exit to Brooklyn* (1966).[250] By the late 1970s, it was also very clear that policing and prosecution practices were being moulded by juries' increasing refusals to accept that pictorial material targeted at an adult heterosexual market warranted criminalisation as 'obscene', and by the sense that increased commercialisation of pornography was inescapable.[251] Police tactics eventually shifted away from jury trials to seizure and destruction of certain – usually termed 'hard-core' – categories of pornography using magistrates' forfeiture powers under section 3 of the 1959 Act. With the advent of video, satellite and cable (and now Internet) distribution and increased industry self-regulation,[252] police resources have shifted even further away from 'adult pornography' and are focused now on targeting material involving children.[253]

The issue which has tended to generate the greatest controversy in discussion about the regulation of pornography is 'harm'. So, for example, the 1979 report of the Home Office-appointed Williams Committee opted for a liberal harm principle and, upon finding no proof of a direct link between pornography and specific harms, recommended abolition of the current obscenity approach.[254] By contrast, the 1980s witnessed a renewed feminist politics on pornography, which claimed to identify a range of negative effects on women flowing from pornography's production, display and consumption, and sparked calls for new legal remedies.[255]

250 See J. Weeks, *Sex, Politics and Society: The Regulation of Sexuality Since 1800* (Longman, 1989), p. 101 (arguing that 'the regulation of pornography and obscenity involved a mix of agencies, procedures and jurisdictions – administrative, judicial, commercial and ethical – which were not bound together by any single force such as a Puritanical will to repress sex and impede enlightenment, but which directed the distribution of various types of publication to different audiences according to limited goals and imperatives'). See also, I. Hunter, D. Saunders and D. Williamson, *On Pornography: Literature, Sexuality and Obscenity Law* (Macmillan, 1993).

251 For more detail, see eg, A. Travis, *Bound and Gagged* (Profile Books, 2000); and B. Thompson, *Soft Core: Moral Crusades against Pornography in Britain and America* (Cassell, 1994).

252 For an account of the range of statutory and non-statutory bodies involved in regulating the content, sale and distribution of magazines, cinema, video and television, see Robertson and Nicol, above n. 24. On the increasing sexual explicitness of the media, see B. NcNair, *Mediated Sex: Pornography and Postmodern Culture* (Arnold, 1996).

253 See M. Hames, *Dirty Squad* (Little Brown, 2000) (describing how Scotland Yard's Obscene Publications Branch has shifted its focus towards countering paedophile activity). See eg, *R v Bowden* [2000] 2 All ER 418 (CA) (re downloading of images to a computer).

254 *Report of the Committee on Obscenity and Film Censorship*, Cmnd. 7772 (HMSO, 1979). It proposed that pictorial material should only be prohibited where there was evidence of physical harm to participants in the production (or where under-16-year-olds were involved); all other material should be 'restricted' to specialist premises. For a feminist 'zoning' argument, see eg, D. Cornell, *The Imaginary Domain* (Routledge, 1995).

255 See C. Smart, *Feminism and the Power of Law* (Routledge, 1989), p. 116 for an argument that 'the feminist concern with pornography has emerged from long-standing campaigns on issues of sexual exploitation (e.g. prostitution) and from the more recent recognition that (hetero)sexuality is a site of conflict and oppression, rather than merely a reflection of 'natural' difference between women and men. It also developed from work on images of women in advertising, literature, film, and the media. This is quite a different 'genesis' and has incorporated into more traditional feminist work on sexual exploitation ideas from semiotics and theories of representation'.

Itzin, for example, has proposed using existing incitement to racial hatred legislation to create an incitement to sexual hatred offence as a template for regulation.[256] The best-known catalyst for a revisioning of the concept of 'obscenity' towards a discourse of harm, however, is Catharine MacKinnon's and Andrea Dworkin's conceptualisation of pornography as a violation of civil rights law – in particular, their attempts in the 1980s to have an anti-pornography ordinance adopted in the state of Minneapolis in the US and, later, in 1992, the imprint of their ideas on the Canadian Supreme Court's decision in *R v Butler*.[257]

In an earlier section, we described Catharine MacKinnon influential conceptualisation of sexual harassment as sex discrimination. It is her views on the legal regulation of pornography, however, which have made her the 'unquestioned theoretical lodestar of the feminist anti-pornography movement':[258] her analysis of pornography has proved unavoidable and, sometimes, inescapable. In essence, MacKinnon isolates pornography as the most potent vehicle of women's subordination:

> Pornography . . . is a form of forced sex, a practice of sexual politics, an institution of gender inequality. . . . [It] is not harmless fantasy or a corrupt and confused misrepresentation of an otherwise natural and healthy sexuality. Along with rape and prostitution in which it participates, pornography institutionalizes the sexuality of male supremacy, which fuses the eroticization of dominance and submission with the social construction of male and female. Gender is sexual. Pornography constitutes the meaning of that sexuality. Men treat women as who they see women as being. Pornography constructs who that is.[259]

In 1983, working with a local residents' campaign in the US state of Minneapolis, MacKinnon and Andrea Dworkin[260] drafted an ordinance in an attempt to establish that pornography was a form of sex discrimination – that is, that it was conduct which exploited and differentially harmed women as a group.[261] The ordinance sought to give civil remedies for harms 'caused' by pornography[262] – for example, having pornography 'forced upon [one] in any place of employment, in education, in a home, or in any public place'. In addition, in line with MacKinnon's argument that 'if a woman is subjected, why should it matter that the work has other value?',[263] the draft ordinance did not allow for pictures or words to be justified on literary, artistic, political or scientific grounds. It was intended that the ordinance should displace the focus of US obscenity

---

256 C. Itzin (ed.), *Pornography: Women, Violence and Civil Liberties* (OUP, 1992). Following the model of ss. 18-19 of the Public Order Act 1986, her proposal would make it unlawful to publish or distribute material which is likely to stir up sexual hatred. For commentary on this proposal, see S. Easton, 'Pornography as Incitement to Sexual Hatred' (1995) 8 FLS 89. Wintemute, above n. 75, has argued for the extension of the existing offence to cover sexual orientation and gender identity.

257 [1992] 1 SCR 452.

258 Ibid.

259 *Feminism Unmodified*, above n. 229, p. 148.

260 See A. Dworkin, *Pornography: Men Possessing Women* (Women's Press, 1982).

261 For background details, see P. Brest and A. Vandenberg, 'Politics, Feminism and the Constitution: The Anti-Pornography Movement in Minneapolis' (1987) 39 Stanford LR 607.

262 Pornography was defined as 'the graphic sexually explicit subordination of women through pictures and/or words portraying the graphic, sexually explicit subordination of women'. The definition provided that '. . . the use of men, children, or transsexuals in the place of women' would also be pornography. This 'add-on' approach to men, children and transsexuals has been criticised, eg by Cornell, above n. 254.

263 C. MacKinnon, 'Pornography, Civil Rights and Speech' (1985) 20 Harv CR-CL L Rev 1, 21.

law on offensiveness and also the implicit acceptance of pornography inherent in the trend for using zoning to keep 'adult' bookshops and cinemas out of residential areas. More importantly, it was intended that it should shift legal discourse about pornography in a progressive direction – namely, away from the terrain of First Amendment free speech to the right to equality protected by the Fourteenth Amendment of the US Constitution.

The Minneapolis ordinance was vetoed, however, while still at the municipal stage. A similar ordinance was adopted subsequently in Indianapolis. But this was soon challenged by an alliance of publishers, distributors and civil libertarian and feminist groups and, in 1985, it was declared unconstitutional on First Amendment grounds in *American Booksellers Association v Hudnut*.[264] Several years later, however, in 1992, the ordinances' analysis of pornography surfaced once again; this time in *R v Butler*, a case before the Canadian Supreme Court concerning the owner of a video store who was appealing against a conviction under Canada's Criminal Code for possession of 'obscene' material for the purposes of sale.[265] Butler's lawyers argued that the Code's obscenity provisions violated the guarantee of 'freedom of thought, belief, opinion and expression' in section 2(b) of the Canadian Charter of Rights and Freedoms. The Court recognised that the obscenity law interfered with the section 2(b) guarantee but, in a parallel to its reasoning in an earlier case, *R v Keegstra*,[266] involving a prohibition on the expression of racist speech, it concluded that the interference was justified under section 1 of the Charter in order to protect other rights and values. In essence, as Kathleen Mahoney has suggested, 'the Court advanced an equality approach using a harm-based rationale to support the regulation of hate propaganda [and pornography] as a practice of inequality'.[267]

The *Butler* court said that a direct link between pornography and violence was not susceptible to exact proof but, as in its earlier hate propaganda cases, it said there was a connection sufficient to uphold the challenged law. The Court's judgment relies upon a three-fold categorisation in order to provide guidance on the meaning of the reference to 'undue exploitation of sex' in the Canadian Criminal Code's obscenity provisions. The Court's first category is pornography showing sex with violence (including threats of violence); this would almost always be prohibited. The second category is explicit sex which is 'degrading and dehumanising'; this would be prohibited if the risk of harm is substantial.[268]

---

264 *American Booksellers Association v Hudnut* 771 F2d 323, 328 (1985). The SCt affirmed the ruling without hearing oral argument: 475 US 1001 (1986). For commentary, see eg, S. Colombo, 'The Legal Battle for the City: Anti-Pornography Municipal Ordinances and Radical Feminism' (1994) 2 FLS 29.

265 [1992] 1 SCR 452. S. 163(8) of the Canadian Criminal Code defined as obscene 'any publication a dominant characteristic of which is the undue exploitation of sex, or of sex and any one or more of the following subjects, namely, crime, horror, cruelty and violence'.

266 [1990] 3 SCR 697. In this case, a majority of the SCt, acknowledging the equality guarantee in s. 15(1) of the Charter, accepted that hate speech causes significant harms, as its targets feel alienated from society and suffer pain and a loss of self-respect, and that it encourages discriminatory attitudes and behaviour between different cultural groups. See also, *R v Andrews and Smith* [1990] 3 SCR 870; and *Human Rights Commission (Canada) v Taylor* [1990] 3 SCR 892.

267 K. Mahoney, '*R. v. Keegstra*: A Rationale for Regulating Pornography?' (1992) 37 McGill LJ 242, 242. Mahoney was co-counsel for the Women's Legal Education and Action Fund (LEAF) in its interventions at the SCt in both *Keegstra* and *Butler*. See eg, B. Cossman et al., *Bad Attitude/s on Trial: Pornography, Feminism, and the 'Butler' Decision* ((Toronto UP, 1996), pp. 42-44 for an argument that the legal regulation of pornography and race-hate speech should not be analogised.

268 That is, if it predisposes individuals to act in an anti-social manner.

In seeking to define the term 'degrading and dehumanising', the court drew an analogy with hate propaganda: 'obscenity wields the power to wreak social damage in that a significant portion of the population is humiliated by its gross misrepresentations'.[269] The third, and final, category identified by the court is sexually explicit materials involving children; these are prohibited. In summary, then, *Butler* upholds the obscenity law but provides that sexually explicit material will not constitute an 'undue exploitation of sex' so long as it does not involve violence, degradation or dehumanisation, or children. Under Canadian law, therefore, sexually explicit materials (especially where they are seen as 'artistic') are protected provided they do not fall within the three categories.[270]

Many count *Butler* as a 'feminist breakthrough'. In particular, it is said to represent 'an extraordinary shift in the traditional rationale for obscenity laws'.[271] The *Butler* analysis rejected traditional approaches to obscenity based on moral disapprobation;[272] it focused instead on the likelihood of harm and the threat to equality flowing from pornography:

> [I]f true equality between male and female is to be achieved, we cannot ignore the threat to equality resulting from exposure to audiences of certain types of violent and degrading materials. Materials portraying women as a class worthy of sexual exploitation and abuse have a negative impact on the individual's sense of self-worth and acceptance.[273]

Progress denied

We turn now to the voices that have been raised against the sorts of developments outlined in the previous two sections. In what follows, we have divided these voices in a crude manner, fashioning only two broad groupings: liberal and postmodern. We are aware that labels generally need to be treated with caution. We appreciate, too, that caution is particularly important if one is using the labels 'liberal' and 'postmodern': that this is made risky, for example, by the

---

269 The SCt also said that: '[a]mong other things, degrading and dehumanizing materials place women (and sometimes men) in positions of subordination, servile submission or humiliation. They run against the principles of equality and dignity of all human beings. In appreciation of whether the material is degrading and dehumanizing, the appearance of consent is not necessarily determinative. Consent cannot save materials that otherwise contain degrading and dehumanizing scenes. Sometimes the very appearance of consent makes the depicted acts even more degrading or dehumanizing'.

270 For recent discussion of 'artistic merit' in the context of a child pornography case, see *R v Sharpe* [2001] 1 SCR 45 (criminalising possession of self-created materials, designed for private use, was not justifiable under the Charter). Speaking about Canada, Dany Lacombe notes that 'throughout the vagaries of the obscenity and pornography debates . . . the artistic defence has remained relatively stable' but that 'the politics of art versus obscenity promises to be volatile in the years to come'; in particular, because of both the ongoing calls for censorship and the increasing emphasis on 'aesthetic values as products of struggle, not gradual enlightenment', we may well have to 'reconceive the aesthetic in a way that integrates it into power relations': see D. Lacombe, *Blue Politics: Pornography and the Law in the Age of Feminism* (Toronto UP, 1994), pp. 156, 162.

271 K. Busby, 'LEAF and Pornography: Litigating on Equality and Sexual Representations' (1994) 9 CJLS 165, 176.

272 It emphasised that '. . . this particular objective is no longer defensible in view of the Charter. . . . The prevention of "dirt for dirt's sake" is not a legitimate objective which would justify the violation of [freedom of expression]'.

273 Above n. 265.

proliferation of liberal positions, ongoing phobias about 'postmodernism', and liberalisms' successes in 'reformulating quarrels and conflicts *with* liberals so that they appear to have become debates *within* liberalism'.[274] We persist with these labels, however, because we believe that they can give us a general sense of broad trends in contemporary thought about the place of recognition-based law reform in societies which purport to be both liberal and multicultural. Specifically, as will be seen below, these broad trends remind us of the need to problematise 'sunny formulations' of rights, such as the one endorsed by the former Home Secretary, Jack Straw, when he described the Human Rights Act 1998 as:

> an ethical language we can all recognise and sign up to, a . . . language which doesn't belong to any particular group or creed but to all of us. One that is based on principles of common humanity. . . . Consider the nature of modern British society. It's a society enriched by different cultures and different faiths. It needs a formal shared understanding of what is fundamentally right and fundamentally wrong if it is to work together in unity and confidence. . . . The Human Rights Act provides that formal shared understanding.[275]

Liberal critics

We begin with the liberal critics. These critics generally portray recognition-based laws as instrinsically illiberal. They argue that such laws jeopardise core democratic goods (notably privacy and freedom of expression) and invite the state into the private sphere. Not surprisingly, many liberals have heaped criticism upon both the US anti-pornography ordinances and the Canadian Supreme Court's opinion in *Butler*. These criticisms have, however, been formulated in slightly different ways. So, for example, Ronald Dworkin's defence of almost completely unrestricted speech rights as a form of negative freedom[276] is different to the US Seventh Circuit's preoccupation with the 'marketplace of ideas' in *American Booksellers Association v Hudnut*.[277] In *Hudnut*, in declaring the Indianapolis anti-pornography ordinance to be unconstitutional, Judge Easterbrook insisted that if pornography could be said to imply or advocate the oppression of women, then it was political speech and, thus, deserving of constitutional protection. In effect, therefore, he rendered Catharine MacKinnon's argument a self-refuting one. That is, 'the very features of pornography that recommend it as a target of regulation also

274 A. MacIntyre, *Whose Justice? Which Rationality?* (Duckworth, 1988) (cited in Brown, above n. 248, p. 51).

275 'Building on a Human Rights Culture', address to the Civil Service College Seminar on 9 Dec. 1999 (cited in Parekh Report, above n. 7, pp. 91, 100).

276 See R. Dworkin, 'Is There a Right to Pornography?' (1981) 1 OJLS 177; and, more recently, Dworkin, above n. 12, pp. 365-370 (which seems to place emphasis on the protection of speech as key to deliberative democracy but also insists that '[c]itizen equality cannot demand that citizens be protected by censorship even from those beliefs, convictions or opinions that make it more difficult to gain attention for their views in an otherwise fair political context, or that damage their own opinion of themselves' (p. 366)).

277 Above n. 264. R. Posner, *Sex and Reason* (Harvard UP, 1992) explains and approves of the decision in the following terms: 'It is true that [pornographic] works . . . often express an ideology of patriarchy and misogyny . . . , but that is no ground for suppression. Rather the contrary, since ideological representations are at the center of the expression that the First Amendment protects' (pp. 381-382).

require its classification as not just expression, but as politically charged expression'.[278]

Despite these differences, it is fair to say that liberal responses to anti-pornography laws generally tend to emphasise that:

> without any proof of the contribution of pornography to overt acts of violence, and without any overt violence or coercion in its production [pornography is] either an instance of expression or a form of sexual practice and hence within the sphere of individuals' privacy.[279]

This sort of position has also been adopted by individuals and groups who describe themselves as feminist.[280] Indeed, as pointed out above, one of the groups spearheading the challenge to the Indianapolis ordinance was feminist – namely, the Feminist Anticensorship Task Force which submitted an amicus brief to the *Hudnut* court.[281] But, the label 'feminists against censorship' is used also to describe a further position in the pornography debates: one which is dissatisfied with both the liberal position and the anti-pornography ordinance/ *Butler* position, and which focuses on cultural representations that eroticise subordination rather than 'pornography' per se.[282] This latter group of 'feminists against censorship' is probably 'best described as indifferent to law' – 'largely because the law seems either irrelevant or too predetermined in its construction of the issues or such a tiny part of the system of the cultural production of meaning'.[283] Yet, as Beverley Brown has pointed out, that indifference to law has allowed (versions of) liberalism to co-opt this feminism as a liberal position. In effect, these liberalisms by adopting '[l]aw, for or against, [as] the sole index of feminisms', see to it that feminists who do not support legislative intervention are 'designated "liberals", their stance incorporated on the basis that their primary commitment must be to the general human values of freedom of the arts or political expression'.[284]

In short, then, 'seeing *speech* through an equality lens'[285] tends to be a bugbear for liberals. As Wojciech Sadurski shows, liberals generally have little time for attempts to show that pornography and hate speech constitute discrimination; moreover, they appear to have even less time for the argument that 'hate-speech bans are affirmative action laws attacking an invidious message'.[286] Liberals,

---

278 F. Michelman, 'Conceptions of Democracy in American Constitutional Argument: The Case of Pornography Regulation' (1989) 56 Tenn LR 291, 301.

279 N. Lacey, 'Theory into Practice? Pornography and the Public/Private Dichotomy' (1993) 20 JLS 93, 104 (reprinted in N. Lacey, *Unspeakable Subjects* (Hart, 1998), pp. 71-97).

280 See eg, A. Assister and A. Carol (eds.), *Bad Girls and Dirty Pictures* (Pluto, 1993); and N. Strossen, *Defending Pornography: Free Speech, Sex, and the Fight for Women's Equality* (Abacus, 1995).

281 For details, see N.D. Hunter and S.A. Law, 'Brief *Amici Curiae* of Feminist Anticensorship Task Force et al., in *American Booksellers Association v. Hudnut*' in F.E. Olsen (ed.), *Feminist Legal Theory* (Dartmouth, 1995).

282 See eg, R. Coward, *Female Desires* (Grove Press, 1985); and S. Kappeler, *Pornography and Representation* (Polity, 1986).

283 Brown, above n. 249, p. 49.

284 Ibid., p. 50. Brown goes on to say: 'In other words, a position whose stance on law might best be characterized as indifference, and whose concerns are with the nature of texts, codings of sexuality, and construction of subject positions is provided with a quite alien foundational perspective and set of concerns.'

285 We take this phrase from W. Sadurski, 'On "Seeing Speech Through an Equality Lens": A Critique of Egalitarian Arguments for Suppression of Hate Speech and Pornography' (1996) 16 OJLS 713 (emphasis added); he, in turn, takes it from C.A. MacKinnon, *Only Words* (Harvard UP, 1993), p. 85.

286 Ibid., p. 714.

however, generally do tend to see laws prohibiting discrimination in employment or education as 'indisputable, unobjectionable and eminently justified'.[287] Thus, the second example of recognition-based law reform looked at earlier – namely, sex harassment law – has taken less of a pounding from liberal critics than anti-pornography laws and is significantly less embattled.[288] That said, harassment law has provoked considerable criticism in the US, in particular on the basis that it represents an unconstitutional infringement of the First Amendment's free speech guarantee. In addition, following a recent court-led expansion in vicarious liability, US commentators have begun to worry about the rise of the 'rational employer': that is, the employer who chooses to over-regulate in an attempt at self-protection – one, for example, who installs 'workplace tsars' to police employees' language and interactions.[289]

It is possible that a similar trend for pitting harassment law against freedom of expression could establish itself in the UK. In a recent essay, Bob Hepple describes freedom of expression as 'the dog that did not bark in the development of UK law on harassment' and goes on to point out that:

> this silent dog may soon bite in the United Kingdom as the incorporation by the Human Rights Act 1998 of Article 10 on the European Convention of Human Rights (ECHR) into domestic law forces government and the courts into an explicit reconciliation of the developing law against harassment with freedom of expression.[290]

The EU's declared ambition to broaden understandings of harassment as discrimination, if combined with a more aggressive approach towards vicarious liability and further recognition of the importance of the subjective perception of the harassee,[291] could also put harassment law in liberals' firing line. It is surely noteworthy, for example, that the EU's attempt (later abandoned) to include a reference to 'disturbing environment' in the Race Directive prompted a warning that overbroad harassment laws may endanger freedom of speech.[292]

Postmodern critics

Questions of 'excess' also preoccupy postmodern critics of the turn towards recognition. In fact, the excesses of state regulation, in particular state regulation via law, is a central theme. Thus, Rick Abel and Allan Hutchinson both seek to remind us of the limitations of legal rules and legal systems. The argument is not that the limitations of law are exclusive to laws regulating expression but, as Abel says, that they are particularly pronounced in such laws:

> Law is the construction of boundaries which are always over- and under-inclusive. But when the state regulates speech, every categorisation is a hard case, not just

287 Ibid., p. 713.
288 But see the US SCt opinion in *RAV v City of St Paul* 505 US 377 (1992) wherein all of the justices purport to protect freedom of expression by striking down a hate-speech law, but where the minority concurrence accuses the majority of adopting a position that endangers anti-discrimination law.
289 Cohen, above n. 230, pp. 450-452.
290 B.A. Hepple, 'Freedom of Expression and the Problem of Harassment' in Beatson and Cripps (eds.), above n. 47, pp. 177-196 at p. 177.
291 See eg, *Reed v Stedman* [1999] IRLR 299 (EAT); and *Driskel v Peninsula Business Services* [2000] IRLR 151 (EAT).
292 Hepple et al., above n. 80, p. 41.

those at the edge. Bans against pornography, hate speech, or blasphemy are forced to admit exceptions for politics, art, literature and scholarship that are capable of engulfing the rule. . . . Context, history, identity, audience, relationship, and motive can invert the moral quality of speech. But law decontextualises, aspires to universalism, and finds motive hopelessly elusive.[293]

Hutchinson bolsters this by alerting us to the uses to which Canadian obscenity law has been put post-*Butler*, in particular the fact that there have been criminal prosecutions involving gay and lesbian publications which depicted not violence or exploitative sex, but consensual sex between people of the same gender.[294] In this way, then, we see how an apparently well-intentioned intensification of juridical control – which was packaged as being about 'seeing speech through an *equality lens*' – can be used against groups who are already the subject of extensive discrimination. The point, as Hutchinson says, is not that either *Butler* or similar anti-pornography stances bring about these prosecutions involving gay and lesbian publications: as he says, seizures and prosecutions of this sort 'have been going on for years'. Rather, the point is that *Butler* 'did tend to validate such practices', which serves as a reminder that:

> [a]ny legal victory can be quickly neutralized by bureaucratic inertia, political intransigence, judicial complacency and rank prejudice. The potential multiplicity of interpretations is reduced to one actual interpretation by official or powerful agents when they fix a law or a ruling's meaning for citizens.[295]

It is sometimes assumed that postmodern critics of the turn towards recognition-based law reform are dismissive of the hatefulness and hurtfulness of hate speech and harassment, or that they fail to see such matters as political. This, however, is a mistaken assumption. As Wendy Brown explains, it is *precisely* because these critics see hate speech and harassment as having these qualities that they urge us to review the turn towards law and to resist further calls for state regulation.[296] The core of the postmodern argument, therefore, is that we need to consider how 'the grammar of recognition itself [has come] to be imposed as the vocabulary in which redress for injuries on the terrain of identity and difference must be pursued',[297] and also whether recognition's dominance creates a politics in which desire for freedom dissolves into moralising and a self-righteous, but fundamentally debilitating, rage.[298] In effect, the argument is that it can be self-defeating:

---

293 Abel, *Speech and Respect*, above n. 61, p. 93. See also, eg E. Jackson, 'The Problem with Pornography: A Critical Survey of the Current Debate' (1995) 3 FLS 49, 69-70 (arguing that '[a] preoccupation with law reform has led to factionalising and a tendency to over-simplify the exceptionally complex relationship between sexual representation and sexual experience. . . . We should be talking about sex and its representation, but to force ourselves to do so in the language of a legal textbook impoverishes the debate').

294 *Little Sisters Book and Art Emporium v Minister for Justice* [2000] 2 SCR 1120.

295 Hutchinson, above n. 17, p. 132. Judicial support for this view emerges from *Little Sisters*, ibid., para. 75: 'while memorandum D9-1-1 requires classifying officers to read books from cover to cover, some officers simply thumb through them or read pages at random. Many officers review videotapes with the assistance of a fast-forward device, stopping only to examine scenes of explicit sex: they do not listen to the soundtrack.'

296 Brown, above n. 216, p. 27.

297 P. Markell, 'The Recognition of Politics: A Comment on Emcke and Tully' (2000) 7 Constellations 496, 504.

298 Brown, above n. 216, p. 27 describes this rage using a Nietzchean concept, '*ressentiment*'.

when the injury that is constitutive of a particular group is thought of primarily in terms of injury to self-esteem rather than in terms of material and structural injustice. Those who organize against symbolic and emotional injury tend to ask not for an equalization of material resources but for symbolic goods to ease the injury, such as hate speech laws or antipornography ordinances. The quest for these symbolic goods, however well intentioned, often ends up endowing the authorities with new legitimation, thus robbing identity politics of its revolutionary potential.[299]

In essence, then, the argument is that we should reflect critically on the 'political *meaning* and *implications* of the turn toward law for resolution of anti-democratic injury'.[300] The US feminist scholar, Judith Butler, is another leading proponent of this sort of postmodern view on recognition-based law reform.[301] Her book, *Excitable Speech*, draws on Marxist concerns about the power of the state and on a Derridean poststructuralist analysis of language, to dispute accounts – such as that provided by Catharine MacKinnon – of pornography and hate speech as illocutionary – that is, as speech-acts which enact what they say in the moment of saying.[302] Butler argues that it is a mistake to close the gap between speech and its effects: we would do better to focus on the 'excitability' of discourse – in other words, on the fact that speech, no matter how hateful, is always out of control or indeterminate and, hence, open to processes of unauthorised reinterpretation. In essence, then, Butler wants us to think more creatively about engendering freedom and equality; that is, to think about recognition outside the realm of courts and legislatures.

There are traces of Judith Butler's and Wendy Brown's arguments in postmodern commentaries on the Canadian Supreme Court's opinion in *Butler* and on trends in sexual harassment law. Thus, the idea of 'progress denied' is central to many postmodern commentaries on *Butler*. For example, *pace* MacKinnon's insistence that *Butler* is about 'politics and power, not morals and manners',[303] the Canadian authors of *Bad Attitude/s* argue that it is moralism in more modern guise. They say that there is 'another story to be told' about *Butler*:

> When we scratch beneath the surface, we find a conservative sexual morality that sees sex as bad, physical, shameful, dangerous, based, guilty until proved innocent, and redeemable only if it transcends its base nature. ... The test for obscenity as reviewed and synthesized by ... *Butler* simply provides a new discourse for what is in fact a very old objective – the legal regulation of sexual morality, and the legal repression of sexual representation. The *Butler* decision and its discourse of harm against women is really just sexual morality in drag.[304]

In support of this position, they point to the post-*Butler* prosecutions involving gay and lesbian publications and, specifically, to the problems thrown up by

---

299 M. Valverde, 'Identity Politics and the Law in the US' (1999) 25 Fem Studies 345, 347.
300 Ibid., p. 28.
301 J. Butler, *Excitable Speech: A Politics of the Performative* (Routledge, 1997).
302 An example of an illocutionary speech-act would be a sign saying 'No travellers allowed'. Illocutionary speech-acts are to distinguished from perlocutionary speech; in the latter, *effects follow from the act of speech*. Examples of texts which argue for pornography and hate speech as illocutionary are C.A. MacKinnon, *Only Words* (Harvard UP, 1993); M. Matsuda, C. Lawrence et al., *Words that Wound: Critical Race Theory, Assaultive Speech, and the First Amendment* (Westview, 1993); and M. Matsuda, *Where Is Your Body? And Other Essays on Race, Gender, and the Law* (Beacon Press, 1996).
303 Hutchinson, above n. 17, p. 131.
304 Cossman et al., above n. 267, p. 107-108.

the reference made in *Butler's* three-fold classification to representations which are 'degrading and dehumanising'.[305] This reference, it is argued, provides a focus for moral crusade by social conservatives.[306] In effect, the argument parallels what Wendy Brown has said about the response of US social conservatives to MacKinnon's anti-pornography law proposals. That is, that for such individuals and groups regulation of pornography, even if not on the basis of offensiveness, provides welcome respite from liberal scorn and offers 'the pleasure of moralizing against the illicit, and the comforts of conservatism – gender is eternal and sexual pleasure is opprobrious – in an era of despair about substantive political transformation'.[307] The end result, it is argued, is that the '"new" public discourse which constructs pornography as an expression and an ideology of sexual violence . . . becomes the constraining norm of the pornography debate'.[308]

A similar argument has surfaced recently in some legal feminist circles in the US in relation to shifting characterisations of the harm of sexual harassment and, hence, of the purpose of sexual harassment law. The principal concern is that, following '[r]ecent front-page publicity given to allegations of sexual misconduct by public figures [which] invites the assumption . . . that the issue is general offensiveness, or transgression of rather traditional norms of civility regarding women',[309] sexual harassment is increasingly being seen not as example of an equality violation but as 'an outrage to the woman's honor, an offence to her sensibilities, and a violation of her purity'.[310] In effect, the shift is to sexual harassment law – and, specifically, the judges who enforce it – as innocent women's 'knights in shining armour' against predatory men. This, then, gives social conservatives a further focus for moral crusade. As Jean Cohen points out:

> [it] plays into the hands of . . . conservatives whose interests are not gender equality, but the reinscription of traditional gender norms at work and at home. It gives them a powerful tool to attack non-conforming men and women while appearing to be on the side of the victim.[311]

305 They provide a list of examples of post-Butler censorship at pp. 4-7. Cossman et al. also emphasise that *Butler* and, more especially, Catharine MacKinnon's general approach to anti-pornography law, promotes a discourse of victimisation which compromises agency. Thus, they ask: might it not be possible for pornography to both constrain and emancipate, and to do so, in particular, in relation to lesbian and gay sexualities which have long been proscribed by law? Cf. D. Herman, 'Law and Morality Re-Visited: The Politics of Regulating Sado-Masochistic Porn/Practice' (1996) 15 Studies in Law, Politics and Society 147; and *Little Sisters*, above n. 294, paras. 63-64 (gay and lesbian culture does not constitute a general exemption from the *Butler* test).

306 See also Carol Harlow and Richard Rawlings, *Pressure Through Law* (Routledge, 1992), p. 218 arguing that the 1970s blasphemy case, *Whitehouse v Lemon* [1979] AC 617, HL, involving a poem published in a gay newspaper prosecution 'did more for its [moral conservative] supporters than merely to relegate "filth" to the underground . . . it provided a valuable focus for a moral crusade'.

307 Brown, above n. 216, p. 91.

308 Cossman et al., above n. 267, p. 3.

309 Cohen, above n. 230, pp. 446-447. The two most prominent public figures against whom such allegations were levelled were Bill Clinton and Supreme Court Justice Clarence Thomas (during his Senate nomination hearings): see N. Fraser, *Justice Interruptus: Critical Reflections on the 'Postsocialist' Condition* (Routledge, 1997), pp. 99-120 and T. Morrison (ed.), *Race-ing Justice, En-Gendering Race: Essays on Anita Hill, Clarence Thomas and the Construction of Social Reality* (Pantheon, 1992).

310 Cohen, above n. 224, pp. 143-144.

311 Ibid.

CONCLUSION: TOWARDS CRITICAL PRAGMATISM AND IMAGINATION

We turn now to the question of how civil liberties law in the Human Rights Act era can best respond to the complex trends, and opposing reactions thereto, described throughout Part III. In so doing, it is tempting to assume that the new human rights culture in the UK (and associated developments such as the inquiry into national identity, and the emphasis on combating institutional racism) will inevitably energise civil liberties thinking on equality. And, more generally, that it also seems to promise a vivacious politics – one characterised by the involvement of a wider range of individuals and groups claiming a plurality of positions. The temptation to fashion such an upbeat conclusion needs, however, to be resisted. We suggest three reasons why this is the case.

The first reason is that, if the liberal and postmodern responses which were outlined above come to dominate the debate on recognition-based law reform, we may end up travelling in full circles.[312] That is to say, although these responses may appear fundamentally different, they are almost as one on the issue of the turn to law:

> [B]oth construe juridification . . . as standing in a zero-sum relationship with personal freedom. To both, where state sovereignty stops, individual liberty begins. . . . Thus, [the postmodern] analysis, like that of the liberals, suffers from the mirror weakness of MacKinnon's: if the latter forgets the repressive and non-neutral aspects of legal regulation, the former ignores the facts of social power which may render counter-speech and efforts to performatively reconfigure harassing [and hate] speech ineffective and dangerous.[313]

The second reason is that, when we add to this 'mix' the calls *for* recognition-based laws, the end-product can be a stand-off. In other words, a set of opposed positions, with each position offering a remedy for what *it* sees as the relevant 'harm'.[314]

The third, and final, reason for downplaying enthusiasm is perhaps the most crucial – at least in the short term. It may be that, in thinking about 'the state we're in' following the coming into force of the Human Rights Act, it is misleading to emphasise problems such as 'stand-off' or moving 'full circle'. The reason for this is that, for all the talk about new voices offering new perspectives on old debates (on topics such as freedom and equality) and on newer ones (such as accommodating liberalism and multiculturalism against a backdrop of conservative nationalism), liberal discourses are singularly ascendant in discussions of human rights law and practice. This ascendancy, we would argue, hints at two potential problems. First, it may mean that liberalism (whatever the version thereof, such as the 'new' liberalism of Third-Way governing, or a rainbow version which emphasises the shared values of variants of liberalism), will get 'to define the conditions of political intelligibility – and render . . . opponents unintelligible'.[315] In other words, it may mean that liberalism(s) will colonise debate and discussion to such an extent that issues will be seen only *within* a liberal frame. This would distort challenges to liberalism

---

312 We take this idea from Cohen, above n. 230.
313 Ibid.
314 Cohen, above n. 230, p. 445.
315 See Brown, above n. 249, p. 51 (developing this argument in relation to pre-HRA pornography debates in the UK).

and the tenets of liberalism itself would also be left largely unquestioned. Second, it suggests the installation of 'a human rights law and practice which is strangely unreflective and generally lacking in "critical bite"'.[316] This is worrying, as Colin Harvey points out, because now that human rights has moved to the mainstream – at both national and international levels – human-rights thinking needs to be even more vigilant about eschewing 'inappropriate versions of legal positivism':

> [I]t is time for scholars to engage in some critical reflection about the process that brought . . . about [this mainstreaming] and what the future holds. In practice this is linked with the question of how the human rights movement can retain a critical edge in a world where human rights is becoming a bureaucratized and totally administered system. . . . [T]he danger is that any critical edge . . . might be lost in a bureaucratized system of monitoring and enforcement that does not deliver on its own promises.[317]

It is these three problems which lead us, then, to our final section. That section will flesh out the argument made in the Introduction to the chapter, where it was suggested that critical pragmatism and imagination ought to be two essential virtues of civil liberties law in the Human Rights Act era. As will become obvious, we believe that these virtues point very clearly to the need for a 'renovation of intellectual habits'[318] within civil liberties law.

Introducing critical pragmatism and imagination

Earlier in the chapter, we described critical pragmatism as an attitude or approach to rights which sees rights as both enabling *and* constraining, and which refuses to participate in the idea of rights-seeking – whether by individuals, groups or national or transnational communities – as a 'treasure hunt'. We also introduced imagination as a key complement to critical pragmatism. In this section, we highlight several issues around freedom of expression and equality, and more generally around liberalism and multiculturalism, which become more transparent when one adopts an approach that is both critically-pragmatic and imaginative.

The first issue we want to address concerns the debate around whether recognition-based law and law reform attempts essentialise identities or (as many liberals prefer to put it) promote a 'groupiness' which undermines individual autonomy. In relation to this debate, critical pragmatism and imagination can assist us in seeing the pros and cons of both practical politics, or activism, and theoretical work on recognition. They can also assist us in seeing that activism and theory do *not* have to speak as one.

Versions of practical politics where 'people wave their race or gender or sexual orientation as if that gave them moral authority and instant knowledge' have been appositely described by one commentator as 'identity all right, but [not] politics'.[319] This form of activism provides easy targets for critics of the drive towards equality through difference. It also tends to submerge differences within groups seeking recognition such that any resulting law reform may

---

316 Harvey, above n. 195, p. 389.
317 Ibid., pp. 389-390.
318 M. Valverde, 'The Law of Breasts and the Risk of Harm' (1999) 8 SLS 181.
319 Valverde, above n. 299, p. 359.

differentially affect group members and thereby foment new inequalities. More fundamentally, it can lead to shallow versions of recognition: it is, in the end, about a form of 'cultural affirmation [that involves] waving one's injury as an identity and making others feel guilty'.[320] In other words, it centres a rights culture wherein rights, and recognition more generally, are principally for 'minorities'. 'The majority', by contrast, is consigned to a dangerous state of liberal shame about both its previous discrimination against 'minorities' and its sense of identity. Furthermore, both 'minorities' and 'the majority' are seen en masse – that is, as without differentiation: the latter because they are alleged to have created and perpetuated the injustice, and the former because successful recognition claims can label group members in one particular way and thereby suppress other aspects of identity. The lessons of this flawed form of recognition, therefore, are that rights activism in the Human Rights Act era needs to place more emphasis on the specificity of identities, and also on the ways in which particular proposals for recognition-based law reform can generate further inequalities as well as greater equality.

It is not just practical politics that needs to reorient itself for the Human Rights Act era. Some theoretical work on identity evinces a converse flaw to that of practical politics and, thereby, misunderstands or downplays the value of 'solidarity-producing politics'[321] and community affirmation to those who have been discriminated against or otherwise excluded or disrespected.[322] We are thinking here not just of liberalism but also, and more especially, of theory which plays up the idea that contemporary life is characterised by a freedom to refashion identity, and which tends also to argue that this freedom is compromised by the turn towards law for recognition.[323] What this work often fails to recognise is that:

> [b]y engaging in disclosing an injustice and displaying an alternative, bringing it about that other members of the society acknowledge this and respond, even if negatively, responding in turn, and gaining less than one hoped for, members of an oppressed minority generate levels of self-empowerment, self-worth, and pride that can overcome the debilitating psychological and sociological effects of misrecognition.[324]

This theoretical work also tends to discount the embedded nature of identity, that is, the way in which membership of groups positions individuals. In talking about groups *positioning* individuals, the argument is not that group membership constitutes an individual's identity, or that groups are prior to individuals – although liberal criticism, which alleges that recognition-based law promotes 'a "groupiness" that is at odds with individualism',[325] often mistakenly makes this assumption. Rather, the argument is that 'a person's identity is her own, [but is]

---

320 Ibid.
321 Young, above n. 199, p. 103.
322 See eg, Valverde, above n. 299, arguing that 'the critique of identity on purely philosophical grounds tends to ignore that oppressed groups do need cultural affirmation, not only as a psychological support but also as a crucial intellectual resource drawing on and affirming the practical community-based efforts that are the lifeblood of critical theory'.
323 We refer here primarily to postmodern scholarship. See similarly, McNay, above n. 15, problematising writing which over-emphasises the opportunities opened up by shifts in social relations, in particular around sexuality and changing roles for women and men.
324 J. Tully, 'Struggles over Recognition and Redistribution' (2000) 7 Constellations 469, 479.
325 Phillips, above n. 70, p. 35.

formed in active relation to social positions, among other things . . .'.[326] It is this argument that the Parekh Report, for example, seem to be driving at when it stresses the need to think of the UK as both 'a community of citizens and a community of communities'.[327] In similar vein, Stuart Hall reminds us that 'identity is not fixed, but it's not nothing either'.[328]

If civil liberties law is to facilitate, rather than obstruct, the development of the UK as both 'a community of citizens and a community of communities', it will need a deeper appreciation of the relationship between individuals and groups, and between groups themselves. Such an understanding is absent not just from civil liberties law but also more generally. Its absence is the reason why the Parekh Report calls for a synergy between liberalism and multiculturalism. In thinking about this synergy, civil liberties law must not see multiculturalism as a concession. Indeed, bringing multiculturalism into relationship with liberalism could be a key vehicle for re-centring equality at a time when New Labour's 'new' liberalism, with its preferred focus on social inclusion, threatens to eliminate equality from the spectrum of democratic objectives. Equality, as Ronald Dworkin has written in relation to this new liberalism or Third Way of governing, 'is the endangered species of political ideals'.[329]

In thinking about the synergy between multiculturalism and liberalism, civil liberties law must also not assume that the former is about cultural equality alone. In its relation to liberalism, multiculturalism must be seen as operating in the same way as the concept of recognition has operated throughout this chapter: that is, it signifies group-conscious claims and laws which are about equality through difference and other values, such as political inclusion. In other words, multiculturalism is not about addressing discrimination against, or disrespect for, cultural difference in isolation from other forms of inequality. Moreover, even where multiculturalism is about apparently simple claims for cultural recognition – for example, language rights or rights to wear religious dress at places of work or in public – such claims are 'usually tied to questions of control over resources, exclusion from benefits of political influence or economic participation, strategic power, or segregation from opportunities':

> [Thus,] even claims for cultural recognition are rarely asserted for their own sake. They are part of demands for political inclusion and equal economic opportunity, where the claimants deny that such equality should entail shedding or privatizing their cultural difference.[330]

But, to what else do critical pragmatism and imagination point? It seems to us that they point to a number of ways in which we might negotiate the endless struggles over 'striking a balance' between freedom of expression and equality. Later we shall address the issue of the struggles themselves, in particular the value of placing these struggles, rather than perfect forms of recognition-based law, at the centre of debate. Here we explain the value of imagination in altering the current equation of freedom of expression *versus* equality. The explanation is based in Jean Cohen's proposal for an oxymoronic approach to legal

---

326 Young, above n. 199, p. 99.
327 Above n. 7, p. xv.
328 S. Hall, 'Interview on Culture and Power' (1997) 86 Radical Philosophy 24, 33.
329 Above n. 12, p. 1.
330 Young, above n. 199, pp. 105, 106.

regulation of issues such as sexual harassment.[331] Cohen argues that we should design and interpret such laws as examples of 'reflexive law'. 'Reflexive law' is a form of law which:

> aims to foster 'self-regulation' within social institutions. . . . [I]t aims to create 'regulated' autonomy, generating new 'subject positions' by institutionalizing procedures in which bargaining power, voice, and standing of the interacting parties is equalized. . . . [R]eflexive law does not dictate outcomes. [T]he state regulates on this paradigm, but indirectly. The idea is to provide legal incentives for self-regulation that will lead social actors to comply with general legislative goals, norms, and constitutional principles. . . . *[It] entails the regulation of self-regulation.*[332]

In effect, then, reflexive law makes it possible to think in terms of 'regulated autonomy' – a concept which, as Cohen points out, is an oxymoron for most ways of thinking about legal regulation and freedom.[333] By centring this paradigm of law, civil liberties law might be able to think a lot less in terms of a choice between legal regulation and freedom, and rather more in terms of how legal regulation could establish 'subject positions' that facilitate agency.[334]

Critical pragmatism and imagination also point to the value of adopting a less structuralist perspective in theoretical work. This proposal has been put forward by the Canadian academic, Mariana Valverde, in relation to understanding Canadian obscenity law in the post-*Butler* era. Valverde recommends that it is best to steer away from the question of whether moralism creeps beneath the surface of this law. The focus, she says, should instead be on asking 'a new set of questions'. These questions would centre the emphasis on 'risk of harm' in post-*Butler* obscenity law, moving out therefrom to other contemporary judicial uses of that concept. Thus, Valverde suggests that we should ask:

> What does the term 'risk' do exactly? What is its pragmatic meaning? How does it govern representations? How does it govern the work of the lower courts? Does risk of harm in obscenity law function in the same way as it does in epidemiology, or in insurance? Does the application of the test by various courts follow a consistent 'actuarial' logic?[335]

Valverde applies her method to recent Canadian obscenity case law, following which she concludes that '"risk of harm" is acting as a veritable joker card'; that is, it is a 'capacious' concept which serves different purposes depending on the context. However – and this is the crucial point – its capaciousness is different to the ambiguity of the old notion of obscenity as an offence to general morality. Specifically, 'risk of harm', although it purports to provide a definitive standard, cannot but open up debate and invite challenge; moreover, this occurs not just because judges cannot control enforcement by customs officers, police and prosecutors but also because:

---

331 Cohen, above n. 230.
332 Ibid., p. 461 (emphasis added). Cohen cites Gunther Teubner and Niklas Luhmann as proponents of reflexive law (see, respectively, 'After Legal Instrumentalism?: Strategic Models of Post-Regulatory Law' in G. Teubner (ed.), *Dilemmas of Law in the Welfare State* (De Gruyter, 1986); and *The Differentiation of Society* (Columbia UP, 1982), pp. 90-121, 324-362). Note, also, that although the term 'reflexive law' is not used, the idea of 'regulation of self-regulation' is also commended by Hepple et al., above n. 80, in its review of UK anti-discrimination legislation.
333 Ibid., p. 444.
334 Ibid., p. 456.
335 Above n. 319, p. 183.

the language of risk and harm is one that many different groups can use and have used authoritatively . . . It is therefore likely that once the language of harm and risk is installed at the heart of the morals offences of the [criminal law], it will be difficult to keep the doors closed against both the experts of risk calculations and the victims who claim to be the main authorities on harm. Making judgements about harm and about risks is not the sort of activity that can be easily monopolized by [courts or legislatures].[336]

In effect, then, Valverde concentrates our attention on the ways in which the post-*Butler* 'risk of harm' test, like rights discourse, provides a site for continuous challenges despite judicial efforts to define its meaning. This, we would suggest, is a more productive understanding of *Butler* and its progeny than stances of euphoria, scepticism or disgust. It reminds us for example that, in a rights culture, there are continual 'opportunity moments', rather than one-off chances.

Valverde's argument about the unconstrainable nature of the 'risk of harm' test might also be used to prompt reflection within civil liberties law on a recent trend in constitutional thought. The trend concerns how to think about and practise democracy in a way that facilitates fair participation by all in an ongoing negotiation and contestation of values, goods and principles. It is commonly referred to as a deliberative, communicative or discussion-based version of democracy, and it has a central relevance for civil liberties law in the Human Rights Act era in relation to both struggles for recognition and, more generally, the conceptualisation of rights.

The way in which it is relevant to recognition has been explained by James Tully. Recognition, Tully says, 'should not be seen as a telos or end state'.[337] In other words, the focus should not be on designing the ultimate form of recognition. Instead, it should be on 'the struggles [for specific forms of recognition] themselves as the primary thing'.[338] Tully's aim is to re-orient us away from the search for definitive theories of justice, or 'end-state' laws, towards what he describes as 'practices of freedom'. Under his proposal:

> [t]he aim of . . . philosophy and corresponding democratic political practice would not be to discover and constitutionalize the just and definitive form of recognition and distribution, but to ensure that ineliminable, agonic democratic games over recognition and distribution, with their rival theories of distribution and recognition, can be played freely, with a minimum of domination.[339]

The proposal is attractive because it reminds us that claims for recognition should not be reduced to a treasure hunt. Struggles for recognition have an independent value: they can, for example, defuse tensions in a non-violent way, provide a positive sense of self for oppressed groups, and produce appropriately-contested understandings of harm. Tully's proposal is also attractive, however, because it foregrounds participation in struggles for recognition as 'practices [which] are, among other things, *processes of citizenization in culturally diverse societies*'.[340] In essence, the argument is that, through the processes of ongoing negotiation and contestation over recognition:

---

336 Ibid., pp. 194-195.
337 Above n. 324, p. 477.
338 Ibid., p. 469.
339 Ibid.
340 Ibid., p. 480 (emphasis added).

[we] become aware of membership in a democratic society which provides the institutions for free play of this democratic activity [of recognition] over time. This form of self-awareness and self-formation that comes into being in the course of the struggles *is* identity as citizens of a free and culturally diverse democracy.[341]

Civil liberties law could benefit considerably from reflection on this aspect of Tully's proposal. In particular, it might ease the tension between national inclusion, or a 'politics of belonging', and currently dominant representations of human rights which tend towards accounts of rights as a toolkit for 'minorities' or 'unpopular causes'. Seeing rights in this way is not without merit. As Colin Harvey has pointed out, it can be exploited by those denied a voice in other forums (for example, refugees and asylum seekers) and it gives judges 'a suitably noble (minority rights protection) justification for their own political activism'.[342] But to see rights in this way alone would be to waste the opportunity moment presented by the new human rights culture. That culture must not be about judges versus representative institutions, or about 'the majority' versus assorted 'minorities', or about rights as a toolkit for individual and group claims.[343] Rather, it should be seen as an opportunity to create institutions – legislatures and courts, and other institutions too – to which individuals and groups feel a sense of belonging. Furthermore, if that opportunity is to be seized, civil liberties law must broach the gulf between its preferred debates (about how the 'constitutional reforms' of a Bill of Rights and devolution will 'modernise' the UK, and whether shifting power to judges is democratic or undemocratic) and other debates. That is, it must listen to the vibrant complexity of discussions in contemporary critical theory about inclusion, exclusion and fair processes for generating 'ongoing provisional agreements open to disagreement, review of the implementation, revision, and struggles all over again . . . '.[344]

---

341 Ibid.

342 Harvey, above n. 195, p. 383. Relatedly, some of the senior judiciary have firmly indicated that they are not interested in the broader notion of the HRA as creating a new dialogue between courts, legislatures and executives: see the comments of Lords Bingham, Woolf and Phillips to the Joint Committee on Human Rights, 26 March 2001, Question 78. Lord Bingham stated: 'I would not myself think in terms of dialogue at all. The business of the judges is to listen to cases and give judgment. . . . I do not myself see it as the role of the judges to engage in dialogue.'

343 Markell, above n. 297, p. 504 asks: '[d]oes the relationship between citizens and the state come to be figured as a relationship of *recognition* – a relatively passive relationship, after all, in which we hope to see our identities mirrored in our political institutions – precisely in response to the felt difficulty of locating spaces for meaningful democratic *action* and *participation* in contemporary public spheres?'

344 Tully, above n. 324, p. 478.

Select bibliography

Abel, R, *Speech and Respect* (Sweet & Maxwell, 1996).

Akdeniz, Y et al, *The Internet, Law and Society* (Longman Pearson, 2000).

Allen, MJ and S Cooper 'Howard's Way – A Farewell to Freedom?' (1995) 58 MLR 364.

Alston, P (ed), *The EU and Human Rights* (OUP, 1999).

Anderson, B, *Imagined Communities* (Verso, 1991).

Anderson, G (ed), *Rights and Democracy: Essays in UK-Canadian Constitutionalism* (Blackstone, 1999).

Ashworth, A, 'Article 6 and the Fairness of Trials' [1999] Crim LR 261.

Assister, A and A Carol (eds), *Bad Girls and Dirty Pictures* (Pluto, 1993).

Bailey, SH, DJ Harris and BL Jones, *Civil Liberties: Cases and Materials* (Butterworths, 1995).

Bakan, J, *Just Words: Constitutional Rights and Social Wrongs* (Toronto UP, 1997).

Bamforth, N, 'The Application of the Human Rights Act 1998 to Public Authorities and Private Bodies' (1999) 58 CLJ 159.

Barendt, E et al, *Libel and the Media: The Chilling Effect* (Clarendon, 1997).

Barnett, A, *This Time: Our Constitutional Revolution* (Vintage, 1997).

Beatson, J and Y Cripps (eds), *Freedom of Expression and Freedom of Information: Essays in Honour of Sir David Williams* (OUP, 2000).

Beck, U, 'The Cosmopolitan Perspective: Sociology of the Second Age of Modernity' (2000) 51 BJ Soc 79.

Bell, C, *Peace Agreements and Human Rights* (OUP, 2000).

Benyon, J (ed), *Scarman and After: Essays Reflecting on Lord Scarman's Report, the Riots and their Aftermath* (Pergamon, 1984).

Bingham MR, T, 'The European Convention on Human Rights: Time to Incorporate' (1993) 109 LQR 390.

Birkinshaw, P, 'An "All Singin' and All Dancin'" Affair: The New Labour Government's Proposals for Freedom of Information' [1998] PL 176.

Birkinshaw, P, *Freedom of Information: The Law, the Practice and the Ideal* (Butterworths, 1996).

Birkinshaw, P, 'Government and the End of its Tether: Matrix Churchill and the Scott Report' (1996) 23 JLS 406.

Blackburn, R and R Plant (eds), *Constitutional Reform: The Labour Government's Constitutional Reform Agenda* (Longman, 1999).

Bogart, WA, *Courts and Country* (OUP, 1994).

Bowling, B, *Violent Racism: Victimisation, Policing and Social Context* (Clarendon, 1998).

Boyd, S (ed), *Challenging the Public/Private Divide: Feminism, Law and Public Policy* (Toronto UP, 1997).

Boyle, J, *Shamans, Software and Spleens: Law and the Construction of the Information Society* (Harvard UP, 1996).

Boyle, K, T Hadden and P Hillyard, *Law and State: The Case of Northern Ireland* (Martin Robertson, 1975).

Braithwaite, J, 'The New Regulatory State and the Transformation of Criminology' (2000) 40 BJ Crim 222.

Brest, P and A Vandenberg, 'Politics, Feminism and the Constitution: The Anti-Pornography Movement in Minneapolis' (1987) 39 Stanford LR 607.

Bridges, L, 'The Lawrence Inquiry: Incompetence, Corruption and Institutional Racism' (1999) 26 JLS 298.

Brown, B, 'Symbolic Politics and Pornography' (1992) 21 Economy and Society 45.

Brown, W, *States of Injury: Power and Freedom in Late Modernity* (Princeton UP, 1995).

Brown, W, 'Suffering Rights as Paradoxes' (2000) 7 Constellations 230.

Brownlee, I, 'New Labour – New Penology? Punitive Rhetoric and the Limits of Manageralism in Criminal Justice Policy' (1998) 25 JLS 313.

Búrca, G de and J Scott (eds), *Constitutional Change in the EU: From Uniformity to Flexibility* (Hart, 2000).

Busby, K, 'LEAF and Pornography: Litigating on Equality and Sexual Representations' (1994) 9 CJLS 165.

Butler, J, *Excitable Speech: A Politics of the Performative* (Routledge, 1997).

Buxton, R, 'The Human Rights Act and Private Law' (2000) 116 LQR 48.

Campbell, C, *Emergency Law in Ireland: 1918-25* (OUP, 1994).

Campbell, C, 'Two Steps Backwards: The Criminal Justice (Terrorism and Conspiracy) Act 1998' [1999] Crim LR 941.

Campbell, T, 'Human Rights: A Culture of Controversy' (1999) 26 JLS 6.

Campbell, T and W Sadurski (eds), *Freedom of Communication* (Dartmouth, 1994).

Carlen, P, *Alternatives to Women's Imprisonment* (Open UP, 1990).

Carne, G, 'Thawing The Big Chill: Reform, Rhetoric and Regression in the Security Intelligence Mandate' (1996) 22 Monash Univ LR 379.

Carrabine, E and B Longhurst, 'Gender and Prison Organisation: Some Comments on Masculinities and Prison Management' (1998) 37 Howard J 161.

Castells, M, *The Rise of Network Society* (Blackwell, 2000).

Chan, J, *Changing Police Culture: Policing in a Multicultural Society* (Cambridge UP, 1997).

Cheney, D, L Dickson, J Fitzpatrick and S Uglow, *Criminal Justice and the Human Rights Act 1998* (Jordans, 1999).

Choongh, S, *Policing as Social Discipline* (Clarendon, 1997).

Clayton, R et al, *The Law of Human Rights* (OUP, 2000).

Cohen, JL, 'Democracy, Difference, and the Right of Privacy' in S Benhabib (ed), *Democracy and Difference: Contesting the Boundaries of the Political* (Princeton UP, 1996), pp 187-217.

Cohen, JL, 'Personal Autonomy and the Law: Sexual Harassment and the Dilemma of Regulating "Intimacy"' (1999) 6 Constellations 443.

Cohen, JL, 'Resdescribing Privacy: Identity, Difference, and the Abortion Controversy' (1992) 3 Col J Gender & Law 43.

Cohen, JL, 'The Hijacking of Sexual Harassment' (1999) 6 Constellations 142.

Coliver, S (ed), *Striking A Balance: Hate Speech, Freedom of Expression and Non-Discrimination* (ARTICLE 19, 1992).

Collier, R, *Masculinities, Crime and Criminology* (Sage, 1998).

Colombo, S, 'The Legal Battle for the City: Anti-Pornography Municipal Ordinances and Radical Feminism' (1994) 2 FLS 29.

Conaghan, J, 'Enhancing Civil Remedies for (Sexual) Harassment: S. 3 of the Protection from Harassment Act 1997' (1999) 7 FLS 203.

Conaghan, J, 'Gendered Harms and the Law of Tort: Remedying (Sexual) Harassment Law' (1996) 16 OJLS 407.

Cooper, D, '"And You Can't Find Me Nowhere": Relocating Identity and Structure within Equality Jurisprudence' (2000) 27 JLS 249.

Cooper, D, *Governing Out Of Order: Space, Law and the Politics of Belonging* (Rivers Oram, 1998).

Cooper, D, *Power in Struggle* (New York UP, 1995).

Cooper, D, 'Regard between Strangers: Diversity, Equality and the Reconstruction of Public Space' (1998) 57 CSP 465.

Cooper, D, *Sexing the City: Lesbian and Gay Politics Within the Activist State* (Rivers Oram, 1994).

Cornell, D, *The Imaginary Domain* (Routledge, 1995).

Cossman, B et al, *Bad Attitude/s on Trial: Pornography, Feminism, and the 'Butler' Decision* (Toronto UP, 1996).

Craig, JDR, 'Privacy in the Workplace and the Impact of European Convention Incorporation on United Kingdom Labour Law' (1998) 19 Comp Lab L&P J 373.

Crawford, A, *The Local Governance of Crime: Appeals to Community and Partnership* (Clarendon, 1997).

Critcher, C and D Waddington (eds), *Policing Public Order: Theoretical and Practical Issues* (Avebury, 1996).

Curran, J and J Seaton, *Power Without Responsibility: The Press and Broadcasting in Britain* (Routledge, 1997).

Curtin, D, 'Citizens' Fundamental Right of Access to EU Information: An Evolving Digital Passepartout' (2000) 37 CMLR 7.

Darian-Smith, E, *Bridging Divides: The Channel Tunnel and English Legal Identity in the New Europe* (California UP, 1999).

Davies, M, *Asking the Law Question* (Sweet & Maxwell, 1994).

Dickson, B (ed), *Civil Liberties in Northern Ireland* (CAJ, 1997).

Dickson, B (ed), *Human Rights and the European Convention* (Sweet & Maxwell, 1997).

Dixon, D, *Law in Policing: Legal Regulation and Police Practices* (Clarendon, 1997).

Dixon, D, 'Legal Regulation and Policing Practice' (1992) SLS 515.

Dorril, S, *MI6: Fifty Years of Special Operations* (Fourth Estate, 2000).

Downes, D and R Morgan, 'Dumping the "Hostages to Fortune"? The Politics of Law and Order in Post-War Britain' in M Maguire, R Morgan and R Reiner (eds), *The Oxford Handbook of Criminology* (OUP, 1997), pp 87-134.

Duff, P and N Hutton (eds), *Criminal Justice in Scotland* (Ashgate, 1999).

Dworkin, R, 'Is There a Right to Pornography?' (1981) 1 OJLS 177.

Dworkin, R, *Sovereign Virtue: Theory and Practice of Equality* (Harvard UP, 2000).

Dzyenhaus, D, *Judging the Judges: Judging Ourselves* (Hart, 1998).

Easton, S, 'Pornography as Incitement to Sexual Hatred' (1995) 8 FLS 89.

Elliott, M, 'The Ultra Vires Doctrine in a Constitutional Setting: Still the Central Principle of Administrative Law' [1999] CLJ 129.

Ellison, G, '"Reflecting All Shades of Opinion": Public Attitudinal Surveys and the Construction of Police Legitimacy in Northern Ireland' (2000) 40 BJ Crim 88.

Elshtain, JB, *Democracy on Trial* (Basic Books, 1995).

Engle Merry, S, 'Global Human Rights and Local Social Movements in a Legally Plural World' (1997) 12 CJLS 247.

Ericson, R and K Haggerty, *Policing the Risk Society* (Clarendon, 1997).

Etzioni, A, *The Limits of Privacy* (Basic Books, 2000).

Ewing, KD, 'Social Rights and Constitutional Law' [1999] PL 104.

Ewing, KD, 'Social Rights and Human Rights: Britain and the Social Charter – the Conservative Legacy [2000] EHRLR 91.

Ewing, KD, 'The Human Rights Act and Parliamentary Democracy' (1999) 62 MLR 79.

Ewing, KD, 'The Politics of the British Constitution' [2000] PL 405.

Ewing, KD and CA Gearty, *Freedom Under Thatcher: Civil Liberties in Modern Britain* (OUP, 1990).

Ewing, KD and CA Gearty, *The Struggle for Civil Liberties: Political Freedom and the Rule of Law in Britain, 1914-1945* (OUP, 2000).

Feldman, D, *Civil Liberties and Human Rights in England and Wales* (Clarendon, 1993).

Feldman, D, 'Human Dignity as a Legal Value – Part II' [2000] PL 61.

Feldman, D, 'Secrecy, Dignity, or Autonomy? Views of Privacy as Civil Liberty' (1994) CLP 41.

Feldman, D, 'The Human Rights Act 1998 and Constitutional Principles' (1999) 19 LS 165.

Fenwick, H, *Civil Liberties* (Cavendish, 1998).

Fenwick, H, *Civil Rights* (Longman, 2000).

Fenwick, H, 'The Right to Protest, the Human Rights Act and the Margin of Appreciation' (1999) 62 MLR 491.

Fish, S, *There's No Such Thing as Free Speech* (OUP, 1994).

Fiss, O, *The Irony of Free Speech* (Harvard UP, 1996).

Fitzpatrick, J, *Human Rights in Crisis: The International System for Protecting Rights During States of Emergency* (Pennsylvania UP, 1994).

Fraser, N, *Adding Insult to Injury* (Verso, 2000).

Fraser, N, *Justice Interruptus: Reflections on the 'Postsocialist' Condition* (Routledge, 1997).

Fredman, S, *A Critical Review of the Concept of Equality in UK Anti-Discrimination Law*, Working Paper No 3 for the Independent Review of the Enforcement of UK Anti-Discrimination Legislation (Centre for Public Law, 1999).

Garland, D, *Punishment and Modern Society: A Study in Social Theory* (OUP, 1990).

Garland, D, 'The Culture of High Crime Societies: Some Preconditions of Recent "Law and Order" Policies' (2000) 40 BJ Crim 347.

Garland, D, 'The Limits of the Sovereign State: Strategies of Crime Control in Contemporary Society' (1996) 36 BJ Crim 445.

Garland, D and R Sparks, 'Criminology, Social Theory and the Challenge of Our Times' (2000) 40 BJ Crim 189.

Gearty, C (ed), *Terrorism* (Dartmouth, 1996).

Gearty, C, 'Terrorism and Human Rights: A Case Study in Impending Legal Realities' (1999) 19 LS 367.

Gearty, C, and A Tomkins, 'Constitutional and Human Rights Law' in D Hayton (ed), *Law's Future(s)* (Hart Publishing, 2000), pp 53-70.

Genders, E and E Player, *Grendon: A Study of a Therapeutic Prison* (OUP, 1994).

Gill, P, *Policing Politics: Security Intelligence and the Liberal Democratic State* (Frank Cass, 1994).

Gilroy, P, *The Black Atlantic: Modernity and Double Consciousness* (Harvard UP, 1993).

Gobert, J and M Punch, 'Whistleblowers, the Public Interest and the Public Interest Disclosure Act' (2000) 63 MLR 25.

Gooding, C, *Blackstone's Guide to the Disability Discrimination Act 1995* (Blackstone, 1995).

Gostin, L (ed), *Civil Liberties in Conflict* (Routledge, 1988).

Griffith, JAG, 'The Brave New World of Sir John Laws' (2000) 63 MLR 150.

Griffith, JAG, *The Politics of the Judiciary* (Fontana, 1997).

Grosz, S, J Beatson and P Duffy, *Human Rights: The 1998 Act and the European Convention* (Sweet & Maxwell, 1999).

Hadfield, B, '*R v. Lord Saville of Newdigate, ex p Anonymous Soldiers*: What is the Purpose of a Tribunal of Inquiry?' [1999] PL 663.

Hall, S (ed), *Representation: Cultural Representations and Signifying Practices* (Sage, 1996).

Hannah-Moffat, K, 'Moral Agent or Actuarial Subject: Risk and Canadian Women's Imprisonment' (1999) 3 Theor Crim 71.

Harding, R, *Private Prisons and Public Accountability* (Open UP, 1997).

Harlow, C, 'Changing the Mindset: The Place of Theory in English Administrative Law' (1994) 14 OJLS 419.

Harlow, C, 'Export, Import. The Ebb and Flow of English Public Law' [2000] PL 240.

Harlow, C and R Rawlings, *Law and Administration* (Butterworths, 1997).

Harlow, C and R Rawlings, *Pressure Through Law* (Routledge, 1992).

Harris, DJ, M O'Boyle and C Warbrick, *Law of the European Convention on Human Rights* (Butterworths, 1995).

Harvey, C, 'Governing after the Rights Revolution' (2000) 27 JLS 61.

Harvey, C, *Seeking Asylum in the UK: Problems and Prospects* (Butterworths, 2000).

Harvey, CJ, 'Dissident Voices: Refugees, Human Rights and Asylum in Europe' (2000) 9 SLS 367.

Harvey, C and S Livingstone, 'Human Rights and the Northern Ireland Peace Process' [1999] EHRLR 162.

Hazell, R (ed), *Constitutional Futures, A History of the Next Ten Years* (OUP, 1999).

Held, D, *Democracy and the Global Order: From the Modern State to Cosmopolitan Governance* (Stanford UP, 1995).

Hepple, B, M Coussey and T Choudhury, *Equality: A New Framework. Report of the Independent Review of UK Anti-Discrimination Legislation* (Hart, 2000).

Hepple, B and E Szyszczak (eds), *Discrimination: The Limits of Law* (Mansell, 1992).

Herman, D, 'Beyond the Rights Debate' (1993) SLS 25.

Herman, D, 'Law and Morality Re-Visited: The Politics of Regulating Sado-Masochistic Porn/Practice' (1996) 15 Studies in Law, Politics and Society 147.

Herman, D, *Rights of Passage: Struggles for Gay and Lesbian Legal Equality* (Toronto UP, 1994).

Herman, D, *The Anti-Gay Agenda and the Christian Right* (Chicago UP, 1997).

Herman, D, 'The Good, the Bad, and the Smugly: Perspectives on the Canadian Charter of Rights and Freedoms' (1994) 14 OJLS 589.

Hillyard, P, *Suspect Community: People's Experience of the Prevention of Terrorism Acts in Britain* (Pluto, 1993).

Hillyard, P, 'The Politics of Criminal Injustice: The Irish Dimension' in M McConville and L Bridges (eds), *Criminal Justice in Crisis* (Edward Elgar, 1994), pp 69-79.

Hillyard, P and D Gordon, 'Arresting Statistics: The Drift to Informal Justice in England and Wales' (1999) 26 JLS 502.

Hirschmann, NJ and C Di Stefano (eds), *Revisioning the Political: Feminist Reconstructions of Traditional Concepts in Western Political Theory* (Westview, 1996).

Hogg, P, *Constitutional Law of Canada* (Carswell, 1997).

Hollingsworth, M and N Fielding, *Defending the Realm: MI5 and the Shayler Affair* (Andre Deutsch, 2000).

Hunt, M, 'The Horizontal Effect of the Human Rights Act' [1998] PL 423.

Hunt, M, 'The Human Rights Act and Legal Culture: The Judiciary and the Legal Profession' (1998) 26 JLS 86.

Hunt, M, *Using Human Rights Law in English Courts* (Hart, 1997).

Hunter, I, D Saunders and D Williamson, *On Pornography: Literature, Sexuality and Obscenity Law* (Macmillan, 1993).

Hutchinson, A, 'In Other Words: Putting Sex and Pornography in Context' (1995) 8 Can J of Law & Juris 107.

Hutchinson, A, *Waiting for Coraf: A Critique of Law and Rights* (Toronto UP, 1995).

Hutchinson, AC, *It's All In The Game: A Nonfoundationalist Account of Law and Adjudication* (Duke UP, 2000).

Hutton, W, *The State We're In* (Cape, 1996).

Hyde, A, *Bodies of Law* (Princeton UP, 1997).

Isin, EF and PK Wood, *Citizenship and Identity* (Sage, 1999).

Itzin, C (ed), *Pornography: Women, Violence and Civil Liberties* (OUP, 1992).

Jackson, J and S Doran, *Judge Without Jury* (Clarendon, 1995).

James, A, K Bottomley, A Liebling and E Clare, *Privatizing Prisons: Rhetoric and Reality* (Sage, 1997).

Jefferson, T, *The Case Against Paramilitary Policing* (Open UP, 1990).

Jennings, A (ed), *Justice Under Fire: The Abuse of Civil Liberties in Northern Ireland* (Pluto, 1988).

Johnston, L, *Policing Britain: Risk, Security and Governance* (Longman, 2000).

Jones, T and T Newburn, *Private Security and Public Policing* (Clarendon, 1998).

Kappeler, S, *Pornography and Representation* (Polity, 1986).

Karpin, I, 'Reimagining Maternal Selfhood: Transgressing Body Boundaries and the Law' (1994) 2 AFLJ 36.

Kennedy, D, *A Critique of Adjudication (Fin De Siecle)* (Harvard UP, 1997).

Kennedy, H, *Eve was Framed: Women and British Justice* (Vintage, 1992).

Klug, F, *Values for a Godless Age: The Story of the UK's New Bill of Rights* (Penguin, 2000).

Klug, F, K Starmer and S Weir, *The Three Pillars of Liberty: Political Rights and Freedoms in the United Kingdom* (Routledge, 1996).

Knightley, P, *The First Casualty: The War Correspondent as Hero and Myth Maker From Crimea to Kosovo* (Prion Books, 2000).

Kymlicka, W, *Multicultural Citizenship: A Liberal Theory of Minority Rights* (Clarendon, 1995).

Lacey, N, 'Criminology, Criminal Law, and Criminalization' in M Maguire, R Morgan and R Reiner (eds), *The Oxford Handbook of Criminology* (Clarendon, 1997), pp. 437-450.

Lacey, N, *Unspeakable Subjects: Feminist Essays in Legal and Social Theory* (Hart, 1998).

Lacey, N and C Wells, *Reconstructing Criminal Law* (Butterworths, 1998).

Lacombe, D, *Blue Politics: Pornography and the Law in the Age of Feminism* (Toronto UP, 1994).

Laws, J, 'Is the High Court the Guardian of Fundamental Constitutional Rights?' [1993] PL 67.

Laws, J, 'Law and Democracy' [1995] PL 72.

Laws, J, 'The Constitution: Morals and Rights' [1996] PL 622.

Laws, J, 'The Limitations of Human Rights' [1998] PL 254.

Lawson-Cruttenden, T and N Addison, *Blackstone's Guide to the Protection from Harassment Act 1997* (Blackstone, 1998).

Leech, M and D Cheney, *The Prisons Handbook 2000* (Waterside, 1999).

Lees, S, *Ruling Passions: Sexual Violence, Reputation and the Law* (Open UP, 1997).

Leigh, I, 'Horizontal Rights, the Human Rights Act and Privacy: Lessons from the Commonwealth?' (1999) 48 ICLQ 57.

Leigh, I, 'Secret Proceedings in Canada' (1996) 34 Osg Hall LJ 113.

Leigh, I, 'Secrets of the Political Constitution' (1999) 62 MLR 298.

Leigh, I and L Lustgarten, 'Five Volumes in Search of Accountability: The Scott Report' (1996) 59 MLR 695.

Leigh, I and L Lustgarten, 'Making Rights Real: The Courts, Remedies, and the Human Rights Act' (1999) 58 CLJ 507.

Leng, R and R Taylor, *Blackstone's Guide to the Criminal Procedure and Investigations Act 1996* (Blackstone, 1996).

Lessig, L, *Code and Other Laws of Cyberspace* (Basic Books, 1999).

Lester, A, 'Equality and UK Law: Past, Present and Future' [2001] PL 77.

Lester, A and D Pannick (eds), *Human Rights: Law and Practice* (Butterworths, 1999).

Lianos, M and M Douglas, 'Dangerization and the End of Deviance' (2000) 40 BJ Crim 261.

Liberty (ed), *Liberating Cyberspace: Civil Liberties, Human Rights and the Internet* (Pluto, 1998).

Liebling, A, 'Doing Research in Prison: Breaking the Silence?' (1999) 3 Theor Crim 147.

Liebling, A, D Price and C Elliott, 'Appreciative Inquiry and Relationships in Prison' (1999) 1 Punishment & Society 71.

Livingston, D, 'Police Discretion and the Quality of Life in Public Places: Courts, Communities and the New Policing' (1997) 97 Col LR 551.

Livingstone, S, 'The House of Lords and the Northern Ireland Conflict' (1994) 57 MLR 333.

Livingstone, S, 'The Northern Ireland Human Rights Commission' (1999) 22 Fordham Int LJ 1465.

Livingstone, S and T Owen, *Prison Law* (OUP, 1999).

Loader, I, 'Democracy, Justice and the Limits of Policing: Rethinking Police Accountability' (1994) 3 SLS 521.

Loader, I, 'Plural Policing and Democratic Governance' (2000) 9 SLS 323.

Loader, I, 'Thinking Normatively About Private Security' (1997) 24 JLS 377.

Loader, I, *Youth, Policing and Democracy* (Macmillan, 1996).

Lord Bingham, 'The Way We Live Now: Human Rights in the New Millennium' [1998] 1 Web JCLI.

Lord Hoffmann, 'Human Rights and the House of Lords' (1999) 62 MLR 159.

Lord Irvine, 'Activism and Restraint: Human Rights and the Interpretative Process' [1999] EHRLR 350.

Lord Steyn, 'Incorporation and Devolution: A Few Reflections on the Changing Scene' [1998] EHRLR 153.

Loughlin, M, *Sword and Scales: An Examination of the Relationship between Law and Politics* (Hart, 2000).

Loveland, I (ed), *A Special Relationship? American Influences on Public Law in the United Kingdom* (Clarendon, 1995).

Loveland, I (ed), *Importing the First Amendment* (Hart, 1998).

Loveland, I, *Political Libels* (Hart, 2000).

Lucy, W, *Understanding and Explaining Adjudication* (OUP, 1999).

Lustgarten, L, 'Constitutional Discipline and the Arms Trade: The Scott Report and Beyond' (1998) 69 Pol Q 422.

Lustgarten, L, 'Racial Inequality and the Limits of Law' (1986) 49 MLR 68.

Lustgarten, L 'The Arms Trade and the Constitution: Beyond the Scott Report' (1998) 61 MLR 499.

Lustgarten, L and I Leigh, *In From the Cold: National Security and Parliamentary Democracy* (Clarendon, 1994).

MacArthur, B (ed), *The Penguin Book of 20th-Century Protest* (Penguin, 1998).

McColgan, A, *Women Under the Law: The False Promise of Human Rights* (Longman, 2000).

McConville, M, J Hodgson, L Bridges and A Pavlovic, *Standing Accused: The Organisation and Practices of Criminal Defence Lawyers in Britain* (Clarendon, 1994).

McConville, M, A Sanders and R Leng, *The Case for the Prosecution: Police Suspects and the Construction of Criminality* (Routledge, 1991).

MacCormick, N, *Questioning Sovereignty: Law, State and Nation in the European Commonwealth* (OUP, 1999).

McCrudden, C (ed), *Anti-Discrimination Law* (Dartmouth, 1991).

McCrudden, C, 'Human Rights Codes for Transnational Corporations: What Can the Sullivan and MacBride Principles Tell Us' (1999) 19 OJLS 167.

McCrudden, C, 'Mainstreaming Equality in the Governance of Northern Ireland' (1999) 22 Fordham Int LJ 1696.

McCrudden, C and G Chambers (eds), *Individual Rights and British Law* (Clarendon, 1994).

McEvoy, K and C White, 'Security Vetting in Northern Ireland: Loyalty, Redress and Citizenship' (1992) 61 MLR 341.

McEvoy, K et al, 'The Home Front: The Families of Politically Motivated Prisoners in Northern Ireland' (1999) 39 BJ Crim 175.

McGarry, J and B O'Leary, *Policing Northern Ireland* (Blackstaff, 1999).

MacKinnon, CA, *Feminism Unmodified: Discourses on Life and Law* (Harvard UP, 1987).

MacKinnon, CA, *Only Words* (Harper Collins, 1994).

MacKinnon, CA, *Sexual Harassment of Working Women* (Yale UP, 1979).

MacKinnon, CA, *Towards a Feminist Theory of the State* (Harvard UP, 1989).

McNay, L, *Gender and Agency: Reconfiguring the Subject in Feminist and Social Theory* (Polity, 2000).

MacPherson Report, *Report of an Inquiry by Sir William MacPherson of Cluny*, Cm 4262-I (HMSO, 1999).

Maguire, M, R Morgan and R Reiner (eds), *The Oxford Handbook of Criminology* (Clarendon, 1997).

Mahoney, K, '*R. v. Keegstra*: A Rationale for Regulating Pornography?' (1992) 37 McGill LJ 242.

Malik, M, 'Governing After the Human Rights Act' (2000) 63 MLR 281.

Markesinis, BS, 'Privacy, Freedom of Expression and the Horizontal Effect of the Human Rights Bill: Lessons from Germany' (1999) 115 LQR 47.

Markesinis, BS (ed), *Protecting Privacy* (OUP, 1999).

Markesinis, BS (ed), *The Impact of the Human Rights Bill on English Law* (OUP, 1998).

Marks, S, 'Civil Liberties at the Margin: The UK Derogation and the European Convention on Human Rights' (1995) 15 OJLS 69.

Marks, S, *The Riddle of All Constitutions: International Law, Democracy, and a Critique of Ideology* (OUP, 2000).

Marquand, D, 'Democracy in Britain' (2000) 71 Pol Q 268.

Marquand, D, *Progressive Dilemma: From Lloyd George to Blair* (Phoenix Grant, 1999).

Martin, D, 'Retribution Revisited: A Reconsideration of Feminist Criminal Law Reform Strategies' (1998) 36 Osg Hall LJ 151.

Matsuda, M et al, *Words that Wound: Critical Race Theory, Assaultive Speech, and the First Amendment* (Westview, 1993).

Miller, D, *On Nationality* (OUP, 1995).

Millns, S and N Whitty (eds), *Feminist Perspectives on Public Law* (Cavendish, 1999).

Milne, S, *The Enemy Within: The Secret War Against the Miners* (Verso, 1994).

Modood, T and P Werbner (eds), *The Politics of Multiculturalism in the New Europe: Racism, Identity and Community* (Zed Books, 1997).

Monbiot, G, *Captive State: The Corporate Takeover of Britain* (Macmillan, 2000).

Moran, LJ, 'The Uses of Homosexuality: Homosexuality for National Security' (1991) 19 Int J Sociology of Law 149.

More, G, 'The Principle of Equal Treatment: From Market Unifier to Fundamental Right?' in P Craig and G de Búrca (eds), *The Evolution of EU Law* (OUP, 1999), pp 517-554.

Morgan, R and M Evans (eds), *Protecting Prisoners: The Standards of the European Committee for the Prevention of Torture in Context* (OUP, 1999).

Morison, J, 'The Case Against Constitutional Reform?' (1998) 25 JLS 510.

Morison, J and S Livingstone, *Reshaping Public Power: Northern Ireland and the British Constitution* (Sweet & Maxwell, 1995).

Morrison, T (ed), *Race-ing Justice, En-Gendering Race: Essays on Anita Hill, Clarence Thomas and the Construction of Social Reality* (Pantheon, 1992).

Morton, FL and R Knoff, *The Charter Revolution and the Court Party* (Broadview, 2000).

Moyle, P, *Profiting from Punishment: Private Prisons in Australia: Reform or Regression?* (Pluto, 2000).

Moynihan, DP, *Secrecy* (Yale UP, 1998).

Mulcahy, A, 'Policing History: The Official Discourse and Organizational Memory of the Royal Ulster Constabulary' (2000) 40 BJ Crim 68.

Mulcahy, A, 'Visions of Normality: Peace and Reconstruction of Policing in Northern Ireland' (1999) 8 SLS 277.

Mullender, R, 'Racial Harassment, Sexual Harassment, and the Expressive Function of Law' (1998) 61 MLR 236.

Murphy, T and N Whitty, 'What is a Fair Trial? Rape Prosecutions, Disclosure and the Human Rights Act' (2000) 8 FLS 1.

Naffine, N and R Owens (eds), *Sexing the Subject of Law* (Law Book Company, 1997).

Nairn, T, *After Britain* (Granta, 2000).

Nedelsky, J, 'Reconceiving Autonomy: Sources, Thoughts and Possibilities' (1989) 1 Yale J Law & Feminism 7.

Nedelsky, J, *Private Property and the Limits of American Constitutionalism* (Chicago UP, 1990).

North, P, *Independent Review of Parades and Marches* (Stationery Office, 1997).

Oliver, D, 'The Frontiers of the State: Public Authorities and Public Functions under the Human Rights Act' [2000] PL 476.

Orford, A, 'Muscular Humanitarianism: Reading the Narratives of the New Interventionism' (1999) 10 EJIL 679.

Palmer, E, 'Resource Allocation, Welfare Rights: Mapping the Boundaries of Judicial Control in Public Administrative Law' (2000) 20 OJLS 63.

Palmer, S, 'The Human Rights Act 1998: Bringing Rights Home' (1998) 1 YELS 125.

Parekh, B, 'Defining British National Identity' (2000) 71 Pol Q 4.

Parekh Report, *The Future of Multi-Ethnic Britain: The Parekh Report* (Profile Books, 2000).

Paton Simpson, E, 'Private Circles and Public Squares: Invasion of Privacy by the Publication of "Private Facts"' (1998) 61 MLR 318.

Patten Report, Independent Commission on Policing for Northern Ireland, *A New Beginning: Policing in Northern Ireland* (HMSO, 1999) (www.belfast.org.uk).

Pearson, G, *Hooligan: A History of Respectable Fears* (Macmillan, 1983).

Phillips, A, *Which Equalities Matter?* (Polity, 1999).

Phillipson, G, 'The Human Rights Act, "Horizontal Effect" and the Common Law: A Bang or a Whimper?' (1999) 62 MLR 824.

Ramsey, I, *Advertising, Culture and the Law* (Sweet & Maxwell, 1996).

Reiner, R, *The Politics of the Police* (OUP, 2000).

Roach, K, *Due Process and Victims' Rights: The New Law and Politics of Criminal Justice* (Toronto UP, 1999).

Robertson, D, *Judicial Discretion in the House of Lords* (Clarendon, 1998).

Robertson, G, *Crimes Against Humanity: The Struggle For Global Justice* (Penguin, 2000).

Robertson, G, *Freedom, The Individual and the Law* (Penguin, 1993).

Robertson, G, *The Justice Game* (Vintage, 1999).

Robertson, G and A Nicol, *Media Law* (Penguin, 1992).

Rock, P, *Reconstructing a Women's Prison: The Holloway Redevelopment Project 1968-88* (Clarendon, 1996).

Rodley, N, *The Treatment of Prisoners Under International Law* (Clarendon, 1999).

Rogers, A, *Secrecy and Power in the British State: A History of the Official Secrets Act, 1911-1989* (Pluto, 1997).

Rose, D, *In the Name of the Law: The Collapse of Criminal Justice* (Vintage, 1996).

Rose, N, 'Government and Control' (2000) 40 BJ Crim 321.

Rose, N, *Powers of Freedom: Reframing Political Thought* (CUP, 1999).

Rose, N, 'The Biology of Culpability: Pathological Identity and Crime Control in a Biological Culture' (2000) 4 Theor Crim 5.

Rosenberg, WA, *The Hollow Hope: Can Courts Bring About Social Change?* (Chicago UP, 1991).

Rowe, M, *The Racialization of Disorder in Twentieth Century Britain* (Ashgate, 1998).

Rumney, P, 'When Rape Isn't Rape: Court of Appeal Sentencing Practices in Cases of Marital and Relationship Rape' (1999) 19 OJLS 243.

Ryder, C, *The RUC: A Force Under Fire* (Mandarin, 1997).

Sadurski, W, 'On "Seeing Speech Through an Equality Lens": A Critique of Egalitarian Arguments for Suppression of Hate Speech and Pornography' (1996) 16 OJLS 713.

Sanders, A, 'Criminal Justice: The Development of Criminal Justice Research in Britain' in PA Thomas (ed), *Socio-Legal Studies* (Dartmouth, 1997), pp 185-205.

Sanders, A and R Young, *Criminal Justice* (Butterworths, 2000).

Sassen, S, *Globalization and Its Discontents: Essays on the New Mobility of People and Money* (New Press, 1999).

Scarman Report, *The Brixton Disorders 10-12 April 1981*, Cmnd 8427 (HMSO, 1981).

Scott, C, 'Accountability in the Regulatory State' (2000) 27 JLS 38.

Sedley, S, *Freedom, Law and Justice* (Sweet & Maxwell, 1999).

Sedley, S, 'Human Rights: A Twenty First Century Agenda' [1995] PL 386.

Sedley, S, 'The Sound of Silence: Constitutional Law without a Constitution' (1994) 110 LQR 270.

Sharpe, SD, 'The European Convention: A Suspects' Charter?' [1997] Crim LR 848.

Shaw, J, 'Constitutionalism in the European Union' (1999) 6 JEPP 579.

Shorts, E and C de Than, *Civil Liberties* (Sweet & Maxwell, 1998).

Simpson, B, *In the Highest Degree Odious: Detention Without Trial in Wartime Britain* (Clarendon, 1992).

Singh, R, 'Privacy and the Media after the Human Rights Act' [1998] EHRLR 712.

Singh, R, M Hunt and M Demetriou, 'Is There a Role For the Margin of Appreciation in National Law After the Human Rights Act?' [1999] EHRLR 15.

Smart, C, *Feminism and the Power of Law* (Routledge, 1989).

Smart, C, 'Law's Power, the Sexed Body, and Feminist Discourse' (1990) 70 JLS 194.

Smith, AM, *New Right Discourses on Race and Sexuality* (Cambridge UP, 1994).

Sparks, R, AE Bottoms and W Hay, *Prisons and the Problem of Order* (Clarendon, 1996).

Stammers, N, *Civil Liberties in Britain During the Second World War: A Political Study* (Croom Helm, 1983).

Starmer, K, *European Human Rights Law* (LAG, 1999).

Stevens, R, 'A Loss of Innocence?: Judicial Independence and the Separation of Powers' (1999) 19 OJLS 365.

Stone, R, *Textbook on Civil Liberties and Human Rights* (Blackstone, 2000).

Strossen, N, *Defending Pornography: Free Speech, Sex, and the Fight for Women's Equality* (Abacus Books, 1995).

Stychin, CF, *A Nation By Rights: National Cultures, Sexual Identity Politics and the Discourse of Rights* (Temple UP, 1998).

Stychin, CF, '"A Stranger to its Laws": Sovereign Bodies, Global Sexualities, and Transnational Citizens' (2000) 27 JLS 601.

Stychin, CF, 'Body Talk: Rethinking Autonomy, Commodification and the Embodied Legal Self' in S Sheldon and M Thomson (eds), *Feminist Perspectives on Health Care Law* (Cavendish, 1998), pp 211-236.

Stychin, CF, '*Grant*-ing Rights: The Politics of Rights, Sexuality and European Union' (2000) 51 NILQ 281.

Stychin, CF, *Law's Desire* (Routledge, 1995).

Stychin, CF, 'New Labour, New "Britain"? Constitutionalism, Sovereignty and Nation/State in Transition' (1999) 19 Studies in Law, Politics and Society 139.

Supperstone, M and J Coppel, 'Judicial Review After the Human Rights Act' [1999] EHRLR 301.

Taggart, M (ed), *The Province of Administrative Law* (Hart, 1997).
Taylor, C, 'Multiculturalism and the Politics of Recognition' in A Gutmann (ed), *Multiculturalism* (Princeton UP, 1992).
Taylor, P, *War and the Media: Propaganda and Persuasion in the Gulf War* (Manchester UP, 1998).
Temkin, J, 'Medical Evidence in Rape Cases: A Continuing Problem for Criminal Justice' (1998) 61 MLR 821.
Temkin, J, 'Reporting Rape in London: A Qualitative Study' (1999) 38 Howard J 17.
Thornton, M (ed), *Public and Private: Feminist Legal Debates* (OUP, 1995).
Thurlow, R, *The Secret State: British Internal Security in the Twentieth Century* (Blackwell, 1994).
Tomkins, A, 'Inventing Human Rights Law and Scholarship' (1996) 16 OJLS 153.
Tomkins, A, *The Constitution After Scott: Government Unwrapped* (Clarendon, 1998).
Townshend, C, *Making the Peace: Public Order and Public Security in Modern Britain* (OUP, 1993).
Tribe, L, *American Constitutional Law* (Foundation Press, 2000).
Tully, J, *Strange Multiplicity: Constitutionalism in an Age of Diversity* (CUP, 1995).
Tully, J, 'Struggles over Recognition and Redistribution' (2000) 7 Constellations 469.
Twining, W, *Blackstone's Tower: The English Law School* (Sweet & Maxwell, 1994).
Twining, W, *Globalisation and Legal Theory* (Butterworths, 2000).

Urban, M, *Big Boys' Rules: The SAS and the Secret Struggle Against the IRA* (Faber & Faber, 1993).

Valverde, M, 'Identity Politics and the Law in the US' (1999) 25 Fem Studies 345.
Valverde, M, 'The Law of Breasts and the Risk of Harm' (1999) 8 SLS 181.
Vickers, L, 'Whistling in the Wind? The Public Interest Disclosure Act 1998' (2000) 20 LS 428.
Vincent, D, *The Culture of Secrecy: Britain 1832-1998* (OUP, 1998).
von Hirsch, A and A Ashworth, 'Law and Order' in A von Hirsch and A Ashworth (eds), *Principled Sentencing* (Hart, 1998), pp 410-424.

Wacks, R, *Personal Information: Privacy and the Law* (Clarendon, 1993).
Wacks, R, *Privacy and Press Freedom* (Blackstone, 1995).
Waddington, D, 'Waddington Versus Waddington: Public Order Theory on Trial' (1998) 2 Theor Crim 373.
Waddington, PAJ, 'Orthodoxy and Advocacy in Criminology' (2000) 4 Theor Crim 93.
Waddington, PAJ, *The Strong Arm of the Law: Armed and Public Order Policing* (Clarendon, 1991).
Wade, W, 'Horizons of Horizontality' (2000) 116 LQR 217.
Wade, W, 'Human Rights and the Judiciary' [1998] EHRLR 520.
Wadham, J and H Mountfield, *Blackstone's Guide to the Human Rights Act 1998* (Blackstone, 1999).
Walker, C, 'The Bombs in Omagh and their Aftermath: The Criminal Justice (Terrorism and Conspiracy) Act 1998' (1999) 62 MLR 879.

Walker, C, 'The Commodity of Justice in States of Emergency' (1999) 50 NILQ 164.

Walker, C, *The Prevention of Terrorism in British Law* (Manchester UP, 1986).

Walker, C and B Fitzpatrick, 'Holding Centres in Northern Ireland, the Independent Commissioner and the Rights of Detainees' [1999] EHRLR 27.

Walker, C and K Starmer (eds), *Miscarriages of Justice: A Review of Justice in Error* (Blackstone, 1999).

Walker, N, *Policing in a Changing Constitutional Culture* (Sweet & Maxwell, 2000).

Walker, N, 'Setting English Judges to Rights' (1999) 19 OJLS 133.

Walker, S, *In Defence of American Liberties: A History of the ACLU* (OUP, 1990).

Wardlaw, G, *Political Terrorism* (CUP, 1989).

Wasik, M and R Taylor, *Blackstone's Guide to the Criminal Justice and Public Order Act 1994* (Blackstone, 1995).

Weeks, J, *Sex, Politics and Society: The Regulation of Sexuality Since 1800* (Longman, 1989).

Weiler, J, *The Constitution of Europe* (CUP, 1999).

Werbner, P, 'Divided Loyalties, Empowered Citizenship? Muslims in Britain' (2000) 4 Citizenship Studies 307.

White, C, 'Security Vetting: Discrimination and the Right to a Fair Trial' [1999] PL 406.

Wilkinson, P, *Terrorism and the Liberal State* (Macmillan, 1995).

Williams, D, 'Bias: The Judges and the Separation of Powers' [2000] PL 45.

Williams, D, *Keeping the Peace: The Police and Public Order* (Hutchinson, 1967).

Williams, D, *Not in the Public Interest: The Problem of Security in Democracy* (Hutchinson, 1965).

Williams, P, *The Alchemy of Race and Rights* (Harvard UP, 1991).

Wintemute, R, 'Lesbian and Gay Inequality 2000: The Potential of the Human Rights Act 1998 and the Need for an Equality Act 2002' [2000] EHRLR 603.

Wright, B, 'Quiescent Leviathan: Citizenship and National Security Measures in Late Modernity' (1998) 25 JLS 213.

Wright, P, *Spycatcher* (Heinemann, 1987).

Young, A, *Femininity in Dissent* (Routledge, 1990).

Young, IM, *Inclusion and Democracy* (OUP, 2000).

Young, IM, *Intersecting Voices: Dilemmas of Gender, Political Philosophy, and Policy* (Princeton UP, 1997).

Young, IM, *Justice and the Politics of Difference* (Princeton UP, 1990).

Young, J, 'Cannibalism and Bulimia: Patterns of Social Control in Late Modernity' (1999) 3 Theor Crim 387.

Young, J, *The Exclusive Society* (Sage, 1999).

Appendix

HUMAN RIGHTS ACT 1998

An Act to give further effect to rights and freedoms guaranteed under the European Convention on Human Rights; to make provision with respect to holders of certain judicial offices who become judges of the European Court of Human Rights; and for connected purposes.

[9th November 1998]

Introduction

1 The Convention Rights

(1)   In this Act "the Convention rights" means the rights and fundamental freedoms set out in—

    (a)   Articles 2 to 12 and 14 of the Convention,
    (b)   Articles 1 to 3 of the First Protocol, and
    (c)   Articles 1 and 2 of the Sixth Protocol,

as read with Articles 16 to 18 of the Convention.

(2)   Those Articles are to have effect for the purposes of this Act subject to any designated derogation or reservation (as to which see sections 14 and 15).

(3)   The Articles are set out in Schedule 1.

(4)   The Secretary of State may by order make such amendments to this Act as he considers appropriate to reflect the effect, in relation to the United Kingdom, of a protocol.

(5)   In subsection (4) "protocol" means a protocol to the Convention—

    (a)   which the United Kingdom has ratified; or
    (b)   which the United Kingdom has signed with a view to ratification.

(6)   No amendment may be made by an order under subsection (4) so as to come into force before the protocol concerned is in force in relation to the United Kingdom.

2 Interpretation of Convention rights

(1)   A court or tribunal determining a question which has arisen in connection with a Convention right must take into account any—

    (a)   judgment, decision, declaration or advisory opinion of the European Court of Human Rights,
    (b)   opinion of the Commission given in a report adopted under Article 31 of the Convention,
    (c)   decision of the Commission in connection with Article 26 or 27(2) of the Convention, or
    (d)   decision of the Committee of Ministers taken under Article 46 of the Convention,

whenever made or given, so far as, in the opinion of the court or tribunal, it is relevant to the proceedings in which that question has arisen.

(2)   Evidence of any judgment, decision, declaration or opinion of which account may have to be taken under this section is to be given in proceedings before any court or tribunal in such manner as may be provided by rules.

(3)   In this section "rules" means rules of court or, in the case of proceedings before a tribunal, rules made for the purposes of this section—

- (a)   by the Lord Chancellor or the Secretary of State, in relation to any proceedings outside Scotland;
- (b)   by the Secretary of State, in relation to proceedings in Scotland; or
- (c)   by a Northern Ireland department, in relation to proceedings before a tribunal in Northern Ireland—
    - (i)   which deals with transferred matters; and
    - (ii) for which no rules made under paragraph (a) are in force.

Legislation

3 Interpretation of legislation

(1)   So far as it is possible to do so, primary legislation and subordinate legislation must be read and given effect in a way which is compatible with the Convention rights.

(2)   This section—

- (a)   applies to primary legislation and subordinate legislation whenever enacted;
- (b)   does not affect the validity, continuing operation or enforcement of any incompatible primary legislation; and
- (c)   does not affect the validity, continuing operation or enforcement of any incompatible subordinate legislation if (disregarding any possibility of revocation) primary legislation prevents removal of the incompatibility.

4 Declaration of incompatibility

(1)   Subsection (2) applies in any proceedings in which a court determines whether a provision of primary legislation is compatible with a Convention right.

(2)   If the court is satisfied that the provision is incompatible with a Convention right, it may make a declaration of that incompatibility.

(3)   Subsection (4) applies in any proceedings in which a court determines whether a provision of subordinate legislation, made in the exercise of a power conferred by primary legislation, is compatible with a Convention right.

(4)   If the court is satisfied—

- (a)   that the provision is incompatible with a Convention right, and
- (b)   that (disregarding any possibility of revocation) the primary legislation concerned prevents removal of the incompatibility,

it may make a declaration of that incompatibility.

(5)   In this section "court" means—

- (a)   the House of Lords;
- (b)   the Judicial Committee of the Privy Council;
- (c)   the Courts-Martial Appeal Court;
- (d)   in Scotland, the High Court of Justiciary sitting otherwise than as a trial court or the Court of Session;
- (e)   in England and Wales or Northern Ireland, the High Court or the Court of Appeal.

(6)   A declaration under this section ("a declaration of incompatibility")—

(a) does not affect the validity, continuing operation or enforcement of the provision in respect of which it is given; and

(b) is not binding on the parties to the proceedings in which it is made.

5 Right of Crown to intervene

(1) Where a court is considering whether to make a declaration of incompatibility, the Crown is entitled to notice in accordance with rules of court.

(2) In any case to which subsection (1) applies—

(a) a Minister of the Crown (or a person nominated by him),
(b) a member of the Scottish Executive,
(c) a Northern Ireland Minister,
(d) a Northern Ireland department,

is entitled, on giving notice in accordance with rules of court, to be joined as a party to the proceedings.

(3) Notice under subsection (2) may be given at any time during the proceedings.

(4) A person who has been made a party to criminal proceedings (other than in Scotland) as the result of a notice under subsection (2) may, with leave, appeal to the House of Lords against any declaration of incompatibility made in the proceedings.

(5) In subsection (4)—

"criminal proceedings" includes all proceedings before the Courts-Martial Appeal Court; and
"leave" means leave granted by the court making the declaration of incompatibility or by the House of Lords.

Public authorities

6 Acts of public authorities

(1) It is unlawful for a public authority to act in a way which is incompatible with a Convention right.

(2) Subsection (1) does not apply to an act if—

(a) as the result of one or more provisions of primary legislation, the authority could not have acted differently; or
(b) in the case of one or more provisions of, or made under, primary legislation which cannot be read or given effect in a way which is compatible with the Convention rights, the authority was acting so as to give effect to or enforce those provisions.

(3) In this section "public authority" includes—

(a) a court or tribunal, and
(b) any person certain of whose functions are functions of a public nature,

but does not include either House of Parliament or a person exercising functions in connection with proceedings in Parliament.

(4) In subsection (3) "Parliament" does not include the House of Lords in its judicial capacity.

(5) In relation to a particular act, a person is not a public authority by virtue only of subsection (3)(b) if the nature of the act is private.

(6) "An act" includes a failure to act but does not include a failure to—

(a) introduce in, or lay before, Parliament a proposal for legislation; or

(b) make any primary legislation or remedial order.

7 Proceedings

(1) A person who claims that a public authority has acted (or proposes to act) in a way which is made unlawful by section 6(1) may—

(a) bring proceedings against the authority under this Act in the appropriate court or tribunal, or

(b) rely on the Convention right or rights concerned in any legal proceedings,

but only if he is (or would be) a victim of the unlawful act.

(2) In subsection (1)(a) "appropriate court or tribunal" means such court or tribunal as may be determined in accordance with rules; and proceedings against an authority include a counterclaim or similar proceeding.

(3) If the proceedings are brought on an application for judicial review, the applicant is to be taken to have a sufficient interest in relation to the unlawful act only if he is, or would be, a victim of that act.

(4) If the proceedings are made by way of a petition for judicial review in Scotland, the applicant shall be taken to have title and interest to sue in relation to the unlawful act only if he is, or would be, a victim of that act.

(5) Proceedings under subsection (1)(a) must be brought before the end of—

(a) the period of one year beginning with the date on which the act complained of took place; or

(b) such longer period as the court or tribunal considers equitable having regard to all the circumstances,

but that is subject to any rule imposing a stricter time limit in relation to the procedure in question.

(6) In subsection (1)(b) "legal proceedings" includes—

(a) proceedings brought by or at the instigation of a public authority; and

(b) an appeal against the decision of a court or tribunal.

(7) For the purposes of this section, a person is a victim of an unlawful act only if he would be a victim for the purposes of Article 34 of the Convention if proceedings were brought in the European Court of Human Rights in respect of that act.

(8) Nothing in this Act creates a criminal offence.

(9) In this section "rules" means—

(a) in relation to proceedings before a court or tribunal outside Scotland, rules made by the Lord Chancellor or the Secretary of State for the purposes of this section or rules of court,

(b) in relation to proceedings before a court or tribunal in Scotland, rules made by the Secretary of State for those purposes,

(c) in relation to proceedings before a tribunal in Northern Ireland—

(i) which deals with transferred matters; and

(ii) for which no rules made under paragraph (a) are in force,

rules made by a Northern Ireland department for those purposes,

and includes provision made by order under section 1 of the Courts and Legal Services Act 1990.

(10) In making rules, regard must be had to section 9.

(11)   The Minister who has power to make rules in relation to a particular tribunal may, to the extent he considers it necessary to ensure that the tribunal can provide an appropriate remedy in relation to an act (or proposed act) of a public authority which is (or would be) unlawful as a result of section 6(1), by order add to—

  (a)   the relief or remedies which the tribunal may grant; or
  (b)   the grounds on which it may grant any of them.

(12)   An order made under subsection (11) may contain such incidental, supplemental, consequential or transitional provision as the Minister making it considers appropriate.

(13)   "The Minister" includes the Northern Ireland department concerned.

8 Judicial remedies

(1)   In relation to any act (or proposed act) of a public authority which the court finds is (or would be) unlawful, it may grant such relief or remedy, or make such order, within its powers as it considers just and appropriate.

(2)   But damages may be awarded only by a court which has power to award damages, or to order the payment of compensation, in civil proceedings.

(3)   No award of damages is to be made unless, taking account of all the circumstances of the case, including—

  (a)   any other relief or remedy granted, or order made, in relation to the act in question (by that or any other court), and
  (b)   the consequences of any decision (of that or any other court) in respect of that act,

the court is satisfied that the award is necessary to afford just satisfaction to the person in whose favour it is made.

(4)   In determining—

  (a)   whether to award damages, or
  (b)   the amount of an award,

the court must take into account the principles applied by the European Court of Human Rights in relation to the award of compensation under Article 41 of the Convention.

(5)   A public authority against which damages are awarded is to be treated—

  (a)   in Scotland, for the purposes of section 3 of the Law Reform (Miscellaneous Provisions) (Scotland) Act 1940 as if the award were made in an action of damages in which the authority has been found liable in respect of loss or damage to the person to whom the award is made;
  (b)   for the purposes of the Civil Liability (Contribution) Act 1978 as liable in respect of damage suffered by the person to whom the award is made.

(6)   In this section—

  "court" includes a tribunal;
  "damages" means damages for an unlawful act of a public authority; and
  "unlawful" means unlawful under section 6(1).

9 Judicial acts

(1)   Proceedings under section 7(1)(a) in respect of a judicial act may be brought only—

  (a)   by exercising a right of appeal;
  (b)   on an application (in Scotland a petition) for judicial review; or
  (c)   in such other forum as may be prescribed by rules.

(2)   That does not affect any rule of law which prevents a court from being the subject of judicial review.

(3)   In proceedings under this Act in respect of a judicial act done in good faith, damages may not be awarded otherwise than to compensate a person to the extent required by Article 5(5) of the Convention.

(4)   An award of damages permitted by subsection (3) is to be made against the Crown; but no award may be made unless the appropriate person, if not a party to the proceedings, is joined.

(5)   In this section—

> "appropriate person" means the Minister responsible for the court concerned, or a person or government department nominated by him;
> "court" includes a tribunal;
> "judge" includes a member of a tribunal, a justice of the peace and a clerk or other officer entitled to exercise the jurisdiction of a court;
> "judicial act" means a judicial act of a court and includes an act done on the instructions, or on behalf, of a judge; and
> "rules" has the same meaning as in section 7(9).

Remedial action

10 Power to take remedial action

(1)   This section applies if—

- (a) a provision of legislation has been declared under section 4 to be incompatible with a Convention right and, if an appeal lies—
  - (i)   all persons who may appeal have stated in writing that they do not intend to do so;
  - (ii) the time for bringing an appeal has expired and no appeal has been brought within that time; or
  - (iii) an appeal brought within that time has been determined or abandoned; or
- (b) it appears to a Minister of the Crown or Her Majesty in Council that, having regard to a finding of the European Court of Human Rights made after the coming into force of this section in proceedings against the United Kingdom, a provision of legislation is incompatible with an obligation of the United Kingdom arising from the Convention.

(2)   If a Minister of the Crown considers that there are compelling reasons for proceeding under this section, he may by order make such amendments to the legislation as he considers necessary to remove the incompatibility.

(3)   If, in the case of subordinate legislation, a Minister of the Crown considers—

- (a) that it is necessary to amend the primary legislation under which the subordinate legislation in question was made, in order to enable the incompatibility to be removed, and
- (b) that there are compelling reasons for proceeding under this section,

he may by order make such amendments to the primary legislation as he considers necessary.

(4)   This section also applies where the provision in question is in subordinate legislation and has been quashed, or declared invalid, by reason of incompatibility with a Convention right and the Minister proposes to proceed under paragraph 2(b) of Schedule 2.

(5)   If the legislation is an Order in Council, the power conferred by subsection (2) or (3) is exercisable by Her Majesty in Council.

(6)   In this section "legislation" does not include a Measure of the Church Assembly or of the General Synod of the Church of England.

(7)   Schedule 2 makes further provision about remedial orders.

Other rights and proceedings

11 Safeguard for existing human rights

A person's reliance on a Convention right does not restrict—

    (a)   any other right or freedom conferred on him by or under any law having effect in any part of the United Kingdom; or

    (b)   his right to make any claim or bring any proceedings which he could make or bring apart from sections 7 to 9.

12 Freedom of expression

(1)   This section applies if a court is considering whether to grant any relief which, if granted, might affect the exercise of the Convention right to freedom of expression.

(2)   If the person against whom the application for relief is made ("the respondent") is neither present nor represented, no such relief is to be granted unless the court is satisfied—

    (a)   that the applicant has taken all practicable steps to notify the respondent; or

    (b)   that there are compelling reasons why the respondent should not be notified.

(3)   No such relief is to be granted so as to restrain publication before trial unless the court is satisfied that the applicant is likely to establish that publication should not be allowed.

(4)   The court must have particular regard to the importance of the Convention right to freedom of expression and, where the proceedings relate to material which the respondent claims, or which appears to the court, to be journalistic, literary or artistic material (or to conduct connected with such material), to—

    (a)   the extent to which—

        (i)   the material has, or is about to, become available to the public; or

        (ii) it is, or would be, in the public interest for the material to be published;

    (b)   any relevant privacy code.

(5)   In this section—

      "court" includes a tribunal; and

      "relief" includes any remedy or order (other than in criminal proceedings).

13 Freedom of thought, conscience and religion

(1)   If a court's determination of any question arising under this Act might affect the exercise by a religious organisation (itself or its members collectively) of the Convention right to freedom of thought, conscience and religion, it must have particular regard to the importance of that right.

(2)   In this section "court" includes a tribunal.

Derogations and reservations

14 Derogations

(1)   In this Act "designated derogation" means—

> . . .
>
> any derogation by the United Kingdom from an Article of the Convention, or of any protocol to the Convention, which is designated for the purposes of this Act in an order made by the Secretary of State.

(2)   . . .

(3)   If a designated derogation is amended or replaced it ceases to be a designated derogation.

(4)   But subsection (3) does not prevent the Secretary of State from exercising his power under subsection (1). . . to make a fresh designation order in respect of the Article concerned.

(5)   The Secretary of State must by order make such amendments to Schedule 3 as he considers appropriate to reflect—

    (a)   any designation order; or
    (b)   the effect of subsection (3).

(6)   A designation order may be made in anticipation of the making by the United Kingdom of a proposed derogation.

15 Reservations

(1)   In this Act "designated reservation" means—

    (a)   the United Kingdom's reservation to Article 2 of the First Protocol to the Convention; and
    (b)   any other reservation by the United Kingdom to an Article of the Convention, or of any protocol to the Convention, which is designated for the purposes of this Act in an order made by the Secretary of State.

(2)   The text of the reservation referred to in subsection (1)(a) is set out in Part II of Schedule 3.

(3)   If a designated reservation is withdrawn wholly or in part it ceases to be a designated reservation.

(4)   But subsection (3) does not prevent the Secretary of State from exercising his power under subsection (1)(b) to make a fresh designation order in respect of the Article concerned.

(5)   The Secretary of State must by order make such amendments to this Act as he considers appropriate to reflect—

    (a)   any designation order; or
    (b)   the effect of subsection (3).

16 Period for which designated derogations have effect

(1)   If it has not already been withdrawn by the United Kingdom, a designated derogation ceases to have effect for the purposes of this Act—

> . . .
>
> at the end of the period of five years beginning with the date on which the order designating it was made.

(2)   At any time before the period—

    (a) fixed by subsection (1). . ., or

    (b) extended by an order under this subsection,

comes to an end, the Secretary of State may by order extend it by a further period of five years.

(3)   An order under section 14(1). . . ceases to have effect at the end of the period for consideration, unless a resolution has been passed by each House approving the order.

(4)   Subsection (3) does not affect—

    (a) anything done in reliance on the order; or

    (b) the power to make a fresh order under section 14(1). . ..

(5)   In subsection (3) "period for consideration" means the period of forty days beginning with the day on which the order was made.

(6)   In calculating the period for consideration, no account is to be taken of any time during which—

    (a) Parliament is dissolved or prorogued; or

    (b) both Houses are adjourned for more than four days.

(7)   If a designated derogation is withdrawn by the United Kingdom, the Secretary of State must by order make such amendments to this Act as he considers are required to reflect that withdrawal.

17 Periodic review of designated reservations

(1)   The appropriate Minister must review the designated reservation referred to in section 15(1)(a)—

    (a) before the end of the period of five years beginning with the date on which section 1(2) came into force; and

    (b) if that designation is still in force, before the end of the period of five years beginning with the date on which the last report relating to it was laid under subsection (3).

(2)   The appropriate Minister must review each of the other designated reservations (if any)—

    (a) before the end of the period of five years beginning with the date on which the order designating the reservation first came into force; and

    (b) if the designation is still in force, before the end of the period of five years beginning with the date on which the last report relating to it was laid under subsection (3).

(3)   The Minister conducting a review under this section must prepare a report on the result of the review and lay a copy of it before each House of Parliament.

Judges of the European Court of Human Rights

18 Appointment to European Court of Human Rights

(1)   In this section "judicial office" means the office of—

    (a) Lord Justice of Appeal, Justice of the High Court or Circuit judge, in England and Wales;

    (b) judge of the Court of Session or sheriff, in Scotland;

(c) Lord Justice of Appeal, judge of the High Court or county court judge, in Northern Ireland.

(2)   The holder of a judicial office may become a judge of the European Court of Human Rights ("the Court") without being required to relinquish his office.

(3)   But he is not required to perform the duties of his judicial office while he is a judge of the Court.

(4)   In respect of any period during which he is a judge of the Court—

(a) a Lord Justice of Appeal or Justice of the High Court is not to count as a judge of the relevant court for the purposes of section 2(1) or 4(1) of the Supreme Court Act 1981 (maximum number of judges) nor as a judge of the Supreme Court for the purposes of section 12(1) to (6) of that Act (salaries etc);

(b) a judge of the Court of Session is not to count as a judge of that court for the purposes of section 1(1) of the Court of Session Act 1988 (maximum number of judges) or of section 9(1)(c) of the Administration of Justice Act 1973 ("the 1973 Act") (salaries etc);

(c) a Lord Justice of Appeal or judge of the High Court in Northern Ireland is not to count as a judge of the relevant court for the purposes of section 2(1) or 3(1) of the Judicature (Northern Ireland) Act 1978 (maximum number of judges) nor as a judge of the Supreme Court of Northern Ireland for the purposes of section 9(1)(d) of the 1973 Act (salaries etc);

(d) a Circuit judge is not to count as such for the purposes of section 18 of the Courts Act 1971 (salaries etc);

(e) a sheriff is not to count as such for the purposes of section 14 of the Sheriff Courts (Scotland) Act 1907 (salaries etc);

(f) a county court judge of Northern Ireland is not to count as such for the purposes of section 106 of the County Courts Act (Northern Ireland) 1959 (salaries etc).

(5)   If a sheriff principal is appointed a judge of the Court, section 11(1) of the Sheriff Courts (Scotland) Act 1971 (temporary appointment of sheriff principal) applies, while he holds that appointment, as if his office is vacant.

(6)   Schedule 4 makes provision about judicial pensions in relation to the holder of a judicial office who serves as a judge of the Court.

(7)   The Lord Chancellor or the Secretary of State may by order make such transitional provision (including, in particular, provision for a temporary increase in the maximum number of judges) as he considers appropriate in relation to any holder of a judicial office who has completed his service as a judge of the Court.

Parliamentary procedure

19 Statements of compatibility

(1)   A Minister of the Crown in charge of a Bill in either House of Parliament must, before Second Reading of the Bill—

(a) make a statement to the effect that in his view the provisions of the Bill are compatible with the Convention rights ("a statement of compatibility"); or

(b) make a statement to the effect that although he is unable to make a statement of compatibility the government nevertheless wishes the House to proceed with the Bill.

(2)   The statement must be in writing and be published in such manner as the Minister making it considers appropriate.

Supplemental

20 Orders etc under this Act

(1) Any power of a Minister of the Crown to make an order under this Act is exercisable by statutory instrument.

(2) The power of the Lord Chancellor or the Secretary of State to make rules (other than rules of court) under section 2(3) or 7(9) is exercisable by statutory instrument.

(3) Any statutory instrument made under section 14, 15 or 16(7) must be laid before Parliament.

(4) No order may be made by the Lord Chancellor or the Secretary of State under section 1(4), 7(11) or 16(2) unless a draft of the order has been laid before, and approved by, each House of Parliament.

(5) Any statutory instrument made under section 18(7) or Schedule 4, or to which subsection (2) applies, shall be subject to annulment in pursuance of a resolution of either House of Parliament.

(6) The power of a Northern Ireland department to make—

(a) rules under section 2(3)(c) or 7(9)(c), or
(b) an order under section 7(11),

is exercisable by statutory rule for the purposes of the Statutory Rules (Northern Ireland) Order 1979.

(7) Any rules made under section 2(3)(c) or 7(9)(c) shall be subject to negative resolution; and section 41(6) of the Interpretation Act (Northern Ireland) 1954 (meaning of "subject to negative resolution") shall apply as if the power to make the rules were conferred by an Act of the Northern Ireland Assembly.

(8) No order may be made by a Northern Ireland department under section 7(11) unless a draft of the order has been laid before, and approved by, the Northern Ireland Assembly.

21 Interpretation, etc

(1) In this Act—

"amend" includes repeal and apply (with or without modifications);
"the appropriate Minister" means the Minister of the Crown having charge of the appropriate authorised government department (within the meaning of the Crown Proceedings Act 1947);
"the Commission" means the European Commission of Human Rights;
"the Convention" means the Convention for the Protection of Human Rights and Fundamental Freedoms, agreed by the Council of Europe at Rome on 4th November 1950 as it has effect for the time being in relation to the United Kingdom;
"declaration of incompatibility" means a declaration under section 4;
"Minister of the Crown" has the same meaning as in the Ministers of the Crown Act 1975;
"Northern Ireland Minister" includes the First Minister and the deputy First Minister in Northern Ireland;
"primary legislation" means any—
(a) public general Act;
(b) local and personal Act;
(c) private Act;
(d) Measure of the Church Assembly;

    (e)   Measure of the General Synod of the Church of England;

    (f)   Order in Council—

        (i)   made in exercise of Her Majesty's Royal Prerogative;

        (ii) made under section 38(1)(a) of the Northern Ireland Constitution Act 1973 or the corresponding provision of the Northern Ireland Act 1998; or

        (iii) amending an Act of a kind mentioned in paragraph (a), (b) or (c);

and includes an order or other instrument made under primary legislation (otherwise than by the National Assembly for Wales, a member of the Scottish Executive, a Northern Ireland Minister or a Northern Ireland department) to the extent to which it operates to bring one or more provisions of that legislation into force or amends any primary legislation;

"the First Protocol" means the protocol to the Convention agreed at Paris on 20th March 1952;

"the Sixth Protocol" means the protocol to the Convention agreed at Strasbourg on 28th April 1983;

"the Eleventh Protocol" means the protocol to the Convention (restructuring the control machinery established by the Convention) agreed at Strasbourg on 11th May 1994;

"remedial order" means an order under section 10;

"subordinate legislation" means any—

    (a)   Order in Council other than one—

        (i)   made in exercise of Her Majesty's Royal Prerogative;

        (ii) made under section 38(1)(a) of the Northern Ireland Constitution Act 1973 or the corresponding provision of the Northern Ireland Act 1998; or

        (iii) amending an Act of a kind mentioned in the definition of primary legislation;

    (b)   Act of the Scottish Parliament;

    (c)   Act of the Parliament of Northern Ireland;

    (d)   Measure of the Assembly established under section 1 of the Northern Ireland Assembly Act 1973;

    (e)   Act of the Northern Ireland Assembly;

    (f)   order, rules, regulations, scheme, warrant, byelaw or other instrument made under primary legislation (except to the extent to which it operates to bring one or more provisions of that legislation into force or amends any primary legislation);

    (g)   order, rules, regulations, scheme, warrant, byelaw or other instrument made under legislation mentioned in paragraph (b), (c), (d) or (e) or made under an Order in Council applying only to Northern Ireland;

    (h)   order, rules, regulations, scheme, warrant, byelaw or other instrument made by a member of the Scottish Executive, a Northern Ireland Minister or a Northern Ireland department in exercise of prerogative or other executive functions of Her Majesty which are exercisable by such a person on behalf of Her Majesty;

"transferred matters" has the same meaning as in the Northern Ireland Act 1998; and

"tribunal" means any tribunal in which legal proceedings may be brought.

(2)   The references in paragraphs (b) and (c) of section 2(1) to Articles are to Articles of the Convention as they had effect immediately before the coming into force of the Eleventh Protocol.

(3)   The reference in paragraph (d) of section 2(1) to Article 46 includes a reference to Articles 32 and 54 of the Convention as they had effect immediately before the coming into force of the Eleventh Protocol.

(4)   The references in section 2(1) to a report or decision of the Commission or a decision of the Committee of Ministers include references to a report or decision made as provided by paragraphs 3, 4 and 6 of Article 5 of the Eleventh Protocol (transitional provisions).

(5)   Any liability under the Army Act 1955, the Air Force Act 1955 or the Naval Discipline Act 1957 to suffer death for an offence is replaced by a liability to imprisonment for life or any less punishment authorised by those Acts; and those Acts shall accordingly have effect with the necessary modifications.

22 Short title, commencement, application and extent

(1)   This Act may be cited as the Human Rights Act 1998.

(2)   Sections 18, 20 and 21(5) and this section come into force on the passing of this Act.

(3)   The other provisions of this Act come into force on such day as the Secretary of State may by order appoint; and different days may be appointed for different purposes.

(4)   Paragraph (b) of subsection (1) of section 7 applies to proceedings brought by or at the instigation of a public authority whenever the act in question took place; but otherwise that subsection does not apply to an act taking place before the coming into force of that section.

(5)   This Act binds the Crown.

(6)   This Act extends to Northern Ireland.

(7)   Section 21(5), so far as it relates to any provision contained in the Army Act 1955, the Air Force Act 1955 or the Naval Discipline Act 1957, extends to any place to which that provision extends.

SCHEDULE 1
The Articles

. . .

PART I
THE CONVENTION: RIGHTS AND FREEDOMS

Article 2
Right to life

1 Everyone's right to life shall be protected by law. No one shall be deprived of his life intentionally save in the execution of a sentence of a court following his conviction of a crime for which this penalty is provided by law.

2 Deprivation of life shall not be regarded as inflicted in contravention of this Article when it results from the use of force which is no more than absolutely necessary:

(a)   in defence of any person from unlawful violence;
(b)   in order to effect a lawful arrest or to prevent the escape of a person lawfully detained;
(c)   in action lawfully taken for the purpose of quelling a riot or insurrection.

Article 3
Prohibition of torture

No one shall be subjected to torture or to inhuman or degrading treatment or punishment.

Article 4
Prohibition of slavery and forced labour

1 No one shall be held in slavery or servitude.

2 No one shall be required to perform forced or compulsory labour.

3 For the purpose of this Article the term "forced or compulsory labour" shall not include:

(a) any work required to be done in the ordinary course of detention imposed according to the provisions of Article 5 of this Convention or during conditional release from such detention;

(b) any service of a military character or, in case of conscientious objectors in countries where they are recognised, service exacted instead of compulsory military service;

(c) any service exacted in case of an emergency or calamity threatening the life or well-being of the community;

(d) any work or service which forms part of normal civic obligations.

Article 5
Right to liberty and security

1 Everyone has the right to liberty and security of person. No one shall be deprived of his liberty save in the following cases and in accordance with a procedure prescribed by law:

(a) the lawful detention of a person after conviction by a competent court;

(b) the lawful arrest or detention of a person for non-compliance with the lawful order of a court or in order to secure the fulfilment of any obligation prescribed by law;

(c) the lawful arrest or detention of a person effected for the purpose of bringing him before the competent legal authority on reasonable suspicion of having committed an offence or when it is reasonably considered necessary to prevent his committing an offence or fleeing after having done so;

(d) the detention of a minor by lawful order for the purpose of educational supervision or his lawful detention for the purpose of bringing him before the competent legal authority;

(e) the lawful detention of persons for the prevention of the spreading of infectious diseases, of persons of unsound mind, alcoholics or drug addicts or vagrants;

(f) the lawful arrest or detention of a person to prevent his effecting an unauthorised entry into the country or of a person against whom action is being taken with a view to deportation or extradition.

2 Everyone who is arrested shall be informed promptly, in a language which he understands, of the reasons for his arrest and of any charge against him.

3 Everyone arrested or detained in accordance with the provisions of paragraph 1(c) of this Article shall be brought promptly before a judge or other officer authorised by law to exercise judicial power and shall be entitled to trial within a reasonable time or to release pending trial. Release may be conditioned by guarantees to appear for trial.

4 Everyone who is deprived of his liberty by arrest or detention shall be entitled to take proceedings by which the lawfulness of his detention shall be decided speedily by a court and his release ordered if the detention is not lawful.

5 Everyone who has been the victim of arrest or detention in contravention of the provisions of this Article shall have an enforceable right to compensation.

Article 6
Right to a fair trial

1 In the determination of his civil rights and obligations or of any criminal charge against him, everyone is entitled to a fair and public hearing within a reasonable time by an independent and impartial tribunal established by law. Judgment shall be pronounced publicly but the press and public may be excluded from all or part of the trial in the interest of morals, public order or national security in a democratic society, where the interests of juveniles or the protection of the private life of the parties so require, or to the extent strictly necessary in the opinion of the court in special circumstances where publicity would prejudice the interests of justice.

2 Everyone charged with a criminal offence shall be presumed innocent until proved guilty according to law.

3 Everyone charged with a criminal offence has the following minimum rights:

    (a) to be informed promptly, in a language which he understands and in detail, of the nature and cause of the accusation against him;
    (b) to have adequate time and facilities for the preparation of his defence;
    (c) to defend himself in person or through legal assistance of his own choosing or, if he has not sufficient means to pay for legal assistance, to be given it free when the interests of justice so require;
    (d) to examine or have examined witnesses against him and to obtain the attendance and examination of witnesses on his behalf under the same conditions as witnesses against him;
    (e) to have the free assistance of an interpreter if he cannot understand or speak the language used in court.

Article 7
No punishment without law

1 No one shall be held guilty of any criminal offence on account of any act or omission which did not constitute a criminal offence under national or international law at the time when it was committed. Nor shall a heavier penalty be imposed than the one that was applicable at the time the criminal offence was committed.

2 This Article shall not prejudice the trial and punishment of any person for any act or omission which, at the time when it was committed, was criminal according to the general principles of law recognised by civilised nations.

Article 8
Right to respect for private and family life

1 Everyone has the right to respect for his private and family life, his home and his correspondence.

2 There shall be no interference by a public authority with the exercise of this right except such as is in accordance with the law and is necessary in a democratic society in the interests of national security, public safety or the economic well-being of the country, for the prevention of disorder or crime, for the protection of health or morals, or for the protection of the rights and freedoms of others.

Article 9
Freedom of thought, conscience and religion

1 Everyone has the right to freedom of thought, conscience and religion; this right includes freedom to change his religion or belief and freedom, either alone or in community with others and in public or private, to manifest his religion or belief, in worship, teaching, practice and observance.

2 Freedom to manifest one's religion or beliefs shall be subject only to such limitations as are prescribed by law and are necessary in a democratic society in the interests of public safety, for the protection of public order, health or morals, or for the protection of the rights and freedoms of others.

Article 10
Freedom of expression

1 Everyone has the right to freedom of expression. This right shall include freedom to hold opinions and to receive and impart information and ideas without interference by public authority and regardless of frontiers. This Article shall not prevent States from requiring the licensing of broadcasting, television or cinema enterprises.

2 The exercise of these freedoms, since it carries with it duties and responsibilities, may be subject to such formalities, conditions, restrictions or penalties as are prescribed by law and are necessary in a democratic society, in the interests of national security, territorial integrity or public safety, for the prevention of disorder or crime, for the protection of health or morals, for the protection of the reputation or rights of others, for preventing the disclosure of information received in confidence, or for maintaining the authority and impartiality of the judiciary.

Article 11
Freedom of assembly and association

1 Everyone has the right to freedom of peaceful assembly and to freedom of association with others, including the right to form and to join trade unions for the protection of his interests.

2 No restrictions shall be placed on the exercise of these rights other than such as are prescribed by law and are necessary in a democratic society in the interests of national security or public safety, for the prevention of disorder or crime, for the protection of health or morals or for the protection of the rights and freedoms of others. This Article shall not prevent the imposition of lawful restrictions on the exercise of these rights by members of the armed forces, of the police or of the administration of the State.

Article 12
Right to marry
Men and women of marriageable age have the right to marry and to found a family, according to the national laws governing the exercise of this right.

Article 14
Prohibition of discrimination
The enjoyment of the rights and freedoms set forth in this Convention shall be secured without discrimination on any ground such as sex, race, colour, language, religion, political or other opinion, national or social origin, association with a national minority, property, birth or other status.

Article 16
Restrictions on political activity of aliens
Nothing in Articles 10, 11 and 14 shall be regarded as preventing the High Contracting Parties from imposing restrictions on the political activity of aliens.

Article 17
Prohibition of abuse of rights
Nothing in this Convention may be interpreted as implying for any State, group or person any right to engage in any activity or perform any act aimed at the destruction of any of the rights and freedoms set forth herein or at their limitation to a greater extent than is provided for in the Convention.

Article 18
Limitation on use of restrictions on rights
The restrictions permitted under this Convention to the said rights and freedoms shall not be applied for any purpose other than those for which they have been prescribed.

PART II
THE FIRST PROTOCOL

Article 1
Protection of property
Every natural or legal person is entitled to the peaceful enjoyment of his possessions. No one shall be deprived of his possessions except in the public interest and subject to the conditions provided for by law and by the general principles of international law.

The preceding provisions shall not, however, in any way impair the right of a State to enforce such laws as it deems necessary to control the use of property in accordance with the general interest or to secure the payment of taxes or other contributions or penalties.

Article 2
Right to education
No person shall be denied the right to education. In the exercise of any functions which it assumes in relation to education and to teaching, the State shall respect the right of parents to ensure such education and teaching in conformity with their own religious and philosophical convictions.

Article 3
Right to free elections
The High Contracting Parties undertake to hold free elections at reasonable intervals by secret ballot, under conditions which will ensure the free expression of the opinion of the people in the choice of the legislature.

PART III
THE SIXTH PROTOCOL

Article 1
Abolition of the death penalty
The death penalty shall be abolished. No one shall be condemned to such penalty or executed.

Article 2
Death penalty in time of war
A State may make provision in its law for the death penalty in respect of acts committed in time of war or of imminent threat of war; such penalty shall be applied only in the instances laid down in the law and in accordance with its provisions. The State shall communicate to the Secretary General of the Council of Europe the relevant provisions of that law.

SCHEDULE 2
Remedial Orders

. . .

Orders

1 (1) A remedial order may—

   (a) contain such incidental, supplemental, consequential or transitional provision as the person making it considers appropriate;
   (b) be made so as to have effect from a date earlier than that on which it is made;
   (c) make provision for the delegation of specific functions;
   (d) make different provision for different cases.

(2)   The power conferred by sub-paragraph (1)(a) includes—

   (a) power to amend primary legislation (including primary legislation other than that which contains the incompatible provision); and
   (b) power to amend or revoke subordinate legislation (including subordinate legislation other than that which contains the incompatible provision).

(3)   A remedial order may be made so as to have the same extent as the legislation which it affects.

(4)   No person is to be guilty of an offence solely as a result of the retrospective effect of a remedial order.

Procedure

2 No remedial order may be made unless—

   (a) a draft of the order has been approved by a resolution of each House of Parliament made after the end of the period of 60 days beginning with the day on which the draft was laid; or
   (b) it is declared in the order that it appears to the person making it that, because of the urgency of the matter, it is necessary to make the order without a draft being so approved.

Orders laid in draft

3 (1) No draft may be laid under paragraph 2(a) unless—

   (a) the person proposing to make the order has laid before Parliament a document which contains a draft of the proposed order and the required information; and
   (b) the period of 60 days, beginning with the day on which the document required by this sub-paragraph was laid, has ended.

(2)   If representations have been made during that period, the draft laid under paragraph 2(a) must be accompanied by a statement containing—

(a) a summary of the representations; and
(b) if, as a result of the representations, the proposed order has been changed, details of the changes.

Urgent cases

4 (1) If a remedial order ("the original order") is made without being approved in draft, the person making it must lay it before Parliament, accompanied by the required information, after it is made.

(2)   If representations have been made during the period of 60 days beginning with the day on which the original order was made, the person making it must (after the end of that period) lay before Parliament a statement containing—

(a) a summary of the representations; and
(b) if, as a result of the representations, he considers it appropriate to make changes to the original order, details of the changes.

(3)   If sub-paragraph (2)(b) applies, the person making the statement must—

(a) make a further remedial order replacing the original order; and
(b) lay the replacement order before Parliament.

(4)   If, at the end of the period of 120 days beginning with the day on which the original order was made, a resolution has not been passed by each House approving the original or replacement order, the order ceases to have effect (but without that affecting anything previously done under either order or the power to make a fresh remedial order).

Definitions

5 In this Schedule—

"representations" means representations about a remedial order (or proposed remedial order) made to the person making (or proposing to make) it and includes any relevant Parliamentary report or resolution; and
"required information" means—
(a) an explanation of the incompatibility which the order (or proposed order) seeks to remove, including particulars of the relevant declaration, finding or order; and
(b) a statement of the reasons for proceeding under section 10 and for making an order in those terms.

Calculating periods

6 In calculating any period for the purposes of this Schedule, no account is to be taken of any time during which—

(a) Parliament is dissolved or prorogued; or
(b) both Houses are adjourned for more than four days.

. . .

SCHEDULE 3
Derogation and Reservation

. . .

PART I
. . .

PART II
RESERVATION

At the time of signing the present (First) Protocol, I declare that, in view of certain provisions of the Education Acts in the United Kingdom, the principle affirmed in the second sentence of Article 2 is accepted by the United Kingdom only so far as it is compatible with the provision of efficient instruction and training, and the avoidance of unreasonable public expenditure.

Dated 20 March 1952. Made by the United Kingdom Permanent Representative to the Council of Europe.

SCHEDULE 4
Judicial Pensions

. . .

Duty to make orders about pensions

1 (1) The appropriate Minister must by order make provision with respect to pensions payable to or in respect of any holder of a judicial office who serves as an ECHR judge.

(2)   A pensions order must include such provision as the Minister making it considers is necessary to secure that—

(a) an ECHR judge who was, immediately before his appointment as an ECHR judge, a member of a judicial pension scheme is entitled to remain as a member of that scheme;

(b) the terms on which he remains a member of the scheme are those which would have been applicable had he not been appointed as an ECHR judge; and

(c) entitlement to benefits payable in accordance with the scheme continues to be determined as if, while serving as an ECHR judge, his salary was that which would (but for section 18(4)) have been payable to him in respect of his continuing service as the holder of his judicial office.

Contributions

2 A pensions order may, in particular, make provision—

(a) for any contributions which are payable by a person who remains a member of a scheme as a result of the order, and which would otherwise be payable by deduction from his salary, to be made otherwise than by deduction from his salary as an ECHR judge; and

(b) for such contributions to be collected in such manner as may be determined by the administrators of the scheme.

Amendments of other enactments

3 A pensions order may amend any provision of, or made under, a pensions Act in such manner and to such extent as the Minister making the order considers necessary or expedient to ensure the proper administration of any scheme to which it relates.

Definitions

4 In this Schedule—

"appropriate Minister" means—

(a) in relation to any judicial office whose jurisdiction is exercisable exclusively in relation to Scotland, the Secretary of State; and

(b) otherwise, the Lord Chancellor;

"ECHR judge" means the holder of a judicial office who is serving as a judge of the Court;

"judicial pension scheme" means a scheme established by and in accordance with a pensions Act;

"pensions Act" means—

(a) the County Courts Act (Northern Ireland) 1959;

(b) the Sheriffs' Pensions (Scotland) Act 1961;

(c) the Judicial Pensions Act 1981; or

(d) the Judicial Pensions and Retirement Act 1993; and

"pensions order" means an order made under paragraph 1.

Index

Footnotes (f) are indexed only if they cover material not mentioned in the text on the same page.

ABC trial, 353-4, 356
Abel, Richard, 386, 424, 425f
Aboriginal Women's Council (Canada), 213
accountability, 2, 24, 87
  democratic, policing, 101
  lethal force, 141-2, 143
  political, 87
  prisons, 217, 219, 239, 245, 278
    establishing, 246-53
    legislation, 247
    political, 250
    prison staff, 232
    privatised prisons, 252-3
  public order, 87
  terrorism prevention, 109, 110-11
accreditation
  legal advisers at police station, 182
'active citizenship', 65, 66, 67, 101, 407-8, 412
adjudication, 52-6
  antifoundationalist view, 53
  foundationalist view, 52-3
  Human Rights Act, 21-2
  judicial, 21-2, 48
  lack of certainty, 55
  nonfoundationalist view, 53
  see also judiciary
advertising
  freedom of expression, 10, 385
  tobacco, 385
Advertising Standards Authority, 34
affray, 78f
ageism, 391
aggravated trespass, 70, 84f
Albright, Madeleine, 373
amicus **briefs**, 31
Amnesty International, 33, 105, 107f, 121, 238

Amnesty International—*contd*
  Northern Ireland, 106, 137, 140, 153, 160, 172
Amsterdam Treaty, 2
Anglo-Irish Agreement (1985), 129, 131
animal rights protest
  as terrorism, 127, 128f
anti-abortion campaigners, 32
anti-foundationalism, 52, 53
anti-pornography campaigns, 33
  see also **pornography**
anti-social behaviour, 66, 67
  orders, 70, 84, 86
anti-terrorism measures *see* **terrorism**
appeals
  terrorist cases, 157-8
Arden, M., 292
'Arms to Iraq' affair, 340, 362-3, 372
assembly *see* **freedom of assembly**
Assisted Prison Visits Unit, 257
association *see* **freedom of association**
asylum
  detention centres, 227
  law, 119
atheoreticism, 8, 9, 11, 14
authoritarian state thesis, 63f

bail
  terrorism offences, 132
Bailey, S.H., 74, 167, 179
Baker , Kenneth, 222
Bamforth, N., 34
Bank of England
  publication of minutes, 333
Bar Council, 34
Barak-Glantz, I., 228
Barlinnie Special Unit, 228
Barnard, C., 87
Barnett, Anthony, 24

'Battle of the Beanfield', 82
Bauman, Zygmunt, 406
Beatson, J., 38
Belfast Agreement 1998, 2
Belmarsh prison, 366
Bennett, C.J., 314
Bennett Inquiry and Report, 137
Bentley, Derek, 163
Between the Lines, 186
The Bill, 186
Bill of Rights, 11f, 18, 24, 31, 42f, 218,
      434
   entrenched, 25
bin Laden, Osama, 108f
binding over, 79, 80
Birch, D., 191
Birkinshaw, P., 364
Birmingham Six, 108, 154, 155, 156,
      163, 171, 238
'black letter' tradition, 8f
Black September, 114
Blair, Tony, 103, 110, 408
   cronies, 3
   see also New Labour
Blake, George, 350
blasphemy, 385
Bloody Sunday, 138
   Inquiry, 40, 52, 155, 331, 368, 376
Blunt, Anthony, 350
Boards of Visitors, 248, 250-1
   disciplinary hearings, 262-3
Booth, Cherie, 290, 321
Bottoms, A., 239, 261
Bowler, Sheila, 164, 171
Boyle, J., 311, 314
breach of confidence
   commercial, 374-5
   contempt of court, 357f, 359, 367
   freedom of speech restriction, 381
   privacy, 287, 289-90, 298
breach of the peace, 70-1, 71f, 77-9
   binding over, 79, 80
   European Court of Human Rights
      support, 79
   police powers, 78-9
   proportionality of powers, 79
Bridgewater Four, 164
Bringing Rights Home, 1, 165
Bristol riots, 63, 64-5, 76
British Academy of Forensic Sciences, 198
'Britishness', 3f
Brittan, Leon, 136, 221, 269, 270
Brixton Prison, 216, 252
Brixton riots, 63, 64-5, 76
broadcasting bans, 47, 117, 129, 152,
      160, 382

Broadcasting Standards Commission
   privacy, 284
Broadwater Farm, 76
Brooke, Lord Justice, 51
Brown, Beverley, 423
Brown, Wendy, 306, 377, 413, 425, 426,
      427
Browne-Wilkinson, Lord, 50-1
Brownlee, I., 177
Bryans, S., 227
Bulger, James, 272, 327
Burgess, Guy, 350
Butler, Judith, 426
Buxton, R., 38

Callan, Kevin, 164
Campaign for Nuclear Disarmament
   security risk, 351, 356
Campbell, Duncan, 352-4
Canada
   Aboriginal Women's Council, 213
   Charter of Rights and Freedoms
      1982, 4f, 10-11, 38, 195
   fair trial post-Charter, 165
   family rights, 11
   import of ideas from, 9
   police managerialism, 97f
   rape case disclosures, 201-5, 209-10,
      213
   standing, 32
   terrorism, 121, 122f
   Women's Legal Education and
      Action Fund (LEAF), 213
capitalism
   collapse of communism and, 15
Cardiff Three, 163, 171
   legal adviser role, 191
Carlos the Jackal, 108f
Castlereagh Holding Centre, 106, 185f
censorship, 381
   prisoner's mail, 253, 254
Chan, J., 187
Charter 88, 24
Chief Inspector of Prisons (CIP), 216,
      218-19, 250, 251, 277, 278
child curfew orders, 84, 86
child safety orders, 80f, 84
Child Support Agency, 313
children
   in adult courts, 174
   Convention on the Rights of the
      Child, 403
   prison visiting, 257, 259
Choongh, S., 171
citizenship, 2, 14-15, 84
   'active', 65, 66, 67, 101, 407-8, 412

citizenship—*contd*
community concept, 65-6, 67, 67f, 68
EU, 408-9
group-differentiated, 410
self-policing, 101
sexual orientation discrimination,
411-12
civil disobedience, 74
civil liberties
British model of rights
incorporation, 5
common law role *see* **civil liberties
tradition**
function variation over time, 11
historic disputes, 3-4
more than human rights, 17-18
reasons for legislation, 5-18
civil liberties tradition, 3, 4
atheoreticism, 14
boundary classifications ignored, 7
common law role, 5
continuity, 6-15
cosmopolitanism, 6, 7, 8
equality rights, 387-405
freedom of expression, 380-7
legalism within, 8
neglect of available resources, 9-10
omissions, 8, 9-11
'oppositional politics', 12
past role, 6
remedies, 7
undermining, 3-4
unpopular causes, 7
weaknesses, 8-9
civil service
class superiority, 343-8, 355
homosexuals as enemy (US), 349-
50
secrecy to maintain status, 343-8
Thatcherism reforms, 345
Clark, Alan, 362
Clarke, Kenneth, 222, 251
Clarke, Liam, 336f
class system
secrecy used to maintain, 343-8, 355
Clinton, President Bill, 319, 414
closed circuit TV cameras, 14, 312
motorway CCTV, 311, 313-14
Code of Minimum Living Standards,
244
**Code of Practice on the Protection of
the Dignity of Women and Men at
Work**, 417
Cohen, Jean, 306-7, 308, 309, 427
reflexive law, 431-2
regulated autonomy, 432

Cold War
defections, 350
commercial confidentiality, 374-5
commercial espionage, 311, 338
Commission for Racial Equality, 393
**Committee on the Administration of
Justice (CAJ)**, 172
Committee of Ministers
enforcement of ECHR awards, 19
common good
recognition and, 412
common law
binding over powers, 77, 79
breach of the peace, 70-1, 77-9
Canadian Charter of Rights and, 38
constitutionalism, 42-3, 47, 52
erosion of rights by government, 41-
4
failing to obey instructions, 78f
foundational role, 43
HRA and, 37-8
public order, 77-9
communism, collapse, 15
Communist Party
repression by security services, 350-1
community concept, 65-6, 67
public order, 67f, 68, 83
community policing, 96
compatibility
constitutional review of legislation,
26
declarations of incompatibility, 22,
26
judicial discretion to ensure, 45
statement, 23
confessions
exclusion, 190
improperly obtained, 156, 157
terrorism offences, 132, 135, 137
constitutionalism
anti-foundationalism, 52, 53
common law, 47, 52
courts and parliament, 5
foundationalism, 52-3
nonfoundationalism, 53-5
constitutions
English, 48-9
contempt of court
breach of confidence, 357f, 359, 367
national security, 367
**Convention on the Elimination of All
Forms of Racial Discrimination**,
402
**Convention on the Elimination of
Discrimination Against Women**,
402

Convention on the Rights of the Child,
      403
Cooper, D., 91
Coppel, J., 28
Cops, 186
corporations
      commercial confidentiality, 374-5
      commercial espionage, 338
      international, 13
      tobacco industry, 13f, 385
correspondence
      prisoners, 295, 297
            family members, 258
            legal adviser, 253-6
      privacy, 294, 296
cosmopolitanism, 2
      civil liberties tradition, 6, 7, 8
Council of Europe, 2, 13
court-martial system, 174
courts
      Convention Rights and law
            development, 37
      discretion, 36-8
      equality in, 393-5
      European Convention and, 35
      horizontal effect of HRA on, 35-8
      judiciary as terrorist targets, 155
      non-discrimination and, 393-5
      non-jury trial
      Criminal Justice (Mode of Trial) Bill,
            171f
      Diplock courts, 132, 135-6, 137, 156,
            171
      parliamentary supremacy and, 44
      as public authorities, 35
      public order, 94-5
      terrorist cases
            appeals, 157-8
            biased summings-up, 156, 170
            confession exclusion, 156, 157
            Diplock courts, 132, 135-6, 137, 156,
                  171
            House of Lords, 158
            judiciary as targets, 155
            Northern Ireland, 155-6
            United Kingdom, 156
covert surveillance, 176, 280, 282-3,
      285-6
      privacy, 295
      see also **surveillance**
Crime and Disorder Act 1998, 68-9, 70,
      83-4, 85
Criminal Bar Association, 198
Criminal Cases Review Commission,
      157, 164, 198
Criminal Defence Service, 189

criminal justice
      politicisation, 217, 220-7
**Criminal Justice and Public Order Act
      1994,** 68, 83-4, 85
**Criminal Justice (Terrorism and
      Conspiracy) Act 1998,** 103
criminal law
      critical theory impact, 177-9
critical pragmatism, 378-9, 429-34
critical theory
      feminist critiques, 177
      governance, 178
      impact, 177-9
Cross, M., 67
cross-examination
      defence tactics, 199-200, 207-9, 211
      fairness, 209-11
      intimidation and insinuation, 207,
            208, 210-11
      'pornographic vignette', 208, 212
      rape cases
            disclosures, 201-5, 209-10, 213
            shield, 208, 209-10
Crown Prosecution Service, 165
The Crying Game, 116
cults, 161
Cumaraswamy, Dato Param, 106
custody see **detention**
custody officer, 180, 181, 189
custody sheets, 180

D-Notices, 352-3, 365
Dalyell, Tam, 357
de la Billiere, General Peter, 334
de Sousa Santos, Boaventura, 379-80
de Than, C., 167
death penalty
      terrorism offences, 134-5
deaths in custody, 185
**Declaration on the Elimination of All
      Forms of Intolerance and of
      Discrimination Based on Religion
      or Belief,** 403
declarations of incompatibility, 22
      delegated legislation, 22f
      remedial action, 22
declaratory relief, 19
defamation, 43, 289, 381
      excessive awards, 382
      privacy, 303
**Defence, Press and Broadcasting
      Committee,** 352f
      D-Notices, 352-3, 365
degrading treatment
      anti-terrorist practices, 106
      pornography, 420-1, 427

degrading treatment—*contd*
prisons, 216, 252, 267
dehumanising treatment
pornography, 420-1, 427
delegated legislation
declarations of incompatibility, 22f
democracy
human rights restrictions in, 27, 248,
295, 296, 332
judicialisation, 47-8
liberal democracy communism, 15
protest value, 57, 58
detention
assault allegations, 185
custody officer, 180, 181, 189
custody sheets, 180
deaths in custody, 185
legal advice access, 166f
mistreatment of suspects, 153, 154
reviews, 180
taping interviews, 180
terrorism offences, 133, 153, 170
time limits, 180
devolution, 1, 13, 407
Dickson, B., 109
Diplock courts, 132, 135-6, 137, 156, 171
disability discrimination
direct, 398
Disability Discrimination Act (1995),
392, 393
indirect, 399-400
justification, 398-9
positive action, 400-1
Disability Discrimination Act (1995),
392, 393
Disability Rights Commission, 393
disclosure, 174, 175
criminal record, 288
discretion of CPS and police, 197-8
equality of arms, 196
fishing expeditions, 197
Guidelines on Disclosure, 198
journalists' sources, 42
Official Secrets Acts lifelong ban,
360
principle, 196-9
prosecution concealment, 197
public interest, 198, 290, 291
rape cases, 201-5, 209-10, 213
complainants' records, 195, 199-
201
counselling centre records, 195,
201-5
fishing expeditions, 203, 204
medical evidence, 199-201, 203,
204-5

disclosure—*contd*
rape cases—*contd*
principle, 196-9
sex abuse allegations, 288-9
third parties, 199
undermining prosecution case, 197
unused material, 197
see also **rape cases**
discretion, 8, 36-8
CPS and police disclosure, 197-8
judicial review, 29
policing, 96-8
prisons, 245-6
discipline, 263
release, 268-9, 271, 275-7
public order, 57, 88, 96-8
to ensure compatibility, 45
discrimination
direct, 398
disability *see* **disability discrimination**
European Convention Article 14,
403-5
indirect, 399-400, 404
justification, 397-401, 404
genuine occupational qualification,
398
insurance policies, 398
national security, 398
private members' clubs, 398
religious, Northern Ireland, 152
sex *see* **sex discrimination**
sexual orientation *see* **sexual
orientation discrimination**
see also **equality**
Dixon, D., 85, 96, 100, 168, 178, 184,
185, 188
domestic violence, 195
see also **rape cases**
Downes, D., 57-8, 64, 76
'Downing Street nanny', 290, 321
Duffy, P., 38
duty solicitors
funding and training, 189
Dworkin, Andrea, 419
Dworkin, Ronald, 403, 422, 431

eco-terrorism, 161
economic espionage, 311, 338
employment vetting, 297, 311
English constitution, 48-9
Equal Opportunities Commission, 392
equality, 377
ageism, 391
anti-discrimination law, 389-96
citizenship *see* **citizenship**
civil liberties tradition, 387-405

equality—contd
as consistent treatment, 398
critical pragmatism, 378-9, 429-34
difference and diversity in UK, 405-6
disability *see* **disability discrimination**
discrimination *see* **discrimination** *and individual types*
'equality mainstreaming', 391
European Charter of Fundamental Rights, 396
European Commission on Human Rights, 404-5
European Convention, 392
Article 14, 403-5
margin of appreciation, 404
European law, 395-6
European Social Charter, 403
gender norms, 427
'groupiness', 410, 413, 429, 430
as moral superiority, 406, 429
hate speech, 423, 425
Hepple Review, 397, 399, 400, 406, 407
Human Rights Act (1998), 392
immigration, 392
international conventions, 402-3
International Labour Organisation, 403
interpretation of legislation, 393-4
judiciary, 393-5
labour lawyers, 403
legislation, 390-3
interpretation, 393-4
marital status, 391
mixophilia, 406
mixophobia, 406
multiculturalism, 378, 410, 413, 431
nationalism *see* **nationalism**
Northern Ireland, 391, 393
Parekh Report, 376, 380, 389, 406, 407, 413, 431
political opinions, 391
politics of belonging, 407-8
positive action, 400-1
racism *see* **racial discrimination**
recognition *see* **recognition**
religious belief, 391, 403, 405
sex *see* **sex discrimination**
sexual orientation *see* **sexual orientation discrimination**
social inclusion and exclusion, 378, 431
through difference, 406-27
see also sexual harassment
equality of arms
disclosure principle, 196
fair trial, 174

Equality Commission Northern Ireland (ECNI), 129, 393
Etzioni, Amitai, 306, 325-6
European Charter of Fundamental Rights, 396
European Commission on Human Rights, 160, 404-5
European Committee for the Prevention of Torture (CPT), 106, 215, 216, 250, 251-2, 278
European Convention on Human Rights, 2, 13, 18-21
Article 6
wording, 173-4
see also **fair trial**
Article 8 privacy, 404
see also **privacy**
Article 14 discrimination, 403-5
justification, 404
margin of appreciation, 404
see also **discrimination**
complainants, 18-19
court, 19
derogation, 160
equality rights, 392
individual petition, 18-19
interpretation, 19-20
judicial discretion to ensure compatibility, 45
legal persons, 19f
limitation on rights, 20, 27
living instruments, 20
margin of appreciation, 21, 28, 37, 296, 332, 404
privacy, 279, 288, 292-8
complexity, 292-3
family life, 294-5
limitations, 295-6
margin of appreciation, 296
positive and negative obligations, 293, 294-5
private life, 293-4
proportionality doctrine, 20, 27, 28-9
public protest rights, 61-2
remedies, 19, 37f
not in HRA, 29-30, 37f
restrictions
legitimate aim, 27, 248
necessary in democratic state, 27, 248, 295, 296, 332
non-discriminatory, 27
prescribed by law, 27
proportionality, 20, 27, 28-9
uniformity across states, 20
'victim', 19

European Convention on the Suppression of Terrorism, 118
European Court of Human Rights, 19, 159-60
  anti-terrorist practices, 106, 107, 151
  breach of the peace, 79
  declaratory relief, 19
  freedom of speech/expression, 384
  just satisfaction award, 19
  membership, 19
  prisons/prisoners, 241, 242, 248
European Prison Rules, 243
European Social Charter
  equality, 403
European Union, 13
  Amsterdam Treaty, 2
  citizenship, 408-9
  Code of Practice on the Protection of the Dignity of Women and Men at Work, 417
  human rights, 2
  Nice Treaty, 2
  tobacco advertising, 385
  UK nation state concerns, 3
evidence
  compelled, 175
  confessions *see* **confessions**
  disclosure *see* **disclosure**
  exclusion, 176
  fabrication, 169
Ewing, K., 47, 48, 83, 167, 337, 348, 354
Excitable Speech **(Butler)**, 426
exclusion orders, 125, 133, 172
exclusion zones, 79
expression *see* **freedom of speech/ expression**

fair trial
  access to legal advice *see* **legal advice**
  Article 6 of European Convention, 173-7
    judiciary attitude to, 176-7
  biased summings-up, 156, 170
  children in adult courts, 174
  civil liberties textbook tradition, 167-79
  compelled evidence, 175
  confession exclusion, 190
  critical theory impact, 177-9
  delay, 174
  disclosure *see* **disclosure**
  equality of arms, 174, 196
  exclusion of unfair evidence, 176
  fabrication of evidence, 169
  guilty pleas, 164
  Human Rights Act and, 165-7

fair trial—*contd*
  independent and impartial tribunal, 174
  judicial powers, 189-91
  legal advice *see* **legal advice**
  military disciplinary hearings, 174
  miscarriages of justice, 163-4, 169-71
  non-jury courts
    Criminal Justice (Mode of Trial) Bill, 171f
    Diplock Courts, 132, 135-6, 137, 156, 171
    Northern Ireland, 171-3
    PACE and, 171
    police powers, 167, 168
  pre-trial stage *see* **detention; Police and Criminal Evidence Act 1998**
  presumption of innocence, 176-7
  prison disciplinary hearings, 174-5
  rape *see* **rape cases**
family life, 294-5
  Canadian Charter and, 11
  children taken into care, 296
Farmer, L., 168
Faulkner, David, 228-9
Feldman, D., 57, 59, 63, 167, 307, 308-9
feminism, 2f
Feminist Anticensorship Task Force, 423
feminist scholarship
  critical theory, 177
  prisoners, 234-5
  privacy, 300, 304-6
    as gender issue, 279
Fenwick, H., 63, 167
Finucane, Pat, 146
Fish, Stanley, 386
Fitzgerald, M., 231
Fitzpatrick, B., 83
football supporters, 69, 407
Fortress Europe, 15, 313
foundationalism, 52-3
Franks Report (1972), 330, 344, 346-7
Fraser, N., 318, 410
Fredman, S., 400
freedom of assembly
  Convention right, 61-2
  marginalisation, 59-60
  meetings, 81-3
  Orange Order parades, 60, 73, 91-3, 148
  parades, 60
  peaceful assembly, 58
  Public Order Act 1986, 68, 69-70
  public order and, 59-60
  right to peaceful assembly, 58

freedom of assembly—*contd*
St Patrick's Day parade, 91, 93
trespassory assemblies, 69, 81
freedom of association, 59, 60
trade union membership ban, 42,
356
freedom of expression *see* **freedom of speech/expression**
freedom of information
2000 Act, 364
exclusions, 372
discetionary scheme, 364
Information Commissioner, 364
ministerial veto, 364-5
national security and, 332, 335, 363-5
secrecy culture, 364
Your Right to Know (White Paper), 364
freedom of movement
population management, 15
Freedom Party (Haider), 396
freedom of speech/expression, 377
actions against, 381
advertising, 10, 385
blasphemy, 385
breach of confidence, 381
broadcasting bans, 47, 117, 129, 152, 160, 382
broadcasting freedom interference, 383
censorship, 381
civil liberties tradition, 380-7
common law right, 382-3, 385-6
defamation, 43, 289, 303, 381, 382
excessive awards, 382
European Court, 384
government information, 382
hate speech, 86f, 423, 425, 426
holocaust denial, 381
Human Rights Act, 387
internet, 381
judiciary in UK, 382-3
libel, 381
limitation necessary in democratic society, 332
material in public domain, 42
media *see* **media**
merits of protecting, 382
Mill, John Stuart, 382
national security, 332
Northern Ireland, 42
obscenity, 381, 385
pornography, 423-4
see also **pornography**
press *see* **media**
privacy, 282, 384
public order, 59, 60, 61, 62-3

freedom of speech/expression—*contd*
racist speech, 381
secrecy, 381
security service memoirs, 334, 336, 366-8
Speakers' Corner, 62
street-corner speaker, 382
tobacco advertising, 385
United States, 9, 386
whistle-blowers *see* **whistle-blowing**
Fry, Elizabeth, 237
The Future of Multi-Ethnic Britain (**Parekh Report**), 376, 380, 389, 406, 407, 413, 431

Gadaffi, Colonel, 366, 367
Galligan, D., 61, 63, 87
Gavison, R., 308
gay rights *see* **sexual orientation discrimination**
gays in the military, 46, 297, 394
GCHQ, 283, 352
in *Spycatcher*, 358
trade union ban, 42, 356
Gearty, C., 47, 48, 83, 119, 121, 123, 126, 167, 337, 348, 354
General Belgrano, 345, 347, 357, 366
genetic information
privacy, 301-2, 307
Geneva Convention on the Status of Refugees, 119
Geraghty, Tony, 336f
Gibraltar
SAS killings, 154-5
Good Friday Agreement 1998, 129
governance, critical theory, 178
government
communism collapse, 15
exercise of power *see* **state power**
parliament influence reduced, 3
Thatcher, 12, 63, 64, 345
erosion of common law liberties, 41-4
see also **New Labour**
Government Technical Assistance Centre, 334
Grant, R., 314
Greenham Common protest, 63-4
Greenpeace, 68, 350f
repression by security services, 351
Grendon Underwood prison, 228
Griffith, J.A.G., 47-8
Grosz, S., 38
Group 4, 217f, 227f
Guidelines on Disclosure, 198
Guildford Four, 108, 155, 163, 171, 197, 238

guilty plea, 164

hacking
  as terrorism, 127
Haider, Jörg, 396
Hall, Stuart, 378, 413, 431
Handsworth riot, 76
harassment, 287, 288
  see also **sexual harassment**
Harding, R., 226
Hare, I., 87
Harris, D.J., 74, 167, 179
Harvey, Colin, 429, 434
hate speech, 86f, 423, 425, 426
Hay, W., 239, 261
Henderson, Paul, 362, 363
Hepple, Bob (B.A.), 424
**Hepple Review (of anti-discrimination
  legislation)**, 397, 399, 400, 406,
  407
Herman, Didi, 379
Hill, Anita, 318
Hill, Paul, 248
Hillyard, P., 110-11, 136
Hindley, Myra, 46, 273-5
Hoffman, Lord, 49
Holloway prison, 216, 228-9, 232, 257
Holloway Redevelopment Group, 228-9
holocaust denial, 381
Hosenball, Mark, 356
housing associations, 34
Howard, John, 237
Howard League for Penal Reform, 234,
  237
Howard, Michael, 84, 172, 220, 223,
  225, 250, 272
Hull prison, 235
  Board of Vistiors, 248
  riot, 248
human body
  as property, 299, 300-2
human rights
  effect of claims, 10-11
  euphoria, 15-16
  experts, 16
  freedom of expression, 384
  gender violence as issue, 195
  institutionalisation, 15
  legal advice, 134, 137
  NATO intervention in Balkans, 118,
    335, 337, 338, 368, 373-4
  as personal possession, 16
  political indeterminancy, 16
  posturing, 16
  prisoners
    final appeal, 242

human rights—*contd*
  prisoners—*contd*
    lack of political will, 244
    limitations, 242-3
    minimum standards, 243, 249
    restrictions, 248
    strategy, 241, 242-4
  privacy, 384
  restrictions
    legitimate aim, 248
    necessary in democratic society,
      27, 248, 295, 296, 332
    prescribed by law, 248
  silence, 105, 129, 130, 134, 136, 153,
    158, 172
  social obligations, 16
  status over-inflated, 15-17
  terrorism offences, 137
  value judgments, 16, 17
  variation over time, 11
  see also **European Convention on
    Human Rights; Human Rights
    Act 1998**
Human Rights Act 1998, 428-9
  common law and, 5, 37-8
  Convention Rights
    incorporation, 4f, 5, 25
    in national courts, 21-2
  criticism, 24-6
  declarations of incompatibility, 22,
    26
  domestic law, 21f
    interpretation in light of, 22-3, 26
  enduring distrust reaction, 47-8
  equality rights, 392
  euphoria, 48
  expectations, 1, 2
  fair trial, 165-7
  freedom of speech/expression, 387
  horizontal effect, 35-9
  individual claimants, 21
  judicial adjudication, 21-2
  judicial pragmatism, 50-2
  judicial review *see* **judicial review**
  legal persons, 24f
  long title, 21
  national security powers, 371-2
  omissions, 25-6
  parliamentary sovereignty and, 49
  positive reviews, 24
  privacy, 282
  private autonomy and power, 35-9
  public authorities *see* **public
    authorities**
  rape prosecutions, 212, 213-14
  reactions to, 47-8

human rights—*contd*
  remedies
    appropriate relief, 30, 37f
    more restrictive than Article 13,
      29-30, 37f
  reviews
    criticism, 24-6
    positive, 24
  standing, 31-3
    non-governmental organisations, 31
    pressure groups, 31, 32
    private individuals, 31-2
    'victims', 31
  text, 449-74
  'victims', 23, 31-3
  'zealots', 50, 52
Human Rights Watch, 106, 160
Hunt, Murray, 36
Hutchinson, Allan, 52, 424-5

identity, 3, 14-15, 412-13
  discounting, 430-1
  specificity, 430
  suppression by groups, 430
  see also **recognition**
imagination, 379-80, 428, 429, 431-2
immigration
  Joint Council for the Welfare of
    Immigrants, 33
  sexual orientation discrimination,
    411-12
imprisonment
  politicisation of policy, 217, 220-7
  see also **prisons/prisoners**
**Incentives and Earned Privileges
  schemes (IEPs)**, 253-4
incorporation of rights
  British model, 4f, 5, 25
**Independent Commissioner for Holding
  Centres**, 107
Independent Television Commission, 284
index of fright, 69-70
information see **disclosure; freedom of
  information**
Information Commissioner, 364
Ingham, Bernard, 345
inhuman and degrading treatment
  anti-terrorist practices, 106
  pornography, 420-1, 427
  prisons, 216, 252, 267
inner city riots, 63, 64, 76
institutional racism, 165, 178-9, 187,
    388-9, 390
intelligence gathering
  terrorism prevention, 143-4, 146-7,
    151-2

interception of communications
  internet, 283
  privacy, 295, 297
  telephone tapping, 284-5, 286, 295, 356
**Interception of Communications
  Tribunal**, 286
international cooperation, 160-1
**International Covenant on Civil and
  Political Rights**, 7, 105, 279, 402
International Labour Organisation
  equality conventions, 403
internet
  crime, 161
  freedom of expression, 381
  privacy, 283, 314-15
    exhibitionism, 321f
Internet Service Providers, 283
interpretation
  European Convention, 19-20
  judicial review and, 27-8
  presumption towards fundamental
    rights, 45
  UK legislation, 19
    HRA consideration in, 22-3, 26
    striking out incompatible law, 22-
      3, 36
interrogations
  terrorist offences, 132, 135
Ireland
  standing, 32
Irish National Liberation Army, 145
Irish Republican Army (IRA), 145
irrationality, 30
Irvine, Lord Chancellor, 49
Irving, David
  holocaust denial, 381

Jenkins, Brian, 113
Jenkins, Roy, 103, 110
Jennings, A., 140
Jockey Club, 34
**Joint Council for the Welfare of
  Immigrants**, 33
Jones, B.L., 74, 167, 179
Jones, Margaret, 82
journalists see **media**
judicial review
  balance, 87
  Convention restrictions and, 27
  discretion, 29
  full and fair hearing, 28
  fundamental rights decisions, 45
  HRA impact, 27-9
  irrationality, 27, 30
  prisons/prisoners, 218, 235, 240-1,
    246, 248-9

judicial review—*contd*
proportionality, 28-9
rights and, 43-4
standing, 31-3
statutory interpretation principle,
27-8
supervisory and appellate courts, 28
ultra vires, 48-9
unreasonableness, 27
judicial supremacism
challenge to parliamentary
sovereignty, 49
judiciary
adjudication, 21-2, 48
'Americanisation', 4
appointment methods, 40
bias, 3
rules of standing, 32
summings-up, 156, 170
chairing inquiries, 40
common law tradition and HRA, 5
constitutional boundaries, 39-40
Convention Rights and law
development, 37
discretion, 36-8
to ensure compatibility, 45
equality and, 393-5
freedom of expression, 382-3
broadcasting ban, 382
HRA horizontal effects on, 35-6
interpretation of legislation, 22-3, 26
national security/secrecy, 354-9
Clive Ponting trial, 357
CND activism, 356
contempt of court, 357f, 359,
367
'gentlemanly class', 355
journalist's sources, 357f
non-interventionist role, 354
Northern Ireland, 355
Public Interest Immunity
certificates, 355, 362-3
sanctioning state policy, 354-5
Spycatcher case, 357-9
telephone tapping, 356
The Zamora, 355
trade union ban at GCHQ, 42, 356
no electoral mandate, 53
non-discrimination and, 393-5
Northern Ireland
background, 156
role, 155-6
as targets, 155
parliamentary supremacy and, 44
politicisation, 48, 53
pragmatism, 50-2

presumption towards fundamental
rights, 45
as rights guardians, 2
role, 39-52
separation of powers, 39-40, 270
striking out incompatible law, 22-3
unelected mandate, 48
jurisdictions
import of ideas from other, 9
JUSTICE, 276-7
Justice in Prisons (**1983 JUSTICE report**),
238

Kaye, Gordon, 284
Keith, M., 178-9
Kelling, George, 85
Kennedy Inquiry, 335
'**KGB Granny**' **affair**, 337
Kimbell, J., 123, 126
King, R., 236
Kiszko, Stefan, 163
Kosovo conflict, 2f
NATO intervention, 118, 335, 337,
338, 368, 373-7

Lacey, N., 60, 75, 178
law and order politics, 57-8, 63-6, 76, 84
community concept, 65-6, 67
see also **public order**
law, reflexive, 431-2
Law Society, 198
Lawless criteria, 124
Lawrence (Stephen) Inquiry, 187, 388-9,
390, 407
Laws, John, 44-5
Lawyers Committee for Human Rights,
106
leaks
culture of, 316, 338, 340, 344, 345
Learmont, John, 223
Learmont Report (1995), 222, 223, 224,
250, 256
Leeds prison, 216, 252
legal advice
access, 166f, 172
delaying, 190, 191
PACE, 180-92
terrorist offences, 134, 137, 153,
157, 190-1
accreditation of advisers, 182
advisers relationship with police, 189
court comments of role of adviser,
190-1
Criminal Defence Service, 189
custody officer, 180
delaying access, 190, 191

legal advice—*contd*
  discouragement by police, 189
  duty solicitors, 189
  empirical findings, 181-2
  minimum duty of adviser, 191
  Police and Criminal Evidence Act
      1998, 180-92
  police station role, 189, 191
  prisoners
    access, 246, 254-6
    confidentiality, 253, 254, 255-6
    disciplinary hearings, 262
    minimum necessary interference,
        255, 256
    Prison rules, 254
    security considerations, 255-6
  quality, 182
  requests ignored, 182
  silence, 191
  silence of adviser, 182
  take-up rate, 181
  telephone advice, 182
legal professional privilege, 296, 297
legalism
  'black letter' tradition, 8f
  civil liberties tradition, 8
  social change, 9-11
legislation
  declarations of incompatibility, 22,
      26
  statement of compatibility, 23
legitimate aim restriction, 27, 248
Leigh, I., 50, 349, 352, 365, 371-2
Leng, Roger, 183
lesbians and gays in forces, 46, 297, 394
Lester, A., 24
lethal force, 106, 107
  accountability of state, 141-2, 143
  European Court of Human Rights,
      141, 142-3
  'shoot to kill' policy, 136, 139-43,
      145-6, 154
Lewinsky, Monica, 319
Lewis, Derek, 221, 224, 231, 251
libel, 289, 381
liberal democracy communism, 15
Liberty, 33, 108, 172
  privacy and, 309-10
Livingston, D., 101
Lloyd, Richard, 82
Loader, I., 179
Lobban, M., 155
local authorities
  elimination of racism, 394
  equality of opportunity, 394
Lockerbie bombing, 120

London Soho bombing, 120
Lustgarten, L., 50, 349, 352, 365, 371-2

MacBride Principles, 160
McColgan, A., 48
McConville, Mike, 183-4, 188
McCrudden, C., 382
McDermott, K., 236
Mackenzie, Compton, 347, 349
MacKinnon, Catharine, 10f, 401, 414-15,
      419, 426, 427
Maclean, Donald, 350
Maguire Seven, 163, 169
Mahoney, Kathleen, 420
Mandela, Nelson, 110
Mandelson, Peter, 366
marches see **processions**
margin of appreciation, 21, 28, 37, 296,
      332, 404
marital rape, 195
marital status discrimination, 391
market intelligence, 374-5
Marquand, David, 368, 369
Marshall, G., 25
martial law, 151
Matrix Churchill affair, 340, 362-3, 372
Mattan, Mahmood Hussein, 163
May Report (1979), 222
Maze Prison, 228, 235, 239
media
  ABC trial, 353-4, 356
  anti-terrorism reporting, 107, 109
  broadcasting bans, 47, 117, 129, 152,
      160, 382
  broadcasting freedom interference,
      383
  contempt of court, 357f, 359, 367
  encouraging reform using, 9
  freedom of expression, 282
  Hindley release campaigns, 273
  investigative journalism, 336, 353-4,
      381
  journalists sources, 42, 172, 357f
  law and order politics, 57-8, 63-6, 76,
      84
  national security/secrecy
    ABC trial, 353-4, 356
    broadcasting bans, 47, 117, 129,
        152, 160, 382
    changing practices, 365-6
    D-Notices, 352-3, 365
    failure to challenge, 350, 352-3
    investigative journalism, 353-4,
        381
    newsworthiness criteria, 366
    prior approval, 367

media—*contd*
  Press Complaints Commission, 34,
      281-2, 284, 384
  press freedom, 384
  prisoner access to, 164, 256, 260
  privacy, 281-2, 315-17
    anti-paparazzi legislation, 322-3
    codes of practice, 284, 322
    constructive invasion of, 322-3
    'live at the scene', 321
    Princess Caroline of Monaco case,
        323-4
    private grief, 321-2
    sensory enhanced technology,
        322-3
  protection of sources, 42, 172, 357f
  public order, 94
  publicity manufactured, 315-17
  terrorism reporting, 112, 114-17,
      153-5, 170
    broadcasting bans, 47, 117, 129,
        152, 160, 382
    demonisation, 115-16
    film coverage, 115-16
    legitimisation, 115, 153-4
    lines of communication, 117
    mistreatment of suspects, 154
    national security mode, 154-5
    pro-state bias, 115
    propaganda role, 155
medical evidence
  rape cases, 199-201
meetings
  public order and, 81-3
memoirs
  national security and, 334, 336, 366-8
  Shayler, 366-8
  Spycatcher, 42, 47, 320, 332-3, 340,
      341, 357-9
Metropolitan police
  institutional racism, 388-9, 390
MI5, 329, 341-2
  computerized Registry, 344
  destruction of evidence, 337
  national security, 334
  official histories, 336-7
  scrutiny in Shayler case, 368
  in *Spycatcher*, 358
  statutory mandate, 360
  surveillance and privacy, 283
MI6, 329, 341-2
  national security, 334
  official histories, 336-7
  scrutiny in Shayler case, 368
  in *Spycatcher*, 358
  surveillance and privacy, 283

Michael Collins, 116
military disciplinary hearings, 174
Mill, John Stuart, 382
Milne, S., 351
miners' disputes, 47, 61, 64, 94
miscarriage of justice, 163-4, 169-71
  biased summings-up, 156, 170
  police malpractice, 170-1
  political expediency, 170
  see also individual cases eg **Birmingham
      Six**
Mitrokhin Archive, 370f
Moloney, Ed, 157
monarchy
  privacy and publicity, 316-17, 328
Moore, John, 301-2, 308
Morgan, R., 57-8, 64, 76, 221, 233, 247
movement, freedom of
  population management, 15
Mulcahy, A., 129-30, 137, 149
multiculturalism, 15, 378, 410, 413
  synergy between liberalism and, 431
multinational corporations, 13

Narodnaya Volya, 119
National Council for Civil Liberties,
    108f
  repression by security services, 351
National Crime Squad (NCS), 334
**National Criminal Intelligence Service
    (NCIS)**, 334
National Health Service
  secrecy in, 335
national security/secrecy
  30-year rule, 338
  access to files, 336-7
  arms exports, 333
  'Arms to Iraq' affair, 340, 362-3, 372
  Bank of England, 333
  Bloody Sunday Inquiry, 40, 52, 155,
      331, 368, 376
  briefings, 340
  citizenship and, 331f
  class superiority, 343-8, 355
  CND as risk, 351, 356
  Cold War obsessions, 350
  commercial espionage, 338
  constitutional vacuum, 368, 370-2
  contemporary scene, 331-9
  culture of secrecy, 339-46, 364, 369-
      70, 371, 374
  current position, 368-75
  democratic conception, 371-2
    challenges to, 374-5
  discrimination justification, 398
  economic espionage, 311

national security/secrecy—*contd*
enemy within, 339-46, 349, 350-2
'European' defence strategy, 335
executive power, 370
external enemy and Glasnost, 361-2
Franks Report (1972), 330, 344, 346-7
freedom of expression and, 332, 381
freedom of information, 332, 335,
    363-5
  2000 Act, 337-8
  exclusions, 372
GCHQ, 352
  in *Spycatcher*, 358
  trade union ban, 42, 356
'gentlemanly secrecy', 343-8
government not State protection,
    340, 348-50, 355-6, 363, 370
Human Rights Act, 371-2
human rights and, 371-4
Information Commissioner, 364
interest of state and government
    policies, 340
investigative journalism, 336, 353-4,
    381
judiciary, 354-9
  Clive Ponting trial, 357
  CND activism, 356
  contempt of court, 357f, 359,
    367
  'gentlemanly class', 355
  journalist's sources, 357f
  non-interventionist role, 354
  Northern Ireland, 355
  Public Interest Immunity
    certificates, 355, 362-3
  sanctioning state policy, 354-5
  Spycatcher case, 357-9
  telephone tapping, 356
  trade union ban at GCHQ, 42, 356
  The Zamora, 355
'KGB Granny' affair, 337
leaks, 316, 338, 340, 344, 345
lesbians and gays in forces, 46, 297,
    394
margin of appreciation, 332
market intelligence, 374-5
Matrix Churchill affair, 340, 362-3, 372
media
  ABC trial, 353-4, 356
  broadcasting bans, 47, 117, 129,
    152, 160, 382
  changing practices, 365-6
  D-Notices, 352-3, 365
  failure to challenge, 350, 352-3
  investigative journalism, 336,
    353-4, 381

national security/secrecy—*contd*
media—*contd*
  newsworthiness criteria, 366
  prior approval, 367
memoirs, 334
  double standards in
    authorisation, 336
  freedom of expression, 367
  Shayler, 366-8
  see also Spycatcher
MI5, 329, 334, 341-2, 358
  computerized Registry, 344
  destruction of evidence, 337
  official histories, 336-7
  scrutiny in Shayler case, 368
  statutory mandate, 360
MI6, 283, 329, 334, 341-2, 358
  official histories, 336-7
  scrutiny in Shayler case, 368
ministerial responsibility to
    parliament, 370-1
National Crime Squad (NCS), 334
National Criminal Intelligence
    Service (NCIS), 334
National Health Service, 335
NATO intervention in Balkans, 118,
    335, 337, 338, 368, 373-4
natural justice and, 340
non-official secrecy, 374
Official Secrets Acts
  1911, 346-8
  1989, 360-1
  Franks Report, 330, 344, 346-7
  human rights and, 332
  media ignoring, 365-6
parliament
  judges State interests, 340, 348-
    50, 355-6, 370
  ministerial responsibility to,
    370-1
Phillips Report on BSE, 338
Ponting, Clive, 345, 347, 357, 366
proportionality, 371, 372
protection of government not State,
    340, 348-50, 355-6, 363, 370
public domain information, 336
Public Interest Immunity (PII)
    certificates, 333, 355, 362-3,
    376
public trust loss, 370-1
Regulation of Investigatory Powers
    Act (2000), 280, 282-3, 334
restriction of rights, 30
Scott Report, 362-3, 372
secret secrecy, 340
Secret State, 348-50, 368

national security/secrecy—*contd*
  security services
    culture of secrecy, 339-46, 364,
      369-70, 371, 374
    enemy within, 350-2
    freedom of information
      exclusion, 372
    secrecy, 349-50
    state repression by, 350-2
    see also MI5; MI6
  Shayler, David, 332-3, 344, 366-8
  social and economic foundations, 10
  Special Air Service, 334
  spin and leaking, 338
  Spycatcher, 42, 47, 320, 357-9
    content of book, 341, 344
    GCHQ, 358
    injunctions, 332-3, 340
    MI5 and MI6 in, 358
  standards and ethics for MPs, 333
  surveillance powers, 334
  Thatcherism and, 345
  'Three Wise Men' panel, 361f
  war-readiness principle, 339-46
  whistle-blowing, 291, 332-3, 345, 357,
    366-8, 372, 381
National Unemployed Workers
  Movement
  repression by security services, 351
nationalism, 378, 406, 407
  'active citizenship', 408
  EU citizenship, 408-9
  football supporters, 407
  politics of belonging, 407-8
  racism and, 406, 407-8
  Scottish, 407
  see also **citizenship; racial**
    discrimination
NATO, 13
  muscular humanitarianism, 118,
    335, 337, 338, 368, 373-7
Nazism, 25
necessary in democratic society
  Convention restriction, 27, 248, 295,
    296, 332
necessity test see **proportionality**
neighbourhood watch, 100
Nelson, Rosemary, 146
Netanyahu, Benjamin, 113
New Labour, 1, 2, 3-4, 127, 177, 224, 226
  active citizenship, 65, 66, 67, 101,
    407-8, 412
  anti-terrorism legislation, 105, 125
  business and entrepreneurship, 375
  constitutional vandalism, 3-4
  control within party, 369

New Labour—*contd*
  dominance of PM and insiders, 3
  ethical foreign policy, 333
  freedom of information, 363-4, 370
  inclusion and exclusion, 378, 431
  tough on crime, tough on the causes
    of crime, 76, 217
'New Penology', 178
Nice Treaty, 2
Nicholls, Patrick, 164
non-governmental organisations, 31
non-legal regulation, 8
nonfoundationalism, 53-5
North Atlantic Treaty Organisation see
  NATO
North Review, 101
Northcote-Trevelyan Report (1854), 343
Northern Ireland, 7
  abuse at Holding Centres, 185f
  Anglo-Irish Agreement (1985), 129,
    131
  appeal courts, 157
  banning speeches by political party,
    42
  Belfast Agreement 1998, 2
  Bloody Sunday, 117f, 138, 142
  Bloody Sunday Inquiry, 40, 52, 155,
    331, 368, 376
  broadcasting bans, 47, 117, 129, 152,
    160, 382
  Castlereagh Holding Centre, 106,
    185f
  Committee on the Administration of
    Justice (CAJ), 172
  Diplock courts, 132, 135-6, 137, 156,
    171
  equality, 391, 393
  Equality Commission, 129, 393
  exclusion orders, 172
  fair employment legislation, 400-1
  fair trial, 171-3
  Good Friday Agreement 1998, 129
  Human Rights Act in, 24
  human rights activism results, 111
  Human Rights Commission, 111,
    129, 173, 393
  Independent Commissioner for
    Holding Centres, 107
  judiciary
    background, 156
    judiciary, role, 155-6
    role, 355
    as targets, 155
  legal advice access delayed, 191
  lethal force *see* **terrorism**, lethal force
  MacBride Principles, 160

Northern Ireland—*contd*
Maze Prison, 228, 235, 239
non-jury (Diplock) courts, 132, 135-6, 137, 156, 171
North Review on processions, 101
Orange Order marches, 60, 73, 91-3, 148
Parades Commission, 92, 102, 129, 148, 173
paramilitarism and policing, 98-9
Patten Report, 102, 104, 147-8, 150, 173
Police Authority for Northern Ireland, 150
Police Service of Northern Ireland, 150
Policing Board, 150
proscribed organisations, 117f, 126, 132, 134, 157
religious discrimination, 152
Review Body, 92
Royal Ulster Constabulary, 129-30
loyalist paramilitaries and, 146
Patten Report, 102, 104, 147-8, 150, 173
sectarian attitudes, 148
special branch, 148
see also **terrorism**, police role
security force prosecutions, 156
'shoot to kill' policy, 136, 139-43, 145-6, 154
silence, inferences from, 105, 129, 130, 134, 136, 153, 158, 172
Standing Advisory Commission on Human Rights (SACHR), 172
supergrasses, 146-7, 172
violence, 64-5
see also **terrorism**
Northern Ireland (Emergency Provisions) Acts 1973-96, 106, 119, 131, 132
Northern Ireland Human Rights Commission, 111, 129, 173, 393
Norwood, Melita, 337
nuclear power
national security and, 351f
nuisance
private, 298
NYPD Blues, 186

obscenity, 381, 385
harm, 432-3
as sex discrimination, 401, 417-21
see also **pornography**
official secrecy *see* **national security/ secrecy**

Official Secrets Acts
1911, 346-8
1989, 360-1
Franks Report (1972), 330, 344, 346-7
government not state protection, 340, 348-50, 355-6, 363, 370
lifelong ban on disclosure, 360
media ignoring, 365-6
notified individuals, 360-1
O'Leary, B., 93
Omagh bombing, 120, 123
ombudsmen, 87
Police Ombudsman, 149
Prisons Ombudsman, 215, 222-3, 245-6, 251, 255, 264, 277, 278
O'Neill, Dairmuid, 146f

parades *see* **processions**
Parades Commission, 102, 148, 173
Parekh Report, 376, 380, 389, 406, 407, 413, 431
Parkhurst prison, 223
Parliament
anti-terrorism policies, 151-3
courting the media, 281
domination by executive, 151
ministerial responsibility to, 370-1
privacy and, 280-1, 282
secrecy protects not state but government, 340, 348-50, 355-6, 363, 370
spin and leaks, 316, 338
standards and behaviour, 333
parliamentary sovereignty
challenge as judicial supremacism, 49
Human Rights Act 1998, 49
parliamentary supremacy
courts and, 44
higher-order law (than parliament), 44-5
Parole Board, 271
Parry, N., 364
Paton-Simpson, E., 321-2
Patten Report, 102, 104, 147-8, 150, 173
Payne, Sarah, 325
peaceful assembly, 58
peaceful protest, 74
Philby, Kim, 350
Phillips, A., 387
Phillips Report on BSE, 338
Phillipson, G., 29, 36, 37, 38
pleas, guilty, 164
police *see* **policing; Royal Ulster Constabulary**
Police Authority for Northern Ireland, 150
Police Complaints Commission, 149

Police and Criminal Evidence Act 1984
  arrest powers, 180
  Codes of Practice, 180
  effects, 164-5, 171
  fair trial, 171
  legal advice right *see* **legal advice**
  police culture and reform strategies,
    184, 185-8
  search and seize property, 180
  stop and search, 180
Police Ombudsman, 149
Police Service of Northern Ireland, 150
policing
  active citizens, 101
  anti-terrorism role *see* **terrorism**
  breach of the peace, 78-9
  brutality, 86
  case construction, 183
  chaperon officers, 193
  citizenship, 101
  community policing, 96
  consent, 89
  consultation, 97
  covert surveillance *see* **surveillance**
  crime control values, 183-4
  culture
    canteen culture, 186
    professionalisation post-PACE,
      186
    and reform strategies, 184, 185-8
    sex discrimination, 186f
    television dramas and, 186-7
  custody officer, 180, 181, 189
  democratic accountability, 101
  discretion, 88, 96-8
  failing to obey instructions, 78f
  flying squads, 99
  gay communities, 286-7
  informers, 175-6
  institutional racism, 165, 178-9, 187,
    388-9, 390
  intelligence gathering, 68, 96, 143-4,
    146-7, 151-2
  malpractice, 170-1
  managerialism, 97f, 165, 177-8
  militarisation, 65
  mission statements, 97
  moment-of-crisis powers, 70
  motivation, 165
  neighbourhood watch, 100
  Northern Ireland *see* **Northern
    Ireland**; **Royal Ulster
    Constabulary**
  ownership and space, 89-91, 95
  PACE, 164-5
  paramilitarism, 98-9

policing—*contd*
  Patten Report, 102, 104, 147-8, 150,
    173
  peacekeeping equipment, 98
  performance indicators, 97
  pre-demonstration negotiation, 89
  prevention practices, 88-9
  private security, 66, 90, 95, 99-100
  public order, 60-1, 65, 68, 78-9, 86-
    91, 95-101
  public participation, 97
  public protection, 165
  quality of service provision, 97-8
  racist patterns, 65
  research, 60-1
  riot gear, 95
  RUC *see* Royal Ulster Constabulary
  self-policing, 100-1
  special constables, 100-1
  structural discretion, 96-8
  surveillance, 68, 96
    privacy and, 295
  telephone tapping, 284-5, 286, 295,
    356
  terrorism, 128, 129-30
    methods transferred, 109
  turn-back powers, 94
  underenforcement, 88-9
  'watching and besetting' powers, 70
  West Midlands Serious Crime Squad,
    164, 171
  zero tolerance, 85-6, 165
Policing Board (of Northern Ireland),
  150
politicisation
  release procedures, 268, 269-70
  separation of powers, 39-40, 270
Ponting, Clive, 345, 347, 357, 366
population management, 15
pornography
  anti-pornography campaigns, 33
  artistic merit, 421f
  degrading and dehumanising
    treatment, 420-1, 427
  harm, 418-19, 432-3
  R v Butler, 420-1, 422, 425, 426-7, 432
  as sex discrimination, 401, 417-21
  violence, 420-1, 423, 427
Porter, B., 374
power, exercise of see **state power**
pragmatism
  critical, 378-9, 429-34
  judicial, 50-2
precedent doctrine, 26
prescribed by law
  Convention restriction, 27

**Preservation of the Rights of Prisoners
(PROP)**, 235
Press Complaints Commission, 34, 281-
2, 284, 384
pressure groups, 6f, 9
adverse impacts on, 10
'law and order' politics, 57-8, 63-6
standing, 31, 32-3
presumption of innocence, 176-7
**Prevention of Terrorism (Temporary
Provisions) Acts**, 103, 106, 118-
19, 125, 131, 132-3
Prime Suspect, 186
Princess Caroline of Monaco **case**
privacy, 323-4
'prior ventilation' rule, 253, 254
Prison Officers Association, 230, 262
Prison Reform Trust, 276-7
Prison Service executive agency, 223-4,
245
Prisons Ombudsman, 215, 222-3, 245-6,
251, 255, 264, 277, 278
prisons/prisoners, 7
access to journalists, 164, 256, 260
access to legal advice, 246, 254-6
accountability, 217, 219, 239, 245,
278
establishing, 246-53
legislation, 247
political, 250
prison staff, 232
privatised prisons, 252-3
Assisted Prison Visits Unit, 257
children, 257, 259
conjugal visits, 257, 258
asylum-seekers, 227
authoritarian management, 228,
229, 239
Barlinnie Special Unit, 228
Belmarsh, 366
Board of Visitors, 248, 250-1
disciplinary powers, 262-3
Brixton, 216, 252
bureaucratic-lawful model, 228, 229
censorship, 253, 254
Chief Inspector of Prisons, 216, 218-
19, 250, 251, 277, 278
child prisoners, 272-3
climate of fear, 216
Code of Minimum Living Standards,
244
Code of Operating Standards, 265
conditions
degrading and inhuman
treatment, 216, 252, 267
health care, 267

prisons/prisoners—*contd*
conditions—*contd*
overcrowding, 217, 218, 221,
245, 265, 267
violence, 267
conjugal visits, 257, 258
contacts with outside world
family members, 257-9
legal advice, 253, 254-6
media, 256, 260
non-family members, 260
non-legal contacts, 257-60
'offence to victims' justification,
260
phone-in radio programmes, 260
Prison Service Order, 257, 259
correspondence, 295, 297
family members, 258
legal adviser, 253-6
degrading and inhuman treatment,
216, 252, 267
Director General role, 224
discipline
Board of Visitors adjudication,
262-3
discretion, 263
false and malicious allegations, 253
hearings, 174-5, 248
informal system, 263-5
legal representation, 262
powers, 261
Prison Discipline Manual, 263
reform strategies, 261
solitary confinement, 264
techniques and policies, 261-5
discretionary powers, 245-6
dispersal prisons, 224-5
drug testing, 240
escapes, 223, 255
European Committee for the
Prevention of Torture (CPT),
215, 216, 250, 251-2, 278
European Court of Human Rights,
241, 242, 248
European Prison Rules, 243
executive influence see politicisation
false and malicious allegations, 253
force, use by prison officers, 230-1
Fresh Start Inititative, 230, 231
'good order and discipline' reasons,
249
governors, 251
demographics, 227-8
management model, 228-9
Grendon Underwood, 228
Group 4, 217f, 227f

prisons/prisoners—*contd*
harassment, 236-7
health care, 267
Holloway, 216, 228-9, 232, 257
Home Secretary role, 220, 224, 275-7
hospital, 267
Howard League, 234, 237
Hull, 235, 248
human rights
final appeal, 242
lack of political will, 244
limitations, 242-3
minimum standards, 243, 249
restrictions, 248
strategy, 241, 242-4
hunger strikes, 235
immigrant detention centres, 227
Incentives and Earned Privileges
schemes (IEPs), 253-4
inhuman and degrading treatment,
216, 252, 267
inmate-control model, 228
journalists, access to, 160, 256, 260
judicial review, 218, 235, 240-1, 246,
248-9
JUSTICE, 276-7
Justice in Prisons, 238
Learmont Report (1995), 222, 223,
224, 250, 256
Leeds, 216, 252
legal advice
access, 246, 254-6
confidentiality, 253, 254, 255-6
disciplinary hearings, 262
minimum necessary interference,
255, 256
Prison rules, 254
security considerations, 255-6
legislation, 217, 247
litigation, 244, 245, 246, 277
local prisons, 225
managerialism, 220, 227, 229-30, 277
May Report (1979), 222
Maze, 228, 235, 239
minimum standards of treatment,
243, 249
Mother and Baby Units, 259
negligence actions, 248
non-legal contacts, 257-60
ombudsman, 215, 222-3, 245-6, 251,
255, 264, 277, 278
open prisons, 225
organisation of system, 223-7
overcrowding, 217, 218, 221, 245,
265, 267
Parkhurst, 223

prisons/prisoners—*contd*
politicisation, 217, 220-7, 278
'prison works' agenda, 217, 223
regimes, 221-3
release procedures, 268, 269-70
separation of powers, 270
population increase, 217, 218, 221,
245, 265, 267
positive obligations, 218
Preservation of the Rights of
Prisoners (PROP), 235
pressure groups, 237, 238
'prior ventilation' rule, 253, 254
prison officers, 230-2
accountability, 232
Fresh Start Inititative, 230, 231
role confusion, 232
use of force, 230, 231
Prison Officers Association, 230, 262
'prison as public body' strategy, 240-
1
Prison Reform Trust, 276-7
Prison Rules, 247-8, 249, 250, 254,
277
Prison Service executive agency, 223-
4, 245
'prison works', 217, 223
prison-industrial complex, 225-6
prisoners, 232-7
complaints, 245-6, 249
feminist research, 234-5
harassment, 236-7
inmate-group abuse, 236
litigation, 244, 245, 246
rights, 7, 175
social problems, 233-4
statistics, 234
subcultures, 236
US, 236, 266
violence, 236-7
women, 234-5, 237
privatisation, 217, 220, 225-7
accountability, 152-3
racism, 216
reformers, 237-8
release procedures, 268-77
case law, 270-7
child defendants, 272-3
discretionary life, 268-9, 271
Home Secretary discretion, 275-7
inconsistent with ECHR, 271
indeterminated sentences, 268-10
legitimate expectation, 274
mandatory life, 269, 271-2
Parole Board recommendations,
271

prisons/prisoners—*contd*
  release procedures—*contd*
    politicians and, 268, 269-70
    retrospective punishment, 275
    tariff stage, 269, 276
    uniquely evil, 273-5
  riots, 220, 235, 248
  rule of law strategy, 238, 239-40, 265
  searches, 247
  security, 223, 277
    legal advice visits, 255-6
    status and function, 224-5
  sexism, 216
  sexual practices, 258f
  shared-powers model, 228
  smuggling of weapons or drugs, 255
  staff
    Fresh Start Inititative, 230, 231
    governors, 227-8
    grades, 227-32
    prison officers, 230-2
    see also accountability
  Strangeways, 220, 235
  strikes, 235
  surveillance, 240
  telephone access, 253
  temporary release, 253
  training prisons, 225
  UN Standard Minimum Rules on the
      Treatment of Prisoners, 243
  US experience, 236, 266
  violence, 236-7
  visits, 253
  Wandsworth, 216, 218, 218f, 252
  Whitemoor, 223, 255
  Wolds, 226
  women prisoners, 225, 228-9
    children visits, 257, 259
    treated as if men, 267
  Woolf Report, 221, 222-3, 235-6, 262,
      263
  Wormword Scrubs, 216
  young offender centres, 225
privacy
  abstract intimacy, 317
  autonomy, 207, 303f, 308
  breach of confidence, 287, 289-90, 298
  Broadcasting Standards Commission,
      284
  Child Support Agency, 313
  common good, 324-6
  companies, 306
  consensual sexual activities, 286-7,
      296-7
  correspondence, 253-6, 258, 294,
      295, 297

privacy—*contd*
  covert surveillance, 176, 280, 282-3,
      285-6, 295
  criminal record disclosure, 288
  customer profiling, 311
  defamation, 289, 303
  developing right to, 287-92
  dignity, 207, 303f, 308
  'Downing Street Nanny', 290, 321
  employment vetting, 297, 311
  encrypted data, 283
  European Convention, 279, 288,
      292-8
    Article 8, 404
    complexity, 292-3
    family life, 294-5
    limitations, 295-6
    margin of appreciation, 296
    positive and negative obligations,
        293, 294-5
    private life, 293-4
  ex-offenders, 288
  family life, 296
  feminist theory and politics, 304-6
  freedom of expression and, 282, 384
  gender inequality and, 279
  genetic information, 301-2, 307
  harassment, 287, 288
  human body as property, 299, 300-2
  Human Rights Act (1998), 282
  Independent Television Commission,
      284
  in information society
    abstract intimacy, 317
    commercial use, 311, 312-13
    internet, 283, 314-15, 321f
    media, 315-17
    publicity, 315-17
    technology, 310-13, 314-15
  interception of communications,
      284-5, 286, 294, 295, 297
  International Covenant on Civil and
      Political Rights, 279
  internet, 283, 314-15, 321f
  intimate associations, 286-7, 296-7,
      309
  judicial record, 283-92
    covert surveillance, 285-6
    media commissions, 284
  leaks, culture of, 316, 338, 340, 344,
      345
  legal professional privilege, 296, 297
  lesbians and gays in forces, 46, 297,
      394
  libel, 289, 381
  liberty, 309-10

privacy—*contd*
limitations
necessary in democratic society,
295, 296
pressing social need, 296
'live at the scene', 321
media, 281-2
anti-paparazzi legislation, 322-3
codes of practice, 284, 322
constructive invasion of, 322-3
in information society, 315-17
'live at the scene', 321
Princess Caroline of Monaco case,
323-4
private grief, 321-2
sensory enhanced technology,
322-3
Venables and Thompson
whereabouts, 327
medical records
personal identity, 291
targeted marketing, 291, 311
Megan's Law, 324-5
motorway CCTV, 311, 313-14
naming and shaming, 324, 325-6
national security, 291, 297
overview, 280-92
parliament, 280-1, 282
spin and leaks, 316, 338
personal information, 289-91, 307-8
centralised accumulation, 312
commercial use, 311, 312-13
deregulation, 311
proof of identity, 312-13
voluntarily given, 312-13
welfare access, 313
place of seclusion, 324
police photographs, 291-2
Press Complaints Commission, 34,
281-2, 284, 384
private nuisance, 298
private telecommunications system,
283
property and
body as property, 299, 300-3
breach of confidence, 298
economic concept, 299
feminist issue, 300
genetic information, 301-2, 307
trespass, 298
proportionality, 287, 288
public domain information, 290
public facts, 320-4
public interest disclosure, 290, 291
in public places, 302, 303-4
public and private divide, 318-19

privacy—*contd*
publicity, 303, 315-17
'consumer-oriented', 319
critical, 319
'democratic publicity', 318-19
monarchy, 316-17, 328
right to one's image, 303, 322
spin and leaks, 316, 338
Regulation of Investigatory Powers
Act (2000), 280, 282-3, 334
reproductive freedom, 328
reputation, 287, 303
sado-masochistic sex, 286-7
sex offences
against children, 324-5
allegations of abuse, 288-9
Megan's Law, 324-5
sexual activities, 286-7, 296-7, 328
spatial zone of protection, 324
Spycatcher see **Spycatcher**
surveillance, 295, 311
accumulation of information, 312
CCTV, 14, 311, 312, 313-14
targeted marketing, 291, 311
telephone communications, 284-5,
286, 294, 356
trespass, 298
unconscionability principle, 290
Universal Declaration of Human
Rights, 279
value, 302-10
disregarded for common good, 326
feminist theory, 304-6
intimate associations, 309
public-private divide, 304-5
violations, 324-6
welfare access, 313
whistle-blowing, 291, 332-3, 345, 357,
366-8, 372, 381
private life, 293-4
anti-abortion campaigners, 32
human rights regulation of, 12, 14
population management, 15
see also **privacy**
private nuisance, 298
private parties
HRA horizontal effect on, 35-6
private schools, 35
private security, 66, 90, 95, 99-100
scope of authority, 100
privilege
legal professional, 296, 297
public interest immunity, 198, 333,
355, 362-3, 376
self-incrimination, 172, 175
see also **silence**

processions, 81-3
  access to highway, 82-3
  banning, 81
  North Review, 101
  Orange Order marches, 60, 73, 91-3,
    148
  Parades Commission, 92, 102, 129,
    148, 173
  police control, 69
  stop and turnback powers, 81-2
property
  as economic concept, 299
  human body as, 299, 300-2
  see also **privacy**
proportionality
  breach of the peace powers, 79
  European Convention
    interpretation, 20
  judicial review, 28-9
  legitimate aim and, 27
  necessity test, 27
  privacy, 287, 288
proscribed organisations, 117f, 126, 132,
    134, 157
protest
  democratic value, 57, 58
public authorities, 23
  contractual functions, 34
  courts, 35
  governmental type powers, 33
  judicial review, 27, 28
  meaning, 33-5
  mixed public private function, 34
  remedies granted against, 36
  standing
    HRA, 34-5
    judicial review, 35
  'substance and nature of act' test, 34
  tribunals, 35
public function, 33-4
public interest immunity
  PII certificates, 333, 355, 362-3, 376
  withholding of evidence, 198
public meetings, 81-3
public order, 76-80
  accountability, 87
  affray, 78f
  aggravated trespass, 70
  anti-social behaviour, 66, 67, 70, 84, 86
  arrest powers, 69
  association, 59, 60
    see also **public protest**
  authoritarian state thesis, 63f
  balance, 79, 80-94
  binding over powers, 79, 80
  breach of the peace, 70-1, 77-9

public order—*contd*
  characteristics, 71-2
  citizenship, 84
  civil disobedience, 74
  common law, 77-9
  community concept, 67f, 68, 83
  competing interests, 91-4
  consensus assumption, 57, 59
  courts, 94-5
  Crime and Disorder Act 1998, 68-9,
    70, 83-4, 85
  Criminal Justice and Public Order
    Act 1994, 68, 83-4, 85
  criminal law and justice, 60
  criminalisation, 65, 67, 85, 94
  decision makers, 94-5
  definition, 71, 77
  discretionary powers, 57
  excluded underclass, 66, 76, 86
  exclusion zones, 79
  expression and, 59, 60
  failing to obey instructions, 78f
  freedom of assembly *see* **freedom of
    assembly**
  freedom of speech/expression, 59,
    60, 61, 62-3
  horseplay offences, 69
  human rights challenges, 94
  index of fright, 69-70
  individual responsibility, 85
  industrial protest, 64
  inner city riots, 63, 64-5, 76
  'law and order' politics, 57-8, 63-6,
    76, 84
  legislation, 68-71
  legitimation of protest, 102
  marches *see* **processions**; **public
    protest**
  media, 94
  meetings, 81-3
  miners' disputes, 47, 61, 64, 94
  moment-of-crisis powers, 70
  morality, 66
  peaceful assembly right, 58
    see also **public protest**
  police state, 72
  policing, 60-1, 65, 68, 87, 95-101
    breach of the peace, 78-9
    brutality, 86
    by consent, 89
    discretion, 88, 96-8
    intelligence gathering, 96
    moment-of-crisis powers, 70
    ownership and space, 89-91, 95
    peacekeeping equipment, 98
    powers, 78-9

public order—*contd*
  policing—*contd*
    pre-demonstration negotiation, 89
    prevention practices, 88-9
    private, 95
    private security, 66, 90, 95, 99-100
    riot gear, 95
    structural discretion, 96-8
    surveillance, 96
    turn-back powers, 94
    underenforcement, 88-9
  private security, 66, 90, 95, 99-100
  privatisation, 66
  processions *see* **processions**
  Public Order Act 1986, 68, 69-70, 83
  'quality of life' crimes, 66
  racially aggravated offences, 70
  raves, 70, 84
  removal of masks, 70
  restriction of rights, 30
  riot *see* **riot**
  safety, 86
  Scarman reports, 80-1
  social breakdown, 72
  space ownership, 89-91, 95
  sporting events, 69, 407
  Thatcherism, 63
  trespass, 65, 70, 84
  'watching and besetting' powers, 70
  weighing competing interests, 91-4
  zero tolerance, 85-6, 165
Public Order Act 1986, 68, 69-70, 83
public protest
  characteristics, 71-2
  civil disobedience, 74
  criminalisation, 65, 67, 67f, 85, 94
  definition, 71, 72-6
  democracy-forcing, 58, 59, 73
  democratic value of protest, 57, 58
  environmental issues, 67
  European Convention and, 61-2
  globalisation, 67
  Greenham Common, 63
  industrial disputes, 94
  legitimation, 102
  miners' disputes, 47, 61, 64, 94
  moral and physical coercion, 74-5
  neo-liberalism, 67
  peaceful, 74
  people power, 73
  on private property, 99-100
  Red Lion Square, 64-5, 81
  riot, 74-6
  social movements, 67-8, 73
    as terrorism, 127-8
  UK rights tradition and, 59-63

publicity
  'consumer-oriented', 319
  critical, 319
  'democratic publicity', 318-19
  monarchy, 316-17, 328
  privacy, 315-19
  right to one's image, 303, 322
  spin and leaks, 316, 338

R v Butler, 420-1, 422, 425, 426-7, 432
Race Relations Act, 390, 391-2
racial discrimination, 378, 391
  Convention on the Elimination of All
    Forms of Racial
    Discrimination, 402
  criminalisation of Afro-Caribbean
    people, 178-9
  direct, 398
  freedom of expression and, 381
  indirect, 399-400
  institutional, 165, 178-9, 187, 388-9,
    390, 407
  institutional racism, 165, 178-9, 187,
    388-9, 390, 407
  local authority duty, 394
  multiculturalism, 15, 378, 410, 413
  nationalism and, 406, 407-8
  police, 7, 165, 187
    see also **institutional racism**
  positive action, 400-1
  prisons, 216
  Race Directive, 395-6
  Race Relations Act, 390, 391-2
  Stephen Lawrence Inquiry, 187, 388-
    9, 390, 407
  UN Committee on the Elimination of
    Racial Discrimination, 408
  see also **nationalism**
Railtrack, 34
Ramsbotham, David, 216f
rape cases, 192-213
  Canadian Supreme Court, 213
    disclosures, 201-5
    rape shield, 208, 209-10
    sexual history evidence, 209
  chaperon officers, 193
  convictions, 193
  counselling centre records, 195, 201-5
  cross-examination
    defence tactics, 199-200
    fairness, 209-11
    intimidation and insinuation,
      207, 208, 210-11
    rape shield, 208, 209-10
    right, 206-7
    sexual history, 195, 201, 206-11

rape cases—*contd*
  cross-examination—*contd*
    tactics, 199-200, 207-9, 211
  defence tactics, 194, 199-200
  defendant's rights, 193-4
  disclosure
    in Canada, 201-5, 208-10
    complainants' records, 195, 199-201
    counselling centre records, 195, 201-5
    fishing expeditions, 203, 204
    medical evidence, 199-201, 203, 204-5
    principle, 196-9
    sexual history, 195, 209
  gender violence as human rights issue, 195
  Human Rights Act and, 212, 213-14
  implied consent defence, 194
  judicial intervention, 195
  marital rape, 195
  medical evidence disclosure, 199-201, 203, 204-5
  myths, 205, 210
  non-stranger rape, 212
  patriarchal assumptions, 211, 212
  rape crisis centres, 195, 201-5
  rights discourse, 211-13
  sexual history
    irrelevance, 210
    see also cross-examination
  third parties
    counselling services, 201-5
    doctors, 199-201, 203, 204-5
    schools, 202
  under reporting, 210, 211
  victim's rights, 193-4
ratio decidendi, 51
raves, 70, 84
Reclaim the Streets, 67
recognition
  common good and, 412
  criticism, 422-4
  cultural, 431
  equality and, 410-14
  excitable speech, 426
  groups, 410, 413, 429, 430
    identity suppression discounting, 430-1
    labelling members, 430
    as moral superiority, 406, 429
    political inclusion, 378, 431
  hate speech, 423, 425, 426
  identity politics, 412-13
  identity suppression/discounting, 430-1

recognition—*contd*
  independent value, 433-4
  liberal criticism, 422-4
  limitations of rules and legal systems, 424-6
  majorities, 430, 434
  minorities, 430, 434
  postmodern criticism, 424-7
  recognition-based law reform, 410-14, 428
  see also **identity**
Red Lion Square protest, 64-5, 81
Redfern Inquiry, 335
reflexive law, 431-2
refugees, 15
  Geneva Convention on status, 119
Regulation of Investigatory Powers Act (2000)
  Commissioners, 283
  complaints tribunal, 283
  internet use, 283
  privacy, 280, 282-3
  see also **surveillance**
Reiner, R., 67, 88, 101
religion
  discrimination, 152, 391, 403, 405
  Northern Ireland, 152
  Sunday working, 405
religious fundamentalists, 127
remedies
  against public authorities, 36
  civil liberties tradition, 7
  European Convention on Human Rights, 19, 37f
  Human Rights Act 1998, 29-30, 37f
reputation, 287, 303
  defamation, 43, 289, 303, 381, 382
  see also **publicity**
Richardson, Genevra, 243
right of silence, 105, 129, 130, 134, 136, 153, 158, 172
Rimmington, Stella, 336
riot, 63, 64-5, 74-6
  determinism, 75
  racialisation, 76
  social conditions, 75-6
Robertson, G., 167-8, 353-4, 381
Rock, P., 232
Rolston, B., 110
Rose, D., 186-7
Rose, N., 326
Royal Commission on Criminal Justice (Runciman Commission), 170
Royal Ulster Constabulary, 129-30
  loyalist paramilitaries and, 146
  Patten Report, 102, 104, 147-8, 150, 173

Royal Ulster Constabulary—*contd*
  sectarian attitudes, 148
  'shoot to kill', 136, 139-43, 145-6,
    154
  special branch, 148
  see also **terrorism**, policing
Runciman Commission, 170
Rusbridger, A., 384

sado-masochistic sex
  privacy and, 286-7, 296-7
Sadurski, Wojciech, 423
Sanders, A., 182, 183-4, 188, 189
Saville Inquiry (Bloody Sunday), 40, 52,
    155, 331, 368, 376
Scales, Ann, 401
Scargill, Arthur, 351
Scarman reports, 80-1, 388
Schauer, F., 318-19
schools, private, 35
Scott Inquiry/Report, 362-3, 372
Scottish nationalism, 407
search and arrest powers, 152
search and seizure of property, 180
searches
  prisoners, 247
secrecy *see* **national security/secrecy**
security services
  culture of secrecy, 339-46, 364, 369-
    70, 371, 374
  enemy within, 350-2
  freedom of information exclusion,
    372
  secrecy, 349-50
  state repression by, 350-2
  see also **MI5**; **MI6**; **national security/
    secrecy**
Sederberg, P., 119-20
self-incrimination freedom, 172
  adverse inferences *see* **silence**
  compelled evidence, 175
separation of powers, 39-40, 270
sex abuse
  disclosure of allegations, 288-9
sex discrimination, 48, 378
  Convention on the Elimination of
    Discrimination Against
    Women, 402
  detriment, 415
  direct, 398, 415
  employer's vicarious liability, 416
  equal pay for equal work, 395
  European law, 395-6
  gender norms, 427
  harassment as, 414-17
  indirect as, 399-400

sex discrimination—*contd*
  obscenity as, 401, 417-21
  part-time workers, 395
  pornography as, 401, 417-21
    violence, 420-1, 423, 427
  positive action, 400-1
  pregnancy, 395
  Sex Discrimination Act, 390
  sexual harassment
    bullying at work, 416
    EU law and policy, 417, 424
    group-based inequality, 415
    harm, 427
    stalking, 416
    in UK, 415-16
    vicarious liability of employer, 416
  within police, 186f
Sex Discrimination Act, 390
sex offences
  against children, 324-5
  Megan's Law, 324-5
  privacy and, 324-5
sexism in prisons, 216
sexual activities, consensual, 286-7, 296-7
sexual harassment
  bullying at work, 416
  EU law and policy, 417, 424
  group-based inequality, 415
  harm, 427
  as sex discrimination, 414-17
  stalking, 416
  in UK, 415-16
  vicarious liability of employer, 416
Sexual Harassment of Working Women
    (MacKinnon), 414-15
sexual orientation
  local authorities and promotion of,
    388
sexual orientation discrimination, 378,
    388, 391-2, 402-3, 411-12, 426-7
  lesbians and gays in military, 46, 297,
    394
Shaw, Stephen, 215f
Shayler, David, 332-3, 344, 366-8
Shearing, C.D., 95
'shoot to kill'
  media reporting, 154
  policy, 136, 139-43, 145-6
  see also **lethal force**
Shorts, E., 167
silence
  inferences from, 105, 129, 130, 134,
    136, 153, 158
  legal advice, 191
  of legal adviser, 182
  self incrimination freedom, 172

Sim, J., 231
Sinn Féin, 117f, 121
Smart, Carol, 212
Smith, A.T.H., 83-4
social inclusion and exclusion, 378, 431
    see also **equality**
social need
    restriction of rights, 30
sovereignty *see* **parliamentary sovereignty**
space
    ownership and public order, 89-91, 95
    public, 90, 95
    rural, 89, 95
    young persons use of, 90-1, 95
Sparks, R., 239, 261
Speakers Corner, 62, 383
Speaking up for Justice (**Home Office**),
    207-8
Special Air Service, 334
speech *see* **freedom of speech/expression**
sporting events
    football supporters, 69, 407
    public order, 69
Spycatcher, 42, 47, 320, 357-9
    content of book, 341, 344
    GCHQ, 358
    injunctions, 332-3, 340
    MI5 and MI6 in, 358
squatters, 84
Stalker, John, 145-6
stalking, 416
standing
    judicial bias and rules of, 32
    judicial review, 31-3
    non-governmental organisations, 31
    pressure groups, 31, 32-3
    private individuals, 31-2
    public authorities
        judicial review, 35
        under HRA, 34-5
Standing Advisory Commission on
    Human Rights (SACHR), 172
state power, 6, 11-14
    administration of state, 13
    contracting state, 12
    control perspective, 13-14
    fixed and legally enforceable
        boundaries, 16
    individuals, 11-12
    internal devolution, 13
    'oppositional politics', 12
    positive obligations, 25
    pressure groups and, 33
    private life, 12, 14
    protection of government not State,
        340, 348-50, 355-6, 363, 370

state power—*contd*
    supranational institutions, 13
    surveillance, 14
    welfare perspective, 13-14
    see also **government**
statement of compatibility, 23
statutory interpretation *see* **interpretation**
Stenning, P.C., 95
Stephen Lawrence Inquiry, 187, 388-9,
    390, 407
Sterling, Claire, 113-14
Stobie, William, 146f
Stock Exchange, 34
Stone, R., 167
stop and search, 180
Strangeways prison, 220, 235
Straw, Jack, 3, 22, 34, 84, 86
    national security, 365, 366
    prisons, 223, 250
    public order, 85f, 86
    Terrorism Act 2000, 103, 125
Stychin, C., 300-1, 411-12
Sunday working, 405
Sunstein, C.R., 59
supergrasses, 146-7, 172
Supperstone, M., 28
Suppression of Terrorism Act 1978, 118-
    19
supranational institutions, 13
surveillance, 14, 178
    accumulation of information, 312
    CCTV, 14, 312, 313-14
    commercial interest justification,
        311
    covert, 176, 280, 282-3, 285-6, 295
    policing public order, 68
    privacy, 280, 282-3, 285-6, 295, 312
    Regulation of Investigatory Powers
        Act (2000), 280, 282-3, 334
    terrorism prevention, 143-4, 146-7
'**Swampy**', 95f
The Sweeney, 186

targeted marketing, 291, 311
Taylor, N., 83
Taylor sisters, 164, 171, 197
telephone tapping, 284-5, 286, 295, 356
Temkin, J., 200-1
terrorism
    abuse of power, 110-11
    academic discourse, 112-14
    access to lawyer, 134, 137, 153, 157,
        191
    accountability, 109, 110-11
    appeals, 157-8
    arrest powers, 136

terrorism—*contd*
asylum law, 119
Birmingham Six, 108, 154, 155, 156, 163, 171, 238
Bloody Sunday, 138, 142
Bloody Sunday Inquiry, 40, 52, 155, 331, 368, 376
broadcasting ban, 47, 117, 129, 152, 160, 382
civil libertarian dilemma, 108-12
confessions, 132, 135, 137
conspiracy to commit acts, 134
courts, 155-9
    appeals, 157-8
    biased summings-up, 156, 170
    confession exclusion, 156, 157
    Diplock courts, 132, 135-6, 137, 156, 171
    House of Lords, 158
    judiciary role, 155-7
    judiciary as targets, 155
    non-jury *see* Diplock courts
    Northern Ireland, 155-6
    United Kingdom, 156
Criminal Justice (Terrorism and Conspiracy) Act 1998, 103
criminal law adequacy, 109
criminal procedure, 134
death penalty, 134-5
definitions, 117-21
democratic mandate requirement, 111
detention, 133, 137, 153
    confessions improperly obtained, 156, 157
    detainee treatment, 105-6, 107
Diplock courts, 132, 135-6, 137, 156, 171
directing terrorism, 134, 135
domestic, 126
eco-terrorism, 161
European Convention on Human Rights, derogation, 107, 123-4
European Convention on the Suppression of Terrorism, 118
European Court, 106, 107, 123, 159-60
exclusion orders, 125, 133
extent of threat in UK, 121-5
extradition, 114, 118
fairness of trials, 106
Gibraltar SAS killings, 154-5
Guildford Four, 108, 155, 163, 171, 197, 238
hacking as, 127
harassment of defence lawyers, 106

terrorism—*contd*
historical legitimacy, 119
homophobic violence, 120
human rights abuses, 137
Human Rights Act, 158
implementing policy see military response
incitement offence, 126
Independent Commissioner for Holding Centres, 107
individual's rights, 108
inhuman and degrading treatment, 106
intelligence based policing, 151-2
intelligence gathering, 138, 143-4, 146-7
international concerns, 105-7
international forums, 159-61
international response, 113-14
international terrorism, 113f
interrogations, 132, 135
legal advice access, 134, 137, 153, 157, 191
legislation, 103, 106, 131-8
    damaging effects, 105-7
    exceptional powers, 105
    permanent, 105
legitimacy of state, 110
legitimate protest as, 127-8
legitimate rebellion, 118
lethal force, 106, 107, 136, 139-43
    accountability of state agencies, 141-2, 143
    planned operations, 139, 141
    prosecutions, 140-1
    'shoot to kill' policy, 136, 139-43, 145-6, 154
limiting principles, 122-5
    credibility of threat, 122-3
    international jurisprudence, 123-5
    overwhelming nature of threat, 123
media coverage, 107, 112, 114-17, 153-5, 170
    broadcasting bans, 47, 117, 129, 152, 160, 382
    demonisation, 115-16
    film coverage, 115-16
    legitimisation, 115
    lines of communication, 117
    pro-state bias, 115
military response, 128-9, 130-1, 138-43
    Bloody Sunday, 138, 142
    bomb disposal, 139

terrorism—*contd*
  policing—*contd*
    intelligence gathering, 138, 139
    lethal force, 139-43
    planned operations, 139, 141
    prosecutions, 140-1
    support for police patrols, 139
  normalisation of exceptional powers,
      105
  Northern Ireland (Emergency
      Provisions) Acts, 106, 119,
      132
  overreaction, 121-2
  parliamentary policy, 151-3
  policing, 126, 143-50
    carding power, 144
    consent, 144-5
    intelligence gathering, 143-4,
        146-7
    methods transfer to other
        activities, 109
    paramilitaries and, 146
    Patten Report, 102, 104, 147-8,
        150, 173
    response, 128, 129-30
    rule of law and, 109, 111
    safeguards, 149-50
    'shoot to kill' policy, 136, 139-43,
        145-6, 154
    special branch, 148
    supergrasses, 146-7, 172
    surveillance, 143-4, 146-7
  political actors, 121
  political solution, 128, 129
  Prevention of Terrorism (Temporary
      Provisions) Acts, 103, 106,
      118-19, 125, 131, 132-3
  proscribed organisations, 117f, 126,
      132, 134, 157
  rejection of state legitimacy, 110
  religious fundamentalists, 127
  repressive powers, 121
  rule of law and, 109, 111
  scheduled offences, 132
  search and arrest powers, 152
  'shoot to kill', 136, 139-43, 145-6
    media reporting, 154
    see also lethal force
  silence right, 105, 129, 130, 134,
      136, 153, 158, 172
  state of emergency, 122
  stop and question powers, 132, 136
  strategy choice, 128-31
  supergrasses, 146-7, 172
  Suppression of Terrorism Act 1978,
      118-19

terrorism—*contd*
  surveillance, 143-4, 146-7
  Terrorism Act 2000 *see* **Terrorism Act
      2000**
  threats in UK, 121-5
    credibility, 122-3
    no evidence for, 126-7
    violence use, 119-20
    war distinguished, 118
  see also individual organisations eg
      Amnesty International
Terrorism Act 2000, 103, 131
  broad definition, 127-8
  international condemnation, 152
  justification, 125-8
  no evidence of threat, 126-7
Thatcher, Margaret, 76, 115, 345
Thatcher government, 12, 41-4, 63, 64,
      345
  'oppositional politics', 12
Thomas, Clarence, 318, 414
Thompson, Robert, 40, 52, 272, 280,
      327, 384
'Three Wise Men' panel, 361f
Time Out, 353
Tisdall, Sarah, 345
tobacco advertising, 385
tobacco industry, 13f
Tomlinson, M., 110
Tomlinson, Richard, 336
Townshend, C., 64-5, 77, 83
trade unions
  banning membership, 42, 356
  miners' disputes, 47, 61, 64, 94
transnational corporations
  information control, 374-5
trespass, 84
  aggravated, 70, 84f
  criminalisation, 65
  privacy and, 298
trespassory assembly, 69, 81
tribunals
  as public authorities, 35
Tully, James, 433-4
Tumim, Stephen, 251
  see also **Woolf Report**
Twining, William, 379-80

ultra vires, 48-9
underclass
  public order and, 66, 76, 86
United Nations, 13
  Committee Against Torture, 105-6
  Committee on the Elimination of
      Racial Discrimination, 408
  Declaration of Human Rights, 402

United Nations—*contd*
Human Rights Committee, 105, 160
Special Rapporteur on the Independence of Judges and Lawyers, 172
Standard Minimum Rules on the Treatment of Prisoners, 243
World Conference on Women (Beijing 1995), 402
United States, 9
anti-pornography strategy, 9f, 10f
free speech, 9, 386
homosexuals as enemies of State, 349-50
imported ideas from, 9
prisoners in, 236, 266
Universal Declaration of Human Rights, 279
unpopular causes, 7
unreasonableness
Wednesbury, 27
Urban, M., 141

value judgments, 17
Valverde, Mariana, 432-3
Venables, Jon, 40, 52, 272, 280, 327, 384
'victim', 19
Human Rights Act 1998, 23, 31-3
rights, 165
standing *see* standing
sufficient interest, 31
Vincent, D., 342, 346, 347
vulnerable witnesses, 193

Wack, Raymond, 307, 308
Waddington, Peter, 60, 88, 95
Wade, W., 24, 25, 35-6, 37, 38, 46
Walker, C., 109, 126
Walker, Neil, 334
Wandsworth prison, 216, 218, 252
Ward, Judith, 163, 169, 197
Wednesbury unreasonableness, 27
welfare access
personal information required for, 313

Wells, C., 60, 75
West Midlands Serious Crime Squad, 164, 171
whistle-blowing, 291, 372
freedom of speech, 381
national security, 332-3
Ponting, 345, 347, 357, 366
Shayler, 332-3, 344, 366-8
Tisdall, 345
Whitemoor Prison, 223, 255
Wilkinson, Paul, 125
Williams Committee Report (1979), 418
Wilson, D., 227
Wilson, W., 290
witnesses
vulnerable, 193
Wolds Prison, 226
Women's Legal Education and Action Fund (LEAF), 213
women's prisons, 225, 228-9
child visits, 257, 259
Holloway Prison, 216, 228-9, 232, 257
Mother and Baby Units, 259
prisoners, 234-5
violence and bullying, 237
women treated as if men, 267
Woolf, LJ, 44, 46f, 51
Woolf Report, 221, 222-3, 235-6
disciplinary procedures, 262, 263
World Trade Organisation protests, 127
Wormword Scrubs Prison, 216
Wright, Peter, 47, 330, 341, 344, 357-9
see also Spycatcher
Wylde, Nigel, 336f

Young, Jock, 85-6, 406
Your Right to Know (White Paper), 364

zero tolerance policing, 85-6, 165
Zizek, Slavoj, 412